The Paradox™ Companion

Bantam Computer Books
Ask your bookseller for the books you have missed

THE AMIGADOS MANUAL
    by Commodore-Amiga, Inc.
ARTIFICIAL INTELLIGENCE ENTERS THE MARKETPLACE
    by Larry R. Harris and Dwight B. Davis
COMMODORE 128 PROGRAMMER'S REFERENCE GUIDE
    by Commodore Business Machines, Inc.
THE COMPUTER AND THE BRAIN
    by Scott Ladd/The Red Feather Press
COMPUTER SENSE: *Developing Personal Computer Literacy*
    by Paul Freiberger and Dan McNeill
EXPLORING ARTIFICIAL INTELLIGENCE ON YOUR IBM PC
    by Tim Hartnell
EXPLORING THE UNIX ENVIRONMENT
    by The Waite Group/Irene Pasternack
FRAMEWORK FROM THE GROUND UP
    by The Waite Group/Cynthia Spoor and Robert Warren
HOW TO GET THE MOST OUT OF COMPUSERVE, 2d ed.
    by Charles Bowen and David Peyton
HOW TO GET THE MOST OUT OF THE SOURCE
    by Charles Bowen and David Peyton
THE NEW *jr*: A GUIDE TO IBM'S PC*jr*
    by Winn L. Rosch
ORCHESTRATING SYMPHONY
    by The Waite Group/Dan Shafer with Mary Johnson
THE PARADOX COMPANION
    by Douglas Cobb, Steven S. Cobb, and Ken E. Richardson/
    The Cobb Group
PC-DOS/MS-DOS
User's Guide to the Most Popular Operating System for Personal Computers
    by Alan M. Boyd
UNDERSTANDING EXPERT SYSTEMS
    by The Waite Group/Mike Van Horn
USER'S GUIDE TO THE AT&T PC 6300 PERSONAL COMPUTER
    by David B. Peatroy, Ricardo A. Anzaldua, H. A. Wohlwend, and
        Datatech Publications Corporation

The Paradox™ Companion

**Douglas Cobb,
Steven S. Cobb, and Ken E. Richardson**

The Cobb Group

BANTAM BOOKS
TORONTO • NEW YORK • LONDON • SYDNEY • AUCKLAND

THE PARADOX COMPANION

A Bantam Book / July 1986

1-2-3 is a trademark of Lotus Development Corporation. Compaq, Compaq Plus, DeskPro, and DeskPro 286 are trademarks of Compaq Computer Corporation. dBASE II is a trademark of Ashton-Tate. Epson MX-80, Epson FX-80, Epson FX-100, and Epson LQ-1500 are trademarks of Epson America, Inc. Hercules Graphics Card is a trademark of Hercules Computer Technology. HP LaserJet is a registered trademark of Hewlett Packard Company. IBM, IBM PC/XT, and IBM PC/AT are trademarks of International Business Machines Corporation. ProWriter is a trademark of C. Itoh Digital Products, Incorporated. Lotus is a trademark of Lotus Development Corporation. Macintosh is a trademark licensed to Apple Computer, Inc. MS-DOS is a trademark of Microsoft, which is a registered trademark of Microsoft Corporation. Okidata is a registered trademark of Oki America, Inc. Paradox is a registered trademark of Ansa Software. PFS: File and PFS: Write are trademarks of Software Publishing. SuperCalc is a trademark of Sorcim, Inc. Symphony is a trademark of Lotus Development Corporation. VisiCalc is a trademark of VisiCorp. WordStar is a trademark of MicroPro, Inc.

Cover design by J. Caroff Associates.
Interior design by Julie Baer Tirpak
Production by Maureen Pawley and Judy Mynhier
Editing by Marjorie Phifer and Linda Baughman

Throughout this book, the trade names and trademarks of many companies and products have been used and no such uses are intended to convey endorsement of or other affiliations with the book.

All rights reserved.
Copyright © 1986 by The Cobb Group, Inc.
Book design by The Cobb Group, Inc.
This book may not be reproduced in whole or in part, by mimeograph or any other means, without permission.
For information address: Bantam Books, Inc.

ISBN 0-553-34361-0

Published simultaneously in the United States and Canada

Bantam Books are published by Bantam Books, Inc. Its trademark, consisting of the words "Bantam Books" and the portrayal of a rooster, is Registered in U.S. Patent and Trademark Office and in other countries. Marca Registrada. Bantam Books, Inc., 666 Fifth Avenue, New York, New York 10103

PRINTED IN THE UNITED STATES OF AMERICA

FG 0 9 8 7 6 5 4 3 2 1

Table of Contents

Dedication/Acknowledgments..vi

Section I
1 Introduction..1

Section II: Paradox Basics
2 Getting Started..5
3 Creating and Viewing Tables...29
4 More on Data Entry and Editing..71
5 Forms..103
6 Managing Tables..149

Section III: Using Paradox
7 Sorting Your Tables..177
8 Queries..191
9 Query by Example...253
10 Multitable Operations...289

Section IV: Reporting
11 Report Fundamentals...329
12 Other Reporting Topics..383

Section V: PAL
13 Simple Scripts..419
14 PAL Basics..449
15 PAL Functions...471
16 Fundamental PAL Techniques..507
17 Other PAL Features..557

Appendix...593
Index..605

To my mother, Ann Ford Cobb, who is always there–DFC

To my father, Westray Stewart Cobb–SSC

To my wife, Jan, who encouraged me to become a writer–KER

Acknowledgments

The authors wish to thank the following people, without whom this book would not have been possible: Tom Cottingham, for putting the deal together; Maureen Pawley, Margie Phifer, Linda Baughman, Julie Tirpak, Judy Mynhier, and Barabara Wells, for making it happen; Ben Rosen, for making the introductions; Steve Dow, Kris Olsen, Richard Schwartz, Robert Shostak, and Ken Einstein of Ansa Software, for helping us at every step along the way; Heather Florence, Kenzi Sugihara, Jono Hardjowirogo, Deborah Aiges, Jim Walsh, and John Kilcullen of Bantam Books, for their confidence in us; Sam Moeller, for his tips and offers of help; Russ Claybrook, for presenting us with some interesting questions; Denise Rogers, Brenda Bankston, Andy Spurgeon, and Patrick Daly, for keeping the ship afloat; and Gena, Jan, and Michelle, for their understanding and encouragement.

Chapter 1
Introduction

Paradox is great software–perhaps the best data base program ever to be introduced for a personal computer. From the first time we saw Paradox, in the summer of 1985, we knew that it was going to be popular. We also knew that it was a product that we wanted to write about. This book is the result of that desire.

Paradox is great because it brings together so many characteristics that have never before been found in one data base manager. Like the old standards, dBASE II and dBASE III, Paradox is a robust data base manager that can handle most any data management task. Also, like those programs, Paradox offers a full-featured applications language (the Paradox Applications Language) that allows you to write complex programs that tie together your table systems.

Like Lotus 1-2-3–and unlike any power data base we know of–Paradox is visual, intuitive software. In Paradox, your data is organized in a simple, understandable row-and-column format. When you're working with a table, your data is displayed on the screen, either in a table or in a form. These characteristics help to make Paradox very easy to learn and use–far easier to learn and use than such old-fashioned, nonvisual programs as dBASE.

Paradox also offers capabilities that are not found in any other popular program. Paradox's unique table-querying system, *query by example*, makes the process of asking questions of your data simpler than in any other program. Instead of *telling* Paradox which data you want it to select, you *show* it which data to choose by defining intuitive examples. In addition, Paradox's report generator lets you create two kinds of reports–tabular and free-form–that can satisfy almost any reporting requirement.

Learning Paradox

The name *Paradox* is very appropriate for this program. While it is easy to learn, it is also very sophisticated and powerful. Although many users will be able to get started with Paradox with little or no help, the program is so extensive you could use it for years without knowing everything there is to know about it.

If you are like most Paradox users, you'll master the program in stages. First, you'll learn to create tables and enter and edit data. Then you'll design basic queries and create simple forms and reports. Next, you'll discover how to write simple scripts and become more adventuresome in your use of queries. Once you reach that point, you'll be an accomplished Paradox user–but you will still have a great deal more to learn. For as long as you work with Paradox, you'll continue to learn new things about the program.

About This Book

We've written *The Paradox Companion* to help you learn Paradox in stages. This book is divided into 17 chapters, which are organized in five sections: "Introduction," "Paradox Basics," "Using Paradox," "Reporting," and "PAL." We've attempted to present the various Paradox concepts in a logical order. Because so many of these concepts interrelate, however, there are places where we present one topic while explaining another. If you come across a concept that isn't familiar to you, you can use the index to find out more about it in another part of the book.

Chapter 1 serves as an introduction to this book. Chapter 2, "Getting Started," covers several fundamental concepts. In this chapter, you'll learn how to load Paradox and configure it for your computer system. You'll also see how Paradox uses the computer's keyboard and screen. In addition, you'll be introduced to terms that have special importance to Paradox and will learn to make selections from menus and lists.

In Chapter 3, "Creating and Viewing Tables," you'll create and enter data into Paradox tables. We'll also show you how to change the entries in a table and how to bring one or more tables into view on your screen. We explain more about data entry and editing in Chapter 4. This chapter teaches you to adjust the appearance of your table images with the Image command and to protect your tables with the ValCheck command. In addition, you'll learn to create and use keyed tables.

You'll learn to use forms to view, edit, and enter data into your Paradox tables in Chapter 5, "Forms." This chapter begins with a discussion of the default form, then explains how to create and use custom forms.

In Chapter 6, "Managing Tables," we show you how to use the commands on the Tools menu to copy, erase, empty, and rename tables and their associated forms and reports. This chapter also explains the [Menu] Modify Restructure command, which lets you change the structure of existing tables.

Chapter 7, "Sorting Your Tables," explains how to define a sort form and execute a sort so you can sort your Paradox tables.

Chapter 8 shows you how to create and use queries. For instance, you'll learn about the [Menu] Ask command, which allows you to create query forms. Moreover, we'll teach you to select fields, define selection conditions, and use special query operators like find, delete, and changeto. Chapter 9, "Query by Example," introduces the concept of examples. Among other things, you'll discover how to use examples to link two tables in a query and make complex calculations. You will also learn to use the powerful calc operator.

Chapter 10, "Multitable Operations," covers several commands that affect more than one table. In this chapter, we explain the [Menu] Tools More Add and [Menu] Tools More Subtract commands, which let you combine tables with identical structures. You'll also learn to enter data into multiple tables through a single form with the [Menu] Modify MultiEntry command. In addition, you'll learn to use the related [Menu] Tools More MultiAdd command, as well as to work with insert queries.

We show you how to create reports from your Paradox tables in Chapter 11, "Report Fundamentals." First, we'll teach you how to use the Instant Report capability to create quick reports. Then we'll show you how to create and use custom tabular and free-form reports. Chapter 12, "Other Reporting Topics," builds on the concepts presented in Chapter 11. In this chapter, you'll learn to use summary fields in reports, group your reports, and use the Custom Configuration Program to change the default report settings.

Chapter 13, "Simple Scripts," is your introduction to the world of scripts and PAL programming. In this chapter, you'll learn what scripts are and how you can create them. You'll also be introduced to the Script Editor and the PAL Debugger.

Chapter 14, "PAL Basics," explains several fundamental PAL concepts. In this chapter, you'll learn about PAL commands, variables, and formulas. The last important building block–Functions–is covered in Chapter 15, "PAL Functions."

If you use PAL, Chapter 16, "Fundamental PAL Techniques," is an especially important chapter for you. You'll learn how to use PAL to write information to the screen, and how to interact with the user of your scripts, create menus, design FOR/NEXT and WHILE/ENDWHILE loops, print from within scripts, and much more. You'll be able to use the information in this chapter as a tool kit to build your own PAL programs.

Chapter 17, "Other PAL Features," covers the remaining PAL topics. In this chapter, you'll discover how to use the Value command to make quick calculations and the MiniScript command to create simple, one-line scripts. This chapter also covers the PAL Debugger, tilde variables, arrays, and procedures.

The Appendix, "Importing and Exporting Files," covers the commands on Paradox's ExportImport menu. These commands allow you to import data from 1-2-3, Symphony, dBASE II and III, PFS: File, and VisiCalc into Paradox, and to export data in Paradox tables to these programs.

Conventions

Throughout this book, we'll use certain conventions which we hope will make the text easier to read and understand. We would like to explain these conventions to you now.

Table names, file names, and function names always appear in capital letters, as in "the CUSTOMER table" and "the CMAX() function." Unless instructed to do so, you are not required to use upper-case letters.

Command names are usually presented in full form, for instance, "the [Menu] Forms Design command." In addition, the names of the individual options in the command name are always capitalized. When you are instructed to issue a command, the first letter of each word in the command is boldfaced, as in the phrase "issue the [**Menu**] **F**orms **D**esign command." This will serve as a reminder that you can issue a command by simply pressing the first letter of the command name.

The names of standard keys like [Esc], [Ctrl], and [Home] are enclosed in square brackets, as are the "nameless" keys on the IBM PC keyboard: [Spacebar], [Backspace], [Tab], and [Shift]. The names of Paradox function keys are also enclosed in brackets, as in [Help], [Do-It!], and [Menu]. In addition, the names of function keys are usually accompanied by a parenthetical reminder of the key location, for example, "press the [**Do-It!**] key ([F2])." Furthermore, the Return/Enter key is represented by the symbol ↵ and the four arrow keys by the symbols →, ←, ↓, and ↑. When two or more keys must be pressed simultaneously, those key names are separated by hyphens, as in "press [**Ctrl**]-[**R**]" or "press [**Alt**]-[**F10**]." You should not type the hyphen.

Additionally, when you are instructed to press a key or type an entry, the characters you should type will be in boldface, as in "press [**Esc**]," "press [**Do-It!**]," and "type **100**."

A Note About Versions

This book is based on Release 1.1 of Paradox. Although it does include discussions of a few topics that are important in Release 1.0 (such as how to use an insert query to enter information into two tables through a single form), most of the discussion assumes that you have upgraded to Release 1.1.

As you will see, Release 1.1 is a vast improvement over Release 1.0 of Paradox. For example, the new release includes several commands, such as [Menu] Modify MultiEntry, that were not part of the earlier release. In addition, Release 1.1 corrects several troublesome bugs in Release 1.0. If you are still using Release 1.0, you should contact Ansa Software as soon as possible to receive your update. Ansa's support number is (415) 595-4851. Their address is 1301 Shoreway Road, Suite 221, Belmont, CA, 94002.

Where to Begin

Exactly where you begin in *The Paradox Companion* depends on how much experience you have with Paradox. If you are just starting out, you should begin with Chapter 2. If you have been working with the program for a while and feel comfortable with the basics, you might want to skip Chapter 2, skim Chapter 3, and begin in earnest with Chapter 4.

Chapter 2
Getting Started

In this chapter, we will show you how to get started using Paradox. We will begin by discussing hardware requirements and showing you how to install the program on your system. Then we will give you an overview of the Paradox program and discuss the Paradox keyboard. Finally, we'll conclude with a discussion of Paradox's context-sensitive help facility.

If you have already installed Paradox on your computer and have begun to work with the program, you may want to skip this chapter and start with Chapter 3. However, if you are new to Paradox, you'll want to read this chapter carefully before you move on to the next chapter.

Hardware Requirements

To use Paradox, you must have the proper computer hardware and peripherals. Paradox is designed to run on the IBM PC, PC/XT, PC/AT, and on 100% compatible systems, such as the Compaq Portable, DeskPro, or the DeskPro 286. If you are not sure whether your computer is 100% compatible, you might want to ask for a demonstration on your machine before you buy the program.

Regardless of your computer configuration, you will need DOS 2.0 or higher to run the program. You also will need a monochrome or color monitor and the appropriate video controller card.

Memory

Paradox requires that your computer have at least 512K of Random Access Memory (RAM). Even with that much memory, however, some of Paradox's features may be limited, especially if you are using Paradox 1.0. When you load Paradox into your computer, most of the available RAM space is consumed by the Paradox program code, which is entirely RAM-resident. As you use Paradox, it imports portions of the tables and other objects that you are using in RAM. As Paradox needs different portions of those tables, it replaces the information in RAM with new information from the disk. The more memory you have, the more information Paradox can hold in memory at once.

The result is a much faster performance. If you have only 512K, Paradox will swap information from disk to memory frequently, thus slowing down the program.

In addition, if you have just 512K of RAM, there are some operations that Paradox may simply be unable to perform. When Paradox thinks that it might run out of room while performing a task, it will display a message telling you it does not have enough memory to perform the task. If Paradox actually does run out of room, it will display a message telling you that a resource limit (memory) has been exceeded. Then it will automatically try to recover memory by clearing the workspace, deleting temporary tables—whatever it can do to keep your tables and data intact. Despite its recovery system, Paradox will return you to DOS in some instances. Although Paradox will save your work before it exits to DOS, it does not take too many of these quick exits to convince you that you need more memory. (This occurs far less frequently in Paradox 1.1.)

For these reasons, we suggest that you install a full 640K of RAM in your computer if you will be using Paradox seriously.

Disk Drives

Paradox will run on a system with two 360K floppy disk drives. However, if you plan to use Paradox seriously, you'll want to get a hard disk.

First, when used on a computer with floppy drives, Paradox is very slow. As you work with Paradox, it is constantly interacting with the disk, loading portions of tables and other objects into memory, and saving information that it no longer needs to disk. This swapping can become quite an irritation when you are using Paradox with floppy drives. The speed of a hard disk helps to cut the time required for swapping dramatically.

Second, as you work with Paradox, you will find that your tables and the family of associated objects (such as forms) will grow rapidly to the point where they will not fit on a floppy disk. Since the smallest hard disks offer more than ten times the storage capacity of a floppy disk, having a hard disk will free you from worrying about running out of space.

For maximum performance, then, your system should have one hard disk with at least 750K bytes of free space to install the program and run the Paradox tutorial, and an additional 1 megabyte (1000K) of free space to manage your data base. Of course, your system should also have one floppy disk drive.

Printer

To take full advantage of Paradox, you will also need a printer. Although you can use Paradox without a printer, you will not be able to use the program's powerful report generator, and you will not be able to create hard-copy reports from your Paradox data. Paradox supports most popular printers, including the entire line of Epson printers, the IBM ProWriter, the Okidata family of printers, and the HP LaserJet printer.

Installing Paradox

The Paradox program (Release 1.1) comes on four disks: System Disk I, System Disk II, the Installation Disk, and a Sample Tables disk. You will use the programs on the Installation Disk to install the program on your system. These installation programs set up a directory, as well as a CONFIG.SYS file that allows you to run the program on your system.

Release 1.0 of Paradox is copy protected; however, a backup copy of System Disk I is provided with the program, and you can make copies of the other program diskettes. Release 1.1 of Paradox is not copy-protected, and you will probably want to use the DOS DiskCopy command to make a backup copy of the program disks before you do anything else. After you do this, you should place the original diskettes in a safe place and use the copies as your working disks.

Since the installation procedure is covered in detail in Chapter 3 of the manual, *Introduction to Paradox*, which comes with the program, we will limit our discussion here to a brief review of the two most common installation procedures—hard disk and two-drive floppy systems. If you have special needs or additional questions, you'll want to read Chapter 3 of the manual.

Release 1.0 Versus Release 1.1

As you may already know, Release 1.0 of Paradox was copy protected, but Release 1.1 is not. Because of the copy-protection system on Release 1.0, there are some minor differences between it and Release 1.1. For the most part, however, you will find the installation procedure to be quick and easy with either version.

In Paradox Release 1.0, System Disk I is copy-protected and may only be installed once. You can, however, uninstall Paradox from either a hard disk or a floppy disk back to the original System Disk I, and then install the program on another system.

You can install Release 1.0 on a hard disk by following the same directions given below. When you do this, Paradox notes the installation on System Disk I and will not allow any additional installations.

If you are installing Release 1.0 on a floppy disk system, you should first use the DOS Format command to format three disks. You will use these disks to make a working copy of System Disks I and II and the Sample Tables disk. You should format the disk that will become System Disk I with the format b:/s DOS command. This will place your system files on the disk. The other two disks need not contain your system files and can be formatted with the format b: command. After you have done this, you can follow the same instructions given below for floppy disk installation.

Hard Disk Installation

If you are using a hard disk drive with one floppy disk drive, you can use the installation programs to copy the Paradox program files to your hard disk. You need to begin the installation procedure from the DOS prompt of the drive on which you want to install Paradox (usually C>). To get to this point, turn your system on, or reboot it by pressing **[Ctrl]-[Alt]-[Del]**. When the DOS prompt appears on the screen (the prompt will probably be C> if you are using a computer with a hard disk), insert the Paradox Installation Disk in drive A, type **a:install c:**, and press ↵. Be sure to insert a blank space between the word *install* and the drive designation. After you do this, Paradox will run the installation program.

In Release 1.1, the installation procedure starts by prompting you to enter your name, your company's name, and the Paradox serial number (you will find this number on the package). This information will be displayed on the screen whenever you start the program. The screen prompts will be slightly different if you are installing Release 1.0.

During the installation procedure, you will need to insert and remove various program disks. Paradox will display instructions on the screen and will prompt you for the disks it needs. After you insert a disk called for by the program, press ↵ to continue the installation procedure.

When you install Paradox on a hard disk, the installation program creates a directory called *paradox* and copies the Paradox program files into that directory. In addition, the program sets up on the root directory of your hard disk a CONFIG.SYS file that contains two commands: Files=16, Buffers=20. This configuration is essential to running the Paradox program. If you already have a CONFIG.SYS file on the root directory of your hard disk, Paradox will modify it as necessary. Although the program will not change any values in your original CONFIG.SYS file that are not relevant to Paradox, it will rename the file CONFIG.PDX.

When the installation procedure is complete, you will be instructed to reboot your system before you run Paradox. If the installation procedure does not work properly, Paradox will display an error message that describes the problem briefly. You will need to correct the problem before you can continue with the installation procedure. The most common problem you are likely to encounter is a lack of sufficient free space on your hard disk. For a detailed discussion of hard disk installation problems, you should refer to Chapter 3 of the book *Introduction to Paradox*.

Once you have the program installed on your system, you can copy the Paradox tutorial onto your hard disk. To do this, start with the DOS prompt on the screen and type **cd\paradox** to change the current directory to \paradox. Next, insert the Paradox Sample Tables disk in drive A, type **a:tutor**, and press ↵. Paradox then will copy all of the files on the Sample Tables disk into the \paradox directory on your hard disk.

Floppy Disk Installation

If you're using a system with two floppy disk drives, start with the DOS prompt for the system drive (usually A>) on the screen. You may need to turn your system on, or press **[Ctrl]-[Alt]-[Del]** to reboot it, to get to this point. When the DOS prompt appears on the screen, insert your DOS disk in drive A and the Paradox Installation Disk in drive B. Then type **b: finstall** and press ↵ (the *f* in *finstall* stands for *floppy*). After you do this, Paradox will display additional instructions on the screen. If you're installing Release 1.1, you'll be required to enter your name, the name of your company, and the Paradox serial number before the initial installation process begins. If you're installing Release 1.0, the prompts will be slightly different. Regardless of the version you're installing, you'll be required to insert and remove various disks during the installation procedure. After you insert a disk called for by the program, you should press ↵ to continue the installation procedure.

The installation procedure automatically transfers your system files from your DOS disk, first to the Installation Disk, then to System Disk I. This makes System Disk I "bootable" on your computer. In addition, when you boot your system with this disk, the values in the CONFIG.SYS file will be in effect.

When the installation procedure is complete, you will see a message on the screen telling you that Paradox has been successfully installed and instructing you to reboot your system. As with hard disk installation, if the installation process does not work properly, Paradox will display an error message. For a detailed discussion of floppy disk installation problems, you should refer to Chapter 3 of the book *Introduction to Paradox*.

Once you have installed the program, you can make a copy of the Paradox tutorial on the Sample Tables disk. This will leave the original disk intact for others who may want to run the tutorial from the beginning.

To copy the Sample Tables disk, start with the DOS prompt on the screen. Then, insert a blank formatted disk in drive B and the Paradox Sample Tables disk in drive A. Now type **ftutor** and press ↵. After you do this, the files on the Sample Tables disk will be copied onto the blank disk in drive B. When the copy process is complete, you'll see the DOS prompt again.

Uninstalling Paradox

If you are using Release 1.0, you can uninstall the program should the need arise. For example, you may want to reinstall it on another disk or computer. To do this, you'll need to run a program on the Installation Disk called **uninstal** (**funstal** if you are using Paradox on a floppy disk system).

To uninstall Paradox from a hard disk, start with the DOS prompt on the screen. Next, insert the Paradox Installation Disk in drive A, type **a:uninstal c:** and press ↵. After you do this, the program will display additional instructions on the screen. You will be required to insert and remove various disks during the uninstall procedure. Once the program has been uninstalled, you can install it again on another disk.

To uninstall Paradox from a floppy disk, start with the DOS prompt on the screen. Next, insert the Paradox Installation Disk in drive A, type **funstal**, and press ↵. After you do this, the program will display additional instructions on the screen. You will be required to insert and remove various disks during the uninstall procedure. Once the program has been uninstalled, you can install it again on another disk.

Loading Paradox

After you have installed Paradox, you are ready to run the program. If you have a hard disk, you should press the **[Ctrl]-[Alt]-[Del]** keys simultaneously to reboot your system before you load the program for the first time. This will ensure that the values in the CONFIG.SYS file, which is set up during the installation procedure, will be in effect. Each time you boot your computer, those values will take effect from that point on.

When the DOS prompt (usually C>) appears on the screen, type **cd\paradox** to change the current directory to \paradox. Then type **paradox** and press ↵ to load the program. After a few moments, the Paradox title screen shown in Figure 2-1 will appear, followed by the screen shown in Figure 2-2.

Figure 2-1   The Title Screen

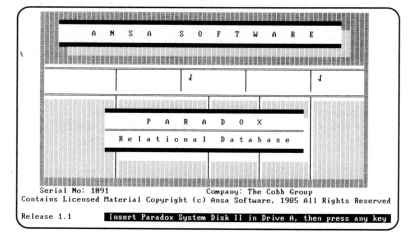

Figure 2-2 The Main Menu

```
View  Ask  Report  Create  Modify  Image  Forms  Tools  Scripts  Help  Exit
View a table.




















     Use -> and <- keys to move around menu, then press <-' to make selection.
```

If you are using a floppy drive system, insert your working copy of System Disk I in drive A and a Paradox data disk in drive B. Then press **[Ctrl]-[Alt]-[Del]** to reboot your system. When the DOS prompt (usually A>) appears, type **paradox** and press ↵. After a few moments, the title screen will appear, along with a message instructing you to insert System Disk II in drive A. When you see this message, remove System Disk I from drive A, insert System Disk II, and press any key. After a few moments, the Paradox Main menu will appear on the screen.

An Overview

Now that you know how to load Paradox, you're ready to take a brief tour of Paradox. In this section, we will talk about the Paradox screen, how Paradox uses the keyboard, and how you issue commands in Paradox. We will also introduce you to the concept of tables and images.

The Screen

When you first load Paradox into your computer, your screen will look like Figure 2-2. As you can see, the main Paradox screen is divided into three areas: the menu area at the top of the screen, the workspace in the middle, and a message area at the bottom.

The Menu Area

The menu area consists of only two lines at the very top of the screen. When you first load Paradox, the Paradox Main menu will appear in this area, as shown in Figure 2-2. The Main menu consists of 11 options, each of which allows you to perform a type of action. The second line in the menu area contains an explanation of the highlighted, or selected, option in the active menu.

As you work with Paradox, you will see different menus in the menu area. Occasionally you will not see any menu at all. If you don't see a menu, and you need to issue a command, you can press the [Menu] key ([F10]). As soon as you press this key, Paradox will display the appropriate menu in the menu area.

In addition to the Paradox menus, you will see status messages and special symbols in the menu area. For example, the symbol ▶ in Figure 2-3 indicates that there are more names in the list being displayed than can be seen at once on the screen. We'll explain these special symbols as we run across them in our discussion.

Figure 2-3 Special Symbols

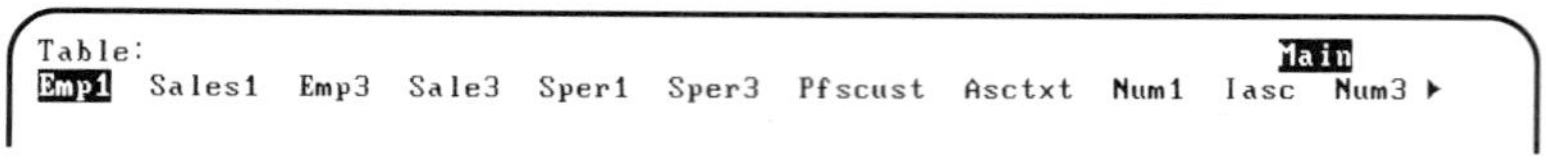

```
Table:                                                            Main
    Emp1  Sales1  Emp3  Sale3  Sper1  Sper3  Pfscust  Asctxt  Num1  Iasc  Num3 ▶
```

The Workspace

The workspace is the large area in the middle of the screen. This is the area that Paradox uses to display images, design forms and reports, and carry out queries. Most of the work you do with Paradox will be carried out in this area.

The Message Area

The message area consists of one line at the bottom of the screen. Paradox uses this area to display error messages and instructions. When you first load Paradox, the message shown in Figure 2-4 will appear in this area.

Figure 2-4 The Message Area

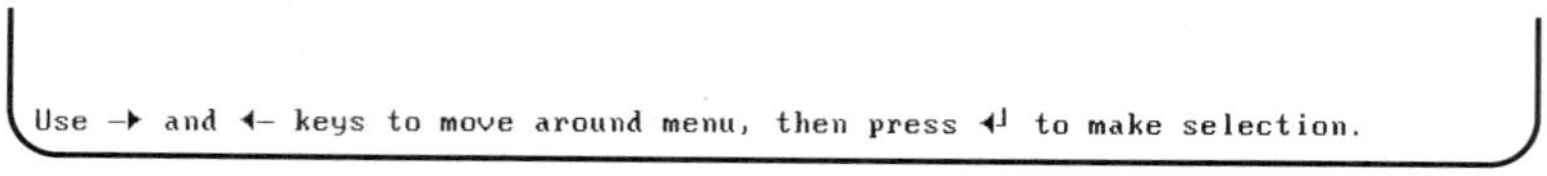

```
Use → and ← keys to move around menu, then press ↵ to make selection.
```

Most of the messages that appear in this area tell you that you have made an error or that something has gone wrong with Paradox. For instance, if you press [Do-It!] ([F2]) when there is nothing ready to be processed, Paradox will display the error message that is shown in Figure 2-5. For a complete list of Paradox error messages, see Appendix A of the *Paradox User's Guide*.

Figure 2-5 An Error Message

```
                                                    Nothing to process now
```

In addition to displaying error messages, Paradox will respond to certain keystrokes with a low-pitched or high-pitched beep. A low-pitched beep usually means that you have tried to move the cursor beyond the boundary of an image. A high-pitched beep usually means that you have pressed the wrong key. You may also occasionally hear a very high-pitched, short beep. This is your computer system's way of telling you that it cannot keep up with your typing; this is not unique to Paradox.

The Keyboard

Like most sophisticated programs, Paradox takes full advantage of the IBM PC keyboard. Although we will cover the purpose of each key in more detail later in this book, let's take a brief look at some of the more important keys before going on.

The Typewriter Keys

The middle portion of the IBM PC keyboard contains the keys found on standard typewriter keyboards. For the most part, you'll use the keys in this part of the keyboard to make entries into your Paradox tables, to type scripts, and so on. However, a few of these keys have special purposes in Paradox.

The [Esc] key is the all-purpose "backup" key. For example, you can use the [Esc] key to move from a submenu to the previous menu. This key lets you backup if you select the wrong option so that you can make another selection.

The ↵ key has several functions in Paradox. You can use ↵ to select options from the menus. When you are viewing a table, ↵ can be used to move the cursor to the next field. ↵ is the key you press to tell Paradox you're finished supplying some requested information, like a table name. In the report generator, the ↵ key lets you insert a line.

The [Ctrl] key also has several uses in Paradox. When used in conjunction with certain other keys, [Ctrl] lets you instantly copy the value from a field of the previous record into the same field of the next record, or change the order of the fields in a table image, among other things. Table 2-1 shows the various uses of the [Ctrl] key in Paradox.

In addition to the uses shown in Table 2-1, the [Ctrl] key can be used in conjunction with the arrow keys and the [Pg Up], [Pg Dn], [Home], and [End] keys to move the cursor around in table images and forms. When it is used in this way, the Paradox manual calls the [Ctrl] key the [Turbo] key. We'll cover these uses for the [Ctrl] key in later chapters.

The last key of interest in this section of the keyboard is [Backspace]. When you are working with a table in the edit mode, pressing [Backspace] erases the character to the left of the cursor in the current field. Pressing [Ctrl]-[Backspace] in the edit mode will erase the entire contents of the field.

Table 2-1 [Ctrl]-Key Combinations

Keys	Paradox Name	Function
[Ctrl]-[Break]		Cancels the current operation and returns to the main workspace.
[Ctrl]-[R]	[Rotate]	Rotates fields to the right of the cursor (table view only).
[Ctrl]-[Y]	[Report Delete Line]	Deletes from the cursor to the end of the line in the report generator.
[Ctrl]-[D]	[Ditto]	In the edit mode, copies the value in the field above the cursor to the current field.
[Ctrl]-[F]		Same as [Field View] ([Alt]-[F5]): enters field view mode.
[Ctrl]-[V]	[Vertical Ruler Toggle]	Shows or hides a vertical ruler in the report generator.
[Ctrl]-[U]	[Undo]	In the edit mode, undoes the last change made.
[Ctrl]-[O]	[ToDOS]	Suspends Paradox and returns to DOS.

Special Function Keys

Paradox uses all ten of the special function keys on the IBM PC keyboard. Table 2-2 shows the name and function that Paradox gives to each of these keys. In addition to the ten basic special function keys, Paradox also supports seven [Alt]-function key combinations. The names and functions of these keys are shown in Table 2-3.

With your Paradox program, you should have received a special keyboard template that shows the Paradox name of each of the special function keys. Because Paradox uses the special function keys so heavily, this template is a very important part of your Paradox program. You'll have a hard time remembering the purposes of all of the function keys without it.

Table 2-2 Special Function Keys

Key	Paradox Name	Function
[F1]	[Help]	Displays a help screen.
[F2]	[DO-IT!]	Completes an operation.
[F3]	[Up Image]	Moves the cursor up one image.
[F4]	[Down Image]	Moves the cursor down one image.
[F5]	[Example]	Enters an example in a query.
[F6]	[Check Mark]	Enters or removes a check mark in a query form.
[F7]	[Form Toggle]	Switches between the table and form view.
[F8]	[Clear Image]	Clears the current image from the workspace.
[F9]	[Edit]	Enters the edit mode.
[F10]	[Menu]	Displays the current Paradox menu.

Table 2-3 [Alt]-Function Key Combinations

Keys	Paradox Name	Function
[Alt]-[F3]	[Instant Script Record]	Begins or ends the recording of an instant script.
[Alt]-[F4]	[Instant Script Play]	Plays an instant script.
[Alt]-[F5]	[Field View]	Enters the field view mode.
[Alt]-[F6]	[Check Plus]	Enters a check plus in a query form.
[Alt]-[F7]	[Instant Report]	Prints an instant report for the current table.
[Alt]-[F8]	[Clear All]	Clears all images from the workspace.
[Alt]-[F10]	[PALMenu]	Displays the PAL menu at the top of the screen.

The Numeric Keypad

As in most IBM PC programs, Paradox uses the keys of the numeric keypad for two purposes. First, in the default condition, the keys in this part of the keyboard are used to move the cursor around the screen. Because the precise effect of these keys depends on where you are in Paradox, we'll save our discussion of them for later chapters.

If you press the [Num Lock] key, the keys on the keypad can be used to enter numbers into tables. While you are using these keys to enter numbers, you can't use them to move the cursor. When you are finished entering numbers and want to use these keys to move the cursor again, you just press [Num Lock] again.

There are a couple of other important keys in this part of the keyboard. When you are working in the edit mode, the [Ins] key allows you to insert a new record into a table. [Ins] can also be used to toggle in and out of the insert mode when you are editing a report, a form, or a script. When you are editing a table, you can use the [Del] key to delete a record.

Paradox Commands

Commands are the tools you'll use to create and work with your Paradox tables. Commands allow you to create tables, enter and edit data, change the structure of tables, create reports, and write and play PAL scripts.

Paradox commands are organized in a "top-to-bottom" system of menus that is very similar in design to the system first used by Lotus 1-2-3. The main, or "top," menu is shown at the top of Figure 2-2.

When you see the Main menu on your screen, you will notice that the first option (View) is highlighted in reverse video. The highlight tells you that View is currently the active choice on the menu. If you press ↵ at this point, you will issue the View command.

Also notice the message on the second line of the screen, *View a table*. This message explains the purpose of the highlighted option. In this case, the message *View a table* explains that the View option allows you to view a table.

We will explain all of the Paradox commands in detail later in this book. However, before we go on, we should show you how to select commands from menus, introduce you to the concept of submenus, and show you how to select files.

Issuing Commands

There are two ways to issue a command in Paradox. First, you can issue any command on the currently visible menu just by typing the first letter in the name of the command. For example, to issue the Report command, you could just press **R**.

Alternatively, you can select a menu option by highlighting it and pressing ↵. To highlight other menu options, press the → or ← keys. Each time you press →, the highlight will move one option to the right. Each time you press ←, it will move one option to the left. As you move the cursor across the screen, the message on the second line will change to tell you what each selection does. For example, if you press → twice, the menu will look like Figure 2-6. To issue the Report command at this point, you would just press ↵.

Figure 2-6 Highlighting Commands

```
View  Ask  Report  Create  Modify  Image  Forms  Tools  Scripts  Help  Exit
Output, design, or change a report specification.
```

If you press ← while the first option in the Main menu, View, is selected, the highlight will wrap around to the last option on the menu, Exit. Similarly, if you press → when the last option on the Main menu is selected, the highlight will scroll back to the View option. All Paradox menus have this wrap-around capability, which you can use to issue commands more quickly. For example, suppose the View option is selected, and you want to issue the Help command. Instead of pressing → nine times to move the Help option, you can press ← just twice.

In addition to using the arrow keys to move through a menu, you can move quickly to the first or last option by pressing the [Home] or [End] keys.

Selecting Tables

When you issue a command from the Main menu, Paradox will do one of several things. First, it may prompt you to enter a file or table name. For example, if you issue the View command, Paradox will prompt you to enter a table name as shown in Figure 2-7.

Figure 2-7   A Paradox Prompt

```
Table:                                                          Main
Enter name of table to view, or press ⏎ to see a list of tables.
```

When you see this prompt, you should type the name of the table you want to view and press ⏎. For example, to view a table named TEST, you would type **TEST** and press ⏎. Immediately, Paradox would bring the table you selected into view. If the table you name is not in the active directory, Paradox will display the message

　　　Cannot find TABLENAME table

If you see this message, you should press **[Backspace]** to erase the name you typed, then retype the name.

If you are not sure of the name of the table you want to view (or if you are a terrible typist and don't want to type the name), you can press ⏎ to see a list of tables stored on the active directory. For example, suppose you have several tables on your data disk and you can't remember the exact name of the table you want to view. If you simply press ⏎ at the prompt, Paradox will show you a list like the one in Figure 2-8.

Figure 2-8   A List of Tables

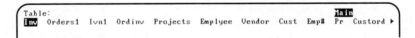

Notice that the first name in this list, Inv, is highlighted. Just as with menus, when you ask Paradox to display a list of table names, it will automatically highlight the first name in the list. You can select any name in the list just as you select options from a menu: either by typing the first letter in the name of the table you want to select or by pointing to its name in the list and pressing ⏎.

The symbol ▶ on the right side of the screen tells you that there are more table names than can be displayed on the screen at one time. To view the hidden table names, you can press → or ← to move the cursor one name at a time to the right or left. If you want to move more quickly, you can use the [Home] and [End] keys to move directly to the first or last name in the list, the ↑ or [Ctrl]-→ keys to scroll one screenful to the right, or the ↓ or [Ctrl]-← keys to scroll one screenful to the left. Once you locate the table you want, highlight it with the cursor and press ⏎.

If you type the first letter in one of the names in the list, Paradox will immediately select the file that begins with that letter. If you type a letter, and there is more than one file in the list whose name begins with that letter, Paradox will "narrow the list" to include just those files whose names begin with that letter. For example, suppose you want to view a table whose name starts with the letter *C*. To find the table name, press **C** (after you press ↵ to see a list of tables) at the prompt. When you do, Paradox will display the names of all tables with names that start with the letter *C*, as shown in Figure 2-9.

Figure 2-9 Selecting a Table

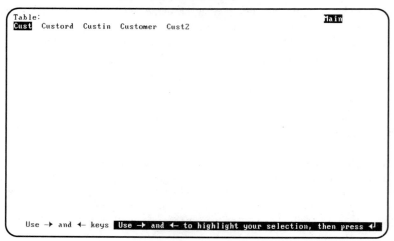

When you look at Figure 2-9, you will notice instructions for selecting the table you want at the bottom of the screen. When you see these instructions, you should press the → or ← key to place the cursor on the table name you want, and then press ↵. Paradox will then display the table you selected on the screen.

Remember–although we used the View command to demonstrate the ways you can select a file, you will be able to select files in this manner whenever Paradox prompts you to enter the name of an existing table.

Submenus

When you issue the Report, Modify, Image, Forms, Tools, or Exit commands, Paradox will display a submenu of additional commands (options). For example, if you issue the Report command, you will see a menu of options that looks like Figure 2-10.

Figure 2-10 The Report Submenu

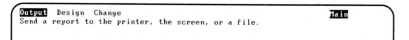

You select commands from a submenu in exactly the same way that you select commands from the Main menu. After you choose a submenu option, Paradox may present another submenu or prompt you for a file name. By working your way down through layer upon layer of submenus, you will finally arrive at the specific command you wish to use.

Paradox Tables

Paradox organizes information in tables. A table is a gridwork of columns (fields) and rows (records) that contains data. Each field (column) in a table contains all of the data of a similar type for each record in the table. For example, you might have a First Name field in a CUSTOMER table that contains the first names of all of your customers, or an Order Number field in an ORDERS table that contains the order number for each order. Every field in a Paradox table has a name.

Each record (row) in a table contains all of the information about one particular person or thing. For example, one row in a CUSTOMER table would contain the name and address for one particular customer. Likewise, each record in an ORDERS table would contain all of the information about one particular order. Each record in a table has a number.

For example, Figure 2-11 shows a table named CUSTOMER. Each row in this table is a complete record on one customer. The field names, Cust number, Last Name, First Name, Address, City, State, and Zip, displayed across the top of the table, identify the type of information contained in each field.

Figure 2-11 The CUSTOMER Table

CUSTOMER	Cust Number	Last Name	First Name	Address	City	State	Zip
1	1245	Priest	Stan	123 Hill St	Louisville	KY	40212
2	1690	Anderson	Harold	45 Mt. Rain	New Albany	IN	47130
3	1888	Jones	William	6610 Willow	Nashville	TN	61215
4	1132	Smith	David	Haven Drive	Louisville	KY	40208
5	1200	Doe	John	Milltown Rd	Louisville	KY	40215
6	1246	Doe	Jane	Crossbuck Dr	Louisville	KY	40215
7	1176	Robinson	Clifford	2323 Vane St	Jeffersonville	IN	47130
8	1509	Carson	Kit	45 Colt St	Clarksville	IN	47132
9	1286	Collins	Richard	1223 Fork Ave	Jeffersontown	KY	40209
10	1751	Ross	Melinda	Apt.12 Fox St	New Albany	IN	47130
11	2376	Baxter	John	# 5 Park Ave	New York	NY	28016
12	3726	Alda	Alan	4077 Mash	Hollywood	CA	90012
13	5171	Conner	Julie	Hopewell Dr	Clarksville	TN	61203
14	5421	Cambridge	Frank	552 B Hill St	Louisville	KY	40212
15	9610	Johnson	Joe	1000 Mob End Rd	Louisville	KY	40204
16	9051	Black	Emma	P.O. Box 397	Dallas	TX	87172
17	1500	Thomas	Tom	RFD 2	Goose Run	KY	40001
18	1136	Winder	Willie	896 Coil St	Jeffersonville	IN	47130
19	1202	Thompson	Zack	111 River Rd	New York	NY	28012
20	3626	O'Grady	Teddy	Limrick St # 3	Paris	KY	40002

A single Paradox table can contain up to 65,000 records and up to 255 fields. A single record can be up to 4000 characters long. However, no one field of any record can contain more than 255 characters.

Every table in Paradox has a unique name. Due to the DOS file name limitation of eight characters, table names can be no longer than eight characters. The name can contain letters, numbers, and special characters, like # and $, but it cannot contain blank spaces. As you will see in the next chapter, Paradox automatically assigns the name extension .DB to every table you create.

Paradox Families and Objects

Every table that you create can have a number of objects associated with it. For example, a single table can have up to ten custom reports and forms. Each report or form is called an *object* and is associated with the table for which it was created. A collection of objects and their associated table are called a *family*.

In addition to custom forms and reports, a table's family can consist of specific image settings, validity checks, a primary index (also known as a key field), and several secondary indexes. Each object you create is automatically assigned the name of the table for which it was created, as well as an extension that identifies the type of object it is. The various objects and their extensions are listed in Table 2-4.

Table 2-4   Paradox Objects and File Name Extensions

Object	Extension
Table	.DB
Form	.F and .F1 through .F9
Report	.R and .R1 through .R9
Image Settings	.SET
Validity Checks	.VAL
Primary Index	.PX
Secondary Indexes	.Y01, .Y02, .Y03, and so on, and .X01, .X02, .X03, and so on

All script files have the file name extension .SC. Script files are not part of a family.

Temporary Tables

In performing the tasks you assign Paradox, the program creates ten different temporary tables: ANSWER, CHANGED, DELETED, ENTRY, FAMILY, INSERTED, KEYVIOL, LIST, PROBLEMS, and STRUCT. Each of these tables is created as a result of a specific operation to hold the information that is generated by that operation. For example, Paradox creates ANSWER tables to hold the results of queries. We'll explain each of these types of tables in more detail later in this book.

Images

When you are viewing or manipulating a table, Paradox displays an image of that table on the screen. Although the image looks like the actual table and contains all of the data that is in the table, it is technically not the table. While you are viewing or editing an image on the screen, the actual table remains secure on the disk. Until you use the [Do-It!] key or the DO-IT! command to make your changes permanent, nothing you do will affect the actual table. If you make changes that you don't want to keep, you can use the Cancel command, which is found on most Paradox menus.

The Table View

The default view in Paradox is the table view. When you look at a table in the table view, you see it as a columnar table, where each field is a column and each record is a row. For example, Figure 2-11 shows a table view image of the CUSTOMER table.

As you can see, the data contained in the table is displayed in columns and rows on the screen. While a table can be quite large, the screen can only show you a small part of it at a time. You can think of your screen as a window through which you can view your tables. For example, if you were to cut a small square hole in a piece of cardboard and place it over this page, you would be able to read through the hole, but you would need to move it around on the page in order to see the entire page. When you are viewing a Paradox table, you can move it around so that you can see all of the data it contains.

In addition, Paradox has a command called Image, which lets you change the way the image is displayed on the screen. Paradox also has a special key combination–[Ctrl]-[R]–which lets you change the order of the fields in the image. We'll explain how to change the image on the screen in Chapter 4.

The Form View

If you wish, you can view, enter, or edit your tables through a form like the one shown in Figure 2-12. Paradox automatically will create a default form for every table in your data base. In addition, you can create custom forms for your tables.

The main difference between the table view and the form view is the amount of information displayed on the screen at one time. In the table view, Paradox displays up to 22 records and as many fields as the screen will allow. In the form view, Paradox displays all of the fields in a record, but can only display one complete record at a time. We'll show you how to create and use forms in chapter 5.

Figure 2-12   The Form View

```
Viewing Customer table with form F: Record 1 of 20           Main  =▼

                                                        Customer  #    1
    Cust Number:       1245
    Last Name:    Priest
    First Name:   Stan
    Address:      123 Hill St
    City:         Louisville
    State:        KY
    Zip:          40212
```

Getting Help

Like the popular Lotus programs 1-2-3 and Symphony, Paradox has an on-line, context-sensitive help facility. To display a help screen at any time, you need only press [Help] ([F1]). For example, if you press [Help] immediately after you load Paradox, you'll see the help screen shown in Figure 2-13.

Figure 2-13   The Main Help Screen

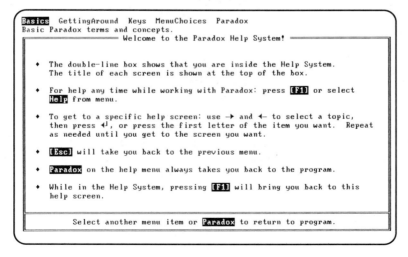

Most help screens have their own submenu that allows you to get more information about a topic. For instance, look at the menu options at the top of the screen in Figure 2-13: Basics, GettingAround, Keys, and MenuChoices. If you select one of these options (you make selections from Help menus in exactly the same way that you make selections from other Paradox menus), Paradox will present a new help screen that contains more information about the selected topic. For example, if you choose Basics from the main Help menu, Paradox will display the help screen shown in Figure 2-14. As you can see, this help screen offers its own menu, which allows you to dig even further into the selected topic. If, after you choose a menu option in the help facility, you want to move back to the previous menu, just press [**Esc**].

Figure 2-14 The Basics Help Screen

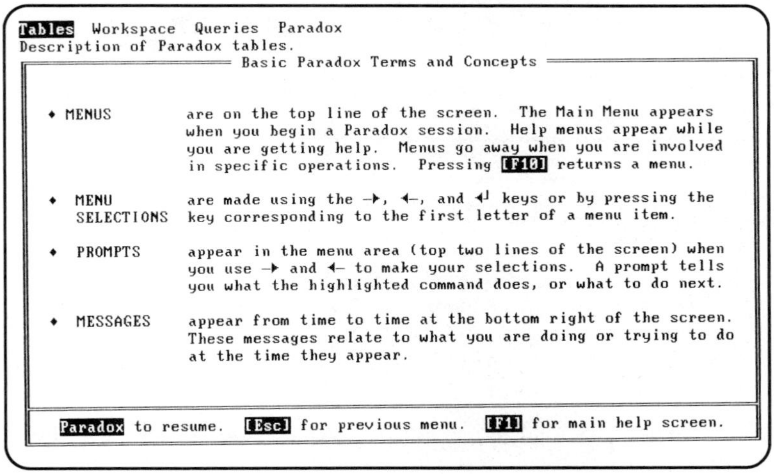

```
Tables  Workspace  Queries  Paradox
Description of Paradox tables.
================ Basic Paradox Terms and Concepts ================

   ♦ MENUS            are on the top line of the screen.  The Main Menu appears
                      when you begin a Paradox session.  Help menus appear while
                      you are getting help.  Menus go away when you are involved
                      in specific operations.  Pressing [F10] returns a menu.

   ♦ MENU             are made using the →, ←, and ↵ keys or by pressing the
     SELECTIONS       key corresponding to the first letter of a menu item.

   ♦ PROMPTS          appear in the menu area (top two lines of the screen) when
                      you use → and ← to make your selections.  A prompt tells
                      you what the highlighted command does, or what to do next.

   ♦ MESSAGES         appear from time to time at the bottom right of the screen.
                      These messages relate to what you are doing or trying to do
                      at the time they appear.


   Paradox to resume.   [Esc] for previous menu.   [F1] for main help screen.
```

Because Paradox's help facility is context-sensitive, the screen that appears when you press this key should offer help that is relevant to what you are currently doing with Paradox. This means that much of the time you won't need to use the Help menus to find the answer to your question. For example, if you press [Help] while you are editing a table, you'll see the help screen shown in Figure 2-15. Notice that this screen offers instructions about how to edit a table.

In addition to the [Help] key, most Paradox menus have a Help command. For example, notice the Help option in the Main menu in Figure 2-2. If you are working with a menu that contains a Help option, you can display a help screen just by choosing the Help option. As with the [Help] key, the screen that appears when you issue a Help command usually will be relevant to what you are doing with Paradox.

To exit from the help facility and return to the program, you can either select **Paradox** from the Help menu or press [**Do-It!**] ([F2]). No matter which method you use, when you exit from Help, Paradox will return you to whatever you were doing before you asked it to help you.

Figure 2-15   The Edit Help Screen

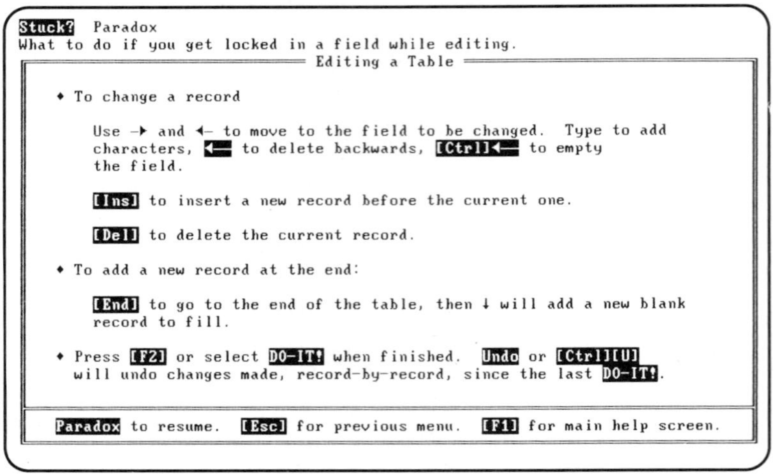

```
Stuck?  Paradox
What to do if you get locked in a field while editing.
═══════════════════ Editing a Table ═══════════════════
  • To change a record

      Use → and ← to move to the field to be changed.  Type to add
      characters, [←] to delete backwards, [Ctrl][←] to empty
      the field.

      [Ins] to insert a new record before the current one.

      [Del] to delete the current record.

  • To add a new record at the end:

      [End] to go to the end of the table, then ↓ will add a new blank
      record to fill.

  • Press [F2] or select DO-IT! when finished.  Undo or [Ctrl][U]
    will undo changes made, record-by-record, since the last DO-IT!.

Paradox to resume.   [Esc] for previous menu.   [F1] for main help screen.
```

The Paradox Tutorial

Another way of getting help is to run the Paradox tutorial on the Sample Tables disk. The tutorial contains several sample tables, scripts, and exercises, which you can perform to help you get acquainted with the program. The tutorial will introduce you to the basic commands and concepts you'll need to understand to get the most out of Paradox.

Earlier in this chapter, we told you how to copy the tutorial. To use it, you should follow the examples and instructions provided in the book *Introduction to Paradox*, which came with your program.

The PCCP

Unlike many programs, Paradox does a good job of configuring itself automatically for the computer hardware you're using. Many users will never need to go through a configuration process before they start using Paradox. However, if you have a black-and-white monitor connected to a color/graphics card, or if you're using a Compaq portable computer, your screen may be hard to read when you first load Paradox. Also, if you're using an IBM color/graphics adapter, you may see interference or "snow" on the screen.

If this is the case, you may need to run a special program, called the Paradox Custom Configuration Program (PCCP), before you do anything else. The PCCP allows you to customize Paradox to your computer system.

Ordinarily, you will not want to run the PCCP until you have become familiar with the program. For that reason, we'll save our main discussion of this tool for later. However, before we go on, let's look at how you can use the PCCP to customize your screen.

Getting Started 25

Loading PCCP

If you are using a hard disk system, the PCCP files were copied to the \paradox directory when you installed the program. To run the PCCP once you have loaded Paradox, issue the [**Menu**] **S**cripts **P**lay command. Next, Paradox will display the prompt that is shown in Figure 2-16.

Figure 2-16   The Script Prompt

```
Script:                                                          Main
Enter name of script to play, or press ← to see a list of scripts.
```

When you see this prompt, you should type **custom** and press ←. (You also can run the PCCP directly from DOS by typing **paradox custom** at the DOS prompt. If you use this method, you won't need to issue the [Menu] Scripts Play command.)

If you are using a floppy disk system, the files for the PCCP will be on the Installation Disk. To run the PCCP program, place the Installation Disk in drive B, then either enter the Paradox program, issue the [**Menu**] **S**cript **P**lay command, and run the custom script, or run the program directly from the DOS prompt. If you run the program from the DOS prompt, be sure to insert System Disk I in drive A.

Next, Paradox will display the prompt shown in Figure 2-17. (If you don't have a color/graphics card in your computer, you won't see this question.)

Figure 2-17   The PCCP Monitor Prompt

```
              Are you using a B&W monitor right now?
                   ( Y ← for yes, N ← for no )
```

If you are using a black-and-white monitor, you now should type **Y** and press ←. This choice automatically corrects the problems with your screen. If you're not using a black-and-white monitor, you should type **N** and press ←. After you make this choice, Paradox will display the menu shown in Figure 2-18.

Figure 2-18   The PCCP Menu

```
Video Reports AsciiConvert SetDirectory DO-IT! Cancel
Monitor, Snow or DisplayColor.
```

Making Changes

If the only reason you ran the PCCP was to tell Paradox that you are using a black-and-white monitor with a color/graphics card, you can issue the **DO-IT!** command at this point without making any additional changes. However, if you are using an IBM color/graphics adapter or a color monitor, you probably will want to make more changes in the video display before you leave the PCCP. For example, you may want to set the background color for Paradox. To do this, issue the **Video** command. After you issue this command, you'll see a submenu that looks like Figure 2-19.

Figure 2-19   The PCCP Video Menu

```
Monitor  Snow  DisplayColor
Mono, B&W, or Color.
```

The Monitor command allows you to select either a monochrome, black-and-white, or color monitor as the default monitor. If you issue the Monitor command, you will see another menu that looks like Figure 2-20.

Figure 2-20   The Monitor Menu

```
Mono  B&W  Color
Black and White monitor.
```

The current default monitor will be highlighted with the cursor. For example, if you entered Y at the monitor prompt earlier, the B&W option would be highlighted now. To change the default monitor, use ← and → to point to the option you want and press ↵. After you do this, the main PCCP menu will again appear on the screen.

The Snow command allows you to eliminate the interference ("snow") you can get when you are using an IBM color/graphics adapter. If you issue the Snow command, you will see the menu shown in Figure 2-21.

Figure 2-21   The Snow Menu

```
No  Yes
Let the snow show.
```

When you see this menu, the default (No) will be highlighted. To change the default, press the → key to place the cursor on Yes, and press ↵. After you do this, the main PCCP menu will appear on the screen.

The DisplayColor command lets you choose the background color for Paradox. After you issue the DisplayColor command, you'll see the menu of options shown in Figure 2-22.

Figure 2-22 The DisplayColor Menu

```
┌─────────────────────────────────────────────────────────────┐
│ DarkBlue  White  Green  Yellow  LightGrey  Cyan  Magenta  Brown │
│ Display Paradox with white text on a dark blue background.     │
└─────────────────────────────────────────────────────────────┘
```

As you can see, there are eight color combinations from which to choose. If you select DarkBlue, Paradox will be displayed with white text on a dark-blue background. If you select White, Paradox will be displayed with white text on a black background. The Green option displays Paradox with green text on a black background. The Yellow option displays Paradox with amber text on a black background. The LightGrey option displays Paradox with white text on a light-grey background. If you select Cyan, Paradox will be displayed with white text on a cyan background. If you select Magenta or Brown, Paradox will be displayed with white text on a magenta or brown background. To select an option, place the cursor on that option and press ↵. After you do this, the main PCCP menu will appear on the screen.

Leaving PCCP

Once you have made all of the changes you want with the Video command, Paradox will return to the main PCCP menu. When it does, you should issue the DO-IT! command to save your changes. After you issue the DO-IT! command, Paradox will ask you if you are using a hard disk. If you are, type **Y** and press ↵. After you do this, the changes you made in the PCCP will be saved to your hard disk. If you are using a floppy disk system, type **N** and press ↵. Paradox then will prompt you to insert System Disk I in drive B and will save the new settings to that disk. After saving your selections, Paradox will return to the DOS prompt. If you want to return to Paradox, you must reload it.

Command Line Configuration

If you do not want to change the default video settings with the PCCP, you can use a command at the DOS prompt to tell Paradox what kind of monitor you are using. For example, suppose you are temporarily using a black-and-white monitor. To tell Paradox about your monitor, you can type **paradox -b&w** at the DOS prompt, and then press ↵. This will set up the proper configuration without going through the PCCP. However, this command does not change the default settings. You will need to enter this command every time you load the program. Table 2-5 shows the command line configurations you can use.

You can use the command line configuration to tell Paradox what type of monitor you are using (-b&w, -mono, -color) or what type of adapter you have (-snow to eliminate interference when using an IBM color/graphics adapter). In addition, you can combine commands. For example, to tell Paradox that you are using a color monitor with an IBM color/graphics adapter, type **paradox -color -snow**, at the DOS prompt, and then press ↵.

Table 2-5 Command Line Configuration

Command	Result
paradox -b&w	Tells Paradox that you are using a black-and-white monitor with a color/graphics adapter.
paradox -mono	Tells Paradox that you are using a monochrome monitor with a monochrome adapter.
paradox -color	Tells Paradox that you are using a color monitor with a color/graphics adapter.
paradox -snow	Tells Paradox to eliminate interference when using an IBM color/graphics adapter.

We will discuss the other options on the PCCP menu in the chapters that deal with related topics, such as the report generator and the ExportImport command. If you need more information at this point, please refer to the index in this book or to Appendix C in the *Paradox User's Guide*.

Leaving Paradox

When you have finished a Paradox session, you should always issue the **[Menu]** **E**xit command to leave the program. When you issue this command, Paradox will present two options: No and Yes. If you do not want to leave Paradox, chose the **N**o option. If you do want to exit, choose **Y**es. When you do this, Paradox automatically will close all the tables you have opened, save any changes you have made, and return to DOS.

You should never turn off your computer without first exiting from Paradox. If you turn off the computer while Paradox is still active, you can damage your tables, resulting in the loss of data. Always use **[Menu]** **E**xit **Y**es to exit from Paradox.

Conclusion

In this chapter, we have given you a broad overview of the Paradox program. We've explained some terminology, introduced you to the concepts of tables and families, and shown you how to issue commands and get help.

In the remainder of the book, we'll build on this basic knowledge as we show you how to use Paradox. We'll begin in the next chapter by showing you how to create a table.

Chapter 3

Creating and Viewing Tables

In this chapter, we will show you how to create tables, how to enter data into tables, and how to edit the data in your tables. We will begin with the [Menu] Create command, which allows you to define the structure of tables. Then we'll show you how to enter data in tables. After that, we'll talk about the [Menu] View command, which allows you to view your tables on the screen. Finally, we'll show you how to edit your tables.

In Chapter 4, we will discuss advanced techniques for editing and data entry. In Chapter 5, we will show you how to design and use forms.

Creating Tables

Before you can do anything with Paradox, you must create one or more tables to hold your data. In this part of the chapter, we'll show you how to use the [Menu] Create command to create tables to store your information.

A Simple Example

Suppose you want to create the EMPLYEE table shown in Figure 3-1 on the next page. To begin, issue the [**Menu**] Create command. After you issue the command, Paradox will prompt you to enter a table name, as shown in Figure 3-2.

Figure 3-2 The Table Prompt

When you see this prompt, you should type the name you want Paradox to give to the new table you are creating. In this case, you should type **EMPLYEE** and press ↵.

Figure 3-1 The EMPLYEE Table

EMPLYEE Emp Number	Last Name	First Name	SS Number	Address	City	State	Zip	Phone	Date of Birth	Date of Hire	Exemptions	Salary
1	Jones	Dave	414-76-3421	4000 St. James Ct.	St. Matthews	KY	40207	(502) 245-6610	10/06/42	6/01/84	3	70,000.00
2	Cameron	Herb	321-65-8765	2331 Elm St.	Louisville	KY	40205	(502) 451-8765	11/24/29	6/01/84	4	58,000.00
4	Jones	Stewart	401-32-8721	4389 Oakbridge Rd.	Lyndon	KY	40222	(502) 452-1040	3/21/50	7/01/84	1	47,000.00
5	Roberts	Darlene	417-43-7777	451 Lone Pine Dr.	Lagrange	KY	40012	(502) 097-3215	9/24/60	11/01/84	3	14,000.00
6	Jones	Jean	414-87-9123	4000 St. James Ct.	St. Matthews	KY	40207	(502) 245-6610	5/14/43	12/01/84	0	33,999.99
8	Williams	Brenda	401-55-1567	555 Court St.	Anchorage	KY	40223	(502) 894-9761	1/12/28	1/01/85	4	40,000.00
9	Myers	Julie	314-38-9452	4512 Parkside Dr.	Louisville	KY	40206	(502) 454-5209	2/06/40	2/01/85	2	32,000.00
10	Link	Julie	345-75-1525	3215 Palm Ct.	Palo Alto	CA	94375	(400) 542-1940	6/03/33	4/01/85	3	30,000.00
12	Jackson	Mary	424-13-7621	7821 Clark Ave.	Clarksville	IN	47130	(012) 200-6754	8/12/56	4/01/85	1	21,000.00
14	Preston	Molly	451-00-3426	321 Indian Hills Rd.	Louisville	KY	40205	(502) 456-3256	4/17/66	7/01/85	0	14,750.00
15	Masters	Ron	317-65-4529	423 W. 72nd St.	New York	NY	10019	(212) 276-5470	12/31/44	7/01/85	2	30,000.00
13	Triplett	Judy	616-10-6610	140 Ashby St.	Clarksville	IN	47130	(012) 200-3301	8/12/50	4/10/85	2	15,750.00
16	Robertson	Kevin	415-24-6710	431 Bardstown Rd.	Elizabethtown	KY	40315	(502) 423-9823	3/16/25	7/15/85	1	37,000.00
17	Garrison	Robert	312-90-1479	55 Wheeler St.	Boston	MA	25607	(617) 543-4124	5/09/45	10/01/85	4	32,125.00
19	Gunn	Barbara	321-97-8632	541 Kentucky St.	New Albany	IN	47132	(012) 325-4709	5/10/50	11/01/85	2	17,500.00

The STRUCT Table

Next, Paradox will display the table STRUCT shown in Figure 3-3. STRUCT is a special temporary table that you use to define the structure of permanent tables. By filling in the STRUCT table, you define the structure of the table you are creating.

Figure 3-3   The STRUCT Table

```
Creating new Emplyee table                              Create
STRUCT        Field Name          Field Type
    1                                        ─── FIELD TYPES ───
                                         A_: Alphanumeric (ex: A25)
                                         Any combination of
                                         characters and spaces
                                         up to specified width.
                                         Maximum width is 255.

                                         N: Numbers with or without
                                            decimal digits.

                                         $: Dollar amounts.

                                         D: Dates in the form
                                            mm/dd/yy or dd-mon-yy.

                                         Use "*" after field type to
                                         show a key field (ex: A4*).
```

The first column under the word *STRUCT* on the left side of the screen is the field number column. You will not enter anything in this column. As you add fields to the table, Paradox will automatically number them consecutively for you.

The next column is the Field Name column. This is where you will enter the names of the fields that you want to include in the table you are creating. By typing the name of a field in this column, you tell Paradox to include a field with that name in the table you are creating.

The last column in the STRUCT table is the Field Type column. You will use this column to specify the field type for each field in the table. To specify the type of a field, you enter a letter in this column that represents the field type: *A* for alphanumeric fields, *N* for numeric fields, *S* for short number fields, *$* for dollar fields, and *D* for date fields. When you designate a field as an alphanumeric field, you must also specify the size, or width, of the field. To specify the width of a field, you must enter a number between 1 and 255 after the letter *A* in the Field Type column.

When you look at Figure 3-3, you will notice that Paradox displays a reminder of the field types on the right side of the screen. This reminder is only displayed when you are creating or restructuring tables.

Defining the Table

Now you are ready to create the EMPLYEE table. To begin, type **Emp Number** in the first and only row of the Field Name column. Next, press the ➡ key to move the cursor to the Field Type column and type **N** to designate this as a number field. After you do this, your screen will look like Figure 3-4.

Figure 3-4 Defining Fields

```
Creating new Emplyee table                                    Create
STRUCT       Field Name         Field Type
    1    Emp Number                N                ── FIELD TYPES ──
                                              A_: Alphanumeric (ex: A25)
                                              Any combination of
                                              characters and spaces
                                              up to specified width.
                                              Maximum width is 255.

                                              N: Numbers with or without
                                                 decimal digits.

                                              $: Dollar amounts.

                                              D: Dates in the form
                                                 mm/dd/yy or dd-mon-yy.

                                              Use "*" after field type to
                                              show a key field (ex: A4*).
```

Now press the ↵ key to move the cursor down one line, type **Last Name** in the Field Name column and **A10** in the Field Type column. The number 10 in this entry specifies the width of the Last Name field. Next, press ↵ again to move to the third row of STRUCT, type the field name **First Name**, press ➡ to move to the Field Type column, and type **A10**. Continue entering field names and field types in this way until your screen looks like Figure 3-5.

Figure 3-5 The Completed STRUCT Table

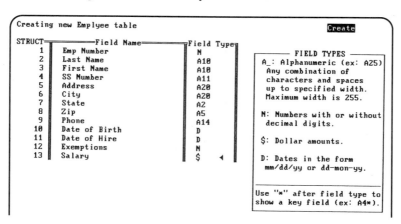

When you have filled in the STRUCT table, press [**Do-It!**] ([F2]), or issue the [**Menu**] DO-IT! command to save the new table. When you do this, Paradox will display the message *Creating Emplyee...* in the lower-right corner of the screen. After a few moments, Paradox will return to the main workspace. The new, empty table will be saved to disk under the name EMPLYEE.DB.

Notes

When Paradox prompts you for the name of the table you want to create, you should specify a name that does not already exist in the current directory. If you enter a name that is the same as the name of an existing table, Paradox will prompt you for confirmation, as shown in Figure 3-6. In addition, the message *TABLENAME table already exists* will appear at the bottom of the screen. If you select Cancel at this point, Paradox will return to the previous prompt so that you can erase the name you entered and enter another name. If you select Replace, Paradox will replace the old table with the new one you are creating. Be careful! All of the data in the old table will be lost if you choose Replace.

Figure 3-6 The Cancel/Replace Menu

```
Cancel  Replace                                              Main
A table with this name already exists, do not reuse name.
```

Field Names

In Paradox, field names can be up to 25 characters long and can include any printable character, except quotation marks ("), brackets ([]), braces ({}), and the combination ->. While field names can include spaces, you cannot begin a field name with a space.

You cannot use the same field name twice in the same table. If you attempt to enter a field name in a table twice, Paradox will display the message *Duplicate field name in the STRUCT table* when you press [Do-It!] to save the structure. Until you remove one of the duplicate field names, you won't be able to save the structure.

You should select field names that describe the contents of the fields they name. For example, the field name *Emp Number* in the EMPLYEE table tells you that that field will contain the unique employee number assigned to each employee in the company. The name *Salary* tells you that the Salary field will contain the salary of each employee.

While your field names can be up to 25 characters long, we suggest that you try to use field names that are as short as possible. When you view a table, Paradox will display the field slightly wider than its field name. By using short field names, you can get more of your table on the screen at one time. One way to achieve short field names is to use abbreviations of long words. If you choose the abbreviations carefully, you can save space without losing the benefit of clarity. For example, notice that we have used the abbreviation *Emp Number* for the name of the field that will contain the employee number data.

Field Types

Paradox recognizes five field types: alphanumeric, number, short number, dollar, and date. Let's look at each of these types in detail.

Alphanumeric (A) Fields

An alphanumeric field can contain entries that are made up of letters, numbers, and special characters. To define a field as an alphanumeric field, you should enter an *A* in the Field Type column of the STRUCT table next to that field's name. In addition, you must specify the width of the field by entering a number between 1 and 255 in this column next to the letter *A*. The number you enter sets the maximum number of characters that can be entered into that field. For example, look at the Last Name row in the STRUCT table in Figure 3-5. The entry A10 in the Field Type column tells Paradox that you want to create an alphanumeric field with a maximum width of ten characters.

If you do not enter a length for an alphanumeric field, Paradox will display the message *Enter length of alphanumeric field; for example A12* at the bottom of the screen when you attempt to move the cursor out of that field. You will not be allowed to leave the Field Type column until you have entered an acceptable width.

Alphanumeric fields are the only fields to which you must assign a length. Paradox will automatically set the length for number, dollar, short number, and date fields.

Since alphanumeric fields can contain numbers, letters, and special characters, you may wonder why you shouldn't make all of your fields alphanumeric. The reasons are simple. While alphanumeric fields will accept any type of entry, Paradox does not allow you to perform math on the entries in alphanumeric fields. Also, making a field alphanumeric restricts the ways that field can be used to make selections. In general, you should only use the alphanumeric field type for fields that contain letters only or letters and numbers.

Number (N) Fields

To designate a field as a number field, enter an **N** in the Field Type column for that field in the STRUCT table. A number field can contain only numbers. Number fields can store numbers as small as 10^{-307} and as large as 10^{308} with up to 15 significant digits. For example, you could enter the numbers 1234, .004356, and 123456789.012345 in a number field. Numbers with more than 15 significant digits are automatically rounded and stored in scientific notation. For example, the number 1234567891234556789 would be stored as 1.23456789123457E+17. It would be displayed on the screen as a series of asterisks. To view the number, you would need to press [Field View] ([Alt]-[F5]). We'll show you how to do this later in this chapter.

By default, Paradox displays number fields without commas and with up to two decimal places. For example, the number 1,234.00 would be displayed as 1234 in a number field. The number 1,234.56 would be displayed as 1234.56, and the number 1,234.50 would be displayed as 1234.5. Negative numbers are preceded by a minus sign (-).

Short Number (S) Fields

To designate a field as a short number field, type an **S** in the Field Type column of the STRUCT table. Short number fields are special number fields that can contain only whole numbers between -32,767 and 32,767. In addition, you cannot use any of Paradox's field formats (which you'll learn about in Chapter 4) in short number fields.

The only advantage to using short number fields instead of number fields is that short number fields require less disk space. In general, because of their limited range, we recommend that you only use short number fields in very large tables where conserving space is important. However, one excellent use of the short number field type is in fields that number the entries in a table. For example, we might have used the short number type for the Emp Number field in EMPLYEE. Since this type of field only contains integers, and rarely contains an entry greater than 32,767, the normal short number type limitations are not a problem.

Dollar ($) Fields

To designate a field as a dollar field, you should enter a dollar sign ($) in the Field Type column of that field in the STRUCT table. Like number and short number fields, dollar fields can contain only numbers.

Dollar fields are similar to number fields, with a couple of important differences. First, numbers in dollar fields are displayed rounded to two decimal places, and commas are inserted in the numbers between the hundreds and thousands places, thousands and millions places, and so on. For example, the number 1234.567 would be displayed as 1,234.57 in a dollar field. If the number does not have a decimal portion, Paradox will add two zeros to the right of the decimal for display purposes. For instance, the number 1234 would be displayed as 1,234.00 in a dollar field. In addition, negative numbers in dollar fields are displayed in parentheses instead of being preceded by a minus sign. For example, the value -1234.56 would be displayed as (1234.56) in a dollar field.

It is important that you understand that the formatting that occurs when you enter a number in a dollar field affects only the display of the number and not the number itself. In other words, although the number 1234.567 would be displayed as 1,234.57 in a dollar field, the actual value in the field would still be 1234.567. If you used this number in a calculation (we'll show you how to do that in a later chapter), Paradox would base the calculation on the full value, 1234.567, and not on the rounded value, 1,234.57.

Date (D) Fields

Date fields allow you to store dates in your Paradox tables. To designate a field as a date field, you should enter a **D** in the Field Type column for that field in the STRUCT table. A date field can contain any valid date between January 1, 100, and December 31, 9999.

You can enter or display dates in two formats. The default date format is MM/DD/YY. To enter the date April 9, 1986, into a table in this form, you would type 4/09/86 or 4/9/86 (you don't need to type the 0 if you don't want to do this). Alternatively, you can enter dates in the form DD-Mon-YY. For example, to enter the date 11/24/86 in this form, you would type 24-Nov-86. No matter how you enter the date, however, Paradox will display it in the form MM/DD/YY. For instance, if you enter the date 24-Nov-86 in a date field, Paradox will display that date as 11/24/86.

Just how you specify the year portion of a date depends on which century that date falls in. For dates between January 1, 1900, and December 31, 1999, you need only type the last two digits of the year. To enter the date May 13, 1987, you would type 31-May-87 or 5/31/87. For dates after December 31, 1999, you must type all four digits. For example, to enter the date March 21, 2001 in a table, you would type 3/21/2001 or 21-Mar-2001. For dates before January 1, 1900, you must type the entire year number. For example, to enter the date June 5, 1895, you'd type 6/5/1895 or 5-Jun-1895.

Paradox automatically checks every date you enter to be sure that it is valid. A valid date is any date that appears on a calendar, including leap days. For instance, both 3/31/45 and 6-Oct-57 are valid dates. An invalid date is one which doesn't appear on a calendar, such as 3/32/86, 2/30/57, or 13/1/85. If you attempt to enter an invalid date into a date field, Paradox will display the message *No such date* at the screen's lower-right corner.

Later in this book, we'll show you how to perform arithmetic using the entries in date fields and how to use date fields in queries to select records.

Moving Around on the Screen

When you are creating a new table, you will use the keys shown in Table 3-1 to move the cursor around in the STRUCT table. For the most part, the effect of pressing each of these keys should be clear from the table. However, there are a couple of quirks that are worth pointing out.

Table 3-1   Cursor Movement Keys

Key	Function
←	Moves the cursor left one column.
→	Moves the cursor right one column.
↑	Moves the cursor up one row.
↓	Moves the cursor down one row.
[Home]	Moves the cursor to the first row in the current column.
[Ctrl]-[Home]	Moves the cursor to the first column on the same row.
[End]	Moves the cursor to the last row in the current column.
[Ctrl]-[End]	Moves the cursor to the last column on the same row.
[Pg Dn]	Moves the cursor down one screen.
[Pg Up]	Moves the cursor up one screen.
[Shift]-[Tab]	Moves the cursor left one column.
[Tab]	Moves the cursor right one column.

First, if the cursor is in the Field Type column of STRUCT, pressing → will wrap the cursor around to the first column of the next row. If the cursor is in the Field Type column of the last row in STRUCT, pressing → will add a new row to STRUCT and position the cursor in the first column of that row. The same is true for the [Tab] and ↵ keys, which have the same effect as → when you are working in STRUCT.

Similarly, pressing ← when the cursor is in the first column of the STRUCT table will move it to the Field Type column of the previous row. If the cursor is in the first column of the first row, pressing ← has no effect.

In addition, if the cursor is in the last row of STRUCT, pressing the ↓ key adds a row to STRUCT and positions the cursor in the Field Name column of that row.

For the most part, cursor control keys work the same way in all Paradox modes. We will point out differences as we explore each feature of the program.

Editing the STRUCT Table

From time to time, you'll make errors as you are making entries in the STRUCT table. Fortunately, it's very easy to edit the contents of the STRUCT table. Let's look at a few examples of how you can use the keys shown in Table 3-1 to edit the STRUCT table.

Changing an Entry

If you make a typing error while making an entry in the STRUCT table, you can press [Backspace] to erase the error and then type the correct character or characters. For example, suppose that, as you are defining the Emp Number field, you type *Emp Numbr* accidentally. Assuming that you haven't moved the cursor, you can press **[Backspace]** once to erase the *r* and then type **er**. If you have moved the cursor, just move it back to the Field Name column for the Emp Number field before you press [Backspace].

If the error is near the beginning of the entry or if the entire entry is an error, you can press [Ctrl]-[Backspace] to erase it entirely and then start over from scratch. For example, suppose that when you are defining the Emp Number field, you absent-mindedly type *Cust Number*. Instead of pressing [Backspace] several times to erase the entry, you could press **[Ctrl]-[Backspace]** once to erase the whole entry and then you could type **Emp Number** in the empty field.

Inserting a Row

If you forget to define a field, you can use the [Ins] key to insert a blank row in the STRUCT table, and then enter the missing field definition in that row. For example, suppose that while you were defining the EMPLYEE table, you left out the Address field. To add the Address field to the table definition, move the cursor to the City row of the

STRUCT table and press **[Ins]** to insert a blank row. Figure 3-7 shows the screen at this point. Now, you can type **Address** in the Field Name column of the new row and **A20** in the Field Type column to define the Address field.

Figure 3-7 Inserting a Row

```
Creating new Emplyee table                                          Create
STRUCT       Field Name       Field Type
  1    Emp Number              N                 FIELD TYPES
  2    Last Name               A10         A_: Alphanumeric (ex: A25)
  3    First Name              A10         Any combination of
  4    SS Number               A11         characters and spaces
  5                                        up to specified width.
  6    City                    A20         Maximum width is 255.
  7    State                   A2
  8    Zip                     A5          N: Numbers with or without
  9    Phone                   A14         decimal digits.
 10    Date of Birth           D
 11    Date of Hire            D           $: Dollar amounts.
 12    Exemptions              N
 13    Salary                  $           D: Dates in the form
 14                                        mm/dd/yy or dd-mon-yy.

                                           Use "*" after field type to
                                           show a key field (ex: A4*).
```

Deleting a Row

If you find that you have entered a field in the STRUCT table by accident, you can delete that field by positioning the cursor on it and pressing [Del]. For example, suppose that in creating EMPLYEE, you accidentally included a field named MI (for middle initial) between the Last Name and First Name fields. Figure 3-8 shows this STRUCT table. To remove this unwanted field, just move the cursor to it and press [Del]. The finished STRUCT table will look just like Figure 3-5.

Figure 3-8 Deleting a Row

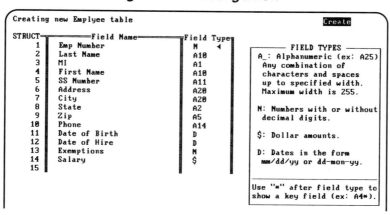

Restructuring Tables

All of the techniques presented so far assume that you catch your mistakes before you press [Do-It!] to save the structure of your table. If you don't realize your mistake until after you have saved the structure, you can still correct the error. To do so, however, you must use the [Menu] Modify Restructure command. We will explain this command in Chapter 6.

The Create Menu

When you press [Menu] ([F10]) while you are creating a table, the Create menu will appear at the top of the screen. Figure 3-9 shows the Create menu.

Figure 3-9 The Create Menu

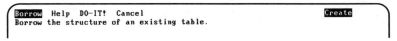

The Help command on this menu should already be familiar to you. As you learned in Chapter 2, most of Paradox's menus offer a Help option. The Help command allows you to access Paradox's context-sensitive help facility. You can also access help by pressing [Help] ([F1]).

The DO-IT! Command

The DO-IT! command also appears on many Paradox menus. Although the precise effect of the DO-IT! command varies from menu to menu, its general purpose is always to process whatever action it is that you are taking. When you choose DO-IT! from the Create menu, Paradox creates the table you have defined in the STRUCT table and returns to the main workspace. Pressing the [Do-It!] key ([F2]) has the same effect as choosing the DO-IT! command.

The Cancel Command

The [Menu] Cancel command lets you leave the Create menu and return to the main workspace without saving your work. When you issue this command, Paradox "forgets" the entries you have made in the STRUCT table and returns to the main workspace without creating a table. Paradox does not prompt you for confirmation before it cancels the creation process. However, the message *Cancelling table creation...* will appear in the lower-right corner of the screen. Pressing [Ctrl]-[Break] has the same effect as issuing the [Menu] Cancel command.

The Borrow Command

The [Menu] Borrow command allows you to borrow the structure of one or more existing tables to create a new table. For example, suppose you want to create a simple table named ADDRESS to store the names, addresses, and phone numbers of your business contacts. You want this table to include eight fields: Last Name, First Name, Spouse, Address, City, State, Zip, and Phone.

To create the ADDRESS table, issue the [**Menu**] Create command and type **ADDRESS** when Paradox asks you for the name of the new table. When the STRUCT table appears on the screen, you can do one of two things. First, you could begin defining the structure of ADDRESS in the same way you defined EMPLYEE: by typing the name of each field in the Field Name column of the STRUCT table and then entering the type for each field in the Field Type column. However, there is an easier way. You might have noticed that all of the fields you want to include in ADDRESS (except for Spouse) are also defined in EMPLYEE. Instead of creating ADDRESS from scratch, therefore, you can create it by borrowing the structure of EMPLYEE.

To do this, issue the [**Menu**] **B**orrow command. After you issue the command, Paradox will prompt you to enter the name of the table whose structure you want to borrow. When you see this prompt, type **EMPLYEE** and press ↵. Paradox will then add the fields from the EMPLYEE table to the STRUCT table as shown in Figure 3-10.

Figure 3-10 Borrowing the Structure of EMPLYEE

```
┌─Creating new Address table─────────────────────────────────────Create─┐
│ STRUCT─────────Field Name───────Field Type                            │
│    1 │ Emp Number         │ N      │      ──── FIELD TYPES ────       │
│    2 │ Last Name          │ A10    │   A_: Alphanumeric (ex: A25)     │
│    3 │ First Name         │ A10    │      Any combination of          │
│    4 │ SS Number          │ A11    │      characters and spaces       │
│    5 │ Address            │ A20    │      up to specified width.      │
│    6 │ City               │ A20    │      Maximum width is 255.       │
│    7 │ State              │ A2     │                                  │
│    8 │ Zip                │ A5     │   N: Numbers with or without     │
│    9 │ Phone              │ A14    │      decimal digits.             │
│   10 │ Date of Birth      │ D      │                                  │
│   11 │ Date of Hire       │ D      │   $: Dollar amounts.             │
│   12 │ Exemptions         │ N      │                                  │
│   13 │ Salary             │ $      │   D: Dates in the form           │
│   14 │                    │        │      mm/dd/yy or dd-mon-yy.      │
│                                    │                                  │
│                                    │   Use "*" after field type to    │
│                                    │   show a key field (ex: A4*).    │
└───────────────────────────────────────────────────────────────────────┘
```

Since ADDRESS and EMPLYEE do not have identical structures, you now need to do a bit of editing. First, move the cursor down to the line of STRUCT that contains the field name *Address* and press [**Ins**] to insert a new row. Then type **Spouse** in the Field Name column and **A10** in the Field Type column to add the Spouse field to the table. Next, move down to the Date of Birth field and press [**Del**] four times to delete the Date of Birth, Date of Hire, Exemptions, and Salary fields.

If you wish, you can also change the type of any field in the STRUCT table or change the length of any alphanumeric field. For example, to change the length of the Last Name field in the ADDRESS definition to 15 characters, just move the cursor to the Field Type column of the Last Name field in STRUCT, press [Backspace] once to erase the 0 in the length definition, type 5, and press ↵. Figure 3-11 shows the completed STRUCT table.

Figure 3-11   The Completed STRUCT Table

```
Creating new Address table                                      Create
STRUCT       Field Name           Field Type
    1    Emp Number                   N              ── FIELD TYPES ──
    2    Last Name                    A15  ◄
    3    First Name                   A10         A_: Alphanumeric (ex: A25)
    4    SS Number                    A11           Any combination of
    5    Spouse                       A10           characters and spaces
    6    Address                      A20           up to specified width.
    7    City                         A20           Maximum width is 255.
    8    State                        A2
    9    Zip                          A5          N: Numbers with or without
   10    Phone                        A14           decimal digits.
   11
                                                  $: Dollar amounts.

                                                  D: Dates in the form
                                                     mm/dd/yy or dd-mon-yy.

                                                  Use "*" after field type to
                                                  show a key field (ex: A4*).
```

When you have made the changes you want, you should press [**Do-It!**] ([F2]) or issue the [**Menu**] DO-IT! command to save the table and return to the main workspace.

Entering Data

When you press [DO-IT!] ([F2]) or issue the [Menu] DO-IT! command to save a newly created table, Paradox saves an empty table and returns to the main workspace. In order to enter data into the table, you must issue the [Menu] Modify DataEntry command. When you issue this command and specify the name of the table into which you want to enter data, Paradox will bring a special temporary table named ENTRY into view. You should type the data you want to store in the main table into the fields of ENTRY. When you have entered all of your data into ENTRY, you should press [Do-It!]. When you press this key, Paradox copies the entries you have made in ENTRY into the permanent table, empties ENTRY, and returns you to the main workspace.

An Example

For example, suppose you want to enter the records shown in Figure 3-1 into the EMPLYEE table you just created. To do this, issue the [**Menu**] Modify DataEntry command. After you issue the command, Paradox will prompt you to enter the name of the table into which you want to enter data. When you see this prompt, type **EMPLYEE**, and press ↵. Paradox then will display the temporary ENTRY table shown in Figure 3-12.

Figure 3-12 The ENTRY Table

The ENTRY Table

When you use the [Menu] Modify DataEntry command to enter records into a table, you will first enter those records into a temporary table named ENTRY. Just as you use the STRUCT table to create permanent tables, you will use the ENTRY table to add records to permanent tables. The purpose of this organization is to protect existing records in the permanent table while you are entering new records.

The structure of ENTRY always matches the structure of whatever table it is that you are entering records into. When you look at Figure 3-12, you will notice that the names of the EMPLYEE table fields are displayed horizontally across the top of the screen. You also will notice a current operation status message (*DataEntry for Emplyee table*), a Cursor Location indicator (*Record 1 of 1*), and a Menu indicator (*DataEntry*).

The leftmost column of the table (under the word ENTRY) is a record number column. Paradox will automatically number the records for you as you enter them–you do not need to enter anything in this column.

Entering Data

When the ENTRY table first appears on the screen, the cursor will be in the first field of the table (in this case, the Emp Number field). To begin entering records, just start typing. For example, to enter the first record, type **1**, and press the → key or the ↵ key. When you do this, Paradox will enter a 1 in the Emp Number column and move to the Last Name column. Now type **Jones** and press → or ↵ again. Paradox will add the name to the field and move the cursor to the next field. Figure 3-13 shows the screen at this point.

Figure 3-13 Adding Records to ENTRY

You should continue to enter information in each column until you have completed the first record. To do this, type **Dave** in the First Name field, press ↵ or →, type **414-76-3421** in the SS Number field, press ↵ or → again, and so on.

Notice that as you move the cursor to the right through the field of EMPLYEE that the leftmost fields disappear off the left side of the screen. This occurs because, like most tables you'll create, EMPLYEE and its ENTRY table are too wide to be viewed in their entirety on the screen at once. When you're viewing the leftmost fields of the EMPLYEE table, the rightmost fields, such as Salary, are out of view. When you press → to move to the right, the leftmost fields disappear as the rightmost fields come into view on the screen.

After you type the information in the Salary column and press the → key, Paradox will move the cursor down one line and back to the Emp Number field. Figure 3-14 shows how your screen will look at this point.

Figure 3-14 Adding Records to ENTRY

You now should enter all of the remaining records from Figure 3-1 into your new table, using the same technique you used to enter the record for Dave Jones.

Cursor Control

Table 3-2 shows the keys you'll use to move the cursor while you are entering data. When you look at the table, you'll notice that it is very similar to Table 3-1. As you work with Paradox, you will discover that most of the keys have the same or very similar functions, regardless of what you're doing in the program. This consistency will help you to learn the basics of the program very quickly.

If the cursor is in the rightmost field of the table, pressing the →, [Tab] or ↵ keys moves the cursor to the first field of the next record. If the cursor is in the last field of the last record, pressing any of these keys will insert a new row in the table and move the cursor to the first field of that row. If the cursor is in the last record of the table, pressing the ↓ key inserts a new record in the table.

Table 3-2   Cursor Control Keys

Key	Function
←	Moves the cursor left one field.
→	Moves the cursor right one field.
↑	Moves the cursor up one record.
↓	Moves the cursor down one record.
[Pg Up]	Moves the cursor up one screenful of records.
[Pg Dn]	Moves the cursor down one screenful of records.
[Home]	Moves the cursor to the first record of the current field.
[End]	Moves the cursor to the last record of the current field.
[Tab]	Moves the cursor right one field (same as →).
[Shift]-[Tab]	Moves the cursor left one field (same as ←).
[Enter]	Moves the cursor right one field (same as →).
[Ctrl]-←	Moves the cursor left one screen.
[Ctrl]-→	Moves the cursor right one screen.
[Ctrl]-[Home]	Moves the cursor to the first field of the current record.

Ending DataEntry

To end a data entry session, either issue the [Menu] DO-IT! command (or press [Do-It!]) or issue the [Menu] Cancel **Y**es command. You cannot end a session in any other way.

[Do-It!] and [Menu] DO-IT!

Pressing [**Do-It!**] ([F2]) or issuing the [Menu] DO-IT! command tells Paradox to end the data entry session, copy the records from the ENTRY table to the permanent table whose name you supplied at the beginning of the data entry session, empty the ENTRY table, and then bring the permanent table into view on the screen. For example, when you have finished entering records into EMPLOYEE, you should press [**Do-It!**] ([F2]) or issue the [**Menu**] DO-IT! command. When you do, Paradox will display the message *Adding records from Entry to Emplyee...* at the bottom of the screen as it adds the records from ENTRY to EMPLYEE. After a few moments, Paradox will display the EMPLYEE table in the workspace, as shown in Figure 3-15.

Figure 3-15   The EMPLYEE Table

```
Viewing Employee table: Record 1 of 15                          Main
┌────────┬─Emp Number─┬─Last Name─┬─First Name─┬─SS Number──┬─────────Addre
│EMPLYEE │            │           │            │            │
│   1    │     1      │  Jones    │  Dave      │ 414-76-3421│ 4000 St. Ja
│   2    │     2      │  Cameron  │  Herb      │ 321-65-8765│ 2331 Elm St
│   3    │     4      │  Jones    │  Stewart   │ 401-32-8721│ 4389 Oakbri
│   4    │     5      │  Roberts  │  Darlene   │ 417-43-7777│ 451 Lone Pi
│   5    │     6      │  Jones    │  Jean      │ 414-07-9123│ 4000 St. Ja
│   6    │     8      │  Williams │  Brenda    │ 401-55-1567│ 555 Court S
│   7    │     9      │  Myers    │  Julie     │ 314-38-9452│ 4512 Parksi
│   8    │    10      │  Link     │  Julie     │ 345-75-1525│ 3215 Palm C
│   9    │    12      │  Jackson  │  Mary      │ 424-13-7621│ 7821 Clark
│  10    │    14      │  Preston  │  Molly     │ 451-00-3426│ 321 Indian
│  11    │    15      │  Masters  │  Ron       │ 317-65-4529│ 423 W. 72nd
│  12    │    13      │  Triplett │  Judy      │ 616-10-6610│ 14D Ashby S
│  13    │    16      │  Robertson│  Kevin     │ 415-24-6710│ 431 Bardsto
│  14    │    17      │  Garrison │  Robert    │ 312-98-1479│ 55 Wheeler
│  15    │    19      │  Gunn     │  Barbara   │ 321-97-8632│ 541 Kentuck
```

The Cancel Command

The Cancel command cancels all of the changes you have made during the current data entry session and returns you to the main workspace. For example, suppose you are adding records to the EMPLYEE table and you discover a large number of errors. You could edit the records in the ENTRY table before adding them to EMPLYEE; however, you may find it easier to cancel the entire data entry operation and start over. To do this, issue the [**Menu**] Cancel command. After you issue the Cancel command, Paradox will prompt you for confirmation, as shown in Figure 3-16.

Figure 3-16   Confirming the Cancel Command

If you issue the No command at this point, Paradox will return to the DataEntry menu so that you can make another selection. If you issue the Yes command, Paradox will cancel all of the changes you have made and return to the main workspace.

You can also cancel the operation by pressing [Ctrl]-[Break]. However, if you use this method, Paradox will not prompt you for confirmation. For this reason, we suggest that you always use the [Menu] Cancel command.

Editing During DataEntry

It is inevitable that you will make errors as you enter records into your tables. As you might expect, Paradox offers you several ways to edit the entries you make in tables. In this section, we'll cover techniques that you can use to edit entries while you are performing data entry. Later in the chapter, we'll show you how to edit records that you have already entered into a permanent table.

Table 3-3 shows the keys you will use to edit entries in a Paradox table. Let's consider a few examples of how these keys work.

Table 3-3   Editing Keys

Key	Function
[Ins]	Inserts a new record in the table.
[Del]	Deletes a record from the table.
[Backspace]	Erases a character in the current field.
[Ctrl]-[Backspace]	Erases all of the characters in the current field.
[Undo] ([Ctrl]-[U])	Undoes the last change made.

Changing an Entry

If you make an error while you are typing an entry, you can press [Backspace] to erase the mistake. For example, suppose you are entering a record into EMPLYEE. As you make the Last Name field entry, you type *Johnsn* instead of *Johnson*, as shown in Figure 3-17. Provided that the cursor is still in the Last Name field, you can correct this error by pressing **[Backspace]** once to erase the letter *n*, and then typing **on**.

Figure 3-17   Changing an Entry

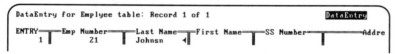

If the error is so great that you want to start from scratch, you can press [Ctrl]-[Backspace] to erase the entire entry, then retype the entry. For example, suppose that as you enter the Address field for the record in Figure 3-18, you type *2134 First St.* instead of *1234 First St.* To correct this error, you could press [Backspace] 14 times to erase the entire entry and then retype it. An easier way, however, would be to press [Ctrl]-[Backspace] once to erase the entire contents of the field, as shown in Figure 3-19, and then retype the entry.

Figure 3-18   Correcting Errors

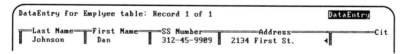

Figure 3-19   Using [Ctrl]-[Backspace]

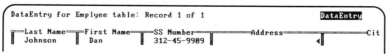

The Field View

If you make an error in an entry, but you don't want to erase the entry to make the correction, you can use the Paradox field view. The field view allows you to edit one entry at a time.

To enter the field view, you position the cursor on the field you want to edit and press [Field View] ([Alt]-[F5]). After you press [Field View], the cursor will change to a rectangular box. When you are using [Field View], the effect of the cursor control keys changes. For example, in the field view, the → key moves the cursor one character to the right and the ← key moves the cursor one character to the left. The [Home] key moves the cursor to the first character in the field, while the [End] key moves the cursor to the last character. In fact, once you are in the field view, you cannot move the cursor out of the current record until you press ↵ to leave the field view. Table 3-4 summarizes the effect of the cursor keys in the field view.

Table 3-4 Cursor Keys in the Field View

Key	Function
←	Moves the cursor left one character.
→	Moves the cursor right one character.
[Home]	Moves the cursor to the beginning of the current entry.
[End]	Moves the cursor to the end of the current entry.
[Ctrl]-←	Moves the cursor one half field to the left.
[Ctrl]-→	Moves the cursor one half field to the right.
[Ctrl]-[Home]	Same as [Home].
[Ctrl]-[End]	Same as [End].
↵	Ends the field view.
[Del]	Deletes the character at the cursor.

The ↑, ↓, [Pg Up], and [Pg Dn] keys have no effect in the field view. Since characters are automatically inserted at the cursor as you type them, the [Ins] key also has no effect in the field view.

For example, suppose that as you enter the City field for the record in Figure 3-19, you type *Phialdelphia* instead of *Philadelphia*. You could correct this error using the [Backspace] or [Ctrl]-[Backspace] techniques, but you might want to use the [Field View] key instead. To do this, first press the **[Field View]** key ([Alt]-[F5]) to enter the field view. Figure 3-20 shows the resulting screen. As you can see, the cursor has changed into a rectangular box.

Figure 3-20 Field View

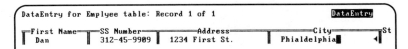

Now, press ← several times. You will notice that the cursor remains in the City field and moves to the left as you press this key. If you press →, the cursor will move to the right, one character at a time, in the City field. If you press [Home], the cursor will move to the beginning of the entry in the field. If you press [End], it will jump to the end of the entry.

Using the cursor movement keys, move the cursor to the first *a* in the entry you typed. Now, press [**Del**] twice to delete the letters *a* and *l*, and then type **la** to complete the entry. Figure 3-21 shows the screen at this point.

Figure 3-21   Correcting Errors with the Field View

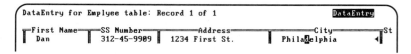

Now, press ↵ to leave the field view. Once you are out of the field view, you can resume moving the cursor and making entries as you normally would.

There are times when you must use [Field View] to view or edit a field. For example, we noted earlier that Paradox will display very large numbers as a series of asterisks. When it does, you must use the field view to view or edit the data in the field. Alternatively, you can issue the [Menu] Image ColumnSize command and make the column wider. We'll show you how to do this later in this chapter.

Deleting a Record

If you make errors in several entries in a record—or if you enter a record that you did not mean to enter—you can delete the entire record by positioning the cursor on any field of that record and pressing [Del]. For example, suppose you have entered the records shown in Figure 3-22 into the ENTRY table for EMPLYEE, then discover that the second record should not have been entered. To remove this record from the table, move the cursor to any field in the second record and press [**Del**]. When you press this key, Paradox will remove the current record from the ENTRY table. The resulting table will look like Figure 3-23.

Figure 3-22   The ENTRY Table

DataEntry for Emplyee table: Record 4 of 4					DataEntry
ENTRY	Emp Number	Last Name	First Name	SS Number	Addre
1	21	Johnson	Dan	312-45-9989	1234 First
2	22	Miller	Glen	414-34-1234	1776 Second
3	23	Samuels	Sam	401-12-5555	#12 Downing
4	24	Diller	Mike	401-00-7654	666 Hall La

Figure 3-23 Deleting a Record

```
DataEntry for Emplyee table: Record 2 of 3              DataEntry
ENTRY    Emp Number    Last Name    First Name    SS Number        Addre
   1         21          Johnson       Dan         312-45-9989    1234 First
   2         23          Samuels       Sam         401-12-5555    #12 Downing
   3         24          Diller        Mike        401-00-7654    666 Hall La
```

Inserting a New Record

If you need to add a record in the middle of the ENTRY table, you can use the [Ins] key to insert a new, blank record in the table. For example, suppose you need to enter a new record between the first two records in Figure 3-23. To do this, move the cursor to any field in what is currently the second record in ENTRY and press **[Ins]**. Immediately, Paradox will insert a blank record in the ENTRY table, as shown in Figure 3-24. Now, you can enter the new record in this blank row.

Figure 3-24 Inserting a Record

```
DataEntry for Emplyee table: Record 2 of 4              DataEntry
ENTRY    Emp Number    Last Name    First Name    SS Number        Addre
   1         21          Johnson       Dan         312-45-9989    1234 First
   2
   3         23          Samuels       Sam         401-12-5555    #12 Downing
   4         24          Diller        Mike        401-00-7654    666 Hall La
```

Although it is perfectly acceptable to insert rows in the ENTRY table, usually there is no need to do so. Usually the order of the records in ENTRY is not really very important.

The Undo Command

Paradox 1.1 offers a command, Undo, that allows you to undo the actions you made one by one. The Undo command can be used to delete from a table entries that you have made accidentally, to undo a change that you made to an entry, or to recover a record that you deleted by mistake (Paradox 1.0 does not offer this capability).

You can issue the Undo command by pressing [Menu] while performing data entry and choosing Undo from the DataEntry menu, or by pressing the [Undo] key ([Ctrl]-[U]). While you are entering data, issuing the Undo command will "undo" the last change you made to the ENTRY table. If the last change you made was to enter a new record, that new record will be deleted. If the last change you made was to edit an entry in the table, that entry will be restored to its previous value. If the last change was to insert or delete a record, then issuing the Undo command will restore the table to its original dimensions. Issuing the Undo command a second time will undo the second-most recent change you made to the table. Issuing the command a third time will undo the third-most recent change, and so on.

Example

For example, suppose you are working in the ENTRY table shown in Figure 3-25, and you accidentally press [Del], thereby deleting a record. Figure 3-26 shows the new ENTRY table with the deleted record. To restore the record to the table, press **[Undo]** ([Ctrl]-[U]). Immediately, Paradox will undo the deletion. The message area at the bottom of the screen will display the message *Record 3 reinserted*.

Figure 3-25 The ENTRY Table

Figure 3-26 Deleting a Record

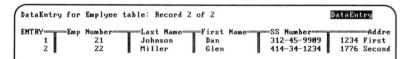

Notes

There are a couple of important things to keep in mind about Undo. First, you can't reverse Undo. Once you've used Undo, the only way to get back to your original is to repeat the action. For example, suppose you use the [Undo] key to delete a record you think was entered erroneously. If you then discover that the record was indeed correct, there's only one way to get it back—by retyping it from scratch.

As you are performing data entry, Paradox maintains a transaction log of your actions. A "transaction" begins when you move the cursor into a new record and ends when you move the cursor out of that record. When you use the Undo command, Paradox simply reverses the effect of the last transaction.

Exactly how many transactions Paradox can record in its log depends on the amount of memory in your computer. In most applications, you will never exceed the capacity of the log. However, in a few cases, it is possible that you will reach the limit. In that event, Paradox will warn you that you have reached a resource limit.

Advanced DataEntry Techniques

As you can see, entering records into a newly created table is extremely simple. However, as you become more experienced with Paradox, you will probably want to take advantage of its advanced data entry features. For example, you may want to change the way the image is displayed on the screen or establish validity checks for certain fields. We will discuss the Image command and validity checks in Chapter 4.

The [Menu] View Command

The [Menu] View command allows you to view your tables on the screen. To view a table on the screen, you issue the [Menu] View command and specify the table you want to view. When you press ↵ to lock in your choice, Paradox will bring the selected table into view on your screen.

For example, suppose you have created the EMPLYEE table discussed earlier, and you now wish to view it. If the table is not already in view, you can bring it to the screen by issuing the [Menu] View command, typing the name of the table you want to view, EMPLYEE, and pressing ↵. Paradox then will bring the table into the workspace, and your screen will look like Figure 3-27. (If EMPLYEE is already in view, you don't need to issue this command.)

Figure 3-27   The Initial View of EMPLYEE

```
Viewing Emplyee table: Record 1 of 15                          Main
EMPLYEE    Emp Number    Last Name     First Name    SS Number     Addre
   1           1         Jones         Dave          414-76-3421   4000 St. Ja
   2           2         Cameron       Herb          321-65-8765   2331 Elm St
   3           4         Jones         Stewart       401-32-8721   4309 Oakbri
   4           5         Roberts       Darlene       417-43-7777   451 Lone Pi
   5           6         Jones         Jean          414-07-9123   4000 St. Ja
   6           8         Williams      Brenda        401-55-1567   555 Court S
   7           9         Myers         Julie         314-38-9452   4512 Parksi
   8          10         Link          Julie         345-75-1525   3215 Palm C
   9          12         Jackson       Mary          424-13-7621   7821 Clark
  10          14         Preston       Molly         451-00-3426   321 Indian
  11          15         Masters       Ron           317-65-4529   423 W. 72nd
  12          13         Triplett      Judy          616-10-6610   14D Ashby S
  13          16         Robertson     Kevin         415-24-6710   431 Bardsto
  14          17         Garrison      Robert        312-98-1479   55 Wheeler
  15          19         Gunn          Barbara       321-97-8632   541 Kentuck
```

When you bring a table into view, you are not looking at the actual table but at an image of the table. While you are viewing the image of the table on the screen, the actual table remains tucked away safely on your data disk. Keep this difference in mind as you work with Paradox: When you view a table, you are looking at an image of that table, not at the table itself. This difference is important because the changes you make in an image do not always affect the actual table.

As you will learn in Chapter 4, Paradox allows you to format the image of a table in a variety of ways. Since the image and the table are distinct, however, making changes to the appearance of the image has no effect on the actual table. Moreover, later in this chapter, you'll learn how to edit a table you are viewing. Since the changes you make are in the image of the table, and not in the table itself, your data is safe from accidents. Paradox will not update the actual table with the changes you have made in the image until you press [Do-It!].

Selecting a Table

When you issue the View command, Paradox displays the prompt shown in Figure 3-28. When you see this prompt, you can type in the name of the table you wish to view and then press ↵ or you can press ↵ to see a list of tables. If you press ↵ to see a list of tables, Paradox will display the names of the tables on the current directory like the one in Figure 3-29.

Figure 3-28 The Table Prompt

```
Table:                                                    Main
Enter name of table to view, or press ↵ to see a list of tables.
```

Figure 3-29 A List of Tables

```
Table:                                                                    Main
123tst  People  Adel  Emplyee  Sales1  Sale3  Sper1  Sper3  Pfscust  Asctxt ▶
```

The symbol ▶ at the end of the line indicates that there are more tables than can be displayed on the screen at one time. To see the hidden table names, you can press the ← key or the → key to move the cursor from name to name, the [End] key to move the cursor to the last table name, the [Home] key to move the cursor to the first table name, the ↑ key or the [Ctrl]-→ sequence to scroll one screen to the right, or the ↓ key or the [Ctrl]-← sequence to scroll one screen to the left.

To select a table to view from the list, just highlight its name with the cursor and press ↵. For example, to view the EMPLYEE table, you would point to its name in the list and press ↵.

You also can select a table by typing the first character of its name. For example, to select the EMPLYEE table, you can press E after you press ↵ at the table prompt.

If more than one table name on the current directory begins with the letter you type, Paradox will narrow the list to include just those tables with names that begin with the letter you typed. For example, suppose there are several tables in the current directory with names that begin with the letter *E*. When you type *E*, Paradox will narrow the list to display just the names of those tables, as shown in Figure 3-30. To select a table from this list, you must point to its name and press ↵.

Figure 3-30   Selecting a Table

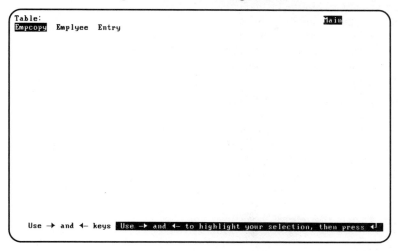

Moving Around in an Image

When you are viewing a table, the cursor control keys on the numeric keypad are used to move to the field or record you wish to view. You can press the cursor control keys by themselves or in combination with other keys that enhance their action. The key combinations and their functions are shown in Table 3-5.

Table 3-5   Cursor Movement Keys

Key	Function
←	Moves the cursor left one field.
→	Moves the cursor right one field.
↑	Moves the cursor up one record.
↓	Moves the cursor down one record.
[Pg Up]	Moves the cursor up one screenful of records.
[Pg Dn]	Moves the cursor down one screenful of records.
[Home]	Moves the cursor to the first record of the current field.
[End]	Moves the cursor to the last record of the current field.
[Tab]	Moves the cursor right one field (same as →).
[Shift]-[Tab]	Moves the cursor left one field (same as ←).
↵	Moves the cursor right one field (sames as →).
[Ctrl]-←	Moves the cursor left one screen.
[Ctrl]-→	Moves the cursor right one screen.
[Ctrl]-[Home]	Moves the cursor to the first field of the current record.
[Ctrl]-[End]	Moves the cursor to the last field of the current record.

When you are viewing a table, pressing →, [Tab], or ↵ moves the cursor to the right one field. If the cursor is in the last column of the image when you press one of these keys, it will move to the first column in the next record. If the cursor is in the last column of the last record when you press →, [Tab], or ↵, you will hear a low-pitched beep. This is Paradox's way of letting you know that you have made an inappropriate selection–there is no field for the cursor to move to.

Viewing More of an Image

Like EMPLYEE, most tables are too large to be displayed in full on the screen at one time. Whenever you use the [Menu] View command to bring a table into view, Paradox will position that table on the screen so that you see the upper-left corner of the table. In most cases, this means that you'll only see the first few records and the leftmost fields in the table. For example, in Figure 3-27 you can see only the first few EMPLYEE fields.

Viewing More Fields

Fortunately, it is easy to move the image around on the screen so that you can view the entire table. For example, to view more of the table, press **[Ctrl]-→**. After you do this, your screen will look like Figure 3-31.

Figure 3-31 Another View of EMPLYEE

```
Viewing Employee table: Record 1 of 15                          Main
     ─────Address─────    ─────City─────   State  ─Zip──  ─────Phone─────
     4000 St. James Ct.   St. Matthews      KY    40207   (502) 245-6610
     2331 Elm St.         Louisville        KY    40205   (502) 451-8765
     4389 Oakbridge Rd.   Lyndon            KY    40222   (502) 452-1040
     451 Lone Pine Dr.    Lagrange          KY    40012   (502) 897-3215
     4000 St. James Ct.   St. Matthews      KY    40207   (502) 245-6610
     555 Court St.        Anchorage         KY    40223   (502) 894-9761
     4512 Parkside Dr.    Louisville        KY    40206   (502) 454-5209
     3215 Palm Ct.        Palo Alto         CA    94375   (408) 542-1948
     7821 Clark Ave.      Clarksville       IN    47130   (812) 288-6754
     321 Indian Hills Rd. Louisville        KY    40205   (502) 456-3256
     423 W. 72nd St.      New York          NY    10019   (212) 276-5478
     14D Ashby St.        Clarksville       IN    47130   (812) 288-3301
     431 Bardstown Rd.    Elizabethtown     KY    40315   (502) 423-9823
     55 Wheeler St.       Boston            MA    25607   (617) 543-4124
     541 Kentucky St.     New Albany        IN    47132   (812) 325-4789
```

Now, to view the remaining fields of the table, press **[Ctrl]-→** again. Now your screen will look like Figure 3-32. As you can see, by moving the image around on the screen, you can easily view all of the records and fields in the table.

Figure 3-32 The Remaining Fields of EMPLYEE

```
Viewing Emplyee table: Record 1 of 15                          Main
┌──────Phone──────┬──Date of Birth──┬──Date of Hire──┬──Exemptions──┬──────Salary──────┐
│   (502) 245-6610│     10/06/42    │    6/01/84     │      3       │     70,000.00    │
│   (502) 451-8765│     11/24/29    │    6/01/84     │      4       │     50,000.00    │
│   (502) 452-1848│      3/21/50    │    7/01/84     │      1       │     47,000.00    │
│   (502) 897-3215│      9/24/60    │   11/01/84     │      3       │     14,000.00    │
│   (502) 245-6610│      5/14/43    │   12/01/84     │      0       │     33,999.99    │
│   (502) 894-9761│      1/12/20    │    1/01/85     │      4       │     40,000.00    │
│   (502) 454-5209│      2/06/48    │    2/01/85     │      1       │     32,000.00    │
│   (408) 542-1948│      6/03/33    │    4/01/85     │      2       │     30,000.00    │
│   (812) 288-6754│      8/12/56    │    4/01/85     │      3       │     21,000.00    │
│   (502) 456-3256│      4/17/66    │    7/01/85     │      1       │     14,750.00    │
│   (212) 276-5478│     12/31/44    │    7/01/85     │      0       │     38,000.00    │
│   (812) 288-3301│      8/12/50    │    4/10/85     │      2       │     15,750.00    │
│   (502) 423-9823│      3/16/25    │    7/15/85     │      1       │     37,000.00    │
│   (617) 543-4124│      5/09/45    │   10/01/85     │      4       │     32,125.00    │
│   (812) 325-4789│      5/18/50    │   11/01/85     │      2       │     17,500.00    │
```

Viewing More Records

Although the EMPLYEE table contains few enough records so that all of them are visible at once on the screen, in most cases your tables will contain hundreds of records. In that event, only a small percentage of the records will be visible at once. As you might expect, however, it is easy to bring other records into view. To move down through a table one record at a time, press ↓. To move down one screen at a time, press [Pg Dn]. To move directly to the last record in the table, press [End].

When you move down through the records in a large table, the first records in the table will disppear off the top of the screen as more records come into view at the bottom. If you want to view the top records again, you need only press ↑, [Pg Up], or [Home].

The [Menu] Image GoTo Command

The [Menu] Image GoTo command allows you to move the cursor instantly to a specific field or record in the current table. For example, suppose you are viewing the EMPLYEE table and the cursor is in the Emp Number field. You want to move to the Exemptions field. To do this, issue the **[Menu] I**mage **G**oTo command. After you issue this command, Paradox will display the GoTo menu, which is shown Figure 3-33.

Figure 3-33 The GoTo Menu

As you can see, you can use the GoTo command to move to a specific field or record. When you issue the **F**ield command, Paradox will display the field names for the current table as shown in Figure 3-34. (You will recall that the ▶ symbol means that there are more options in the list that are not currently in view.)

Figure 3-34 Selecting a Field to Go To

```
Select a field to move to.                                           Main
 Emp Number  Last Name  First Name  SS Number  Address  City  State  Zip  Phone ▶
```

To select the field to which you want to go, either point to its name in the list and press ↵, or press the key corresponding to the first character in the name of the field to which you want to go. To select the Exemptions field, for example, simply press **E**. If you have two or more field names that start with the same character, Paradox will prompt you to choose between them.

Once you select a field name, Paradox will move to the field instantly. For example, if you select the Exemptions field, Paradox will move the cursor to that field, as shown in Figure 3-35.

Figure 3-35 Using the GoTo Command

```
Viewing Emplyee table: Record 1 of 15                    Main
 ┌─Exemptions─┬─Salary─┐
 │     3      │ 70,000.00 │
 │     4      │ 50,000.00 │
 │     1      │ 47,000.00 │
 │     3      │ 14,000.00 │
 │     0      │ 33,999.99 │
 │     4      │ 40,000.00 │
 │     1      │ 32,000.00 │
 │     2      │ 30,000.00 │
 │     3      │ 21,000.00 │
 │     1      │ 14,750.00 │
 │     0      │ 38,000.00 │
 │     2      │ 15,750.00 │
 │     1      │ 37,000.00 │
 │     4      │ 32,125.00 │
 │     2      │ 17,500.00 │
```

You also can use the GoTo command to move to a specific record in the current table. For example, suppose the cursor is in record 1 of EMPLYEE and you want to move it to record number 15. To move to record number 15, issue the **[Menu] I**mage **G**oTo **R**ecord command. After you issue this command, Paradox will display the prompt shown in Figure 3-36.

Figure 3-36 The Record Number Prompt

When you see this prompt, type **15** and press ↵. When you do, Paradox will move the cursor directly to record number 15. The cursor will be in the same field it was in when you issued the command.

Typing and Editing

You cannot make any changes to the data in a table you are viewing unless you first press the [Edit] key ([F9]) to enter the edit mode. This feature of Paradox is designed to protect your data from being changed accidentally.

For instance, suppose you want to change the entry in the First Name field of the first record in the EMPLYEE table from *Dave* to *David*. You might try to move to that field and press [Ctrl]-[Backspace] to erase the current entry. When you do this, however, Paradox will display the message *Press the Edit key [F9] if you want to make changes* and will not erase the entry. If you want to change the entry, you must first press [Edit] to enter the edit mode. We'll show you how to edit tables in the next part of this chapter.

Viewing More Than One Image

Paradox allows you to have more than one image on the screen at one time. In fact, you can have more than one image of a single table in view, or images of several different tables, or both. The number of images you can view at once is limited only by the memory capacity of your computer.

Viewing Two Images of the Same Table

If you want to view two parts of a single table at the same time, you can bring two images of that table into view simultaneously. For example, suppose you are viewing the EMPLYEE table as shown in Figure 3-27, and you want to view more fields without changing the current image. To do this, issue the **[Menu] V**iew command again, type **EMPLYEE**, and press ↵. After you do this, your screen will look like Figure 3-37.

Figure 3-37   Two Views of EMPLYEE

```
Viewing Emplyee table: Record 1 of 15                            Main
 EMPLYEE   Emp Number    Last Name    First Name    SS Number      Addre
    12        13          Triplett     Judy         616-10-6610    14D Ashby S
    13        16          Robertson    Kevin        415-24-6710    431 Bardsto
    14        17          Garrison     Robert       312-98-1479    55 Wheeler
    15        19          Gunn         Barbara      321-97-8632    541 Kentuck

 EMPLYEE   Emp Number    Last Name    First Name    SS Number      Addre
     1         1          Jones        Dave         414-76-3421    4000 St. Ja
     2         2          Cameron      Herb         321-65-8765    2331 Elm St
     3         4          Jones        Stewart      401-32-8721    4389 Oakbri
     4         5          Roberts      Darlene      417-43-7777    451 Lone Pi
     5         6          Jones        Jean         414-07-9123    4000 St. Ja
     6         8          Williams     Brenda       401-55-1567    555 Court S
     7         9          Myers        Julie        314-38-9452    4512 Parksi
     8        10          Link         Julie        345-75-1525    3215 Palm C
     9        12          Jackson      Mary         424-13-7621    7821 Clark
    10        14          Preston      Molly        451-00-3426    321 Indian
    11        15          Masters      Ron          317-65-4529    423 W. 72nd
    12        13          Triplett     Judy         616-10-6610    14D Ashby S
    13        16          Robertson    Kevin        415-24-6710    431 Bardsto
    14        17          Garrison     Robert       312-98-1479    55 Wheeler
    15        19          Gunn         Barbara      321-97-8632    541 Kentuck
```

You now can adjust the two images to display the fields and records you wish to view. For example, suppose you want to change the bottom image of EMPLYEE to display the rightmost fields in the table. To do this, press **[Ctrl]-→** twice. After you do this, your screen will look like Figure 3-38.

Figure 3-38   Changing the Fields Displayed

EMPLYEE	Emp Number	Last Name	First Name	SS Number	Addre
12	13	Triplett	Judy	616-18-6610	14D Ashby S
13	16	Robertson	Kevin	415-24-6710	431 Bardsto
14	17	Garrison	Robert	312-98-1479	55 Wheeler
15	19	Gunn	Barbara	321-97-8632	541 Kentuck

Viewing Emplyee table: Record 1 of 15   Main

Phone	Date of Birth	Date of Hire	Exemptions	Salary
(502) 245-6610	10/06/42	6/01/84	3	70,000.00
(502) 451-8765	11/24/29	6/01/84	4	50,000.00
(502) 452-1848	3/21/50	7/01/84	1	47,000.00
(502) 897-3215	9/24/60	11/01/84	3	14,000.00
(502) 245-6610	5/14/43	12/01/84	0	33,999.99
(502) 894-9761	1/12/20	1/01/85	4	40,000.00
(502) 454-5209	2/06/48	2/01/85	1	32,000.00
(408) 542-1948	6/03/33	4/01/85	2	30,000.00
(812) 288-6754	8/12/56	4/01/85	3	21,000.00
(502) 456-3256	4/17/66	7/01/85	1	14,750.00
(212) 276-5478	12/31/44	7/01/85	0	30,000.00
(812) 288-3301	8/12/50	4/10/85	2	15,750.00
(502) 423-9823	3/16/25	7/15/85	1	37,000.00
(617) 543-4124	5/09/45	10/01/85	4	32,125.00
(812) 325-4789	5/18/50	11/01/85	2	17,500.00

Notes

Notice that pressing [Ctrl]-→ while the cursor is in the lower image of EMPLYEE affects only that image. When you have more than one image displayed on the screen at a time, the image containing the cursor is called the current image. All of your keystrokes refer to and affect the current image. For example, you have just seen that pressing [Ctrl]-→ when the cursor was in the bottom image affected that image, but not the top one.

In addition, the name of the table that is represented by the current image will always be the first name in any list of names that Paradox displays when you issue a command. For example, if you issue the [Menu] View command while the current image is an image of the EMPLYEE table, then press ↵ to see a list of table names, the name EMPLYEE will be the first name in the list. The same is true of the [Menu] Query command and any other command that offers a list of table names.

Also notice that the second image of EMPLYEE came into view below the first image on the screen. The second table image you bring into view will always appear on the screen below the first, the third image will appear below the second, and so on.

In addition, notice that Paradox moved most of the first image of EMPLYEE out of view when you brought the second image into view. When you bring a second image to the screen, Paradox will display that image in full on the screen. If there are other images in view, Paradox will shift those images out of view off the top of the screen.

Whenever there is an image on the workspace that is not fully in view on the screen, Paradox will display a symbol in the upper-right corner of the screen. For example, notice the symbol ▲= at the top of the screen in Figure 3-37. This tells you that a part of the upper image of EMPLYEE is not visible. Now glance at the symbol =▼ in the upper-right corner of Figure 3-39. This tells you that a portion of the lower image of EMPLYEE is not in view. If there are images out of view at both the top and the bottom of the screen, Paradox will display the symbol ▲=▼.

Moving between Images

Of course, whenever there is more than one image on the screen, you will need a way to move between images. Moving between images is controlled by two keys: [Up Image] ([F3]) and [Down Image] ([F4]). [Up Image] moves the cursor up from the current image to the image above the current image. [Down Image] moves the cursor from the current image to the image below.

For example, suppose you want to move to the top image of the EMPLYEE table. To do this, press **[Up Image]**. After you do this, the screen will look like Figure 3-39.

Figure 3-39 Moving between Images

```
┌Viewing Emplyee table: Record 1 of 15                          Main  =▼
│EMPLYEE┬─Emp Number─┬─Last Name─┬─First Name─┬─SS Number─┬──────Addre
│   1   │     1      │  Jones    │  Dave      │ 414-76-3421│ 4000 St. Ja
│   2   │     2      │  Cameron  │  Herb      │ 321-65-8765│ 2331 Elm St
│   3   │     4      │  Jones    │  Stewart   │ 401-32-8721│ 4389 Oakbri
│   4   │     5      │  Roberts  │  Darlene   │ 417-43-7777│ 451 Lone Pi
│   5   │     6      │  Jones    │  Jean      │ 414-07-9123│ 4000 St. Ja
│   6   │     8      │  Williams │  Brenda    │ 401-55-1567│ 555 Court S
│   7   │     9      │  Myers    │  Julie     │ 314-38-9452│ 4512 Parksi
│   8   │    10      │  Link     │  Julie     │ 345-75-1525│ 3215 Palm C
│   9   │    12      │  Jackson  │  Mary      │ 424-13-7621│ 7821 Clark
│  10   │    14      │  Preston  │  Molly     │ 451-00-3426│ 321 Indian
│  11   │    15      │  Masters  │  Ron       │ 317-65-4529│ 423 W. 72nd
│  12   │    13      │  Triplett │  Judy      │ 616-10-6610│ 14D Ashby S
│  13   │    16      │  Robertson│  Kevin     │ 415-24-6710│ 431 Bardsto
│  14   │    17      │  Garrison │  Robert    │ 312-98-1479│ 55 Wheeler
│  15   │    19      │  Gunn     │  Barbara   │ 321-97-8632│ 541 Kentuck
│
│       ┬──Phone─────┬─Date of Birth─┬─Date of Hire─┬─Exemptions─┬──Salary──
│       │(502) 245-6610│  10/06/42   │   6/01/84    │     3      │ 70,000.00
│       │(502) 451-8765│  11/24/29   │   6/01/84    │     4      │ 50,000.00
│       │(502) 452-1048│   3/21/50   │   7/01/84    │     1      │ 47,000.00
│       │(502) 897-3215│   9/24/60   │  11/01/84    │     3      │ 14,000.00
```

In this example, the cursor is in the upper EMPLYEE image. Since the upper image is now the current image, all of your keystrokes will affect that image. Also notice that the symbol in the upper-right corner of the screen has changed to =▼, indicating that a portion of the lower image of EMPLYEE is not visible.

To move back to the lower image, you would press [Down Image]. When you press this key, Paradox will shift the upper image of EMPLYEE off the top of the screeen, bringing the lower image into view again, as shown in Figure 3-38.

When you move the cursor back into a table, it will return to the field and record that it occupied the last time it was in that table. For example, when you press [Down Image] to move the cursor back into the second EMPLYEE table, it will return to the same postion it was in before you moved it out of the table.

As you might expect, you cannot move up beyond the top image on the workspace or down below the bottom image. If you press [Down Image] while the cursor is in the last image, Paradox will simply beep. The same thing will happen if you press [Up Image] while the cursor is in the top image.

Viewing Images of Several Tables

In addition to being able to view more than one image of a table, you can view more than one table at the same time. In fact, you are far more likely to have several images of different tables on the screen at once than you are to have two or more images of the same table in view.

For example, suppose you are viewing two images of the EMPLYEE table, and you want to bring the ADDRESS table into view. To do this, issue the [**Menu**] View command, type **ADDRESS** at the prompt, and press ↵. Figure 3-40 shows the results.

Figure 3-40   Viewing Two Tables

```
┌─────────────────────────────────────────────────────────────────────────┐
│ Viewing Address table: Table is empty                       Main  ▲═    │
│    EMPLYEE══Emp Number══╤══Last Name══╤══First Name══╤══SS Number══╤══Addre│
│      15 │        19     │    Gunn     │   Barbara    │  321-97-8632 │ 541 Kentuck│
│                                                                         │
│        ══Phone══╤══Date of Birth══╤══Date of Hire══╤══Exemptions══╤══Salary══│
│     (502) 245-6610│   10/06/42    │    6/01/84     │      3       │  70,000.00│
│     (502) 451-8765│   11/24/29    │    6/01/84     │      4       │  50,000.00│
│     (502) 452-1848│    3/21/50    │    7/01/84     │      1       │  47,000.00│
│     (502) 897-3215│    9/24/60    │   11/01/84     │      3       │  14,000.00│
│     (502) 245-6610│    5/14/43    │   12/01/84     │      0       │  33,999.99│
│     (502) 894-9761│    1/12/20    │    1/01/85     │      4       │  40,000.00│
│     (502) 454-5209│    2/06/48    │    2/01/85     │      1       │  32,000.00│
│     (408) 542-1948│    6/03/33    │    4/01/85     │      2       │  30,000.00│
│     (812) 288-6754│    8/12/56    │    4/01/85     │      3       │  21,000.00│
│     (502) 456-3256│    4/17/66    │    7/01/85     │      1       │  14,750.00│
│     (212) 276-5478│   12/31/44    │    7/01/85     │      0       │  38,000.00│
│     (812) 288-3301│    8/12/50    │    4/10/85     │      2       │  15,750.00│
│     (502) 423-9823│    3/16/25    │    7/15/85     │      1       │  37,000.00│
│     (617) 543-4124│    5/09/45    │   10/01/85     │      4       │  32,125.00│
│     (812) 325-4789│    5/18/50    │   11/01/85     │      2       │  17,500.00│
│                                                                         │
│    ADDRESS══╤══Emp Number══╤══Last Name══╤══First Name══╤══SS Number══╤══Spou│
└─────────────────────────────────────────────────────────────────────────┘
```

Notice that in Figure 3-40 the top image of EMPLYEE has been shifted so much that only one of its records is visible. Also notice the symbol ▲= in the top-right corner of the screen, which alerts you to this fact. The ADDRESS table appears as it does on the screen because it is an empty table. If it had contained any records, Paradox would have displayed as many of those records as possible when you brought the table into view.

To move between the images in Figure 3-40, you need only press [Up Image] and [Down Image]. For instance, to move to the lower EMPLYEE image, you would press **[Up Image]** once. To move to the upper EMPLYEE image, you would press **[Up Image]** again. Figure 3-41 shows the screen as it would look when you move the cursor into the upper image of EMPLYEE. Notice that the ADDRESS table has disappeared from view and that the symbol in the upper-right corner of the screen has changed to =▼.

Figure 3-41   Using [Up Image]

```
Viewing Emplyee table: Record 1 of 15                              Main  =▼
 EMPLYEE  Emp Number    Last Name    First Name    SS Number       Addre
     1         1        Jones         Dave          414-76-3421    4000 St. Ja
     2         2        Cameron       Herb          321-65-8765    2331 Elm St
     3         4        Jones         Stewart       401-32-8721    4389 Oakbri
     4         5        Roberts       Darlene       417-43-7777    451 Lone Pi
     5         6        Jones         Jean          414-07-9123    4000 St. Ja
     6         8        Williams      Brenda        401-55-1567    555 Court S
     7         9        Myers         Julie         314-38-9452    4512 Parksi
     8        10        Link          Julie         345-75-1525    3215 Palm C
     9        12        Jackson       Mary          424-13-7621    7821 Clark
    10        14        Preston       Molly         451-00-3426    321 Indian
    11        15        Masters       Ron           317-65-4529    423 W. 72nd
    12        13        Triplett      Judy          616-10-6610    14D Ashby S
    13        16        Robertson     Kevin         415-24-6710    431 Bardsto
    14        17        Garrison      Robert        312-98-1479    55 Wheeler
    15        19        Gunn          Barbara       321-97-8632    541 Kentuck

      Phone        Date of Birth  Date of Hire   Exemptions    Salary
  (502) 245-6610    10/06/42        6/01/84           3        70,000.00
  (502) 451-8765    11/24/29        6/01/84           4        50,000.00
  (502) 452-1048     3/21/50        7/01/84           1        47,000.00
  (502) 897-3215     9/24/60       11/01/84           3        14,000.00
```

This figure shows that, try as it might, Paradox is not always able to display even a small part of every table image that is in view. In fact, once you bring more than three or four tables to the screen, it is extremely unlikely that all of them will be visible at once. As you can imagine, the symbols in the upper-right corner of the screen are extremely important to help you remember what is where on the workspace.

The only limitation to the number of images you can bring into view at once is the memory of your computer. As you become more comfortable with Paradox, you are likely to encounter situations where you will have four, five, six or more images in view at once. No matter how many images are in view, the same simple rules discussed in this section will apply.

Removing Images from the Screen

To remove an image from the screen, move the cursor into that image and press **[Clear Image]** ([F8]). For example, suppose you want to remove the second EMPLYEE table image from the screen. To do this, use [Up Image] or [Down Image] to move the cursor into this image, then press [**Clear Image**]. Figure 3-42 shows the resulting screen.

Figure 3-42 Clearing an Image

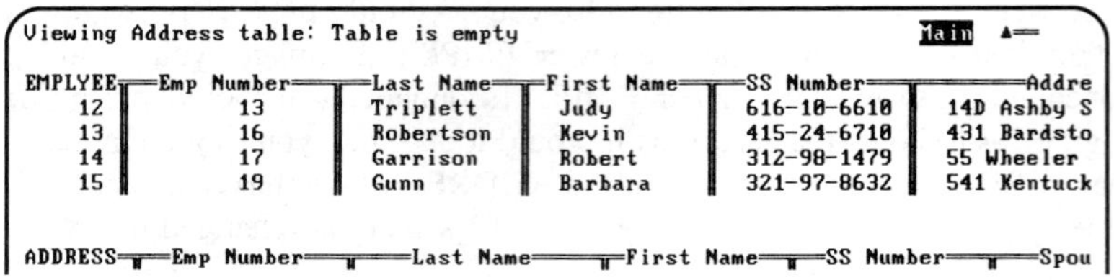

```
 Viewing Address table: Table is empty                        Main

   EMPLYEE  Emp Number   Last Name   First Name   SS Number      Addre
      12       13         Triplett    Judy         616-10-6610   14D Ashby S
      13       16         Robertson   Kevin        415-24-6710   431 Bardsto
      14       17         Garrison    Robert       312-98-1479   55 Wheeler
      15       19         Gunn        Barbara      321-97-8632   541 Kentuck

   ADDRESS   Emp Number      Last Name       First Name   SS Number     Spou
```

To remove all of the images from the workspace, press [Clear All] ([Alt]-[F8]). For example, suppose you have several images in the workspace and you need to free some memory to perform an operation. You should press [**Clear All**] to clear the workspace and return to the Main menu.

It is important to understand that clearing an image does not erase or delete the table with which that image is associated. Clearing an image simply removes the image from view. The table with which the image is associated remains on the disk, safe and sound.

Editing Entries

You have just seen how easy it is to create a table and then enter data into it. You have also seen how easy it is to make changes to the entries in the ENTRY table before you press [Do-It!] to add those entries to a permanent table. In this section, we'll show you how to edit the records that are already stored in a permanent table.

In fact, the techniques you use to edit the entries in a table are exactly the same as the ones you used to edit the entries in the ENTRY and STRUCT tables. All you have to do to edit a table is enter the edit mode and use the editing keys in Table 3-3 on page 46 to edit the data in the table. While you are editing a table, you can change entries, insert and delete records, and even enter new records. When you have made the changes you want to make, you should press [Do-It!] to save the changes. If you want to cancel the edit, you can issue the [Menu] Cancel command.

Examples

Before you can edit a table, you must first enter the edit mode. To enter the edit mode, you issue the [Menu] Modify Edit command and select the name of the table you want to edit. When you do this, Paradox will bring the table you specify into view and will enter the edit mode. Once you are in the edit mode, you can enter the table.

For example, to edit the EMPLYEE table, you should issue the [**Menu**] **M**odify **E**dit command, type **EMPLYEE**, and press ↵. You can also enter the mode by pressing the [Edit] key while the table you want to edit is in view. We'll show you how to do this in a few pages.

Changing Entries

Suppose you want to change the First Name field entry of the first record in the EMPLYEE table from *Dave* to *David*. To make this change, first issue the [**Menu**] Modify Edit command, type **EMPLYEE**, and press ↵. When the EMPLYEE table appears on the screen, move the cursor to the First Name field of the first record. When the cursor is in place, press [**Backspace**] once to erase the *e* in *Dave*, and then type **id**. Figure 3-43 shows the screen after this correction has been made.

Figure 3-43 Making Corrections

```
Editing Emplyee table: Record 1 of 15                        Edit
EMPLYEE  Emp Number   Last Name   First Name   SS Number      Addre
   1          1         Jones       David    ◄  414-76-3421   4000 St. Ja
   2          2         Cameron     Herb        321-65-8765   2331 Elm St
   3          4         Jones       Stewart     401-32-8721   4389 Oakbri
   4          5         Roberts     Darlene     417-43-7777   451 Lone Pi
   5          6         Jones       Jean        414-07-9123   4000 St. Ja
   6          8         Williams    Brenda      401-55-1567   555 Court S
   7          9         Myers       Julie       314-38-9452   4512 Parksi
   8         10         Link        Julie       345-75-1525   3215 Palm C
   9         12         Jackson     Mary        424-13-7621   7821 Clark
  10         14         Preston     Molly       451-00-3426   321 Indian
  11         15         Masters     Ron         317-65-4529   423 W. 72nd
  12         13         Triplett    Judy        616-10-6610   14D Ashby S
  13         16         Robertson   Kevin       415-24-6710   431 Bardsto
  14         17         Garrison    Robert      312-98-1479   55 Wheeler
  15         19         Gunn        Barbara     321-97-8632   541 Kentuck
```

If the change you need to make is so great that you would be better off starting from scratch, you can press [Ctrl]-[Backspace] to erase the entire entry, then type the new entry. For example, suppose you want to change the Address field entry of the record for employee 8, Brenda Williams, from *555 Court St.* to *100 Owl Creek Rd.* To make this change, move the cursor to the Address field of record number 6 and press [**Ctrl**]-[**Backspace**] to erase the current entry. Then type **100 Owl Creek Rd.** and press ↵ to lock in the entry. Figure 3-44 shows the resulting EMPLYEE table.

Figure 3-44 Changing an Entry

```
Editing Emplyee table: Record 6 of 15                          Edit
 First Name   SS Number     Address             City          St
  David       414-76-3421   4000 St. James Ct.  St. Matthews
  Herb        321-65-8765   2331 Elm St.        Louisville
  Stewart     401-32-8721   4389 Oakbridge Rd.  Lyndon
  Darlene     417-43-7777   451 Lone Pine Dr.   Lagrange
  Jean        414-07-9123   4000 St. James Ct.  St. Matthews
  Brenda      401-55-1567   100 Owl Creek Rd.   Anchorage     ◄
  Julie       314-38-9452   4512 Parkside Dr.   Louisville
  Julie       345-75-1525   3215 Palm Ct.       Palo Alto
  Mary        424-13-7621   7821 Clark Ave.     Clarksville
  Molly       451-00-3426   321 Indian Hills Rd. Louisville
  Ron         317-65-4529   423 W. 72nd         New York
  Judy        616-10-6610   14D Ashby St.       Clarksville
  Kevin       415-24-6710   431 Bardstown Rd.   Elizabethtown
  Robert      312-98-1479   55 Wheeler St.      Boston
  Barbara     321-97-8632   541 Kentucky St.    New Albany
```

The Field View

You can also use the field view to edit the entries in a table. To enter the field view, you position the cursor on the field you want to edit and press [Field View] ([Alt]-[F5]). After you press [Field View], the cursor will change to a box, and you will be able to move around in that field to make changes.

As when you are editing records in the ENTRY table, entering the field view restricts the movement of the cursor to the one field you are editing. When you are in the field view, the cursor movement keys move the cursor from character to character within the field you are editing, rather than moving it from field to field within the table. Table 3-4 on page 47 shows the effect of each of the cursor movement keys in the field view.

For example, suppose that you want to change the SS Number field entry for employee number 6, Jean Jones, from 414-07-9123 to 413-07-9123. To make this change, move the cursor to record number 5 and press [**Field View**] to enter the Field View. Now, press ← to move the field view cursor to the second 4 in the entry. Figure 3-45 shows the screen at this point. Now, press [**Del**] to delete the 4, and type **3**. Finally, press ↵ to exit from the field view.

Figure 3-45   Using the Field View

```
Editing Emplyee table: Record 5 of 15                          Edit
┌─Emp Number─┬─Last Name─┬─First Name─┬─SS Number──┬─Address──────────┐
       1      Jones       David        414-76-3421   4000 St. James Ct.
       2      Cameron     Herb         321-65-8765   2331 Elm St.
       4      Jones       Stewart      401-32-8721   4389 Oakbridge Rd.
       5      Roberts     Darlene      417-43-7777   451 Lone Pine Dr.
       6      Jones       Jean         41█-07-9123   4000 St. James Ct.
       8      Williams    Brenda       401-55-1567   100 Owl Creek Rd.
       9      Myers       Julie        314-38-9452   4512 Parkside Dr.
      10      Link        Julie        345-75-1525   3215 Palm Ct.
      12      Jackson     Mary         424-13-7621   7821 Clark Ave.
      14      Preston     Molly        451-00-3426   321 Indian Hills R
      15      Masters     Ron          317-65-4529   423 W. 72nd St.
      13      Triplett    Judy         616-10-6610   14D Ashby St.
      16      Robertson   Kevin        415-24-6710   431 Bardstown Rd.
      17      Garrison    Robert       312-98-1479   55 Wheeler St.
      19      Gunn        Barbara      321-97-8632   541 Kentucky St.
```

Deleting a Record

If you want to delete the record, you can do so by positioning the cursor in any field of the record you want to delete and pressing [Del]. For example, suppose you want to delete the record for Judy Triplett from the EMPLYEE table. To remove this record from the table, move the cursor to any field in the record and press [**Del**]. The resulting table will look like Figure 3-46.

Figure 3-46 Deleting a Record

```
Editing Emplyee table: Record 12 of 14                    Edit
┌─Emp Number─┬─Last Name─┬─First Name─┬─SS Number──┬─Address────────────┐
       1      Jones       David        414-76-3421   4000 St. James Ct.
       2      Cameron     Herb         321-65-8765   2331 Elm St.
       4      Jones       Stewart      401-32-8721   4389 Oakbridge Rd.
       5      Roberts     Darlene      417-43-7777   451 Lone Pine Dr.
       6      Jones       Jean         413-07-9123   4000 St. James Ct.
       8      Williams    Brenda       401-55-1567   100 Owl Creek Rd.
       9      Myers       Julie        314-38-9452   4512 Parkside Dr.
      10      Link        Julie        345-75-1525   3215 Palm Ct.
      12      Jackson     Mary         424-13-7621   7821 Clark Ave.
      14      Preston     Molly        451-00-3426   321 Indian Hills R
      15      Masters     Ron          317-65-4529   423 W. 72nd St.
      16      Robertson   Kevin       ◄415-24-6710   431 Bardstown Rd.
      17      Garrison    Robert       312-98-1479   55 Wheeler St.
      19      Gunn        Barbara      321-97-8632   541 Kentucky St.
```

Adding Records

You can also add new records to your tables using the edit mode. You can either append the new records to the end of the table or use the [Ins] key to insert a new record in the middle of the table.

Appending Records

To append a new record to a table, you use the cursor keys to move the cursor to the last record in the table, then press ↓ to add a new record to the table. Once the new record is in place, you can fill it in just as you normally would.

For example, suppose you want to add a new record at the end of EMPLYEE. To add the record, press ↓ to move the cursor to the last record in the table, and then once more to add a new record. Now, enter the information for employee number 20 from Table 3-6 on page 66 into the new record. Figure 3-47 shows the completed table.

Figure 3-47 Adding a Record

```
Editing Emplyee table: Record 15 of 15                    Edit
EMPLYEE┬─Emp Number─┬─Last Name─┬─First Name─┬─SS Number──┬─Addre─────
   1         1        Jones       David        414-76-3421   4000 St. Ja
   2         2        Cameron     Herb         321-65-8765   2331 Elm St
   3         4        Jones       Stewart      401-32-8721   4389 Oakbri
   4         5        Roberts     Darlene      417-43-7777   451 Lone Pi
   5         6        Jones       Jean         413-07-9123   4000 St. Ja
   6         8        Williams    Brenda       401-55-1567   100 Owl Cre
   7         9        Myers       Julie        314-38-9452   4512 Parksi
   8        10        Link        Julie        345-75-1525   3215 Palm C
   9        12        Jackson     Mary         424-13-7621   7821 Clark
  10        14        Preston     Molly        451-00-3426   321 Indian
  11        15        Masters     Ron          317-65-4529   423 W. 72nd
  12        16        Robertson   Kevin        415-24-6710   431 Bardsto
  13        17        Garrison    Robert       312-98-1479   55 Wheeler
  14        19        Gunn        Barbara      321-97-8632   541 Kentuck
  15        20      ◄ Emerson     Cheryl       401-65-1820   800 River R
```

You can use this technique to add as many records as you wish to a table. However, we suggest that you use the [Menu] Modify DataEntry command if you are going to enter more than one or two records. Using this command will keep existing records safe from accidental alteration when you are entering records.

Table 3-6 Sample Data

Emp Number	20	13
Last Name	Emerson	Jakes, Jr.
First Name	Cheryl	Sal
SS Number	401-65-1820	321-65-9151
Address	800 River Rd.	3451 Michigan Ave.
City	Prospect	Dallas
State	KY	TX
Zip	40222	65987
Phone	(502) 896-5139	(214) 398-1987
Date of Birth	7/30/66	5/23/59
Date of Hire	1/01/86	5/01/85
Exemptions	2	6
Salary	12,000.00	34,000.00

Inserting a Record

You can also insert a record in the middle of a table in the edit mode. All you have to do is move the cursor to the place in the table where you want the new record to be, press [Ins] to insert a new record, and then fill that record with new data.

For example, suppose you want to add a new record between the records for employees 12 (Mary Jackson) and 14 (Molly Preston). To make this entry, move the cursor to any field in record number 10 (Molly Preston) and press **[Ins]** to insert a new record. Now enter the data for employee number 13 that is shown in Table 3-6 into the new record. Figure 3-48 shows the completed table.

Figure 3-48 Adding the Data

```
Editing Emplyee table: Record 11 of 16                    Edit
EMPLYEE==Emp Number==-Last Name==First Name==SS Number==========Addre
   1        1         Jones       David       414-76-3421   4000 St. Ja
   2        2         Cameron     Herb        321-65-8765   2331 Elm St
   3        4         Jones       Stewart     401-32-8721   4389 Oakbri
   4        5         Roberts     Darlene     417-43-7777   451 Lone Pi
   5        6         Jones       Jean        413-07-9123   4000 St. Ja
   6        8         Williams    Brenda      401-55-1567   100 Owl Cre
   7        9         Myers       Julie       314-38-9452   4512 Parksi
   8       10         Link        Julie       345-75-1525   3215 Palm C
   9       12         Jackson     Mary        424-13-7621   7821 Clark
  10       13         Jakes, Jr.  Sal         321-65-9151   3451 Michig
  11       14         Preston     Molly       451-00-3426   321 Indian
  12       15         Masters     Ron         317-65-4529   423 W. 72nd
  13       16         Robertson   Kevin       415-24-6710   431 Bardsto
  14       17         Garrison    Robert      312-98-1479   55 Wheeler
  15       19         Gunn        Barbara     321-97-8632   541 Kentuck
  16       20         Emerson     Cheryl      401-65-1820   800 River R
```

The Undo Command

If you make a mistake while you are editing a table in Paradox Release 1.1, you can use the [Menu] Undo command or the [Undo] key ([Ctrl]-[U]) to reverse your error. As when you are entering records, the Undo command always undoes the last change you made to the table you are editing. If the last change you made was to edit an entry in the table, that entry will be restored to its previous value. If the last change was to delete a record, then issuing the Undo command will restore the record to the table. If you issue this command again, Paradox will undo your second-most recent action, and so on.

For example, suppose you accidentally press the [Del] key while you are editing the EMPLYEE table, deleting the record for Molly Preston from the table. To recover this error, you could press **[Undo]**. Immediately, Paradox will restore the deleted record to the table. In addition, the message *Record 11 reinserted* will appear at the bottom of the screen. (If you issue the [Menu] Undo command instead of pressing [Undo], Paradox will prompt you for confirmation before it restores the deleted record. You must choose Yes to bring the record back into the table.)

Leaving the Edit Mode

When you are finished editing, you can either press the [Do-It!] key or issue the [Menu] DO-IT! command to save the changes you have made. After you do this, Paradox will save the changes you have made in the table. The message *Ending edit...* will appear briefly at the bottom of the screen, and Paradox will return to the main workspace.

If you don't want to save the changes you have made, you can issue the [Menu] Cancel command to end the editing session without saving your work. After you issue the Cancel command, Paradox will prompt you for confirmation. If you issue the No command at this point, Paradox will return to the Edit menu so that you can make another selection. If you issue the Yes command, Paradox will cancel all of the changes you have made and return to the main workspace.

You can also cancel the operation by pressing [Ctrl]-[Break]. However, if you use this method, Paradox will not prompt you for confirmation. For this reason, we suggest that you always use the [Menu] Cancel command.

Using the [Edit] Key

In the previous example, we used the [Menu] Modify Edit command to enter the edit mode. You can also enter the edit mode, however, by bringing the table you want to edit into view and pressing the [Edit] key ([F9]). When you press [Edit] ([F9]) to enter the edit mode, Paradox assumes that you want to edit a table in the workspace and does not prompt you for a table name.

For example, suppose you want to edit the EMPLYEE table. Rather than issuing the [Menu] Modify Edit command, you could issue the [Menu] View command to bring the

EMPLYEE table into view, and then press [Edit] to enter the edit mode. Once you are in the edit mode, it doesn't matter how you got there–everything works the same way whether you issue the [Menu] Modify Edit command or press [Edit]. After you have made the changes you want to make, you can press [Do-It!] or issue the [Menu] DO-IT! command to save the changes you have made, or issue the [Menu] Cancel command to cancel the changes and return to the view mode.

If there is more than one image in view when you press [Edit], you will be able to edit the records in all of the tables in view. For example, suppose both the EMPLYEE table and the ADDRESS tables are in view, as shown in Figure 3-40. If you press [Edit] at this point, you can edit the entries in either table. As always, you can use the [Up Image] and [Down Image] keys to move the cursor from table to table.

If there are two images of the same table in view when you press [Edit], one of the images will disappear. Paradox makes this change to avoid the problems that could arise from having two images of the same table, one of which contained edited entries and the other of which did not.

A Word About Tables

Before you begin to create your own tables, you should take some time to consider the types of information you normally use and plan your tables accordingly. For example, consider the way you now use your paper filing (data storage) system. You probably have files on people and things like your employees, your customers, your company's products, and a host of other topics that you need to conduct your business. Your files are most likely organized in a way that groups similar types of information together and provides easy accessibility. Your Paradox tables should be organized the same way.

For example, suppose you want to create a table to track the projects to which your employees are assigned. You may at first feel compelled to include every scrap of information you can think of in the table and create a table structured like the one shown in Figure 3-49. However, you will quickly discover that it is better to create several smaller tables than it is to put everything into a "super table."

For example, you can break the large table PROJS into two smaller tables. Figures 3-5 and 3-50 show the structure of two tables–EMPLYEE (with which you are already familiar) and PROJECTS–that together contain every field from PROJS. The EMPLYEE contains basic data about employees. The PROJECTS table tracks the various projects to which the employees are assigned.

By splitting the one table into two, you make the data base system more efficient and easier to use. As a general rule, you should strive to create small tables that contain the information you need, without duplicating information found in a related table.

Figure 3-49   A Poorly Structured Table

```
Creating new Projs table                              Create
STRUCT      Field Name           Field Type
   1    Emp Number                   N           ── FIELD TYPES ──
   2    Last Name                   A10          A_: Alphanumeric (ex: A25)
   3    First Name                  A10          Any combination of
   4    SS Number                   A11          characters and spaces
   5    Address                     A20          up to specified width.
   6    City                        A20          Maximum width is 255.
   7    State                        A2
   8    Zip                          A5          N: Numbers with or without
   9    Phone                       A14             decimal digits.
  10    Date of Birth                D
  11    Date of Hire                 D           $: Dollar amounts.
  12    Exemptions                   N
  13    Salary                       $           D: Dates in the form
  14    Job Number                   N              mm/dd/yy or dd-mon-yy.
  15    Client Number                N
  16    Job Type                     N
  17    Description                 A30          Use "*" after field type to
  18    Manager                      N           show a key field (ex: A4*).
  19    Estimated Completion Date    D
  20    Actual Completion Date       D
```

Figure 3-50   The Structure of the PROJECTS Table

```
Viewing Struct table: Record 1 of 7                    Main
STRUCT      Field Name           Field Type
   1    Job Number                   N*
   2    Client Number                N
   3    Job Type                     N
   4    Description                 A30
   5    Manager                      N
   6    Estimated Completion Date    D
   7    Actual Completion Date       D




                                              projects table has 0 records
```

When you break a large table like PROJS into several smaller tables, you need some way to link the tables so that you can recombine the information they contain. This is accomplished by including a common field in the two tables. The linking fields don't need to have the same name, but they do need to contain the same kind of information. For example, the linking fields in EMPLYEE and PROJECTS are the Emp Number field in the EMPLYEE table and the Manager field in the PROJECTS table. Although these two fields don't have the same name, they contain the same information. The Manager field in the PROJECTS table contains the employee number (from the EMPLYEE table) of the employee assigned to manage that project. Because of this common field, the tables can be easily linked with a query. We'll show how to do this in Chapter 9.

Conclusion

In this chapter, we have shown you how to create tables, enter data, and edit the data in your tables. In addition, we have shown you how to view tables.

In Chapter 4, we will show you how to change the appearance of images and how to set validity checks for your tables. We also will discuss advanced techniques for editing and data entry. In Chapter 5, "Forms," we will show you how to design and use forms.

Chapter 4

More on Data Entry and Editing

In the preceding chapter, we showed you how to create tables, enter data into tables, and edit the records in a table. In this chapter, you'll learn more about entering and editing data. First, you'll learn about key fields. Then we'll show you how to use the Image command to change the way the image is displayed on the screen. In addition, we will discuss the ValCheck command, which allows you to define validity checks.

Keyed Tables

A keyed table is a table that has one or more key fields. A key field is a field that you designate as a primary index for a table. When you designate a key field, Paradox will arrange the records in the table so that the entries in the key field are in ascending order. In addition, Paradox will check every entry you make into the key field and will not allow you to make an entry in that field that duplicates an existing entry. Designating key fields helps to give your table order, builds a simple level of validity checking into your table, and makes queries work faster.

Key fields are strictly optional–you do not need to designate any field in any table as a key field. However, once you become familiar with Paradox, we think you'll find many uses for key fields.

Defining Key Fields

To designate a field as a key field, you type an asterisk (*) after the field type in the Field Type column of the STRUCT table as you define the table. You can enter the asterisk by typing an asterisk or by pressing the [Spacebar] after you enter the field type.

The field you use as the key field in a table must be the first field in the table. Paradox will not let you save the structure of a table that has a key field anywhere but the top of the table's structure.

An Example

For example, suppose you want to create the PROJECTS table with the structure shown in Figure 4-1. Notice that the Job Number field has been designated as a key field. To do this, issue the [**Menu**] Create command, type **PROJECTS**, and press ↵. When the STRUCT table appears on the screen, type **Job Number** in the Field Name column. Then, to designate the Job Number field as a key field, move to the Field Type column, type **N**, and then either type an asterisk (*) or press the [**Spacebar**]. Once you've defined this field, enter the remaining field names and types shown in Figure 4-1.

Figure 4-1 The PROJECTS Table

```
Viewing Struct table: Record 1 of 7                         Main
 STRUCT          Field Name           Field Type
    1      Job Number                  N*
    2      Client Number               N
    3      Job Type                    N
    4      Description                 A30
    5      Manager                     N
    6      Estimated Completion Date   D
    7      Actual Completion Date      D
```

Now, press [**Do-It!**] to save the new table and return to the main workspace. As you can see, creating keyed tables is not very different from creating other tables; however, as you will soon see, there is a big difference in the way Paradox manages keyed tables.

Notes

You can designate any field type as a key field. If you designate an alphanumeric field as a key field, the records in the table will be sorted so that the key field entries are arranged alphabetically. If you designate a date field as a key field, the records will be sorted so that the entries in that field are in order from the earliest to the most recent date. If you designate a number, short number, or dollar field as a key field, the records will be sorted so that the entries in the key field are in ascending numeric order.

One disadvantage of using key fields is that they reduce the total number of characters you can enter per record. For example, in non-keyed tables you can enter up to 4000 characters per record in the table. On the other hand, keyed tables can contain no more than 1350 characters per record.

Entering Records into Keyed Tables

Figure 4-2 shows the records we entered in the PROJECTS table for this example. Notice that the records are arranged so that the entries in the key field, Job Number, are in ascending numeric order. Regardless of the order in which records are entered in this table, Paradox will always sort them into ascending order based on the entries in the Job Number field.

Figure 4-2 A Keyed Table

PROJECTS	Job Number	Client Number	Job Type	Description	Manager	Estimated Completion Date	Actual Completion Date
1	100	1001	1	Install PC AT/Paradox/1-2-3	1	3/01/86	4/11/86
2	101	1001	3	AT/Paradox/1-2-3 Intro	1	5/01/86	
3	102	1002	2	Paradox A/R System	1	6/01/86	
4	103	1003	1	Install Compaq Plus/Symphony	1	11/01/86	
5	104	1003	2	Symphony Intro Course	4	2/21/86	2/15/86
6	105	1003	4	Recommend AR System	4	3/21/86	
7	106	1004	2	Paradox Time Accounting System	1	9/01/85	9/01/85
8	107	1004	3	1986 Compilation/Review	8	3/15/85	
9	108	1005	3	1986 Compilation/Review	8	10/15/85	10/15/85
10	109	1006	3	1986 Compilation/Review	8	9/15/85	9/15/85
11	110	1007	5	Tax Consultation		11/15/85	11/15/85
12	111	1008	2	1986 Tax Return		12/15/85	12/22/85
13	112	1009	2	1986 Tax Return	16	1/15/86	

To enter the records from Figure 4-2 into your PROJECTS table, issue the [**Menu**] Modify DataEntry command, type **PROJECTS**, and press ↵. When the ENTRY table for PROJECTS comes into view, simply type the records from Figure 4-2 into the table. When you are finished, press [**Do-It!**] or issue the [**Menu**] DO-IT! command to store the contents of ENTRY in PROJECTS.

Key Violations

By now, you are probably wondering what is so different about keyed tables. Everything we've done so far has been pretty simple. But suppose you now want to add the records shown in Table 4-1 to the PROJECTS table.

Table 4-1 Sample Data

Job Number	112	114	115
Client Number	1007	1013	1014
Job Type	1	2	1
Description	1986 Tax Return	1986 Tax Return	Install PC AT/Paradox/1-2-3
Manager	16	7	1
Estimated Completion Date	4/15/86	4/15/86	5/15/86

To do this, issue the [**Menu**] Modify DataEntry command, type **PROJECTS**, and press ↵. When the ENTRY table appears on the screen, you should enter the new data from Table 4-1. Figure 4-3 shows the completed ENTRY table. Notice that the Job Number field entry for the first record in this table conflicts with the Job Number field entry for record number 13 in PROJECTS.

Figure 4-3 The Completed ENTRY Table

```
DataEntry for Projects table: Record 1 of 3                    DataEntry
ENTRY     Job Number    Client Number    Job Type    Description
  1          112           1007             1         1986 Tax Return
  2          114           1013             2         1986 Tax Return
  3          115           1014             1         Install PC AT/Paradox
```

Now press [**Do-It!**] ([F2]). After you do this, Paradox will add the records from ENTRY to PROJECTS as usual; however, the record in ENTRY that you assigned the job number 112 will not be entered in PROJECTS. Instead, this record will be copied to the temporary KEYVIOL table. Figure 4-4 shows the screen at this point.

Figure 4-4   The KEYVIOL Table

```
Viewing Keyviol table: Record 1 of 1                            Main
  PROJECTS    Job Number    Client Number    Job Type             Description
     1           100            1001             1         Install PC AT/Paradox
     2           101            1001             3         AT/Paradox/1-2-3 Intr
     3           102            1002             2         Paradox A/R System
     4           103            1003             1         Install Compaq Plus/S
     5           104            1003             2         Symphony Intro Course
     6           105            1003             4         Recommend AR System
     7           106            1004             2         Paradox Time Accounti
     8           107            1004             3         1986 Compilation/Revi
     9           108            1005             3         1986 Compilation/Revi
    10           109            1006             3         1986 Compilation/Revi
    11           110            1007             5         Tax Consultation
    12           111            1008             2         1986 Tax Return
    13           112            1009             2         1986 Tax Return
    14           114            1013             2         1986 Tax Return
    15           115            1014             1         Install PC AT/Paradox

  KEYVIOL     Job Number    Client Number    Job Type             Description
     1           112            1007             1         1986 Tax Return
```

This happened because there already is a job number 112 in the PROJECTS table. Any time you enter records in a keyed table, Paradox will check your entries to make sure that they do not duplicate an existing entry in the key field of the permanent table. If there is a conflict, a key violation will occur when Paradox attempts to copy the records from ENTRY into the permanent table. When a key violation occurs, Paradox will place the offending records in a KEYVIOL table for editing.

Editing the KEYVIOL Table

To add this record to the PROJECTS table, you must first edit the KEYVIOL table and change the Job Number entry for the record. To do this, press [**Edit**] ([F9]) to enter the edit mode. Once you are in the edit mode, position the cursor in the Job Number field of KEYVIOL, press [**Ctrl**]-[**Backspace**] to erase the Job Number entry, and type a new entry, like **113**. Figure 4-5 shows the screen after you make this change. Next, press ↵ to lock in the new Job Number entry, then press [**Do-It!**] ([F2]) or issue the [**Menu**] DO-IT! command to leave the edit mode and save the change.

Figure 4-5   The Edited KEYVIOL Table

```
Editing Keyviol table: Record 1 of 1                           Edit
PROJECTS ─Job Number─ ─Client Number─ ─Job Type─ ─────Description─────
    1         100          1001           1       Install PC AT/Paradox
    2         101          1001           3       AT/Paradox/1-2-3 Intr
    3         102          1002           2       Paradox A/R System
    4         103          1003           1       Install Compaq Plus/S
    5         104          1003           2       Symphony Intro Course
    6         105          1003           4       Recommend AR System
    7         106          1004           2       Paradox Time Accounti
    8         107          1004           3       1986 Compilation/Revi
    9         108          1005           3       1986 Compilation/Revi
   10         109          1006           3       1986 Compilation/Revi
   11         110          1007           5       Tax Consultation
   12         111          1008           2       1986 Tax Return
   13         112          1009           2       1986 Tax Return
   14         114          1013           2       1986 Tax Return
   15         115          1014           1       Install PC AT/Paradox

KEYVIOL ─Job Number─ ─Client Number─ ─Job Type─ ─────Description─────
    1        113          1007           1       1986 Tax Return
```

Adding KEYVIOL to PROJECTS

Now, to add the record in the KEYVIOL table to the PROJECTS table, issue the [**Menu**] Tools More Add command. This command allows you to add the records in one table (called the source table) to another table (the target table). Although we will discuss this command in detail in Chapter 10, we will explain enough about it here to let you recover from key violations.

After you issue this command, Paradox will prompt you to enter the name of the source table–that is, the table that contains the records you want to add. When you see this prompt, type **KEYVIOL**, and press ↵. Paradox then will prompt you to enter the name of the table to which the records should be added–the target table. You now should type **PROJECTS** and press ↵. When you do, Paradox will display the menu in Figure 4-6.

Figure 4-6   The NewEntries/Update Menu

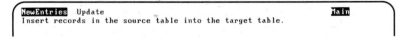

```
NewEntries  Update                                              Main
Insert records in the source table into the target table.
```

This menu tells Paradox how to treat the records you are adding to the table. The NewEntries option tells Paradox to append the records from the source table to the target table. The Update option tells Paradox to update the records in the target table, using the entries in the source table.

Since you want to add the records from the KEYVIOL table to those that are already in the PROJECTS table, you should issue the NewEntries command. Paradox then will add the records from the KEYVIOL table to the PROJECTS table and display it in the workspace. Figure 4-7 shows the new PROJECTS table.

Figure 4-7   The New PROJECTS Table

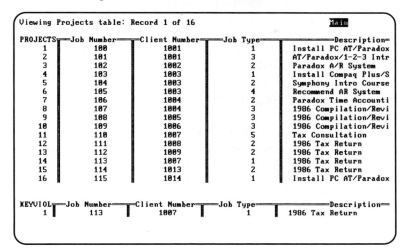

If you use the NewEntries option to add records from a KEYVIOL table to a permanent table, and you have not corrected the key violations in the KEYVIOL table, Paradox will not enter any record that still contains a key violation in the permanent table. Instead, Paradox will once again place the erroneous records in a KEYVIOL table.

Editing Keyed Tables

Editing keyed tables is a bit tricky. Because Paradox does not check for key violations during an edit, it is possible to overwrite records accidentally.

For example, suppose you are viewing the PROJECTS table, and you want to change the job number 112 to the job number 120. To do this, you would press [Edit], move to the Job Number field entry for record 13, press [Ctrl]-[Backspace] to erase the current entry, and type the new entry. However, suppose that you type 102 instead of 120. When you press [Do-It!] to end the edit and save the change, Paradox will replace the original job number 102 with the renamed job number 112. Moreover, the replaced record will not be placed in any temporary table–it is gone forever.

You can avoid this trap by editing keyed tables through the [Menu] Modify DataEntry command. For example, instead of pressing [Edit] to make the change in the job number, issue the [**Menu**] **M**odify **D**ataEntry command, type **PROJECTS**, and press ↵. When the ENTRY table appears on the screen, type in the complete record for the job number 120 and press [**Do-It!**]. Now, if you've typed 102 instead of 120, the record will be placed in a KEYVIOL table. You then can edit the KEYVIOL table and add the record to the PROJECTS table. Of course, you still will need to delete the old record 112 from the PROJECTS table, but this way you'll have a chance to make sure the changes are correct.

Another way to minimize any potential loss of data is to make sure that you always make a backup copy of important tables. We'll show you how to do this with the [Menu] Tools Copy command in Chapter 6, "Managing Tables."

Except for the potential trap discussed above, editing a keyed table is exactly the same as editing any other table. Remember, though–use caution when editing your keyed tables.

Tables with Two Key Fields

If you wish, you can designate more than one key field in a table. When you do this, Paradox will allow duplicate entries in each individual key field but will not allow any two records to have the same entries in all the key fields. This is useful when you have a table with two fields, which individually can contain duplicate entries, but when considered together, must be unique.

For example, suppose you are using Paradox for order entry. You want to create a table named ORDLOG that records every order you write. Let's assume that each order you write may include three or four different lines, each of which represents an order for a different product. For example, order 1001 may include three lines: an order for three widgets, an order for two wombats, and an order for one woofer. So that you can track your orders accurately, you need to record two pieces of information about each item ordered: the order number and the line number. Figure 4-8 shows the structure of a table that will do the trick. You will notice that the first two fields in this table are Ord Num and Line.

Figure 4-8 The Structure of ORDLOG

```
Viewing Struct table: Record 1 of 4                         Main
 STRUCT        Field Name        Field Type
    1      Ord Num               N*
    2      Line                  N*
    3      Description           A20
    4      Price                 $




                                              Ordlog table has 10 records
```

By designating both the Ord Num and Line fields as keys, you make it possible for both fields to contain duplicate entries, but impossible for any two records to have the same entry in both fields. In other words, while there might be several 1001 entries in the Ord Num field, and several 1 entries in the Line field, there could be only one record with the Ord Num field entry 1001 and the Line field entry 1. If you attempted to enter a second record with these entries, Paradox would copy that record into a KEYVIOL table.

Designating just one key field, in this case, won't work. You already know that each order may have several lines, and thus will occupy several records in the table. For example, order 1001 described above would occupy three records: order 1001, line 1; order 1001, line 2; and order 1001, line 3. Since each of these records will have the same Ord Num field entry, you can't make Ord Num alone a key field. Similarly, since every order will have at least one line 1, there will be many duplicate entries in the Line field.

If you designate more than one key field, you still must place the key fields at the top of the table. If the table has several key fields, then all of the key fields must be at the top of the table's structure, before any non-key fields.

When a table contains more than one key field, Paradox will arrange the table so that the entries in the primary (first) key field are in ascending numeric order. If there are duplicate entries in the primary key field (as there will usually be), then Paradox uses the entries in the secondary key field to break the ties. For example, Figure 4-9 shows the ORDLOG table as it will look after a few records have been entered. Notice that the records are arranged in ascending Ord Num field order and that the records in each Ord Num group are arranged by the Line field entries.

Figure 4-9   The ORDLOG Table

```
Viewing Ordlog table: Record 1 of 10                            Main
ORDLOG    Ord Num      Line      Description         Price
   1       1001         1        Widgets              34.95
   2       1001         2        Wombats              56.00
   3       1001         3        Woofer               75.00
   4       1002         1        Woofer               75.00
   5       1003         1        Wombats              56.00
   6       1003         2        Wombats              56.00
   7       1004         1        Wombats              56.00
   8       1004         3        Widgets              34.95
   9       1004         4        Wombats              56.00
  10       1005         1        Wombats              56.00
```

Key Fields and Queries

In Chapter 8, we'll show you how to create queries. Queries are special tools that allow you to select information from a table. One of the advantages of key fields is that they make your queries work faster. Although that probably does not make much sense to you right now, later on it will be very important.

Changing the Image

The Image command allows you to make changes in the way information is displayed on the screen, without affecting the actual table upon which the image is based. The Image command is on three different menus: Main, DataEntry, and Edit. Except for the KeepSettings option, which appears only when you issue the Image command from the Main menu, the Image commands on all three menus offer the same capabilities.

The Image Menu

Suppose you are viewing the EMPLYEE table, and you want to change the way the image is displayed on the screen. To do this, issue the **[Menu]** Image command. After you issue the command, Paradox will display the menu shown in Figure 4-10.

Figure 4-10 The Image Menu

```
TableSize  ColumnSize  Format  GoTo  Move  PickForm  KeepSettings  Main
Change the number of records to show in the current image.
```

If you are viewing the table through a form, the menu will look like Figure 4-11. Notice that the TableSize, ColumnSize, and Move options are not available on the Form View image menu; however, the remaining options work the same in the form view as they do in the table view.

Figure 4-11 The Image Menu for Forms

```
Format  GoTo  PickForm  KeepSettings                        Main  =▼
Change the format of a field.
```

Changing the Number of Records Showing

Normally, Paradox can display up to 22 records of a table on the screen at one time. (Of course, if there is more than one image on the screen, you are unlikely to see the full 22 records.) However, you can change the number of records displayed by issuing the [Menu] Image TableSize command.

For example, suppose you are viewing the EMPLYEE table. Since the EMPLYEE table contains just 16 records, its on-screen image is only 16 rows deep. But suppose you want to reduce the image to display only ten records at a time. To do this, issue the **[Menu]** Image TableSize command. After you issue this command, the cursor will change to a blinking box (sometimes referred to as the pointing cursor) in the last record of the table. At this point, you can press ↑, ↓, [Home], or [End] to change the size of the EMPLYEE image. Pressing the ↑ key reduces the number of records shown on the screen. Each time you press ↑, the size of the image shrinks by one row. You can reduce the number of records in the image to a minimum of two. If you want to shrink the image to the two-record minimum, you can simply press [Home].

To increase the number of records showing, press the ↓ key. You can press the [End] key to move quickly to the maximum allowable display (22 records) or the total number of records in the table, whichever is smaller.

To reduce the size of the EMPLYEE image from 16 records to ten records, press ↑ six times, then press ↵ to lock in the change. Figure 4-12 shows the EMPLYEE table image as it will look after you make this change. Notice that only ten records are in view. When you've set the table size, you can view and manipulate the records as before. The only difference will be the number of records displayed on the screen at one time.

Figure 4-12 Changing the Number of Records Displayed

```
Viewing Employee table: Record 10 of 16                              Main
  EMPLYEE==Emp Number==---Last Name===T=First Name===SS Number===========Addre
      1         1         Jones         David         414-76-3421    4000 St. Ja
      2         2         Cameron       Herb          321-65-8765    2331 Elm St
      3         4         Jones         Stewart       401-32-8721    4389 Oakbri
      4         5         Roberts       Darlene       417-43-7777    451 Lone Pi
      5         6         Jones         Jean          413-07-9123    4000 St. Ja
      6         8         Williams      Brenda        401-55-1567    100 Owl Cre
      7         9         Myers         Julie         314-38-9452    4512 Parksi
      8        10         Link          Julie         345-75-1525    3215 Palm C
      9        12         Jackson       Mary          424-13-7621    7821 Clark
     10        13         Jakes, Jr.    Sal           321-65-9151    3451 Michig
```

Changing the Column (Field) Size

You can use the ColumnSize option on the Image menu to increase or decrease the width of a column (field). One application of this command is to reduce the size of the columns in the image so that you can see more columns at once.

For example, when you look at Figure 4-12, you'll notice that the Address column is partially hidden. If you want to view the entire Address column, you can reduce the width of one or more of the columns to its left. To do this, issue the **[Menu] I**mage ColumnSize command. After you issue this command, the cursor will change to a box, and Paradox will display the instructions shown in Figure 4-13 at the top of the screen.

When you see these instructions, you should press the → and ← keys to position the pointing cursor in the Emp Number column, and press ↵. Paradox then will display the instructions for sizing the column shown in Figure 4-14.

Figure 4-13 The ColumnSize Prompt

```
Use → and ← to move to the column you want to resize...    Main
then press ↵ to select it...
EMPLYEE═══Emp Number═══════Last Name═══════First Name═══════SS Number═══════════Addre
     1         1            Jones           David           414-76-3421        4000 St. Ja
     2         2            Cameron         Herb            321-65-8765        2331 Elm St
     3         4            Jones           Stewart         401-32-8721        4389 Oakbri
     4         5            Roberts         Darlene         417-43-7777        451 Lone Pi
     5         6            Jones           Jean            413-07-9123        4000 St. Ja
     6         8            Williams        Brenda          401-55-1567        100 Owl Cre
     7         9            Myers           Julie           314-38-9452        4512 Parksi
     8        10            Link            Julie           345-75-1525        3215 Palm C
     9        12            Jackson         Mary            424-13-7621        7821 Clark
    10        13            Jakes, Jr.      Sal             321-65-9151        3451 Michig
```

Figure 4-14 Defining the Column Size

```
Now use → to increase column width, ← to decrease...    Main
press ↵ when finished.
```

At this point, you can press ← or → to narrow or widen the current column. Each time you press ←, the column will become one character narrower. Pressing → will make the column wider, one character at a time. You can decrease the width of a column to one character or increase its width to be as wide as its field name, up to 25 characters. If you want to reduce the width of a field to one character, just press [Home]. If you want to make it as wide as possible, press [End].

To reduce the size of the Emp Number field to one character, press the ← key several times or the [Home] key once. Notice that as you press ← or [Home] to decrease the width of Emp Number, the columns to its right are pulled to the left, and the entire Address field comes into view. When you have the column size adjusted, press ↵. Figure 4-15 shows the new image of the EMPLYEE table.

Figure 4-15 The New Image of EMPLYEE

```
Viewing Emplyee table: Record 10 of 16                   Main
EMPLYEE═Emp ═Last Name══════First Name═════SS Number═══════════Address═══════════
     1   *   Jones           David          414-76-3421        4000 St. James Ct.
     2   *   Cameron         Herb           321-65-8765        2331 Elm St.
     3   *   Jones           Stewart        401-32-8721        4389 Oakbridge Rd.
     4   *   Roberts         Darlene        417-43-7777        451 Lone Pine Dr.
     5   *   Jones           Jean           413-07-9123        4000 St. James Ct.
     6   *   Williams        Brenda         401-55-1567        100 Owl Creek Rd.
     7   *   Myers           Julie          314-38-9452        4512 Parkside Dr.
     8   *   Link            Julie          345-75-1525        3215 Palm Ct.
     9   *   Jackson         Mary           424-13-7621        7821 Clark Ave.
    10   *   Jakes, Jr.      Sal            321-65-9151        3451 Michigan Ave.
```

When you look at Figure 4-15, you will notice that the numerical values in the Emp Number field have been replaced with asterisks. This occurred because we made the column too small to display the values in the field. If you use 1-2-3, this format may be familiar to you.

Whenever you reduce the width of a number, dollar, or short number field so much that Paradox cannot display the values in the field in full, it will display them as a series of asterisks instead. This does not mean that the values in your table now contain asterisks–only the image is affected. Reducing the width of an alphanumeric or date field does not have the same effect. When you reduce the width of alphanumeric or date fields, Paradox simply displays as many characters as will fit in the narrow column.

Field View

If you want to view the entries in a narrow field, you can enter the field view. To do this, position the cursor on a record in the narrow column and press [**Field View**] ([Alt]-[F5] or [Ctrl]-[F]). After you press [Field View], the cursor will change to a box, and the field value will be displayed. For example, Figure 4-16 shows the first record in the Emp Number field after we have entered the field view.

Figure 4-16   A Field View

```
Viewing Emplyee table: Record 1 of 16                                Main
EMPLYEE┬Emp  ┬─Last Name─┬─First Name─┬─SS Number─┬────Address────────┐
    1  │ 1  │ Jones     │ David      │ 414-76-3421│ 4000 St. James Ct.│
    2  │ *  │ Cameron   │ Herb       │ 321-65-8765│ 2331 Elm St.      │
    3  │ *  │ Jones     │ Stewart    │ 401-32-8721│ 4389 Oakbridge Rd.│
    4  │ *  │ Roberts   │ Darlene    │ 417-43-7777│ 451 Lone Pine Dr. │
    5  │ *  │ Jones     │ Jean       │ 413-07-9123│ 4000 St. James Ct.│
    6  │ *  │ Williams  │ Brenda     │ 401-55-1567│ 100 Owl Creek Rd. │
    7  │ *  │ Myers     │ Julie      │ 314-38-9452│ 4512 Parkside Dr. │
    8  │ *  │ Link      │ Julie      │ 345-75-1525│ 3215 Palm Ct.     │
    9  │ *  │ Jackson   │ Mary       │ 424-13-7621│ 7821 Clark Ave.   │
   10  │ *  │ Jakes, Jr.│ Sal        │ 321-65-9151│ 3451 Michigan Ave.│
```

As you learned in Chapter 3, when you are in the field view, the functions of the cursor movement keys change. For example, in the field view the → and ← keys move the cursor one character to the right or left, respectively. The [Home] key moves the cursor to the first character in the field, while the [End] key moves the cursor to the last character. You can use these keys to scroll through the entry in the narrow field. Although you can only see a few characters at a time (in the example, only one character at a time), by scrolling though the field, you can eventually see the entire entry.

Although you can use the field view to view the contents of fields in narrow columns, normally you will not want to leave any column in an image so narrow that you can't see at least most of the values it contains. For instance, you would probably not want to leave the width of the Emp Number field at one character. To widen this field to six characters (wide enough to view all of the entries the field contains), issue the [**Menu**] Image ColumnSize command, point to the Emp Number field, press → five times, and press ↵. Figure 4-17 shows the EMPLYEE table at this point. Notice that all of the field values are now displayed, but the field name remains partially hidden.

Figure 4-17 The EMPLYEE Table

```
Viewing Employee table: Record 1 of 16                              Main
 EMPLYEE Emp Number  Last Name    First Name    SS Number       Address
   1       1         Jones        David         414-76-3421     4000 St. James Ct
   2       2         Cameron      Herb          321-65-8765     2331 Elm St.
   3       4         Jones        Stewart       401-32-8721     4389 Oakbridge Rd
   4       5         Roberts      Darlene       417-43-7777     451 Lone Pine Dr.
   5       6         Jones        Jean          413-07-9123     4000 St. James Ct
   6       8         Williams     Brenda        401-55-1567     100 Owl Creek Rd.
   7       9         Myers        Julie         314-38-9452     4512 Parkside Dr.
   8      10         Link         Julie         345-75-1525     3215 Palm Ct.
   9      12         Jackson      Mary          424-13-7621     7821 Clark Ave.
  10      13         Jakes, Jr.   Sal           321-65-9151     3451 Michigan Ave
```

Changing the Field Format

The Image menu also offers a command, Format, that allows you to change the display format of number, dollar, and date fields. Field formats in Paradox are very much like cell formats in Lotus 1-2-3.

To change the format of a field, you issue the [Menu] Image Format command and select the field you want to format. After you have told Paradox which field you want to format, it will present a menu of format options that are appropriate to the type of field you have selected. You choose the option you want from the menu to format the field.

Date Formats

Paradox allows you to display dates in two different forms: MM/DD/YY or DD-Mon-YY. As you learned in Chapter 3, you can enter date values in either of these forms. However, in the default state, Paradox will always display dates in the form MM/DD/YY. If you want to display the dates in a date field in DD-Mon-YY form, you must format that field.

For example, suppose you want to change the format of the Date of Birth field in the sample EMPLYEE table. To do this, first issue the [Menu] Image Format command. After you issue this command, the cursor will change to a box, and Paradox will instruct you to select the field you want to format. When you see this prompt, you should move the cursor to the Date of Birth field and press ↵. Paradox will recognize the field as a date field and will display the format options shown in Figure 4-18.

Figure 4-18 Format Options for Date Fields

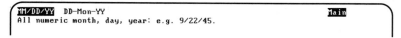

The first option, MM/DD/YY, is the default display for date fields. The other option displays dates in the form DD-Mon-YY so that the date January 13, 1986, would be displayed as 13-Jan-86. You should select the format you prefer by highlighting it with the cursor and pressing ↵. After you do this, Paradox will reformat all of the values in the column. For example, Figure 4-19 shows how the screen will look after you change the format for the Date of Birth field.

Figure 4-19   Changing the Default Date Format

```
Viewing Emplyee table: Record 1 of 16                    Main
┌─City────────┬─State─┬─Zip───┬─Phone────────┬─Date of Birth─┬─Date o─
│ St. Matthews│  KY   │ 40207 │ (502) 245-6610│  6-Oct-42    │  6/01
│ Louisville  │  KY   │ 40205 │ (502) 451-8765│ 24-Nov-29    │  6/01
│ Lyndon      │  KY   │ 40222 │ (502) 452-1848│ 21-Mar-50    │  7/01
│ Lagrange    │  KY   │ 40012 │ (502) 897-3215│ 24-Sep-60    │ 11/01
│ St. Matthews│  KY   │ 40207 │ (502) 245-6610│ 14-May-43    │ 12/01
│ Anchorage   │  KY   │ 40223 │ (502) 894-9761│ 12-Jan-20    │  1/01
│ Louisville  │  KY   │ 40206 │ (502) 454-5209│  6-Feb-48    │  2/01
│ Palo Alto   │  CA   │ 94375 │ (408) 542-1948│  3-Jun-33    │  4/01
│ Clarksville │  IN   │ 47130 │ (812) 288-6754│ 12-Aug-56    │  4/01
│ Dallas      │  TX   │ 65987 │ (214) 398-1987│ 23-May-59    │  5/01
```

Number and Dollar Fields

As you know, Paradox treats number and dollar fields in much the same way. In fact, the only difference between the two is their default display format. The default format for a number field is Paradox's General format. The default format for a dollar field is Comma. As you might expect, you can change the format of either dollar or number fields. In fact, the format options for these two types of fields are identical.

For example, suppose you want to reformat the Salary field in the EMPLYEE table. To do this, issue the **[Menu] I**mage **F**ormat command, select the Salary field, and press ↵. Paradox will recognize the field as a dollar field and will display the menu shown in Figure 4-20. The current format for the field, Comma, will be highlighted with the cursor. The other options are the available formats for number and dollar fields.

Figure 4-20   Format Options for Number and Dollar Fields

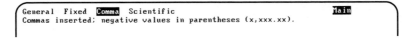

The Format Options

The General format is the default format for number fields. In this format, numbers are displayed without commas and with up to two decimal places, if necessary. For example, the number 1,234.00 will be displayed as 1234 in the General format. The number 1,234.56 will be displayed as 1234.56, the number 1,234.50 will be displayed as 1234.5, the number 1234.5678 will be displayed as 1234.5678, and so on. In the General format, negative numbers are preceded by a minus sign (-). For instance, the number -1,234.56 will be displayed as -1234.56. Large numbers are displayed as a series of asterisks. In the General format, numbers are aligned as though they have two decimal places, even if they have no decimals at all.

The Fixed format displays a set number of decimal places for the displayed values. For example, if you select Fixed and set the number of decimal places to 2, the number 1,234 will be displayed as 1234.00. The number 1234.567 will be displayed as 1234.57 in this format. Negative numbers are preceded by a minus sign in the Fixed format.

You can specify from zero to 15 decimal places. If you specify more decimal places than there are digits in the number being formatted, Paradox will append zeros to the number. For instance, the number 1234.5 would be displayed as 1234.50000 in the Fixed format with five decimal places. If the number of decimals you specify is less than the number of decimals in the number being formatted, Paradox will round the number for display purposes. For example, the number 1234.5678 would be displayed as 1235 in the Fixed format with zero decimal places.

The Comma format is the default format for dollar fields. In the Comma format, numbers are displayed with commas between the hundreds and thousands, thousands and millions, and so on. You can tell Paradox to include from zero to 15 decimal places in the display (the default is two decimal places). Negative numbers are displayed enclosed in parentheses in the Comma format. For example, the value 33,999.99 will be displayed as 33,999.99 in the Comma format with two decimal places. The value -33,999.99 will be displayed as (33,999.99). The value 1234.567 will be displayed as 1,234.5670 in the Comma format with four decimal places and as 1,235 in the Comma format with zero decimal places.

The Scientific format displays values in exponential notation with from zero to 15 decimal places. For example, the number 70,000.00 will be displayed as 7.00E+04 and the number 1,234,567.89 will be displayed as 1.23E+06 in the Scientific format with two decimal places. Negative numbers are preceded by a minus sign. For example, the number -1,234,567.89 will be displayed as -1.235E+06 in the Scientific format with three decimal places.

Changing the Format

To change the format of the selected field, position the cursor on the format you prefer, and press ↵. For example, suppose you want to change the format of the Salary field from Comma with two decimal places to Comma with zero decimal places. To do this, point to the Comma option and press ↵. After you select the format you prefer, Paradox will prompt you to set the number of decimal places. The default setting (2) is already filled in for you. If you want to accept this setting, just press ↵. To change this setting, press the [Backspace] key to erase the default setting, then type a number from zero to 15. For instance, to change the setting to 0, press [**Backspace**], type **0**, and then press ↵.

How Paradox Displays Formatted Numbers

It is important that you understand that the number of decimals you specify when you format a number or dollar field does not affect the actual values stored in that field. The format only changes the way the numbers appear in the image of the table. Even though the numbers are rounded for display purposes, the actual numbers remain unchanged.

Working with Formatted Fields

When you edit a rounded field, the cursor will appear at the left of the field, rather than the right, to remind you that the value has been rounded. In addition, an asterisk will appear at the end of the field, as shown in Figure 4-21.

Figure 4-21   Editing a Rounded Field

```
Editing Emplyee table: Record 5 of 16                    Edit
─Date of Hire─┬─Exemptions─┬─────Salary─
    6/01/84   │     3      │     70,000
    6/01/84   │     4      │     50,000
    7/01/84   │     1      │     47,000
   11/01/84   │     3      │     14,000
   12/01/84   │     0      │ -   34,000* ◄
    1/01/85   │     4      │     40,000
    2/01/85   │     1      │     32,000
    4/01/85   │     2      │     30,000
    4/01/85   │     3      │     21,000
    5/01/85   │     6      │     34,000
```

If you want to edit a rounded field, you must use [Field View] or reformat the field.

Alphanumeric and Short Number Fields

You cannot change the format for alphanumeric or short number fields. If you try to format an alphanumeric or short number field, Paradox will display the message *Only N, $, and D fields may be formatted* at the bottom of the screen.

The Move Command

The Move command allows you to change the order of the fields in the image of a table without affecting the arrangement of the fields in the actual table. For example, suppose you want the State field to be the first field in the image of the EMPLYEE table. To make this change, issue the **[Menu] I**mage **M**ove command. After you issue the command, Paradox will display a list of the fields in the table and will prompt you to select a field to move, as shown in Figure 4-22.

Figure 4-22 Selecting a Field to Move

```
Name of field to move:                                           Main
Emp Number  Last Name  First Name  SS Number  Address  City  State  Zip  Phone ►
```

When you see this prompt, you should select the State field and press ↵. When you do, the cursor will change to a box, and Paradox will instruct you to point to the place where you want to insert the field. Exactly where you point depends on whether you are moving the column to the left or right of its original position. If you are moving a column to the left, it will be inserted to the left of the column in which you place the pointing cursor. If you are moving a column to the right, it will be inserted to the right of the column in which you place the pointing cursor.

Since you are moving the State field to the left and you want it to appear to the left of the Emp Number field, you should move the pointing cursor to the Emp Number column. When the cursor is in place, press ↵. After you do this, Paradox will move the column to its new location and shift all other columns automatically. Figure 4-23 shows the screen after you move the column.

Figure 4-23 The New Field Order for EMPLYEE

```
Viewing Emplyee table: Record 1 of 16                    Main
EMPLYEE State  Emp Number  Last Name    First Name   SS Number     Addre
    1    KY         1      Jones        David        414-76-3421   4000 St. Ja
    2    KY         2      Cameron      Herb         321-65-8765   2331 Elm St
    3    KY         4      Jones        Stewart      401-32-8721   4389 Oakbri
    4    KY         5      Roberts      Darlene      417-43-7777   451 Lone Pi
    5    KY         6      Jones        Jean         413-07-9123   4000 St. Ja
    6    KY         8      Williams     Brenda       401-55-1567   100 Owl Cre
    7    KY         9      Myers        Julie        314-38-9452   4512 Parksi
    8    CA        10      Link         Julie        345-75-1525   3215 Palm C
    9    IN        12      Jackson      Mary         424-13-7621   7821 Clark
   10    TX        13      Jakes, Jr.   Sal          321-65-9151   3451 Michig
```

The [Rotate] Key [Ctrl]-[R]

You can also move columns by pressing [Rotate] ([Ctrl]-[R]). However, unlike the Move command, [Rotate] doesn't allow you to move a field to a specific location. Instead, [Rotate] always moves the current field to the end of the table so that it is the last field.

For example, suppose you now want to move the Emp Number field to the end of the table image. First position the cursor in the Emp Number field, then press **[Rotate]** ([Ctrl]-[R]). Figure 4-24 shows the screen after you move the Emp Number column.

Figure 4-24 Using [Rotate]

```
Viewing Emplyee table: Record 1 of 16                    Main
EMPLYEE State  Last Name    First Name   SS Number      Address
    1    KY    Jones        David        414-76-3421    4000 St. James Ct.
    2    KY    Cameron      Herb         321-65-8765    2331 Elm St.
    3    KY    Jones        Stewart      401-32-8721    4389 Oakbridge Rd.
    4    KY    Roberts      Darlene      417-43-7777    451 Lone Pine Dr.
    5    KY    Jones        Jean         413-07-9123    4000 St. James Ct.
    6    KY    Williams     Brenda       401-55-1567    100 Owl Creek Rd.
    7    KY    Myers        Julie        314-38-9452    4512 Parkside Dr.
    8    CA    Link         Julie        345-75-1525    3215 Palm Ct.
    9    IN    Jackson      Mary         424-13-7621    7821 Clark Ave.
   10    TX    Jakes, Jr.   Sal          321-65-9151    3451 Michigan Ave.
```

[Rotate] is most useful in situations where you want to scroll through the fields in a table but don't want to permanently alter the image. If you keep pressing [Rotate], the fields in the image will rotate toward the left edge of the image, enabling you to view each one without moving the cursor. If you press [Rotate] enough times, the original order of the columns will be restored.

The KeepSettings Command

The KeepSettings command tells Paradox to remember the image settings you have established for a particular table and to make them the default settings for viewing, entering data into, or editing that table. Unless you issue this command, none of the changes made in the image are permanent. Once you end the current session, the default settings will be restored.

For example, suppose you have used every command discussed in this chapter to define just the right image for your table. You certainly don't want to go through the same process every time you view the table. To avoid such frustration, you should issue the [Menu] Image KeepSettings command. When you do, Paradox will save the image settings for the current table in a file with the name EMPLYEE.SET and will display the message *Settings recorded...* at the bottom of the screen. If you already have a .SET file associated with the table, Paradox will replace the existing file with the new one. The next time you view the table, enter data, or edit the records, the table image will be displayed with the image settings you saved.

You will recall that the Image command can be found in three locations: on the Main menu, on the DataEntry menu, and on the Edit menu. Ansa put this command in three places so that you would have the flexibility to change the image you are working with during any activity. However, when you are entering or editing records, if you issue the Image command, you will notice that there is no KeepSettings option. The Image command on these menus allows you to change the image, but the changes you make cannot be saved.

You can delete the Settings file for a table with the [Menu] Tools Delete KeepSettings command. For example, suppose you decide that you don't want to keep the settings you just saved for the EMPLYEE table. To delete the settings, issue the [Menu] Tools Delete KeepSettings command. When Paradox prompts you to enter the name of the table whose settings you wish to delete, type **EMPLYEE** and press ↵. After you do this, Paradox will delete the file and return to the main workspace. Once you delete the .SET file, Paradox will display the table with the default settings. (For more on the Tools command, please refer to Chapter 6, "Managing Tables.")

The ValCheck Command

The ValCheck command allows you to establish validity checks for your tables. As you know, Paradox does some validity checking automatically. For example, it won't let you enter letters in a number field or make an entry in an alphanumeric field that is longer than the field width. In addition, you've seen how key fields can be used to prevent duplicate entries in certain fields. However, ValCheck takes you one step further than these basic tools.

You will find the ValCheck command on both the DataEntry and Edit menus. When you issue the ValCheck command, Paradox will display the menu shown in Figure 4-25.

Figure 4-25 The ValCheck Menu

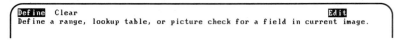

The ValCheck menu has two options: Define and Clear. The Define command lets you set the validity checks you want for the current image. The Clear command lets you clear validity checks for all, or individual fields in the current image. If you choose the **D**efine command, the cursor will change to a small, blinking box, and Paradox will prompt you to select the field for which you want to establish a validity check. You should move the cursor to the appropriate field and press ↵. Paradox then will display the menu shown in Figure 4-26, which lists the types of validity checks you can establish. We will review each of these options in the examples that follow.

Figure 4-26 Validity Checks

Setting a Low Value

The LowValue option allows you to set a minimum value for the entries in a field. Once you define a low value for a field, you will not be able to make an entry in the field that has a value lower than the low value.

For example, suppose you are viewing the EMPLYEE table, and you want to set a validity check for the Salary field that will not allow entries of less than $5,000.00. To do this, first press **[Edit]** ([F9]) to enter the edit mode, then issue the **[Menu]** **V**alCheck command. After you issue the ValCheck command, you will see the menu shown in Figure 4-25. Since you want to define a validity check, you should choose **D**efine. When Paradox prompts you to specify the field to which you want to assign a validity check, move the cursor to the Salary field and press ↵. Paradox then will display the menu shown in Figure 4-26. To set a low value for the Salary field, choose the **L**owValue command.

Next, Paradox will prompt you to specify the low value for the field. When you see this prompt, type **5000,** and press ↵. After you do this, the message *Low value recorded* will appear in the lower-right corner of the screen. The message will disappear when you press any key.

From now on, Paradox will check any value that you enter in the Salary field to ensure that it is greater than or equal to 5000. If you try to enter a value that is less than 5000, Paradox will not accept the entry and will not allow you to move the cursor out of the field. For example, if you try to enter the value 4999 in the Salary field after defining the low value 5000, your screen will look like Figure 4-27.

Figure 4-27 An Invalid Entry

```
Editing Emplyee table: Record 1 of 16                    Edit
╔Date of Birth╤═Date of Hire═╤═Exemptions═╤═════Salary═════╗
    10/06/42      6/01/84         3        4999
    11/24/29      6/01/84         4        50,000.00
     3/21/50      7/01/84         1        47,000.00
     9/24/60     11/01/84         3        14,000.00
     5/14/43     12/01/84         0        33,999.99
     1/12/20      1/01/85         4        40,000.00
     2/06/48      2/01/85         1        32,000.00
     6/03/33      4/01/85         2        30,000.00
     8/12/56      4/01/85         3        21,000.00
     5/23/59      5/01/85         6        34,000.00
     4/17/66      7/01/85         1        14,750.00
    12/31/44      7/01/85         0        38,000.00
     3/16/25      7/15/85         1        37,000.00
     5/09/45     10/01/85         4        32,125.00
     5/18/50     11/01/85         2        17,500.00
     7/30/66      1/01/86         2        12,000.00


                                    Value no less than 5000.00 is expected
```

To correct the entry, press **[Ctrl]-[Backspace]** to clear the field, then type a number greater than or equal to 5000. Once you have made an appropriate response, you can leave the field and continue with the edit.

Although we used a dollar field to demonstrate the use of the LowValue command, you can also use the LowValue command in number and short number fields. In addition, the LowValue command can be used in date fields. For example, suppose you want to make sure that no Date of Hire field entry is less than 6/1/84, the date your company was founded. To set this validity check, issue the **[Menu]** ValCheck Define command and select the Date of Hire field at the prompt. Next, issue the LowValue command, type **6/1/84** at the prompt, and press ↵. Now Paradox will not let you enter any date in the field that comes before 6/1/84.

You can even use LowValue in alphanumeric fields if you wish. If you define a low value for an alphanumeric field, Paradox will not allow any entry in that field that has an ASCII value lower than the ASCII value of the LowValue setting. For the most part, you will not find this particular validity check very useful for alphanumeric fields.

Setting a High Value

You can also establish an upper limit for the values entered in a field. For example, suppose you want to set a high value for the Exemptions field in EMPLOYEE so that no number greater than nine is entered. To do this, first you must issue the **[Menu]** View command to bring **EMPLYEE** into view (if it is not already in view) and press **[Edit]** to enter the edit mode. Next, issue the **[Menu]** Val**C**heck **D**efine command. When Paradox prompts you to define the high value field, select the **E**xemptions field. Next, issue the **H**igh**V**alue command.

Paradox will then prompt you for the high value. When you see this prompt, type **9** and press ↵. After you do this, the message *High value recorded* will appear at the bottom of the screen. The message will disappear when you press any key.

From now on, if you try to enter a value greater than nine in the Exemptions field, Paradox will display the message *Value no greater than 9 is expected* at the bottom of the screen and will not let you leave the field until you make an acceptable response.

Like the LowValue command, the HighValue command can be used with any type of field. When you set a high value for a date field, Paradox will not allow you to enter a date in that field that is greater than (after) the high value date. If you set a high value for an alphanumeric field, Paradox will not allow you to enter a value in that field that has an ASCII value greater than the ASCII value of the high value you specify.

Setting a Default Value

The Default command on the ValCheck menu allows you to set a default value for a field. When you specify a default value for a field, Paradox will enter that value in that field of every record, unless you specifically tell it otherwise. If you want Paradox to enter the default value in the field, all you have to do is leave the field empty. This is an extremely useful feature that can save you a lot of time.

For example, suppose that most of your employees live in the same city, like Louisville. If you set *Louisville* as the default value for the City field, Paradox will automatically enter Louisville in the City field of every record, unless you type a different entry.

To set Louisville as the default value for the City field in EMPLYEE, first bring EMPLYEE into view and enter the edit mode. Next, issue the **[Menu]** Val**C**heck **D**efine command and select the City field when Paradox tells you to specify the field to which you want to assign a validity check. Next, issue the **D**efault command. When you do, Paradox will prompt you to enter a default value. You should type **Louisville** and press ↵. When you do this, the message *Default value recorded* will appear at the bottom of the screen.

From this point on, if the user leaves the City field of any record blank as he is entering records, Paradox will automatically enter the value *Louisville* into that blank field.

Of course, you can set a default value for date and number fields as well as alphanumeric fields. For example, suppose you want to set the default for the Exemptions field at 1. To do this, issue the **[Menu]** Val**C**heck **D**efine command, select the Exemptions field, issue the **D**efault command, and type **1**. Once you have set this default, Pardox will enter a 1 in the Exemptions field of any record for which you do not specify a different number.

When you establish a default validity check, be sure to type the default value exactly as you want it entered. The value Paradox enters into your table will be identical to the default value you specify. If you mistype the default value, every entry that Paradox makes for you will also be mistyped.

The Picture Command

The Picture option on the ValCheck menu allows you to establish a "picture" for the entries in a field. Once you set a picture for a field, all of the entries in that field must conform to the picture.

Pictures perform three basic functions. First, they define the type of characters that an entry may contain. Second, they define the number of characters that an entry must contain. Third, they allow you to define the position of literal characters (such as the dashes in a Social Secuity number or the slashes in a date) in an entry.

There are several different symbols you can use to define pictures. The basic building blocks for pictures are shown in Table 4-2. Each of these picture characters tells Paradox to accept a particular type of character. In addition to these simple symbols, there is another group of special symbols that you can use in pictures. We'll cover those symbols in the next part of this chapter.

Table 4-2 Picture Characters

Picture	Function
#	Accepts a number only.
?	Accepts a letter only (upper or lower case).
@	Accepts any character.
&	Accepts only a letter and converts it to upper case.
!	Accepts any character and converts it to upper case.

The # Character

The # character accepts only numbers. You can use this character to define pictures for alphanumeric fields that should only contain number entries–fields like Zip and SS Number. For example, suppose you want to be sure that every entry made in the Zip field of EMPLYEE will be entered in the form 12345. To do this, issue the **[Menu]** ValCheck Define command. When Paradox prompts you to supply the field to which you want to assign the validity check, specify the Zip field. Next, issue the **Picture** command. When you do, Paradox will prompt you to enter the picture for this field. To define the appropriate picture for this field, type ##### and press ↵. Paradox will then display the message *Picture specification recorded* at the bottom of the screen.

The picture ##### specifies an entry made up of five numbers. Once you assign this picture to the Zip field, Paradox will only allow entries in that field that match the picture. For one thing, this picture restricts the types of characters you can enter in the

Zip field. If you try to enter a character other than a number in this field, Paradox will respond with a low-pitched beep. This occurs because the symbol #, which you used throughout the picture, only matches numeric characters.

Second, this picture tells Paradox that Zip field entries must contain five characters. If you try to leave the field before you have typed five numbers, Paradox will display the message *Incomplete field* at the bottom of the screen. You will not be able to leave the field until you complete the entry.

The ? Character

The picture character ? tells Paradox to accept only letters. You might use this character in a picture in an alphanumeric field to restrict the field to letters. For example, suppose that you have a table named CLIENTS that contains a field named CODE that, in turn, contains three-letter abbreviations of your clients' names. Every Code field entry must be three characters long. You could use the picture ??? to force the user to enter three characters each time he or she makes an entry in the Code field. Since ? only accepts letters, the picture ??? would also prevent the user from entering a number in this field.

The @ Character

The @ character will accept any character, number, or letter. Since Paradox will normally accept any character in an alphanumeric field, this symbol has the effect of requiring a character. For instance, the picture @@@ will accept any three-character entry. The difference between this picture and no picture is that the @@@ picture requires a three-character entry.

The & Character

The & symbol accepts only letters and converts any lower-case letter you type into upper case. This picture character is very useful in fields, like the State field in EMPLYEE, that contain abbreviations in all upper case. For example, suppose you want to define a picture for the State field of EMPLYEE that will accept only two letters and that will convert whatever you type into upper case. To create this picture, issue the **[Menu]** **V**alCheck **D**efine command and specify the State field. Next, choose **P**icture from the ValCheck menu and type **&&** when Paradox prompts you for the picture. When you press ↵, Paradox will assign this picture to the field and will display the message *Picture specification recorded* at the bottom of the screen.

Once you have defined this picture, Paradox will accept only two-character letter entries in the State field. If you attempt to enter a number in the field, or if you attempt to enter just a single letter, Paradox will not accept the entry. You will have to correct the entry before going on.

If the letters you type are in lower case, Paradox will convert them to upper case. For instance, if you make the entry *ky* in the State field after you have defined this picture, Paradox will convert the entry to *KY* before storing it in the table.

The ! Character

The ! character is a hybrid of the & and @ characters. Like @, ! will accept any type of character. Like &, however, ! will convert any letter you type into upper case. You might use this symbol in a field that contains both numbers and letters, and in which you want the letters to be capitalized. For instance, suppose you have a table named DRIVERS that includes a field called Tag. This field stores the license tag number for every driver listed in the table. In most states, tag numbers are made up of letters and numbers, as in NXX 478 and NYS 475. You could use a picture like *!!! !!!* to accept this type of entry. Since this picture will accept both numbers and letters, it will accept any six-character license number. Furthermore, since it will convert letters to upper case, you don't have to press [Shift] to enter a letter.

Literal Characters

You can also use literal characters in pictures. When you enter a literal character in a picture, Paradox will automatically type the literal character for you.

For example, suppose you want to be sure that every entry in the SS Number field will be made in the form 123-45-6789. To do this, issue the **[Menu]** **V**alCheck **D**efine command and select the SS Number field. Next, issue the **P**icture command. When Paradox prompts you to supply the picture for this field, type ###-##-#### and press ↵. After you do this, Paradox will display the message *Picture specification recorded* at the bottom of the screen.

The picture ###-##-#### specifies an entry made up of nine numbers separated by two dashes. Once you assign this picture to the SS Number field, Paradox will only allow entries in the SS Number field that contain nine numbers. In addition, as you make entries in the SS Number field, Paradox will supply the dashes (-) between the digits for you. For example, suppose you want to enter the number 123-45-6789 in the SS Number field. When you type **123**, Paradox will display 123-. After you type two more numbers, Paradox will insert the next dash, and the display will read 124-45-. Now all you need to do to complete the entry is enter the last four digits.

In addition to punctuation marks like -, you may include literal spaces, letters, and numbers in your pictures. For example, the picture *!!! !!!*, which we showed you a few paragraphs ago, contains a literal space. If you use this picture, Paradox will automatically type a space for you after you type three characters.

Similarly, the picture *1986###-#* contains several literal characters. Even though this picture begins with a literal character, Paradox will not type the characters 1986 automatically as soon as you move the cursor into a field that is governed by this pattern.

Instead, Paradox will wait for you to either type a 1 or press the [Spacebar] before doing anything. If you do either of these things, Pardox will immediately type 1986, then wait for you to type three digits. After you type these characters, Paradox will type a hyphen and then wait for you to type one more number. If you type a character that does not conform to the picture, Paradox will respond with a low-pitched beep.

Other Picture Symbols

In addition to the characters above, there are five characters that have special meanings when you are designing a picture: *;, *, [], {},* and *,*. These symbols are modifiers; that is, they modify the function of the basic picture characters in your pictures.

The ; character tells Paradox to accept the picture character that follows it literally. For example, if you use the character # in a PAL picture, Paradox will only accept a number in that field. This can cause a problem if you want to include a number sign (#) in the actual entry in the field but still want to use a picture for that field.

However, if you precede the # symbol with a semicolon (;), Paradox will include the literal character # in the field entry, rather than using the symbol # as a picture for a number. For example, suppose your company uses a three-digit code followed by a number sign for its inventory control number (for example, 123# or 999#). You could use the picture ###;# in that field. This picture tells Paradox to accept any three digits followed by the literal symbol #.

The * character tells Paradox to repeat a picture symbol a specified number of times. This symbol is followed by a number, which represents the number of times you want the picture symbol repeated, and by the symbol itself. For example, the picture *123*3#* tells Paradox to enter the characters 123, then accept any three digits entered by the user. The characters *3#* tell Paradox to repeat the symbol # three times, making it the equivalent of the picture *123###*.

If you do not enter a number after the * , Paradox will accept any number of characters of the specified type, from zero to the maximum number of characters allowed in the field. For example, while the picture *2# tells Paradox to accept only two digits, the picture *# tells Paradox to accept as many digits as the user types. If you forget the * symbol, Paradox will interpret the number literally. For instance, the picture *1233#* tells Paradox to accept the characters 1233, followed by a numeric character.

The characters *{}* are called the grouping operator. They can be used with other special characters to define a group. For example, the picture *2{#?}##*, which is equivalent to #?#?##, tells Paradox to accept a number followed by a letter, then another number followed by another letter, and then two more numbers. The expression *{#?}* in this picture tells Paradox to treat the characters *#?* as a group.

The { } characters have another purpose. Earlier we noted that when you include literal characters in your pictures, Paradox will automatically type those characters for you. For example, we said that the picture ###-##-#### will cause Paradox to type the dashes between the sections of a Social Security number automatically. If you want to, you can use the { } characters to suppress this automatic feature. For example, suppose you do not want Paradox to fill in the dashes for you in the SS Number field. To suppress the automatic fill-in, place the dashes inside curly braces, as in ###{-}##{-}####. Now the dashes will only be filled in if the user types them or presses the [Spacebar] after entering the digits.

The comma (,) is used in pictures to define a set of alternatives. You could use the comma and the { } characters together to allow a given character in an entry to be any one of a group of characters. For example, suppose the items in your inventory start with two variable digits, followed by one of four possible three-digit combinations, and end in two fixed digits. You could define a picture like ##{1,2,3,4}23 for this field. This picture tells Paradox that the user will enter two variable digits, followed by either a 1, a 2, a 3, or a 4. After the user enters one of those digits, Paradox will automatically enter 23 to complete the entry.

The [] characters tell Paradox that the entry they enclose is optional. For example, suppose you want to define a picture for the First Name field in the EMPLYEE table that will automatically convert the first letter to upper case. To do this, you could define a picture that looks like this: &[?][?][?][?][?][?][?][?]. This picture tells Paradox to accept only a letter for the first character and to convert that letter to upper case. The user then can enter up to nine optional letters to complete the entry. (This picture could also be defined as &*9[?].)

A Note

Some picture characters are inappropriate for some fields. For example, you should not use the character ?, which accepts a letter, in a number field. Unfortunately, Paradox does not warn you when a picture is inappropriate for a given field. For example, suppose you define a picture like &### for a number field. This picture tells Paradox to accept only a letter for the first character, convert it to upper case, and then accept three digits to complete the entry. Paradox will let you define this picture for a number field. When you try to use the picture to enter data, however, Paradox won't allow you to enter anything in the field. If you try to enter a letter, Paradox will not accept it because of the field type. If you try to enter a number, Paradox will not accept it because of the picture.

Pictures can make data entry quicker and more accurate. The examples we've shown you here really only scratch the surface of this powerful feature of Paradox. However, you should remember that creating and defining pictures can be tricky, especially when you move beyond the basics and begin to create pictures that are more flexible. You will want to take the time to practice with pictures before you begin relying on them in your important tables.

The Required Command

The Required command tells Paradox that a field must have a value–blanks are not allowed. When you set a required validity check on a field, during data entry you will not be able to move the cursor out of a record that has a blank in that field.

For example, suppose you want to make sure that every employee has a value entered in the Salary field. To establish this requirement, issue the **[Menu]** Val**C**heck **D**efine command and select the Salary field. Next, issue the **R**equired command. After you issue the command, Paradox will prompt you for confirmation. To confirm the command, you should choose the **Y**es command. When you do, Paradox will display the message *Required status recorded* at the bottom of the screen. (If you do not want to put the required status in effect, you should choose No.)

Once you use the Required command, Paradox will not let you leave the Required field without entering a value. If you try to leave the field without entering a value, the message *A value must be provided in this field; press [F1] for help* will appear at the bottom of the screen. You must enter a value before you can leave the field. If there already is a blank value in a record when you set the Required ValCheck, you can leave it blank. However, if you subsequently edit the field, Paradox will then insist that you enter a value.

Setting a TableLookup Validity Check

The TableLookup command causes Paradox to check the values entered in a given field of a table against the values in a field of another table. If the entry you make in the field with the Lookup validity check does not exist in the specified field of the other table, Paradox will not accept the entry.

For example, you might have noticed that the entries in the Manager field of the PROJECTS table are, in fact, the employee numbers of the managers of each of the jobs in PROJECTS. Since only employees who actually exist can manage jobs, it would make sense to set up a lookup validity check on the Manager field of PROJECTS that would check any entry in that field against the entries in the Emp Number field of the EMPLYEE table.

To set this check, first you issue the **[Menu]** **M**odify **E**dit command to bring PROJECTS to the screen in the edit mode. Next, you issue the **[Menu]** Val**C**heck **D**efine command and select the Manager field. When the ValCheck menu appears, you must issue the **T**ableLookup command.

After you do this, Paradox will prompt you to enter the name of the table that contains the lookup values. You should type EMPLYEE and press ↵. Next, Paradox will display the message *Table lookup recorded* at the bottom of the screen.

From now on, any value entered in the Manager field in the PROJECTS table will be checked against the employee numbers in the Emp Number field of EMPLYEE. If you enter an invalid number, Paradox will display the message *Not one of the possible values for this field* at the bottom of the screen. You must correct the error before Paradox will let you leave the field.

The check field in the lookup table must be the first field of that table. For example, Emp Number is the first field in EMPLYEE. In fact, you will notice that Paradox does not even prompt you for the name of the field that contains the check values; it merely asks for the name of the table and looks in the first field of that table for the match values. (Of course, the field to which you assign the lookup validity check can be anywhere in the table.)

Also note that, since Paradox must compare every entry you make with the values in the lookup table, the editing and data entry process will be slower. However, you can speed up the process by making the field in the lookup table a keyed field.

Although we used a number field to demonstrate this validity check, it is equally applicable to date and alphanumeric fields. For example, you could use a lookup validity check to verify the dates entered in a date field, or an alphanumeric string used as part numbers in an inventory table.

When you define the lookup table, you must tell Paradox the directory in which the table is located, unless it is on the active directory. For example, suppose the EMPLYEE table is on a directory called c:\paradox\people, and the PROJECTS table is on a directory called c:\paradox\numbers. Then, when Paradox prompts you to enter the name of the lookup table, you should type **c:\paradox\people\emplyee** and press ↵.

Notes

Validity checks should be established for a table as soon as possible. Since the ValCheck command is on the DataEntry menu, the ideal time to establish validity checks is when you issue the [Menu] Modify DataEntry command to enter your first set of records in a newly created table.

By establishing validity checks early, you can minimize the potential for errors during data entry and editing. This is especially important if several different people will be entering data or editing the records in your tables.

When you are setting up validity checks for a table, those checks will take effect immediately after you define them. Any existing records in the table will not be affected. For example, suppose you set the Required check for the SS Number field in the EMPLYEE table. Any pre-existing blanks in the field may be left blank; however, if you then decide to edit those records, Paradox will not let you leave the field until you have entered a value.

Saving Validity Checks

If you are using Version 1.1 of Paradox, the validity checks you set will be saved automatically when you press [Do-It!] ([F2]) or issue the [Menu] DO-IT! command to end editing or data entry. When you do this, Paradox sets up a file with a .VAL extension and saves your checks to the file. If there is an existing .VAL file for the table, Paradox will replace it with the updated version.

In Version 1.0, Paradox does not automatically save the validity checks you set. Instead, if you want to create a .VAL file, you must issue the Keep command before you press [Do-It!] to end the session. Keep is a command on the Paradox 1.0 ValCheck menu (shown in Figure 4-28) that is not found in Version 1.1.

Figure 4-28 The ValCheck Menu for Version 1.0

After you issue the Keep command, Paradox will prompt you for confirmation. This prompt alerts you to the fact that existing validity checks will be replaced if you issue the Replace command. If you issue the Cancel command, Pardox will return to the previous prompt without replacing the existing .VAL file.

Clearing Validity Checks

You can use the [Menu] ValCheck Clear command to clear any validity checks that you have assigned to a table. This command allows you to clear the validity checks for just a single field or for the table as a whole.

For example, suppose that after setting a validity check for the Salary field, you want to clear just the check for that field. To do this, issue the **[Menu]** **ValCheck** **Clear** command. After you issue this command, Paradox will display the menu shown in Figure 4-29. Since you want to clear the validity checks from one field, in this case, Salary, you should choose **Field**.

Figure 4-29 Clearing Validity Checks

Next, Paradox will prompt you to specify the field whose validity checks you want to clear. When you see this prompt, move the cursor to the Salary field and press ↵. Paradox then will remove the checks from the Salary field and display the message *Validity checks removed from field* at the bottom of the screen. Entries made in the field will not be checked except for the routine checking automatically performed by Paradox.

If you wish to remove the validity checks from all of the fields in the table, issue the **[Menu]** **V**alCheck **C**lear **A**ll command. After you issue the command, Paradox will display the message *All validity checks removed* at the bottom of the screen. When you issue this command, Paradox suspends all validity checks for the duration of the current data entry or edit session. When you press [Do-It!] or issue the [Menu] DO-IT! command to end the session, Paradox deletes the .VAL file from disk. From that point on, the default validity check settings will be in effect. If you issue the [Menu] Cancel command to end the date entry or edit session, however, Paradox will not delete the .VAL file.

Deleting a .VAL File

You can also delete a .VAL file with the [Menu] Tools Delete ValCheck command. For example, suppose you established and saved validity checks for the EMPLYEE table, which you now want to delete. To do this, issue the **[Menu]** **T**ools **D**elete **V**alCheck command. After you issue the command, Paradox will prompt you to enter a table name. When you see this prompt, type **EMPLYEE** and press ↵. Paradox then will delete the .VAL file and return to the main workspace.

Special Tricks for Data Entry

By taking advantage of a few special tricks, you can reduce the amount of time you spend entering and editing data. We'll cover those topics next.

The Ditto Key ([Ctrl]-[D])

The [Ditto] key allows you to copy to the current field in one record the entry from that same field in the previous record. For example, suppose you are entering a few new records into the PROJECTS table, as shown in Figure 4-30. Now suppose that the Client Number field entry for the second record is identical to the Client Number field entry for the first record. Instead of typing the Client Number entry for record 2, you could move the cursor to the Client Number field of the second record and press [Ditto] ([Ctrl]-[D]). Figure 4-31 shows the result. As you can see, Paradox has copied the entry from the Client Number field of record 1 into record 2.

Figure 4-30 The ENTRY Table for PROJECTS

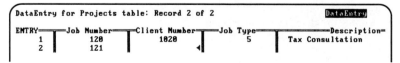

Figure 4-31 Using the [Ditto] Key

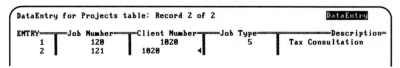

Whenever you have identical entries in a field in two or more consecutive records, you can use [Ditto] to save you a lot of time during data entry and editing.

Number and Dollar Fields

While you are entering a number in a number or dollar field, you can use commas to separate the hundreds from the thousands, the thousands from the millions, and so on, in the numbers you type. For example, you could enter the number 9123456 as **9,123,456**.

Paradox allows you to use the [Spacebar] to perform a wide variety of tasks during data entry and editing. For instance, when you are entering data into a number field, you can press the [Spacebar], instead of typing a period, to enter a decimal point. For example, to enter the number 1234.56, you could type **1234[Spacebar]56**.

You can enter a negative number by enclosing it in parentheses. For example, you could enter the number -1234.56 as (1234.56). If you use parentheses to enter negative numbers, you can use the [Spacebar] to add the second parenthesis automatically. For instance, to enter the number -35 in a number or dollar field, type **(35**, then press the **[Spacebar]** to enter the closing parenthesis.

Date Fields

Paradox will try to guess the date you want while you are entering a date. For example, suppose you want to enter the date 2/21/86. To do this, type **21-f**. When you do, Paradox will automatically capitalize the letter *F* for you. Now, press **[Spacebar]**. When you do this, Paradox will automatically supply the second letter in the month name, *e*. If you press **[Spacebar]** again, Paradox will complete the month name by typing a *b*. If the first letter you type is common to several months, Paradox will supply the second letter in the name of the earliest month of the year that begins with the first letter you typed.

If you press the **[Spacebar]** while you are entering a date, Paradox will define the current portion of the date as equal to that component of today's date. For example, suppose that today is March 1, 1986. If you press the **[Spacebar]** to begin a date field entry, Paradox will type *3*–the month portion of today's date.

If you leave out the year portion of a date, Paradox will assume that the date is in the current year. For example, assuming that the current year is 1986, if you type **12/25↵**, Paradox will enter the date into your table as 12/25/86.

Conclusion

In this chapter, we have introduced you to a few advanced data entry and editing concepts. First, we showed you how to create a keyed table and how to deal with key field violations. Then we showed you how to change the appearance of your tables using the Image command. Next, we showed you how to create validity checks. Finally, we offered a few tips that may help to make your data entry faster and easier.

Chapter 5
Forms

So far, we have shown you how to create tables and enter and edit the records in a table, as well as several ways to view your tables. In this chapter, we will show you how to custom design forms that can be used to view, edit, or enter data into your tables.

As you will see, Paradox's capacity to create forms gives you considerable flexibility for viewing and editing the records in your tables. For example, the default table view displays up to 22 records on the screen at the same time, but a very limited number of fields. On the other hand, the form view displays one record at a time, but as many fields as will fit on the screen. The table view always shows the fields in columns and rows, while the form view can display fields any way you choose. In addition, the form view can contain calculated fields that aren't actually in the table.

The Default Form

Paradox automatically creates a default form for every table. To view a table through this default form, you simply press [Form Toggle] ([F7]) while you are viewing the table. For example, to view EMPLYEE through its default form, you would issue the **[Menu]** View command to bring EMPLYEE into view and then press **[Form Toggle]** to enter the form view. Figure 5-1 shows this form on the screen.

Notice that the fields in the default form are placed vertically down the left side of the screen. Also notice that Paradox automatically draws a double-line border around the screen. In the upper-right corner of the screen, Paradox displays the table name, EMPLYEE, in reverse video, as well as a record number field that tells you which record from the table you are viewing through the form. All default forms contain these same basic elements.

The message *Viewing Emplyee Table with form F: Record 1 of 16,* which appears at the top of the screen, tells you which table you are viewing, which of that table's forms you are using, and which record is currently displayed in the form. A message like this one will always appear at the top of the screen while you are working in a form.

Figure 5-1   The Default Form for EMPLYEE

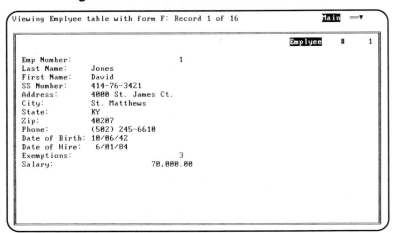

Also notice the symbol =▼ in the upper-right corner of the screen. This symbol tells you that there are more records in the table following this record. If you were viewing a record in the middle of the table (instead of record 1), the symbol would be ▲=▼. This symbol tells you that there are records above and below the current record in the table. Similarly, if you were viewing the last record in the table (record 16, in this case) the symbol would be ▲=. This symbol tells you that there are more records in the table and that they are all above the record you are viewing.

If a table has more than 19 fields, Paradox automatically will create a multipage form for the table. We'll cover multipage forms later in this chapter.

Using Forms

You can use forms to view, edit, or add to the records in the table. Using a form to perform these tasks is very similar to using the default table view. The only difference is the way the records are displayed on the screen.

Moving Around in a Form

The cursor control keys work differently when you are using a form than they do when you are in the table view. However, you will find that, overall, using a form is not very different from using the default table view. Table 5-1 shows the effect of each of the cursor movement keys in a form.

Table 5-1 Cursor Movement in Forms

Key(s)	Function
↑	Moves the cursor up one field in the current record or up to the last field of the previous record.
→	Moves the cursor to the next field (right or down).
←	Moves the cursor to the previous field (left or up).
↓	Moves the cursor down one field in the current record or to the first field of the next record.
↵	Moves the cursor to the next record.
[Home]	Moves the cursor to the first record of the table.
[Ctrl]-[Home]	Moves the cursor to the first field of the current record.
[End]	Moves the cursor to the last record in the table.
[Ctrl]-[End]	Moves the cursor to the last field of the current record.
[Pg Up]	Moves the cursor to the previous page in a multipage form or up to the previous record in a single-page form.
[Pg Dn]	Moves the cursor to the next page in a multipage form or to the next page in a single-page form.
[Ctrl]-[Pg Up]	Moves the cursor to the same field of the previous record.
[Ctrl]-[Pg Dn]	Moves the cursor to the same field of the next record.

Cursor Control within a Record

To demonstrate how the cursor control keys work, let's look at a few examples. In Figure 5-1 the cursor is in the first field of the first record (Emp Number). To move it to the next field, Last Name, press ↓ once. If you now continue to press ↓, the cursor will move through the remaining fields of the form. When you reach the last field, Salary, pressing ↓ again moves the cursor to the first field of the next record. Instead of pressing ↓, you could press ↵ or →. Pressing any of these keys will move the cursor to the next field in the record.

To move up to the previous field of a record, press either ↑ or ←. For example, to move from the Salary field back to the Exemptions field of record 1, press ↑. If you now continue to press the ↑ key, the cursor will move up through the remaining fields of the form. If the cursor is on the first field of a record, pressing the ↑ key moves it to the last field of the previous record. If there is no previous record for the cursor to move to, Paradox will respond with a low-pitched beep.

You can move the cursor to the last field of a record quickly by pressing [Ctrl]-[End]. For example, if the cursor is on the Emp Number field of the first record and you press [Ctrl]-[End], it will move instantly to the Salary field. You can move quickly from the last field of the form to the first field by pressing [Ctrl]-[Home]. For example, if the cursor is on the Salary field of a record and you press [Ctrl]-[Home], it will move instantly to the Emp Number field.

Moving between Records

In the preceding examples, you learned that pressing ↓ or → with the cursor in the last field of a record moves it to the first field of the next record. Conversely, pressing ↑ or ← with the cursor in the first field of a record moves it to the last field of the previous record (assuming there is a previous record).

You can also use the [Pg Up] and [Pg Dn] keys and the [Ctrl]-[Pg Up] and [Ctrl]-[Pg Dn] combinations to move between records. For example, suppose you are viewing the first record in the EMPLYEE table and you want to move to the next record. To do this, press **[Pg Dn]**. After you do this, your screen will look like Figure 5-2.

Figure 5-2 Moving between Records

```
Viewing Emplyee table with form F: Record 2 of 16           Main  ▲=▼

                                                          Emplyee  #  2
    Emp Number:                 2
    Last Name:       Cameron
    First Name:      Herb
    SS Number:       321-65-8765
    Address:         2331 Elm St.
    City:            Louisville
    State:           KY
    Zip:             40205
    Phone:           (502) 451-8765
    Date of Birth:   11/24/29
    Date of Hire:    6/01/84
    Exemptions:                 4
    Salary:              50,000.00
```

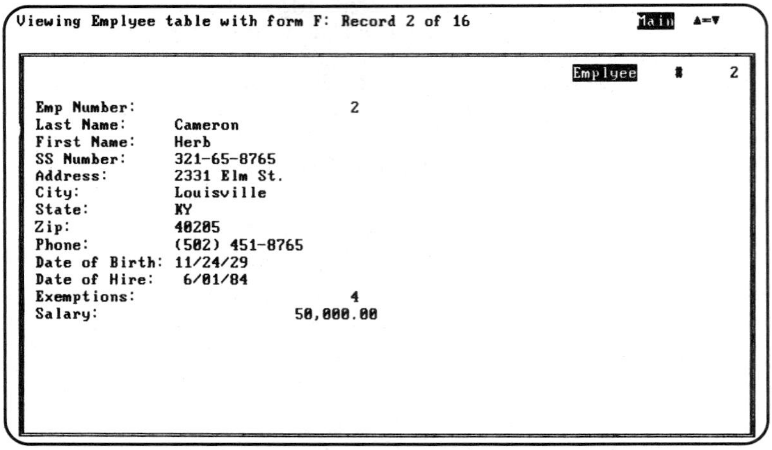

Notice in Figure 5-2 that the record number at the top of the page has changed to 2. In addition, the cursor location message at the top of the page now reads *Record 2 of 16,* and the symbol on the far-right side of the screen, ▲=▼, now indicates that there are records above and below the current record.

To move back to the previous record, press **[Pg Up]**. When you press this key, Paradox will bring the first record back into view, as shown in Figure 5-1.

When you press [Pg Up] or [Pg Dn] to move between the records in a table, the cursor will be placed in the first field of the record to which you are moving. If you press [Ctrl]-[Pg Up] or [Ctrl]-[Pg Dn] instead, however, the cursor will move to the same field in the new record that it was in when you pressed the key. For example, if you position the cursor on the First Name field of the first record and press [Ctrl]-[Pg Dn], the cursor will move to the First Name field of record number 2.

To move the cursor to the last record in the table, you could press [Pg Dn] repeatedly; however, you can move quickly to the last record in a table by pressing the [End] key. For example, to move to the last record (record 16) in the EMPLYEE table, you can press [End]. If you now want to move back to the first record in the table, just press [Home]. Paradox will move instantly to record number 1.

Entering Records

Entering records through a form is very similar to entering records through a table view. To enter records into a table through a form, first issue the **[Menu] M**odify **D**ataEntry command and type the name of the table with which you want to work. When the ENTRY table for that table comes into view, press **[Form Toggle]** to switch to the form view. Immediately, the default form for the table will come into view. Once the form is on the screen, you can make entries into it just as you would when entering data through the table view. When the entries are all in place, press **[Do-It!]** to copy the new data into the permanent table.

An Example

For example, suppose you want to enter a new record into the EMPLYEE table through the default form. Table 5-2 shows the record you want to enter into the table.

Table 5-2 A Sample Record

Emp Number	21
Last Name	Ross
First Name	Melinda
SS Number	256-41-1984
Address	607 Montana Ave.
City	Shively
State	KY
Zip	40208
Phone	(502) 636-0068
Date of Birth	4/1/52
Date of Hire	5/1/86
Exemptions	1
Salary	35000

To enter this record, issue the **[Menu] M**odify **D**ataEntry command. When Paradox prompts you to enter a table name, type **EMPLYEE** and press ↵. After you do this, Paradox will display the ENTRY table in the table view. Now, to use the default form, press **[Form Toggle]**. When you do this, Paradox will use that form for data entry. Your screen will look like Figure 5-3.

Figure 5-3 Using the Default Form

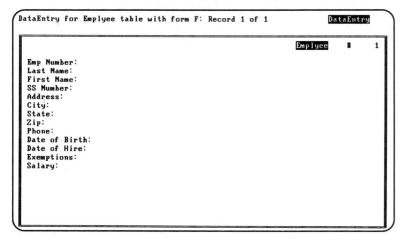

To begin entering the record, type **21** and press ↓ to move the cursor to the Last Name field. Next, type **Ross** and press ↓ again. Now type **Melinda**, press ↓ to move the cursor to the SS Number field, type **256-41-1984**, and press ↓. You can continue in this way–typing entries and pressing ↓–until you have entered all of the information for Melinda Ross. When you finish, your screen will look like Figure 5-4.

Figure 5-4 The Completed Form

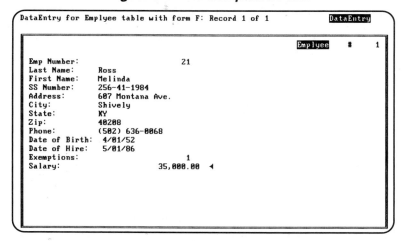

Now press ↓. After you do this, Paradox will once again display a blank entry form and will wait for you to enter a new record. If you wanted to enter a new record at this point, you could do so by using the techniques just demonstrated.

To end data entry and add the record in ENTRY to EMPLYEE, press **[Do-It!]** ([F2]) or issue the **[Menu]** DO-IT! command. Paradox then will add the new record to EMPLYEE and will display that table in the workspace in the table view. Whenever Paradox brings a table into the workspace, it will be in the default table view. To switch to the form view, you must press [Form Toggle] ([F7]) or issue the [Menu] Image PickForm command and select a form.

Editing in Data Entry

If you make a mistake during data entry (as you almost certainly will from time to time), you can correct that mistake in much the same way you corrected mistakes during data entry through a table. All you need to do is move to the field you want to correct, erase the error, and type in the correct information. Table 5-3 shows the keys you will use to edit a form.

Table 5-3   Editing Keys

Key	Function
[Backspace]	Deletes one character in the current field.
[Ctrl]-[Backspace]	Deletes the contents of the current field.
[Ins]	Inserts a new record in the table.
[Del]	Deletes a record in the table.
[Undo]	Undoes the last action.

For example, suppose you are entering a new record into EMPLYEE through a form and you notice that Mr. Rogers' name was entered as *Rgoers* and that his social security number was entered as *321-45-6789* as shown in Figure 5-5, instead of *321-54-6789*.

Figure 5-5   Editing during Data Entry

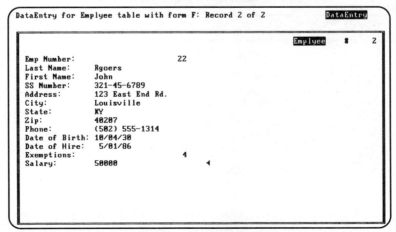

To correct the first error, move the cursor to the Last Name field and press [**Ctrl**]-[**Backspace**] to clear the field. Then type **Rogers** in the blank field and press ↵. Figure 5-6 shows the corrected entry.

Figure 5-6   The Corrected Entry

```
DataEntry for Emplyee table with form F: Record 2 of 2        DataEntry

                                                         Emplyee   #   2
    Emp Number:                    22
    Last Name:      Rogers      ◄
    First Name:     John
    SS Number:      321-45-6789
    Address:        123 East End Rd.
    City:           Louisville
    State:          KY
    Zip:            40207
    Phone:          (502) 555-1314
    Date of Birth:  10/04/30
    Date of Hire:   5/01/86
    Exemptions:                     4
    Salary:                    50,000.00
```

Using the Field View

To correct the entry in the SS Number field, you could use the same technique; however, you may find it easier to edit this field in the field view. To do this, position the cursor on the SS Number field and press [**Field View**] ([Alt]-[F5]). After you do this, Paradox will switch to the field view, as shown in Figure 5-7.

Figure 5-7   Field View

```
DataEntry for Emplyee table with form F: Record 2 of 2        DataEntry

                                                         Emplyee   #   2
    Emp Number:                    22
    Last Name:      Rogers
    First Name:     John
    SS Number:      321-45-6789█◄
    Address:        123 East End Rd.
    City:           Louisville
    State:          KY
    Zip:            40207
    Phone:          (502) 555-1314
    Date of Birth:  10/04/30
    Date of Hire:   5/01/86
    Exemptions:                     4
    Salary:                    50,000.00
```

Using the field view to edit a form is the same as using it to edit from within the table view. To correct the error in the SS Number field, press ← to move the cursor to the number 4, then press **[Del]** twice to delete the incorrect characters and type **54**. After you do this, your screen will look like Figure 5-8. Now, to end the field view, press ↵.

Figure 5-8 Correcting Entries

```
DataEntry for Emplyee table with form F: Record 1 of 1        DataEntry

                                                        Emplyee    #    1
       Emp Number:              22
       Last Name:       Rogers
       First Name:      John
       SS Number:       321-54 6789 ◄
       Address:         123 East End Rd.
       City:            Louisville
       State:           KY
       Zip:             40207
       Phone:           (502) 555-1314
       Date of Birth:   10/04/30
       Date of Hire:    5/01/86
       Exemptions:                    4
       Salary:                50,000.00
```

Deleting and Inserting Records

When you are entering records through a form, you can insert and delete records just as you do in the table view. For example, to insert a new record in the ENTRY form, just place the cursor where you want the new record to be inserted and press [Ins].

To delete a record during data entry, position the cursor on any field in the record and press [Del]. For example, suppose you decide not to add the record for Mr. Rogers to EMPLYEE. To delete this record, just position the cursor on any field in the record and press **[Del]**.

Editing an Existing Table through a Form

Editing an existing table through a form is essentially the same as editing records that you are entering into a table through a form. To edit a table through a form, you first bring the table into the workspace in the edit mode, either by issuing the [Menu] Modify Edit command or by issuing the [Menu] View command to bring the table into view, then pressing [Edit] ([F9]) to enter the edit mode. Next, you press [Form Toggle] to enter the form view.

Once you have the table in the edit mode, you can make changes in the records in much the same way as described in the preceding example. In fact, if you have followed the examples in Chapters 3 and 4, and in the first part of this chapter, you already know how to edit through a form. When you are editing through a form, you can press [Backspace] to erase characters in the current field or [Ctrl]-[Backspace] to erase the entire field. You also can press [Ins] to insert a blank record or [Del] to delete a record. You can use the field view to edit a field. You can also use the Undo command to undo an error.

For example, suppose you are viewing the EMPLYEE table through the default form and you want to delete the record for Melinda Ross entered in the previous example. To do this, press [**Edit**] ([F9]) to enter the edit mode. Then, press [**End**] to position the cursor on record number 17 and press [**Del**] to delete the record.

Once you have made all of the changes you want in the table, press [**Do-It!**] or issue the [**Menu**] DO-IT! command to save your changes and return to the main workspace.

The DataEntry and Edit Menus

When you are entering data or editing records through a form, pressing [Menu] ([F10]) causes the active menu (DataEntry or Edit) to appear at the top of the screen. You will recall that these menus are exactly the same. This menu is shown in Figure 5-9.

Figure 5-9   The DataEntry and Edit Menus

As you can see, this menu is the same as when you're entering records through the default table view, which is explained in Chapters 3 and 4. In fact, the only difference you will notice involves the Image command. If you issue the Image command, you'll see the menu shown in Figure 5-10.

Figure 5-10   The Image Menu for Forms

This menu contains only three commands: Format, GoTo, and PickForm. You may recall that when you are entering records through a table, the Image menu you see includes three additional commands: TableSize, ColumnSize, and Move.

The functions of the Format and GoTo commands in a form are identical to their functions in a table view. The Format command allows you to format a field, the GoTo command allows you to move the cursor to a named field or record, and the PickForm command lets you select a custom form. For more about the Image commands, see Chapter 4. We'll cover the PickForm command later in this chapter.

Creating Custom Forms

The default form may be perfectly adequate for most of your needs; however, you will undoubtedly encounter situations where you will want to use a custom-designed form. For example, you may want to design a custom form for the EMPLYEE table that displays only the names and addresses of your employees. Or you might want to design a form that includes prompts for the user or one that uses special calculated fields. Paradox allows you to design the form you want quickly and easily.

An Example

Suppose you want to design a custom form for EMPLYEE, like the one shown in Figure 5-11. This form displays only the names and addresses of the employees in the table.

Figure 5-11 A Custom Form

```
Viewing Emplyee table with form F1: Record 1 of 16          Main  —▼

                        ABC Company
                    Employee Address Form

                 Name: David      Jones

                 Address: 4000 St. James Ct.

                 City: St. Matthews

                 State: KY

                 Zip: 40207
```

To design this form, issue the **[Menu] F**orms command. The next menu you see will look like Figure 5-12. As you can see, this menu has two commands: Design and Change. The Design command allows you to design a new form for a table. The Change command allows you to redesign an existing form.

Figure 5-12 The Design/Change Menu

Since you want to design a form, you should issue the **Design** command. After you issue the Design command, Paradox will prompt you to enter the name of the table for which you want to design a form. You should type **EMPLYEE** and press ↵.

Next, Paradox will prompt you to assign a number to the form, as shown in Figure 5-13. A table can have up to ten different forms: the default form, F, and up to nine custom forms that you design. Whenever you create a custom form for a table, you must give that form a number between 1 and 9 (you can also use the letter *F* to designate a custom form, but we'll save that concept for later). To assign a number to a form, just point to the form number you want to use and press ↵ or press the key corresponding to the form number. For example, to assign form number 1 to our sample form, you could point to the number 1 in the list and press ↵ or simply type **1** from the keyboard.

Figure 5-13   The Form Number Prompt

After you assign a number to the form, Paradox will prompt you to enter a form description. Every form you create should have a description. Paradox uses this description as the second line prompt that appears whenever you point to the form's number in a form number list. You should make sure the description clearly defines the contents of the form.

When you see this prompt, type **Employee Addresses** and press ↵. After you do this, Paradox will display the forms design screen shown in Figure 5-14.

Figure 5-14   The Forms Design Screen

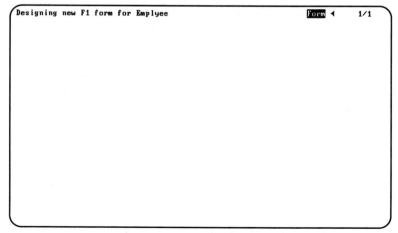

As you can see, the forms design screen starts out completely empty. The only information displayed on the screen is the current operation reminder (*Designing new F1 form for Emplyee*), the menu reminder (*Form*), a Style indicator (◄), and the page indicator (*1/1*). As you will learn later in this chapter, the Style indicator helps to remind you of the style settings that are in effect for the form. The Page indicator tells you which page of the form you are working on and the total number of pages in the form. For example, the Page indicator in the example, 1/1, tells you that you are working on the first page of a one-page form.

The actual work area of the form design screen is 22 lines long and 80 characters wide. You'll want to keep these numbers in mind as you design your form.

Adding a Border

To begin designing our sample form, issue the **[Menu] B**order command. After you issue this command, Paradox will display the types of borders you can create, as shown in Figure 5-15. We will discuss each of these commands in detail later in this chapter.

Figure 5-15   The Border Menu

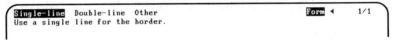

For now, you should issue the **D**ouble-line command. When you do, Paradox will prompt you to indicate where the border should begin. When you see this prompt, press ↵. This will start the border in the upper-left corner of the screen. Paradox then will prompt you to move the cursor to the diagonal corner of the border. When this prompt appears, press the ↑ |key. This will "wrap" the border around the screen. Now press ← to define the entire screen in the border, as shown in Figure 5-16, and press ↵ to set the border. Your screen will look like Figure 5-17.

Figure 5-16   Defining the Screen in the Border

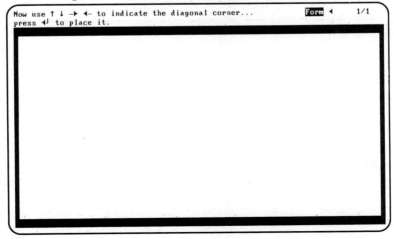

Figure 5-17 The Completed Border

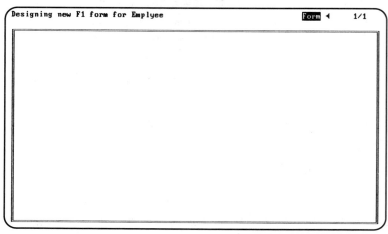

After you set the border, the cursor will be in the lower-right corner of the screen. To move it to the top-left side of the screen, press [**Home**], followed by [**Ctrl**]-[**Home**].

Adding a Title

Now you are ready to add a title to the form. To add the title shown on the finished form in Figure 5-11 to the form, press ➡ several times to move the cursor to the center of the screen, followed by ⬇, which moves it down one line. Now type **ABC Company**. Next, press the ↵ key to move the cursor down one line and then press the ➡ key repeatedly to move back toward the center of the screen. Next, type **Employee Address Form**. Your screen will now look like Figure 5-18. (Don't worry if you didn't get the title exactly in the center of the screen; we'll show you how to make adjustments later.)

Figure 5-18 Adding a Title

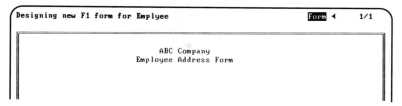

The characters that you type from the keyboard are called literals since what you type on the screen is exactly (literally) what you will see in the form. If you want all capital letters, for example, you must use the [Shift] or [Caps Lock] key as you type.

Placing Fields

Now you are ready to place the fields from EMPLYEE onto the form. To begin, use the arrow keys to move the cursor down two lines and position it under the title. Then type **Name:** and press the **[Spacebar]** once. Figure 5-19 shows the screen at this point. Next, issue the **[Menu] P**ut command. After you issue this command, Paradox will display the types of fields you can put on the form, as shown in Figure 5-20. When you see this menu, issue the **R**egular command. Paradox then will display a list of the fields in EMPLYEE and prompt you to select one, as shown in Figure 5-21.

Figure 5-19   The Custom Form

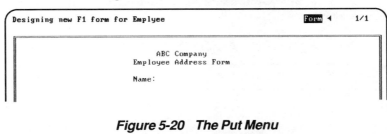

Figure 5-20   The Put Menu

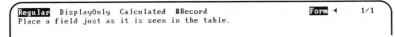

Figure 5-21   Selecting a Regular Field

When you see this prompt, press the ➡ key twice to position the cursor on the First Name field and press ↵. After you do this, the cursor will change to a small box, and Paradox will prompt you to place the field. If you've been following this example, the cursor will already be positioned next to the word *Name*. To place the First Name field on the form, then, all you need to do is press ↵. (If the cursor is not next to the word *Name*, you should use the arrow keys to move it there, then press ↵.)

Next, Paradox will prompt you to adjust the size of the field. To make the field the same size as its length in the table, just press ↵. After you do this, Paradox will place the field on the form. It will be represented by a series of dashed lines, like those you see in Figure 5-22.

Figure 5-22 The First Name Field in Place

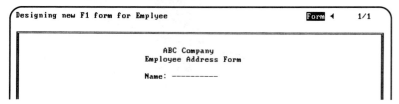

Now, press ➡ to move the cursor one space to the right, issue the [**Menu**] **Pu**t **R**egular command again, select the **L**ast **N**ame field from the list, press ↵ to place it next to the First Name field, then press ↵ to accept the default length. After you do this, your screen will look like Figure 5-23.

Figure 5-23 Adding the Last Name Field

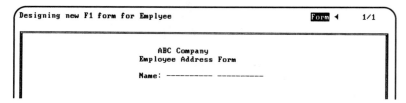

Notice that we have now entered two fields on the same line of the form. Although the default form has only one field per line, you can enter two or more fields on the same line of a custom form. In fact, you can place as many fields on a line as will fit.

Now press ↵ twice to move the cursor down two lines, then move the cursor to the center of the screen and type **Address:** followed by a single space. Next, issue the [**Menu**] **P**ut **R**egular command, select the Address field, and place it next to the word you just typed. You can continue in this way–positioning the cursor, typing the field name prompts, issuing the [Menu] Put Regular command to select the field name, and pressing ↵ to accept the default length–until your screen looks like Figure 5-24.

Now, to save your new form, press [**Do-It!**] ([F2]) or issue the [**Menu**] DO-IT! command. Paradox then will save the form and return to the main workspace.

Using the PickForm Command

Once you create a form, you can use it immediately to view, edit, or enter records into the table. For example, to use the form you just created, first issue the [**Menu**] **V**iew command to bring the EMPLYEE table into the workspace (if it is not already there). When the table appears in the workspace, issue the [**Menu**] **I**mage PickForm command. After you issue this command, Paradox will display a Form Number menu, as shown in Figure 5-25.

Figure 5-24   The Completed Design Screen

```
Designing new F1 form for Emplyee                    Form ◄   1/1

                        ABC Company
                     Employee Address Form

                   Name: ---------- ----------

                   Address: --------------------

                   City: --------------------

                   State: --

                   Zip: -----
```

Figure 5-25   The Form Number Menu

As you can see, this menu shows you the forms you have associated with the table. In this case, you only have two forms: F, the default form, and 1, the form you just created. As you create forms for the table, Paradox will add them to this menu.

To select your custom form, highlight it with the cursor and press ↵ or just press **1**. After you do this, Paradox will display the records in the table through the form. Your screen will look like Figure 5-11.

You now can use your form for viewing, editing, or data entry. All of the things you learned about the default form apply equally to custom forms.

Form Creation Basics

Now that you have created your first custom form, we need to go back and cover in detail the concepts we breezed by as you were creating the form.

Form Numbers

As we have said, you can design up to ten different forms for every table. When you create a new form, you must assign a number to the form. Paradox uses this number to identify the form. For example, you used the number 1 to identify the form you just created. From now on, Paradox will use the name F1 when it refers to this form.

Normally, you'll give the first custom form you create for a table the number 1, the second form the number 2, and so on. If you wish, however, you can skip a number. For instance, you could call the first form you create number 5, if you wish. Numbering your forms in order is a lot simpler, though.

You can also assign the name F to a custom form. As you know, Paradox stores the default form that it creates for each table under this name. If you do give a custom form the name F, that form will replace the standard default form. From that point on, you'll see your custom form, and not the Paradox default form, whenever you press [**Form Toggle**] while viewing the associated table.

You can also give a new custom form a number that has already been assigned to an existing form. For instance, suppose you are creating a new form for the EMPLYEE table. When Paradox presents the list shown in Figure 5-13, you choose number 1. When you do this, Paradox will display a Cancel/Replace menu and will display the message *F1 already exists* in the lower-right corner of the screen. If you issue the Cancel command, Paradox will return to the Form Number prompt so that you can assign another number to the form. If you issue the Replace command, however, Paradox will replace the existing form with the one you are creating.

The *Paradox User's Guide* and certain Paradox menus refer to the form number as the form name. The terms *form name* and *form number* can be used interchangeably.

Form Descriptions

After you assign a number to the form, Paradox prompts you to enter a form description. The description you enter can be up to 40 characters long and should be specific so that you will be able to remember the purpose of the form. For example, *Employee Addresses* describes the form we created in the example. You can leave the form description blank if you wish. To do this, simply press ↵ at the prompt.

Once entered, the form description will appear on the Form Number menu whenever the corresponding form number is highlighted. For example, if you issue the [Menu] Image Pickform command and point to option 1, Paradox will display the description *Employee Addresses* in the second line of the menu, as shown in Figure 5-26.

Figure 5-26 The Form Description

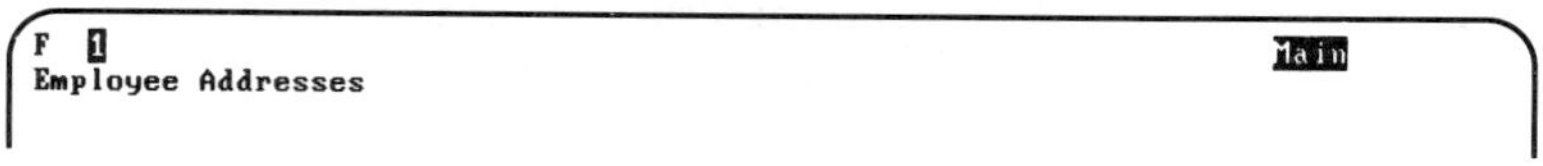

```
F 1                                                        Main
Employee Addresses
```

The Forms Editor

The Forms Editor is the tool you use to design forms. Although you have some experience with the Editor already, there are several important characteristics of the Editor that you will need to understand before you begin designing your own forms. As you will learn, the concepts of creating and editing a form are closely related.

Moving Around on the Screen

Table 5-4 shows the function of each of the cursor movement keys in the Forms Editor. As you can see, for the most part, these keys do what you would expect them to do. About the only tricky part of moving the cursor in the Forms Editor is the way it will "wrap around" whenever it reaches the edge of the workspace. For example, if the cursor is in the first row of the Editor, pressing ↑ will move it to the last row of the same column in the workspace. Similarly, if the cursor is in the last (rightmost) column of the workspace, pressing → will move it to the first column of the same row.

You can use this characteristic of the Forms Editor to your advantage. For example, when we created the custom form shown in Figure 5-11, we added a border around the entire form. To do this, we had to point to the upper-left corner of the screen, then press ↵ and point to the lower-right corner. Rather than pressing ↓ 21 times and → 79 times to point to the lower-right corner, we took advantage of the Editor's cursor wrap. To point to the lower-right corner of the screen, we pressed ↑ once and then ← once. Pressing ↑ moved the cursor to the bottom of the first column of the screen. Pressing ← then moved it to the last column in the last row.

Table 5-4 Moving the Cursor in the Forms Editor

Key(s)	Function
↑	Moves the cursor up one line. If the cursor is at the top of the screen, it will move to the last line in the same column.
→	Moves the cursor to the right. If the cursor is at the rightmost column on the screen, it will wrap around to the left on the same line.
←	Moves the cursor to the left. If the cursor is at the leftmost column of the screen, it will wrap around to the right on the same line.
↓	Moves the cursor down one line. If the cursor is at the bottom of the screen, it will move to the top in the same column.
[Home]	Moves the cursor to the first line of the screen.
[Ctrl]-[Home]	Moves the cursor to the beginning of a line.
[End]	Moves the cursor to the last line of the screen.
[Ctrl]-[End]	Moves the cursor to the end of a line.
[Pg Up]	Moves the cursor to the previous page in a multipage form.
[Pg Dn]	Moves the cursor to the next page in a multipage form.
↵	Moves the cursor down to the beginning of the next line.

Replace and Insert Modes

Like most text editors, the Paradox Forms Editor offers two modes of operation: the insert mode and the replace (or overwrite) mode. When the forms design screen first appears, it is in the replace mode. In the replace mode, characters that you type from the keyboard will overwrite and replace existing characters. For example, suppose you are designing a new form for the EMPLYEE table, like the one shown in Figure 5-27.

Figure 5-27   A New Form

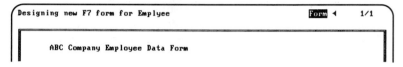

Now suppose that you want to change the word *Data* in the title to the word *Information*. To do this, position the cursor on the *D* in *Data* and type **Information Form**. After you do this, your screen will look like Figure 5-28.

Figure 5-28   Changing a Form Title

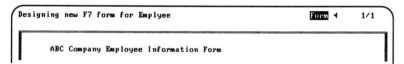

In the insert mode, the characters you type are inserted between existing characters, and those existing characters are moved to the right. To enter the insert mode, you simply press [Ins]. Since the [Ins] key is a toggle key, if you press it a second time, you will return to the replace mode. For example, suppose you want to add the word *Incorporated* after the company name in the title. To do this, position the cursor on the *E* in *Employee*, press [**Ins**], and type **Incorporated.** As you type the word, Paradox will insert it and move the existing characters to the right, as shown in Figure 5-29.

Figure 5-29   Inserting a Word

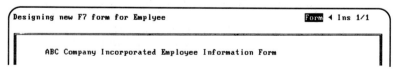

Notice the word *Ins* displayed in the upper-right corner of the screen in Figure 5-29. When you are working in the insert mode, the reminder *Ins* is displayed in the upper-right corner of the screen, between the Style indicator and the Page indicator.

You can take advantage of the insert mode to center text on the screen. For example, to center the title in the above example, position the cursor on the letter *A* in *ABC* and, if the Editor is not already in the insert mode, press [**Ins**]. Now, press the [**Spacebar**] several times. Each time you press the [Spacebar], the title will move one space to the right. Figure 5-30 shows the title centered on the screen.

Figure 5-30   Centering the Title

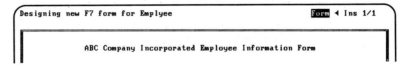

Deleting Characters

You can also delete characters from forms. For example, suppose you want to change the word *Incorporated* in the report title to *Inc*. To do this, position the cursor on the first *o* in *Incorporated* and press [**Del**]. When you do this, Paradox will delete the character at the cursor and move to the next character. You now can continue to press [**Del**] until all of the unwanted characters have been deleted. After you do this, your screen will look like Figure 5-31.

Figure 5-31   Deleting Characters

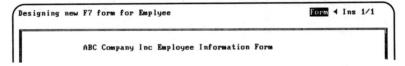

You can also use the [Backspace] key to delete characters. For example, you could change the word *Incorporated* to *Inc* by placing the cursor on the space after the *d* in *Incorporated* and pressing the [**Backspace**] key nine times.

In the above examples, the Forms Editor was in the insert mode. As you saw, when you delete a character with the [Backspace] key while the Editor is in the insert mode, Paradox pulls any remaining characters on the same line to the left. When you are in the replace mode, however, the [Backspace] key merely erases characters to its left–it does not adjust the remaining characters.

Word Wrap

The Forms Editor does not offer conventional "word wrap." If you type beyond the right margin of the screen, the characters you type will wrap around to the left edge of the screen; however, the wrapped characters are not automatically moved down one line, as you might expect.

For example, look at the screen shown in Figure 5-32. We created this screen by moving the cursor a few characters from the left edge of the screen and typing *This example of....* When we reached the right side of the screen, the last few characters wrapped around to the beginning of the same line. Should you run into this kind of problem, the only thing you can do is delete the characters and start over.

Figure 5-32   The Word Wrap Problem

```
Designing new F3 form for Emplyee                    Form ◄    1/1
┌─────────────────────────────────────────────────────────────────┐
│en, as This  example of the "word wrap" problem in the Paradox forms design scre│
│                                                                 │
```

If the Editor is in the insert mode, you will not be able to type past the right edge of the screen. If you continue typing when the cursor is at the right edge, the message *Cannot move line further to right* will appear in the lower-right corner of the screen.

The Cancel Command

If you decide not to save a form you have begun to design, you can issue the [Menu] Cancel command. The Cancel command returns you to the main workspace without saving the form. After you issue this command, Paradox will prompt you for confirmation with a No/Yes menu. If you issue the No command, Paradox will return you to the forms design screen. Issuing the Yes command causes Paradox to return to the main workspace without saving your work. The message *Ending form design* will appear at the bottom of the screen.

Placing Fields

To create the EMPLYEE custom form in Figure 5-11, you placed several of the fields from EMPLYEE into the form. There are four kinds of fields you can place on a form: regular, calculated, display-only, and record number. As you can see in Figure 5-33, the four options Regular, DisplayOnly, Calculated, and #Record are displayed on the menu after you issue the [Menu] Put command.

Figure 5-33   Field Types

Let's suppose that you want to create the form shown in Figure 5-34. This form includes five fields: Last Name (a regular field), Emp Number (a regular field), Salary (a display-only field), Hourly rate (a calculated field), and Record Number (a record number field). To create this form, first issue the [Menu] Forms Design command. When Paradox prompts you for a table name, type **EMPLYEE** and press ↵. When Paradox prompts you to specify a number for the form, choose an unused number (we'll use **2**) and then enter a description for the form (we'll use **Field Type Example**). When the form design screen is in view, you are ready to place fields.

Figure 5-34   A Sample Form

```
┌─────────────────────────────────────────────────────────────────┐
│ Designing new F2 form for Emplyee                  Form ◄  1/1  │
│                                                                 │
│                                                                 │
│       Last Name: ----------                                     │
│       Employee Number: ------                                   │
│       Salary: ----------------------                            │
│       Hourly Rate: ----------------------                       │
│                                                                 │
│                                         Record Number: ------   │
│                                                                 │
└─────────────────────────────────────────────────────────────────┘
```

Regular Fields

A regular field is any field that appears in the table on which you are working. For example, the regular fields in the EMPLOYEE table are Emp Number, Last Name, First Name, SS Number, Address, City, State, Zip, Phone, Date of Birth, Date of Hire, Exemptions, and Salary.

To place a regular field in a form, you issue the [Menu] Put Regular command. After you issue this command, Paradox will display a list of field names and will prompt you to indicate the field you want to place. You can select a field in one of two ways: either by positioning the cursor on the field name and pressing ↵ or by pressing the key corresponding to the first character in the field name. If you have two or more fields that start with the same character, Paradox will prompt you to place the cursor on the one you want to place and select it by pressing ↵.

Placing an Alphanumeric Field

For example, suppose you are creating the form shown in Figure 5-34 and you want to place the Last Name field in the form. To do this, first use the arrow keys to position the cursor, then type the literal **Last Name:** followed by a space. (This literal is not required, but it helps you remember the function of the field.) Then issue the **[Menu] P**ut **R**egular command, point to the Last Name field in the list and press ↵.

Once you select a field, the cursor will change to a small blinking box called the pointing cursor, and Paradox will prompt you to indicate where you want to place the field. You should point to the place in the form where you want the field to begin and press ↵. You can place the field anywhere on the screen you choose.

In the example, you should position the cursor next to the word *Name:* and press ↵. After you do this, your screen will look like Figure 5-35.

Figure 5-35 Positioning the Field

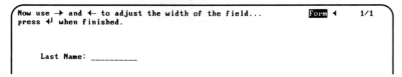

After you press ↵ to place the field, Paradox will display the field as a series of dashed lines and will prompt you to adjust its width. The default length for the field is the same as the field's width in the table for which you are creating a form. Each dash that you see on the screen represents one character in the field. You can reduce the width of the field by pressing the ← key at the field-width prompt. Once the field is the desired width, you can press ↵ to lock it in place. Alternatively, you can accept the default width by pressing ↵ without pressing ←.

You can reduce the size of a field to a minimum of one character. To do this, you could press the ← key several times to reach the minimum or press the [Home] key once. If you accidentally make the field too small, before you press ↵, press the → key to increase its width or the [End] key to return it to the default width.

If you make a field too small, Paradox will display only part of the entry (if it's an alphanumeric field) or a series of asterisks (if it's a number field) when you view the records in the table. To view the entire entry, you must press [Field View] ([Alt]-[F5]).

You cannot increase the width of an alphanumeric field beyond its width in the table–the default width. Normally, you will not want to shorten alphanumeric fields, either. To accept the default width in the example, then, you should press ↵. Figure 5-36 shows this field in place in the form.

Figure 5-36 Placing an Alphanumeric Field

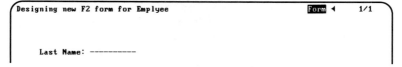

Placing a Number Field

Now, let's place the Number field Emp Number on the form. First move the cursor down two lines and type the literal text **Employee Number:**, then issue the **[Menu] P**ut **R**egular command and choose Emp Number from the list. When Paradox prompts you to define the position of the Emp Number field on the form, point to the character after the word *Number:* and press ↵. Figure 5-37 shows the screen at this point.

Figure 5-37   Placing a Number Field

```
Now use → and ← to adjust the width of the field...      Form ◄    1/1
press ↵ when finished.



      Last Name: ----------
      Employee Number: _____
```

Now, Paradox will prompt you to define the length of the Emp Number field in the form. As before, you can use the ← and [Home] keys to narrow the field. Normally, you will want to change the width of the numeric fields you place on a form. For example, notice how much space Paradox has allotted to the Emp Number field in the form, even though this field contains only one and two-digit numbers. Since you don't need all of this space, you will probably want to narrow the Emp Number field. To do this, press the ← key until the Emp Number field is just five characters wide, and then press ↵. Your screen will now look like Figure 5-38. From now on when you use this form to work with the EMPLYEE table, the Emp Number field will display only five characters.

Figure 5-38   Reducing the Field Length

```
Designing new F2 form for Emplyee                         Form ◄    1/1



      Last Name: ----------
      Employee Number: -----
```

Notes

You can place each regular field only once on the form. In fact, after you place a field, it is automatically removed from the list of fields that you see after you issue the [Menu] Put Regular command.

Once you place a field on the screen, you can type a literal to its left or right; however, you cannot type over it. If you try to type over a field, Paradox will display the message *Cannot place text on top of a field* at the bottom of the screen. If you are in the insert mode, and you add literal text to the left of a field, the field will move to the right as you type. When the right edge of the field reaches the right edge of the form, Paradox will not allow you to continue typing.

You don't have to place every field in a table on a form. When you are designing forms, you can place only those fields you want to see in the form. However, you must place at least one regular field on each page of the form. Paradox will not let you save a form unless it has at least one regular field on each page.

Display-only Fields

Display-only fields are like regular fields, except that they cannot be edited in any way; they are for show only. Unlike regular fields, which can only be placed once per form, display-only fields can be placed on a single form as many times as you want.

To place a display-only field on a form, you should issue the [Menu] Put DisplayOnly command. Paradox then will prompt you to select a field just as it does when you place a regular field on the form. After you select a field, Paradox will prompt you to place it and adjust its width as if you were placing a regular field.

For example, suppose you are designing the form for the EMPLYEE table shown in Figure 5-34, and you want to place the Salary field on the form as a display-only field. To do this, first move the cursor to the appropriate place and type the literal **Salary:**, then issue the [**Menu**] **P**ut **D**isplayOnly command. After you issue this command, Paradox will prompt you to select a field, just as it does when you place a regular field on the form. When you see this prompt, select the Salary field. Next, Paradox will prompt you to place the field on the form. You now should position the pointing cursor next to the literal *Salary:* and press ↵. Now, to accept the default width for the field, press ↵. Figure 5-39 shows the form at this point.

Figure 5-39   A Display-only Field

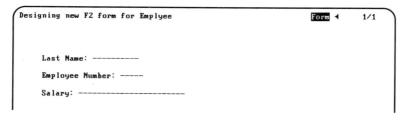

Display-only fields are very useful in situations where you want to display a field on a form, but you don't want to allow changes to be made in that field. Display-only fields also are useful if you have a multipage form and you want to keep track of a specific field on each page. By entering a given field as a display-only field on each page of the form, you can keep track of which record you are working with. For example, suppose you design a form for the EMPLYEE table that is five pages long. You could place the Emp Number field on each page as a display-only field to help you keep track of the records.

Calculated Fields

A calculated field shows the result of mathematical calculations based on other fields in the table. For example, suppose you want to place the calculated field *Hourly Rate* on the form in Figure 5-39. This field will show the employee's hourly rate (calculated by dividing the Salary field entry by 2080).

To place the Hourly Rate field in the form, first type the literal **Hourly Rate:** into the form at the appropriate place. Next, issue the **[Menu] P**ut **C**alculated command. Paradox then will prompt you to enter a mathematical expression. When you see this prompt, type **[Salary]/2080** and press ↵. The expression *[Salary]* in this formula tells Paradox to use the Salary field entry of the current record as the dividend in the division.

Next, Paradox will prompt you to place the field on the form. When it does, place the cursor next to the literal *Hourly Rate:* and press ↵. Next, Paradox will prompt you to adjust the width of the field. When it does, press ↵ to accept the default width. After you do this, your screen will look like Figure 5-40.

Figure 5-40   A Calculated Field

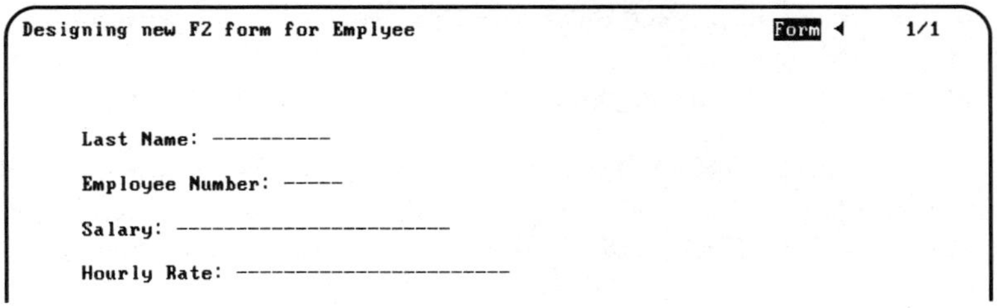

```
Designing new F2 form for Emplyee                    Form ◄    1/1



    Last Name: ----------

    Employee Number: -----

    Salary: ----------------------

    Hourly Rate: ----------------------
```

The expression you use in a calculated field can be up to 48 characters long. It can contain field names that are enclosed in square brackets ([ ]), mathematical operators like +, -, *, /, and ( ), or constant values like .10, 30, and 1.5. You also can enter dates and literals as constant values. For example, the expression *7/1/86 + 30* would return the date *31-Jul-86*. The expression *Employee + [Last Name]* would display *Employee Jones*.

Whenever you include a field name in an expression, it must be enclosed in square brackets. For example, to include the Salary field in the expression, you typed *[Salary]*, not *Salary*. If you do not include the brackets, Paradox will not recognize it as a field. Instead, it will be interpreted as a literal.

Paradox automatically checks the expression you enter to be sure it is valid. If you enter an invalid expression, Paradox will display the message *Invalid expression* at the bottom of the screen. You also will occassionally see the message *Syntax error in expression* at the bottom of the screen. This usually means that the expression has been entered incorrectly. When you see either of these messages, press [Backspace] or [Ctrl]-[Backspace] to erase the entry and type in the correct expression.

Note that calculated fields are record-oriented. For example, while you can include a reference to any field in the current record in a calculated field expression, you cannot place a calculated field that will compute the total number of hours worked by all employees or the total salary paid to all employees.

Record Number Fields

When Paradox creates a default form, it automatically puts a record number field in the upper-right corner of the form (see Figure 5-1). This field displays the number of the record you are viewing through the form. As you might expect, you can also include record number fields in your custom forms.

For example, suppose you are designing the form shown in Figure 5-34 on page 125, and you want to display the record number for each record on the form. To do this, type the literal **Record Number:** into the form, then issue the **[Menu]** **P**ut #Record command. After you issue this command, Paradox will prompt you to place the field, just as it does whenever you place a regular field. When you see this prompt, move the cursor to the lower-right corner of the screen and press ↵. Then, when Paradox prompts you to adjust the width of the field, press ↵ to accept the default width. After you press ↵, Paradox will place the field on the form. Figure 5-34 shows the completed form.

You can place a record number field anywhere you choose. You probably will want to place a record number field on each page of a multipage form to help you keep track of the records in your table. We'll show you how to do this later in this chapter.

Using the Form

When you have finished designing the form, press **[Do-It!]** to save your work and return to the main workspace. Now, let's edit the table through the form to see how each field type works. To do this, issue the **[Menu]** **M**odify **E**dit command and type **EMPLYEE** to identify the table you want to edit. When the table comes into view, issue the **[Menu]** **I**mage **P**ickForm command and select the form number assigned to the form you just created. (If you followed the example exactly, the new form will be form 2.)

Figure 5-41 shows the first record of EMPLYEE in the form. As you can see, the Last Name and Salary fields display the entries from those fields in the first record of EMPLYEE. The calculated field *Hourly Rate* shows the result of dividing the value in the Salary field of the current record by 2080: 33.6538461538462. The record number field Record Number displays a 1, the current record number.

Figure 5-41 Using the Form

```
┌─────────────────────────────────────────────────────────────────────┐
│  Editing Emplyee table with form F2: Record 1 of 16      Edit   ═▼ │
│                                                                     │
│                                                                     │
│         Last Name:  Jones                                           │
│         Employee Number:  1                                         │
│         Salary:            70,000.00                                │
│         Hourly Rate:       33.6538461538462                         │
│                                                                     │
│                                      Record Number:    1            │
│                                                                     │
│                                                                     │
└─────────────────────────────────────────────────────────────────────┘
```

Paradox does not allow you to move the cursor into calculated, display-only, or record number fields. Since there are only two regular fields in this table, in fact, if you press →, ↓, or ↵ twice, the cursor will jump past the Salary, Hourly Rate, and Record Number fields directly into the second record. As you view different records in the table, the fields will change to the current record number.

Notice that the Hourly Rate field uses the default format for number fields (General), which allows up to 15 digits (including decimal places) to be displayed. Paradox always assigns the General format to calculated fields. In this case, it would probably be more meaningful to display just the first two or three decimal places, instead of all 15. Unfortunately, there is no way to format a calculated field after you have placed it.

Erasing Fields

To erase a field after you have placed it on a form, you issue the [Menu] Erase command, position the cursor on the field you want to erase, and press ↵. For example, suppose you are designing the form shown in Figure 5-42. Now suppose that you decide you don't want to include a record number field on the form. To erase this field, issue the [Menu] Erase command. After you issue this command, Paradox will display the menu shown in Figure 5-43.

Figure 5-42   A Custom Form

```
┌─────────────────────────────────────────────────────────────────────┐
│ Designing new F3 form for Emplyee                        Form ◄ Ins 1/1 │
├─────────────────────────────────────────────────────────────────────┤
│                                                                     │
│                                           Record Number: ------     │
│                                                                     │
│             Employee Number: ----------------------                 │
│             Last Name: ----------                                   │
│             First Name: ----------                                  │
│             Salary: ----------------------                          │
│             Exemptions: ----------------------                      │
│                                                                     │
└─────────────────────────────────────────────────────────────────────┘
```

Figure 5-43   The Erase Menu

```
┌─────────────────────────────────────────────────────────────────────┐
│ Field  Border  Area                                      Form ◄  1/1 │
│ Remove a field from the form.                                        │
└─────────────────────────────────────────────────────────────────────┘
```

As you can see, this menu has three options: Field, Border, and Area. To erase a field, issue the Field command. Paradox then will prompt you to indicate the field you want to erase. When you see this prompt, position the cursor anywhere on the record number field, and press ↵. Paradox then will remove the field from the form. Figure 5-44 shows the changed form.

Figure 5-44 Erasing a Field

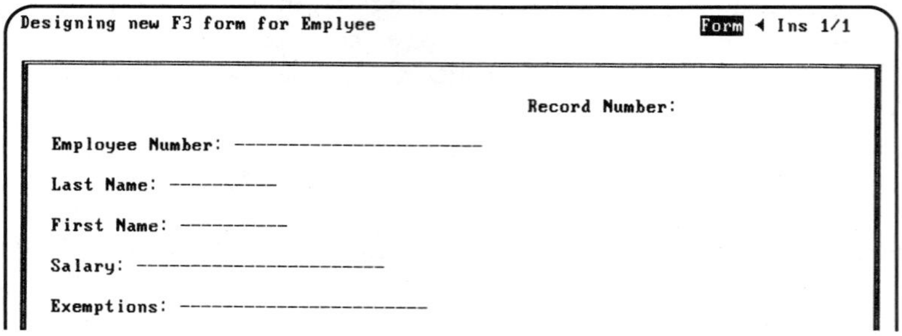

```
Designing new F3 form for Emplyee                    Form ◄ Ins 1/1

                                      Record Number:
        Employee Number: ------------------------
        Last Name: ----------
        First Name: ----------
        Salary: ----------------------
        Exemptions: ----------------------
```

If the cursor is not positioned on a field when you press ↵, the message *No field here* will appear in the lower-right corner of the screen. Once you have the cursor positioned correctly, press ↵ to erase the field.

Notice that the literal text *Record Number:* was not erased when you erased the record number field from the form. To erase the literal, position the cursor on the letter *R* and press [**Del**] 14 times.

Moving Fields

You also can move fields after they have been placed on the form. For example, suppose you have placed a record number field in the upper-right corner of a form you are designing, as shown in Figure 5-42.

Now suppose you want to move the field and the associated literal text *Record Number:* to the lower-right corner of the screen. You could erase the field and then put it back where you want it, but it's easier to move the field. To do this, issue the [**Menu**] **M**ove command. After you issue this command, Paradox will prompt you to indicate the area to be moved. When you see this prompt, position the cursor on the *R* in *Record* and press ↵. Paradox then will prompt you to move to the diagonal corner of the area. When it does, press → until the literal *Record Number:* and the field itself are highlighted, as shown in Figure 5-45, and then press ↵.

Figure 5-45 The Highlighted Area

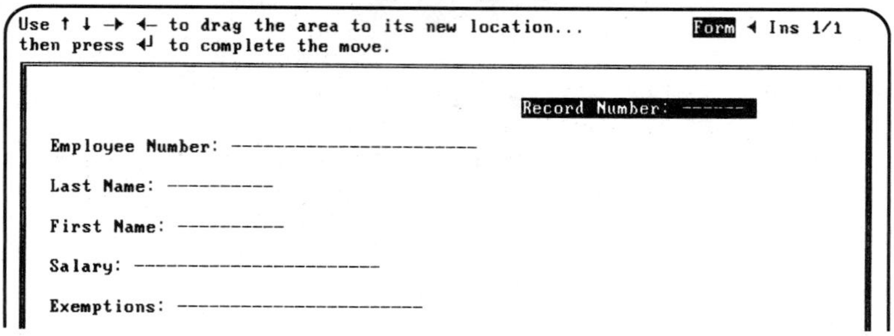

```
Use ↑ ↓ → ← to drag the area to its new location...     Form ◄ Ins 1/1
then press ↵ to complete the move.

                                      Record Number: ------
        Employee Number: ------------------------
        Last Name: ----------
        First Name: ----------
        Salary: ----------------------
        Exemptions: ----------------------
```

Notice the instructions at the top of the screen in Figure 5-45. These instructions tell you to use the cursor keys to move the field. You now should press ↓ to move the cursor to the bottom of the screen. As you move the cursor down the screen, the highlighted area "drags" to the new location. When you reach the desired location and press ↵, the field is moved instantly as shown in Figure 5-46.

Figure 5-46 Completing the Move

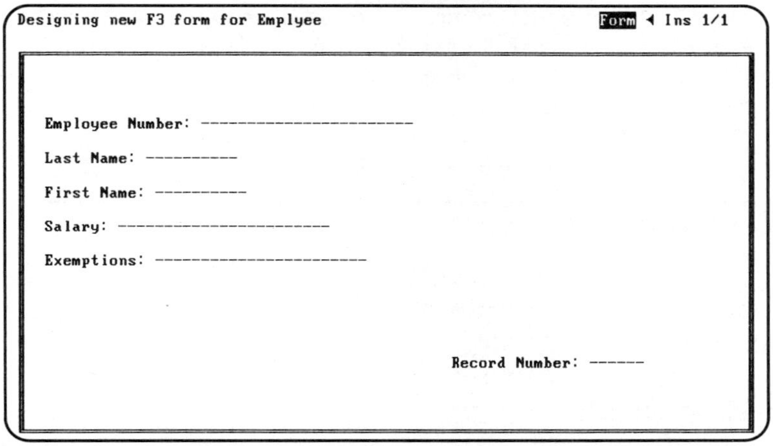

```
┌Designing new F3 form for Emplyee─────────────Form ◄ Ins 1/1─┐
│ ┌─────────────────────────────────────────────────────────┐ │
│ │                                                         │ │
│ │    Employee Number: ------------------------            │ │
│ │    Last Name: ----------                                │ │
│ │    First Name: ----------                               │ │
│ │    Salary: ------------------------                     │ │
│ │    Exemptions: ------------------------                 │ │
│ │                                                         │ │
│ │                                                         │ │
│ │                              Record Number: ------      │ │
│ │                                                         │ │
│ └─────────────────────────────────────────────────────────┘ │
└─────────────────────────────────────────────────────────────┘
```

Although we used the Move command to move a record number field in this example, you can use this command to reposition any field of any type.

Notice that there is no menu under the Move command as described in the *Paradox User's Guide*. The Move command is not specific for fields, borders, or text. Anything that you define as an area can be moved with this command.

Borders

As you know, Paradox allows you to place borders around your forms. We've placed double-line borders around the forms we've designed so far. However, Paradox allows you to place many different kinds of borders around your forms. We'll show you how to create different types of borders in this section.

When you issue the [Menu] Border command during the creation of a form, Paradox displays three options: Single-line, Double-line, and Other. The Single-line command lets you place a single-line border around your form. The Double-line command lets you place a double-line border around a form (the default form has a double-line border). The Other command lets you design your own border, using either keyboard characters or ASCII characters.

Single-line Borders

A Single-line border is exactly what you'd expect–a border drawn with a single line. For example, suppose you are designing the form shown in Figure 5-47, and you want to place a single-line border around it. To do this, issue the **[Menu] B**order Single-line command. After you issue this command, Paradox will prompt you to point to one corner of the area around which you want to draw the form. When you see this prompt, move the cursor to the upper-left corner of the screen and press ↵. Paradox then will prompt you to indicate the diagonal (opposite) corner of the border. When it does, press the ↑ key, followed by the ← key to move the cursor to the lower-right corner of the screen. Now, press ↵ to place the border, as shown in Figure 5-48.

Figure 5-47 A Sample Form

```
Designing new F3 form for Emplyee                    Form ◄    1/1

                         ABC Company Inc.
                        Employee Update Form
           Name: ----------  ----------

           Emp Number: ------   Date of Hire: -----------

           Exemptions: ----------------------

           Salary: ----------------------

           Hourly Rate: ----------------------




                                        Record: ------
```

Figure 5-48 A Single-line Border

```
Designing new F3 form for Emplyee                    Form ◄    1/1
  ┌──────────────────────────────────────────────────────────────┐
  │                      ABC Company Inc.                        │
  │                     Employee Update Form                     │
  │        Name: ----------  ----------                          │
  │                                                              │
  │        Emp Number: ------   Date of Hire: -----------        │
  │                                                              │
  │        Exemptions: ----------------------                    │
  │                                                              │
  │        Salary: ----------------------                        │
  │                                                              │
  │        Hourly Rate: ----------------------                   │
  │                                                              │
  │                                                              │
  │                                     Record: ------           │
  └──────────────────────────────────────────────────────────────┘
```

Special Character Borders

In addition to single-line and double-line borders, you can also create a border that is made up of any printable character. For example, suppose you want to place a border made up of dollar signs ($) around the form shown in Figure 5-47. To make this border, issue the **[Menu] B**order **O**ther command. After you issue this command, Paradox will prompt you to enter the character that you want to use for the border. When you see this prompt, type $ and press ↵. Paradox then will prompt you to define the border. Since you want to position the form around the entire screen, you should press ↵ , then ↑, followed by ←, and then ↵ to place the border. Figure 5-49 shows the new form.

Figure 5-49   A $ Border

```
┌─────────────────────────────────────────────────────────────────────────┐
│ Designing new F3 form for Emplyee                          Form ◄   1/1 │
├─────────────────────────────────────────────────────────────────────────┤
│ $$$$$$$$$$$$$$$$$$$$$$$$$$$$$$$$$$$$$$$$$$$$$$$$$$$$$$$$$$$$$$$$$$$$$$$ │
│ $                                                                     $ │
│ $                         ABC Company Inc.                            $ │
│ $                        Employee Update Form                         $ │
│ $                                                                     $ │
│ $   Name: ----------  ----------                                      $ │
│ $                                                                     $ │
│ $   Emp Number: ------   Date of Hire: -----------                    $ │
│ $                                                                     $ │
│ $   Exemptions: ----------------------                                $ │
│ $                                                                     $ │
│ $   Salary: -------------------------                                 $ │
│ $                                                                     $ │
│ $   Hourly Rate: ---------------------                                $ │
│ $                                                                     $ │
│ $                                                                     $ │
│ $                                                                     $ │
│ $                                                                     $ │
│ $                                          Record: ------             $ │
│ $                                                                     $ │
│ $                                                                     $ │
│ $$$$$$$$$$$$$$$$$$$$$$$$$$$$$$$$$$$$$$$$$$$$$$$$$$$$$$$$$$$$$$$$$$$$$$$ │
└─────────────────────────────────────────────────────────────────────────┘
```

Notice that the new border in Figure 5-49 replaces the border that was on the form in Figure 5-48. Whenever you place one border on top of another, the new border will replace the old one. If the new border only partially overlaps the old border, only that portion of the old border that is under the new one will be replaced.

Although you can use any character on the keyboard as a border character, you can only use one character in a border. For example, you cannot place a border made up of *$* and *A*. If you enter more than one character, Paradox will display the message *Only a single character can be used for borders* at the bottom of the screen. When you see this message, you must press the [Backspace] key to erase the entry, then type in a single character.

In addition to keyboard characters, you can use characters from your computer's extended character set (ASCII codes 128-254) to draw borders. For example, suppose you want to create the border shown in Figure 5-50. This border uses ASCII character 176 as the border character.

To do this, issue the **[Menu] B**order **O**ther command. When Paradox prompts you for a character, press the **[Alt]** key while typing the ASCII code, **176**, on the numeric keypad, then press ↵. Next, Paradox will prompt you to place the border. When you see this prompt, place the border around the form as described above and press ↵. After you do this, your screen will look like Figure 5-50.

Figure 5-50   An ASCII Character Border

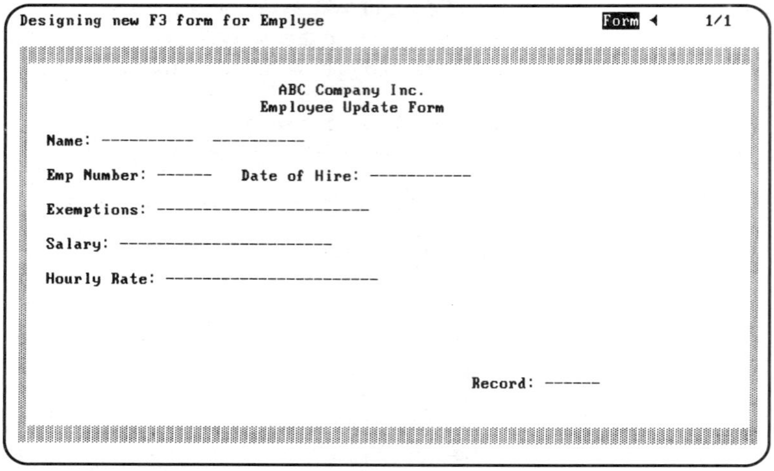

```
Designing new F3 form for Emplyee                    Form ◄    1/1

       ABC Company Inc.
       Employee Update Form

   Name: ----------  ----------

   Emp Number: ------    Date of Hire: -----------

   Exemptions: ----------------------

   Salary: ----------------------

   Hourly Rate: ----------------------



                                          Record: ------
```

Note that you must use the numeric keypad on the right side of the keyboard to define the ASCII code of the character you want to use in the border. If you press the number keys across the top of the keyboard, Paradox will respond with a high-pitched beep. (There is a table of ASCII codes and characters in Appendix A of the *PAL User's Guide*, which came with your program.)

When you want to use a special character border, you should place all the fields and literals you want on the form before you add the border. If you don't, you may not be able to adjust your fields and literals on the screen. For example, suppose you design a form using ASCII character number 247 as a border, then you type a title, like ABC COMPANY INC., on the screen. To center the title on the screen, you would position the cursor in front of it, press [Ins], followed by the [Spacebar]. However, when you do this, Paradox will display the message *Cannot move line further to the right* at the bottom of the screen. Apparently, there is a bug in Paradox that causes it to treat the line as if it were full of characters when you use certain ASCII characters for borders. If you get caught in this trap, all you need to do is erase the border and start over.

Erasing Borders

If you place a border on the form that you later discover you don't really want, you can erase it with the [Menu] Erase Border command. For example, suppose you want to erase the border you just placed on the form in the previous example. To do this, you issue the [**Menu**] **E**rase **B**order command. After you issue this command, Paradox will prompt you to position the cursor on a corner of the border you want to erase, just as it does when you place the border. When you see this prompt, position the cursor on a corner of the border and press ↵. Paradox then will prompt you to move the cursor to the diagonal corner. When it does, move the cursor to the diagonal corner and press ↵. After you do this, Paradox will erase the border. Your screen will again look like Figure 5-47.

You can also erase a border by typing over it, or you can delete part of it with the [Del] key or the [Backspace] key. You also can erase a border (or a section of a border) if it is part of an area that you define after you issue the [Menu] Erase Area command.

Erasing an Area

So far, we have shown you how to erase fields and borders with the [Menu] Erase commands. You can also use this command to erase a rectangular area in a form. For example, suppose you are designing the form shown in Figure 5-47, and you decide you want to start over. All you want to retain from the work you've done so far is the form title and the name fields. You could issue the [Menu] Cancel Yes command and then start over from scratch, but it's easier to erase the area of the form you no longer want.

To do this, issue the [**Menu**] **E**rase **A**rea command. After you issue this command, Paradox will prompt you to place the cursor on a corner of the area you want to erase. When you see this prompt, move the cursor to the space just before the *E* in the literal *Emp Number* and press ↵. Paradox then will prompt you to move the cursor to the diagonal corner of the area you want to erase. When it does, press ← until the cursor appears on the right side of the screen. Then press ↓ to move the cursor to the bottom-right corner of the screen. Figure 5-51 shows the screen at this point. Now just press ↵ to erase the screen. Figure 5-52 shows the resulting form.

Figure 5-51   Defining the Area to Erase

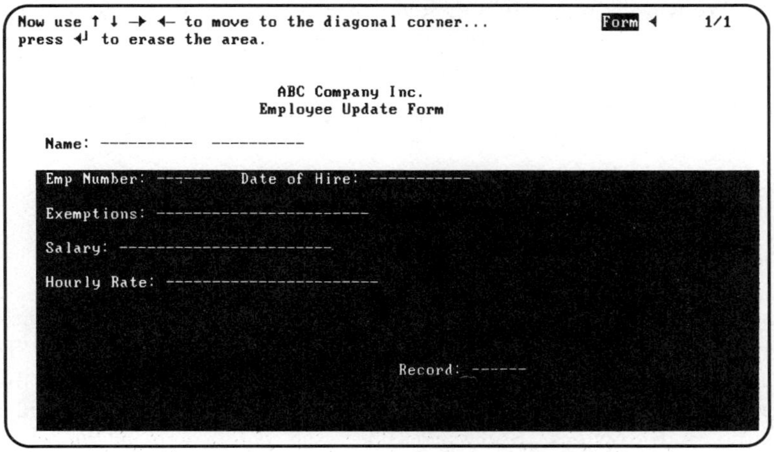

Figure 5-52   Erasing an Area

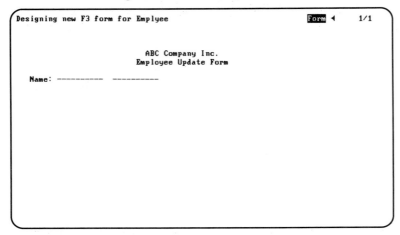

Usually, you'll want to erase an area that is part of the screen. However, you can also use the [Menu] Erase Area command to erase the entire screen if you wish. Regardless of the size of the area you want to erase, however, the steps are the same.

Setting the Style for Your Form

The [Menu] Style command allows you to control whether or not field names are displayed on a form and how text and borders are displayed on the screen. For example, you can use this command to display the text in your forms in high intensity or reverse video, or to make text and borders blink.

When you issue the [Menu] Style command, Paradox will display the Style menu shown in Figure 5-53. As you can see, this menu has several commands for setting the style of your form. We will discuss each of these commands in the sections that follow.

Figure 5-53   The Style Menu

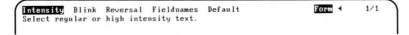

Displaying Field Names

When you place a field on the forms design screen, the field name is not automatically shown. For example, Figure 5-54 shows a sample form without field names. To display the field names on the form, you should issue the **[Menu] S**tyle command. When you see this menu, issue the Fieldnames command. When you do, Paradox will display a menu that offers two options: Show and Hide. The Show command causes Paradox to display field names on the screen. The Hide command hides the field names. The Hide option is the default. If you issue the **Hide** command, your screen will not change–it will look like Figure 5-54.

Figure 5-54   A Sample Form

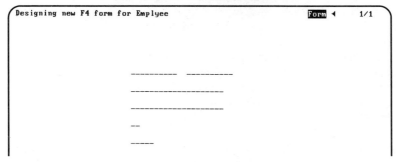

To bring the field names into view, you must issue the **Show** command. When you do this, the dashes that represent the fields on the form will be partially or completely replaced by the names of the fields they represent. This is shown in Figure 5-55.

Figure 5-55   Displaying the Field Names

Notice the style setting message at the bottom of the screen shown in Figure 5-55. This message will appear whenever you change a style setting. It will disappear when you press a key.

It is important that you understand that the Fieldnames Show command causes the field names to be displayed only when you are working in the Forms Editor. The field names will not be displayed when you use this form to view, edit, or enter records. The only way to have the field names displayed when you are using the form is to include them as literal characters in the form.

Setting Styles for Text and Borders

The other options on the Style menu allow you to control the display of literal text and borders in your forms. The Intensity option lets you display text and borders in high or normal intensity. Blink lets you create blinking text and borders. Reversal lets you display text and borders in normal or reverse video. The Default option sets all of the style settings to the default—the style we've used throughout this chapter.

When you select a style setting, it goes into effect immediately. Any literal text or borders that you enter from that point on will be displayed in the specified format. However, any text or borders that are already in place will not be affected by the new style you set. Fields, however, are not affected by the style settings. They will always be displayed in the default style.

Once you set a new style, it will remain in effect until you specifically change it. After you have entered all of the text (or defined the border) that you wanted to display in the special style, use the [Menu] Style command to restore the default style. Otherwise, all of the text that you enter in the form will be displayed in the selected style.

If you change the default style settings, a style setting message will be displayed at the bottom of the screen. This message will remain in view until you press a key. In addition, the Style indicator at the top of the screen will change to the style you set. For example, if you choose the Blink style, the Style indicator will blink.

Setting the Intensity

For example, suppose you are designing the form shown in Figure 5-54, and you want to enter the field name prompts into the form in intense video. To do this, you issue the [Menu] Style Intensity command. After you issue the command, you will see a menu that offers two options: High and Regular. The High command sets the display at high intensity. The Regular command turns off High Intensity and returns the display to normal. When you see this menu, issue the High command. When you do, the style message will change to reflect the new style.

Any text and borders you place on the screen after you issue this command will be displayed in high intensity. If you enter the field name prompts (Name:, Address:, City:, State:, and Zip:) into the form, they will automatically be displayed in intense video. (You'll have to take our word for this; High Intensity does not show up in a figure.)

Once you have entered the field name prompts, you can use the [Menu] Style Intensity Regular command to restore the High Intensity setting to the default.

The Blink Attribute

The [Menu] Style Blink command causes text and borders to blink on the screen. For example, suppose you are designing the form shown in Figure 5-55, and you want to enter the message *All fields must be completed* in the form. To draw the user's attention to this message, you want it to be displayed in blinking video. To do this, you should issue the [Menu] Style Blink command. After you issue this command, Paradox will display a menu with two options, Blink and NoBlink, which turn the Blink style setting on and off. When you see this menu, choose Blink to activate the Blink style attribute.

Now move the cursor toward the lower-right corner of the form and type **All fields must be completed.** As you type, the characters will come into view in blinking video. (You'll have to take our word for this; like High Intensity, there's no way for us to illustrate blinking text in a figure.)

Once you have entered the message, you can use the [Menu] Style Blink NoBlink command to restore the Blink setting to the default.

The Reverse Attribute

The [Menu] Style Reversal command lets you display text and borders in reverse video. For example, suppose you are designing the form shown in Figure 5-55, and you want to display the title *ABC Company Employee Address Form* in reverse video. To do this, you issue the [Menu] Style Reversal command. After you issue this command, Paradox will display a menu that offers two options, ReverseVideo and Normal, which turn the Reverse Video style setting on and off. You should choose the ReverseVideo command. Now, any new text and borders that you place on the form will be displayed in reverse video. If you enter the title, the form will look like Figure 5-56.

*Figure 5-56 **The Reverse Attribute***

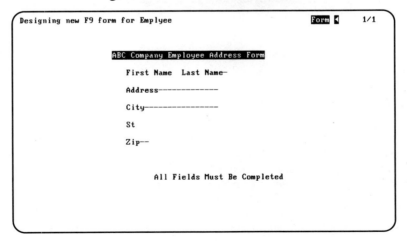

Once you have entered the title, you can use the [Menu] Style Reversal Normal command to restore the Reverse setting to the default.

Mixing Styles

You can mix any or all of the styles we've talked about. For example, suppose you are designing the form shown in Figure 5-56, and you want to design a reverse video, blinking border around your form. To do this, issue the **[Menu]** Style **B**link **B**link command. Next, to add reverse video, issue the **[Menu]** Style **R**eversal **R**everseVideo command. Now, you can use the **[Menu]** **B**orders command to add a reverse video, blinking border to the form. Figure 5-57 shows the completed form. Of course, the border on your form will blink.

Figure 5-57 Mixing Attributes

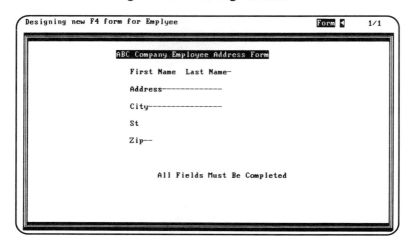

Once you have entered the border, you can use the [Menu] Style Reversal Normal command and [Menu] Style Blink NoBlink command to restore the default settings.

Multipage Forms

Throughout this chapter, we've used single-page forms to illustrate how to design forms. There may be times, however, when you want to design a multipage form. For example, if you have a large table with more than 19 or 20 fields and you want to place all of them on a form, you may need to design a multipage form. In addition, if your table has more than 19 fields, its default form will be a multipage form.

Designing and using a multipage form is really no different than designing and using a single-page form, except, of course, for the extra pages. You'll be able to use all of the techniques and commands you learned earlier in this chapter to design multipage forms.

A form can have up to 15 pages. When you design a multipage form, you must design each page individually. A "page" in this case refers to the screen, not a printed page. For example, if you want a double-line border around each page of the form, you must place the border on each page individually. Each page of the form must have at least one regular field on it.

An Example

Suppose you are designing the form shown in Figure 5-57, and you want to add a second page to the form. To do this, you issue the **[Menu]** Form command. After you issue this command, Paradox will display a menu that offers two options: Insert and Delete. The Insert command allows you to insert a page in the form. The Delete command deletes the current page from the form.

When you see this menu, issue the Insert command. Paradox then will ask you if you want the page inserted before or after the current page. If you choose the Before option, Paradox will add a page in front of the current page and move the cursor to it. If you choose the After command, Paradox will add a page to the form and make it the current page. Since in the example you want to add the new page after the current page, you should choose After. Paradox then will add the page and make it the current page.

Figure 5-58 shows the new, blank page on the screen. The only indication you have that you are on the second page of the form is the status message at the top-right corner of the screen. It now reads: *2/2*.

Figure 5-58 A Second Page

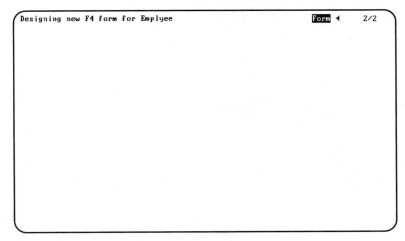

At this point, designing the second page of the form is just like designing the first page. You can place a border around the screen, set the style, place fields, and add literals. You cannot, however, place a regular field that appears on the first page on the second page. Remember—you can only place a regular field once per form. Of course, you can always erase the field from the first page and then place it on the second page.

For example, suppose you want to place a border around the second page of our sample form and then place the Salary, Exemptions, and Date of Hire fields on it. To do this, issue the [**Menu**] **B**order **D**ouble-line command and place the border around the page. Then use the [**Menu**] **P**ut **R**egular command to place the Salary, Exemptions, and Date of Hire fields on the page and identify the fields with literals. Since the pages of a multipage form are not well identified, you might want to place a record number field on the page and add the literal *Page 2 of 2*. Your screen should now look like Figure 5-59.

Figure 5-59   Identifying the Page

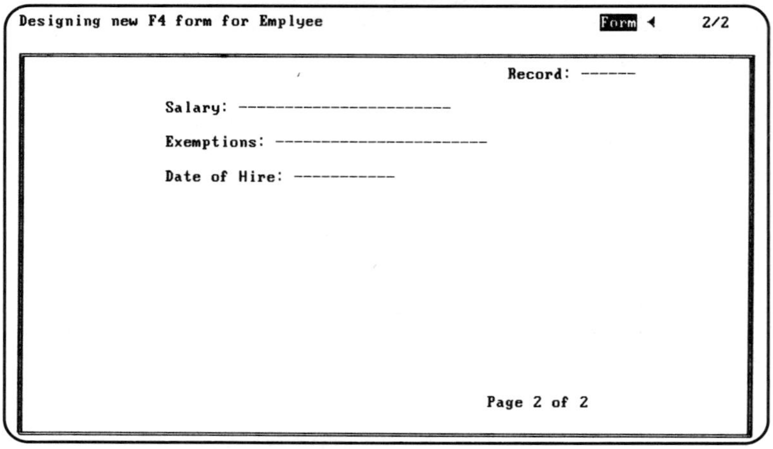

```
Designing new F4 form for Emplyee                    Form ◄    2/2

                                       Record: ------
            Salary: ----------------------
            Exemptions: -------------------
            Date of Hire: -----------




                                              Page 2 of 2
```

Instead of using a record number field to identify the second page, you also could use a field from the form. For example, in the EMPLYEE table form you might use the Emp Number field to help you remember at which record you are looking. Since you can only place a regular field in a form once, the occurrences of the field on the second and subsequent pages will have to be display-only fields.

Moving between Pages

The [Pg Up] and [Pg Dn] keys let you move between the pages of a form. To move up from one page to the previous page, press [Pg Up]. Pressing [Pg Dn] moves the cursor from one page to the following page. For example, to move from page 1 of the sample form to page 2, press [**Pg Dn**]. To move back to the first page, press [**Pg Up**].

As you move between pages, the Page indicator at the top of the screen will change. For example, when the cursor is on page 1 of a two-page form, the indicator will read *1/2*. When you press [Pg Dn] to move to the next page, the indicator will read *2/2*.

Moving Areas between Pages

Moving an area from one page to another in a multipage form is just like moving an area from one location to another on a single-page form. To move an area to a different page, you issue the [Menu] Move command, use the cursor keys to define the area to be moved, and press ↵. When Paradox prompts you to indicate the new location for the area, press [Pg Up] or [Pg Dn] to move the cursor to the upper-left corner of the page to which you want to move the area, and then use the arrow keys to move the cursor to the point on the page where you want the area placed. Finally, press ↵ to complete the move.

For example, suppose you are designing the form from the previous example, and you want to move the Date of Hire field from the second page to the first page. To do this, issue the **[Menu] M**ove command, and define the Date of Hire field as the area to move. After you do this, your screen will look like Figure 5-60.

Figure 5-60   Defining the Area

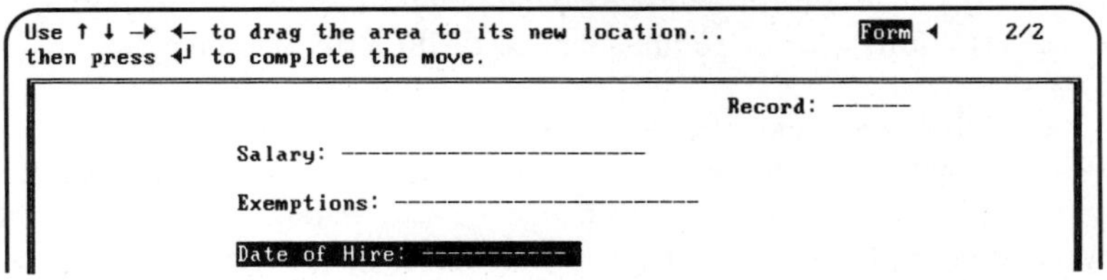

Now press **[Pg Up]**. After you do this, Paradox will move the cursor to the first page of the form. Now, use the arrow keys to position the area on the form, and then press ↵. After you do this, your screen will look like Figure 5-61.

Figure 5-61   Completing the Move

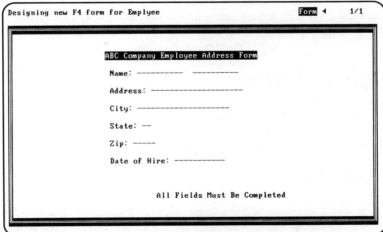

Deleting Pages from a Form

You can use the [Menu] Form Delete command to delete a page from a form. This command deletes the current page of the form (the page the cursor is on). You need to be sure that the cursor is on the page that you want to delete before you issue this command.

The Delete command is very unforgiving. If you accidentally delete a page, the only thing you can do is insert a new page and start over.

If you're working on page 1 of a single-page form and you issue the [Menu] Form Delete command, Paradox will delete everything on the form and display an empty page 1.

Changing Forms

After you have designed and saved a form, you can make changes in it by issuing the [Menu] Forms Change command. After you issue this command, Paradox will prompt you to specify the name of the table that is associated with the form you wish to change. For example, to change a form that is associated with the EMPLYEE table, you would issue the [Menu] Forms Change command, type EMPLYEE, and press ↵.

After you issue this command, Paradox will display a Form Number menu that lists the forms associated with the specified table. When you see the Form Number menu, select the number of the form you wish to change. Next, Paradox will display the form's description and prompt you to change it. To do this, you can press [Backspace] to erase it and then type a new one, or you can press ↵ to retain the current description.

After you specify the description, Paradox will display the form on the screen. At this point, making changes in the form is exactly like designing a new form. You can erase and place fields, move fields, add pages, design borders, and select different styles.

After you have made the changes you want, you can press [Do-It!] or issue the [Menu] DO-IT! command to save the form and return to the main workspace. If you decide you don't want to save your changes, issue the [Menu] Cancel Yes command. Paradox will save the original form and return you to the main workspace.

Managing Forms

Once you've created a number of custom forms, you'll want to know how to manage them effectively. For example, you may want to make a copy of a form, or rename a form, or delete an obsolete form.

Copying Forms

As you work with forms, you will no doubt discover that designing a complicated form can be a time-consuming and tedious task. The task can become even more onerous if you need two similar, but slightly different forms for the same table. You might think that you will need to design each form individually, but, fortunately, there is an easy way to create two or more similar forms for the same table. After you have designed the first form, you can use the [Menu] Tools Copy Form command to make a copy of it, then make changes in the copy with the [Menu] Forms Change command.

For example, suppose you designed the form shown in Figure 5-61 for the EMPLYEE table. Now suppose you need a similar but slightly different form. To create the second form, first issue the [Menu] Tools Copy Form command. After you issue this command, Paradox will prompt you to enter the name of the table with the form to be copied. When it does, type **EMPLYEE** and press ↵.

Next, Paradox will display the form numbers associated with the specified table. When you see this prompt, select the number of the form you wish to copy. Since in the example, the form you want to copy is form F4, you should select form number **4**.

Now Paradox will prompt you to enter a form number for the copy. To store the copy of the form under the name F5, type **5**. Once you select a form number for the copy, the message *Copying form F4 for Emplyee to F5...* will appear at the bottom of the screen. When the copying process is complete, Paradox will return you to the main workspace. Now you can issue the [Menu] Forms Change command to edit the copied form.

As you may have noticed, Paradox automatically removes the number of the form you are copying from the menu of forms to which you can copy. For example, when you copied form 4 for EMPLYEE, the number 4 was not included in the list of destination form names. This prevents you from assigning the same number to two forms.

If you select a number for the copy that already has a form assigned to it, Paradox will prompt you to confirm your choice by displaying a Cancel/Replace menu. If you issue the Cancel command, Paradox will return to the form number menu so that you can select another number. If you issue the Replace command, Paradox will replace the existing form with the copy.

If you wish, you can store the copy of a form under the name F. Saving the copy under this name defines it as the default form. From that point on, pressing [Form Toggle] will display the copy of the form. Of course, saving the copy under the name F will replace the current default form with the copy.

You cannot copy a form from one table to another unless the tables involved have identical structures. (We'll show you how to copy a form from one table to another with the same structure in Chapter 6.)

When you design a custom form, it becomes part of the table's family, and is, therefore, tied to the table. Changes you make in the table, such as restructuring it, will affect the form. (We'll show you how to restructure tables in Chapter 6.)

Deleting Forms

You can delete a form with the [Menu] Tools Delete Form command. For example, suppose you design a form for the EMPLYEE table that subsequently becomes obsolete. To delete this form, issue the [Menu] Tools Delete Form command. After you issue this command, Paradox will prompt you to enter the name of the table associated with the form you want to delete. When you see this prompt, type **EMPLYEE** and press ↵. Paradox then will display the forms (by form number) associated with the table and will prompt you to select the one to be deleted.

You can now enter the number of the form you want to delete. For example, to delete form number 1, select number **1**. As Paradox deletes the form, the message *Deleting F1 form for Emplyee...* will appear at the bottom of the screen. When the deletion is complete, Paradox will return you to the main workspace.

You should exercise caution when you delete forms. Paradox does not present a Cancel/Ok menu when it deletes forms. Once you specify the number of the form you want to delete, the form is gone.

Changing Form Names

You can change the name (number) of a form by issuing the [Menu] Tools Rename Form command. For example, suppose you design a form for the EMPLYEE table and store it under the name 4. Now suppose you want to rename it F, making it the default form.

To do this, issue the **[Menu] T**ools **R**ename Form command. After you issue the command, Paradox will prompt you to enter the name of the table associated with the form you wish to rename. When you see this prompt, type **EMPLYEE** and press ↵. Next, Paradox will display the form numbers associated with the table and prompt you to select the one to be renamed. You now should select form **4**. After you select the form to be renamed, Paradox will prompt you to assign a new name (number) to the form for copying a form. When you see this prompt, type **F**.

If the number you select as the new name for the form you're renaming does not already have a form stored under it, Paradox will simply rename the form. Since F already has a form assigned to it, however, Paradox will display a Cancel/Replace menu. To replace the current form F with the form whose name you are changing, select **R**eplace. After you do this, the message *Renaming F4 form for Emplyee to F...* will appear at the bottom of the screen. After a moment, Paradox will return to the main workspace.

If you do not want to replace the current default form, you can choose Cancel from the Cancel/Replace menu. When you do this, Paradox will return to the previous prompt so that you can select another number.

Conclusion

In this chapter, we showed you how to design and use forms. We began with a discussion of the default form and showed you how to use that form to enter and edit data. Then we showed you how to design custom forms. Next, we covered the various options in the Forms menu. Finally, we showed you various ways to manage forms.

Chapter 6

Managing Tables

In Chapters 3, 4, and 5, we showed you how to create tables and enter data into tables. We also showed you how to edit the information in your tables, create validity checks, change the appearance of table images on the screen, and use forms.

In this chapter, we'll show you how to use several commands that affect tables as a whole. We'll begin with the Tools menu commands, which allow you to rename, copy, erase, and empty tables and other objects. We'll also cover the ToDOS command, which allows you to exit from Paradox to DOS, use DOS programs, and then return to Paradox in the exact spot from which you left. Finally, we'll cover the [Menu] Modify Restructure command, which allows you to change the structure of your Paradox tables.

The Tools Menu

When you issue the [Menu] Tools command, Paradox will display the Tools menu shown in Figure 6-1. This menu contains a number of useful "utility" commands, which you can use to perform certain housekeeping chores, such as renaming, copying, and emptying tables. In this chapter, we'll look at the Rename, Copy, Delete, and Info options. We'll cover the QuerySpeedup command in Chapter 8 and the ExportImport command in the appendix.

Figure 6-1 The Tools Menu

```
Rename  QuerySpeedup  ExportImport  Copy  Delete  Info  More        Main
Rename a table, custom form, report, or script.
```

If you choose the More command from the Tools menu, Paradox will display the submenu shown in Figure 6-2. We will discuss the Add, MultiAdd, and Subtract commands in detail in Chapter 10. We will limit our discussion here to the Empty, Protect, Directory, and ToDOS commands.

Figure 6-2 The Tools More Menu

```
Add  MultiAdd  Subtract  Empty  Protect  Directory  ToDOS           Main
Add records in one table to those in another.
```

Many of the commands on the Tools menu offer options that allow you to operate on objects other than tables. For instance, the Copy command offers options that allow you to copy forms, scripts, and reports, as well as tables. We'll show you how to use these commands with objects other than tables throughout the book when we cover the various types of objects.

Renaming Tables

The [Menu] Tools Rename command can be used to rename Paradox tables, forms, reports, and scripts. When you issue this command, Paradox will display the menu in Figure 6-3, which lists the different objects that you can rename. To rename a table, you choose the Table option from this menu, then specify the name of the table you want to rename and the new name for the table. When you press ↵, Paradox will rename the table as you have instructed.

Figure 6-3   The Tools Rename Menu

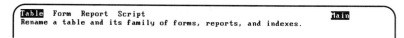

You will probably use the [Menu] Tools Rename Table command frequently to rename and save temporary tables, like the ANSWER table (discussed in Chapter 8) or the KEYVIOL table (covered in Chapter 4). You'll see more examples of this command in those chapters.

An Example

Suppose you want to change the name of the table TASKS to JOBS. To begin, issue the **[Menu]** **T**ools **R**ename command. Since you want to rename a table, when Paradox presents the menu in Figure 6-3, you should choose **T**able. Next, Paradox will prompt you to enter the current name of the table you want to rename. At this point, you can type the name of the table you want to rename, **TASKS**, and press ↵. Alternatively, you can press ↵ to see a list of the tables in the current directory and select the name from this list. Once you've specified the name of the table you want to rename, Paradox will prompt you to enter the new name for the table. When you see this prompt, type the new name for the table: **JOBS**. When you press ↵, Paradox will display the message *Renaming TASKS to JOBS...* in the lower-right corner of the screen.

Notes

When you rename a table, all of the objects associated with the table (reports, forms, indexes, etc.) will be transferred to the new name. This means that you won't lose any of the forms or reports you created when you rename a table.

If you enter a new name that duplicates the name of an existing table, Paradox will prompt you for confirmation and will display the message *TABLENAME exists* at the bottom of the screen. If you issue the Cancel command, Paradox will return to the previous prompt so that you can erase the entry with the [Backspace] key and enter another name for the table. If you choose Replace, Paradox will replace the existing table with the table you are renaming.

If you supply the name of a nonexistent table when Paradox asks you to specify the table you want to rename, Paradox will display the message *Cannot find TABLENAME table*.

Copying Tables

The [Menu] Tools Copy command allows you to make copies of existing Paradox objects, like tables, forms, and reports. When you issue the [Menu] Tools Copy command, Paradox will display the menu shown in Figure 6-4. This menu, which is similar to the one you see when you issue the Rename command, allows you to choose the type of object you want to copy. To copy a table, you should choose the **T**able option, then type the name of the table you want to copy, followed by the name under which you want to store the copy. When you press ↵, Paradox will copy the contents and structure of the table you specify and will create a new table with the name you selected. The original table will remain intact after the copy is completed.

Figure 6-4 The Copy Menu

```
Table  Form  Report  Script  JustFamily                       Main
Copy a table and its family of forms, reports, and index files.
```

An Example

For example, suppose you want to make a copy of the table EMPLYEE. Also suppose you want to save the copy under the name PEOPLE. To do this, issue the **[Menu] T**ools **C**opy command. When you see the menu in Figure 6-4, choose the **T**able option. Next, Paradox will prompt you to enter the name of the table you wish to copy. You should type the name of the table to be copied, **EMPLYEE**, and press ↵. When you do this, Paradox will prompt you to enter a name for the copy of the table. You should type the new name, **PEOPLE**, and press ↵.

After you press ↵, Paradox will copy the structure and contents of the EMPLYEE table into a new table named PEOPLE. As it does this, the message *Copying from EMPLYEE to PEOPLE* will appear at the bottom of the screen. After a few moments, Paradox will return you to the main workspace.

Notes

When you copy a table, all of the objects associated with the table (reports, forms, indexes, etc.) will be copied with the data to the new table. This means that you won't need to recreate the forms or reports you have defined for the new table.

If the name you supply as the destination of the copy duplicates the name of an existing table, Paradox will prompt you for confirmation and will display the message *TABLENAME exists* at the bottom of the screen. If you issue the Cancel command, Paradox will return to the previous prompt so that you can erase the entry and enter another name for the table. If you choose Replace, Paradox will replace the existing table with the table you are copying.

If you specify the same table as the source and destination of the copy (in other words, if you ask Paradox to copy a table onto itself), Paradox will display the message *Cannot copy a table to itself*. If you supply the name of a nonexistent table when Paradox asks you to specify the source for the copy, Paradox will display the message *Cannot find TABLENAME table*.

Copying JustFamily

The [Menu] Tools Copy JustFamily command lets you copy a table's family of objects (reports, forms, validity checks, and image settings) from one table to another without copying the table itself. When you issue this command, Paradox will prompt you to enter the name of the table whose family you wish to copy, followed by the name of the destination table. Since copying JustFamily from one table to another may overwrite part of the existing family of the destination table, Paradox then will prompt you to confirm the command. If you issue the Cancel command, Paradox will return to the previous prompt so that you can reenter the name of the destination table. However, if you issue the Replace command instead, Paradox will copy the family to the destination table. The message *Copying family members from TABLENAME to TABLENAME...* will appear at the bottom of the screen. After a few moments, Paradox will return to the main workspace.

An Example

Suppose you have a table called CUSTOMER, which lists all of your customers, and you have spent considerable time creating various forms, reports, and validity checks for the table. Now suppose you have created a query that copies all of the information for customers who live in the state of Indiana to an ANSWER table, and you have used the [Menu] Tools Rename Table command to save the ANSWER table under the name INDIANA. (We'll discuss queries in detail in Chapters 8 and 9.)

As a result of these steps, you'll have a table, INDIANA, which contains just the records you requested from CUSTOMER. However, none of the "family members" of related objects from the CUSTOMER table, such as forms and report definitions, will be associated with the new table. To copy the CUSTOMER table family to the new table INDIANA, issue the **[Menu]** **T**ools **C**opy **J**ustFamily command. When Paradox prompts you for the table whose family you want to copy, type **CUSTOMER** and press ↵. At the next prompt, type the name of the destination table, **INDIANA**, and press ↵. When Paradox prompts you to confirm the command, you should select **R**eplace from the menu. After a few moments, all of the family members from CUSTOMER will be copied to the new table. Now you can use the various objects you have created for both tables.

Notes

When you use the [Menu] Tools Copy JustFamily command, you must already have a destination table in place to receive the copied objects. If the target table you specify does not exist, Paradox will display the message *Cannot find TABLENAME table*.

In addition, the source and destination tables must have identical structures. If the source and destination tables do not have compatible structures, Paradox will display the message *TABLENAME and TABLENAME have incompatible structures*.

Deleting Tables

The [Menu] Tools Delete command allows you to delete tables, reports, and other Paradox objects. When you issue the [Menu] Tools Delete command, Paradox will display the menu shown in Figure 6-5. This menu lists the various objects you can delete with this command. To delete a table and its related objects, choose the **T**able option. When you make this selection, Paradox will prompt you for the name of the table to delete.

Figure 6-5 The Tools Delete Menu

```
Table  Form  Report  Script  QuerySpeedup  KeepSettings  ValCheck  Main
Delete a table and its family of forms, reports and indexes.
```

When you type the name and press ↵, Paradox will prompt you to confirm the deletion. In addition, the message *If you select OK, TABLENAME and its family will be deleted* will appear at the bottom of the screen. If you choose Cancel, Paradox will return you to the previous prompt. If you want to erase a different table, you can erase the current entry and type a different name. If you want to cancel the command, just press [Esc] several times to return to the Main menu.

If you choose OK, Paradox will delete the table you have specified and its family of forms, reports, and indexes. As it deletes the table, Paradox will display the message *Deleting TABLENAME and its associated family* at the bottom of the screen. After a few moments, Paradox will return to the main workspace.

For example, suppose you want to delete a table named JOBS and its family. To do this, issue the [**Menu**] **T**ools **D**elete **T**able command. When Paradox prompts you to enter a table name, type **JOBS** and press ↵. Next, Paradox will prompt you for confirmation. If everything is correct, you should choose **OK**. When you do, Paradox will delete the table and its family. If you have made a mistake (such as mistyping the table name or typing the name of the wrong table) or have decided that you don't want to delete the table after all, choose Cancel.

Remember that the [Menu] Tools Delete command is very unforgiving. Once you have selected the OK option from the Confirmation menu, the table or other object you asked Paradox to delete is gone forever. Needless to say, you always should use this command with caution.

The [Menu] Tools Info Command

The [Menu] Tools Info command allows you to obtain some basic information about your data bases. For one thing, this command can be used to review the structure of a table. It can also be used to obtain an inventory of the tables, scripts, and other files on any directory, or a listing of the family of objects that are associated with a table.

When you issue the [Menu] Tools Info command, Paradox will display the menu shown in Figure 6-6. Notice that this menu offers three options: Structure, Inventory, and Family. The Structure option allows you to review the structure of any table. The Inventory option allows you to obtain an inventory, or directory, of the tables, scripts, or files on a directory. The Family option allows you to obtain a listing of the objects that are associated with a particular table.

Figure 6-6   The Info Menu

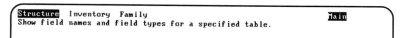

Reviewing the Structure

Suppose you want to check the structure of the table EMPLYEE. To do this, issue the [**Menu**] **T**ools **I**nfo command and select the **S**tructure option. Next, Paradox will prompt you to enter the name of the table whose structure you want to review. When you see this prompt, type **EMPLYEE** and press ↵. After a few moments, Paradox will display the structure of the table on the screen, as shown in Figure 6-7.

Notice that the STRUCT table in Figure 6-7 is almost identical to the STRUCT table that you use to create or restructure a table. (See Chapter 3 for more information on creating tables.) Unlike the Create and Modify Restructure commands, however, the [Menu] Tools Info Structure command allows you only to review the structure of the table; it won't let you make any changes to the table.

Figure 6-7 The STRUCT Table

```
Viewing Struct table: Record 1 of 13                    Main
STRUCT       Field Name        Field Type
   1    Emp Number             N
   2    Last Name              A10
   3    First Name             A10
   4    SS Number              A11
   5    Address                A20
   6    City                   A20
   7    State                  A2
   8    Zip                    A5
   9    Phone                  A14
  10    Date of Birth          D
  11    Date of Hire           D
  12    Exemptions             N
  13    Salary                 $

                                    EMPLYEE table has 16 records
```

Since the STRUCT table is a temporary table, you may want to print a copy of it for future reference before you remove it from view. To do this, simply get your printer ready and then press **[Instant Report]** ([Alt]-[F7]) with the cursor on the table. (We'll cover reporting in detail in Chapters 11 and 12).

Inventory

The [Menu] Tools Info Inventory command lets you view an inventory of the tables, scripts, or other files stored in a directory. When you choose the Inventory option from the [Menu] Tools Info menu, Paradox will display the submenu shown in Figure 6-8. If you choose Tables from this menu, Paradox will display an inventory of table names only. Similarly, if you choose Scripts, Paradox will display a list of script files. Selecting Files tells Paradox to display a list of all files of all types.

Figure 6-8 The Inventory Menu

After you choose one of these three options, Paradox will prompt you to specify the name of the directory from which you want to obtain the inventory. When you see this prompt, you should type the name of the directory with which you want to work, and press ↵. Alternatively, you could just press ↵ without typing anything else to view an inventory of the files on the current directory. When you do either of these things, Paradox will present a temporary table named LIST. This table contains the names and creation dates of all of the files of the specified type on the indicated directory.

An Example

For example, suppose you want to see a list of the tables that are stored on the current directory. To obtain this inventory, issue the [Menu] Tools Info Inventory command. When Paradox presents this menu, choose Tables. Next, when Paradox prompts you to specify the directory from which you want to obtain the inventory, press ↵ to select the current directory.

After you press ↵, Paradox will display a LIST table like the one shown in Figure 6-9. As you can see, the LIST table contains two fields: Name and Date. The Name field contains the name of the files of the type you've selected (in this case, Tables) on the selected directory. The Date field contains the creation dates of each of the files.

Figure 6-9 The LIST Table

```
Viewing List table: Record 1 of 18                          Main
LIST          Name                          Date
   1    Answer                            4/09/86
   2    Changed                           4/09/86
   3    Client                            3/24/86
   4    Customer                          4/09/86
   5    Emplyee                           4/09/86
   6    Entry                             4/09/86
   7    Jobs                              1/05/86
   8    Johntime                          4/07/86
   9    Orddfc                           10/31/85
  10    People                            4/09/86
  11    Products                         10/26/85
  12    Projdel                           4/06/86
  13    Projects                          4/06/86
  14    Prospect                          4/07/86
  15    Sortemp                           3/27/86
  16    Struct                            4/09/86
  17    Tasks                            10/26/85
  18    Time                              4/07/86
```

The Scripts Option

If you issue the [Menu] Tools Info Inventory Scripts command, Paradox will create a LIST table that contains the names of the script files (.SC files) on the specified directory. Since we have not yet created any script files, if you issue this command now, Paradox probably will create an empty LIST table. Later, after you have created scripts, you can use this command to obtain an inventory of those scripts.

The Files Option

The [Menu] Tools Info Inventory Files command produces a LIST table that contains the names of all the files on the specified directory, or just those files that conform to a pattern you define. After you issue this command, Paradox will display the prompt in Figure 6-10. When you see this prompt, you should enter a directory and a DOS pattern, then press ↵. For example, if you want to obtain an inventory of the 1-2-3 worksheet files on the disk in drive A, type **A:*.WKS**. If you want to obtain a list of the dBASE III files on the directory c:\dbase\data, type **c:\dbase\data*.DBF**.

Figure 6-10 The Files Prompt

```
Pattern:                                                    Main
Enter DOS directory pattern (e.g. *.TXT, or ↵ for working directory).
```

After you supply the directory and DOS pattern, Paradox will create a LIST table that contains all of the files on the selected directory that match the pattern you defined.

Notes

Like the STRUCT table, the LIST table you see when you issue the [Menu] Tools Info command is a temporary table. If you wish, you can rename it as a permanent table with the [Menu] Tools Rename command. If you want to obtain a printout of the inventory, you can press [Instant Report] ([Alt]-[F7]).

If there are no files of the specified type on the directory you specify, Paradox will create an empty LIST table. If you feel certain that there are files of the specified type on the directory, check to make sure that you selected the correct option (Tables, Scripts, or Files), that you specified the right directory, and, if you selected the Files option, that your pattern was defined correctly.

The Family Option

The [Menu] Tools Info Family command allows you to view an inventory of the family of objects that are associated with a particular table. When you issue this command, Paradox will prompt you to enter the name of the table whose family you want to review. When you type a table name and press ↵, Paradox will display a temporary table named FAMILY, which displays the family associated with a Paradox table.

For example, suppose you want to review the family of objects that are associated with the table EMPLYEE. To review this list, issue the **[Menu] Tools Info Family** command and type the name **EMPLYEE** when you see the Table Name prompt. After a moment, Paradox will display the FAMILY table shown in Figure 6-11.

Figure 6-11 The EMPLYEE Family

```
Viewing Family table: Record 1 of 6                         Main
FAMILY━━━━━━━━━━━━━━━━━Name━━━━━━━━━━━━━━━━━━━━━━━━━━━━━Date━━━━━
   1 │ Emplyee                                           │ 4/27/86
   2 │ Form F                                            │ 4/27/86
   3 │ Form F1                                           │ 4/25/86
   4 │ Form F2                                           │ 4/24/86
   5 │ Form F3                                           │ 4/24/86
   6 │ Form F4                                           │ 4/26/86
```

Like the LIST table, the FAMILY table includes only two fields: Name and Date. As you can see, the FAMILY table for EMPLYEE contains the table itself and the forms we created in Chapter 5. If you did not delete the .SET and .VAL files created in Chapter 4, your FAMILY table will also show those files. Notice that the first record shows the name and creation date of the table whose family you are reviewing. The second record shows the name and creation date of the standard form for this table, F, and so on. As in this case, the name of the table you are investigating will always be the first record in the FAMILY table.

Also like the LIST table, the FAMILY table is a temporary table. If you wish, you can rename it as a permanent table with the [Menu] Tools Rename command. If you want to obtain a printout, you can press [Instant Report] ([Alt]-[F7]).

Emptying Tables

The [Menu] Tools More Empty command allows you to delete the records in a table without deleting the table itself. When you issue the [Menu] Tools More Empty command, Paradox will prompt you to enter the name of the table you want to empty. When you see this prompt, enter a table name and press ↵. Next, Paradox will display a Cancel/OK menu, which prompts you for confirmation. Also, the message *All records will be deleted from TABLENAME* will appear at the bottom of the screen.

If you issue the Cancel command at this point, Paradox will return to the previous prompt. You can either erase the current entry and type a different name or press [Esc] or [Ctrl]-[Break] to cancel the command. If you choose OK, Paradox will delete every record from the table, and the message *Emptying table...* will appear briefly in the lower-right corner of the screen. After a few moments, Paradox will return to the main workspace.

An Example

For example, suppose you have a table named STOCK that lists the stock numbers and descriptions of all the items in your inventory. Figure 6-12 shows this table on the screen. Now suppose you have just reorganized your inventory and you want to change the SKU and Description entries in the table. You could edit the table and make the changes you want; however, you may find it easier to empty the table and start over.

Figure 6-12 The STOCK Table

```
Viewing Stock table: Record 1 of 5                          Main
   STOCK     SKU       Description        Price      Quantity
      1    123A499    Widget              50.00         10
      2    234B066    Wombat              50.00          4
      3    311A473    Woofer             200.00         17
      4    345C111    Zither              75.00        100
      5    215W778    Xylophone          100.00         54
```

Managing Tables   159

To empty the table, issue the **[Menu] T**ools **M**ore **E**mpty command. When Paradox prompts you for the name of the table to be emptied, type **STOCK** and press ↵. Then, when Paradox presents the Confirmation menu, choose **OK**. Immediately, Paradox will display the *Emptying table...* message and will delete every record from STOCK.

Notes

Like the [Menu] Tools Delete command, the [Menu] Tools More Empty command can be very destructive. Once you choose OK to confirm the command, Paradox will immediately delete every record in the specified table. There is no way to restore the deleted records. Be careful!

However, there is one way to insure against accidentally destroying a table with this command. You can use the [Menu] Tools Copy command to copy all of the records from the table you're about to empty into a new table before you use the [Menu] Tools More Empty command. Then, if you discover that you've made an error, you can use the [Menu] Tools Add command to add the records back to the table that you just emptied.

Emptying a table has no effect on the objects associated with the table (reports, forms, indexes, etc.). Any object that existed before you empty the table will exist after you empty the table.

Protecting Your Tables

The [Menu] Tools More Protect command allows you to establish a security system for the tables in your data base. By using this command, you can assign a password to a table or script, or write-protect a table or other object. When you issue the [Menu] Tools More Protect command, Paradox will present the submenu shown in Figure 6-13.

Figure 6-13 The Protect Menu

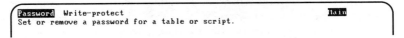

Password Protection

The Password option allows you to assign a password to a table (or a script). After you have assigned a password to a table, anyone trying to view or edit the table will be prompted to supply the password. If the person does not supply the correct password, he or she will not be able to view or edit the table.

An Example

For example, suppose you want to assign the password *CESSNA* to the EMPLYEE table. To do this, issue the **[Menu] T**ools **M**ore **P**rotect command and choose the

Password option. When you do, Paradox will display the menu shown in Figure 6-14, which offers two options: Table and Script.

Figure 6-14 The Password Menu

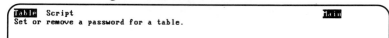

Since you want to protect a table, choose the Table option. Next, Paradox will prompt you to enter the name of the table you want to protect. You should type **EMPLYEE** and press ↵. Finally, Paradox will prompt you to specify the password you want to use to protect this table. You now should type the password **CESSNA** and press ↵. After you enter a password, Paradox will prompt you to confirm the password by typing it a second time. When you see this prompt, you should retype the password and press ↵. If you type the same password both times, Paradox will accept the password and display the message *Encrypting...* at the bottom of the screen as it password-protects your table. After a few moments, Paradox will return to the main workspace.

If you do not type the same password the second time, Paradox will display the error message *Password was originally entered as firstword*, where *firstword* is the original spelling of the password. If this happens, press the **[Backspace]** key to erase the entry, type the correct password, and press ↵. This step is included to prevent you from permanently locking a table with a mistyped password.

Working with Passwords

Once you've assigned a password to a table, you'll be prompted to enter that password before you can do anything to or with the table. As soon as you issue a command and select the name of a protected table, Paradox will prompt you to enter the password.

The password you enter must be identical to the password you used to protect the table (including upper/lower case and spacing) before Paradox will allow access to the table. If the password you type is correct, Paradox will then allow you to proceed with the command. If you type the wrong password, Pardox will display the message *Invalid password* in the lower-right corner of the screen.

For example, suppose you have password-protected the EMPLYEE table with the password CESSNA. If you issue the [Menu] View command and supply the name EMPLYEE as the table you want to view, Paradox will prompt you to supply the password for the table. You should type **CESSNA** (remember, case counts) and press ↵ to view the table.

Although we used the [Menu] View command in the example, you would have to supply the password before you could do anything to the table, including edit it, enter records into it, restructure it, or even view its structure. However, once you have supplied the proper password for a table, you won't need to supply it again for the remainder of that work session.

Notes

Your passwords can be up to 50 characters long and may include alphabetic characters, spaces, punctuation marks like !, numerals, and special symbols like @ and #. For example, 12345, ABCDE, 10/6/57, Piper, PIPER, Beech2, !!!!!, and @@@@@ are all acceptable passwords.

You should try to choose passwords for your tables that are easy to remember. For example, I used CESSNA as the password in the previous example because that is the brand of the first airplane I learned to fly. You might want to use technical terms, brand names from your hobby, the names of your grade school teachers, or any other distinct, unique, memorable word as your password. In addition to choosing memorable words, you should always write your passwords down and store them in a secure place. Remember: once you assign a password to a table, there is no way to access the table without the password.

Removing or Changing a Password

The process of removing or changing a password is essentially the same as the process for establishing a password for the first time. However, to remove or change a password, you must know the existing password. For example, suppose the EMPLYEE table is password protected and you want to remove the password. To do this, issue the **[Menu] Tools More Protect Password Table** command. When Paradox prompts you to enter a table name, type **EMPLYEE** and press ↵. After you do this, Paradox will prompt you to enter the password. You then should type the current password, **CESSNA**, and press ↵. Next, Paradox will prompt you to enter the new password for the table. If you just want to remove the existing password, all you need to do is press ↵. If you want to change the password, type in the new password and press ↵. Paradox then will prompt you to confirm the new password. Once you confirm the new password, Paradox will encrypt the table.

Write-protecting Your Tables

The [Menu] Tools More Protect Write-Protect command allows you to protect a table from being overwritten, modified, or deleted. Write-protecting a table locks the table so that no changes can be made to its contents or structure.

When you issue this command, Paradox will prompt you for the name of the table you want to write-protect. When you type the name and press ↵, Paradox will display the menu in Figure 6-15. (If the table is password protected, you will need to supply the password before you see this menu.) To write-protect the table, choose Set. If the table is already protected, you can unprotect it by choosing Clear.

Figure 6-15 The Write-Protect Menu

An Example

For example, suppose that you want to write-protect the EMPLYEE table. To do this, issue the [Menu] Tools More Protect Write-Protect command. After you issue this command, Paradox will prompt you to enter the name of the table that you want to protect. When you see this prompt, type **EMPLYEE** and press ↵. When you do, Paradox will display the Write-Protect menu. Since you want to write-protect the table, you should issue the Set command. When you make this selection, Paradox will write-protect the table and display the message *EMPLYEE is now write-protected* at the bottom of the screen.

From now on, whenever a user attempts to modify the table, Paradox will display a message at the bottom of the screen to remind him that the table is write-protected, and it will not permit the alteration to occur.

If you need to change a protected table, you can unprotect the table by issuing the [Menu] Tools More Protect Write-Protect command, entering the name of the table, and then issuing the Clear command. For example, to unprotect the EMPLYEE table, issue the [Menu] Tools More Protect Write-Protect command, type **EMPLYEE**, press ↵, and choose the Clear option.

Since a write-protected table can be easily unprotected, it is not a foolproof form of protection. Probably the biggest advantage of write-protecting important tables is that doing so prevents you from accidentally destroying a table or the data it contains. Because you would need to unlock the table to make any changes, there is no chance of mistakenly deleting or emptying the table.

The [Menu] Tools More Directory Command

The [Menu] Tools More Directory command allows you to change the current working directory during a Paradox session. When you issue this command, Paradox will display a prompt that shows the current directory. To change the active directory, just press **[Backspace]** to erase all or part of the existing setting, and then type in the name of the new directory.

Since changing the active directory causes the workspace to be cleared and deletes all temporary tables, when you press ↵, Paradox will display a Cancel/OK menu that prompts you to confirm the change. If you issue the Cancel command, Paradox will return to the previous prompt. If you issue the OK command, Paradox will clear the workspace and change the working directory.

An Example

For example, suppose you are using a hard disk system and your working directory is c:\paradox\data. Now suppose you want to work with a few tables that are stored on a floppy disk in drive A. To do this, issue the **[Menu] T**ools **M**ore **D**irectory command. After you issue this command, Paradox will display the current directory and prompt you to change it, as shown in Figure 6-16.

Figure 6-16 The Directory Prompt

When you see this prompt, you should press **[Ctrl]-[Backspace]** to erase the current directory, then type **a:**, press ↵, and choose **OK** from the Confirmation menu. When you do this, Paradox will clear the workspace and change the working directory. In addition, the message *Working directory is now a:* will appear at the bottom of the screen. The message will disappear when you press any key from the keyboard.

Changing the Default Directory

If you wish, you can change the default working directory through the Paradox Custom Configuration Program (PCCP). To do this, issue the **[Menu] S**cripts **P**lay command, type **custom**, and press ↵. If you are using a floppy disk system, you will need to insert the Installation Disk in drive B before you issue the command. After you issue the command, Paradox will display the main PCCP menu shown in Figure 6-17.

Figure 6-17 The PCCP Menu

```
Video  Reports  AsciiConvert  SetDirectory  DO-IT!  Cancel
Monitor, Snow or DisplayColor.
```

When you see this menu, issue the SetDirectory command. Paradox then will display the current working directory and prompt you to change it. To change the current default, press the **[Ctrl]-[Backspace]** key to erase it, type the new directory, and press ↵. After you do this, Paradox will return to the main PCCP menu. When it does, issue the DO-IT! command to exit from the PCCP and save the new default directory specification.

The [Menu] Tools More ToDOS Command

The [Menu] Tools More ToDOS command allows you to suspend Paradox temporarily and access DOS. This lets you use DOS utility programs, such as DISKCOPY, FORMAT, and CHKDSK, without exiting from Paradox.

When you issue the [Menu] Tools More ToDOS command or press the [ToDOS] key ([Ctrl]-[O]), Paradox will suspend its operation, and the DOS prompt will appear on the screen. At this point, your screen will look like Figure 6-18. Once the DOS prompt appears on the screen, you can use any of the DOS utilities or run any other program (except for memory-resident programs).

Figure 6-18   The ToDOS Screen

```
WARNING! Do not delete or edit Paradox objects, or load RAM-resident programs.
To return to Paradox, type exit.

The COMPAQ Personal Computer MS-DOS
Version 2.02

(C) Copyright COMPAQ Computer Corp. 1982, 83
(C) Copyright Microsoft 1981, 82, 83

C:\paradox\data>
```

Once you've done whatever it was you wanted to do, you can return to Paradox by typing **exit** and pressing ↵. When the Paradox screen reappears, everything will be just as you left it when you exited to DOS. Any tables that were in view before will be in view now, and any temporary tables that existed when you exited from Paradox will still exist.

An Example

For example, suppose you are working in Paradox and your screen currently looks like Figure 6-19. This screen shows a query form and ANSWER table based on the EMPLYEE table.

Figure 6-19   A Query Form and ANSWER Table

```
Viewing Answer table: Record 1 of 16                              Main
EMPLYEE    Emp Number      Last Name       First Name      SS Number
              9                9                9

ANSWER    Emp Number      Last Name       First Name
   1          1            Jones           David
   2          2            Cameron         Herb
   3          4            Jones           Stewart
   4          5            Roberts         Darlene
   5          6            Jones           Jean
   6          8            Williams        Brenda
   7          9            Myers           Julie
   8         10            Link            Julie
   9         12            Jackson         Mary
  10         13            Jakes, Jr.      Sal
  11         14            Preston         Molly
  12         15            Masters         Ron
  13         16            Robertson       Kevin
  14         17            Garrison        Robert
  15         19            Gunn            Barbara
  16         20            Emerson         Cheryl
```

Now suppose further that you need to format a floppy disk during a Paradox session. To do this, issue the **[Menu]** **T**ools **M**ore **T**oDOS command or press **[ToDOS]** [Ctrl]-[O]. When the DOS prompt appears, you should type **Format a:** and press ↵. When DOS prompts you to insert a new disk in drive A, place the disk you want to format in A and press ↵.

When the disk is formatted, you can type **exit** and press ↵ to return to Paradox. When you return to the program, your screen will look just like Figure 6-19. The ANSWER table that was on the screen when you issued the ToDOS command will still be there when you return.

Notes

If you are using a system with two floppy disk drives, you will need to remove the Paradox System Disk II from drive A and insert your DOS disk. When you type **exit** to return to Paradox, Paradox will prompt you to insert System Disk II in drive A.

Notice the message *WARNING! Do not delete or edit Paradox objects, or load RAM-resident programs* at the top of the screen in Figure 6-18. Believe it! As we have told you several times, Paradox makes full use of the memory in your computer. While you are using ToDOS, Paradox freezes the contents of its memory so that nothing is lost while you're at the DOS level. If you run any memory-resident program while you're at the DOS level (Sidekick and 1-2-3 are both memory-resident), you could lose data.

When you are in DOS, the automatic mechanisms built into Paradox to prevent data loss cannot function. Therefore, you must exercise caution when you are using DOS. For example, never delete or edit Paradox objects or load RAM-resident programs while you are in DOS. If you change disks while in DOS, you must restore the original configuration before you return to Paradox. Never turn off your computer or press [Ctrl]-[Alt]-[Del] to reboot while Paradox is suspended!

As a general rule, it is safer to issue the [Menu] Exit Yes command to exit from Paradox, and then use DOS. The biggest advantage of using ToDOS is that it allows you to leave Paradox temporarily without losing all of your temporary tables. If you use the ToDOS command carefully, it can save you some time.

Restructuring Tables

As you become more experienced in designing and manipulating tables, you will probably want to make changes in the structures of your tables. For example, you may want to add or delete fields, designate key fields, or even change a field type in a table that you have already created. Paradox allows you to make such changes with the [Menu] Modify Restructure command.

Restructure Basics

Although Paradox has some built-in features to protect against data loss when you are restructuring a table, we recommend that you always use the [Menu] Tools Copy Table command to make a copy of the table you want to change before you begin restructuring. This ensures that you will not lose any data if you make an error.

Once you have made a copy of the table, issue the **[Menu] M**odify **R**estructure command. After you issue this command, Paradox will prompt you to enter the name of the table to be restructured. When you see this prompt, you should type the name of the table you want to restructure.

When you press ↵, Paradox will display a STRUCT table for the table you are restructuring. If you type **EMPLYEE** when Paradox prompts you for the name of the table to restructure, Paradox will bring a STRUCT table for EMPLYEE to the screen, as shown in Figure 6-20. As you can see, this STRUCT table lists the name and type of every field in the table being restructured. This table is very similar to the STRUCT table you see when you use the [Menu] Create command to define a new table. In fact, the process of restructuring a table is fundamentally the same as creating a new table.

Figure 6-20   The STRUCT Table for EMPLYEE

```
┌─────────────────────────────────────────────────────────────────────────┐
│ Restructuring Emplyee table                                 Restructure │
│ STRUCT╤════════Field Name═════╤═Field Type╕                             │
│    1  │ Emp Number            │ N         │    ┌──── FIELD TYPES ────┐  │
│    2  │ Last Name             │ A18       │    │ A_: Alphanumeric (ex: A25) │
│    3  │ First Name            │ A18       │    │ Any combination of   │  │
│    4  │ SS Number             │ A11       │    │ characters and spaces│  │
│    5  │ Address               │ A28       │    │ up to specified width.│ │
│    6  │ City                  │ A28       │    │ Maximum width is 255.│  │
│    7  │ State                 │ A2        │    │                      │  │
│    8  │ Zip                   │ A5        │    │ N: Numbers with or without │
│    9  │ Phone                 │ A14       │    │    decimal digits.   │  │
│   10  │ Date of Birth         │ D         │    │                      │  │
│   11  │ Date of Hire          │ D         │    │ $: Dollar amounts.   │  │
│   12  │ Exemptions            │ N         │    │                      │  │
│   13  │ Salary                │ $         │    │ D: Dates in the form │  │
│       │                       │           │    │    mm/dd/yy or dd-mon-yy. │
│                                                │                      │  │
│                                                │ Use "*" after field type to │
│                                                │ show a key field (ex: A4*). │
└─────────────────────────────────────────────────────────────────────────┘
```

You can edit the STRUCT table using the same techniques you learned in Chapters 3 and 4 for editing regular Paradox tables. For example, you can use the ↓ key to move to the bottom of STRUCT, add a new, blank row, and enter a new field. Or you can press [Ins] to insert a new row in STRUCT at the current cursor location and define a new field there. You can use the [Del] key to delete fields from the table. You can even move a field to a different location in the STRUCT table and change the name or the type of any field. Since most of the techniques you use to restructure a table are identical to the ones you used to edit a table's structure during its creation, we won't cover them here. We'll only cover a few techniques that are unique to restructuring.

When you have made the desired changes to the table, you can press [Do-It!] to make the changes permanent. If you make an error, or decide not to make changes after all, you can issue the [Menu] Cancel command to stop the restructure.

Deleting Fields

When you are restructuring a table, you can delete a field in the same way you can while creating the table: by placing the cursor on that field and pressing [Del]. As soon as you press [Del], the field will be deleted from the image of STRUCT.

Since deleting a field from an existing table will usually result in the loss of data, Paradox will prompt you to confirm the deletion. When you press [Do-It!] ([F2]) or issue the [Menu] DO-IT! command to save the new table, Paradox will display a menu that offers two options: Delete and Oops! If you choose the Delete command at this point, Paradox will delete the field (and all of the information it contains) as it saves the restructured table, and will return to the main workspace. If you choose Oops! Paradox will return to the restructure screen so that you can restore the field to the table.

If you delete more than one field from the table during one restructure operation, Paradox will prompt you to confirm the deletion of each field individually. If you choose the Oops! option for any deleted field, Paradox will return you to the restructure screen so that you can make any needed corrections.

Changing the Field Order

As you learned in Chapter 4, you can change the order of the fields in the image of a table and can make that change permanent with the [Menu] Image KeepSettings command. Once you have established the order of the fields in the actual table, however, the only way to change the order is to restructure the table.

For example, the original order of the fields in the EMPLYEE table is: Emp Number, Last Name, First Name, SS Number, Address, City, State, Zip, Phone, Date of Birth, Date of Hire, Exemptions, and Salary. Suppose you want to rearrange the fields in the following order: Emp Number, Last Name, First Name, Address, City, State, Zip, Phone, Date of Birth, SS Number, Date of Hire, Exemptions, and Salary.

To begin, issue the **[Menu]** Tools Copy command and copy the records in EMPLYEE into a table called **TEMP**. When the copy is complete, issue the **[Menu]** Modify Restructure command, type **EMPLYEE** to identify the table you want to restructure, and press ↵.

To begin changing the order of the fields, move the cursor down to the Date of Hire field and press **[Ins]** to insert a blank line above it. Next, type **SS Number** in the Field Name column and press ↓ to move the cursor out of the new row. When you do this, Paradox will recognize that you want to move the SS Number field and will complete the move for you. You do not need to enter anything in the Field Type column or delete the SS Number field from its previous location. As Paradox makes the change, the message *Moving SS Number field...* will appear briefly in the lower-right corner of the screen. Figure 6-21 shows the STRUCT table after the change is made. Notice that the SS Number field is now between the Date of Birth and Date of Hire fields.

Figure 6-21 Moving a Field

```
Restructuring Emplyee table                                    Restructure
STRUCT         Field Name             Field Type
  1     Emp Number                    N           ── FIELD TYPES ──
  2     Last Name                     A10        A_: Alphanumeric (ex: A25)
  3     First Name                    A10         Any combination of
  4     Address                       A20         characters and spaces
  5     City                          A20         up to specified width.
  6     State                         A2          Maximum width is 255.
  7     Zip                           A5
  8     Phone                         A14        N: Numbers with or without
  9     Date of Birth                 D           decimal digits.
 10     SS Number                     A11
 11     Date of Hire              ◄   D          $: Dollar amounts.
 12     Exemptions                    N
 13     Salary                        $          D: Dates in the form
                                                  mm/dd/yy or dd-mon-yy.

                                                 Use "*" after field type to
                                                 show a key field (ex: A4*).
```

You must type the field name exactly as it appears in the table in order for Paradox to recognize it and move the field. If you do not duplicate an existing name exactly, Paradox will assume that you are adding a new field to the table.

When you have finished rearranging the table, press **[Do-It!]** ([F2]) or issue the **[Menu]** **DO**-IT! command to save the new table. After a few moments, Paradox will display the new table, EMPLYEE, in the workspace.

Changing the Field Size

When you are restructuring a table, you can expand or contract the length of any alphanumeric field in the table. (The length of number, dollar, and date fields are set by Paradox and cannot be changed.) To change the length of a field, first issue the **[Menu]** **M**odify **R**estructure command to bring the STRUCT table into view. Next, move to the Field Type column for the field you want to change, erase the current Length setting, and type a new length. When you press **[Do-It!]**, Paradox will make the change permanent.

An Example

For example, suppose you want to expand the size of the Last Name field in the EMPLYEE table from 10 to 15 characters. To do this, issue the **[Menu]** **M**odify **R**estructure command, type **EMPLYEE**, and press ↵. When the STRUCT table for EMPLYEE appears, move the cursor to the Field Type column for the Last Name field, press the [**Backspace**] key twice to erase the existing entry, 10, and type **15**. After you do this, your screen will look like Figure 6-22. If you press [Do-It!] at this point, Paradox will permanently change the length of the Last Name field to 15 characters.

Figure 6-22   Increasing the Field Size

```
Restructuring Emplyee table                                    Restructure
STRUCT        Field Name       Field Type
    1   Emp Number             N                    FIELD TYPES
    2   Last Name              A15  ◀        A_: Alphanumeric (ex: A25)
    3   First Name             A10           Any combination of
    4   SS Number              A11           characters and spaces
    5   Address                A20           up to specified width.
    6   City                   A20           Maximum width is 255.
    7   State                  A2
    8   Zip                    A5            N: Numbers with or without
    9   Phone                  A14              decimal digits.
   10   Date of Birth          D
   11   Date of Hire           D             $: Dollar amounts.
   12   Exemptions             N
   13   Salary                 $             D: Dates in the form
                                                mm/dd/yy or dd-mon-yy.

                                             Use "*" after field type to
                                             show a key field (ex: A4*).
```

Shortening a Field

You can also reduce the length of an alphanumeric field. For example, suppose you decide to reduce the length of the First Name field in EMPLYEE from 10 to 5 characters. To do this, issue the [**Menu**] **M**odify **R**estructure command, type **EMPLYEE**, and press ↵. When the STRUCT table for EMPLYEE appears, move the cursor to the Field Type column of the First Name field, press the [**Backspace**] key to erase the current length, and type **5**. Figure 6-23 shows the screen at this point.

Figure 6-23   Reducing the Field Size

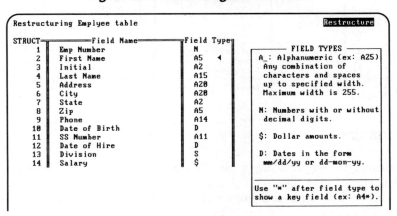

If any entry in the alphanumeric field you shorten is longer than the new length you have specified, you run the risk of losing data. Therefore, when you press [Do-It!] ([F2]) or issue the [Menu] DO-IT! command after shortening a field, Paradox will display the menu shown in Figure 6-24. In addition, the message *Possible data loss for the Fieldname field* will appear in the message area.

Figure 6-24   The Trimming/No-Trimming/Oops! Menu

If you issue the Oops! command, Paradox will return to the restructure screen so that you can adjust the field size. If you issue the [Menu] Cancel command after you choose Oops!, Paradox will disregard all of the changes you have made.

Trimming

If you issue the Trimming command at this point, Paradox will "chop off" the characters that don't fit the new field size and will save the new table. For example, Figure 6-25 shows the EMPLYEE table as it will look if you now choose the Trimming option and press ↵. Notice that some of the entries in the First Name field have been truncated ("trimmed") to fit within the new, shorter field.

Figure 6-25   Shortened First Name Field

```
Viewing Emplyee table: Record 1 of 16                              Main
 EMPLYEE=Emp Number=====Last Name==First Name=SS Number=====Address=
    1        1          Jones      David      414-76-3421   4000 St. James
    2        2          Cameron    Herb       321-65-8765   2331 Elm St.
    3        4          Jones      Stewa      401-32-8721   4389 Oakbridge
    4        5          Roberts    Darle      417-43-7777   451 Lone Pine
    5        6          Jones      Jean       413-07-9123   4000 St. James
    6        8          Williams   Brend      401-55-1567   100 Owl Creek
    7        9          Myers      Julie      314-38-9452   4512 Parkside
    8       10          Link       Julie      345-75-1525   3215 Palm Ct.
    9       12          Jackson    Mary       424-13-7621   7821 Clark Ave
   10       13          Jakes, Jr. Sal        321-65-9151   3451 Michigan
   11       14          Preston    Molly      451-00-3426   321 Indian Hil
   12       15          Masters    Ron        317-65-4529   423 W. 72nd St
   13       16          Robertson  Kevin      415-24-6710   431 Bardstown
   14       17          Garrison   Rober      312-98-1479   55 Wheeler St.
   15       19          Gunn       Barba      321-97-8632   541 Kentucky S
   16       20          Emerson    Chery      401-65-1898   800 River Rd.
```

No-Trimming

If you choose the No-Trimming option, Paradox will restructure the table according to your instructions, shortening the fields you have told it to shorten. Any records that include entries that don't fit in the newly shortened fields will be stored in a special table named PROBLEMS. The PROBLEMS table is a temporary table that has a structure identical to the original structure of the table you are restructuring. PROBLEMS temporarily preserves the records you might otherwise lose until you decide what to do with them. Choosing No-Trimming assures that you, and not Paradox, will have control over the trimming process.

For example, suppose you restructure EMPLYEE, shortening the First Name field from 10 to 5 characters. There are six records in EMPLYEE with First Name field entries that will not fit in the new, five-character-wide First Name field: employee numbers 4, 5, 8, 17, 19, and 20. If you choose the No-Trimming option, Paradox will remove those records from EMPLYEE and enter them into a PROBLEMS table like the one shown in Figure 6-26. Notice that PROBLEMS and EMPLYEE have the same structure.

Figure 6-26   The PROBLEMS Table

```
Viewing Problems table: Record 1 of 6                          Main
     EMPLYEE┬─Emp Number─┬──Last Name─┬─First Name─┬─SS Number──┬──────Address=
        1   │     1      │   Jones    │   David    │ 414-76-3421│ 4000 St. James
        2   │     2      │   Cameron  │   Herb     │ 321-65-8765│ 2331 Elm St.
        3   │     6      │   Jones    │   Jean     │ 413-87-9123│ 4000 St. James
        4   │     9      │   Myers    │   Julie    │ 314-38-9452│ 4512 Parkside
        5   │    10      │   Link     │   Julie    │ 345-75-1525│ 3215 Palm Ct.
        6   │    12      │   Jackson  │   Mary     │ 424-13-7621│ 7821 Clark Ave
        7   │    13      │   Jakes, Jr.│  Sal      │ 321-65-9151│ 3451 Michigan
        8   │    14      │   Preston  │   Molly    │ 451-00-3426│ 321 Indian Hil
        9   │    15      │   Masters  │   Ron      │ 317-65-4529│ 423 W. 72nd St
       10   │    16      │   Robertson│   Kevin    │ 415-24-6710│ 431 Bardstown

     PROBLEMS┬─Emp Number─┬──Last Name─┬─First Name─┬─SS Number──┬──────Addr
        1   │     4      │   Jones    │   Stewart  │ 401-32-8721│ 4389 Oakbr
        2   │     5      │   Roberts  │   Darlene  │ 417-43-7777│ 451 Lone P
        3   │     8      │   Williams │   Brenda   │ 401-55-1567│ 100 Owl Cr
        4   │    17      │   Garrison │   Robert   │ 312-98-1479│ 55 Wheeler
        5   │    19      │   Gunn     │   Barbara  │ 321-97-8632│ 541 Kentuc
        6   │    20      │   Emerson  │   Cheryl   │ 401-65-1898│ 800 River
```

To preserve the records in PROBLEMS, you can edit the PROBLEMS table to make the records fit the new field size, then add them to the restructured table. In this case, you must reduce the length of the entries in that field to no more than five characters, so they will fit in the new table. You might want to shorten the entry to an initial or abbreviate the entry in some other way. On the other hand, you might simply want to press [Backspace] to erase the excess characters.

Once all of the entries have been shortened sufficiently, you must add the edited records in the PROBLEMS table to the restructured EMPLYEE table. To do this, issue the **[Menu] Tools More Add** command. When Paradox prompts you to enter the name of the source table (the table that contains the records you want to add), type **PROBLEMS** and press ↵. Then, when Paradox prompts you for the name of the table to which the records should be added, type **EMPLYEE** and press ↵. After you do this, Paradox will display the message *Adding Problems to Emplyee...* at the bottom of the screen. After a few moments, Paradox will display the EMPLYEE table (with the added records) in the workspace. Figure 6-27 shows the completed EMPLYEE table.

Figure 6-27 Adding PROBLEMS to EMPLYEE

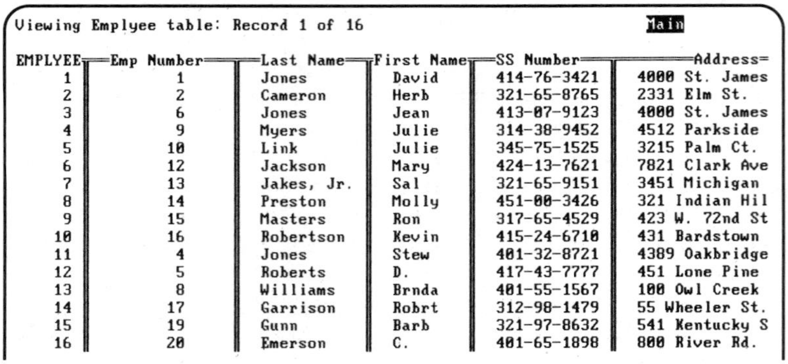

```
Viewing Emplyee table: Record 1 of 16                    Main
EMPLYEE┬─Emp Number─┬─Last Name─┬─First Name─┬─SS Number──┬──Address═
   1   │      1     │ Jones     │ David      │ 414-76-3421│ 4000 St. James
   2   │      2     │ Cameron   │ Herb       │ 321-65-8765│ 2331 Elm St.
   3   │      6     │ Jones     │ Jean       │ 413-07-9123│ 4000 St. James
   4   │      9     │ Myers     │ Julie      │ 314-38-9452│ 4512 Parkside
   5   │     10     │ Link      │ Julie      │ 345-75-1525│ 3215 Palm Ct.
   6   │     12     │ Jackson   │ Mary       │ 424-13-7621│ 7821 Clark Ave
   7   │     13     │ Jakes, Jr.│ Sal        │ 321-65-9151│ 3451 Michigan
   8   │     14     │ Preston   │ Molly      │ 451-00-3426│ 321 Indian Hil
   9   │     15     │ Masters   │ Ron        │ 317-65-4529│ 423 W. 72nd St
  10   │     16     │ Robertson │ Kevin      │ 415-24-6710│ 431 Bardstown
  11   │      4     │ Jones     │ Stew       │ 401-32-8721│ 4389 Oakbridge
  12   │      5     │ Roberts   │ D.         │ 417-43-7777│ 451 Lone Pine
  13   │      8     │ Williams  │ Brnda      │ 401-55-1567│ 100 Owl Creek
  14   │     17     │ Garrison  │ Robrt      │ 312-98-1479│ 55 Wheeler St.
  15   │     19     │ Gunn      │ Barb       │ 321-97-8632│ 541 Kentucky S
  16   │     20     │ Emerson   │ C.         │ 401-65-1898│ 800 River Rd.
```

The [Menu] Tools More Add command will work only if the two tables have compatible field types in the *same* order. In the example, the only change we made in the structure of the EMPLYEE table was to reduce the size of a field. In this case, the Tools More Add command worked just fine. However, if you make other changes in the structure of the table–such as adding a field or changing the type of the field–you may not be able to add records from the PROBLEMS table to the newly restructured table. Should you fall into this trap, you may be able to construct an insert query to insert the records from PROBLEMS into EMPLYEE. We will discuss insert queries and the Tools More Add command in detail in Chapter 10, "Multitable Operations."

Since the PROBLEMS table is a temporary table, Paradox will warn you if you are about to perform an operation that could cause the data in PROBLEMS to be lost. For example, if a PROBLEMS table exists and you issue the [Menu] Restructure command, Paradox will display a Cancel/OK prompt that asks you to confirm the loss of the PROBLEMS table. If you choose Cancel at this point, Paradox will cancel the restructure operation so that you can edit or rename the PROBLEMS table. If you choose OK, Paradox will continue with the restructure operation and will overwrite the PROBLEMS table if necessary.

Changing Field Types

You may encounter situations where you need to change a field type in a table. To change the type of a field, issue the [Menu] Modify Restructure command to bring the STRUCT table for the table you want to modify into view. Then move to the Field Type entry for the field whose type you want to change, press [Backspace] or [Ctrl]-[Backspace] to erase the existing type entry, and insert the new field type.

Converting Any Field Type to an Alphanumeric Field

You can change any field type to an alphanumeric field. When you convert a field to an alphanumeric field, the entries in that field will be converted into strings in the same form as the original entry. For instance, if you convert a date type field that contains the entry 6/01/86 into an alphanumeric field, the entry will appear in the new field as the string 6/01/86. Similarly, if you convert a $ field that contains the entry 1,234.56 into an alphanumeric field, the entry in the new field will be the string 1234.56.

When you convert a field of any type to an alphanumeric field, you should make sure that the length of the converted field is adequate to contain the data in the original field. For example, if you are converting a date field to an alphanumeric field, you should set the length of the resulting alphanumeric field to at least 8. If you are converting a $ type field that contains the entry 1,234.56 to an alphanumeric field, you should set the length of the field to at least 7. If you set the field length too short, you will have an opportunity to place those records into a PROBLEMS table where they can be edited.

Although you can convert any field to an alphanumeric field, you must remember that doing so will destroy the special properties of the entries in that field. For instance, if you convert a number field to an alphanumeric field, you will not be able to use Paradox's mathematical capabilites to compute statistics on the new alphanumeric field. You should be very careful about converting numbers or dates to alphanumeric data.

Converting Alphanumeric Fields

You can convert an alphanumeric field to a number field or to a dollar field. However, only the entries limited to numerals (0 through 9), decimals, and commas will be converted. Any entry that contains any other character will not be converted and will be entered into a PROBLEMS table.

For example, the Zip field in the EMPLYEE table is an A-type field with a length of 5. Since it contains numeric information, you can easily convert it to an N field. On the other hand, the Address field in EMPLYEE is also an A-type field. However, because this field contains mixed data (both numerals and alphabetic characters), if you try to convert it to a number field, all of the records in the table will be placed in a PROBLEMS table.

Similarly, you can convert an alphanumeric field to a date field, but only entries that are in a recognized date form (MM/DD/YY or DD-Mon-YY) will be converted. Any entry that contains any other character will not be converted and will be entered into a PROBLEMS table.

Converting a Date Field to a Number Field

Although the *Paradox User's Guide* says that you can convert a date field to a number field, if you try to do this, you will get an error message. If you try to do so, Paradox will display the message *New type specified for Fieldname isn't compatible with old type* at the bottom of the screen. When this happens, you must respecify the field as a date or alphanumeric field. Conversely, you cannot change a number field to a date field. If you try to do this, you will see the same error message.

Converting One Type of Number Field to Another

You can change any type of number field (N, $, or S) to another type. However, if you're converting to a short number field (S), you could lose some data. Remember that short number fields can accept only integer values between -32767 and 32767. If you convert a number or dollar ($) field to a short number field, and that field contains data that will be lost in the conversion, you can place those entries in a PROBLEMS table by selecting No-Trimming from the menu.

Notes

Now that you've seen how to perform the most common types of restructure chores, you should be aware of a few other topics.

The Restructure Menu

When you are restructuring a table, pressing [Menu] ([F10]) causes the Restructure menu to be displayed at the top of the screen. Figure 6-28 shows this menu.

Figure 6-28 The Restructure Menu

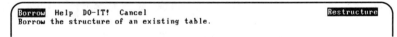

Notice that the Restructure menu is exactly like the Create menu discussed in Chapter 3. In fact, the Borrow, Help, DO-IT!, and Cancel commands perform the same functions in both menus. The Help command displays a Paradox help screen and is equivalent to pressing [Help] ([F1]). The DO-IT! command saves the restructured table and returns you to the main workspace. Issuing the [Menu] DO-IT! command is the same as pressing [Do-It!] ([F2]).

The Borrow command allows you to borrow the structure of one or more existing tables. This command works just like the Borrow command on the menu you see when you are creating a table.

The Cancel command cancels the restructuring process and returns you to the main workspace without saving any of the changes you've made. When you issue the [Menu] Cancel command, Paradox does not prompt you for confirmation. However, the message *Cancelling restructure...* will appear briefly in the lower-right corner of the screen. Issuing the Cancel command is equivalent to pressing [Ctrl]-[Break].

Other Paradox Objects

When you restructure a table, Paradox will update the standard form and the standard report for that table. However, any altered fields are automatically deleted from custom reports and forms. Therefore, when you restructure a table, you will need to modify any custom reports or forms that are part of the table's family. When you press [Do-It!] ([F2]) or issue the [Menu] DO-IT! command to complete the restructuring of a table, Paradox will display various messages at the bottom of the screen to remind you of the changes made in the objects associated with the table.

After you have restructured a table, you can use the [Menu] Report Change command (discussed in Chapters 11 and 12) to update your custom reports and the [Menu] Forms Change command (discussed in Chapter 5) to update your custom forms.

Restructuring Keyed Tables

You can restructure keyed tables just as easily as non-keyed tables. However, there are some important differences you should remember. For one thing, while you can rearrange and change the key fields in a table, you must place all key fields at the top of the STRUCT table. If you try to process a STRUCT table in which the key fields are not at the top of STRUCT, Paradox will display the error message *Non-consecutive key found for fieldname*.

Second, you must be careful not to define a field that contains duplicate entries as a key field while you are restructuring a table. If you designate a field with duplicate entries as the primary key while you're restructuring a table, Paradox will place records with duplicate values in a KEYVIOL table. As you learned in Chapter 4, when you see a KEYVIOL table, you can edit the entries in that table to remove the key field conflict, then use the [Menu] Tools Add command to add the contents of the KEYVIOL table to the main table.

Often when you see a KEYVIOL table after you've restructured a table, it means that you've made an error. Either you have mistakenly selected the wrong field to be a key field, or you have selected a field that is not an appropriate key field. Fortunately, this type of error is easy to correct. If you made a copy of the original table before you started restructuring, you can just erase both the restructured table and the KEYVIOL table and begin again. If you did not copy the original table, you should restructure the newly restructured table to remove the key field, then use the [Menu] Tools More Add command to add the data in KEYVIOL to that table.

Recovering Disk Space

When you delete a record from a table, the space occupied by that record is not automatically "recovered" on the disk and, therefore, becomes wasted space. To recover this space for future use, issue the **[Menu] M**odify **R**estructure command, type the table name, and press ↵. When the STRUCT table appears on the screen, press **[Do-It!]** ([F2]) or issue the **[Menu]** DO-IT! command without making any changes in the table's structure. After you do this, Paradox will "clean up" the table and reclaim the space that was occupied by the deleted records.

Conclusion

In this chapter, we've shown you how to copy, empty, rename and otherwise work with tables. (We'll show you specific instances where you should use a Tools command throughout the remainder of this book.) In addition, we have shown you how to change the structure of a table and have pointed out some of the traps you should avoid when restructuring a table.

In the next chapter, we'll show you how to sort your tables.

Chapter 7

Sorting Your Tables

So far, we have shown you how to create tables and how to enter and edit data. This chapter begins the section of *The Paradox Companion* in which we'll tell you how to use the data in your tables. We'll begin this chapter with a discussion of the [Menu] Modify Sort command. In the next two chapters, we'll show you how to query, or ask questions of, your tables. In Chapter 10, we'll consider tools that will let you work on more than one table at a time.

The [Menu] Modify Sort command allows you to rearrange the records in your tables based on the entries in certain selected fields. You can sort a table on any type of field in ascending or descending order. You can choose to store the sorted records in a new table or have the sorted records overwrite the original, unsorted table. If you wish, you can sort a table on more than one field. In fact, Paradox is one of the few programs that allows you to sort a table on up to as many fields as there are in the table.

A Simple Example

The EMPLYEE table shown in Figure 7-1 on the next page contains no key fields and, therefore, stores records in the order in which they were entered. Suppose you want to sort the records in the table alphabetically by the entries in the Last Name field, then save the resulting sorted table under the name SORTEMP. To begin, issue the **[Menu] Modify Sort** command. After you issue this command, Paradox will prompt you to enter the name of the table you want to sort. When you see this prompt, you should type **EMPLYEE** and press ↵.

Specifying the Destination

When you supply the name of the table you want to sort and press ↵, Paradox will display the menu shown in Figure 7-2. This menu lets you choose where Paradox will store the result of the sort.

Figure 7-1   The EMPLYEE Table

```
Viewing Emplyee table: Record 15 of 16                        Main
 EMPLYEE┬──Emp Number──┬──Last Name──┬─First Name─┬──SS Number──┬──────────Addre
    1   │      1       │  Jones      │  David     │ 414-76-3421 │ 4000 St. Ja
    2   │      2       │  Cameron    │  Herb      │ 321-65-8765 │ 2331 Elm St
    3   │      4       │  Jones      │  Stewart   │ 401-32-8721 │ 4389 Oakbri
    4   │      5       │  Roberts    │  Darlene   │ 417-43-7777 │ 451 Lone Pi
    5   │      6       │  Jones      │  Jean      │ 413-07-9123 │ 4000 St. Ja
    6   │      8       │  Williams   │  Brenda    │ 401-55-1567 │ 100 Owl Cre
    7   │      9       │  Myers      │  Julie     │ 314-38-9452 │ 4512 Parksi
    8   │     10       │  Link       │  Julie     │ 345-75-1525 │ 3215 Palm C
    9   │     12       │  Jackson    │  Mary      │ 424-13-7621 │ 7821 Clark
   10   │     13       │  Jakes, Jr. │  Sal       │ 321-65-9151 │ 3451 Michig
   11   │     14       │  Preston    │  Molly     │ 451-00-3426 │ 321 Indian
   12   │     15       │  Masters    │  Ron       │ 317-65-4529 │ 423 W. 72nd
   13   │     16       │  Robertson  │  Kevin     │ 415-24-6710 │ 431 Bardsto
   14   │     17       │  Garrison   │  Robert    │ 312-98-1479 │ 55 Wheeler
   15   │     19       │  Gunn       │  Barbara   │ 321-97-8632 │ 541 Kentuck
   16   │     20       │  Emerson    │  Cheryl    │ 401-65-1898 │ 800 River R
```

Figure 7-2   Specifying the Sort Destination

```
 Same  New                                                      Main
 Place results of the sort in the same table.
```

If you choose the Same option, Paradox will overwrite the existing table with the sorted table as it performs the sort. As a result, the original order of the records will be lost. If you choose New, Paradox will place the sorted records in a new table. When you choose New, the records are sorted from the original table to a new table, and the original table remains intact after the sort is completed. Since in this case you want the sorted records to be stored in a new table, you should choose New. When you choose this option, Paradox will prompt you to enter a name for the new (destination) table. When you see this prompt, you should type **SORTEMP** and press ↵.

Defining the Sort Form

After you choose the destination, Paradox will display the sort form shown in Figure 7-3. The sort form lists the fields in the table and allows you to tell Paradox which fields you want to use to arrange the table. Notice that the first line on the screen contains the operation message *Sorting Emplyee table into new Sortemp table,* as well as the name of the current menu, *Sort*. The next few lines contain the instructions for defining the sort. Notice also that the names of the fields from the EMPLYEE table are displayed vertically down the left side of the screen.

To sort the table alphabetically by last name, you should press the ↓ key once to position the cursor on the Last Name field, then type the number **1**. This number tells Paradox to use the Last Name field as the primary (first) sort key field when it performs the sort. Figure 7-4 shows the screen at this point. Since in this case you want to sort the table on only one field, and you want to sort in ascending order, you don't need to make any more entries in the sort form.

Figure 7-3 The Sort Form Screen

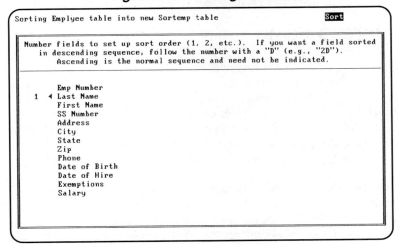

Figure 7-4 Defining the Sort

Sorting

Once you've defined the sort for the EMPLYEE table, either press **[Do-It!]** ([F2]) or issue the **[Menu]** DO-IT! command to sort the table. When you do either of these things, Paradox will sort the table according to the forms you defined, will store the result in the table SORTEMP, and will bring that table to the screen. Figure 7-5 shows the SORTEMP table.

Figure 7-5 The SORTEMP Table

```
Viewing Sortemp table: Record 1 of 16                    Main
SORTEMP  Emp Number   Last Name     First Name   SS Number    Addre
   1         2        Cameron       Herb         321-65-8765  2331 Elm St
   2        20        Emerson       Cheryl       401-65-1898  800 River R
   3        17        Garrison      Robert       312-98-1479  55 Wheeler
   4        19        Gunn          Barbara      321-97-8632  541 Kentuck
   5        12        Jackson       Mary         424-13-7621  7821 Clark
   6        13        Jakes, Jr.    Sal          321-65-9151  3451 Michig
   7         1        Jones         David        414-76-3421  4000 St. Ja
   8         4        Jones         Stewart      401-32-8721  4389 Oakbri
   9         6        Jones         Jean         413-07-9123  4000 St. Ja
  10        10        Link          Julie        345-75-1525  3215 Palm C
  11        15        Masters       Ron          317-65-4529  423 W. 72nd
  12         9        Myers         Julie        314-38-9452  4512 Parksi
  13        14        Preston       Molly        451-00-3426  321 Indian
  14         5        Roberts       Darlene      417-43-7777  451 Lone Pi
  15        16        Robertson     Kevin        415-24-6710  431 Bardsto
  16         8        Williams      Brenda       401-55-1567  100 Owl Cre
```

Sort Basics

Now that you have seen one example of a sort, let's go back and cover a few basics. After we cover these important points, we'll show you how to sort on more than one field and then how to sort a keyed table.

New Versus Same

As you saw in the example, the first option you'll see after you issue the Sort command and specify the name of the table to sort is Same/New. This menu allows you to set the destination of the sort. Although you will occasionally choose Same, there are a couple of good reasons to choose New. First, choosing New ensures that you won't lose any data if something goes wrong while Paradox is performing the sort. When you choose the Same option, Paradox actually overwrites the original table as it performs the sort. Because of this, any problem, such as a power failure, could be a disaster.

Second, by choosing New, you make sure that the original table will be available if you need it for any reason. In some cases, it is difficult to re-sort the records in a sorted table into their original order. Unless you use the New option, you might find that you cannot recreate the original table when you need it. If you later decide you really don't need the original table, you can always delete it with the [Menu] Tools Delete Table command.

In the example, we selected the New option, and Paradox asked us to supply the name of the destination table for the sort. If you choose Same, Paradox will display the sort form immediately. Since the sorted records will be stored in the original table, you don't need to supply a name for the destination.

If you choose the New option, then supply the name of an existing table, Paradox will display the Cancel/Replace menu shown in Figure 7-6. If you choose Cancel from this menu, Paradox will back-up to the previous prompt so that you can erase the table name with the [Backspace] key and can type in a different name for the destination table. If you choose Replace, Paradox will replace the existing table that has the specified name with the sorted table.

Figure 7-6   The Cancel/Replace Menu

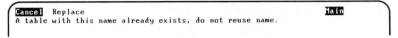

Sort Order

By default, Paradox sorts into ascending order. This means that number and dollar fields are sorted into ascending numeric order, and date fields are sorted so that the earlier dates come before the later dates. Alphanumeric fields that contain only alphabetic characters (a, b, c, and so on) are sorted into alphabetical order. Alphanumeric fields that contain only numeric entries (such as zip codes) are sorted into ascending numeric order.

Alphanumeric fields that contain mixed entries (like *123 Main Street* or *#43A345*) are a bit trickier. In alphanumeric fields like this, Paradox will perform the sort based on the ASCII order of the characters. For example, *123 Main Street* comes before *426 Market Street*. Similarly, #43A345 comes before #77B555, but after !43A345. If you are sorting an alphanumeric field in which the entries start with both upper and lower-case letters, Paradox will sort the table so that the entries that start with the upper-case letters are at the top of the table.

You can also ask Paradox to sort tables in descending order. Descending order sorts number and dollar fields in descending numeric order (highest numbers first) and date fields so that the most recent dates appear before the earlier dates. Alphanumeric fields that contain only alphabetic characters are sorted in reverse alphabetical order (z before y, b before a). If the alphanumeric field contains mixed entries, it is sorted into descending order using the same rules Paradox follows in sorting into ascending order.

To change the sort order of a field from ascending to descending, you simply type a *D* (for *Descending*) next to the field name in the sort form. For example, suppose you want to sort again the EMPLYEE table into reverse alphabetical order on the Last Name field. To begin, issue the **[Menu]** Modify Sort command, type **EMPLYEE**, and press ↵. When Paradox displays the Same/New menu, choose New and then specify SORTEMP2 as the target table. After you press ↵, Paradox will display the sort form shown in Figure 7-7. Notice that Paradox has not retained the previous sort definition.

Figure 7-7 Defining the Sort for SORTEMP2 Table

```
Sorting Emplyee table into new Sortemp2 table              Sort
┌─────────────────────────────────────────────────────────────────┐
│ Number fields to set up sort order (1, 2, etc.).  If you want  │
│ a field sorted in descending sequence, follow the number with  │
│ a "D" (e.g., "2D").                                            │
│    Ascending is the normal sequence and need not be indicated. │
├─────────────────────────────────────────────────────────────────┤
│        ◄ Emp Number                                             │
│          Last Name                                              │
│          First Name                                             │
│          SS Number                                              │
│          Address                                                │
│          City                                                   │
│          State                                                  │
│          Zip                                                    │
│          Phone                                                  │
│          Date of Birth                                          │
│          Date of Hire                                           │
│          Exemptions                                             │
│          Salary                                                 │
└─────────────────────────────────────────────────────────────────┘
```

To specify a descending sort on the Last Name field, you should move the cursor to that field in the specification form and type **1D** next to the field name. As before, the *1* tells Paradox that you want to use the Last Name field as the primary key when you sort the table. The *D* tells Paradox to sort this field into descending order. Figure 7-8 shows the completed sort form.

Figure 7-8 The Completed Sort Form

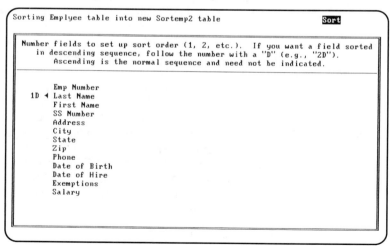

Now press **[Do-It!]** to sort the table. When you press this key, Paradox will sort the table into descending order based on the Last Name field and will store the result in the table SORTEMP2. Figure 7-9 shows the table which results from these instructions.

Figure 7-9 The SORTEMP2 Table

```
Viewing Sortemp2 table: Record 1 of 16                          Main
SORTEMP2   Emp Number    Last Name     First Name   SS Number      Addr
    1           8        Williams      Brenda       401-55-1567    100 Owl Cr
    2          16        Robertson     Kevin        415-24-6710    431 Bardst
    3           5        Roberts       Darlene      417-43-7777    451 Lone P
    4          14        Preston       Molly        451-00-3426    321 Indian
    5           9        Myers         Julie        314-38-9452    4512 Parks
    6          15        Masters       Ron          317-65-4529    423 W. 72n
    7          10        Link          Julie        345-75-1525    3215 Palm
    8           1        Jones         David        414-76-3421    4000 St. J
    9           4        Jones         Stewart      401-32-8721    4389 Oakbr
   10           6        Jones         Jean         413-07-9123    4000 St. J
   11          13        Jakes, Jr.    Sal          321-65-9151    3451 Michi
   12          12        Jackson       Mary         424-13-7621    7821 Clark
   13          19        Gunn          Barbara      321-97-8632    541 Kentuc
   14          17        Garrison      Robert       312-98-1479    55 Wheeler
   15          20        Emerson       Cheryl       401-65-1898    800 River
   16           2        Cameron       Herb         321-65-8765    2331 Elm S
```

Sorting Over and Over

As evidenced by the previous example, you can sort your tables as many times as you wish and in as many different ways as you need. All you have to do each time you want to sort a table is issue the [Menu] Modify Sort command, define the correct sort forms, and press [Do-It!].

There may be times when you'll define a particularly complex or important sort form and will want to save that form for future use. Unfortunately, there is no way to save sort forms in Paradox. Each time you want to sort a table, you must redefine the sort form. The only way to preserve sort forms is to write a PAL program that sorts the table in the desired way. We'll show you how to do this in Chapter 14.

Reversing a Sort

As long as you choose the New option from the Same/New menu, you don't need to worry about reversing a sort. Since Paradox will not change the original table as it performs the sort, the records in that table will still be in their original order.

If you choose the Same option, however, things can be a good deal more difficult. When you choose Same, the records are sorted back into the original table, and the original order of the records is lost. Unless the table has a field that identifies the original order of the records, it will be impossible to reverse the sort.

For example, the Emp Number field in the EMPLYEE table identifies the original order of the table and could be used to reverse a sort on any other field. As long as the table has a field of this type, you can reverse the sort easily enough just by sorting again the table onto itself. For example, suppose you used the [Menu] Modify Sort Same command to sort the EMPLYEE table into ascending order by the entries in the Last Name field. Figure 7-10 shows the sorted table. Now you want to restore the table to its original order. To begin, issue the [**Menu**] Modify Sort command, specify **EMPLYEE** as the table to sort, and choose the **S**ame option. When the sort form appears, move to the Emp Number field and type **1**.

Figure 7-10 The Sorted EMPLYEE Table

```
Viewing Emplyee table: Record 1 of 16                        Main
EMPLYEE   Emp Number    Last Name    First Name    SS Number       Addre
   1           2         Cameron      Herb          321-65-8765    2331 Elm St
   2          20         Emerson      Cheryl        401-65-1898    800 River R
   3          17         Garrison     Robert        312-98-1479    55 Wheeler
   4          19         Gunn         Barbara       321-97-8632    541 Kentuck
   5          12         Jackson      Mary          424-13-7621    7821 Clark
   6          13         Jakes, Jr.   Sal           321-65-9151    3451 Michig
   7           1         Jones        David         414-76-3421    4000 St. Ja
   8           4         Jones        Stewart       401-32-8721    4389 Oakbri
   9           6         Jones        Jean          413-07-9123    4000 St. Ja
  10          10         Link         Julie         345-75-1525    3215 Palm C
  11          15         Masters      Ron           317-65-4529    423 W. 72nd
  12           9         Myers        Julie         314-38-9452    4512 Parksi
  13          14         Preston      Molly         451-00-3426    321 Indian
  14           5         Roberts      Darlene       417-43-7777    451 Lone Pi
  15          16         Robertson    Kevin         415-24-6710    431 Bardsto
  16           8         Williams     Brenda        401-55-1567    100 Owl Cre
```

After the form is completed, press [**Do-It!**] to process the sort. Figure 7-11 shows the sorted EMPLYEE table. Notice that the records are now in the same order as shown in Figure 7-1.

Figure 7-11 The Re-sorted EMPLYEE Table

```
Viewing Emplyee table: Record 1 of 16                        Main
EMPLYEE   Emp Number    Last Name    First Name    SS Number       Addre
   1           1         Jones        David         414-76-3421    4000 St. Ja
   2           2         Cameron      Herb          321-65-8765    2331 Elm St
   3           4         Jones        Stewart       401-32-8721    4389 Oakbri
   4           5         Roberts      Darlene       417-43-7777    451 Lone Pi
   5           6         Jones        Jean          413-07-9123    4000 St. Ja
   6           8         Williams     Brenda        401-55-1567    100 Owl Cre
   7           9         Myers        Julie         314-38-9452    4512 Parksi
   8          10         Link         Julie         345-75-1525    3215 Palm C
   9          12         Jackson      Mary          424-13-7621    7821 Clark
  10          13         Jakes, Jr.   Sal           321-65-9151    3451 Michig
  11          14         Preston      Molly         451-00-3426    321 Indian
  12          15         Masters      Ron           317-65-4529    423 W. 72nd
  13          16         Robertson    Kevin         415-24-6710    431 Bardsto
  14          17         Garrison     Robert        312-98-1479    55 Wheeler
  15          19         Gunn         Barbara       321-97-8632    541 Kentuck
  16          20         Emerson      Cheryl        401-65-1898    800 River R
```

The Sort Menu

If you press [Menu] ([F10]) while you are defining a sort form, Paradox will display the Sort menu shown in Figure 7-12. As you can see, this menu has only three options. The Help command, which is equivalent to pressing [Help] ([F1]), displays Paradox's context-sensitive help screen. The DO-IT! command, which is equivalent to pressing [Do-It!] ([F2]), tells Paradox to perform the sort and display the sorted table in the workspace.

The Cancel command tells Paradox to cancel the sort form and return to the main workspace. When you issue the Cancel command, Paradox does not prompt you for confirmation. However, the message

> Cancelling sort...

will appear in the lower-right corner of the screen. You can also cancel a sort by pressing [Ctrl]-[Break].

Figure 7-12 The Sort Menu

```
Help  DO-IT!  Cancel                                    Sort
Help with sorting a table.
```

Copying JustFamily

When you sort the records in a table into a new table, Paradox does not automatically copy the family (reports, forms, validity checks, etc.) of the original table to the new table. However, you can use the [Menu] Tools Copy JustFamily command to copy those objects after you complete the sort. This command copies a table's family without copying the table itself.

For example, suppose you want to copy the family of objects of EMPLYEE to the new table SORTEMP. To begin, issue the [Menu] Tools Copy JustFamily command. After you issue this command, Paradox will prompt you for the name of the original table. When you see this prompt, you should type **EMPLYEE** and press ↵. Next, Paradox will prompt you for the name of the target table. You should type the name of the sorted table, in this case **SORTEMP**, and press ↵. Since the objects you are copying will replace any existing objects associated with the target table, Paradox will prompt you for confirmation with the menu in Figure 7-13.

Figure 7-13 The Cancel/Replace Menu

```
Cancel  Replace                                          Main
Do not continue with the family copy.
```

If you issue the Cancel command at this point, Paradox will return to the previous prompt and wait for you to specify a different target file name. If you issue the Replace command, Paradox will copy the family from the original table to the target table. You will see the message

> Copying family members from TABLENAME to TABLENAME...

displayed at the bottom of the screen.

When you use the [Menu] Tools Copy JustFamily command, there must be a target table ready to receive the family. This means that you should sort first, then use the Copy JustFamily command to copy the related objects. In addition, both the source and target tables must have the same structure. If you used the [Menu] Modify Sort command to create the target table, you can be sure that both tables have the same structure.

Sorting on More Than One Field

In the examples we've considered so far, we've asked Paradox to sort tables on only a single field. You can, however, designate more than one field to sort on if you wish. In fact, you can ask Paradox to sort on as many fields as there are fields in the table.

Why Sort on Multiple Fields?

The need for multiple-field sorts arises when there are identical records in a table's primary sort field. If there are duplicate entries in the primary sort field, then the records in the sorted table may still appear to be "out of order." For example, Figure 7-5 shows the sorted table SORTEMP. To create this table, we asked Paradox to sort the EMPLYEE table into ascending order based on the Last Name field. Notice the three records with the Last Name field entry *Jones* in the SORTEMP table. Although these records are in proper order in relation to the other records in the table, notice that the names in the First Name field are not in alphabetical order.

If you want both the First Name and Last Name fields to be sorted, you'll need to perform a two-field sort. When you perform a two-field sort, Paradox will first sort the table on the field you designate as the primary sort key. Then, if there are duplicate entries in the primary sort field, Paradox will sort those records based on the entries in the secondary sort field. The secondary sort will serve as a "tie-breaker" for any duplicate entries in the primary field.

An Example

To sort the EMPLYEE table on two fields, first issue the [Menu] Modify Sort command, type **EMPLYEE** when Paradox asks for the name of the table to sort, choose New, and specify **SORTEMP3** as the name of the table to receive the sorted records. When the sort form appears, move to the Last Name field and type the number **1**. This number tells Paradox that you want to use the Last Name field as the primary sort field for the table. Next, move the cursor to the First Name field and type the number **2**. This entry tells Paradox to use First Name as the secondary sort field for EMPLYEE. Figure 7-14 shows the completed form.

Figure 7-14 A Two-field Sort

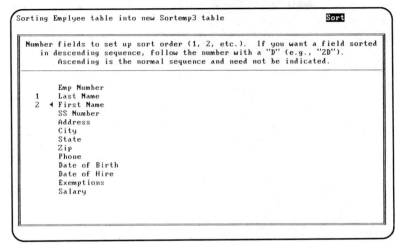

When you press **[Do-It!]**, Paradox will sort the EMPLYEE table and store the results in the table SORTEMP3. Figure 7-15 shows this table. Notice that, as in the SORTEMP table, the records in SORTEMP3 are arranged in alphabetical order according to the entries in the Last Name field. However, notice that the three records with the Last Name entry *Jones* are now arranged in alphabetical order according to the entries in the First Name field. Since the First Name field was designated as the secondary sort field, Paradox used that field to decide which Jones should be placed first in the table.

Figure 7-15 The SORTEMP3 Table

```
Viewing Sortemp3 table: Record 1 of 16                         Main
SORTEMP3   Emp Number    Last Name      First Name    SS Number       Addr
    1           2        Cameron        Herb          321-65-8765    2331 Elm S
    2          20        Emerson        Cheryl        401-65-1898    800 River
    3          17        Garrison       Robert        312-98-1479    55 Wheeler
    4          19        Gunn           Barbara       321-97-8632    541 Kentuc
    5          12        Jackson        Mary          424-13-7621    7821 Clark
    6          13        Jakes, Jr.     Sal           321-65-9151    3451 Michi
    7           1        Jones          David         414-76-3421    4000 St. J
    8           6        Jones          Jean          413-07-9123    4000 St. J
    9           4        Jones          Stewart       401-32-8721    4389 Oakbr
   10          10        Link           Julie         345-75-1525    3215 Palm
   11          15        Masters        Ron           317-65-4529    423 W. 72n
   12           9        Myers          Julie         314-38-9452    4512 Parks
   13          14        Preston        Molly         451-00-3426    321 Indian
   14           5        Roberts        Darlene       417-43-7777    451 Lone P
   15          16        Robertson      Kevin         415-24-6710    431 Bardst
   16           8        Williams       Brenda        401-55-1567    100 Owl Cr
```

Notes

As we have said, Paradox does not limit you to just two-field sorts. You can continue to designate fields for the sort, up to the total number of fields in that table. To designate the third sort field, you'd type a 3 in the sort specification field next to that field. To designate the fourth, fifth, and subsequent sort fields, you would enter the appropriate number next to those fields. For example, you could define a sort specification for the EMPLYEE table like the one shown in Figure 7-16.

Figure 7-16 Defining Three Sort Fields

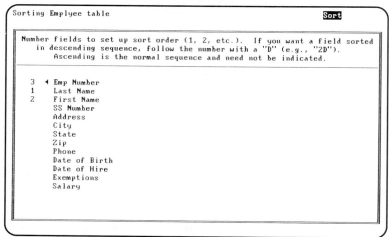

However, there is not much point in performing a three-field sort on a table that does not have duplicate entries in the secondary sort field, or a four-field sort on a table that does not have duplicate entries in the tertiary (third) sort field. In fact, if you processed the sort specification in Figure 7-16, the resulting sorted table would be identical to the one shown in Figure 7-15. In most cases, you will not need to use more than two or three sort fields.

If you do not define the sort order on the sort form, Paradox will sort the records by field in ascending order. For example, suppose you issue the [Menu] Modify Sort command, type EMPLYEE, choose New, and specify SORTEMP4 as the destination table. When the sort form appears, you press [Do-It!] without making any entries. Paradox will perform the sort in ascending order by Emp Number, followed by Last Name, First Name, SS Number, and so on.

You can mix ascending and descending sorts in a single sort form. For example, you could ask Paradox to sort the EMPLYEE table into ascending order on the Last Name field by placing a 1 next to that field in the form, and then ask it to sort the First Name entries in each Last Name group into decending order by typing 2D next to that field.

If you do not define the sort in numerical order, Paradox will not perform the sort. Instead, it will display the message

> Sort key X is missing

where X is the number you omitted. For example, notice that the number 2 is missing from the sort specification in Figure 7-17. If you try to process this sort, Paradox will display the message

Sort key 2 is missing

Figure 7-17 Definition of Sort Omitting Numerical Sequence

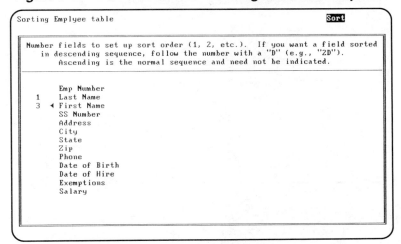

If you enter a number next to a field in the sort specification by mistake, you can erase it just by pressing [Backspace]. For example, suppose you entered the number 3 next to the First Name field in the sort specification in Figure 7-17 by mistake. To erase the error, just move the cursor to the First Name field and press [Backspace]. Once you have erased the mistake, you can type a new number or move to a different field.

Sorting Keyed Tables

You will recall from our previous discussion of key fields that designating a key field in a table automatically establishes a sort order for the records in that table. Since Paradox will not let you violate the sort order in a keyed table, you cannot sort a keyed table onto itself. If you are sorting a keyed table, therefore, you will not see the Same/New option. Instead, Paradox will prompt you to enter a name for the new table.

For example, suppose you want to sort the records in the PROJECTS table in descending order by client number. To begin, issue the **[Menu] M**odify **S**ort command, type **PROJECTS**, and press ↵. When you do this, Paradox will recognize the key field in the table and prompt you to supply the name of the destination table. When you see this prompt, you should type a name for the new table (we called ours Sortprj) and press ↵. When the sort form shown in Figure 7-18 appears, you should press the ↓ key to position the cursor on the Client Number field, then type **1D**.

*Figure 7-18 The Sort Form
for the PROJECTS Table*

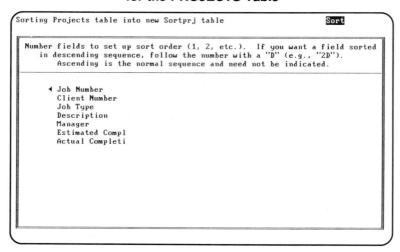

Next, press **[Do-It!]** ([F2]). After you do this, Paradox will perform the sort and display the new table in the workspace, as shown in Figure 7-19.

Figure 7-19 The Sorted PROJECTS Table

```
Viewing Sortprj table: Record 1 of 16                              Main
 SORTPRJ══Job Number══╤══Client Number══╤══Job Type══╤══════Description══
    1          115           1011             6         Assist with Loan Appli
    2          113           1010             1         1986 Audit
    3          114           1010             3         1986 Compilation/Revie
    4          112           1009             2         1986 Tax Return
    5          111           1008             2         1986 Tax Return
    6          110           1007             5         Tax Consultation
    7          109           1006             3         1986 Compilation/Revie
    8          108           1005             3         1986 Compilation/Revie
    9          106           1004             2         Paradox Time Accountin
   10          107           1004             3         1986 Compilation/Revie
   11          103           1003             1         Install Compaq Plus/Sy
   12          104           1003             2         Symphony Intro Course
   13          105           1003             4         Recommend AR System
   14          102           1002             2         Paradox A/R System
   15          100           1001             1         Install PC AT/Paradox/
   16          101           1001             3         AT/Paradox/1-2-3 Intro
```

Conclusion

In this chapter, we've shown you how to sort your Paradox tables. We showed you how to choose the destination for the sorted records, how to define the fields on which you want to sort, and how to define the order of the sort. You'll find that sorting will be an important part of your work with Paradox.

In the next chapter, "Queries," we will begin to show you how to query, or ask questions of, your Paradox tables.

Chapter 8

Queries

In the first chapters of this book, we showed you how to create Paradox tables, how to modify the structure of those tables, and how to enter data into tables. However, if all you could do with Paradox were to create tables and type entries into those tables, the program would not be very useful. The real power of Paradox lies in its ability to answer questions about your tables.

In Paradox, the tools you use to locate information that is stored in a table are called queries. The word "query" means "to ask." You can use queries to ask Paradox to extract selected information from a table, to delete information from a table, to change selected data, or even to combine two tables into a single table.

In this chapter, we'll show you how to query, or ask questions of, your Paradox tables. We'll begin with some very simple examples and build up to more complex ones. Along the way, we'll offer notes, hints, and cautions that you can apply to your own queries.

A Simple Example

Suppose you have created the table named EMPLYEE, whose structure is shown in Figure 8-1, and have entered the information shown in Figure 8-2 on page 193 into the table. Figure 8-3 shows this table in view on the screen. Now suppose that you want to extract from this table all of the records that have the entry KY in the State field. To do this, you'll want to create a query on the EMPLYEE table.

Creating a Query Form

Before you can define a query for any table, you must create a query form for that table. To create a query form for the EMPLYEE table, first press [Clear All] ([Alt]-[F8]) to clear the screen, then issue the [Menu] Ask command and supply the name of the table that you want to query. In this case, when Paradox asks you for the name of the table you want to query, either type the table name **EMPLYEE** or press ↵ and point to the table name EMPLYEE in the list that Paradox provides.

Figure 8-1 The Structure of EMPLYEE

```
Viewing Struct table: Record 1 of 13                    Main
 STRUCT     Field Name          Field Type
   1     Emp Number              N
   2     Last Name               A10
   3     First Name              A10
   4     SS Number               A11
   5     Address                 A20
   6     City                    A20
   7     State                   A2
   8     Zip                     A5
   9     Phone                   A14
  10     Date of Birth           D
  11     Date of Hire            D
  12     Exemptions              N
  13     Salary                  $
```

Figure 8-3 The EMPLYEE Table

```
Viewing Emplyee table: Record 1 of 16                   Main
 EMPLYEE  Emp Number   Last Name     First Name   SS Number     Addre
    1         1        Jones         David        414-76-3421   4000 St. Ja
    2         2        Cameron       Herb         321-65-8765   2321 Elm St
    3         4        Jones         Stewart      401-32-8721   4389 Oakbri
    4         5        Roberts       Darlene      417-43-7777   451 Lone Pi
    5         6        Jones         Jean         413-07-9123   4000 St. Ja
    6         8        Williams      Brenda       401-55-1567   100 Owl Cre
    7         9        Myers         Julie        314-38-9452   4512 Parksi
    8        10        Link          Julie        345-75-1525   3215 Palm C
    9        12        Jackson       Mary         424-13-7621   7821 Clark
   10        13        Jakes, Jr.    Sal          321-65-9151   3451 Michig
   11        14        Preston       Molly        451-00-3426   321 Indian
   12        15        Masters       Ron          317-65-4529   423 W. 72nd
   13        16        Robertson     Kevin        415-24-6710   431 Bardsto
   14        17        Garrison      Robert       312-98-1479   55 Wheeler
   15        19        Gunn          Barbara      321-97-8632   541 Kentuck
   16        20        Emerson       Cheryl       404-14-1422   8100 River
```

When you have specified the table you want to query, Paradox will present a new image, called a query form, for that table. Figure 8-4 on the next page shows a query form for the EMPLYEE table. Figure 8-5 shows this form on the screen. You'll use this query form to tell Paradox on which fields and records you want to operate.

Figure 8-5 A Query Form for EMPLYEE

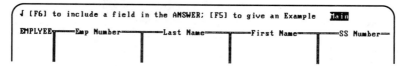

Filling in the Query Form

Once you have created a query form, you will usually make entries in that form that define the query you want Paradox to perform. At this stage, you can select the fields that you want Paradox to include in the result of the query, and you can define selection conditions that select records based on the entries in those records.

Queries   193

Figure 8-2 The EMPLYEE Table

Emp Number	Last Name	First Name	SS Number	Address	City	State	Zip	Phone	Date of Birth	Date of Hire	Exemptions	Salary
1	Jones	David	414-76-3421	4000 St. James Ct.	St. Matthews	KY	40207	(502) 245-6610	10/06/42	6/01/84	3	78,000.00
2	Cameron	Herb	321-65-8765	2321 Elm St.	Louisville	KY	40205	(502) 451-8765	11/24/29	6/01/84	4	58,000.00
3	Jones	Stewart	401-32-8721	4389 Oakbridge Rd.	Lyndon	KY	40222	(502) 452-1048	3/21/50	7/01/84	1	47,000.00
4	Roberts	Darlene	417-43-7777	451 Lone Pine Dr.	Lagrange	KY	40012	(502) 897-3215	9/24/60	12/01/84	3	14,000.00
5	Jones	Jean	413-07-9123	4000 St. James Ct.	St. Matthews	KY	40207	(502) 245-6610	5/14/43	7/01/84	0	33,999.99
6	Williams	Brenda	401-55-1567	100 Owl Creek Rd.	Anchorage	KY	40223	(502) 894-9761	1/12/28	1/01/85	5	48,000.00
7	Myers	Julie	314-38-9452	4512 Parkside Dr.	Louisville	KY	40206	(502) 454-5289	2/06/48	2/01/85	1	32,000.00
8	Link	Julie	345-75-1525	3215 Palm Ct.	Palo Alto	CA	94375	(408) 542-1948	6/03/33	4/01/85	2	30,000.00
9	Jackson	Mary	424-13-7621	7821 Clark Ave.	Clarksville	IN	47138	(812) 288-6754	8/12/56	4/01/85	3	21,000.00
10	Jakes, Jr.	Sal	321-65-9151	3451 Michigan Ave.	Dallas	TX	65987	(214) 398-1987	5/23/59	5/01/85	6	34,000.00
11	Preston	Molly	451-00-3426	321 Indian Hills Rd.	Louisville	KY	40205	(502) 456-3256	4/17/66	7/01/85	8	14,750.00
12	Masters	Ron	317-65-4529	423 W. 72nd St.	New York	NY	10019	(212) 276-5478	12/30/44	7/01/85	0	38,000.00
13	Robertson	Kevin	415-24-6718	431 Bardstown Rd.	Elizabethtown	KY	40315	(502) 423-9823	3/16/25	7/15/85	1	37,000.00
14	Garrison	Robert	312-90-1479	55 Wheeler St.	Boston	MA	25687	(617) 543-4124	5/09/45	10/01/85	4	32,000.00
15	Gunn	Barbara	321-97-8632	541 Kentucky St.	New Albany	IN	47132	(812) 325-4709	5/10/58	11/01/85	2	17,500.00
16	Emerson	Cheryl	404-14-1422	8100 River Rd.	Prospect	KY	40222	(502) 896-5139	7/30/66	1/01/86	2	12,000.00

Figure 8-4 A Query Form for EMPLYEE

EMPLYEE | Emp Number | Last Name | First Name | SS Number | Address | City | State | Zip | Phone | Date of Birth | Date of Hire | Exemptions | Salary |

In the example, we want to extract all of the information (that is, the data stored in each field) for all of the records that have the entry KY in the State field. To fill in this query form, press the **[Check Mark]** key ([F6]) while the cursor is still in the area under the query form name. Pressing [Check Mark] causes Paradox to place a check mark in each field of the query, as shown in Figure 8-6. When you process this query, Paradox will include every selected field (that is, every field that includes a check mark) in the result.

Figure 8-6 Selecting Fields

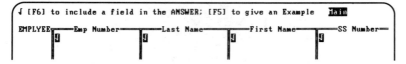

Now you must enter a selection condition in the form that tells Paradox to select only those records that have the entry KY in the State field. To do this, press → seven times to move the cursor to the State field of the query form. Now, type **KY**. Notice that you don't need to press [Edit] before you type. Figure 8-7 shows the screen at this point, and Figure 8-8 shows the entire completed query.

Figure 8-7 The Completed Query

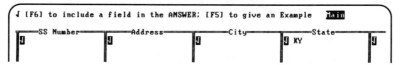

Processing the Query

To process the query, press **[Do-It!]** ([F2]). When you press this key, Paradox will display the message *Processing query...* in the lower-right corner of the screen. (If the query is improperly defined, Paradox will display one of a variety of error messages.)

Figure 8-9 on page 196 shows the screen as it will look after you process the query. As you can see, Paradox has created a new table, ANSWER, which includes only those records that have the entry KY in the State field. Figure 8-10 shows the entire ANSWER table. Because you selected every field in the query form, the ANSWER table includes every field from the EMPLYEE table. In other words, the ANSWER table contains the information that answers your query.

Of course, this is a very simple query. Paradox queries can be far more complex than this one. In the remainder of this chapter, we'll show you how to build more sophisticated queries in Paradox.

Figure 8-8 The Completed Query

EMPLOYEE	Emp Number	Last Name	First Name	SS Number	Address	City	State	Zip	Phone	Date of Birth	Date of Hire	Exemptions	Salary
							KY						

Figure 8-10 The ANSWER Table

ANSWER	Emp Number	Last Name	First Name	SS Number	Address	City	State	Zip	Phone	Date of Birth	Date of Hire	Exemptions	Salary
	1	Jones	David	414-76-3421	4000 St. James Ct.	St. Matthews	KY	40207	(502) 245-6610	10/06/42	6/01/84	3	70,000.00
	2	Cameron	Herb	321-65-8765	2321 Elm St.	Louisville	KY	40205	(502) 451-8765	11/24/29	6/01/84	4	58,000.00
	4	Jones	Stewart	401-32-8721	4389 Oakbridge Rd.	Lyndon	KY	40222	(502) 452-1040	3/21/50	7/01/84	1	47,000.00
	5	Roberts	Darlene	417-43-7777	451 Lone Pine Dr.	Lagrange	KY	40012	(502) 897-3215	9/24/60	11/01/84	3	14,000.00
	6	Jones	Jean	413-87-9123	4000 St. James Ct.	St. Matthews	KY	40207	(502) 245-6610	5/14/43	12/01/84	8	33,999.99
	8	Williams	Brenda	401-55-1567	100 Owl Creek Rd.	Anchorage	KY	40223	(502) 894-9761	1/12/28	1/01/85	5	40,000.00
	9	Myers	Julie	314-38-9452	4512 Parkside Dr.	Louisville	KY	40206	(502) 454-5209	2/06/40	2/01/85	1	32,000.00
	14	Preston	Molly	451-80-3426	321 Indian Hills Rd.	Louisville	KY	40205	(502) 456-3256	4/17/66	7/01/85	1	14,750.00
	16	Robertson	Kevin	415-24-6710	431 Bardstown Rd.	Elizabethtown	KY	40315	(502) 423-9823	3/16/25	7/15/85	1	37,000.00
	20	Emerson	Cheryl	404-14-1422	0100 River Rd.	Prospect	KY	40222	(502) 896-5139	7/30/66	1/01/86	2	12,000.00

Figure 8-9 The ANSWER Table

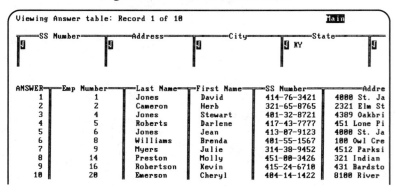

Query Basics

Now that you have seen an example of a query, we should go back and cover a few basics about queries. We'll start with some notes about query forms and then look in detail at ANSWER tables.

Query Form Notes

Before you can define a query for a table, you must create a query form for that table. This step is always required since without a query form there can be no query. As you have seen, you create a query form for a table by issuing the [Menu] Ask command and specifying the name of the table.

The query form that Paradox creates for a table always has the same structure as that table. For example, the query form you created for EMPLYEE has the same structure as the table EMPLYEE. It includes all of the fields that are in EMPLYEE; furthermore, the fields in the query form are in the same order as the fields in the table. In fact, the query form even has the name EMPLYEE.

You will notice that the query form in Figure 8-5 appears at the top of the screen. Whenever you create a new query form, it will always appear at the top of the screen, above normal table images.

Notice that the EMPLYEE table was not in view when we created the query in Figure 8-7. Paradox does not require that you view a table in order to create a query form for that table. If you are viewing a table when you create a query form, the query form will appear above the table image at the top of the screen. The table you are querying does not need to be in view when you process the query. If the table is not in view when you press [Do-It!], Paradox will not bring it into view. If the table is in view, the ANSWER table will appear below it on the screen.

More than one query form can be active at once. In fact, some types of queries require you to create several different query forms. To create a second and third query form, you just repeat the [Menu] Ask command and specify the name of the table for which you want to create a form. If there are already other query forms on the screen when you create a new query form, the new form will appear below the existing forms on the screen, but above any normal table images.

Although there can be query forms for several different tables on the screen at once, you can only create one query form at a time for a given table. If there is already one query form for a table on the screen when you issue the [Menu] Ask command to create another form for that same table, Paradox will simply ignore the command.

Moving the Cursor

If there are other images on the screen with a query form, you can move the cursor from image to image with the [Up Image] ([F3]) and [Down Image] ([F4]) keys. For example, to move the cursor from the ANSWER table in Figure 8-9 to the EMPLYEE query form, press **[Up Image]**.

You can move the flashing cursor around within a query form in exactly the same way that you move it around in a table image. The → and ← keys move the cursor right and left from field to field. If you move far enough to the right, the query form will shift so that new fields come into view at the right side of the screen, and other fields will disappear to the left.

Just as in a table image, the [Ctrl]-→ and [Ctrl]-← keys move the cursor one screen to the right or left. The [Ctrl]-[Home] combination will move the cursor to the far-left edge of the query form, and the [Ctrl]-[End] combination will move it to the far-right edge.

You can use the ↑ and ↓ keys to move the cursor from row to row in the query form. However, Paradox will not allow you to move the cursor to the second row of a query form until you have made an entry in the first row. If you press ↓ before you make an entry in the first row of a form, Paradox will just beep. We'll begin to use these keys in a few pages when we talk about OR queries.

Making Entries

In the example, you made two kinds of entries in the query form. First, you used the [Check Mark] key to enter checks in all the fields of the form. These check marks select the fields that you want Paradox to include in the ANSWER table.

As a rule, you must select at least one field in a query form before you process a query. If you press [Do-It!] to process a query form in which no fields are selected, Paradox will deliver one of two messages. If the query is completely blank, Paradox will return the message *Nothing to process now*. If the query contains a selection condition, but no selected fields, Paradox will return the message *Query has no checked fields* when you press [Do-It!].

Second, in our example, we entered the letters KY in the State field of the form. This entry is an example of a selection condition. By entering these characters in the State field of the query form, we asked Paradox to select those records in EMPLYEE that have the State field entry KY.

As you saw, making an entry in a query form is as easy as moving the cursor to the field where you want the entry to be stored, and typing the entry. The big difference between making an entry in a query form and making an entry in a table is that you don't need to press [Edit] or issue any commands before you make an entry in a query form.

Of course, the simple entry KY is just one small example of the types of entries you can make in query forms. We will look at many more query form entries in the remainder of this chapter.

Reusing Query Forms

You don't need to start from scratch each time you want to construct a query on a table. If you have previously queried the table, and the query form you used is still on the workspace, you can use that existing query form to perform the new query. All you need to do is change the form so that it defines the new query, and then press [Do-It!].

For example, suppose that you now want to select all of the records from the EMPLYEE table that have the entry IN in the State field. To do this, you would move the cursor to the query form, then move to the State field. When the cursor is in place, press **[Ctrl]-[Backspace]** to erase the existing entry, KY. Then just type **IN**. Figure 8-11 shows the completed query form.

Figure 8-11

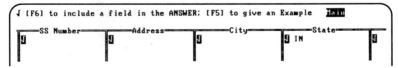

Now press **[Do-It!]** to process the query. Figure 8-12 shows the resulting ANSWER table. This table includes all of the fields from EMPLYEE, but only two records. The records in ANSWER are the only records in the table that meet the selection condition you described.

By the way, when you processed this query, Paradox replaced the original ANSWER table with the new ANSWER table. Unless you renamed the original ANSWER table, its contents are now lost. The only way to recreate the old ANSWER table would be to redefine and process the query shown in Figure 8-7 on page 194.

Figure 8-12

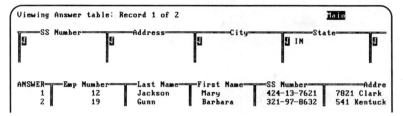

Clearing a Query Form

You can clear a query form from the workspace in exactly the same way that you clear any other image. To clear a query form, you just move the cursor to that form and press [Clear Image]. For example, to clear the query form that you created in the previous example, you would press **[Up Image]** to move the cursor into the form, and then press **[Clear Image]** to clear the query form from view. As you might expect, if you press [Clear All] ([Alt]-[F8]) while a query form is on the workspace, it will be cleared away along with all of the other images on the workspace.

Query forms are temporary. When you clear a query form from the screen, that query form ceases to exist. Any entries that you have made in the query form are lost. If you want to reuse a query form that you have cleared from the screen, you must recreate it from scratch with the [Menu] Ask command.

There is one exception to this rule. You can use the [Menu] Scripts QuerySave command to save your queries into special query scripts. We'll cover this command at the end of this chapter.

Creating a New Query Form

Suppose you want to define a new query on a table for which a query form already exists, but the new query you want to create is vastly different from the existing query. You might find it easier to clear the existing query and start from scratch than to edit the existing query. To create a new, blank query for a table, first use the [Clear] or [Clear All] key to clear the existing query form. Then use the [Menu] Ask command to create a form for the table.

Throughout this chapter, we'll ask you to begin an example by creating a new, blank query form for a table. When we ask you to do this, use the technique you just learned to create the form.

The Answer Table

In general, when you perform a query, Paradox will copy the information you have requested from the table you are querying into a temporary table called ANSWER and will display that table on the screen. (In certain cases, Paradox may copy the information to other places as well, or may not create an ANSWER table.) In most situations, ANSWER is a perfectly normal Paradox table. However, there are a couple of things you need to know about these ANSWER tables.

First, if you look at Figure 8-10 on page 195, you'll notice that the entries in ANSWER are arranged in ascending order based on the entries in the Emp Number field. As a rule, Paradox will arrange the entries in the ANSWER tables it creates in ascending order, based on the entries in the first field of ANSWER. For example, if the first field of ANSWER is an A-type (alphanumeric) field, the entries will be in alphabetic order. If the first field is an N-type (numeric) field, the records will be in ascending numeric order.

Also notice that in Figure 8-9 on page 196 the cursor is in the ANSWER table. No matter where the cursor is when you process a query, it will be in the first field of the first record in ANSWER when the query is completed.

If the ANSWER table that results from a query is large, it may push the query form, and perhaps other images as well, off the top of the screen. The hidden images still exist; they're simply out of view. If you want to look at them, press the **[Up Image]** key.

Editing ANSWER

You can edit the contents of an ANSWER table just as you edit the contents of any other Paradox table. However, you must keep in mind that the ANSWER table that results from a query is completely independent from the table that you queried to produce the ANSWER table. Changes that you make to the data in an ANSWER table do not affect the entries in the original, permanent table.

Querying ANSWER

Because ANSWER tables are perfectly normal Paradox tables, they can be queried like any other table. For example, suppose that you have created the ANSWER table shown in Figure 8-13. Remember that this table includes only those records from EMPLYEE that have the State field entry IN. Now suppose that you want to query the ANSWER table to locate those records with the City field entry *New Albany*.

To make this selection, first press **[Clear Image]** to clear the EMPLYEE query form, then use the **[Menu] A**sk command to create a new query form for the ANSWER table. Next, press **[Check Mark]** with the cursor in the space under the form name to select every field in the form. Then move to the City field and type **New Albany**. Figure 8-13 shows the completed query.

Figure 8-13

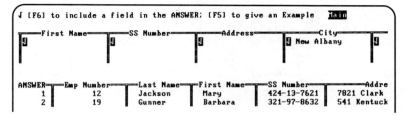

To process the query, press **[Do-It!]**. As before, pressing [Do-It!] will cause Paradox to select the requested records from the table you are querying (in this case, ANSWER) and to write them into a table called ANSWER. Figure 8-14 shows the new ANSWER table. This table includes only the one record from the original ANSWER table (shown in Figure 8-13) that has the City field entry *New Albany*.

Figure 8-14

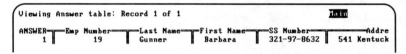

Since the table you are querying in this example is an ANSWER table, it will be overwritten by the new ANSWER table as the query is processed. In addition, Paradox will erase the query form for the original ANSWER table as you perform the query. This only makes sense–after all, how could a query form exist for a table that has been replaced with a new table? Whenever you perform a query on the ANSWER table, both the previous ANSWER table and the ANSWER query form will be erased when you press [Do-It!]. If you want to preserve the first ANSWER table, you should rename it before you create the second query.

Saving ANSWER

Only one ANSWER table can exist at any time. Whenever you perform a query, the ANSWER table created by that query will overwrite the existing ANSWER table, if there is one. Any information stored in the first ANSWER table will be lost.

As a result, if you want to preserve the results of a query, you'll need to rename the ANSWER table that is produced by the query before you perform another query. You can rename an ANSWER table (or any other table, for that matter) by issuing the [Menu] Tools Rename Table command, supplying the name of the table to be renamed, and supplying the new name you want to give the table. For example, to change the name of the ANSWER table you just created to NEWALB, you would issue the **[Menu] Tools Rename Table** command, type **ANSWER**, press ↵, type **NEWALB**, and then press ↵ once again.

Selecting Fields

As you have learned, when you process a query, Paradox creates a special table, called ANSWER, that contains the information that you requested. Although the structure of ANSWER will always be related to the structure of the table that you are querying, ANSWER can include all or only some of the fields (and all or only some of the records) from the table you are querying. You tell Paradox which fields to include in ANSWER by selecting fields in the query form.

You select fields in query forms by pressing either [Check Mark] or [Check Plus] while the cursor is in the appropriate place in the form. In the first few examples, you selected every field in the query form by pressing [Check Mark] while the cursor was in the space under the query form name. This action placed a check mark in every field of the form. When the form was processed, Paradox included every field from the query form in the ANSWER table.

You don't need to select every field in a query form, however. You can select just one field or several fields, depending on how you want the ANSWER table to look.

Selecting One Field

To select a field in a query form, you should use the arrow keys to move the cursor into that field in the query form, and then press the [Check Mark] key ([F6]). For example, suppose you want to select the Last Name field in an EMPLYEE query form. To begin, press **[Clear All]** to clear the screen, then use the **[Menu] A**sk command to create a new query form for EMPLYEE. To select the Last Name field, press ➡ twice to move the cursor into that field of the query form, and then press **[Check Mark]** ([F6]). Figure 8-15 shows the completed query. As you can see, Paradox has marked the selected field in the query form with a check mark.

Figure 8-15

Once you have selected a field, you can deselect it by pressing the **[Check Mark]** key a second time. For example, to deselect the Last Name field, you would move the cursor to the Last Name field in the query form (it should already be there) and press **[Check Mark]** again. As soon as you press [Check Mark], Paradox will remove the check mark from the field, indicating that it has been deselected. If you then want to reselect the field, you need only press **[Check Mark]** again.

If you press **[Do-It!]** to process this query when only the Last Name field is selected, Paradox will create the ANSWER table shown in Figure 8-16. As always, this table includes the records from the table that were selected by the query you have defined. Since you selected only one field in the query form, the ANSWER table includes only one field. The records in this field are arranged in alphabetical order.

Figure 8-16

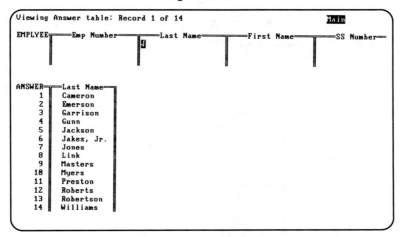

Notice that there are only 14 records in ANSWER, while there are 16 records in EMPLYEE. This occurs because several of the records in EMPLYEE have the same entry in the Last Name field and because (without knowing it) you asked Paradox to copy only unique entries to the ANSWER table. We will discuss the concept of duplicate entries in a few pages.

There's one more thing worth pointing out about this query. Notice that we didn't enter any selection conditions into the query form; we merely selected a field and pressed [Do-It!]. You don't need to use selection conditions in queries. If you don't include selection conditions in a query, Paradox will include every unique record from the table in the ANSWER table.

Selecting More Fields

As you might expect, you can select more than one field in a query form. To select additional fields, you need only enter checks or check pluses in those fields. For example, suppose you want to include not only the last name, but also the address of each employee in EMPLYEE in the ANSWER table. To do this, press **[Up Image]** to move to the EMPLYEE query form. Then move the cursor to the Address field. When the cursor is in place, press **[Check Mark]** to select the field. Figure 8-17 shows the completed query.

When you press **[Do-It!]**, Paradox will create a new ANSWER table like the one shown in Figure 8-18. Notice that this new table includes the contents of both the Last Name and the Address fields of EMPLYEE.

Figure 8-17

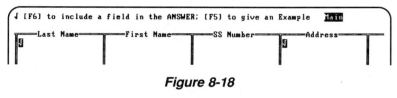

Figure 8-18

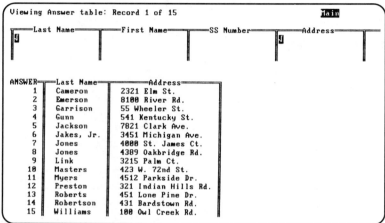

Of course, you can use this technique to select as many of the fields in a query form as you wish. Paradox will always include all of the fields that you have selected in the ANSWER table. For example, Figure 8-19 shows a query form in which the Last Name, First Name, and Address fields in the EMPLYEE table are selected, and also the ANSWER table that Paradox will produce when you process that query.

Figure 8-19

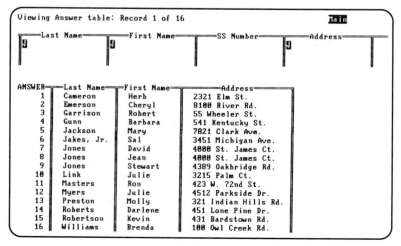

Selecting Every Field

If you want to select every field in a query form, just move the cursor to the area under the query form name (the space at the left edge of the query form) and press [Check Mark]. This is the technique we used in the first example to select every field in EMPLYEE. When you do this, Paradox will place check marks in every field of the query form. As you might expect, when you process a query in which every field is selected, the ANSWER table will include every field that appears in the query form.

Selecting Unselected Fields

Suppose you have selected one or more fields in a form and you now want to select the remaining fields. All you need to do is move the cursor to the space under the query form name and press [Check Mark]. When you press [Check Mark], Paradox will select all of the unselected fields in the query form. As before, the result will be a query form with every field selected.

For example, suppose you had selected every field in the EMPLYEE query form except for the Emp Number field. If you move the cursor to the space under the query form's name and press **[Check Mark]**, Paradox will enter a check mark in the Emp Number field. The check marks in the other fields will not be affected by this action.

Deselecting All Fields

As you might expect, you can also use this technique to deselect all of the fields in a query form. If all of the fields in a query form are selected, then you can deselect all of the fields in one step by pressing [Check Mark] while the cursor is in the space under the query form name at the left edge of the image.

If at least one field in the form is not selected, pressing [Check Mark] while the cursor is in the space under the query form name won't deselect the selected fields. Instead, pressing [Check Mark] in this case will select the fields that were previously unselected. Of course, after you have pressed [Check Mark] once to select every field, you can deselect every field simply by pressing [Check Mark] again.

Notes

As you have seen, when every field in a query form is selected, Paradox will include every field from the form in the ANSWER table. There will be times when you'll want to include all of the fields in a table in the ANSWER table when you perform a query. Usually, though, when you select every field in a query form, you'll also create selection conditions in the form that select only certain records for the ANSWER table. Otherwise, the ANSWER table will be an exact copy of the table that you are querying. (One exception to this rule occurs when you want to use a query to make a copy of a table. By selecting every field in the table's query form and pressing [Do-It!], you can create an exact copy of a table very quickly.)

You can also use the "select all" technique when you want to select most, but not all, of the fields in a form. All you need to do is press [Check Mark] while the cursor is in the space under the query name to select every field, and then move through the form pressing [Check Mark] to deselect certain fields. For example, suppose you want to select every field in the EMPLYEE query form except for the Emp Number field. You could do this by moving the cursor to each of the fields in the form individually and pressing [Check Mark]. As an alternative, however, you could move to the space under the query form name, press [Check Mark] once to select every field, then move to the Emp Number field and press [Check Mark] to deselect that one field.

Including Duplicate Records

As we mentioned earlier, the ANSWER table in Figure 8-16 includes only 14 records, while the EMPLYEE table includes 16. This difference occurs because some of the entries in the Last Name field of EMPLYEE are duplicates. When you use the [Check Mark] key to select the field or fields that you want Paradox to include in the ANSWER table, Paradox will include in the ANSWER table only one copy of any records that have the same entry in all selected fields. In the example, three records in EMPLYEE had the same entry–Jones–in the only field you selected–Last Name–so Paradox included only one of these three records in the ANSWER table in Figure 8-16.

What Is a Duplicate Record?

It is important that you understand that, for purposes of querying, Paradox considers records to be duplicates only if they have exactly the same entry in all of the fields that you select in the query form. If two records have identical entries in the fields you have selected, Paradox will always consider them to be duplicates–even if they have different entries in the unselected fields. This means that it is possible that two records that are really quite different will be considered as duplicates by a query that includes only one or two fields.

For instance, the records for David Jones, Jean Jones, and Stewart Jones in the EMPLYEE table are clearly not identical in most regards. However, since the first query we created included only one field, and since these three records have the same entry in that one field, Paradox considered them to be duplicates.

On the other hand, if two records have the same entries in all but one selected field, then they will not be considered duplicates. As a general rule, the more fields you select, the less chance there is that any two records will have exactly the same entry in all of the selected fields.

For example, look back at the query shown in Figure 8-17. This query uses check marks to select both the Last Name and Address fields. Now look at Figure 8-18, which shows the ANSWER table that was created when we processed the query. As you can see, Paradox included two Jones records in this ANSWER table–one with the entry *4000 St. James Ct.* in the Address field, and one with the entry *4389 Oakbridge Rd.* in that field.

If you look back at the original EMPLYEE table, in Figure 8-2, you'll see why this occurred. Notice that the records for David Jones and Jean Jones have the same entries in both the Last Name and Address fields, but that the record for Stewart Jones has a different entry in the Address field. Since the records for David Jones and Jean Jones in the EMPLYEE table have the same entries in the two selected fields, only one of these two duplicate records was included in the ANSWER table. Since the record for Stewart Jones had a different entry in the Address field, that record was also included in the ANSWER table.

As you might expect, selecting yet another field in the query form would cause Paradox to cease considering David Jones and Jean Jones as duplicates. For example, Figure 8-19 shows the ANSWER table that Paradox produced when you selected the First Name field in addition to the Last Name and Address fields. Notice that there are now three records in the ANSWER table that have the entry *Jones* in the Last Name field. Because all three Joneses have different first names, and since the First Name field is now selected in the query form, Paradox no longer considers these records to be duplicates.

Using [Check Plus]

If you want to include all instances of duplicate records in your ANSWER table, you must use the [Check Plus] key ([Alt]-[F6]) instead of the [Check Mark] key to select at least one of the fields you want to include in ANSWER. When you use [Check Plus] to select a field in the query form, Paradox will include all of the entries from the selected fields–including duplicates–in the ANSWER table.

Let's look at how this works. Suppose you want to select the Last Name field from every record in the EMPLYEE table, including duplicate records. To begin, create a new, empty EMPLYEE query form. Now, use the arrow keys to move the cursor to the Last Name field and press **[Check Plus]** ([Alt]-[F6]) to select the field. Figure 8-20 shows the completed query. Notice the check mark and plus sign in the Last Name field.

Figure 8-20

Once you have entered a check plus in the Last Name field, press **[Do-It!]** to process the query. Figure 8-21 shows the resulting ANSWER table. Notice that ANSWER now includes 16 records–the same number as EMPLYEE–and that there are three different Jones entries in the Last Name field of ANSWER. Because you used the [Check Plus] key, and not the [Check Mark] key, to select the Last Name field, Paradox has included all of the entries from that field, including duplicates, in the ANSWER table.

Figure 8-21

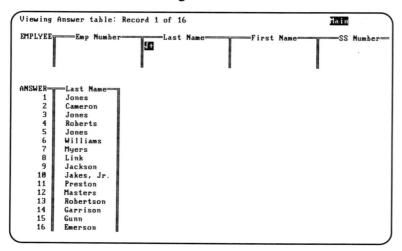

Also notice that the ANSWER table in Figure 8-21 is not sorted. Instead, the entries in ANSWER appear in the same order as the corresponding entries in EMPLYEE. Whenever you use [Check Plus], Paradox will not sort the ANSWER table.

Check Plus and Multifield Queries

When you are defining a query in which several fields are selected and you want to include duplicate records in the ANSWER table, you need to mark only one of the fields in the query form with a check plus. The rest of the fields can be marked with simple checks. This is true even if some of the records have the same entries in two or more of the selected fields. As long as one field in the query contains a check plus, all duplicates will be included in the ANSWER table.

For example, suppose that you want to include both the Last Name and Address fields in ANSWER, and that you want all three Jones records to appear in ANSWER. You might think that you need to enter a check plus in both the Last Name and Address fields to achieve the desired result. However, you can create the ANSWER table you want just by entering a check plus in the Last Name field and a check in the Address field.

Changing a Check to a Check Plus

What if you want to enter a check plus in a field that already contains a check? For example, suppose the Last Name field of an EMPLYEE query form already contains a check mark. To replace this check with a check plus, move the cursor to the Last Name field and press **[Check Mark]** or **[Check Plus]** to deselect the Last Name field. Then, without moving the cursor, press **[Check Plus]** to reselect the field with a check plus.

Unfortunately, Paradox requires you to use two keystrokes to replace a check with a check plus. You must first press **[Check Mark]** or **[Check Plus]** to deselect the field, and then press **[Check Plus]** to reselect it. You cannot both remove an existing check mark and replace it with a check plus just by pressing [Check Plus].

Defining Selection Conditions

So far, we have shown you how to create query forms, how to select fields, and how to process queries. Now we're ready to look at the next step in defining queries: defining selection conditions. In general, selection conditions tell Paradox which records you want it to include in the ANSWER table, much like checks and check pluses tell Paradox which fields to include in ANSWER. Selection conditions are like filters, or tests, that select records based on the entries in one or more fields.

You've already seen several examples of simple selection conditions. For instance, in the first example, we entered the condition KY in the State field of a query form. This condition told Paradox to include only those records with the State field entry KY in the ANSWER table.

Selection conditions are entered in the fields of query forms. The position of the selection condition in the query form tells Paradox which field you want to test. That is, when you enter a selection condition in the Last Name field of a table, Paradox will test the entries in the Last Name field of the table against that condition.

When you process a query that contains a selection condition, Paradox will compare the entries in the indicated field of the table you are querying to the entry in that field of the query form. If the entry from the table passes the test (that is, if it satisfies the condition), then the record will be a part of the ANSWER table. Otherwise, it will not be included in ANSWER.

There are many different types of selection conditions. You can create selection conditions for alphabetic, numeric, and date fields. These conditions will select a record that meets either of two or more tests, or the conditions will select a record only if it meets all of two or more conditions. You can even create selection conditions that will select a record that is similar to the condition.

Exact-match Conditions

Suppose you want to look at the records of all employees in EMPLYEE that have the entry *Jones* in the Last Name field. To begin, create a new, empty query form for EMPLYEE. Now, move the cursor to the space under the query form name and press **[Check Mark]** to select all the fields in the form.

Now you are ready to define the selection condition. To do this, move the cursor to the Last Name field and type the word **Jones**. Next, press **[Do-It!]** to create the ANSWER table shown in Figure 8-22. As you can see, since there are only three records in the EMPLYEE table that have the entry *Jones* in the Last Name field, the ANSWER table includes just three records. Since you selected every field in the query form, the ANSWER table includes all the fields from EMPLYEE.

Figure 8-22

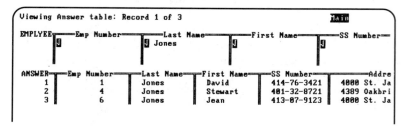

(By the way, are you surprised that Paradox copied the records for all three Joneses to the ANSWER table? Remember that records are duplicates only if they have the same entry in all selected fields. Since the Jones entries all have different first names, employee numbers, and so on, Paradox does not think of them as duplicates.)

Exact-match Condition Basics

All exact-match selection conditions work like this simple example. To select records that are exactly like a condition, just type the selection condition into that field of the query form. When you press [**Do-It!**], Paradox will compare the entries in that field of the table to the condition you entered in the query form. If the entry in the field matches the entry in the query form exactly, the entries from the appropriate fields of that record will be included in ANSWER. If not, Paradox will not include the record in ANSWER.

If it helps, you can use the following device to help you remember the meaning of exact-match selection conditions. When you enter the selection condition in a field, imagine that there is an equal sign between the field name and the condition. For example, you could think of the condition you just created in this way: *Last Name = Jones*. As you can see, this way of thinking about alphabetic selection conditions helps to make plain the meaning of the condition. This condition says: If the entry in the Last Name field of the table equals Jones, then the record will be selected. Otherwise, it will not be included in ANSWER.

In fact, you can include an equal sign in your exact-match conditions if you like. For example, the selection condition you just defined could have been entered as *=Jones*, as shown in Figure 8-23. To Paradox, this condition and the one in Figure 8-25 are identical. However, since including the equal sign in the condition forces you to type one extra character, and since the equal sign is not required, we suggest that you do not use it.

Figure 8-23

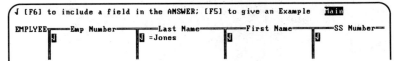

Exact-match conditions are extremely literal. If an entry in the indicated field is different from the condition in any way, the record will not be selected. The entry must even agree with the condition in capitalization. For example, if the Last Name field of one of the records in EMPLYEE contained the entry *jones, JONES, or JOnes*, it would not be selected by the selection condition Jones. Similarly, if you had defined the condition as *JONES*, none of the records in the table would have been selected.

If the selection conditions you define do not select any records, then the ANSWER table that Paradox creates will be empty. For example, suppose you create the query shown in Figure 8-24. The selection condition James in the Last Name field of the query tells Paradox to select all records that have the entry *James* in the Last Name field. Because there are no records in EMPLYEE with the Last Name field entry *James*, when you press this query, Paradox will create an empty ANSWER table if you process this query.

Figure 8-24

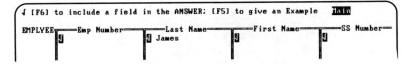

You can remove an exact-match condition from a field by moving the cursor to that field and pressing [Ctrl]-[Backspace]. For example, to remove the condition *James* from the Last Name field of the query form, move the cursor to the Last Name field and press **[Ctrl]-[Backspace]**.

Using Quotation Marks in Exact-match Conditions

Because commas have a special purpose in queries, if the exact-match condition you want to define refers to an entry that contains a comma, you'll need to enclose the condition in quotation marks. For example, suppose you want to extract the record for Sal Jakes, Jr., from EMPLYEE. To make this search, you would enter the condition **"Jakes, Jr."** (the quotation marks are required) in the Last Name field of the EMPLYEE query form. When you press **[Do-It!]** to process this query, Paradox will create the ANSWER table shown in Figure 8-25.

If you use a condition that includes a comma and do not enclose it in quotation marks, the query will not produce the desired result. You will learn more about why this happens in a few pages.

Figure 8-25

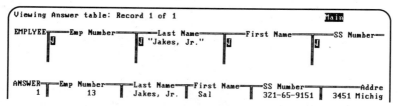

There is at least one other case in which you may need to use quotation marks in an exact-match condition. On rare occasions, you may have an entry in a table that looks to Paradox like the name of an operator. For example, you might have a record in EMPLYEE with the last name entry *Blank*. If you want to use that name as a condition, you would need to enclose it in quotation marks like this: "Blank".

If an entry in a table includes quotation marks, and you want to use that entry as a selection condition, you must precede the quotation marks in the condition with a backslash (\). For example, suppose one of the entries in the Last Name field of the EMPLYEE table is *"Hot Rocks" Ford*. If you want to create an exact-match selection condition to find this entry, it will look like this: *"Hot Rocks" Ford*.

Exact-match Conditions in Numeric Fields

Suppose you want to select all of the records for individuals that have the entry 0 in the Exemption field. To do this, first create a new, empty EMPLYEE query form and select all of the fields in the form. Next, move to the Exemptions field and type **0**. Now, press **[Do-It!]** to process the query. Figure 8-26 shows the query and the resulting ANSWER table. This table contains two records–Jean Jones and Ron Masters–both of which have the entry 0 in the Exemptions field.

Figure 8-26

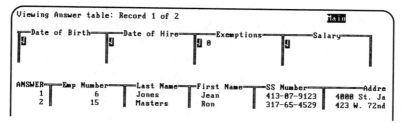

Exact-match Conditions in Dollar ($) Fields

Creating exact-match conditions for dollar ($) fields is no different than creating exact-match conditions for numeric fields. For example, suppose you want to see all of the records from EMPLYEE with the Salary field entry 32,000.00. To do this, first create a new, blank query form for EMPLYEE and select all of the fields in the form. Next, move to the Salary field and type **32000**. Now, press **[Do-It!]**. Figure 8-27 shows the result. Because there are only two records in the EMPLYEE table with the Salary field entry 32000. (the records for Julie Myers and Robert Garrison), this new ANSWER table includes only those two records.

Figure 8-27

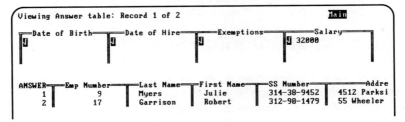

Exact-match Conditions in Date Fields

As you have probably guessed, you can also create exact-match conditions for date fields. For instance, suppose that you want to select those records in the EMPLYEE table that have the Date of Hire field entry 7/01/85. To do this, first create a new, blank EMPLYEE query form and select all of the fields in the form. Then move to the Date of Hire field and type the date **7/01/85** or **7/1/85** (you don't need to include the zero). Now press **[Do-It!]**. Figure 8-28 shows the query and resulting ANSWER table. As you can see, Paradox has included two records in the ANSWER table. If you look at the EMPLYEE table, you will see that these are the only two records that have the entry 7/01/85 in the Date of Hire field.

Figure 8-28

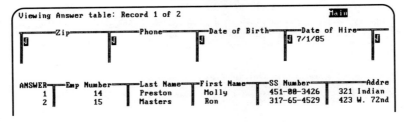

As you learned in Chapter 4, Paradox allows you to assign two different formats to dates: DD/MM/YY (the default) and DD-Mon-YY. Paradox recognizes exact-match conditions for date fields that are in either form. The form of the condition does not even need to match the form of the dates in the table you are querying. For instance, in the example, you could have used the condition 1-Jul-85 instead of 7/01/85 without changing the meaning of the condition.

A Note

Although you can create exact-match criteria for number, dollar, and date fields, you are not likely to do so very often. When you are working with these types of fields, you'll more often be interested in looking at groups of records–for instance, all the records with a number greater than 60 in the Age field or all the records with a value between 30,000 and 40,000 in the Salary field. We'll cover this type of search in an upcoming section.

Selection Conditions and Selecting Fields

You don't need to select every field in the query form if you intend to use selection conditions. You can use a condition even if you select only one or two fields. For example, suppose you only wanted to look at the First Name, Last Name, and Employee Number entries of all employees that have the entry *Jones* in the Last Name field.

To begin, create a new, empty EMPLYEE query form. Next, move to the Last Name field and make the entry **Jones**. Now, move to the Emp Number field, press **[Check Mark]**, then move to the First Name field, press **[Check Mark]** again, and finally move to the Last Name field and press **[Check Mark]** a third time.

When you press **[Do-It!]**, Paradox will create the ANSWER table in Figure 8-29. As before, the ANSWER table includes only the three records that have the entry *Jones* in the Last Name field. And this time, since you only selected the Emp Number, Last Name, and First Name fields in the query form, the ANSWER table includes only those three fields.

Figure 8-29

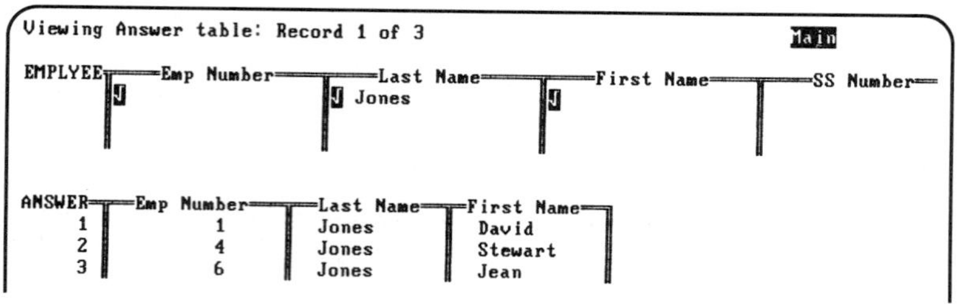

```
Viewing Answer table: Record 1 of 3                              Main
 EMPLYEE┬──Emp Number──────┬──Last Name──────┬──First Name──────┬──SS Number──
        │√                 │√ Jones          │√                 │


 ANSWER─┬──Emp Number──────┬──Last Name──────┬──First Name──────
     1  │        1         │  Jones          │  David
     2  │        4         │  Jones          │  Stewart
     3  │        6         │  Jones          │  Jean
```

Not Selecting the Condition Field

As you can see, you don't need to select every field in the query form when you use a selection condition. In fact, you don't even need to select the field that contains the selection condition. For example, suppose you want to create an ANSWER table that contains just two fields–Employee Number and First Name–and that includes only those records with the last name Jones.

To create this query, move the cursor back to the EMPLYEE query form and then move it into the Last Name field. Now, press **[Check Mark]** to deselect the field. Figure 8-30 shows the query form at this point (notice that the First Name and Address fields are still selected). As you can see, deselecting the Last Name field did not affect the condition in that field.

Figure 8-30

Now press **[Do-It!]** to process the query. Figure 8-31 shows the resulting ANSWER table. Notice that Paradox has included just those records that have the entry *Jones* in the Last Name field in the ANSWER table, even though the Last Name field itself was not selected and is not included in ANSWER.

Figure 8-31

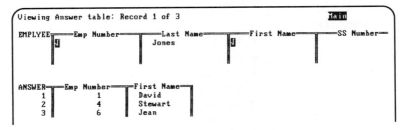

Selecting Duplicate Records

If you want the ANSWER table to include duplicate records, you must use a check plus to select at least one of the fields in the query form. For example, suppose you want to extract the last name and address for all of the individuals in the table with the Last Name entry *Jones*. To create a query that will do the trick, first create a new, empty EMPLYEE query form. Next, use the **[Check Plus]** key to select the Last Name field and either **[Check Mark]** or **[Check Plus]** to select the Address fields. Then, enter the exact-match condition **Jones** in the Last Name field.

When you process this query, Paradox will create the ANSWER table that is shown in Figure 8-32. Notice that this table includes three records, two of which are identical. These duplicate records are included in ANSWER because we used a check plus to select the Last Name field.

Figure 8-32

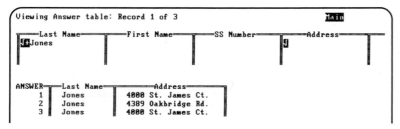

Patterns

Like most other data base programs, Paradox offers special operators, called wildcards, that can be used in place of other characters in selection conditions. Because wildcard operators match any character, you can use them when you need to create one condition to select records that are alike in some regards and different in others. In Paradox, conditions that contain wildcards are called patterns. Paradox offers two different wildcard operators: .. and @.

The .. Operator

The .. operator, which is sometimes called the series wildcard operator, can be used to represent a series of any number of characters in a condition. For example, the condition Rob.. would match any entry that began with the letters *Rob*, including *Rob, Robert, Roberts, Robertson, Roberson, Robbie,* and so on.

You can enter this operator in a condition just by typing two periods. For example, to enter the condition Rob.. in a query form, you would type the letters **Rob** and then type two periods.

Let's use the condition Rob.. in an EMPLYEE query. To begin, create a new, blank query form for the EMPLYEE table and select every field in the form. Next, move to the Last Name field and type **Rob...** Now press **[Do-It!]** to process the query. Figure 8-33 shows the query and the resulting ANSWER table. Notice that this table contains two records–one for Darlene *Rob*erts, and one for Kevin *Rob*ertson–both of which begin with the characters *Rob*.

Figure 8-33

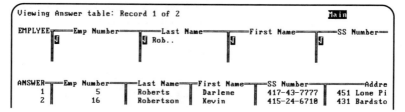

You can use the .. wildcard at any position in a condition. For example, the condition ..n would match any entry that ends with an *n*. If you entered the condition ..n in the Last Name field of the EMPLYEE query form, the resulting ANSWER table would include the records for Herb Camero*n*, Mary Jackso*n*, Molly Presto*n*, Kevin Robertso*n*, Robert Garriso*n*, Barbara Gun*n,* and Cheryl Emerso*n*–all of which end with an *n*.

Similarly, the condition G..n will match any entry that begins with a *G* and ends with an *n*. For example, if you entered the condition G..n in the Last Name field of the EMPLYEE query form, the resulting ANSWER table would include the records for Robert *G*arriso*n* and Barbara *G*un*n*.

Interestingly, capitalization does not count when you use wildcards. For instance, Paradox would consider the conditions g..n, G..N, and g..N to be the same as G..n. Any of these conditions would select the same two records from EMPLYEE.

Furthermore, you can use the .. operator more than once in a single condition. For example, the condition G..r..n will select any record that begins with a *g*, has an *r* somewhere in the middle, and ends with an *n*. This condition would select the record for Robert *G*a*r*riso*n* from the EMPLYEE table.

The @ Operator

The second wildcard operator, @, can be used to match any single character in a condition. Unlike the .. operator, which can stand for a series of characters of any length, the @ operator takes the place of only a single character. For example, the condition M@sters would match the entries *Masters, Misters, Mosters, Musters,* or any other entry that begins with *M*, ends with *sters*, and has one character in between. Similarly, the condition J@@@@ matches the entries *Jones, Johns, Jakes,* or any entry that begins with the letter *J* and includes any four other characters.

It is important that you understand that the condition J@@@@ would not match the entries *Job, Jackson,* or *Jehoshaphat,* even though the condition J.. would. The @ operator represents only a single character. Each @ operator that you include in a condition can match only one character in an entry. If a condition contains four @ operators, then those four operators represent exactly four characters–no more and no less.

You can enter this operator in a condition just by typing the character @ ([Shift]-2). For example, to enter the condition M@sters in a query form, you would type the letter **M**, then the symbol **@**, then the characters **sters**.

If you enter the condition **J@@@@** in the Last Name field of an EMPLYEE query form and press **[Do-It!]**, Paradox will create the ANSWER table shown in Figure 8-34. As you can see, this table contains three records: David *J*ones, Stewart *J*ones, and Jean *J*ones–all of whose last names are made up of a *J* followed by four characters. You will notice, however, that the record for Mary Jackson is not included in ANSWER since there are more than four letters following the *J* in her last name.

Figure 8-34

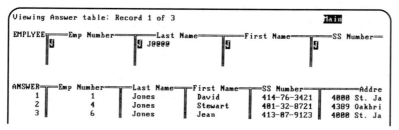

As with the .. operator, capitalization does not count when you use the @ operator. In addition, you can use the @ operator more than once in a single pattern and at any position in a pattern. You can even use the @ operator as the first or last character in a pattern. However, remember that the @ operator does not match noncharacters. For a match to occur, there must be a letter in the entry being matched for every @ operator in the pattern. For example, the pattern J@@@@ would match the names *Jones* and *Jakes*, but not the entry *Jobs*, since there are only three letters following the *J* in *Jobs* but four @ operators in the pattern.

If you need to include an @ symbol in a pattern, but don't want Paradox to regard the character as a wildcard operator, you'll need to enclose it in quotation marks. For example, suppose that you have created a table with a field named *Code*. The Code field contains these entries:

@13451
#17643
@17690
&12340
@14169

You want to select only the records with Code field entries that begin with an @ symbol. To do this, you would need to enter the pattern

"@"..

in the Code field of the query form. If you did not enclose the @ symbol in quotes, Paradox would consider it to be a wildcard character and would select all five records.

Wildcards and Numeric Fields

Unlike most data base programs, Paradox allows you to use wildcards in numeric and dollar field conditions. For example, the pattern 3.. would match the numbers 30, 35, 300, 350, 366, 3000, 3300033, and any other numbers that began with the digit 3.

For example, Figure 3-35 shows a query and the ANSWER table that Paradox created when we processed that query. Notice the selection condition pattern 3.. in the Salary field of this query. As you can see, the ANSWER table includes all of the records for employees with an income that begins with a 3.

Figure 8-35

```
Viewing Answer table: Record 1 of 7                                  Main
  ┌─Date of Birth─┬─Date of Hire─┬─Exemptions─┬─Salary─
  │               │              │            │ 3..
  │               │              │            │

  ANSWER─┬─Emp Number─┬─Last Name──┬─First Name─┬─SS Number──┬─Addre
     1   │     6      │  Jones     │  Jean      │ 413-87-9123│ 4000 St. Ja
     2   │     9      │  Myers     │  Julie     │ 314-38-9452│ 4512 Parksi
     3   │    10      │  Link      │  Julie     │ 345-75-1525│ 3215 Palm C
     4   │    13      │  Jakes, Jr.│  Sal       │ 321-65-9151│ 3451 Michig
     5   │    15      │  Masters   │  Ron       │ 317-65-4529│ 423 W. 72nd
     6   │    16      │  Robertson │  Kevin     │ 415-24-6710│ 431 Bardsto
     7   │    17      │  Garrison  │  Robert    │ 312-98-1479│ 55 Wheeler
```

You can also use the @ wildcard operator in numeric fields. For example, suppose you wanted to select all of the employees that have salaries that begin with a 3, followed by any four digits, a decimal, and any two digits. You could do this by entering the pattern 3@@@@.@@ in the Salary field of the EMPLYEE query form.

Wildcards and Date Fields

Paradox also allows you to use wildcards in conditions that you create for date fields. For instance, the pattern 7/../85 would match the entries 7/01/85, 7/10/85, 7/14/85, and 7/22/85, and any other date entries that have 7 in the month position and also have 85 in the year position.

For example, suppose you enter the pattern 7/../85 in the Date of Hire field of an EMPLYEE table query form. When you process this query, Paradox will create the ANSWER table shown in Figure 8-36. Notice that this table includes the records for the three employees who were hired in July, 1985: Molly Preston, Ron Masters, and Kevin Robertson. The same result would be achieved by the pattern 7/@@/85.

Figure 8-36

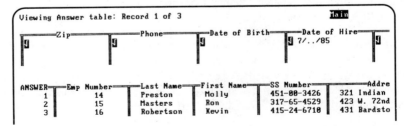

When you use wildcard operators in date fields, the pattern you define must be in the same form as the entries in the selected field of the table. If the entries are in the MM/DD/YY form, the pattern must also be in that form. If the entries are in the DD-Mon-YY form, the pattern must also be in that form. If the pattern is in a different form than the entries, the query will not select any records. For instance, if you entered the pattern ..-Jul-85 in the Date of Hire field and pressed [Do-It!], Paradox would create an empty ANSWER table. Likewise, the same thing would happen if you entered the pattern 15-J@@-85 in the query form. If the pattern has a different form than the entries, then the pattern will not match any records.

Selecting Ranges of Records

Frequently you will want to select records that have entries that fall within a certain range. This is particularly true when you are selecting records based on the entries in numeric, dollar, or date fields. For example, you might want to locate all of the entries with a Salary field entry that is greater than 30,000, or all of the records with a Date of Hire field entry that is less than (before) July 1, 1985.

Paradox includes a set of operators, called range operators, that allow you to create this kind of query. Table 8-1 shows the five range operators. These operators allow you to create conditions that will match entries that are greater than, less than, greater than or equal to, less than or equal to, or not equal to a stated value. Let's look at how they work.

Table 8-1   Range Operators

Operator	Meaning
>	Greater Than
<	Less Than
>=	Greater Than or Equal To
<=	Less Than or Equal To

Greater Than (>)

Suppose you want to select all records that have an entry greater than 30,000 in the Salary field. To do this, you would select all of the fields in an empty EMPLYEE query form, move to the Salary field, and enter the condition **>30000**. When you press **[Do-It!]** to process the query, Paradox will create the ANSWER table shown in Figure 8-37. Notice that this table includes every entry from the EMPLYEE table that has an entry greater than 30,000 in the Salary field.

Notice, however, that the ANSWER table does not include the record for Julie Link, whose salary is exactly $30,000. When you use the greater than range operator (>) in a condition, Paradox will select only those records with entries in the indicated field that are greater than the value specified in the condition. If an entry in the indicated field is equal to the value specified by the condition, that record will not be selected.

Figure 8-37

```
Viewing Answer table: Record 1 of 10                              Main
┌─Date of Birth─┬─Date of Hire─┬─Exemptions─┬─Salary──────────
│               │              │            │ >30000
│               │              │            │

┌ANSWER─┬─Emp Number─┬─Last Name─┬─First Name─┬─SS Number──┬──────Addre
│   1   │     1      │ Jones     │ David      │ 414-76-3421│ 4000 St. Ja
│   2   │     2      │ Cameron   │ Herb       │ 321-65-8765│ 2321 Elm St
│   3   │     4      │ Jones     │ Stewart    │ 401-32-8721│ 4389 Oakbri
│   4   │     6      │ Jones     │ Jean       │ 413-07-9123│ 4000 St. Ja
│   5   │     8      │ Williams  │ Brenda     │ 401-55-1567│ 100 Owl Cre
│   6   │     9      │ Myers     │ Julie      │ 314-38-9452│ 4512 Parksi
│   7   │    13      │ Jakes, Jr.│ Sal        │ 321-65-9151│ 3451 Michig
│   8   │    15      │ Masters   │ Ron        │ 317-65-4529│ 423 W. 72nd
│   9   │    16      │ Robertson │ Kevin      │ 415-24-6710│ 431 Bardsto
```

Greater Than or Equal To (>=)

If you want to select all of the records with entries that are greater than or equal to a stated value, you should use the greater than or equal to operator (>=). For example, Figure 8-38 shows a query on the EMPLYEE table that will select every record with a Salary field entry that is greater than or equal to 30,000, and the ANSWER table that Paradox will create when you process this query. Notice that the record for Julie Link is included in this new ANSWER table.

Figure 8-38

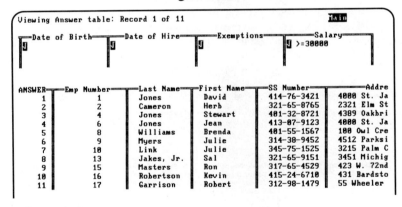

Less Than (<)

To select all of the records with an entry that is less than a given value, you'll need to use the less than operator (<). For example, suppose you want to select all of the records that have a Salary field entry less than 50,000. To make this selection, replace the entry in the Salary field of the EMPLYEE query form with the entry <50000. Notice the entry **<50000** in the Salary field. When you press **[Do-It!]** to process this query, Paradox will create the ANSWER table shown in Figure 8-39. As you can see, this table includes all of the records from EMPLYEE with Salary field entries less than 50,000.

Figure 8-39

```
Viewing Answer table: Record 1 of 14                    Main
┌─Date of Birth──┬─Date of Hire─┬─Exemptions─┬─Salary────
│ 9              │ 9            │ 9          │ 9  <50000

ANSWER──┬─Emp Number─┬─Last Name──┬─First Name─┬─SS Number──┬────────Addre
  1     │    4       │ Jones      │ Stewart    │ 401-32-8721│ 4389 Oakbri
  2     │    5       │ Roberts    │ Darlene    │ 417-43-7777│ 451 Lone Pi
  3     │    6       │ Jones      │ Jean       │ 413-07-9123│ 4000 St. Ja
  4     │    8       │ Williams   │ Brenda     │ 401-55-1567│ 100 Owl Cre
  5     │    9       │ Myers      │ Julie      │ 314-38-9452│ 4512 Parksi
  6     │   10       │ Link       │ Julie      │ 345-75-1525│ 3215 Palm C
  7     │   12       │ Jackson    │ Mary       │ 424-13-7621│ 7821 Clark
  8     │   13       │ Jakes, Jr. │ Sal        │ 321-65-9151│ 3451 Michig
  9     │   14       │ Preston    │ Molly      │ 451-00-3426│ 321 Indian
 10     │   15       │ Masters    │ Ron        │ 317-65-4529│ 423 W. 72nd
 11     │   16       │ Robertson  │ Kevin      │ 415-24-6710│ 431 Bardsto
 12     │   17       │ Garrison   │ Robert     │ 312-90-1479│ 55 Wheeler
 13     │   19       │ Gunn       │ Barbara    │ 321-97-8632│ 541 Kentuck
 14     │   20       │ Emerson    │ Cheryl     │ 404-14-1422│ 8100 River
```

Less Than or Equal To (<=)

If you want to select every record with an entry that is less than or equal to a given value, you'll need to use the less than or equal to operator (<=). For example, suppose you want to select every record that has a Salary field entry less than or equal to 50,000. Figure 8-40 shows a query that will make this selection and the ANSWER table that Paradox will produce when you process the query. As you can see, this table is similar to the ANSWER table created by the previous query, except that it includes the record for Herb Cameron, whose salary is exactly 50,000.

Figure 8-40

```
Viewing Answer table: Record 1 of 15                    Main
┌─Date of Birth──┬─Date of Hire─┬─Exemptions─┬─Salary─────
│ 9              │ 9            │ 9          │ 9  <=50000

ANSWER──┬─Emp Number─┬─Last Name──┬─First Name─┬─SS Number──┬────────Addre
  1     │    2       │ Cameron    │ Herb       │ 321-65-8765│ 2321 Elm St
  2     │    4       │ Jones      │ Stewart    │ 401-32-8721│ 4389 Oakbri
  3     │    5       │ Roberts    │ Darlene    │ 417-43-7777│ 451 Lone Pi
  4     │    6       │ Jones      │ Jean       │ 413-07-9123│ 4000 St. Ja
  5     │    8       │ Williams   │ Brenda     │ 401-55-1567│ 100 Owl Cre
  6     │    9       │ Myers      │ Julie      │ 314-38-9452│ 4512 Parksi
  7     │   10       │ Link       │ Julie      │ 345-75-1525│ 3215 Palm C
  8     │   12       │ Jackson    │ Mary       │ 424-13-7621│ 7821 Clark
  9     │   13       │ Jakes, Jr. │ Sal        │ 321-65-9151│ 3451 Michig
 10     │   14       │ Preston    │ Molly      │ 451-00-3426│ 321 Indian
 11     │   15       │ Masters    │ Ron        │ 317-65-4529│ 423 W. 72nd
 12     │   16       │ Robertson  │ Kevin      │ 415-24-6710│ 431 Bardsto
 13     │   17       │ Garrison   │ Robert     │ 312-90-1479│ 55 Wheeler
 14     │   19       │ Gunn       │ Barbara    │ 321-97-8632│ 541 Kentuck
 15     │   20       │ Emerson    │ Cheryl     │ 404-14-1422│ 8100 River
```

Using Range Operators in Date Fields

Now suppose that you want to select all of those records with a Date of Hire field entry that is less than 7/01/85 (July 1, 1985). To do this, enter the condition **<7/1/85** in the Date of Hire field of an EMPLYEE query form. Now, when you press **[Do-It!]** to process the query, Paradox will create the ANSWER table shown in Figure 8-41. As you can see, this table contains every record with a Date of Hire field entry that is "less than" 7/01/85.

Figure 8-41

```
Viewing Answer table: Record 1 of 10                                Main
    ┌─Zip─────┬─Phone──────┬─Date of Birth──┬─Date of Hire──┬
    │         │            │                │ <7/1/85       │

ANSWER─┬─Emp Number─┬─Last Name──┬─First Name──┬─SS Number──┬──────Addre
   1   │     1      │ Jones      │ David       │ 414-76-3421│ 4000 St. Ja
   2   │     2      │ Cameron    │ Herb        │ 321-65-8765│ 2321 Elm St
   3   │     4      │ Jones      │ Stewart     │ 401-32-8721│ 4389 Oakbri
   4   │     5      │ Roberts    │ Darlene     │ 417-43-7777│ 451 Lone Pi
   5   │     6      │ Jones      │ Jean        │ 413-07-9123│ 4000 St. Ja
   6   │     8      │ Williams   │ Brenda      │ 401-55-1567│ 100 Owl Cre
   7   │     9      │ Myers      │ Julie       │ 314-38-9452│ 4512 Parksi
   8   │    10      │ Link       │ Julie       │ 345-75-1525│ 3215 Palm C
   9   │    12      │ Jackson    │ Mary        │ 424-13-7621│ 7821 Clark
  10   │    13      │ Jakes, Jr. │ Sal         │ 321-65-9151│ 3451 Michig
```

Notice that, when used in a date field, the less than operator (<) matches entries that are before the date specified by the condition. That is, the condition <1/01/85 selects dates that are before January 1, 1985. Similarly, when you use the greater than operator (>) in a date field condition, the condition matches entries that come after the specified date. For instance, the condition >1/01/85 selects dates that are after January 1, 1985.

You can also use the <=, >=, and <> operators in date fields. When you use range operators in date field conditions, you can specify the date in either the MM/DD/YY or the DD-Mon-YY form. For example, the conditions >7/01/85 and >1-Jul-85 are identical to Paradox. Either condition will match all the entries in the indicated field that are greater than July 1, 1985.

Using Range Operators in Alphanumeric Fields

Paradox also allows you to use range operators in alphanumeric fields. When used in alphabetic fields, range operators match entries that have an ASCII character code that is less than or greater than the code for a specified entry. In the ASCII system, numerals like 1, 2, and 3 have code values "less than" upper-case letters like *A, B,* and *C.* Lower-case letters, like *a, b,* and *c,* come after upper-case letters. The > operator selects entries that have an ASCII value that is greater than the word or phrase specified by the condition. Similarly, the < operator selects entries that have an ASCII value that is less than the specified word or phrase.

Range Operators and Patterns

You cannot use any of Paradox's range operators with patterns. In most cases, it just doesn't make sense to use a range operator with a pattern. For example, what does the condition >@Smith mean? Since the @ wildcard can stand for any character, this condition could select any entry. Similarly, the condition <=1.. is meaningless since the expression 1.. could represent any number from 1 to infinity. If you try to process a query that contains conditions like these, Paradox will display the message *Expression makes no sense*.

The Like Operator

There will be times in your work with Paradox when you'll want to use a condition to select records, but you won't remember the exact spelling or capitalization of the entry you want to match. This is especially true when you are working with larger tables. As we have said, normally Paradox will not select records unless they match the selection condition exactly, so not knowing the exact form of the entry you want to match could be a real problem.

Fortunately, Paradox includes a special operator, called like, that lets you select records that are only similar to, and not exact duplicates of, the selection condition you specify. This unique tool makes it possible to find information in your tables even when you are not sure of the spelling, capitalization, or other characteristics of the entry for which you are looking.

An Example

For example, suppose you want to look at the record for the employee named Myers, but you can't remember whether the name is spelled *Meyers, Miers,* or *Myers*. Instead of guessing, you could create a like condition. To do this, first create a new, blank query form for EMPLYEE and select every field in the form. Next, move to the Last Name field and enter the phrase **like Meyers**. Figure 8-42 shows the completed query.

Figure 8-42

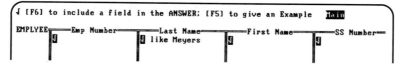

When you press **[Do-It!]**, Paradox will create the ANSWER table shown in Figure 8-43. As you can see, the table includes the record for Julie Myers. Thanks to the like operator, we were able to locate this record, even though we didn't know the exact spelling of her name.

Figure 8-43

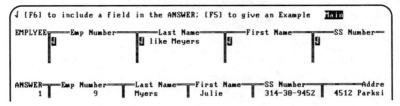

You will probably find yourself using the like operator most often when you have failed to locate a record using a conventional exact-match query. For example, suppose you have just tried to locate the record for Julie Myers, using the selection condition Meyers. The result was an empty ANSWER table. Rather than continuing to try to match the name exactly, at this point you would be better off to use a like condition to try to find the entry.

Like Rules

Like is a very powerful tool, but it does have a few restrictions. The condition that you use with like must begin with the same letter as the entry for which you are searching. In other words, the condition **like Byers** would not select the record for Julie Myers. In addition, the condition you use with like must bear some resemblance to the entry for which you are searching. For example, the condition **like Myth** would not select the record for Julie Myers, even though the word *Myth* begins with the letters *My*.

Perhaps these two restrictions are best summarized by saying that you should use like when you can make a good, but not perfect, guess at the correct spelling of the entry for which you are looking. If you're just guessing wildly, the like condition probably won't be much help.

The like operator ignores case. For example, the selection condition **like MEYERS** would select the entry for Julie Myers. This means that you can use like to locate entries when you are not sure if the entries are in upper or lower case.

Of course, if the condition you use with like matches an entry in the table exactly, the record will be selected. For example, the selection condition **like Myers** would select the entry for Julie Myers.

The Not Operator

The not operator allows you to select entries that are not equal to some specified number or string or characters. For example, suppose you want to select every record in the EMPLOYEE table except for those with the entry *Jones* in the Last Name field. To make this selection, create a new, blank query form for EMPLOYEE and select every field in that form. Next, enter the condition **not Jones** in the Last Name field of the EMPLOYEE query form. When you press **[Do-It!]** to process this query, Paradox will create the ANSWER table shown in Figure 8-44. As you can see, this table includes every record from EMPLYEE, except for those with the Last Name field entry *Jones*.

Figure 8-44

```
Viewing Answer table: Record 1 of 13                    Main
  EMPLYEE  ─Emp Number─   ─Last Name─    ─First Name─   ─SS Number─
           |              | not Jones    |              |

ANSWER  ─Emp Number─  ─Last Name─   ─First Name─  ─SS Number─      ─Addre
   1           2      Cameron       Herb          321-65-8765      2321 Elm St
   2           5      Roberts       Darlene       417-43-7777      451 Lone Pi
   3           8      Williams      Brenda        401-55-1567      100 Owl Cre
   4           9      Myers         Julie         314-38-9452      4512 Parksi
   5          10      Link          Julie         345-75-1525      3215 Palm C
   6          12      Jackson       Mary          424-13-7621      7821 Clark
   7          13      Jakes, Jr.    Sal           321-65-9151      3451 Michig
   8          14      Preston       Molly         451-00-3426      321 Indian
   9          15      Masters       Ron           317-65-4529      423 W. 72nd
  10          16      Robertson     Kevin         415-24-6710      431 Bardsto
  11          17      Garrison      Robert        312-98-1479      55 Wheeler
  12          19      Gunn          Barbara       321-97-8632      541 Kentuck
  13          20      Emerson       Cheryl        404-14-1422      8100 River
```

You can use the not operator with wildcard and range operators, if you wish. For example, the Date of Hire field in the query form in Figure 8-45 contains the condition not ../../84. As you can see, when you process this query, Paradox will select all of the records that do not have a 1984 date entry in the Date of Hire field. Similarly, the condition not R.. in the Last Name field of the query in Figure 8-46 will cause Paradox to select all records that do not begin with an *R*. If you enter the condition **not >30000** in the Salary field of an EMPLYEE query form, as shown in Figure 8-47, Paradox will select all records that have a Salary field entry that is not greater than $30,000. (Of course, you could also state the condition as <=30000, which is probably simpler.)

Figure 8-45

```
Viewing Answer table: Record 1 of 11                    Main
  ─Zip─       ─Phone─       ─Date of Birth─   ─Date of Hire─
  |           |             |                 | not ../../84 |

ANSWER  ─Emp Number─  ─Last Name─   ─First Name─  ─SS Number─      ─Addre
   1           8      Williams      Brenda        401-55-1567      100 Owl Cre
   2           9      Myers         Julie         314-38-9452      4512 Parksi
   3          10      Link          Julie         345-75-1525      3215 Palm C
   4          12      Jackson       Mary          424-13-7621      7821 Clark
   5          13      Jakes, Jr.    Sal           321-65-9151      3451 Michig
   6          14      Preston       Molly         451-00-3426      321 Indian
   7          15      Masters       Ron           317-65-4529      423 W. 72nd
   8          16      Robertson     Kevin         415-24-6710      431 Bardsto
   9          17      Garrison      Robert        312-98-1479      55 Wheeler
  10          19      Gunn          Barbara       321-97-8632      541 Kentuck
  11          20      Emerson       Cheryl        404-14-1422      8100 River
```

Figure 8-46

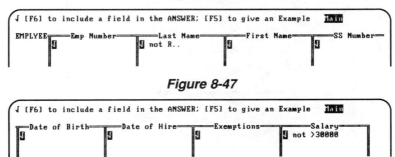

Figure 8-47

The Blank Operator

The blank operator allows you to select records that do not have entries in a specified field. This useful operator allows you to identify the records in a table that is missing certain information.

To demonstrate this operator, we'll use the PROJECTS table. Figure 8-48 shows the structure of PROJECTS, and Figure 8-49 on page 228 shows the data we've entered into the table. Notice that only some records have entries in the Actual Completion Date field. Those records with entries in this field are complete; the others are still in progress.

Figure 8-48

Suppose that you want to look at those records that do not have an entry in the Actual Completion Date field. To make this selection, first use the **[Menu]** **A**sk command to create a new query form for PROJECTS, then press **[Check Mark]** while the cursor is under the query form name to select every field in the form. Next, move to the Actual Completion Date field and type the word **blank**.

Now, press **[Do-It!]** to process the query. Figure 8-50 on page 229 shows the resulting ANSWER table. As you can see, Paradox has included only those records with blank Actual Completion Date fields in ANSWER.

You can also use the blank operator with the not operator to select all records except those with a blank in the selected field. For example, suppose you now want to look at all of the records in PROJECTS that do contain an entry (in other words, the projects that are completed). To do this, you could replace the entry in the Actual Completion Date

Figure 8-49

PROJECTS	Job Number	Client Number	Job Type	Description	Manager	Estimated Completion Date	Actual Completion Date
1	100	1001	1	Install PC AT/Paradox/1-2-3	1	3/01/86	4/11/86
2	101	1001	3	AT/Paradox/1-2-3 Intro	1	5/01/86	
3	102	1002	2	Paradox A/R System	1	6/01/86	
4	103	1003	1	Install Compaq Plus/Symphony	1	11/01/86	
5	104	1003	2	Symphony Intro Course	4	2/21/86	2/15/86
6	105	1003	4	Recommend AR System	4	3/21/86	
7	106	1004	2	Paradox Time Accounting System	1	9/01/85	9/01/85
8	107	1004	3	1986 Compilation/Review	8	3/15/85	
9	108	1005	3	1986 Compilation/Review	8	10/15/85	10/15/85
10	109	1006	3	1986 Compilation/Review	8	9/15/85	9/15/85
11	110	1007	5	Tax Consultation		11/15/85	11/15/85
12	111	1008	2	1986 Tax Return		12/15/85	12/22/85
13	112	1009	2	1986 Tax Return	16	1/15/86	
14	113	1010	1	1986 Audit	16	2/15/86	
15	114	1010	3	1986 Compilation/Review	1	3/15/86	
16	115	1011	6	Assist with Loan Applicat	4	9/30/85	11/30/85

Figure 8-50

```
Viewing Answer table: Record 1 of 8                          Main
    ┌─Manager──────┬─Estimated Completion Date┬Actual Completion Date┐
    │9             │9                         │9 blank               │
    │              │                          │                      │


ANSWER─┬─Job Number─┬─Client Number─┬─Job Type─┬─────────Description═
   1   │   101      │   1001        │   3      │ AT/Paradox/1-2-3 Intro
   2   │   102      │   1002        │   2      │ Paradox A/R System
   3   │   103      │   1003        │   1      │ Install Compaq Plus/Sy
   4   │   105      │   1003        │   4      │ Recommend AR System
   5   │   107      │   1004        │   3      │ 1986 Compilation/Revie
   6   │   112      │   1009        │   2      │ 1986 Tax Return
   7   │   113      │   1010        │   1      │ 1986 Audit
   8   │   114      │   1010        │   3      │ 1986 Compilation/Revie
```

field of the query form in Figure 8-50 with the entry **not blank**. Figure 8-51 shows the completed query. When you press **[Do-It!]**, Paradox will create the ANSWER table shown in Figure 8-51.

Figure 8-51

```
Viewing Answer table: Record 1 of 8                          Main
    ┌─Manager──────┬─Estimated Completion Date┬Actual Completion Date┐
    │9             │9                         │9 not blank           │


ANSWER─┬─Job Number─┬─Client Number─┬─Job Type─┬─────────Description═
   1   │   100      │   1001        │   1      │ Install PC AT/Paradox/
   2   │   104      │   1003        │   2      │ Symphony Intro Course
   3   │   106      │   1004        │   2      │ Paradox Time Accountin
   4   │   108      │   1005        │   3      │ 1986 Compilation/Revie
   5   │   109      │   1006        │   3      │ 1986 Compilation/Revie
   6   │   110      │   1007        │   5      │ Tax Consultation
   7   │   111      │   1008        │   2      │ 1986 Tax Return
   8   │   115      │   1011        │   6      │ Assist with Loan Appli
```

As you might expect, you can use the blank operator in any type of field. For example, suppose you want to determine whether or not there are any projects in PROJECTS that have not been assigned a manager (in other words, whether there are any records with a blank in the Manager field). To make this selection, erase the condition in the Actual Completion Date field and enter the condition **blank** in the Manager field.

Be sure that you understand the difference between entering the blank operator in a field of a query form and leaving that field of the query form blank. Entering the blank operator in a field tells Paradox to select only those records from the table being queried that have a blank in that field. Leaving the field blank, however, does not create a selection condition. When you leave a field in a query form blank (that is, when you do not enter a selection condition in the field), Paradox will not use that field as a basis for selecting records. In other words, leaving a field in a query form blank tells Paradox that you don't care what is in the field.

The Today Operator

The today operator allows you to enter the current date into a query form as a condition with a minimum of effort. The today operator always stands for the current date and is always used in a date-type field. Let's look at how this operator works.

We'll use the PROJECTS table to demonstrate this function. Suppose that today is February 1, 1986. You want to look at all of the records from PROJECTS that have an Estimated Completion Date field entry that is less than today's date. In other words, you want to look at all of the projects that should be finished.

To begin, create a new, empty query form for PROJECTS and select every field in the form. Next, move to the Estimated Completion Date field and make the entry **<Today**. Assuming that today is really February 1, 1986, when you process this query, Paradox will create the ANSWER table shown in Figure 8-52. As you can see, this table includes only those records with estimated completion dates less than February 1, 1986. Of course, the results you get will depend upon the day on which you perform the query.

Figure 8-52

```
√ [F6] to include a field in the ANSWER; [F5] to give an Example   Main
┌─Description──────┬─Manager──────┬─Estimated Completion Date─┬─Actual Completi
│ √                │ √            │ √ <Today                  │ √

ANSWER─┬─Job Number─┬─Client Number─┬─Job Type─┬──────Description═
   1   │    106     │     1004      │    2     │ Paradox Time Accountin
   2   │    107     │     1004      │    3     │ 1986 Compilation/Revie
   3   │    108     │     1005      │    3     │ 1986 Compilation/Revie
   4   │    109     │     1006      │    3     │ 1986 Compilation/Revie
   5   │    110     │     1007      │    5     │ Tax Consultation
   6   │    111     │     1008      │    2     │ 1986 Tax Return
   7   │    112     │     1009      │    2     │ 1986 Tax Return
   8   │    115     │     1011      │    6     │ Assist with Loan Appli
```

Paradox derives the value of today from the system clock of your computer. If the system clock date isn't accurate, then the today operator will not be accurate. You can change the system clock date by issuing the DOS Date command when you're at the system level.

Today can also be used as a base date in a mathematical selection condition. For example, suppose that your company has a policy of placing new employees on probation for 90 days after their date of hire, and that today is February 1, 1986. Also suppose that you want to select the records for all employees that are still in the probationary period.

To make this selection, first clear the PROJECTS query form and then create a new, blank query form for EMPLYEE. When the new form appears, select every field in the form, then move to the Date of Hire field and enter the condition **>Today-90**. Now press **[Do-It!]** to process the query. Figure 8-53 shows the resulting ANSWER table.

Figure 8-53

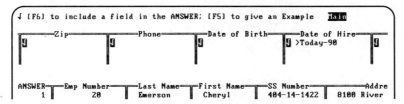

Logical ANDS and ORS

So far, we have considered only queries that select records that meet a single conditional test. In addition to these simple queries, however, Paradox also allows you to create queries that select records that meet all or one of several different conditions. When you want to select records that meet all of several conditions, you should create an AND query. When you want to select records that meet one or more of several conditions, you should create an OR query.

OR Queries

To create an OR query, you just select fields and enter selection conditions on more than one row of the query form. For instance, suppose you want to select the records from the EMPLYEE table that have either the entry KY or the entry IN in the State field. To do this, first create a blank query form for the EMPLYEE table. Next, press **[Check Mark]** while the cursor is in the space under the query form name EMPLYEE to select every field in the form. Then move to the State field in this query form and type **KY**. Figure 8-54 shows the query form at this point. If you pressed **[Do-It!]** at this point, Paradox would select all of the records with the State field entry KY.

Figure 8-54

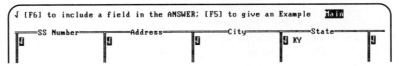

Next, press the ↓ key to move down one row and type **IN** in the second row of the State field. Then move to the far-left of the second row and press **[Check Mark]** to select every field in this second row of the query. Figure 8-55 shows the completed query.

Figure 8-55

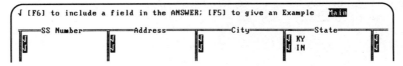

Now press **[Do-It!]** to process the query. Figure 8-56 shows the resulting ANSWER table. As you can see, Paradox has selected all of the records from the EMPLYEE table that have the entry KY or the entry IN in the State field. In effect, Paradox has joined the two conditions with a logical OR so that the query can be translated into English like this: *Select every field of every record with the State field entry KY or the State field entry IN.*

Figure 8-56

```
Viewing Answer table: Record 1 of 12                            Main
 ┌─SS Number─┐ ┌─Address─┐ ┌─City─┐ ┌─State─┐
 │           │ │         │ │      │ │ KY    │
 │           │ │         │ │      │ │ IN    │

ANSWER┬─Emp Number─┬─Last Name─┬─First Name─┬─SS Number──┬─Addre
  1   │     1      │  Jones    │  David     │ 414-76-3421│ 4000 St. Ja
  2   │     2      │  Cameron  │  Herb      │ 321-65-8765│ 2321 Elm St
  3   │     4      │  Jones    │  Stewart   │ 401-32-8721│ 4389 Oakbri
  4   │     5      │  Roberts  │  Darlene   │ 417-43-7777│ 451 Lone Pi
  5   │     6      │  Jones    │  Jean      │ 413-07-9123│ 4000 St. Ja
  6   │     8      │  Williams │  Brenda    │ 401-55-1567│ 100 Owl Cre
  7   │     9      │  Myers    │  Julie     │ 314-30-9452│ 4512 Parksi
  8   │    12      │  Jackson  │  Mary      │ 424-13-7621│ 7821 Clark
  9   │    14      │  Preston  │  Molly     │ 451-00-3426│ 321 Indian
 10   │    16      │  Robertson│  Kevin     │ 415-24-6710│ 431 Bardsto
 11   │    19      │  Gunn     │  Barbara   │ 321-97-8632│ 541 Kentuck
 12   │    20      │  Emerson  │  Cheryl    │ 404-14-1422│ 8100 River
```

In this example, we made entries on two lines of the query form. However, you can make entries on up to 22 lines in a single query form, if you wish. A query form with 22 lines would have 22 separate sets of conditions, all joined with logical ORs. In reality, however, your query forms will rarely include more than two or three lines.

Selecting Fields in OR Queries

In the example, we selected every field in both rows of the ANSWER table. As you might expect, Paradox does not require you to select every field in an OR query. You can select as many fields, or as few, as you want, as long as you meet two conditions. First, you must select at least one field in each row of the query form that contains a selection condition. If you don't meet this restriction, Paradox will display the error message *One or more query rows do not contribute to ANSWER* when you press [Do-It!].

Second, Paradox requires that you select the same fields in every row of the query form that contains a selection condition. For example, if you select just the Last Name and State field in the first row of a query, you must select just those fields—no more and no less—in the second and subsequent rows. If you try to process a query that breaks this rule, Paradox will display the error message *Query appears to ask two unrelated questions* when you press **[Do-It!]**.

The Effect of Blank Rows

If you select fields in a row of the query form that does not include a selection condition, Paradox will include the selected fields from every record in the ANSWER table. For example, suppose you use the [Check Mark] key to select every field in the third row of the query form in Figure 8-63 so that it looks like Figure 8-57. Remember, the third row of this query does not contain a selection condition. If you press [Do-It!] to process this query, Paradox will create an ANSWER table that includes every field of every record from EMPLYEE.

Figure 8-57

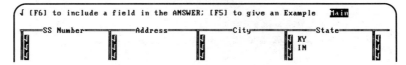

Here's why this occurs: As you saw in the very first part of this chapter, a row in a query form that does not contain a selection condition will select every record from the table. It doesn't matter whether the query form has just one row, as in our earliest examples, or several rows, as in this case. If the table contains several rows, then the blank row is joined to the conditions in the other rows with a logical OR. For example, in this case, the query could be translated in this way: *Select every record with the State field entry KY or the State field entry IN or with any entry in any field.* Obviously, this query will select every record in the table.

ORs on Different Fields

In the simple examples we've considered so far, we have created OR conditions within a single field. You can, however, create OR conditions that involve several fields. For example, suppose you want to select from EMPLYEE all records that have the entry *Jones* in the Last Name field or a number greater than 35,000 in the Salary field. Figure 8-58 shows a query that would make this selection. To create this query, begin with a new, empty query form for EMPLYEE, select every field, and enter the selection condition **Jones** in the first row of the Last Name field of the query form, and the condition **>35000** in the second row of the Salary field.

Figure 8-59 shows the ANSWER table that Paradox will create when you process this table. Notice that the table includes all of the records from the EMPLYEE table that have either the entry *Jones* in the Last Name field or an entry greater than 35,000 in the Salary field.

Notice also that a few records in EMPLYEE meet both of these conditions; that is, the Last Name field entry is *Jones* and the Salary field entry is greater than 35,000. However, notice that these records only appear in the ANSWER table once. As in this case, when a record meets more than one condition in an OR query, the record will appear in the ANSWER table only once.

Figure 8-58

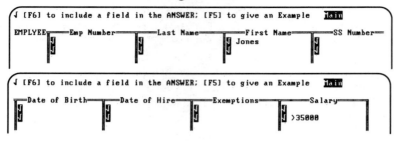

Figure 8-59

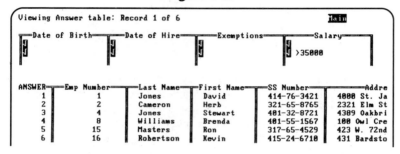

AND Queries

As you have seen, OR queries allow you to select records that meet one of several selection conditions. AND queries, on the other hand, allow you to select records that meet all of several conditions. AND conditions are created by entering more than one selection condition in a single row of a query form.

For example, suppose you want to select those records from EMPLYEE with an entry less than ten in the Emp Number field and a number greater than 35,000 in the Salary field. Figure 8-60 shows a completed query that will make this selection.

Notice that there are two selection conditions in the first row of this query: the formula **<10** in the Emp Number field, and the entry **>35000** in the Salary field. These two conditions are joined by a logical AND so that the query could be translated into English like this: *Select every record that has an Emp Number field entry that is less than 10 AND a Salary field entry that is greater than 35000.*

Figure 8-61 shows the ANSWER table that Paradox will create when you process this query. As you can see, the table includes only those records that satisfy both selection conditions: David Jones, Herb Cameron, Stewart Jones, and Brenda Williams.

Figure 8-60

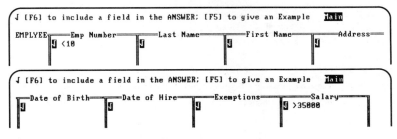

Figure 8-61

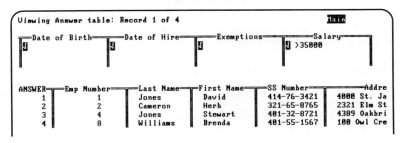

ANDs in One Field

The method shown in the previous example works fine if the selection conditions you specify apply to different fields. But what if you want to link two conditions that apply to the same field with a logical AND? For example, suppose you want to select every record from the table that has a Salary field entry greater than $20,000 AND less than 40,000. To do this, create a new, empty query form for EMPLYEE and select every field in the form. Then move the cursor to the first row of the Salary field and type **>20000,<40000.**

Whenever you enter two or more conditions in a single field of a query form, Paradox joins those conditions with a logical AND. For example, this query can be translated like this: *Select every field of every record that has a Salary field greater than 20000 and a Salary field entry less than 40000.*

Figure 8-62 shows the ANSWER table that will result from this table. Notice that this table includes only those records from EMPLYEE that have a Salary field entry between 20,000 and 40,000. Notice that the two conditions in the query in Figure 8-62 are separated by a comma. Whenever you enter two or more conditions into a single field of a query form, you must separate the individual conditions with commas.

The only limit on the number of conditions you can enter in a single field of a query form is the overall Paradox limit of 255 characters in a single entry. In most cases, this limitation will not cause you any difficulty.

Figure 8-62

```
Viewing Answer table: Record 1 of 8                          Main
 ┌─Date of Birth─┐┌─Date of Hire─┐┌─Exemptions─┐┌─Salary──────┐
 │               ││              ││            ││ >20000,<40000│


 ┌ANSWER┬─Emp Number─┬─Last Name──┬─First Name─┬─SS Number──┬──────Addre
 │   1  │     6      │ Jones      │ Jean       │ 413-07-9123│ 4000 St. Ja
 │   2  │     9      │ Myers      │ Julie      │ 314-30-9452│ 4512 Parksi
 │   3  │    10      │ Link       │ Julie      │ 345-75-1525│ 3215 Palm C
 │   4  │    12      │ Jackson    │ Mary       │ 424-13-7621│ 7821 Clark
 │   5  │    13      │ Jakes, Jr. │ Sal        │ 321-65-9151│ 3451 Michig
 │   6  │    15      │ Masters    │ Ron        │ 317-65-4529│ 423 W. 72nd
 │   7  │    16      │ Robertson  │ Kevin      │ 415-24-6710│ 431 Bardsto
 │   8  │    17      │ Garrison   │ Robert     │ 312-98-1479│ 55 Wheeler
```

Combining AND and OR Queries

So far, we've created OR queries and AND queries. As you might expect, however, you can also create combined AND/OR queries. For example, suppose you want to select those records that have a Date of Birth field entry that is less than (before) January 1, 1950 AND an Emp Number field entry that is less than 10, OR that have the entry *Jones* in the Last Name field.

Figure 8-63 shows a completed query that will do the trick. Notice that this query contains three selection conditions. The first row of the Emp Number field contains the condition <10. The first row of the Date of Birth field contains the condition <1/1/50. These two conditions combine to select only those records with a Date of Birth field entry that is less than January 1, 1950, and an Emp Number field entry that is less than 10. The second row of the Last Name field contains the condition Jones.

Figure 8-64 shows the ANSWER table that was created by processing this query. As you can see, this table includes all of the records from the table that have the Last Name field entry *Jones*, or a Date of Birth field entry that is less than 1/1/50 and an Emp Number field entry that is less than 10.

Figure 8-63

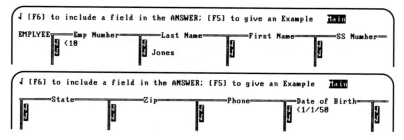

Figure 8-64

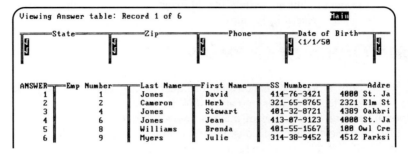

Now suppose that you want to select all of the records that have an entry greater than 45,000 in the Salary field AND a Date of Birth field entry that is less than January 1, 1940, OR an entry greater than 45,000 in the Salary field and a Date of Hire field entry that is less than 9/1/84. Figure 8-65 shows a query that will perform this selection.

Notice that there are selection conditions in two rows of this query form. The conditions in the first row—<1/1/40 in the Date of Birth field and >45000 in the Salary field—combine to select only those records with a Date of Birth field entry that is before January 1, 1940, and a Salary field entry greater than 45,000. The conditions in the second row—<9/1/84 in the Date of Hire field and >45000 in the Salary field—combine to select only those records with a Date of Hire field entry that is before September 1, 1984, and a Salary field entry greater than 45,000. When taken together, the conditions on the two rows of the form will select any record that meets the condition specified by the entries on either row. As you can see, Figure 8-66 shows the ANSWER table that results from this query.

Figure 8-65

Figure 8-66

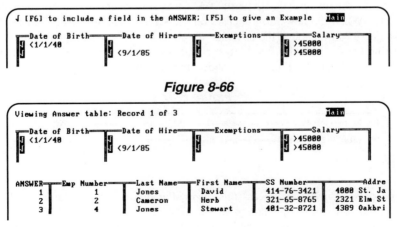

Figuring out just how to create a complex AND/OR query can take a bit of thinking. If you get confused, you might try writing the query as a sentence, complete with *ands* and *ors*, before you try to create it in Paradox.

Other Types of Queries

So far, we've only worked with conventional queries that copy the information from selected fields of selected records into an ANSWER table. However, Paradox is capable of performing several other types of queries, including queries that allow you to delete records that match selection conditions, find matching records in a table without copying them to an ANSWER table, or change entries in records that match selection conditions.

Find Queries

Find queries allow you to find the first record in a table which matches the selection conditions you specify. This type of query is useful when you need to view or edit a specific record in a table, and you don't have time to browse through the table to locate the record.

To create a find query, you first create a query form and enter the word **find** in the space under the form name at the left edge of the form. Next, you enter the appropriate selection conditions (if any) into that form. When you process a find query, Paradox will bring the table being queried into view (if it is not already on the screen) and will move the cursor to the first record in the table being queried that meets the conditions you have defined. In addition, Paradox will copy all of the records that match the condition you have defined into an ANSWER table.

For example, suppose you need to take a peek at the record for Julie Meyers, employee number 9. To begin, use the **[Menu] Ask** command to create a new query form for EMPLYEE. When the new form appears on the screen, type the word **find** in the space under the query form name at the left edge of the table. This word signals to Paradox that this is a find query. Finally, move to the first row of the Emp Number field and enter the selection condition **9**. Figure 8-67 shows the completed query.

Figure 8-67

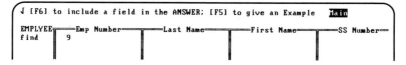

When you press **[Do-It!]** to process this query, Paradox will bring the EMPLYEE table into view and will move the cursor to the first record in the table that matches the selection conditions you have defined. In this case, Paradox will move the cursor to the record for Julie Meyers, as shown in Figure 8-68.

Figure 8-68

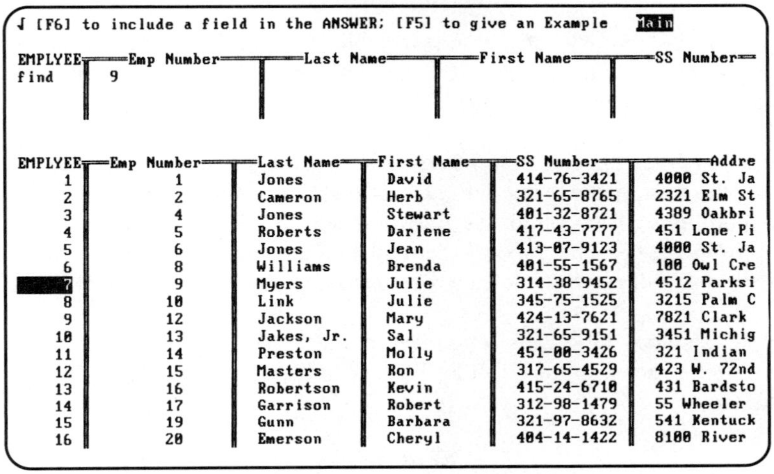

```
√ [F6] to include a field in the ANSWER; [F5] to give an Example    Main
EMPLYEE┬═══Emp Number═══╤═══Last Name═══╤═══First Name═══╤═══SS Number═══
find   │        9       │               │                │



EMPLYEE┬═Emp Number═╤═Last Name═╤═First Name═╤═SS Number═╤═══════Addre
   1   │     1      │  Jones    │  David     │ 414-76-3421│ 4000 St. Ja
   2   │     2      │  Cameron  │  Herb      │ 321-65-8765│ 2321 Elm St
   3   │     4      │  Jones    │  Stewart   │ 401-32-8721│ 4389 Oakbri
   4   │     5      │  Roberts  │  Darlene   │ 417-43-7777│ 451 Lone Pi
   5   │     6      │  Jones    │  Jean      │ 413-07-9123│ 4000 St. Ja
   6   │     8      │  Williams │  Brenda    │ 401-55-1567│ 100 Owl Cre
   7   │     9      │  Myers    │  Julie     │ 314-38-9452│ 4512 Parksi
   8   │    10      │  Link     │  Julie     │ 345-75-1525│ 3215 Palm C
   9   │    12      │  Jackson  │  Mary      │ 424-13-7621│ 7821 Clark
  10   │    13      │  Jakes, Jr.│ Sal       │ 321-65-9151│ 3451 Michig
  11   │    14      │  Preston  │  Molly     │ 451-00-3426│ 321 Indian
  12   │    15      │  Masters  │  Ron       │ 317-65-4529│ 423 W. 72nd
  13   │    16      │  Robertson│  Kevin     │ 415-24-6710│ 431 Bardsto
  14   │    17      │  Garrison │  Robert    │ 312-98-1479│ 55 Wheeler
  15   │    19      │  Gunn     │  Barbara   │ 321-97-8632│ 541 Kentuck
  16   │    20      │  Emerson  │  Cheryl    │ 404-14-1422│ 8100 River
```

Notice that we said that Paradox will bring the EMPLYEE table into view when you process this query. Whenever you perform a find query, if the table being queried is not in view, Paradox will bring it into view when you process the query. As you may recall, most conventional queries do not bring the table being queried into view.

After Paradox moves the cursor to the first matching record in the table, Paradox returns to the normal viewing mode. If you want to edit the record that Paradox has located, you must press the **[Edit]** key to enter the edit mode. If you want to review the surrounding records, you can press ↑, ↓, or any of the other movement keys.

In addition to moving the cursor to the first record that matches the defined conditions, Paradox also copies any records that match the conditions you have defined into an ANSWER table. However, this table will not appear on the screen, as it will when you process conventional queries. If you want to view the ANSWER table, just issue the View command.

The ANSWER table that is created by a find query is different from conventional ANSWER tables in another way. In most ANSWER tables, the records are arranged in ascending order based on the entries in the first record of the table. In find query ANSWER tables, however, the records appear in the same order as they were arranged in the queried table.

If there is not a record in the table being queried that matches the condition you have defined, Paradox will display the message *No record matches Find query*.

Notice that we didn't select any fields when we created the query in Figure 8-67. Because find queries operate on entire records, and not on specified fields, there is no need to select fields in a find query. In fact, if you attempt to process a find query that includes checked fields, Paradox will display the message *Fields in Find rows cannot be checkmarked*.

Delete Queries

Delete queries allow you to delete from a table those records that match the selection conditions you specify. In addition to being deleted from the table, the deleted records are stored in a temporary table called DELETED.

To create a delete query, you first create a query form and enter the word **delete** in the space under the form name at the left edge of the form. Next, you enter the appropriate selection conditions (if any) into that form. When you process a delete query, Paradox will delete from the table the records that matched the specified selection conditions. In addition, Paradox will copy the deleted records to a temporary table called DELETED.

For example, suppose Julie Link, employee number 10, has resigned from her job and you want to delete her from the EMPLYEE table. Figure 8-69 shows a delete query that will do the trick.

Figure 8-69

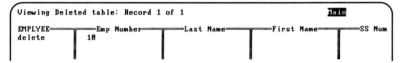

To create this query, make a new, blank query form for EMPLYEE. When the new form appears on the screen, type the word **delete** in the space under the query form name at the left edge of the table. This word signals to Paradox that this is a delete query. Now move to the first row of the Emp Number field and type the number **10**, the Emp Number field entry of the record you want to delete.

When you press **[Do-It!]** to process this query, Paradox will copy the record for Julie Link to a DELETED table and will delete her record from EMPLYEE. Figure 8-70 shows the screen as it will look after the query is processed.

Figure 8-70

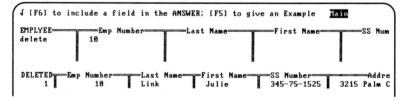

When you process a delete query, you won't see the revised table on the screen unless it was in view when you processed the query. If the table is not in view when you press [Do-It!], it will not be in view after the query is processed. The DELETED table, however, always comes into view when you process a delete query.

Like ANSWER, DELETED is a temporary table. Each time you perform a delete query, Paradox overwrites the existing DELETED table (if there is one) with the DELETED table for the new query. If you want to preserve the contents of the DELETED table, you should rename it before you process another delete query.

Notice that we didn't select any fields when we created the query in Figure 8-69. Because delete queries operate on entire records, and not on specified fields, there is no need to select fields in a delete query. In fact, if you attempt to process a delete query that includes selected fields, Paradox will display the message *Insert, Delete, and Changeto rows may not be checkmarked.*

When you process a delete query, Paradox will delete those records that match the selection conditions you have defined. If you do not define any conditions before you process the query, Paradox will delete every record from the table. Be careful! Although you can restore deleted records to a table, it is easy to destroy a great deal of data by making a simple mistake with delete queries.

An Alternative Method

Of course, you can also delete records from a table with the [Del] key. There are two major advantages to using delete queries instead of the [Del] key to delete records. First, as you have seen, when you use a delete query to delete records, the deleted records are copied to a temporary DELETED table. As you'll see in chapter 10, you can restore deleted records from the DELETED table by using an insert query. Second, delete queries make it possible to delete all of the records that meet a given set of conditions at once.

Reversing a Deletion

As you know, when you process a delete query, Paradox copies the records it deletes into a temporary table named DELETED. By viewing this table, you can determine whether or not Paradox operated on the correct records when you processed the query. The DELETED table also makes it possible to reverse the effects of the delete query. If you must restore those records to the table from which they were deleted, you can use the [Menu] Tools More Add command.

For example, suppose you want to restore the record you just deleted to EMPLYEE. To do this, issue the [Menu] Tools More Add command, specify **DELETED** as the table that contains the records you want to add and **EMPLYEE** as the table to which to add the records. When you press ⏎, Paradox will add the one record from DELETED to EMPLYEE and will bring EMPLYEE into view. Figure 8-71 shows the resulting EMPLYEE table.

You can also use a special kind of query, called an insert query, to restore deleted records from DELETED. We'll show you how to create and use insert queries in Chapter 10.

Figure 8-71

```
Viewing Emplyee table: Record 1 of 16                    Main

DELETED   Emp Number   Last Name   First Name   SS Number      Addre
   1         10         Link        Julie       345-75-1525    3215 Palm C


EMPLYEE   Emp Number   Last Name   First Name   SS Number      Addre
   1          1         Jones       David       414-76-3421    4000 St. Ja
   2          2         Cameron     Herb        321-65-8765    2321 Elm St
   3          4         Jones       Stewart     401-32-8721    4389 Oakbri
   4          5         Roberts     Darlene     417-43-7777    451 Lone Pi
   5          6         Jones       Jean        413-07-9123    4000 St. Ja
   6          8         Williams    Brenda      401-55-1567    100 Owl Cre
   7          9         Myers       Julie       314-30-9452    4512 Parksi
   8         12         Jackson     Mary        424-13-7621    7821 Clark
   9         13         Jakes, Jr.  Sal         321-65-9151    3451 Michig
  10         14         Preston     Molly       451-00-3426    321 Indian
  11         15         Masters     Ron         317-65-4529    423 W. 72nd
  12         16         Robertson   Kevin       415-24-6710    431 Bardsto
  13         17         Garrison    Robert      312-98-1479    55 Wheeler
  14         19         Gunn        Barbara     321-97-8632    541 Kentuck
  15         20         Emerson     Cheryl      404-14-1422    8100 River
  16         10         Link        Julie       345-75-1525    3215 Palm C
```

Changeto Queries

Changeto queries allow you to change the entries in a given field for all of the records in a table that match your selection conditions. Changeto queries are similar to the search and replace capability of most word processors.

To define a changeto query, you first create a query form and enter the appropriate selection conditions (if any) into that form. Then you enter the word **changeto** into the field of the query form that you want to change, followed by the new value that you want to assign to the entries in that field. When you process a changeto query, Paradox will change the entries in the appropriate field of the selected records to the specified changeto value. In addition, Paradox will copy the original version of any changed records to a temporary table called CHANGED.

For example, suppose Brenda Williams, employee number 8, has just changed the number of exemptions she wishes to claim from 5 to 6. Let's use a changeto query to make this change. To begin, bring the EMPLYEE table into view and move to the Exemptions field. Next, create a new, blank query for EMPLYEE, then enter the selection condition **8** in the first row of the Emp Number field of the query form.

Now you need to tell Paradox which field you want it to change and how you want it changed. To do this, move the cursor to the first row of the Exemptions field and type **changeto 6**. Figure 8-72 shows the completed query and the EMPLYEE table. Now, press **[Do-It!]** to process the query. Figure 8-73 shows the screen as it will look after the query has been processed. Notice that the Exemptions field entry for Brenda Williams has changed from 5 to 6, just as you requested, and that the original record for Brenda Williams has been copied into a CHANGED table.

Figure 8-72

```
√ [F6] to include a field in the ANSWER; [F5] to give an Example  Main
  EMPLOYEE┬═Emp Number═┬══════Last Name══════┬══════First Name══════┬══SS Number══
          │     8      │                     │                      │
```

Zip	Phone	Date of Birth	Date of Hire	Exemptions	
40207	(502) 245-6610	10/06/42	6/01/84	3	****
40205	(502) 451-8765	11/24/29	6/01/84	4	****
40222	(502) 452-1048	3/21/50	7/01/84	1	****
40012	(502) 897-3215	9/24/60	11/01/84	3	****
40207	(502) 245-6610	5/14/43	12/01/84	0	****
40223	(502) 894-9761	1/12/20	1/01/85	5	****
40206	(502) 454-5209	2/06/48	2/01/85	1	****
47130	(812) 288-6754	8/12/56	4/01/85	3	****
65987	(214) 398-1987	5/23/59	5/01/85	6	****
40205	(502) 456-3256	4/17/66	7/01/85	1	****
10019	(212) 276-5478	12/30/44	7/01/85	0	****
40315	(502) 423-9823	3/16/25	7/15/85	1	****
25687	(617) 543-4124	5/09/45	10/01/85	4	****
47132	(812) 325-4789	5/18/50	11/01/85	2	****
40222	(502) 896-5139	7/30/66	1/01/86	2	****
94375	(408) 542-1948	6/03/33	4/01/85	2	****

```
√ [F6] to include a field in the ANSWER; [F5] to give an Example  Main
  ┬══Phone══┬══Date of Birth══┬══Date of Hire══┬══Exemptions══
  │         │                 │                │  changeto 6
```

Zip	Phone	Date of Birth	Date of Hire	Exemptions	
40207	(502) 245-6610	10/06/42	6/01/84	3	****
40205	(502) 451-8765	11/24/29	6/01/84	4	****
40222	(502) 452-1048	3/21/50	7/01/84	1	****
40012	(502) 897-3215	9/24/60	11/01/84	3	****
40207	(502) 245-6610	5/14/43	12/01/84	0	****
40223	(502) 894-9761	1/12/20	1/01/85	5	****
40206	(502) 454-5209	2/06/48	2/01/85	1	****
47130	(812) 288-6754	8/12/56	4/01/85	3	****
65987	(214) 398-1987	5/23/59	5/01/85	6	****
40205	(502) 456-3256	4/17/66	7/01/85	1	****
10019	(212) 276-5478	12/30/44	7/01/85	0	****
40315	(502) 423-9823	3/16/25	7/15/85	1	****
25687	(617) 543-4124	5/09/45	10/01/85	4	****
47132	(812) 325-4789	5/18/50	11/01/85	2	****
40222	(502) 896-5139	7/30/66	1/01/86	2	****
94375	(408) 542-1948	6/03/33	4/01/85	2	****

The CHANGED Table

Whenever you process a changeto query, Paradox will copy the original versions of all the records that are changed to a CHANGED table. By viewing this table, you can determine whether Paradox operated on the correct records when you processed the query.

The CHANGED table also allows you to reverse the effects of the changeto query. To reverse a changeto query, you must delete the records or record that was changed incorrectly from the original table, and then use the [Menu] Tools More Add command to add the contents of CHANGED to the original table.

Figure 8-73

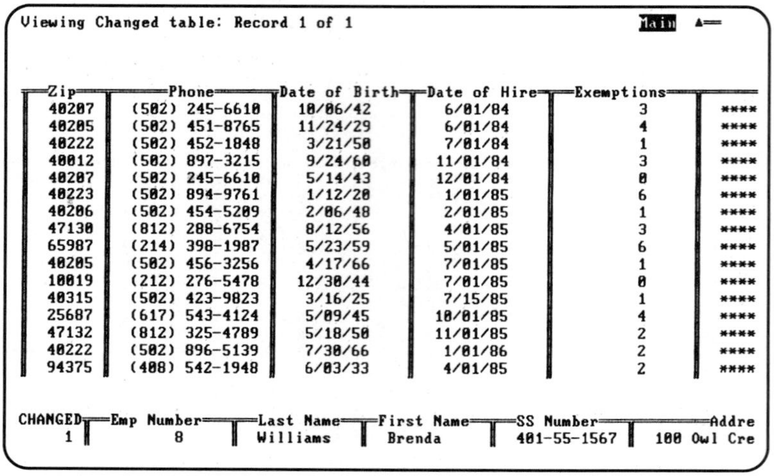

```
Viewing Changed table: Record 1 of 1                          Main  ▲=
┌─Zip───┬───Phone─────┬─Date of Birth─┬─Date of Hire─┬─Exemptions─┬──────
│ 40207 │ (502) 245-6610 │ 10/06/42   │ 6/01/84    │     3      │ ****
│ 40205 │ (502) 451-8765 │ 11/24/29   │ 6/01/84    │     4      │ ****
│ 40222 │ (502) 452-1848 │  3/21/50   │ 7/01/84    │     1      │ ****
│ 40012 │ (502) 897-3215 │  9/24/60   │ 11/01/84   │     3      │ ****
│ 40207 │ (502) 245-6610 │  5/14/43   │ 12/01/84   │     0      │ ****
│ 40223 │ (502) 894-9761 │  1/12/20   │ 1/01/85    │     6      │ ****
│ 40206 │ (502) 454-5209 │  2/06/48   │ 2/01/85    │     1      │ ****
│ 47130 │ (812) 288-6754 │  8/12/56   │ 4/01/85    │     3      │ ****
│ 65987 │ (214) 398-1987 │  5/23/59   │ 5/01/85    │     6      │ ****
│ 40205 │ (502) 456-3256 │  4/17/66   │ 7/01/85    │     1      │ ****
│ 10019 │ (212) 276-5478 │ 12/30/44   │ 7/01/85    │     0      │ ****
│ 40315 │ (502) 423-9823 │  3/16/25   │ 7/15/85    │     1      │ ****
│ 25687 │ (617) 543-4124 │  5/09/45   │ 10/01/85   │     4      │ ****
│ 47132 │ (812) 325-4789 │  5/18/50   │ 11/01/85   │     2      │ ****
│ 40222 │ (502) 896-5139 │  7/30/66   │ 1/01/86    │     2      │ ****
│ 94375 │ (408) 542-1948 │  6/03/33   │ 4/01/85    │     2      │ ****

┌CHANGED─┬Emp Number─┬─Last Name─┬─First Name─┬─SS Number──┬─────Addre
│   1    │    8      │ Williams  │  Brenda    │ 401-55-1567│ 100 Owl Cre
```

Like ANSWER, CHANGED is a temporary table. Each time you perform a changeto query, Paradox overwrites the existing CHANGED table (if there is one) with the CHANGED table for the new query. If you want to preserve the contents of the CHANGED table, you should rename it before you process another changeto query.

Changing Several Records

Up to this point, we have used Changeto to change the entries in the fields of one record. In many cases, you can make that kind of change just as easily by using the edit mode. Changeto queries are most valuable when you want to change the entries in a given field in several records.

If you use a changeto operator in a query form that does not contain any selection conditions, Paradox will make the requested change to every record in the table. For example, if you created the query in Figure 8-72 but did not enter the selection condition 8 in the Emp Number field, Paradox would change the Exemptions field entry for every record in the table to 5. In a more practical application, you could use this type of query to increase the salary of every employee in the table by 10%. (In fact, we'll show you how to do just that in the next chapter.)

If you use the changeto operator in a query form that includes selection conditions that will select several records, Paradox will change the entry in the indicated fields of all matching records. Let's use the PROJECTS table to demonstrate. Suppose you want to change the Manager field entry to 2 for every project with the Manager field entry 4. To begin, create a new, blank query form for PROJECTS, then move to the first row of the Manager field and type **4, changeto 2**. Figure 8-74 shows the result. As you can see, Paradox has changed the Manager field entry to 2 for every record with the Manager field entry 4 and has copied the unchanged versions of those records to a CHANGED table.

Figure 8-74

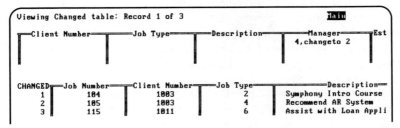

The QuerySave Command

Earlier in the chapter, we explained that queries are temporary. When you clear a query from the screen, it ceases to exist. The only way to recover the query is to recreate the query from scratch. Since most of your queries will be ad hoc queries (queries that are designed to perform a particular task that is unlikely to be repeated), this characteristic will not be a problem in most cases.

However, there will be a few queries that you use over and over and that you would rather not recreate each time you need to use them. Fortunately, Paradox includes a command, [Menu] Scripts QuerySave, that you can use to save your queries into special script files. When you have saved a query into a script file, you can bring it back to the screen with the [Menu] Scripts Play command. Once it is on the screen, you can process it by pressing [Do-It!].

An Example

Suppose you have created the query shown in Figure 8-75. This query selects those records that have an Estimated Date of Completion field entry that is less than Today+90 but greater than Today; in other words, this query will select those projects that are forecast to be completed in the next 90 days. Suppose you use this query nearly every month and you don't want to recreate it from scratch every time you need it.

Figure 8-75

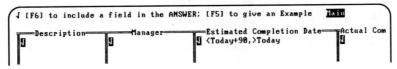

To save this query, simply issue the **[Menu]** Scripts QuerySave command. When Paradox prompts you for a name for the saved query, choose a name that will help you remember the function of the query. For instance, in this case you might choose a name like 90DAYS. Once you supply the name and press ↵, Paradox will save the query into a script file. The query will not be removed from the screen, so if you want to process it after you save it, all you need to do is press **[Do-It!]**.

Now suppose that a week has gone by and you want to reuse the query. To begin, press **[Clear All]** to clear the screen. (This step is not required; we include it so that you can see more easily the effect of playing the query script.) Next, issue the **[Menu]** Scripts Play command and type the name of the query—in this case, **90DAYS**. When you press ↵, Paradox will bring the saved query to the screen. Now, to process the query, just press **[Do-It!]**. When you press this key, Paradox will process the query just as if you had created it from scratch.

Most of the queries you save will be more complex than this one. After all, if you can redefine the query from scratch as easily as you can retrieve it from a script, it doesn't make much sense to save that query in a script. However, this query demonstrates all of the steps involved in saving queries.

Notes

If the active query includes several query forms (we'll see some queries like this in the next chapter), all the query forms will be saved when you issue the QuerySave command. When you play the saved query, all the forms will be retrieved to the screen.

In the example, we cleared the screen before we played the saved script 90DAYS. You don't need to clear the screen before you can retrieve a saved query, however. If there is a query on the screen when you play a saved query, the query you are playing will replace the existing query. If there are other images on the screen, the query being played will appear above those images at the top of the screen.

In Chapter 13, "Scripts," we will explore the QuerySave command in more detail. In that chapter, we'll pay special attention to the nature of the script files that are created when you issue three Querysave commands.

Speeding Up Queries

Because the queries that we have used as examples in this chapter refer to tables that contain only a few records, Paradox was able to process them very quickly. In the real world, however, your tables are likely to contain many more records than our example tables. When you are querying tables that contain hundreds or thousands instead of just a dozen or so records, queries can take a great deal longer to execute.

Fortunately, Paradox offers two tools—key fields and the [Menu] Tools QuerySpeedup command—that you can use to speed up the processing of your queries. Let's look at both of these useful tools.

Key Fields

As you learned in Chapter 13, Paradox lets you to create key fields in your tables. These key fields have several purposes, one of which is to speed up the processing of queries.

Key Field Review

To create a key field, you type an asterisk next to the field type entry in the Field Type field when you create the table. For example, Figure 8-76 shows the STRUCT table for the PROJECTS table. Notice the asterisk in the Field Type field of the Job Number record in this table.

Figure 8-76

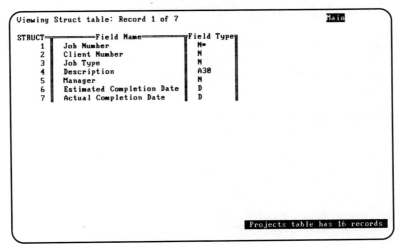

When you designate a key field for a table, Paradox will allow you to make only unique entries into that field. If you attempt to enter into a keyed table a record that contains a key field entry that is identical to an existing key field entry, Paradox will place that record in a table called KEYVIOL.

In addition, when you designate a key field, the records in the table will always be sorted according to the key field. For example, in the PROJECTS table, Job Number is a key field. When you look at the PROJECTS table, it will always be sorted on the Job Number field.

The one disadvantage of creating key fields is that they significantly reduce the capacity of each record in the table. A record in a nonkeyed table has a capacity of 4000 bytes. A record in a keyed table, on the other hand, has a capacity of only 1350 bytes.

You can have as many key fields as you wish in a Paradox table, provided that all of the key fields are adjacent to one another and that the first key field is the first field in the table. You designate the second and subsequent key fields just as you do the first: by typing an asterisk in the Field Type column of the STRUCT table for that table as you create it. If you designate more than one key field, then each key field can contain duplicate entries, just as long as no two records have exactly the same entries in all of the key fields.

Key Fields and Queries

Another important purpose for key fields is speeding up your queries. When you designate a key field, Paradox creates a *primary index* for that table on the key field. When you query the table, and use a selection condition in the key field, Paradox will use the index to locate the matching records. If the table contains a large number of records, the query will be processed much more quickly than it could without the key field.

The QuerySpeedup Command

Although key fields are very helpful, there may be times when you won't be able to make a field a key field, but would still like to speed up queries that refer to that field. In those cases, you can use the [Menu] Tools QuerySpeedup command to create a secondary index on the selected field.

Query Speedup Basics

To take advantage of the [Menu] Tools QuerySpeedup command, you first create a query on the table that you want to index. This query should include selection conditions in the fields on which you want to index the table. After you create the query, you issue the **[Menu] T**ools **Q**uerySpeedup command. When you issue this command, Paradox will display the message *Processing query speedup* as it builds the secondary indexes. Once the secondary indexes have been created, Paradox will use them to speed up any query that refers to one of the indexed fields.

An Example

For example, suppose you frequently create queries that refer to the Salary field in EMPLYEE. To speed up these queries, you want to create a secondary index on the Salary field.

To begin, use the **[Menu] A**sk command to create a new query form for the EMPLYEE table. When the new form appears, press **[Check Mark]** to select every field, then move to the Salary field and enter the selection condition **30000**. Figure 8-77 shows the complete query.

Figure 8-77

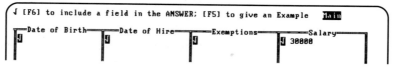

Now, issue the **[Menu] T**ools **Q**uerySpeedup command. When you issue the command, Paradox will display the message *Processing query speedup* and will build a secondary index on the Salary field for the EMPLYEE table. The next time you create a query that refers to this field, Paradox will use the index to speed up the query.

Notes

Once you have created secondary indexes, you do not have to do anything to keep them up to date. Paradox automatically updates all of the secondary indexes for a table when you perform a query on that table. (Notice that the update occurs not during data entry, but when you process a query.)

Defining the Query

Although we used the selection condition 30,000 in the Salary field of the example query, we could have used any numeric condition in that field. As long as the condition you use has the correct type (dates in date fields, numbers in number fields, and so on), the actual condition you enter in the query form to create a secondary index doesn't matter to Paradox. All that Paradox looks for is a selection condition. When it finds a condition–any condition–in the form, Paradox creates an index on the field that contains the condition.

If the condition you use has the wrong type, Paradox will display the error message *Expression in this field has the wrong type* when you issue the [Menu] Tools QuerySpeedup command.

The QuerySpeedup command will create a separate index for each field for which you have defined a selection condition. If you want to create several secondary indexes for a table, you can do so by creating one query for the table and entering a selection condition in each field in the form on which you want to index the table. Once again, remember that you can use any selection condition of the appropriate type in the fields of the query form–the query does not have to make sense.

For example, if you create the query shown in Figure 8-78 and issue the **[Menu] T**ools **Q**uerySpeedup command, Paradox will create indexes for the Date of Hire, Date of Birth, and Exemptions fields.

Figure 8-78

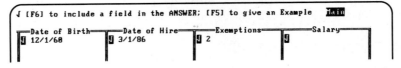

You must select at least one field in the query form you use to create indexes. If no fields in the query are selected, Paradox will display the message *Query has no checked fields* when you issue the [Menu] Tools QuerySpeedup command.

The Index Files

When you issue the **[Menu] T**ools **Q**uerySpeedup command, Paradox creates a pair of files on disk for every field in the active query that contains a selection condition. These files have the same root name as the table to which they relate and have extensions like .X01 and .Y01, .X02 and .Y02, and .X0C and .Y0C. The amount of space consumed by these files depends on the size of the table you are indexing.

Deleting Indexes

You can delete all of the secondary indexes for a table by issuing the [Menu] Tools Delete QuerySpeedup command and specifying the name of the table whose indexes you want to delete. For example, to delete the indexes for the EMPLYEE table, you'd issue the **[Menu] Tools D**elete **Q**uerySpeedup command and type EMPLYEE. When you press ↵, Paradox will display the message *Deleting speedup files for EMPLYEE table* as it deletes every secondary index for EMPLYEE from the active directory.

The [Menu] Tools Delete QuerySpeedup command has no effect on key field indexes. If a table has a key field, the key field indexes will be intact after you issue the Delete QuerySpeedup command.

You cannot delete individual indexes from within Paradox. If you want to delete one set of secondary index files, you can try to do so using the DOS erase command. However, it is difficult to identify which index files relate to which field. Our suggestion is that you use the Delete QuerySpeedup command to delete all of the indexes, and then recreate those that you want to retain.

The No Speedup Possible Message

Sometimes when you issue the [Menu] Tools QuerySpeedup command, Paradox will display the message *No speedup possible* in the message area. You'll see this message if you try to create a secondary index on a key field or on a field for which a secondary index already exists, or if you issue the [Menu] Tools QuerySpeedup command when the active query does not contain any selection conditions.

This message also appears when you create a selection condition that contains a range operator (>, <, <=, >=, or <>) and then use the [Menu] Tools QuerySpeedup command. No indexes will be created in the field. Strangely, however, if you change the selection condition in that field into an exact-match condition, Paradox will create indexes.

When to use QuerySpeedup

Secondary indexes are most useful when you need to perform a specific query that refers to non-keyed fields over and over. In those situations, the time required to create and maintain the secondary indexes is more than offset by the increased speed of your queries. On the other hand, it is probably not worthwhile to create secondary indexes for ad hoc queries or for queries that you only perform once in a while.

In addition, you should keep in mind that indexes are not free. For one thing, index files consume disk space. Moreover, Paradox automatically updates every index file for a table each time you process any query on that table. To avoid wasting valuable disk space and time, you should avoid creating unnecessary indexes on your tables.

Finally, because Paradox automatically updates indexes every time you process a query, indexes are not much help with small tables. In fact, in some cases, indexes can actually slow down queries in very small tables. If the time required to update the index, plus the time required to process the query, equals or exceeds the time required to process the query without an index, you're better off not having an index.

The best advice we can give about secondary indexes is that you should experiment with them in your tables. If you find that your queries work better with secondary indexes, use them; if not, get rid of them.

Key Fields Versus Query Speedup

One of the primary advantages of the QuerySpeedup command over key fields is that QuerySpeedup does not require that the field in which you are indexing contain only unique entries. This means that you can use QuerySpeedup to create indexes on fields that you refer to a great deal in queries but which are likely to contain duplicate entries. The Salary field in the EMPLYEE table is such a field. On the other hand, creating an index on a field that contains many duplicate entries will not do much to speed up queries that refer to that field.

In addition, QuerySpeedup does not require that the field in which you index be the first field in the table. This makes QuerySpeedup more flexible than key fields.

Key fields, on the other hand, are great when you have a field that logically should be the first field in a table and which will always contain unique entries. The Emp Number field in EMPLYEE and the Job Number field in PROJECTS are examples of this type of field. Remember that when you make these fields key fields, you not only speed up your queries, you also guarantee the order of the records in your table and avoid the problem of duplicate entries.

Conclusion

In this chapter, you've learned how to build and use simple queries. You've seen how to create query forms, how to select fields using [Check Mark] and [Check Plus], and how to define selection conditions. You've also seen how to use several of Paradox's special query operators, like find, delete, and changeto.

In the next chapter, we'll introduce the one remaining query topic: examples. In that chapter, you'll learn what examples are, how they are created, and how they can be used.

Chapter 9
Query by Example

In the previous chapter, you learned how to create queries in Paradox. There is still one more important concept that you must learn, however, before you will fully understand queries: Examples. Examples are special tools that allow you to relate the entries in one field of a table to the entries in other fields of the same table, or to fields in other tables. You can use examples to link one table to another, to perform calculations and to make selections. The power of these tools is virtually unlimited.

A Simple Example

Figure 9-1 shows a query form that contains two examples, which are the highlighted *E*s in the Estimated Completion Date and the Actual Completion Date fields. This query tells Paradox to select every record with an Actual Completion Date field entry that is greater than the Estimated Completion Date field entry for the same record. In other words, this query tells Paradox to select every project that was completed behind schedule.

Figure 9-1

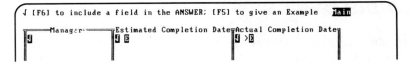

To create this query, first use the **[Menu] A**sk command to create a new query form for PROJECTS, and then use the **[Check Mark]** key to select every field in the form. To enter the example *E* in the Estimated Completion Date field, move to the Estimated Completion Date field, press **[Example]** ([F5]), and type the letter **E**. To enter the second example, move the cursor to the Actual Completion Date field, type >, press **[Example]** ([F5]), and type **E**.

When you process this query, Paradox will create the ANSWER table that is shown in Figure 9-2. As you can see, this query results in only the three records from PROJECTS that have an Actual Completion Date field entry greater than the Estimated Completion Date field entry.

Figure 9-2

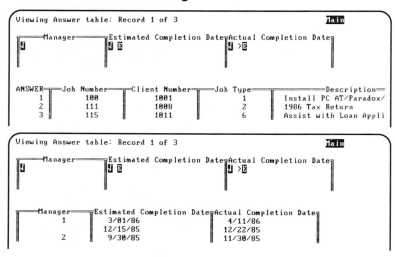

Let's consider how this query works. The example *E* in this query is a symbol, or a placeholder, for the entries in the Estimated Completion Date field of each record. This example allows you to relate the contents of the Estimated Completion Date field to the contents of other fields, in this case, to the entries in the Actual Completion Date field.

The selection condition >E tells Paradox to make the selection by comparing the entries in the Actual Completion Date field to the value of the example *E*. As a result of this condition, the query will select any record that has an Actual Completion Date field entry that is greater than the Estimated Completion Date field entry for the same record.

Example Basics

Although the previous illustration is very simple, it points out many important characteristics of examples. First, this illustration shows how to enter examples into query forms. To enter an example into a query form, you move the cursor to the appropriate field of the form, press **[Example]** ([F5]), and type the example. As soon as you begin typing, the highlight will appear around the characters you type.

Second, as in this case, examples always come in groups of at least two. You will never use just one example in a query. If you think about it for a moment, you'll realize that this makes sense. Since examples are tools that allow you to relate one field to another, there would be no point in using one example without using another.

Editing Examples

You can erase and edit examples in the same way that you erase other entries in query forms. To erase an example, just move the cursor to the field that contains the example and press [Ctrl]-[Backspace]. If you want to replace the example with another example, you must press the [Example] key after you erase the old example and before you begin typing the new example. If you don't press [Example], the characters you type will be entered as a selection condition.

To erase a part of an example, just move the cursor to the field that contains the example and press [Backspace]. Each time you press [Backspace], Paradox will erase one character from the example. If you want to replace the characters you erase, you can simply type the characters. Unless you erase every character in the old example, Paradox will automatically include the characters you type in the example. If you use [Backspace] to erase the entire example, and then want to enter another example, you must press the [Example] key before you begin typing.

You can also edit examples (although you will rarely do so). You can use the [Backspace] key to erase the characters you want to change, and then replace those characters by typing the new characters. You can also use the [Field View] key ([Alt]-[F5]) to enter the field view when you edit examples.

Examples Are Not Conditions

It is important that you do not confuse examples with selection conditions. When you enter the example *E* into the Estimated Completion Date field, you are not telling Paradox to select those records that have the entry *E* in the Estimated Completion Date field. Instead, you are telling Paradox to use the letter *E* as an example for the entries in the Estimated Completion Date field.

Of course, you can use examples in selection conditions. The entry *>E* is an example of a selection condition that contains an example. Even in this case, however, the role of the example is symbolic, not literal. This selection condition does not ask Paradox to select those records with an Actual Completion Date field entry that is greater than the letter *E*. Instead, it asks Paradox to select those entries with an Actual Completion Date field entry that is greater than the value represented by *E*, the Estimated Completion Date field entry for that same record.

Remember, examples are not literal like conditions. Examples are representations, or symbols, or placeholders, for the contents of a given field.

Examples Can Be Any Character

It is important that you understand that the actual example you use for any field is completely up to you. All that is important is that you use the same example in each field in the group of fields you want to relate. Although examples can contain only numbers and letters, you can use letters in number fields, numbers in alphabetic fields, single digits, groups of digits, single letters, groups of letters, real words, or nonsense words, as long as you use the same example in all of the fields in the group of fields you want to relate.

For instance, you could have just as easily used the number 123 in the previous example, creating a query like the one in Figure 9-3. To create this query, just create a new, empty query for PROJECTS, select every field, move to the Estimated Completion Date field, press [**Example**], and type **123**. To enter the second example, move the cursor to the Actual Completion Date field, type >, press [**Example**], and type **123**. To Paradox, this query and the one in Figure 9-1 are identical.

Figure 9-3

As long as you use the same example in each field of the group of fields you want to relate, Paradox doesn't care what type of entry you use as the example. If you use different examples in fields that you want to relate, however, Paradox will be unable to process the query. For example, suppose that you created the query form shown in Figure 9-4. As you can see, we've entered the example *123* in the Estimated Completion Date field of this query, and the example *E* in the Actual Completion Date field. When you process this query, Paradox will display the error message *Example element E has no defining occurrence.*

Figure 9-4

The one important exception to this rule is that Paradox does not care if examples agree in case. For instance, consider the query in Figure 9-5. Notice that the Estimated Completion Date field contains the example *e*, while the Actual Completion Date field contains the example *E*. To Paradox, these two examples are the same, and this query is identical to the one in Figure 9-1.

Figure 9-5

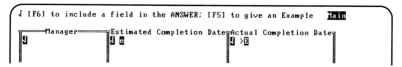

Using Examples in Single-table Queries

In the previous example, we used an example in a single-table query. Before we go on to show how examples can be used to relate different tables, let's consider several more examples of single-table queries that use examples.

An Example

Suppose you want to select all records from the EMPLYEE table that have a Salary field entry that is greater than or equal to 50% of the salary for David Jones. Figure 9-6 shows a query that will do the trick. To define this query, create a new query form for EMPLYEE. Next, enter the condition **Jones** in the first row of the Last Name field and the condition **David** in the first row of the First Name field. Then move to the Salary field, press **[Example]**, and enter the example **123**. Next, move the cursor to the second row of the form and select every field. Then move to the Salary field and type

>[Example]123*.5

Notice that Paradox stops highlighting characters as soon as you type the asterisk. Since Paradox allows you to use only letters and numbers in examples, as soon as you type a character other than a letter or a number, Paradox assumes that you are finished with the example. Remember that the characters > and *.5 are not a part of the example. The example is just the highlighted characters *123*.

Figure 9-6

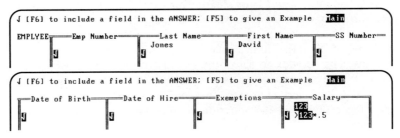

This condition says: *Select all records that have a Salary field entry that is greater than 50% of the example salary.* When you process this query, Paradox will create the ANSWER table shown in Figure 9-7. As you can see, this table includes every field with a Salary field entry that is greater than 50% of David Jones' salary.

Figure 9-7

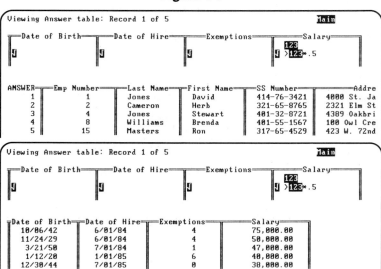

How It Works

The form of this query may be a little bit confusing to you. In the last chapter, you learned that when you enter selection conditions on two rows of a query form, those conditions are joined with a logical OR. In the example query, however, the two rows are not connected in this way. In this query, the first row of the query defines the example. This line says: *Use 123 as the example for the Salary field entry for the record that has the entries* David *in the First Name field and* Jones *in the Last Name field*.

The second row of the query form contains a selection condition that uses the example 123. This row tells Paradox to select the records in EMPLYEE with a salary that is greater than 50% of the example salary—in other words, David Jones' salary. When Paradox processes this query, it uses the first row of the query to define the example, and then it uses the example in the selection condition in the second row to select the appropriate records.

In the query shown in Figure 9-1, both the defining statement and the selection condition are in the same row. That is possible in the query in Figure 9-1 because the defining statement and the condition that uses the example are in different fields. As long as the defining statement and the condition that uses the example are in different fields, both expressions can be in the same row. If, as in the query shown in Figure 9-6, both expressions must be entered in the same field, the defining statement and the condition that uses the example must be in different rows.

Notice that we did not select any fields in the first row of this query form. If we had selected fields in that row, Paradox would have included any record that matched the conditions specified on that row in the ANSWER table. Since we don't want to use the first row to select records, but only to define the example, we didn't select any fields in that row.

The "Query may take a long time ..." Message

Did you notice the message *Query may take a long time to process*, which appeared at the bottom-right corner of the screen when you processed the query? This message is Paradox's way of telling you that the query you have defined is particularly complex and may require a long time to complete. Sometimes, as in this case, the message really doesn't mean much. In other cases, however, this message may signal that Paradox will require several minutes–or perhaps longer–to process the query.

This message can be a big help. Were it not for this message, you would have no way to know how long a query might take to process. You could end up sitting in front of your computer for several minutes waiting for the query to finish. Thanks to the message, however, you can do something else while the query is running, and come back in a few minutes to check on its progress.

A Fine Point

In the example, there was only one record in EMPLYEE that met the conditions stated in the query: First Name equals David, Last Name equals Jones. But suppose there had been two or more records that satisfied the condition. For example, suppose you had not entered the name *David* in the First Name field of the query form. As you recall, there are several records in EMPLYEE that satisfy the condition: Last Name equals Jones.

When you press [**Do-It!**], Paradox will create the ANSWER table shown in Figure 9-8 on the next page. If you study this table for a moment, you may notice that it contains every record from EMPLYEE that has a Salary field entry greater than 50% of the Salary field entry of any of the Jones' records. In other words, since the selection condition in the first row of the query form selected several records, the second row of the query used the Salary field entry of each of those records in selecting records.

Another Example

Suppose you want to find all of the records for people who are older than David Jones. To make this selection, first create a new, empty query form for the EMPLYEE table and select every field in that form. Next, move to the Emp Number field and enter the selection condition **1**, David Jones' employee number. Now, move to the Date of Birth field, press [**Example**], and type **DOB**. Next, move to the second row of the Date of Birth field and type

>[Example]DOB

Finally, move to the space under the form name in the second row and press [**Check Mark**] to select every field in this row. Figure 9-9 shows the completed query. In this query, the first row of the query defines the condition DOB. Because you have entered the number 1 in the Emp Number field of this row, DOB is used to represent the Date of Birth field entry for David Jones, the employee with employee number 1. The second row of the query uses the example DOB to select records. If the entry in the Date of Birth field for a given record is greater than the value of the example DOB, then that record will be included in ANSWER.

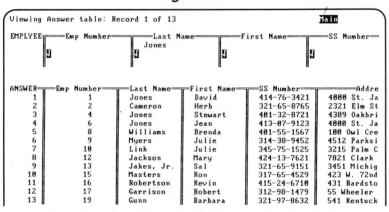

Figure 9-8

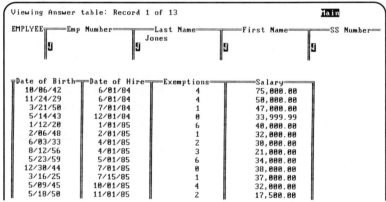

Figure 9-9

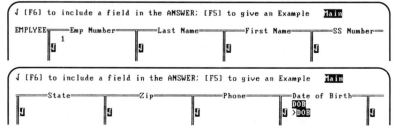

When you process this query, Paradox will create the ANSWER table that is shown in Figure 9-10. As you can see, this table includes only those records with Date of Birth field entries that are greater than that of David Jones.

Figure 9-10

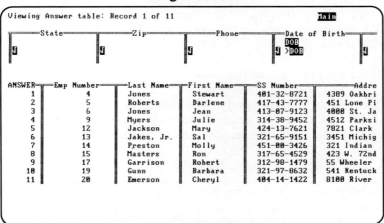

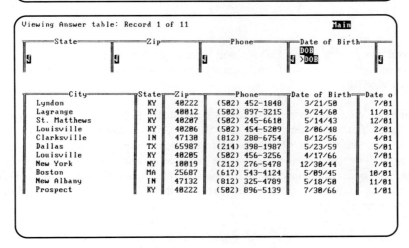

Using Examples in Changeto Queries

You can also use examples in changeto queries. When used in this way, examples allow you to make changes to the entries in a field based on the entries in that field or in other fields of the same record. For example, suppose you want to increase every Salary field entry in EMPLYEE by 10%. To create a query that will make this change, first use the **[Menu] A**sk command to create a new query form for EMPLYEE. Then move to the Salary field and type

[Example]123,changeto [Example]123*1.1

Figure 9-11 shows the completed query. The first part of the entry in the Salary field sets up 123 as the example for the entries in the Salary field. The second part uses the example *E* to tell Paradox to increase each entry in the Salary field by 1.1 times.

Figure 9-11

When you process this query, Paradox will increase each entry in the Salary field entry by 10%. In addition, the original, unchanged records will be copied to the temporary table named CHANGED.

Now suppose you want to increase by 10% the Salary field entry for just those records with a Salary field entry that is less than $25,000. To create this query, just move the cursor to the Salary field of the query form, type a comma, and type the selection condition **<25000**. Figure 9-12 shows the completed query. If you process the query, Paradox will once again increase the values in the Salary field by 10%. This time, however, Paradox will change only those records that currently have a Salary field entry that is less than $25,000.

Figure 9-12

Now suppose you want to push back by ten days the Estimated Completion Date for every project in PROJECTS that is not already complete. Figure 9-13 shows a query that will accomplish this task. To create this query, first make a new query form for PROJECTS. Next, move to the Actual Completion Date field and enter the selection condition **blank**. This condition assures that the query will operate only on records that do not have an entry in the Actual Completion Date field (that is, those projects that are not yet complete). Now, move to the Estimated Completion Date field and type

[Example]E,changeto [Example]E+10

The first part of this entry sets up E as the example for the entries in the selected records of the Estimated Completion Date field. The second part of the entry uses the example E to instruct Paradox to increase the value of each Estimated Completion Date field by 10.

Figure 9-13

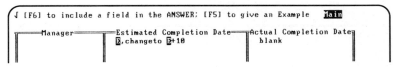

When you process this query, Paradox will add 10 to the Estimated Completion Date field entry for every record with a blank Actual Completion Date field.

Using Examples in Other Types of Queries

Although examples are most useful in changeto queries, you can also use them to find queries, delete queries, and with the not and like operators. In general, you will use examples in this type of query in exactly the same way you use them in other one-table queries: to let you make selections in one field based on entries in some other field. So that you can see how useful examples are in these kinds of queries, however, we'll look at a few examples.

Using Examples with Not

Suppose you want to locate all of the entries in the EMPLYEE table that have a State field entry that is different from the State field entry for David Jones. Figure 9-14 shows a query that will make this selection. To define this query, first create a new, blank query form for the EMPLYEE table. Next, move to the Emp Number field and type **1**, the employee number for David Jones. Then move to the State field, press **[Example]**, and type **ST**.

Now, move down to the second row of the query form and select every field in that row. Then move to the State field, type **not**, press **[Example]**, and type **ST**.

Figure 9-14

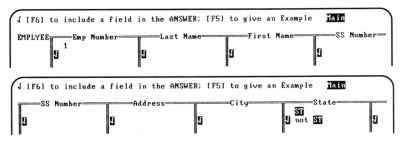

Now press **[Do-It!]** to create the ANSWER table shown in Figure 9-15. As you can see, this table includes only those records from EMPLYEE that have a State field entry that is different from the State field entry for David Jones, employee number 1.

Figure 9-15

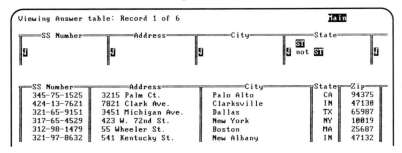

As in the earlier examples, the first row of this query defines the example, and the second row of the query uses the example to select records. In this example, the first row tells Paradox that the example *ST* stands for the State field entry for the record with the Emp Number field entry 1.

A Delete Query Example

You can also use examples in delete queries. For example, suppose you want to delete from the PROJECTS table any projects that have the same Client Number field entry as job number 103. To begin, create a new, blank query form for the PROJECT table. Next, move to the Job Number field and type **103**. Then move to the Client Number field, press **[Example]**, and type **ABC**.

Next, you should move down to the second row of the query form, and type the word **delete** in the space under the form name. Then move to the Client Number field, press **[Example]**, and type **ABC**. Since this will be a delete query, you will not select any fields in any row of the form.

When you press [Do-It!] to process the query, Paradox will delete from PROJECTS any project that has a Client Number field entry that is the same as the Client Number field entry for job number 103. These records will be copied to a DELETED table. As you can see, Figure 9-16 shows the query and the DELETED table on the screen.

Figure 9-16

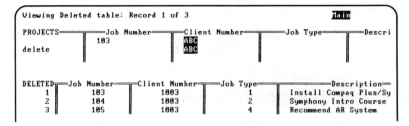

As in the previous example, the first row of the query form in Figure 9-16 defines the example. However, in this case, the first row tells Paradox that the example *ABC* represents the Client Number field entry for the record in PROJECTS that has the Job Number field entry 103. The second row of the query uses this example to delete records from the table.

Two-table Operations

In Chapter 3, we introduced the concept of normalized tables. In that chapter, we showed you how you can make your data bases more efficient if you create groups of related, normalized tables, and divide your data among these tables. In that chapter, we also introduced the concept of common fields–fields that are common to two or more related tables, which contain the same type of data in all of the tables, and which can be used to relate the data stored in those tables. However, we stopped short of showing you how to use the common fields to relate normalized tables.

As you have probably guessed, examples are the tools that you use to link two or more related tables that you want to query or join. In fact, this is probably the most common and most important use of these tools. When used in this way, examples tell Paradox on which field or fields it should link the tables you want to relate. Let's look at several instances of how examples can be used to link related tables.

An Example

Suppose that you want to create a new table that includes the job number and job type fields from PROJECTS and the description field from a table called JOBS. The JOBS table contains the job number and description of each type of job our hypothetical company performs: audits, compilation, tax return preparation, and so on. Figures 9-17 and 9-18 show the contents and structure of JOBS.

Figure 9-17

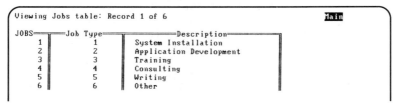

Figure 9-18

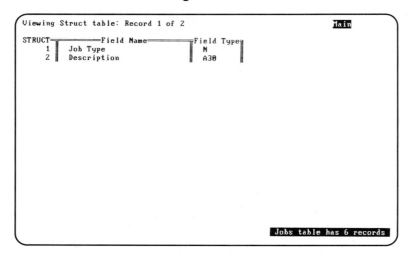

To create the new table, you'll need to define a fairly complex query. To begin, use the **[Menu] A**sk command to create a new query form for PROJECTS. Next, select the Job Number and Job Type fields in this query form. Now, with the cursor in the Job Type field, press **[Example]**, and type **123**.

Now issue the **[Menu] A**sk command again and create a new query form for JOBS. When this query appears, move to the Description field and press **[Check Mark]**. Then move to the Job Type field, press **[Example]**, and type **123**. Figure 9-19 shows the query.

Figure 9-19

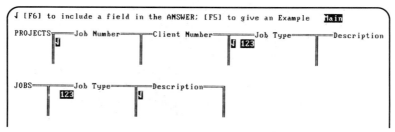

Notice that the three fields we've selected are the fields we want Paradox to include in the ANSWER table. Also notice the examples in the Job Number fields. These examples link the two tables in the Job Number field. In other words, the examples tell Paradox that it should match the numbers in the Job Number field of PROJECTS to the numbers in the Job Number field of JOBS as it processes the query.

Now press **[Do-It!]** to process the query. Figure 9-20 shows the result. As you can see, Paradox has created a new ANSWER table which contains the Job Number and Job Type fields from PROJECTS and the Description field from JOBS.

Figure 9-20

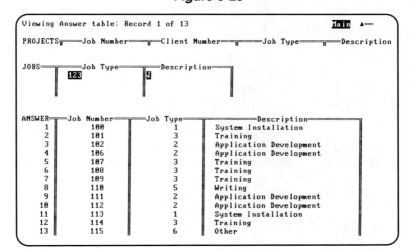

Notes

There is no absolute limit to the number of tables that you can link through a query. The precise number that you'll be able to relate depends on the configuration of your computer and the size of the tables that you will be relating. Since most of your multitable queries will involve only two or three tables, you are unlikely to ever encounter the limit.

About Multiple Query Forms

As you have seen, a query that you use to relate two or more tables must contain one query form for each of those tables. Creating the second and subsequent query forms is like creating the first: You just issue the **[Menu]** Ask command and specify the name of the table for which you want to create a query form. The second and subsequent forms appear on the screen below the first form. To move from one form to another, just press **[Up Image]** or **[Down Image]**.

Keep in mind that any query form that is visible is active. If there are three query forms on the screen, the conditions in all three forms will be considered by Paradox when you press **[Do-It!]**. There is no way to exclude a visible query form from being processed. If you have created a query form, and do not need it any longer, you should clear it.

If there are two or more query forms in view when you press [Do-It!], and those forms are unrelated, Paradox will display the error message

> Query appears to ask two unrelated questions

The Order of ANSWER

Notice the order of the fields in the ANSWER table in Figure 9-20. Specifically, notice that the fields you selected in PROJECTS, the first query form in the query, appear in ANSWER ahead of the field you selected in JOBS, the second query form in the query. When you create a query that operates on more than one table, the fields in the resulting ANSWER table will always be arranged in this way. All of the selected fields from the first query form in the query will appear first in ANSWER, followed by the fields from the second query form, then the third, and so on.

You'll want to keep this rule in mind when you create multitable queries. Although you can use the [Menu] Image command to rearrange the columns in ANSWER after you process the query, it is easier to arrange the query forms in the query so that the fields in ANSWER are in the desired order.

Normalizing Tables

It is important that you understand that examples can only be used to link tables that have some relationship to one another. In other words, if the PROJECTS table did not include a Job Type field, there would not be any way to link that table to the JOBS table. Only because we designed these tables to be related can we link them using examples.

Now you see how the principle of normalization, which we explained for the first time in Chapter 3, works. JOBS and PROJECTS are examples of normalized tables. Rather than including the description of each job type in PROJECTS, we placed the various job descriptions in a separate table, JOBS. So that we could easily relate these two tables, we included a code field, Job Type, in both tables. Since both tables include this field, they can be related easily using examples.

As you work with Paradox, you'll find more and more places where it makes sense to create normalized sets of tables instead of storing all the data about a particular thing in one huge table. As you use this technique more, you'll find yourself using examples in two-table queries more often. In the remainder of this section, we'll show other examples of normalized sets of tables, and we'll explain the use of examples to link tables.

Another Example

Now suppose you want to create a table that contains the Job Number and Description fields from the PROJECTS table and the Last Name and First Name fields from EMPLYEE. The Last Name and First Name portion of each record in this new table would be the last and first names of the project manager. This table would let you determine at a glance the manager of each project.

To begin, create a new, blank query on PROJECTS. When the query comes into view, use **[Check Mark]** to select the Job Number and Description fields. Then move to the Manager field, press **[Example]**, and type **123**. Now, create a new query form for EMPLYEE. When the form appears on the screen, use the **[Check Mark]** key to select the Last Name and First Name fields. Then move to the Emp Number field, press **[Example]**, and type **123**.

Figure 9-21 shows the completed query. Notice that the four fields that we've selected are the four fields we want Paradox to include in the ANSWER table. Also notice the examples in the Manager and Emp Number fields. These examples link the two tables on these two fields. In other words, the examples tell Paradox that it should match the numbers in the Manager field of PROJECTS to the contents of the Emp Number field of EMPLYEE as it processes the query.

Figure 9-21

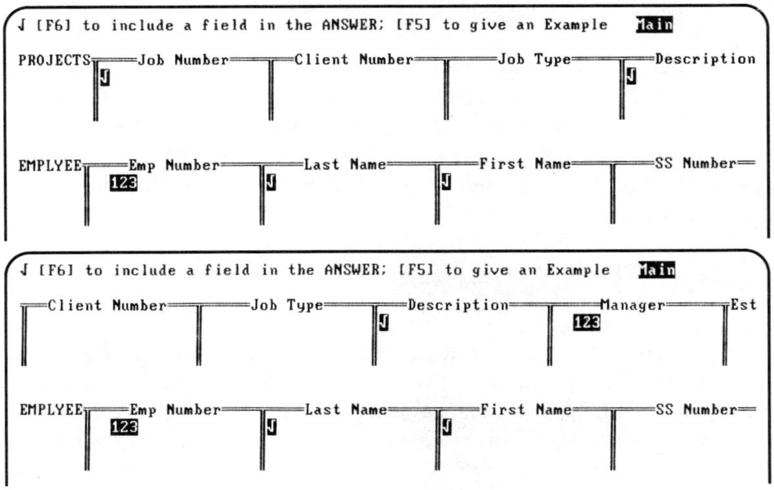

```
√ [F6] to include a field in the ANSWER; [F5] to give an Example   Main
   PROJECTS    Job Number    Client Number    Job Type    Description
                    √                                          √

   EMPLYEE     Emp Number    Last Name    First Name    SS Number
                   123           √            √
```

```
√ [F6] to include a field in the ANSWER; [F5] to give an Example   Main
          Client Number    Job Type    Description    Manager    Est
                                           √            123

   EMPLYEE     Emp Number    Last Name    First Name    SS Number
                  123           √             √
```

Now press **[Do-It!]** to process the query. Figure 9-22 shows the result. As you can see, Paradox has created a new ANSWER table, which contains the Job Number and Description fields from the PROJECTS table and the First Name and Last Name fields from the EMPLYEE table.

Figure 9-22

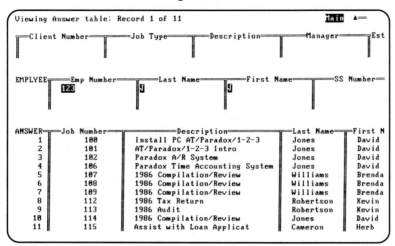

Notice also that, although the fields we used to relate EMPLYEE and PROJECTS have the same type and length, they do not have the same name. In some data base programs, like dBASE III, you can only relate tables on fields that have the same name. This restriction can be a real problem. In Paradox, the fields that you use to relate tables should have the same type and length, but they do not need to have the same name.

Of course, although the fields that you choose to relate two tables do not need to have the same name, they should contain related data. In the example, it made sense to use the Manager and Emp Number fields to relate PROJECTS and EMPLYEE since both of these fields contain employee number data. It would not make sense to try to relate these tables on other fields, however, since there are no other fields in the two tables that contain related data.

Two-table Find Queries

Suppose you want to look at the employee record for the manager of Project 108. Figure 9-23 shows a query that will do the trick. To create this query, first create a new, blank query form for the EMPLYEE table. When the query form comes into view, type the word **find** in the space under the form name. Next, move to the Emp Number field, press **[Example]**, and type **123**.

Now create a new, blank query form for the PROJECTS table. Next, move to the Job Number field and type **108**, the number of the job in which you are interested. Finally, move to the Manager field, press **[Example]**, and type **123**.

Figure 9-23

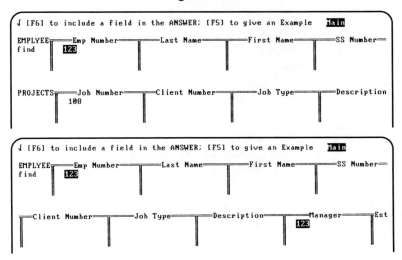

This query tells Paradox to find in EMPLYEE the record which has the same manager number as the record that is selected by the condition 108 in the Job Number field. The example *123* represents the manager number of the project that matches the condition which you selected.

When you process this query, Paradox will bring the EMPLYEE table into view, and will move the cursor to the record for employee number 6. Figure 9-24 shows the screen at this point.

Figure 9-24

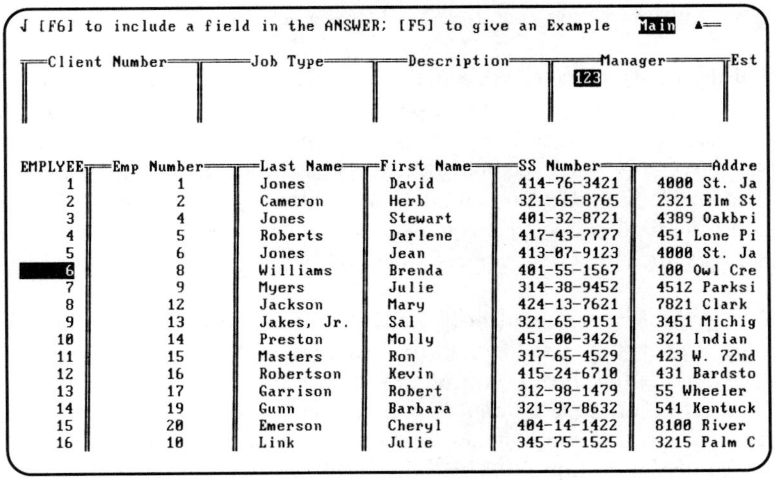

A More Complex Example

Let's look at a more complex example of two-table queries. Suppose you want to see the following information about each job that was completed after the Estimated Completion Date: the manager's employee number and name, and the job number, client number, description, estimated completion date, and actual completion date for the project itself. Figure 9-25 shows a query that will make this selection.

Figure 9-25

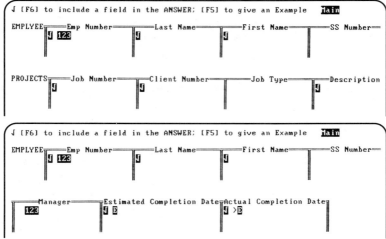

To create this query, first make new query forms for EMPLYEE and PROJECTS. Use the **[Check Mark]** key to select the Emp Number, Last Name, and First Name fields in EMPLYEE, and the Job Number, Client Number, Description, Estimated Completion Date, and Actual Completion Date fields in PROJECTS.

Once all of the fields are selected, move to the Estimated Completion Date field in the PROJECTS query form, press **[Example]**, and type **E**. Then move to the Actual Completion Date field, type **>**, press **[Example]**, and type **E**. These two examples work together to select only those records with an Actual Completion Date field entry that is greater than the Estimated Completion Date field entry. The entry in the Estimated Completion Date field defines the example, and the entry in the Actual Completion Date field uses the example in a selection condition.

Next, move to the Manager field in PROJECTS, press **[Example]**, and type **123**. Then move to the Emp Number field in EMPLYEE, press **[Example]**, and type **123** again. These two examples link EMPLYEE and PROJECTS on the Manager and Emp Number fields. The effect of these examples is to cause Paradox to select any record from EMPLYEE that has an Emp Number field entry that matches the entry in the Manager field of a record selected from PROJECTS.

When you process this query, Paradox will create the ANSWER table, which is shown in Figure 9-26. As you can see, Paradox has created an ANSWER table that contains the selected fields from both EMPLYEE and PROJECTS, and which contains only those records for which the Actual Completion Date field entry is greater than the Estimated Completion Date entry.

Figure 9-26

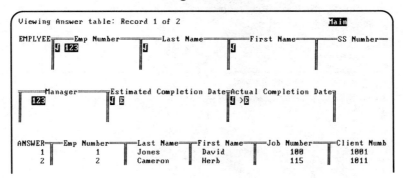

Calc Queries

The calc operator is a powerful tool that lets you make calculations based on the entries in the fields of a table. Paradox stores the results of the calculations in special fields that it adds to the ANSWER table. You can use the calc operator to compute statistics about your tables or to use the data in one or several fields to make computations.

An Example

Let's look at an example of a calc query. Suppose you want to compute the hourly wage rate for every employee in the EMPLYEE table. Figure 9-27 shows a query that makes this calculation.

Figure 9-27

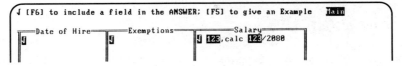

To create this query, first make a new query form for EMPLYEE. When the query form is in view, use the **[Check Mark]** key to select every field in the form. Next, move the cursor to the Salary field and type

[Example]123,calc [Example]123/2080

This query sets 123 as the example for the contents of the Salary field and tells Paradox to divide the contents of this field for every record by 2080. (We chose 2080 because there are 2080 working hours in a year.)

When you press **[Do-It!]** to process this table, Paradox will create the ANSWER table shown in Figure 9-28. As you can see, this table includes a field, Salary / 2080, which did not exist in the EMPLYEE table. This new field contains the results of the calc query. If you check, you'll see that each entry in this field is equal to the corresponding entry in the Salary field, divided by 2080.

Figure 9-28

```
Viewing Answer table: Record 1 of 16                    Main
    ┌─Date of Hire──┐┌─Exemptions──┐┌──────Salary──────┐
    │ J             ││ J           ││ J 123, calc 123/2080
    │               ││             ││                   │

┌─Date of Hire─┬─Exemptions─┬──Salary──┬─Salary / 2080─┐
│   6/01/84    │     4      │ 82,500.00│     39.66     │
│   6/01/84    │     4      │ 55,000.00│     26.44     │
│   7/01/84    │     1      │ 51,700.00│     24.86     │
│  11/01/84    │     3      │ 16,940.00│      8.14     │
│  12/01/84    │     0      │ 37,399.99│     17.98     │
│   1/01/85    │     6      │ 44,000.00│     21.15     │
│   2/01/85    │     1      │ 35,200.00│     16.92     │
│   4/01/85    │     2      │ 33,000.00│     15.87     │
│   4/01/85    │     3      │ 25,410.00│     12.22     │
│   5/01/85    │     6      │ 37,400.00│     17.98     │
│   7/01/85    │     1      │ 17,847.50│      8.58     │
│   7/01/85    │     0      │ 41,800.00│     20.10     │
│   7/15/85    │     1      │ 40,700.00│     19.57     │
│  10/01/85    │     4      │ 35,200.00│     16.92     │
│  11/01/85    │     2      │ 21,175.00│     10.18     │
│   1/01/86    │     2      │ 14,520.00│      6.98     │
```

This example illustrates one of the most important practical benefits of the calc operator. If the calc operator did not exist, you might have felt the need to include an Hourly Wage field in the structure of EMPLYEE. Thanks to calc, however, you don't need to store this information in your table permanently. Instead, you can simply calculate the hourly rate whenever you need it. By using calc cleverly, you may eliminate certain fields from your tables, thus saving space and increasing the performance of Paradox.

Another Example

Let's consider another example. Suppose you want to calculate the difference between the Actual Completion Date and the Estimated Completion Date for all completed projects. To begin, clear the screen, then create a new query form for PROJECTS and select every field in the first row of the form. Then move to the Estimated Completion Date field, press **[Example]**, and type **E**. This entry sets *E* as the example for the entries in the Estimated Completion Date field.

Next, move to the Actual Completion Date field and type

> [Example]A,not blank,calc [Example]A-[Example]E

This entry sets A as the example for the entries in the Actual Completion Date field, tells Paradox to select only those records that do not have a blank entry in the Actual Completion Date field, and tells Paradox to create a new, calculated field whose contents will equal A-E, or Actual Completion Date minus Estimated Completion Date.

When you process this query, Paradox will create the ANSWER table that is shown in Figure 9-29. As you can see, Paradox has created a new field, *Actual Completion Date–Estimated Completion Date*, in ANSWER and has stored the results of the calculations in that field.

Figure 9-29

```
Viewing Answer table: Record 1 of 7                                    Main
┌─Manager──────┬─Estimated Completion Date─┬─Actual Completion Date───┐
│ᚘ             │ᚘ E                        │ᚘ A,not blank,calc A-E    │
│              │                           │                          │


  ┌─Estimated Completion Date─┬─Actual Completion Date─┬─Actual Completion Date─┐
  │ 3/01/86                   │ 4/11/86                │ 41                     │
  │ 9/01/85                   │ 9/01/85                │ 0                      │
  │ 10/15/85                  │ 10/15/85               │ 0                      │
  │ 9/15/85                   │ 9/15/85                │ 0                      │
  │ 11/15/85                  │ 11/15/85               │ 0                      │
  │ 12/15/85                  │ 12/22/85               │ 7                      │
  │ 9/30/85                   │ 11/30/85               │ 61                     │
```

Also notice that ANSWER includes only those records from PROJECTS that did not have a blank in the Actual Completion Date field. This example shows how easy it is to use selection conditions in calc queries.

Calc Queries on Alphanumeric Fields

You can use the calc operator to concatenate, or string together, the entries in two text fields. For example, in EMPLYEE the first name and last name of each employee are in different fields. Suppose you want to create a new field that contains each employee's full name in normal form (as in David Jones).

To begin, create a new, empty query form for EMPLYEE and select every field in the form. Next, move to the Last Name field, press **[Example]**, and type **L**. Now move to the First Name field and type

> [Example]F, calc [Example]F+" "+[Example]L

This query sets *L* as the example for the entries in the Last Name field and *F* as the example for the entries in the First Name field. The formula

    calc F+" "+L

tells Paradox to concatenate the contents of the First Name field (F) and the Last Name field (L) and to place a space between the two. The space is represented in the formula by a space surrounded by quotation marks.

Figure 9-30 shows the query and the ANSWER table that Paradox will create when you process this query. Notice the new field, *First Name + Blank + Last Name*, which contains the new entries Paradox has created. As you can see, this new field contains the full names of all the employees in EMPLYEE.

Figure 9-30

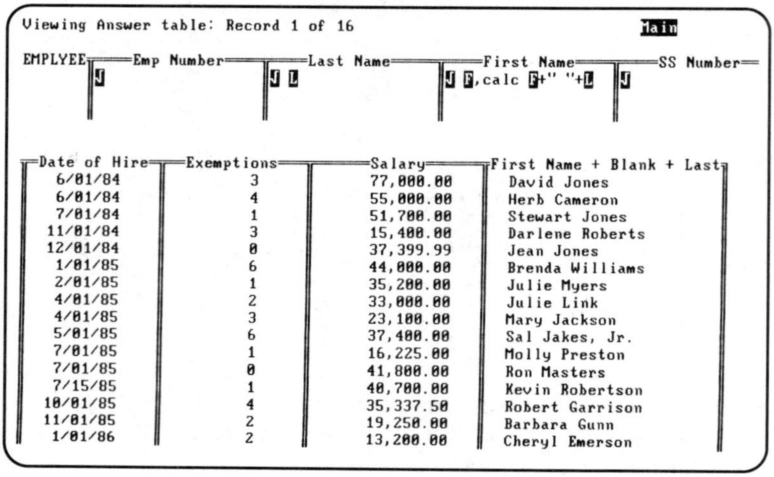

```
Viewing Answer table: Record 1 of 16                                    Main
EMPLYEE    Emp Number      Last Name       First Name         SS Number
                                            ,calc F+" "+L

   Date of Hire  Exemptions      Salary      First Name + Blank + Last
     6/01/84        3           77,000.00    David Jones
     6/01/84        4           55,000.00    Herb Cameron
     7/01/84        1           51,700.00    Stewart Jones
    11/01/84        3           15,400.00    Darlene Roberts
    12/01/84        0           37,399.99    Jean Jones
     1/01/85        6           44,000.00    Brenda Williams
     2/01/85        1           35,200.00    Julie Myers
     4/01/85        2           33,000.00    Julie Link
     4/01/85        3           23,100.00    Mary Jackson
     5/01/85        6           37,400.00    Sal Jakes, Jr.
     7/01/85        1           16,225.00    Molly Preston
     7/01/85        0           41,800.00    Ron Masters
     7/15/85        1           40,700.00    Kevin Robertson
    10/01/85        4           35,337.50    Robert Garrison
    11/01/85        2           19,250.00    Barbara Gunn
     1/01/86        2           13,200.00    Cheryl Emerson
```

In the example, we used the expression

    +" "+

to add a single blank space between the first name and last name. In fact, Paradox allows you to include any literal characters that you wish between quotation marks. For instance, look at the query and ANSWER table in Figure 9-31. The query includes the expression

    calc "Dear "+F+" "+L

which tells Paradox to concatenate the word *Dear* to each employee's full name. If you look at the resulting ANSWER table, you'll notice the word *Dear* before the names in the calculated field of this table.

Figure 9-31

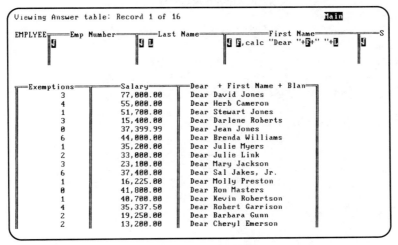

Notes

Just like other ANSWER tables, the ANSWER table that results from a calc query is a temporary table. If you want to save the contents of the new field, you must rename the ANSWER table. If you want the new field to be a part of the main table, you might want to assign ANSWER the name of the table you just queried. If you want to retain the results of the calculation without including them in the main table, you should choose a different name.

Some Paradox users become confused about the difference between the calc and changeto operators. *Changeto* queries cause Paradox to change the actual values in the fields of the table being queried. Calc queries, on the other hand, use the entries in the fields of the table being queried as the basis for a calculation; the result of the calculation is stored in a separate field.

For example, the query in Figure 9-32 is identical to the query in Figure 9-27 on page 273, except it uses the changeto operator instead of the calc operator. When you process this query, it will change the entries in the Salary field by dividing them by 2080. As a result, the new Salary field entry for David Jones will be 37.02, the Salary field entry for Julie Myers will be 16.92, and so on.

Figure 9-32

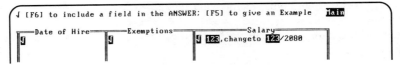

You cannot use a calc query to relate an alphanumeric field to any other type of field. For example, consider the calc query in Figure 9-33. The expression

   calc DOH/S

uses the examples *DOH* and *S* to attempt to link the Date of Hire and Salary fields. If you try to process this query, Paradox will highlight the entry in the Salary field of the query form and will display the error message

   calc expression has type error

Figure 9-33

The same thing will happen if you try to use calc to link an alphanumeric field with a date or dollar ($) field. You can, however, use calc to link a numeric field with a dollar field or a date field. For example, the query in Figure 9-34 uses the expression

   calc S/E

to link the Exemptions field in EMPLYEE to the Salary field. Although Salary has the type $ and Exemptions has the type N, this query is perfectly acceptable to Paradox.

Figure 9-34

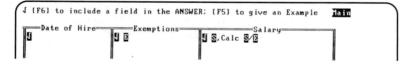

Calculating Summary Statistics

You can also use calc to calculate summary statistics on the entries in numeric and date fields. Paradox offers five special statistical operators–Sum, Average, Max, Min, and Count–that you can use in conjunction with calc to compute statistics. Each of these statistical operators computes a different statistic, based upon the other entries you make in the query form. Sum computes the sum of the entries you specify. Max and Min compute the maximum and minimum values of the specified entries. Average computes the arithmetic mean, or average, of the selected entries. Count computes the count of the specified entries.

Let's consider a few examples of these operators. Suppose you want to know the total annual salary paid by your company (in other words, the total of the Salary field in EMPLYEE). To make this calculation, you'll use the Sum operator in a calc query.

To begin, create a new query form for EMPLYEE. When the form appears, move to the Salary field and type **calc sum**. Now press **[Do-It!]** to process the query and create the ANSWER table shown in Figure 9-35. As you can see, this table contains just one field–Sum of Salary–and just one record. The one entry in the table, 589,792.49 is the sum of the entries in the Salary field of EMPLYEE.

Figure 9-35

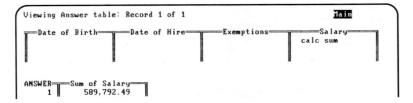

The Average operator works in the same way as Sum. For example, suppose you want to know the average of the Salary field entries. To calculate this statistic, just move the cursor to the Salary field of the query form, and change the word *sum* to **average**. When the change is made, press **[Do-It!]**. Figure 9-36 shows the resulting ANSWER table. The one entry in this table, 36,862.03, is the AVERAGE of the Salary field entries.

Figure 9-36

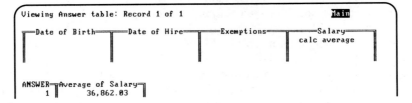

Notice that we did not select any fields in either of these queries. When you select fields in a query that uses statistical operators, Paradox will compute group statistics for the field or fields you select. Since at this point you want to compute statistics for the table as a whole, you don't need to select any fields. We'll show you how to create group summaries in a few pages.

Now suppose that you want to compute the total number, or count, of the entries in the Salary field. To do this, enter the expression **calc count** in the Salary field of the query form. When you process this query, Paradox will create the ANSWER table shown in Figure 9-37. As you can see, this table includes just one field, Count of Salary. The single entry in that field, 15, is the total number of entries in the Salary field.

Figure 9-37

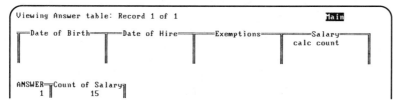

Scope and Field Compatibility

There are two concepts that you must keep in mind when you use statistical operators: Scope and Field Compatibility. The scope of an operator determines whether or not it will operate on all the records in a field, or only on the unique records. The field compatibility of an operator determines in which types of fields that operator can be used.

Scope of Statistical Operators

Since there are 16 records in EMPLYEE, and each of these records has a Salary field entry, you may wonder why the expression *calc count* in the previous example returned the number 15. The answer involves the concept of scope. The scope of an operator determines whether it will operate on all of the records in a table, or just upon those records that have a unique entry in the specified column.

Each of Paradox's statistical operators has a default scope. Sum and Average will operate on all of the records in the specified column, even if there are duplicate entries. Count, Max, and Min operate only on the unique entries in the specified field.

If you look at the Salary field in EMPLYEE (Figure 9-38 shows this table), you'll notice that there are two identical 35,200.00 entries in this field. When Paradox evaluated the *calc count* expression, it counted only one of these two duplicate entries. The result, 15, is the number of unique entries in the Salary field. On the other hand, when Paradox computed the Sum and Average of the Salary field entries in the two previous examples, it evaluated both of these records. The Sum and Average returned by those queries include all 16 entries in the field.

If you wish, you can override the default scope of any of Paradox's statistical operators by using the words *all* and *unique*. For example, suppose you want to compute the count of all of the entries in the Salary field. To make this calculation, you would add the word **all** to the expression **calc count** in the Salary field, as shown in Figure 9-39. When you process this query, Paradox will create the ANSWER table shown in Figure 9-40. As you can see, the result in this table, 16, includes all entries in the Salary field.

Figure 9-38

```
Viewing Emplyee table: Record 1 of 16                    Main
 Date of Birth   Date of Hire    Exemptions      Salary
   10/06/42        6/01/84           4           82,500.00
   11/24/29        6/01/84           4           55,000.00
    3/21/50        7/01/84           1           51,700.00
    9/24/60       11/01/84           3           16,940.00
    5/14/43       12/01/84           0           37,399.99
    1/12/20        1/01/85           6           44,000.00
    2/06/48        2/01/85           1           35,200.00
    6/03/33        4/01/85           2           33,000.00
    8/12/56        4/01/85           3           25,410.00
    5/23/59        5/01/85           6           37,400.00
    4/17/66        7/01/85           1           17,847.50
   12/30/44        7/01/85           0           41,800.00
    3/16/25        7/15/85           1           40,700.00
    5/09/45       10/01/85           4           35,200.00
    5/18/50       11/01/85           2           21,175.00
    7/30/66        1/01/86           2           14,520.00
```

Figure 9-39

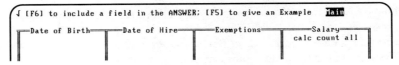

Figure 9-40

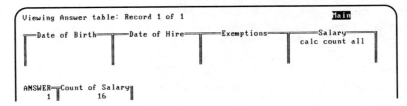

On the other hand, suppose you want to compute the sum of just the unique entries in the Salary field. To make this calculation, you would enter the expression **calc sum unique** in the Salary field of an otherwise empty EMPLOYEE query form. When you process this query, Paradox will create the ANSWER table shown in Figure 9-41. Notice that the result in this table, which shows the sum of only the unique entries, is 35,200.00 less than the result in the earlier example. (Although this example may not seem very realistic, it demonstrates the effect of the unique operator. We'll look at a more realistic example of the unique operator in a few pages.)

Figure 9-41

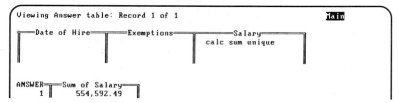

As you create more and more sophisticated statistical queries, you'll need to pay more and more attention to the concept of scope. In general, the default scope that Ansa has chosen for each of the statistical operators is the best choice. Occasionally, though, you'll need to use Unique and All to alter the scope.

Field Compatibility

Field compatibility is another important characteristic of statistical operators. Simply put, not every operator will work in every type of field. While you can use the Count, Max, and Min operators in all types of fields, you can only use Average in number, short number, dollar, and date fields. Sum can only be used in number, short number, and dollar fields.

If you attempt to use an operator in the wrong type of field, Paradox will display an error message that describes the error you have made. For instance, if you try to calculate the average of an alphanumeric field, Paradox will display the error message

> Only numeric and date fields may be averaged

If you try to compute the sum of a date field, Paradox will display the message

> Only numeric fields may be summed

Other Examples

You can enter statistical operators in two or more fields of a query form. For example, Figure 9-42 shows a query form that will calculate the average salary and average number of exemptions from EMPLYEE and the ANSWER table Paradox will create when you process this query. As you can see, this table includes two fields: Average of Exemptions and Average of Salary. The results in this table are the averages of the values in those two fields.

Figure 9-42

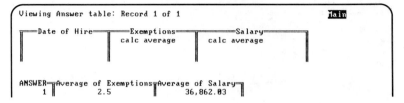

You can also enter two statistical operators in one field. For example, the query in Figure 9-43 computes the maximum and minimum values from the Salary field. To define this query, just create a new query form for EMPLYEE and type the entry

calc max,calc min

in the Salary field. When you process this query, Paradox will create the ANSWER table shown in Figure 9-43. As you can see, this table includes two fields, Max of Salary and Min of Salary, and two entries, the maximum and minimum values from the Salary field.

Figure 9-43

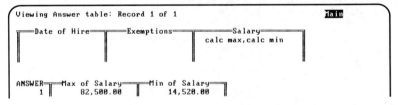

You can also use statistical operators in queries that include selection conditions. For example, suppose you want to know how many employees are paid more than 30,000.00 per year. To make this computation, you would create the query shown in Figure 9-44. Notice the selection condition **>30000** in the Salary field and the entry **calc count** in the Emp Number field. When you press **[Do-It!]** to process this query, Paradox will create the ANSWER table shown in Figure 9-45. As you can see, this table has just one entry, 11, which is the number of employees in EMPLYEE who earn more than 30,000.00.

Figure 9-44

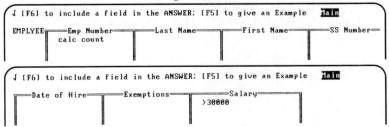

Figure 9-45

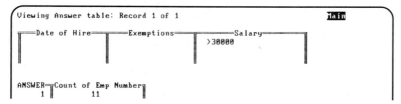

Do you wonder why we entered the formula *calc count* in the Emp Number field? We chose this field because we were sure that there was a unique entry in it for each record in the table. In fact, we could have entered the function in the Social Security Number field and achieved essentially the same result. If we had entered the function in the Last Name field, however, as shown in Figure 9-46, the result would have been different. As you can see, the number in the table is now 9 and not 11. Since there are three Jones entries in the Last Name field, there are only nine unique names that meet the condition.

Figure 9-46

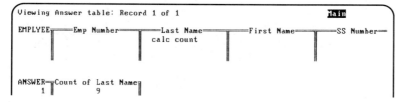

Computing Group Statistics

Paradox's statistical operators can also be used to compute group statistics. To compute a group statistic, you use [Check Mark] to select the field on which you want Paradox to group the table and enter a statistical operator in the field or fields on which you want to compute statistics.

For example, suppose you want to calculate the number of projects that each manager is responsible for; in other words, you want to calculate the number of times each manager's employee number appears in the Manager field of PROJECTS. To make this calculation, first create a new query form for PROJECTS. Next, move to the Manager field and press **[Check Mark]** to select the field. Finally, move to the Job Number field and type the formula **calc count**. Figure 9-47 shows the completed query form.

Figure 9-47

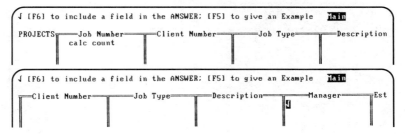

When you process this query, Paradox will create the ANSWER table that is shown in Figure 9-48. Notice that this table includes two fields, Manager and Count of Job Number, and five records, one for each unique employee number in the Manager field of PROJECTS. The entries in the Manager field of ANSWER are the employee numbers from the Manager field of PROJECTS. The entries in the Count of Job Number field represent the number of jobs for which each manager is responsible. In other words, the 5 in the Count of Job Number field of the second record in ANSWER means that manager number 1 is responsible for five different jobs.

Figure 9-48

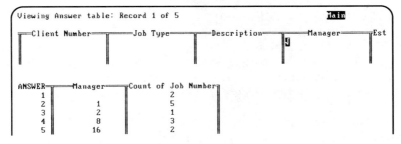

Notice that the first record in ANSWER has a blank in the Manager field. This occurs because a few of the records in ANSWER do not have Manager field entries. Whenever you compute group statistics, and the field on which you're grouping has blanks, Paradox will lump together all of the blanks and present them at the top of the ANSWER table.

The Location of the Formula

In the example, we entered the formula *calc count* in the Job Number field, so Paradox computed the total of different Job Numbers associated with each manager. If, on the other hand, we entered the formula in the Client Number field, Paradox would create the ANSWER table shown in Figure 9-49. The entries in the Count of Client Number field in this ANSWER table represent the number of different *clients* with which each manager is associated. As you can see, the entries in this table differ from those in the first ANSWER table.

Figure 9-49

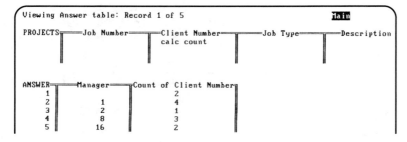

Grouping on More Than One Field

If you enter checks in more than one field of a group summary query, Paradox will compute group statistics on both fields. For example, suppose you want to know how many jobs of each type each manager is responsible for. To calculate this statistic, first create a new, empty query form for the PROJECTS table. When the form is in view, move to the Job Type field and press **[Check Mark]**, then move to the Manager field and press **[Check Mark]**. Finally, move to the Job Number field (again, the field that is sure to have a unique entry for every record in the table) and enter the expression **calc count**.

Now press **[Do-It!]** to process the query. Figure 9-50 shows the resulting ANSWER table. As you can see, this table includes three fields: Job Type, Manager, and Count of Job Number. Notice that there is a record in this table for each job type/manager pair. The Count of Job Type field for each record shows the number of jobs of the indicated type that belong to the indicated manager. For instance, the first record shows that manager 1 has one job of type 1. The seventh record shows that manager 8 has three jobs of type 3.

Figure 9-50

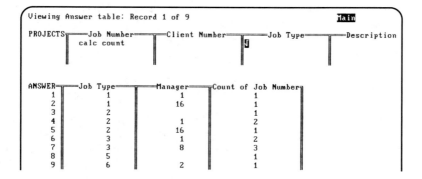

Using Computed Statistics to Make Selections

You can use Paradox's statistical operators to make selections from tables. For example, suppose you want to look at all the records in EMPLYEE that have a Salary field entry greater than 120% of the average salary. Performing this query is a two-step operation.

To begin, create a new query form for the EMPLYEE table. When the form appears, move to the Salary field and type **calc average**. Now press **[Do-It!]** to create the ANSWER table shown in Figure 9-51. The single entry in this table is the average of the Salary field entries.

Figure 9-51

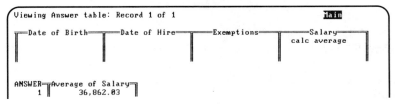

Now, press **[Up Image]** to move back to the EMPLYEE query form, press **[Clear Image]** to erase the existing form, and then use the **[Menu]** Ask command to create two new query forms: one for EMPLYEE and one for ANSWER. Next, select every field in the EMPLYEE query form, move to the Salary field, and type

>[Example]123*1.2

Finally, move to the Average of Salary field in the ANSWER query form and type

[Example]123

Figure 9-52 shows the completed query. This query tells Paradox to select those records from EMPLYEE that have a Salary field entry greater than 120% of the entry in the Average of Salary field in ANSWER. The example *123* links the Average of Salary field to the Salary field.

Figure 9-52

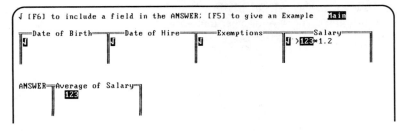

When you press **[Do-It!]** to process the query, Paradox will create the ANSWER table shown in Figure 9-53. As you can see, this table contains only the records from EMPLYEE that have a Salary field entry that is greater than 1.2 times the average salary.

Figure 9-53

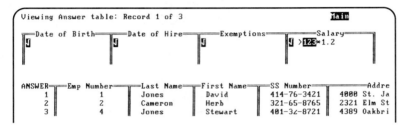

Remember that whenever you perform a query on the ANSWER table, both the previous ANSWER table and the ANSWER query form will be erased when you press [Do-It!]. If you want to preserve the first ANSWER table, you should rename it before you create the second query.

There is another way to use statistics to make selections. You can use the PAL calculator to compute a statistic and store the value of that statistic in a variable. Then you can enter that variable into a query form to make your selection. We'll show you how to use the PAL calculator in this way in Chapter 14, "PAL Basics."

Conclusion

In this chapter, you've learned how to use examples in your queries. As you have seen, examples are extremely powerful tools that allow you to create relationships between the fields in your queries. You can use examples to make selections by comparing the entries in one field of a table to the entries in another field of that same table. You can use examples to relate the fields in two different tables and create combined tables. You can also use examples in calc queries to make calculations on the entries in your tables.

Although you now know about the most important uses for examples, there are several other applications for these tools. Examples can be used in special queries, called insert queries, that insert the entries from the fields of one table into another table. Examples can also be used with the [Menu] Modify MultiEntry Setup command. We'll look at these uses of examples, and several other important Paradox topics, in the next chapter.

Chapter 10

Multitable Operations

In the previous chapters, you learned how to use queries to create new tables, and how to use examples to link related tables. In this chapter, we'll cover several commands that allow you to update one table using the records in another table. We'll begin with a thorough discussion of the [Menu] Tools More Add command, which you've seen before. Then we'll cover the [Menu] Tools More Subtract command, which allows you to subtract the records in one table from those in another table. Next, we'll look at two related commands, [Menu] Modify MultiEntry and [Menu] Tools More MultiAdd, which allow you to divide the records that are in one table into two or more related tables. Finally, we'll look at Paradox's most flexible multitable tool, the insert query.

The [Menu] Tools More Add Command

The [Menu] Tools More Add command allows you to add the records in one table to the records in another table with an identical structure. One of the primary uses for the Add command is to accumulate data from several batches of tables into one master table. In addition, this command can be used to add back records that have been placed by the DataEntry command in a KEYVIOL table or by the Restructure command in a PROBLEMS table. Add can also be used when you want to reinsert records that you have extracted with a query and edited.

Basics

When you issue the [Menu] Tools More Add command, Paradox first prompts you for the name of the source table, which is the table that contains the records you want to add. Next, Paradox asks you to supply the name of the target table, which is the table to which you want to add records. Remember: The source and target tables must have identical structures.

What happens after you specify the source and target tables depends on the version of Paradox you are using and whether the target table is keyed. If you are using the first release of Paradox, or if you are using Paradox 1.1 and the target table is not keyed, then Paradox will immediately append the records from the source table to the target table below any records that are already in that table. If you are using Paradox 1.1 and the target table is keyed, Paradox will offer you two options: NewEntries and Update. (Paradox 1.0 does not offer these options.) The effect of the Add command depends on which of these options you select.

Using Add with Non-keyed Tables

If you are using the first release of Paradox, or if you are using Paradox 1.1 and the table to which you want to add records does not have a key field, Paradox will add the records in the source table to the target table as soon as you specify both table names and press ↵. The records from the source table will be appended to the target table below any records that are already in the target table.

For example, suppose you have created a table called TIME. You use this table to maintain a record of how each employee spends his or her time. Figure 10-1 shows the structure of this table. Notice that it contains no key fields.

Figure 10-1

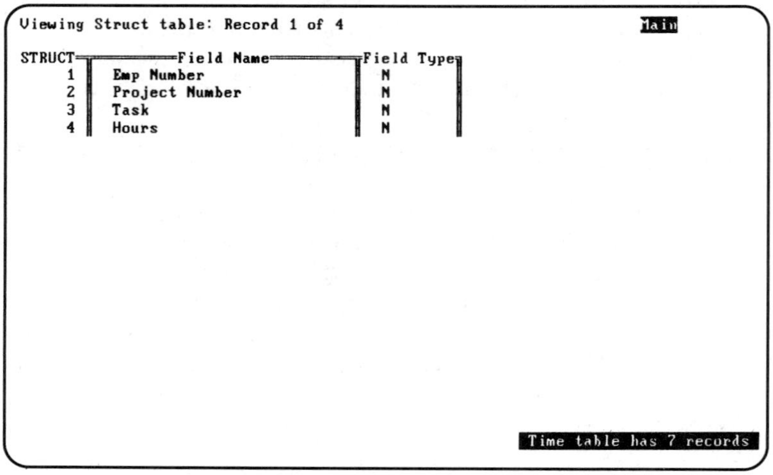

```
Viewing Struct table: Record 1 of 4                          Main
STRUCT          Field Name          Field Type
   1     Emp Number                   N
   2     Project Number               N
   3     Task                         N
   4     Hours                        N




                                          Time table has 7 records
```

To simplify data entry, each employee keeps his or her own time records in a personal copy of the TIME table. At the end of each week, you consolidate the records from the individual employee tables into the table, TIME. As you'll see, this is a perfect application for the Add command.

For example, suppose that you want to add the contents of a table called JOHNTIME to the TIME table. Figure 10-2 shows the contents of JOHNTIME, and Figure 10-3 shows the current contents of TIME. To begin, issue the [Menu] Tools More Add command. When Paradox asks for the name of the source table (the table that contains the records you want to add), type the table name **JOHNTIME**. When Paradox asks you to identify the target table (the table to which you want to add the records), type **TIME**.

Figure 10-2

```
Viewing Johntime table: Record 3 of 3                    Main
JOHNTIME   Emp Number   Project Number   Task    Hours
    1           3            100           8       10
    2           3            115           8       20
    3           3            104           5       25
```

Figure 10-3

```
Viewing Time table: Record 1 of 7                        Main
TIME   Emp Number   Project Number   Task    Hours
  1         1            100           3       8
  2         1            100           5       12
  3         1            100           2       6
  4         1            125           1       1
  5         2            100           3       24
  6         2            116           5       4
  7         2            110           2       40
```

When you press ↵, Paradox will display the message

Adding records from JOHNTIME to TIME

as it adds the records from JOHNTIME to TIME. When the records are added, Paradox will bring the TIME table (the table to which you added the records) into view. Figure 10-4 shows the TIME table with the records from JOHNTIME.

Figure 10-4

```
Viewing Time table: Record 1 of 10                       Main
TIME   Emp Number   Project Number   Task    Hours
  1         1            100           3       8
  2         1            100           5       12
  3         1            100           2       6
  4         1            125           1       1
  5         2            100           3       24
  6         2            116           5       4
  7         2            110           2       40
  8         3            100           8       10
  9         3            115           8       20
 10         3            104           5       25
```

Notes

The [Menu] Tools More Add command does not have any effect on the contents of the source table. The records that are in the table when you issue the command will be in the table when the command is completed. If you want to empty the source table after you have added its contents to the target table, you can use the [Menu] Tools More Empty command to do this.

If the source and target tables do not have the same structures, then Paradox will display the message

> TABLENAME and TABLENAME have incompatible structures

If you see this message, you should check the structures of the source and target tables to identify the incompatibility in their structures. For tables to have identical structures, they must have the same number of fields, and each field in the target table must be of the same type as the corresponding field in the source. For instance, if the first field in the target table is an alphanumeric field, then the first field in the source table must be alphanumeric. If the third field in the target table is a numeric field, then the third field in the source must be numeric, too.

Interestingly, the Add command does not care about the length of alphanumeric fields. If an alphanumeric field in the target table is shorter than the corresponding field in the source table, Paradox will trim the contents of that field as it adds them to the target.

Also, the Add command does not mind if the fields in the two tables have the same names, as long as the two tables have the same structures. That is, as long as the source and target tables have the same type of fields in the same order, you can add records from one to another, even if the names of the fields in the two tables are different.

If either the source table or the target table is password protected, Paradox will prompt you for the password when you issue the [Menu] Tools More Add command. You must provide the correct password before you can add any records.

The source and target tables do not need to be on the same disk or on the same directory. If one or both of the files are on a directory other than the default directory, you should tell Paradox where the files are located when you specify the source and target table names. For example, suppose you want to add the contents of a table named MARYTIME, which is on the directory *c:\paradox\data\mary* to the table named TIME, which is on the default directory. When Paradox asks you to specify the name of the source table, you should type

> **c:\paradox\data\mary\MARYTIME**

Using Add with Keyed Tables

If you are using Paradox 1.1, and the target table has one or more key fields, Paradox will present you with two options when you use the Add command: NewEntries and Update. Exactly how the Add command affects the target table depends on which of these options you select.

If you are using Paradox 1.0, then you will not see these options. Instead, Paradox will attempt to add the records in the source table to the target table, just as in the previous example. If key violations occur as a result of the Add command, Paradox will place those records in a KEYVIOL table. We'll cover KEYVIOL tables and the Add command in a few pages.

The NewEntries Option

If you choose the NewEntries option, Paradox will append the records in the source table to the target table. The records from the source table will be appended to the target table below any records that are already in the target table. If key violations occur as a result of the Add command, Paradox will place those records in a KEYVIOL table.

An Example

For example, suppose you have created a table called PROSPECT. You use this table to collect the names and addresses of people who call or write to request information on your company's products. Figure 10-5 shows the structure of this table. Notice that the Prospect Number field is a key field.

Figure 10-5

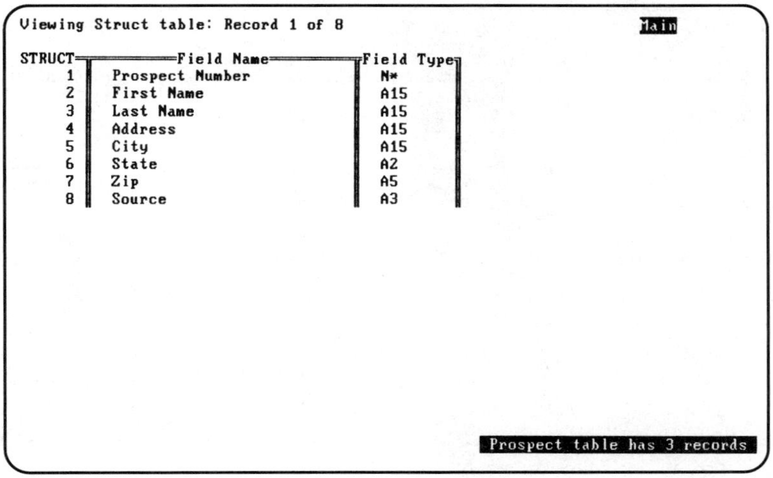

```
Viewing Struct table: Record 1 of 8                    Main
STRUCT        Field Name          Field Type
   1    Prospect Number              N*
   2    First Name                   A15
   3    Last Name                    A15
   4    Address                      A15
   5    City                         A15
   6    State                        A2
   7    Zip                          A5
   8    Source                       A3




                                          Prospect table has 3 records
```

Now suppose further that you have two employees, Mary and John, who answer the telephone and open mail. Both of these employees have their own copy of the PROSPECT table, which contains the names they have collected. Mary's file is called FONEPROS and John's is called MAILPROS. Both MAILPROS and FONEPROS have the same structure as PROSPECT (in fact, these tables could be created easily by borrowing the structure of the PROSPECT table). Every so often, you must combine the records from these two files into one master PROSPECT table. This is a perfect application for the Add command.

For example, suppose that PROSPECT, FONEPROS, and MAILPROS contain the records shown in Figure 10-6. You want to combine the records from FONEPROS and MAILPROS into PROSPECT. To begin, issue the [**Menu**] **T**ools **M**ore **A**dd command. When Paradox prompts you for the name of the source table (the table that contains the records you want to add), type **FONEPROS**. Then, when Paradox prompts you for the name of the target table (the table to which you want to add the records), type **PROSPECT**.

Figure 10-6

```
Viewing Prospect table: Record 1 of 3                            Main
 PROSPECT Prospect Number   First Name    Last Name      Address
    1         1              John          Smith         111 Any Street
    2         2              Sally         Struthers     999 Maple St.
    3         3              Mike          Murphy        9876 Dixie Hy.

 FONEPROS Prospect Number   First Name    Last Name      Address
    1         4              Jim           Morrison      100 W. 73rd St.
    2         6              Fred          Foote         123 Brattle St.

 MAILPROS Prospect Number   First Name    Last Name      Address
    1         5              Bill          Johnson       42 Old Rock Rd.
    2         7              Dave          Jones         123 Yale Ct.

Viewing Prospect table: Record 1 of 3                            Main
   Last Name    Address            City          State  Zip     Source
   Smith        111 Any Street     Louisville    KY     40205   WSJ
   Struthers    999 Maple St.      Indianapolis  IN     35801   NYT
   Murphy       9876 Dixie Hy.     Radcliff      KY     40322   TEL

   Last Name    Address            City          State  Zip     Source
   Morrison     100 W. 73rd St     New York      NY     10026   NYT
   Foote        123 Brattle St     Cambridge     MA     02165   WSJ

   Last Name    Address            City          State  Zip     Source
   Johnson      42 Old Rock Rd.    Memphis       TN     12345   TEL
   Jones        123 Yale Ct.       New Haven     CN     98765   NYT
```

When you press ↵, Paradox will present two options: New Entries and Update. Since in this case you want to add the records in the FONEPROS table to the records that are already in the PROSPECT table, you should choose **N**ewEntries. After you make this choice, Paradox will display the message

Adding records from FONEPROS to PROSPECT

When the records are added, Paradox will bring the PROSPECT table into view. Figure 10-7 shows the PROSPECT table with the records from FONEPROS.

Now you're ready to add the records from MAILPROS to PROSPECT. To do this, repeat the [**Menu**] **T**ools **M**ore **A**dd command, specify **MAILPROS** as the source table and **PROSPECT** as the target table. When you press ↵, Paradox will display the *Adding records...* message, will add the records from MAILPROS to PROSPECT, and will bring the PROSPECT table into view.

Figure 10-7

```
Viewing Prospect table: Record 1 of 5                    Main
PROSPECT  Prospect Number   First Name    Last Name    Address
   1            1           John          Smith        111 Any Street
   2            2           Sally         Struthers    999 Maple St.
   3            3           Mike          Murphy       9876 Dixie Hy.
   4            4           Jim           Morrison     100 W. 73rd St.
   5            6           Fred          Foote        123 Brattle St.
```

Figure 10-8 shows the PROSPECT table with the records from both FONEPROS and MAILPROS. Notice that Paradox has arranged the records in PROSPECT into ascending Prospect Number order. This occurs because the Prospect Number field in PROSPECT is a key field.

Figure 10-8

```
Viewing Prospect table: Record 1 of 7                    Main
PROSPECT  Prospect Number   First Name    Last Name    Address
   1            1           John          Smith        111 Any Street
   2            2           Sally         Struthers    999 Maple St.
   3            3           Mike          Murphy       9876 Dixie Hy.
   4            4           Jim           Morrison     100 W. 73rd St.
   5            5           Bill          Johnson      42 Old Rock Rd.
   6            6           Fred          Foote        123 Brattle St.
   7            7           Dave          Jones        123 Yale Ct.
```

Using Add to Overcome Key Violations

Another important use of the Add NewEntries command is to overcome key violation errors. For example, suppose you have used the [Menu] Modify DataEntry command to enter a few new records directly into the PROSPECT table. Figure 10-9 shows these entries in the ENTRY table. In making these entries, suppose you mistyped one prospect number. Instead of typing 10, the correct number, you typed 1, the number in the Prospect Number field of the first record in PROSPECT. Because of this typo, a key violation occurred when the Entry command was executed, causing Paradox to enter one of the records from ENTRY in the KEYVIOL table shown in Figure 10-10.

Figure 10-9

```
DataEntry for Prospect table: Record 1 of 3              DataEntry
ENTRY    Prospect Number   First Name    Last Name    Address
   1            8           Billy       ◄ Thompson     1234 S. 3rd St.
   2            9           Rodney        McCray       9999 Easy St.
   3            1           William       Bedford      222 N.E. Pkwy.

         Last Name      Address           City          State   Zip     Source
         Thompson       1234 S. 3rd St.   Louisville    KY      40000   TSN
         McCray         9999 Easy St.     Houston       TX      54321   BBW
         Bedford        222 N.E. Pkwy     Memphis       TN      36502   WSJ
```

Figure 10-10

```
Viewing Keyviol table: Record 1 of 1                    Main
PROSPECT┬Prospect Number┬──First Name──┬──Last Name──┬──Address──
    1   │       1       │  John        │  Smith      │  111 Any Street
    2   │       2       │  Sally       │  Struthers  │  999 Maple St.
    3   │       3       │  Mike        │  Murphy     │  9876 Dixie Hy.
    4   │       4       │  Jim         │  Morrison   │  100 W. 73rd St.
    5   │       5       │  Bill        │  Johnson    │  42 Old Rock Rd.
    6   │       6       │  Fred        │  Foote      │  123 Brattle St.
    7   │       7       │  Dave        │  Jones      │  123 Yale Ct.
    8   │       8       │  Billy       │  Thompson   │  1234 S. 3rd St.
    9   │       9       │  Rodney      │  McCray     │  9999 Easy St.

KEYVIOL┬Prospect Number┬──First Name──┬──Last Name──┬──Address──
    1   │       1       │  William     │  Bedford    │  222 N.E. Pkwy
```

At this point, you need to edit the contents of the KEYVIOL table to eliminate the key conflict, and then add the records from KEYVIOL to the target table. To correct the error in this example, bring KEYVIOL into view, press **[Edit]**, move to the Prospect Number field, press **[Backspace]** to erase the erroneous entry, type **10**, and press **[Do-It!]**. Figure 10-11 shows the corrected table.

Figure 10-11

```
Viewing Keyviol table: Record 1 of 1                    Main
PROSPECT┬Prospect Number┬──First Name──┬──Last Name──┬──Address──
    1   │       1       │  John        │  Smith      │  111 Any Street
    2   │       2       │  Sally       │  Struthers  │  999 Maple St.
    3   │       3       │  Mike        │  Murphy     │  9876 Dixie Hy.
    4   │       4       │  Jim         │  Morrison   │  100 W. 73rd St.
    5   │       5       │  Bill        │  Johnson    │  42 Old Rock Rd.
    6   │       6       │  Fred        │  Foote      │  123 Brattle St.
    7   │       7       │  Dave        │  Jones      │  123 Yale Ct.
    8   │       8       │  Billy       │  Thompson   │  1234 S. 3rd St.
    9   │       9       │  Rodney      │  McCray     │  9999 Easy St.

KEYVIOL┬Prospect Number┬──First Name──┬──Last Name──┬──Address──
    1   │      10       │  William     │  Bedford    │  222 N.E. Pkwy
```

Once the error is corrected, Paradox will allow you to enter the record from KEYVIOL into PROSPECT. To begin, issue the **[Menu] T**ools **M**ore **A**dd command. When Paradox prompts you for the name of the source table, supply the name of the table that contains the record you want to add–in this case, **KEYVIOL**. When Paradox prompts you for the name of the target table, type **PROSPECT**.

After you type the name of the target table, Paradox will present the two Add options: NewEntries and Update. In this case, because you want to add the records in the source table to the target table, you should choose NewEntries. When you make this selection, Paradox will add the records from the source table to the target table. The records from the source table will be appended to the target table below any records that are already in the target table.

Figure 10-12 shows the PROSPECT table after the Add command is completed. As you can see, the single record from KEYVIOL has been added to the records in PROSPECT.

Figure 10-12

```
Viewing Prospect table: Record 1 of 10                        Main
  PROSPECT─Prospect Number────First Name────Last Name────Address────
     1          1            John          Smith         111 Any Street
     2          2            Sally         Struthers     999 Maple St.
     3          3            Mike          Murphy        9876 Dixie Hy.
     4          4            Jim           Morrison      100 W. 73rd St.
     5          5            Bill          Johnson       42 Old Rock Rd.
     6          6            Fred          Foote         123 Brattle St.
     7          7            Dave          Jones         123 Yale Ct.
     8          8            Billy         Thompson      1234 S. 3rd St.
     9          9            Rodney        McCray        9999 Easy St.
    10         10            William       Bedford       222 N.E. Pkwy
```

The Add NewEntries Command and Key Fields

It's possible that key violation errors will occur when you use either the Add NewEntries command in Paradox 1.1 or the regular Add command in Paradox 1.0. A key violation occurs when the target table has a key field, and a record in the source table has a key field entry that is the same as a key field entry in a target table. When this occurs, Paradox will enter that record in a KEYVIOL table but will not enter it in the target table. (Whether or not the source table has a key field has no effect on the command.)

For example, suppose you want to add the records from the table FONEPROS, shown in Figure 10-13, to PROSPECT. Notice that the second record in FONEPROS has a key field entry that conflicts with the key field entry for the fifth record in PROSPECT. When you use the [Menu] Tools More Add NewEntries command to add the records in FONEPROS to PROSPECT, Paradox will not add the second record from FONEPROS to PROSPECT, but instead will enter that record in a KEYVIOL table. Figure 10-14 shows this table. Of course, the first record from FONEPROS, ENTRY, will be added to PROSPECT properly.

Figure 10-13

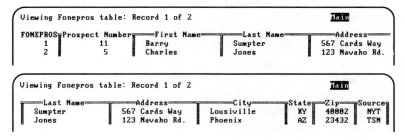

Figure 10-14

```
Viewing Keyviol table: Record 1 of 1                          Main
PROSPECT╤Prospect Number══╤═First Name═══╤═Last Name═══╤═Address═══════
    1   │       1         │   John       │   Smith     │ 111 Any Street
    2   │       2         │   Sally      │   Struthers │ 999 Maple St.
    3   │       3         │   Mike       │   Murphy    │ 9876 Dixie Hy.
    4   │       4         │   Jim        │   Morrison  │ 100 W. 73rd St.
    5   │       5         │   Bill       │   Johnson   │ 42 Old Rock Rd.
    6   │       6         │   Fred       │   Foote     │ 123 Brattle St.
    7   │       7         │   Dave       │   Jones     │ 123 Yale Ct.
    8   │       8         │   Billy      │   Thompson  │ 1234 S. 3rd St.
    9   │       9         │   Rodney     │   McCray    │ 9999 Easy St.
   10   │      10         │   William    │   Bedford   │ 222 N.E. Pkwy.
   11   │      11         │   Barry      │   Sumpter   │ 567 Cards Way

KEYVIOL╤Prospect Number══╤═First Name═══╤═Last Name═══╤═Address═══════
    1  │       5         │   Charles    │   Jones     │ 123 Navaho Rd.
```

If a key violation occurs, you will need to edit the entries in the KEYVIOL table to remove the conflict, then use the Add command to add the KEYVIOL table to the appropriate target table. In this case, you would edit the Prospect Number field of the record in KEYVIOL to remove the conflict, then use Add to add the records from KEYVIOL to PROSPECT.

If a record in the source table has a key field entry that is the same as a key field entry in a target table, and the entries in the other fields of the source record are also identical to the entries in that field of the target, then no key violation will occur. In that case, the record from the source table will not be added to the target table nor placed in a KEYVIOL table.

The Update Option

If you use the [Menu] Tools More Add command to add records to a keyed table, and choose the Update option, Paradox will use the records in the source table to update the records in the target table. (Paradox 1.0 does not offer an Update option and has no command that can duplicate the effects of this option.) Exactly how this occurs depends on whether or not there are records in the source table that contain key field entries that conflict with key field entries in the target table.

If there is not a conflict between the entries in the key field of the target table and the corresponding field of the source table, Paradox will insert the records from the source table into the target table in key field order. That is, the records from the source table will be inserted between the records in the target table so that the entries in the key field of the target table are in ascending key field order.

If there is a conflict between the entries in the key field of the target table and the corresponding field of the source table, Paradox will use the data from the non-key fields of the source table to update the record with the conflicting key field entry in the target table. Any records that are changed as a result of the Add Update operation are copied to a CHANGED table.

An Example: Using Update to Edit Tables

In Chapters 2 and 3, you learned about the [Menu] Modify Edit command, which allows you to edit the contents in your tables. In those chapters, we cautioned you that the Edit command is one of the few Paradox commands that allow you to affect directly the entries in your tables. Other commands operate on intermediate tables, and this feature helps to protect the integrity of your data. For example, the DataEntry command enters records into a table called ENTRY. Only when you press [Do-It!] are those records transferred to the permanent table.

Thanks to the Update option, you can use a similar approach to editing your tables. Instead of editing your primary table directly, you can use a query to copy all of the records in a table to an ANSWER table, edit the records in that table, and then use the Add Update command to update the original table.

For example, suppose you want to make a few changes to the PROSPECT table. Rather than editing the table directly, you decide to copy the records from PROSPECT into an ANSWER table, edit the ANSWER table, and then use the [Menu] Tools More Add Update command to add the records from ANSWER back into PROSPECT.

To begin, use the [Menu] Ask command to create a query form for PROSPECT. When the form appears, press [Check Mark] to select every field. When you press [Do-It!] to process this table, Paradox will copy every record from PROSPECT into an ANSWER table. Figure 10-15 shows this table.

Figure 10-15

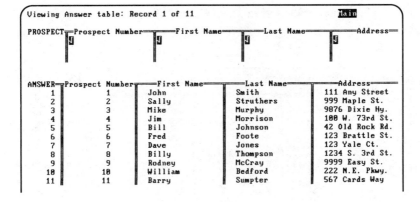

Once the ANSWER table has been created, you can press [Edit] to enter the edit mode and then make the following changes: (1) Change the First Name field entry for record 7 from *Dave* to **David**, (2) Change the Address field entry for record 1 from *111 Any Street* to **555 Main Street**, and (3) Add a record for **Guy Greene, 123 Park Place, Louisville, KY 40205**, source **CJT**, prospect number **12**.

When you have made these changes, press **[Do-It!]** to process the changes and return to the view mode. Figure 10-16 shows the edited ANSWER table.

Figure 10-16

ANSWER	Prospect Number	First Name	Last Name	Address
1	1	John	Smith	555 Main Street
2	2	Sally	Struthers	999 Maple St.
3	3	Mike	Murphy	9876 Dixie Hy.
4	4	Jim	Morrison	100 W. 73rd St.
5	5	Bill	Johnson	42 Old Rock Rd.
6	6	Fred	Foote	123 Brattle St.
7	7	David	Jones	123 Yale Ct.
8	8	Billy	Thompson	1234 S. 3rd St.
9	9	Rodney	McCray	9999 Easy St.
10	10	William	Bedford	222 N.E. Pkwy.
11	11	Barry	Sumpter	567 Cards Way
12	12	Guy	Greene	123 Park Place

Viewing Answer table: Record 1 of 12

Now you are ready to use ANSWER to update PROSPECT. To do this, issue the **[Menu] T**ools **M**ore **A**dd command and specify **ANSWER** as the source table and **PROSPECT** as the target table. Because you want to use the records in ANSWER to update PROSPECT, when Paradox presents the NewEntries and Update options, you should choose **U**pdate.

When you make this choice, Paradox will use the records in ANSWER to update PROSPECT, will copy any changed records from PROSPECT to a CHANGED table, and will display both the CHANGED table and the new PROSPECT table on the screen. As it does these things, Paradox will display the message

    Updating from ANSWER to PROSPECT

in the lower-right corner of the screen. Figure 10-17 shows the screen after the command is finished.

Figure 10-17

Viewing Prospect table: Record 1 of 12

PROSPECT	Prospect Number	First Name	Last Name	Address
1	1	John	Smith	555 Main Street
2	2	Sally	Struthers	999 Maple St.
3	3	Mike	Murphy	9876 Dixie Hy.
4	4	Jim	Morrison	100 W. 73rd St.
5	5	Bill	Johnson	42 Old Rock Rd.
6	6	Fred	Foote	123 Brattle St.
7	7	David	Jones	123 Yale Ct.
8	8	Billy	Thompson	1234 S. 3rd St.
9	9	Rodney	McCray	9999 Easy St.
10	10	William	Bedford	222 N.E. Pkwy.
11	11	Barry	Sumpter	567 Cards Way
12	12	Guy	Greene	123 Park Place

CHANGED	Prospect Number	First Name	Last Name	Address
1	1	John	Smith	111 Any Street
2	2	Sally	Struthers	999 Maple St.
3	3	Mike	Murphy	9876 Dixie Hy.
4	4	Jim	Morrison	100 W. 73rd St.
5	5	Bill	Johnson	42 Old Rock Rd.
6	6	Fred	Foote	123 Brattle St.
7	7	Dave	Jones	123 Yale Ct.

If you take a close look at the PROSPECT table, you'll see that the changes you made to the ANSWER table have now been brought into the PROSPECT table. For example, notice that the Address field entry for record number 1 in PROSPECT is now *555 Main Street*, not *111 Any Street*. Also notice that the First Name field entry for record number 7 in now *David*, not *Dave*.

Here's what happened: When Paradox processed the Add command, it found records in PROSPECT that had the same key field entry as the records you changed in ANSWER. Since you selected the Update option, Paradox used the entries from ANSWER to update, or change, the entries in the corresponding records in PROSPECT.

In addition, notice that Paradox has added to PROSPECT the new record that you added to ANSWER. Because the entry in the Prospect Number field of this new record did not conflict with the Prospect Number field entry for any record in PROSPECT, Paradox simply added it to PROSPECT.

Although you cannot see them all in Figure 10-17, the CHANGED table includes every record from the original PROSPECT table. Because there was a record in ANSWER for every record in PROSPECT, when you issued the Add Update command, Paradox updated every record in PROSPECT. Of course, since most of the records in ANSWER were identical to the corresponding records in PROSPECT, most of the records in PROSPECT were not really changed by the Add Update command. Paradox, however, thinks that all the records in PROSPECT were changed, so it copied all the records to CHANGED.

Although this method of editing takes a bit more effort than just pressing the [Edit] key, it is far safer. For one thing, no changes are made to the main table until you issue the [Menu] Tools More Add Update command. This means that if you make an error in editing, you can just start over without risking your data. Even after you have used the Add Update command, the records from the main table that were changed will appear in a CHANGED table. This means that you can reverse the effects of the edit even after you use the Add command.

The Tools More Subtract Command

The Tools More Subtract command allows you to subtract one table from another table with the same structure. When you subtract one table from another, Paradox will delete from the table you are subtracting all of the records that also appear in the table you are subtracting. In other words, this command allows you to delete from one table all of the records that it has in common with another table of identical structure. As you might expect, this command is the opposite of the [Menu] Tools Add command.

An Example

For example, suppose you have created the PROSPECT table shown in the previous examples. After you do a few promotional mailings, you receive several requests from people on the prospect list who want to remove their names from that list. Therefore, you need to remove these names from PROSPECT.

To process these requests, you could create a new table, called REMOVE, that has exactly the same structure as PROSPECT. (You could create this table easily by issuing the [Menu] Create command, specifying the name REMOVE, then pressing [Menu] again, choosing the Borrow option, and specifying the name of the table whose structure you want to borrow: PROSPECT. You could also create the table using a query.) Once you have created the table, you should enter the records shown in Figure 10-18 into it. These are the records for the individuals who have asked to be removed from your list.

Figure 10-18

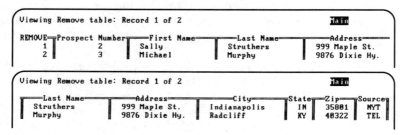

Once the records are in REMOVE, you can use the Subtract command to remove the names from PROSPECT. To begin, issue the [Menu] Tools More Subtract command. When Paradox prompts you for the name of the table that contains the records you want to subtract, type REMOVE and press ↵. Then, when Paradox prompts you for the name of the table from which you want to remove records, type PROSPECT.

When you press ↵, Paradox will display the message

Subtracting REMOVE from PROSPECT

and will delete from PROSPECT every record for which there is an identical record in REMOVE. When the command is finished, Paradox will bring PROSPECT, the table from which you subtracted records, into view. Figure 10-19 shows the screen as it should look after the command has run its course.

Figure 10-19

Notes

If you attempt to use Subtract to subtract tables that do not have the same structure, Paradox will display the message

> TABLENAME and TABLENAME have incompatible structures

If you see this message, you should check the structures of the tables to identify the incompatibility in their structures. As with the Add command, for tables to have identical structures, they must have the same number of fields, and each field in the target table must be of the same type as the corresponding field in the source. Like the Add command, Subtract does not care about the length of alphanumeric fields, nor about the names of the fields in the two tables.

If either the source table or the target table is password protected, Paradox will prompt you for the password when you issue the [Menu] Tools More Add command. You must provide the correct password before you can add records.

The source and target tables do not need to be on the same disk or directory. If one or both of the files are on a directory other than the default directory, you should tell Paradox where the files are located when you specify the source and target table names.

In general, for a record to be deleted by the Subtract command, there must be identical occurrences of the record in both the table from which you want to subtract and the table that contains the records you want to subtract. If a record in the table that contains the records you want to subtract is similar, but not identical to, a record in the table from which you want to subtract, that record will not be removed.

If either table is a keyed table, however, things work a bit differently. In that event, any record in the target table with a key field entry that is the same as the key field entry of a record in the source table will be subtracted—even if the other entries in the two records are not identical.

For example, look at the second record in the REMOVE table in Figure 10-18. Notice that this record is almost identical to the third record in PROSPECT, except that the First Name field entry for this record in REMOVE is Michael and the First Name field entry for the corresponding record in PROSPECT in Figure 10-17 is Mike. Now notice that when you used the Subtract command to subtract REMOVE from PROSPECT, Paradox removed the record for Mike Murphy from PROSPECT. Because PROSPECT is a keyed table, Paradox used the record in REMOVE to delete the similar record in PROSPECT, even though these two records are not completely identical. Had both REMOVE and PROSPECT been non-keyed tables, however, Paradox would not have deleted the record for Mike Murphy from PROSPECT.

The [Menu] Tools More Subtract command has no effect on the contents of the source table (the table that contains the records you want to subtract). For instance, in the example, the source table REMOVE contained two records before you issued the [Menu] Tools More Subtract command. After you issue the command, this table will still contain two records.

MultiEntry and MultiAdd

Sooner or later in your work with Paradox, you will encounter an application that requires you to enter information into two tables through a single form. This will be especially true if you organize your data into groups of related normal tables. Since in Paradox every form is attached to a single table, it might seem impossible to come up with a form that will allow you to enter data into two tables at once. Release 1.1 of Paradox, however, includes two commands, MultiEntry and MultiAdd, that allow you to do this both quickly and easily.

(Paradox 1.0 does not offer either of these commands. If you are using Paradox 1.0, you must use insert queries to accomplish this same result. We'll show you how to use insert queries in the next section.)

The [Menu] Modify MultiEntry Command

The [Menu] Modify MultiEntry command makes it easy to enter data into two or more tables at one time. In fact, this command is very similar to the [Menu] Modify DataEntry command, except that it is used when you need to enter data into more than one table at once.

The MultiEntry command offers two options: Entry and Setup. The Setup option allows you to create two special tables, a source table and a map table, that make it possible to enter data into two or more tables through the same form. The source table includes all of the relevant fields from the tables into which you want to make entries (we'll call these the target tables). The map table tells Paradox how to divide the data in the source table into the permanent tables.

The Entry option lets you use the multitable system that you've created with Setup to enter data into the target tables through the source table. When you use this command to enter data into the source table and press **[Do-It!]**, Paradox will distribute the data to the target tables automatically, using the relationships that are defined by the map table.

An Example

For example, suppose you have created the two tables whose structures are shown in Figures 10-20 and 10-21. The first table, CUSTOMER, is used to record the name, address, and so on of your customers. Notice that the Cust Number field in this table is a key field. The second table, ORDER, records the information about what was ordered.

Figure 10-20

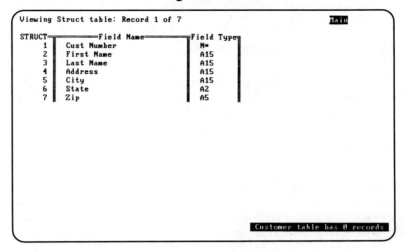

Figure 10-21

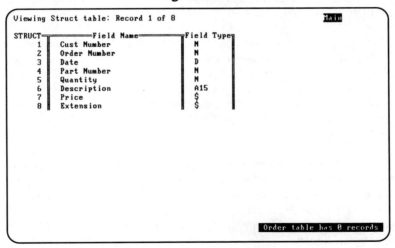

These two tables are an excellent example of a normalized data base. Rather than storing all the information about each order and each customer in one huge table, the data is stored in two separate but related tables. In this case, the tables are related on the Cust Number field. Because the tables are separate, the data is stored efficiently. Because they are related, it is easy to reconstruct the data, for instance, so you can look at all of the orders that relate to a particular customer.

The problem with normalized table groups like this one is that you will usually want to enter data into all of the tables in the group at once. For example, in this case, you want to enter order and customer information into the system at the same time whenever you receive an order. Without the MultiEntry command, you would need to enter the data in these tables one table at a time. Thanks to the MultiEntry command, however, you can do the whole job in one step.

Creating the Source and Map Tables

To begin, you must create the source and map tables. Creating these tables is a two-step process. First, you construct a query on the target tables that tells Paradox which fields from each table should be included in the source table and how the data from the source table should be divided between the target tables. Then you must issue the [Menu] Modify MultiEntry Setup command both to process the query and to create the source and map tables.

The query you use to create the source and map tables should include a query form for every table into which you want to make entries. In the example, the query will include two query forms: one for CUSTOMER and one for ORDER. Once you create the query, you should select every field in both query forms that you want Paradox to include in the source and map tables. Any field that you select in the query will be included in the source and map table. In addition, you should use examples to link the related fields in the two tables. Any pair of fields that you link with examples will be represented by a single field in the source table.

To create the query in the example, first use the [**Menu**] **A**sk command to create new, blank query forms for the CUSTOMER and ORDER tables. When these query forms are in view, use the [**Check Mark**] key to specify the fields that you want to include in the source table. You should select every field in CUSTOMER and every field in ORDER except for the Cust Number field. Since this field is selected in CUSTOMER, and will be linked to the Cust Number field in CUSTOMER by an example, it should not be selected in the ORDER table.

Once you have selected the fields in the query forms, you must enter examples in the forms that tell Paradox on which fields to relate the two tables ORDER and CUSTOMER. To do this, move to the Cust Number field in CUSTOMER, press [**Example**], and type **123**. Next, press [**Down Image**] to move down to the ORDER query form; then move to the Cust Number field, press [**Example**], and type **123**. Figure 10-22 shows the completed query.

Figure 10-22

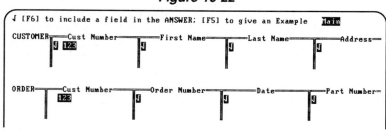

Multitable Operations

Now you are ready to process the query. To do this, issue the [**Menu**] **M**odify **M**ulti**E**ntry **S**etup command. This command will use the active query to create the source and map tables. When you issue the command, Paradox will prompt you to enter the name of the source and map tables. In the example, we'll use the name **NEWORD** for the source table and **ORDMAP** for the map table.

When you press ↵ after entering the map table name, Paradox will create the source table NEWORD and the map table ORDMAP. Figure 10-23 shows the screen as it will look after the command is completed. Figure 10-24 shows the structure of the source table NEWORD, and Figure 10-25 shows the structure of the map table ORDMAP. Both the source table and the map table are regular, permanent Paradox tables.

Figure 10-23

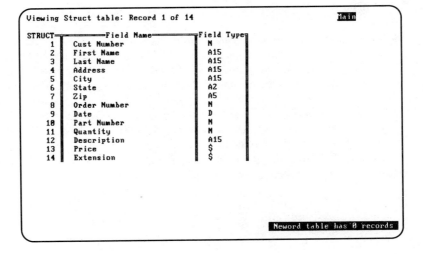

Figure 10-24

Figure 10-25

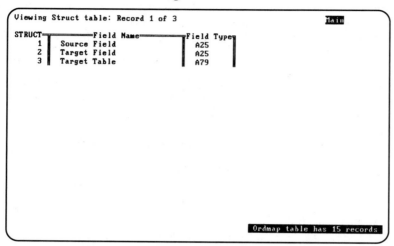

You will enter your data into the multitable system through the source table. Notice that the source table includes all of the fields from the two tables ORDER and CUSTOMER. In fact, the source table has exactly the same structure as the ANSWER table Paradox would create if you processed the query in Figure 10-22 with the [Do-It!] key.

The map table tells Paradox how to distribute entries from the source table to the target tables. You will notice that the map table ORDMAP has three fields: Source Field, Target Field, and Target Table. All map tables share this structure. Source Field lists each of the fields in the source table. Target Field and Target Table identify the target table (CUSTOMER or ORDER) and the field to which the contents of that field should be distributed.

Entering Data

Once you have created the source and map tables, you are ready to use the multientry system. To enter data into the system, issue the [Menu] Modify MultiEntry Entry command. After you issue the command, Paradox will prompt you to enter the name of the source table, **NEWORD**, and the name of the map table, **ORDMAP**. When you press ↵, Paradox will display the ENTRY table for NEWORD, just as it does when you issue the [Menu] Modify DataEntry command to enter data into individual tables. You can either begin typing immediately or press [**Form Toggle**] ([F7]) to view the ENTRY table through a form. If you are working along with the example, go ahead and enter the three orders shown in Table 10-1 into the table. Figure 10-26 shows the ENTRY table for NEWORD after these records have been entered.

Table 10-1 Sample Data

Cust Number	1	2	3
First Name	John	David	Barbara
Last Name	Smith	Jones	Williams
Address	111 Main St.	1234 Elm St.	321 4th St.
City	Peru	Pikeville	New York
State	IN	KY	NY
Zip	35710	40999	10001
Order Number	100	101	102
Date	11/22/85	11/23/85	11/24/85
Part Number	1234	1000	2000
Quantity	4	1	2
Description	Red Widget	Blue Wombat	Brown Bat
Price	$100.00	$50.00	$75.00
Extension	$400.00	$50.00	$150.00

Figure 10-26

```
DataEntry for Neword table: Record 1 of 3                    DataEntry
  ENTRY    Cust Number      First Name      Last Name      Address
    1           1             John            Smith         111 Main St.
    2           2             David           Jones         1234 Elm St.
    3           3             Barbara         Williams      321 4th St.
```

Distributing the Data

Once you have entered the data, press **[Do-It!]**. When you press [Do-It!], Paradox will automatically distribute the data to the appropriate fields in the CUSTOMER and ORDER tables. At the same time, the message

> Adding records from Entry to targets in map table ORDMAP

will appear at the bottom of the screen. Figure 10-27 shows the resulting tables.

Figure 10-27

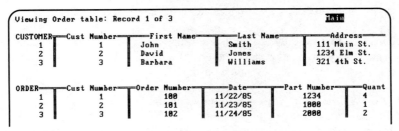

Paradox uses the map table to distribute the records from the source table to the target tables. When you press [Do-It!], Paradox copies the entries from each field of the source table to the destination tables, using the relationships defined in the map table. For instance, the map table tells Paradox that the First Name field in the source table NEWORD is related to the First Name field of the target table CUSTOMER.

Notes

There are several fine points that you should keep in mind when you use the MultiEntry command. We will cover these points in this section.

Creating the Map and Source Tables

When you use the MultiEntry command to create a source table, Paradox expects that you will select only one occurrence of any field that you use to relate the two tables. The fields that you link with examples in the query form will receive data from a single field in the source table. In the example, we used the Cust Number field to relate the two tables. Because we entered examples in this field in both tables, Paradox only expects one occurrence to be selected. In fact, if you selected both Cust Number fields, Paradox would return the message

> Only one use of 123 example may be checkmarked

Although only one occurrence of the Cust Number field is selected in the query, and the Cust Number field occurs only once in the source table, the map table includes two Cust Number fields. The first occurrence is linked to the Cust Number field in the CUSTOMER target table and the second to the Cust Number field in the ORDER table.

In addition, the query you use to create the source and map tables can contain only check marks and examples. You cannot enter any selection conditions or special operators like delete, insert, calc, or changeto in the query.

You can use any name you want for the source and map tables. However, we suggest that you choose names for the source and map tables that will make it easy to remember that they are related. For instance, the names NEWORD and ORDMAP in the example make it easy to remember that these tables are designed to work together.

If you choose a name for either table that has already been assigned to a table, Paradox will ask whether you want to replace the existing table with the new one, or cancel the name you have selected and choose a new name.

Although you will nearly always use a query and the [Menu] Modify MultiEntry Setup command to define the source table and the map table, you don't need to do this. If you wish, you can create these tables with the [Menu] Modify Create command. Keep in mind that all map tables have the same three fields and include one record for each field in both target tables.

More Than Two Tables

You can use the MultiEntry command to enter data into more than two related tables. As in the two-table example, you would begin by creating a source table and a map table for the table system. The query you use to create these tables should include query forms for all of the target tables. Each query form should include an example that tells Paradox how to relate the data in the table system.

Once you've created a source and map table, the process of using MultiEntry for a three-or-more-table system is identical to the process demonstrated in the previous example.

Reusing the Multientry System

After distributing the data to the target tables, Paradox empties the source table and saves it as a regular table. The map table is also saved as a regular Paradox table. You can reuse these tables as many times as you wish. If you want to reuse a multientry system that you have previously defined, you don't need to redefine the source and map tables. Instead, you can simply issue the [Menu] Modify MultiEntry Entry command, specify the source and map tables you want to use, and begin entering data.

It is important to note that the source and map tables are *not* part of the family of the tables upon which they are based. If you restructure the target tables, the change will not be passed through to the source and map tables. If you do restructure a target table, you may also need to create a new query to redefine the source and map tables.

The Entry Menu

If you press [Menu] while you are entering records using the [Menu] Modify MultiEntry Entry command, Paradox will display the Entry menu shown in Figure 10-28. This menu is identical to the menu you see when you press [Menu] while entering records using the standard [Menu] Modify DataEntry command.

Figure 10-28

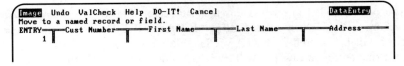

The MultiEntry Command and Key Fields

If one or more of the target tables have key fields, it is possible that key violation errors will occur when you use the MultiEntry command. A key violation occurs when a record that you enter through the source table has a key field entry that is the same as a key field entry in a target table, but the entries in the other fields of the source record are not the same as the entries in those fields of the target. When this occurs, Paradox will enter that record in a KEYVIOL table. The record will not be entered in any target table. This is true even if the key violation only affects one of the target tables.

For example, suppose you have issued the [Menu] Modify MultiEntry Entry command and have entered the records shown in Table 10-2 into the NEWORD table. Figure 10-29 shows these records in the ENTRY table for NEWORD. Notice that the Cust Number field entry for the second record in ENTRY is the same as the entry in the Cust Number field of the third record in CUSTOMER shown in Figure 10-27.

Table 10-2 Sample Data

Cust Number	4	3
First Name	Don	Julia
Last Name	Johnson	Baker
Address	123 Beach Road	2 River Road
City	Miami	Cincinnati
State	FL	OH
Zip	23689	23789
Order Number	103	104
Date	3/1/86	6/1/86
Part Number	1000	1000
Quantity	4	5
Description	Blue Wombat	Blue Wombat
Price	$50	$50.00
Extension	$200.00	$250.00

Figure 10-29

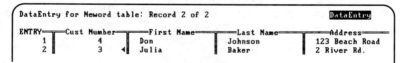

When you press [Do-It!] to process this table, Paradox will not insert any data from the second record in ENTRY in either CUSTOMER or ORDER. Instead, all of the data in that record will be entered in a KEYVIOL table. Figure 10-30 shows this table. Of course, the first record in ENTRY will be properly divided between the CUSTOMER and ORDER tables.

Figure 10-30

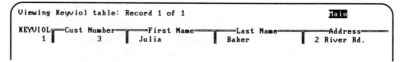

If a key violation occurs, you'll need to edit the entries in the KEYVIOL table to remove the conflict, then distribute the record to the appropriate target tables. The best way to distribute the corrected data is the MultiAdd command, which we'll cover in a few pages.

If a record that you enter through the source table has a key field entry that is the same as a key field entry in a target table, and the entries in the other fields of the source record are also identical to the entries in that field of the target, then no key violation will occur. In that event, the new record will simply disappear. It will neither be added to the target table, placed in a KEYVIOL table, nor retained in the source table.

This rule may seem strange, but there is an important reason that MultiEntry works this way. In many cases when you use MultiEntry, there will be several records in one target table for each record in the other target table. For instance, in an order entry system, it is likely that each customer will order several different items. This means that in the CUSTOMER/ORDER table system, there are likely to be several records in ORDER for each record in CUSTOMER.

For instance, suppose that you've issued the [Menu] Modify MultiEntry Entry command and have entered the records shown in Table 10-3 into NEWORD. Figure 10-31 shows these entries in the ENTRY table. Notice that the CUSTOMER field entries for the first record in ENTRY exactly duplicate the third record in CUSTOMER in Figure 10-27, and that the second and third records in ENTRY have exactly the same entries in all of the CUSTOMER table fields.

Table 10-3 Sample Data

Cust Number	3	6	6
First Name	Barbara	John	John
Last Name	Williams	Dawkins	Dawkins
Address	321 4th St.	123 E. St.	123 E. St.
City	New York	Washington	Washington
State	NY	DC	DC
Zip	10001	20001	20001
Order Number	105	106	107
Date	7/1/86	7/2/86	7/5/86
Part Number	1234	1000	2000
Quantity	1	3	4
Description	Red Widget	Blue Wombat	Brown Bat
Price	$100.00	$50.00	$75.00
Extension	$100.00	$150.00	$300.00

Figure 10-31

```
DataEntry for Neword table: Record 1 of 3                         DataEntry
ENTRY====Cust Number======First Name======Last Name======Address=======
   1        3         ◄  Barbara          Williams        321 4th St.
   2        6            John             Dawkins         123 E. St.
   3        6            John             Dawkins         123 E. St.
```

When you press **[Do-It!]** to process this table, Paradox will enter three records in ORDERS–one for each item ordered–but will enter only one record in CUSTOMER–the record for the new customer. Because the CUSTOMER field entries for the first record in ENTRY duplicate the third record in CUSTOMER, Paradox will not insert the information from those fields in CUSTOMER. In addition, since the data in the CUSTOMER table fields of the second and third records in ENTRY have exactly the same entries, Paradox will enter only one of those records in the CUSTOMER table. Figure 10-32 shows the CUSTOMER and ORDER tables at this point.

Figure 10-32

```
Viewing Order table: Record 1 of 7                                  Main
 CUSTOMER─┬─Cust Number─┬─First Name─┬─Last Name─┬─Address─────
    1    │      1      │   John     │   Smith   │ 111 Main St.
    2    │      2      │   David    │   Jones   │ 1234 Elm St.
    3    │      3      │   Barbara  │   Williams│ 321 4th St.
    4    │      4      │   Don      │   Johnson │ 123 Beach Road
    5    │      6      │   John     │   Dawkins │ 123 E. St.

 ORDER────┬─Cust Number─┬─Order Number─┬─Date────┬─Part Number─┬─Quant
    1    │      1      │     100      │ 11/22/85│    1234     │   4
    2    │      2      │     101      │ 11/23/85│    1000     │   1
    3    │      3      │     102      │ 11/24/85│    2000     │   2
    4    │      4      │     103      │ 3/01/86 │    1000     │   4
    5    │      3      │     105      │ 7/01/86 │    1234     │   1
    6    │      6      │     106      │ 7/02/86 │    1000     │   3
    7    │      6      │     107      │ 7/05/86 │    2000     │   4
```

Keep in mind that this rule occurs only if you have specified a key field in one or both of the target tables. If the target tables do not have key fields, Paradox will enter duplicate records in the tables. Also remember that this rule applies only when all of the entries in the target table fields of the source table have the same entries as the fields of a record that is already in the target table. If the two sets of entries are not identical, but the key field entries are, the record from the source table will be entered in a KEYVIOL table.

Password Protection

If you wish, you can assign a password to the source table after it has been created. If you do assign a password to the source table, Paradox will prompt you for the password when you issue the [Menu] Modify MultiEntry Entry command before it will allow you to make any entries.

If either of the target tables, or the map table, is password protected, Paradox will not prompt you for the target or map table password when you issue the [Menu] Modify MultiEntry Entry command. Instead, it will simply deliver the message

> Password not given for target table TABLENAME

and terminate the MultiEntry operation without allowing you to enter any records. In other words, Paradox checks the target tables for protection but does not allow you to specify a password for these tables directly.

If you want to password-protect a multientry table system, you should assign the same password to every table in the system. Then, when you issue the [Menu] Modify MultiEntry Entry command and supply the password, Paradox will use the password you type to unlock both the source table and all of the target tables. Remember: If you use a different password for even one of the target tables, Paradox will not allow you to add records with the MultiEntry Entry command.

The [Menu] Tools More MultiAdd Command

The [Menu] Tools More MultiAdd command is closely related to the [Menu] Modify MultiEntry command and to the [Menu] Tools More Add command. Like the Add command, [Menu] Tools More MultiAdd allows you to add records from one table to another table. Like the MultiEntry command, MultiAdd allows you to distribute the records from a single table (the source table) into two or more target tables, using the relationships defined in a map table.

The MultiAdd command assumes that the records you want to distribute are already in the source table when you issue the command. This command does not allow you to enter records before distribution. The MultiEntry command, on the other hand, first asks you to enter records into the source table, then distributes those records to the target tables.

Like the MultiEntry command, the MultiAdd command requires that you define a source table and a map table. These tables serve precisely the same function with MultiAdd that they serve with MultiEntry. Interestingly, however, the MultiAdd command does not have a Setup option that allows you to define the source and map tables. You'll need to use the [Menu] Modify MultiEntry Setup command to define the source and map tables that you'll use with the MultiAdd command.

Although you probably will use the MultiAdd command less often than the MultiEntry command, it has several important applications. One of the primary uses for the MultiAdd command is distributing records to the appropriate target tables that have been placed by the MultiEntry command in a KEYVIOL table. Another application for the MultiAdd command is distributing the records that you import from a non-normalized dBASE III or 1-2-3 data base into normalized Paradox tables. MultiAdd can also be used when you want to redistribute to the original tables records that you have merged with a query and have modified.

The [Menu] Tools More MultiAdd command offers two options: New Entries and Update. These options are similar to the NewEntries and Update options of the [Menu] Tools More Add command. The effect of the MultiAdd command depends on which of these options you select and on whether or not the target tables include key fields.

The NewEntries Option

The NewEntries option causes the MultiAdd command to behave almost exactly like the MultiEntry command. If you choose NewEntries, Paradox will add the records from the source table to each of the target tables. The records from the source table will be appended to the target tables below any records that are already in the target tables.

An Example

For example, suppose you have used the [Menu] Modify MultiEntry command to enter a few new records into the CUSTOMER and ORDER tables through the source table NEWORD. Figure 10-29 shows these entries in the ENTRY table. Let's suppose that in making these entries, you simply mistyped one customer number. Instead of typing 5, the correct number, you typed 3, the number of the third customer in CUSTOMER. Because of this typo, a key violation occurred when the MultiEntry command was executed, causing Paradox to enter one of the records from ORDENTRY in the KEYVIOL table shown in Figure 10-30.

At this point, you need to edit the contents of the KEYVIOL table to eliminate the key conflict, and then distribute the entries to the appropriate target tables. To correct the error in this example, bring KEYVIOL into view, press [**Edit**], move to the Cust Number field, press [**Backspace**] to erase the erroneous entry, type **5**, and press [**Do-It!**]. As you can see, Figure 10-33 shows the corrected table.

Figure 10-33

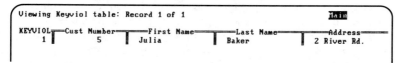

The easiest way to make this distribution from KEYVIOL into CUSTOMER and ORDER is to use the MultiAdd NewEntries command. To begin, issue the [**Menu**] **Tools More MultiAdd** command. When Paradox prompts you for the name of the source table, you should supply the name of the table that contains the record you want to distribute—in this case, KEYVIOL.

When Paradox prompts you for the name of the map table, you should supply the name of an existing map table that defines the relationship between the source table and the target tables. In this case, you already have a map table, ORDMAP, which will do the trick perfectly. ORDMAP works because the KEYVIOL table has exactly the same structure as the source table NEWORD, which you created in the previous section. If the map table you specify in this step does not match the structure of the source table you have specified, Paradox will display an error message when you execute the command.

After you type the name of the map table, ORDMAP, Paradox will present the two MultiAdd options: NewEntries and Update. In this case, because you want to add the records in the source table to the target tables, you should choose **NewEntries**. When you make this selection, Paradox will add the records from the source table to each of the target tables.

Figure 10-34 shows the CUSTOMER and ORDER table after the MultiAdd command is completed. As you can see, the single record from KEYVIOL has been divided into two records—one for CUSTOMER and one for ORDER—each of which has been entered into the appropriate table.

Figure 10-34

```
Viewing Order table: Record 1 of 8                              Main
  KEYVIOL ══Cust Number══ ══First Name══ ══Last Name══ ══Address══
     1           5           Julia          Baker        2 River Rd.


  CUSTOMER ══Cust Number══ ══First Name══ ══Last Name══ ══Address══
     1           1           John           Smith        111 Main St.
     2           2           David          Jones        1234 Elm St.
     3           3           Barbara        Williams     321 4th St.
     4           4           Don            Johnson      123 Beach Road
     5           5           Julia          Baker        2 River Rd.
     6           6           John           Dawkins      123 E. St.


  ORDER ══Cust Number══ ══Order Number══ ══Date══ ══Part Number══ ══Quant══
     1        1              100         11/22/85      1234            4
     2        2              101         11/23/85      1000            1
     3        3              102         11/24/85      2000            2
     4        4              103         3/01/86       1000            4
     5        3              105         7/01/86       1234            1
     6        6              106         7/02/86       1000            3
     7        6              107         7/05/86       2000            4
     8        5              104         6/01/86       1000            5
```

The MultiAdd NewEntries Command and Key Fields

If you look closely at Figure 10-34, you'll see that Paradox has added the records from KEYVIOL to CUSTOMER and ORDER differently. The portion of the record from KEYVIOL that was added to CUSTOMER was inserted into CUSTOMER in key field order. This occurred because the Cust Number field in CUSTOMER is a key field. In general, if one or both of the target tables in a MultiAdd NewEntries operation has a key field, and there is not a conflict between the entries in the key field of the target table and the corresponding field of the source table, Paradox will insert the records from the source table into the target table in key field order. That is, the records from the source table will be inserted between the records in the target table so that the entries in the key field of the resulting target table are in ascending order.

On the other hand, notice that the portion of the record from KEYVIOL that was added to the ORDER table was appended to the end of that table. This occurred because ORDER has no key fields. In general, when you use the MultiAdd NewEntries command to add records to a non-keyed table, Paradox will append the records from the source table to the target table below any records that are already in the target table.

If one or more of the target tables have key fields, it is possible that key violation errors will occur when you use the MultiAdd NewEntries command. These violations are handled by MultiAdd in exactly the same way that they are handled by MultiEntry.

A key violation occurs when a record that you enter through the source table has a key field entry that is the same as a key field entry in a target table, but the entries in the other fields of the source record are not the same as the entries in that field of the target. When this occurs, Paradox will enter that record in a KEYVIOL table. The record will not be entered in any target table. This is true even if the key violation affects only one of the target tables. If a key violation occurs, you'll need to edit the entries in the KEYVIOL table to remove the conflict, then distribute the record to the appropriate target tables by repeating the MultiAdd command.

If a record that you enter through the source table has a key field entry that is the same as a key field entry in a target table, and the entries in the other fields of the source record are also identical to the entries in that field of the target, then no key violation will occur. In that event, the new record will simply disappear. It will neither be added to the target table nor placed in a KEYVIOL table.

The Update Option

If you choose the Update option from the MultiAdd menu, Paradox will use the records in the source table to update the records in the target tables. Exactly how this occurs depends on whether or not the target tables are keyed. If a target table is not keyed, the records from the source table will be appended to the target table below any existing records, just as if you had selected the NewEntries option.

If a target table is keyed, but there is not a conflict between the entries in the key field of the target table and the corresponding field of the source table, Paradox will insert the records from the source table into the target table in key field order. That is, the records from the source table will be inserted between the records in the target table so that the entries in the key field of the resulting target table are in ascending order.

If a target table is keyed, and there is a conflict between the entries in the key field of the target table and the corresponding field of the source table, Paradox will use the data from the non-key fields of the source table to update the record with the conflicting key field entry in the target table. This last case is by far the most important use of the Update option. Let's consider an example of how it works.

An Example

Suppose that you receive an order from a customer who is already in your customer table, but the customer's address has changed since she last placed an order. You have issued the MultiEntry Entry command and have entered the record shown in Table 10-4 into the NEWORD table. Figure 10-35 shows this record in place. Notice that this record has the same entry in the Cust Number field as the second entry in the CUSTOMER table, and that most of the other entries in the CUSTOMER fields of ENTRY agree with the entries in the second record in CUSTOMER, but that the Address and Zip field entries are different. When you press **[Do-It!]** to execute the MultiEntry command, Paradox will detect a key violation and will place this record in a KEYVIOL table. Figure 10-36 shows this table.

Table 10-4 Sample Data

Cust Number	2
First Name	David
Last Name	Jones
Address	555 Oak St.
City	Lexington
State	KY
Zip	40555
Order Number	108
Date	8/15/86
Part Number	1234
Quantity	1
Description	Red Widget
Price	$100.00
Extension	$100.00

Figure 10-35

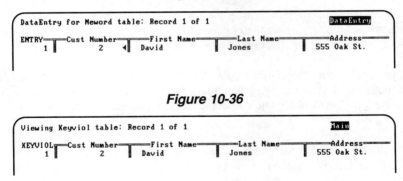

Figure 10-36

Unlike the previous example, in this case you don't want to add the record from KEYVIOL to CUSTOMER. Instead, you want to update the record for customer number 2 in the CUSTOMER table by replacing it with the record from KEYVIOL. You can do this with the Update option of the MultiAdd command.

To update the CUSTOMER and ORDER tables, issue the **[Menu] T**ools **M**ore **M**ultiAdd command, then specify **KEYVIOL** as the source table and **ORDMAP** as the map table. Next, choose the **U**pdate option. Since the entry in the key field of the second record in CUSTOMER is the same as the entry in the corresponding field of KEYVIOL, Paradox will use the record in KEYVIOL to update the second record in CUSTOMER. As you can see, Figure 10-37 shows the CUSTOMER and ORDER tables as they will look after the MultiAdd command is finished. Notice that the Address field entry for the second record in CUSTOMER has been changed to agree with the entry from KEYVIOL.

Figure 10-37

```
Viewing Customer table: Record 1 of 6                                    Main
    ┌─First Name─┬─Last Name─┬─Address────────┬─City────────┬─Sta
    │ John       │ Smith     │ 111 Main St.   │ Peru        │ I
    │ David      │ Jones     │ 555 Oak St.    │ Lexington   │ K
    │ Barbara    │ Williams  │ 321 4th St.    │ New York    │ N
    │ Don        │ Johnson   │ 123 Beach Road │ Miami       │ F
    │ Julia      │ Baker     │ 2 River Rd.    │ Cincinatti  │ O
    │ John       │ Dawkins   │ 123 E. St.     │ Washington  │ D

ORDER─┬─Cust Number─┬─Order Number─┬─Date────┬─Part Number─┬─Quant
  1   │      1      │     100      │11/22/85 │    1234     │   4
  2   │      2      │     101      │11/23/85 │    1000     │   1
  3   │      3      │     102      │11/24/85 │    2000     │   2
  4   │      4      │     103      │ 3/01/86 │    1000     │   4
  5   │      3      │     105      │ 7/01/86 │    1234     │   1
  6   │      6      │     106      │ 7/02/86 │    1000     │   3
  7   │      6      │     107      │ 7/05/86 │    2000     │   4
  8   │      5      │     104      │ 6/01/86 │    1000     │   5
  9   │      2      │     108      │ 8/15/86 │    1234     │   1
```

Notes

The contents of the source table do not change when you use the [Menu] Tools More MultiAdd command. Whatever was in the source table before you issued the command will be in the source table after the command is completed. Whether or not the source table has a key field has no effect on the command.

Unlike the Menu Tools More Add Update command, the [Menu] Tools More MultiAdd Update command does not create a temporary CHANGED table. This means that once you execute the MultiAdd Update command, the original records in the target table will be lost for good.

As with the MultiEntry command, if the source table in a MultiAdd operation is password protected, Paradox will prompt you to supply the password before it executes the command. Paradox will check the target tables and the map table for protection but will not allow you to specify a password for these tables directly. If you want to password-protect a multientry table system, you should assign the same password to every table in the system. Then, when you issue the [Menu] Modify MultiEntry Entry command and supply the password, Paradox will use the password you type to unlock both the source table and all of the target tables.

Insert Queries

In Chapter 8, you learned about the special query operators find and delete. There is one more special operator, insert. The insert operator allows you to insert the data from one or more tables into a different table.

Insert queries are the most flexible of Paradox's multitable tools. Although you can use the insert operator to create queries that duplicate the function of the Add, MultiAdd, and MultiEntry commands, it is more flexible than those tools. You can use insert queries to insert information into a table from another table that has a completely unrelated structure, to insert just a few fields of data from one table into another, or to insert data from several tables into one.

The importance of insert queries in your work with Paradox depends on which version of the program you are using. If you are using Version 1.0, which does not offer a MultiAdd or MultiEntry capability, you will probably need to use insert queries more often. If you are using Paradox 1.1, you will probably use insert queries only when an Add, MultiAdd, or MultiEntry command will not work.

Insert Query Basics

To perform an insert query, you must create a query that contains a form for every table from which you want to insert records (the source tables) and a form for the table into which you want to insert records (the target table). Once the query is created, you enter the word *insert* in the space under the form name of the query form for the table into which you want to insert the records. Next, you use examples to link the common fields in the query forms.

When you process the query, the contents of the specified fields of the source table or tables will be added to the corresponding fields of the target table. The new data will appear in the target table below any records that are already in that table. At the same time, Paradox will copy the data from the source tables into a special temporary table called INSERTED. This table will be brought into view when the query is completed.

An Example

Suppose you are about to undertake a large promotional mailing. You want to send the mail to all of the people in both your PROSPECT and CUSTOMER tables. So that you can operate on the data more easily, you decide to add the records from CUSTOMER to PROSPECT before you begin creating mailing labels.

Instead of combining the CUSTOMER table directly into PROSPECT, we'll use a third table, MAILLIST, to receive data from both tables. Although there are several ways to create this table, the easiest is to build a simple query on the PROSPECT table. To do this, use the [Menu] Ask command to create a new query form for PROSPECT and use

[**Check Mark**] to select the First Name, Last Name, Address, City, State, and Zip fields in the form. When you process this query, Paradox will create the ANSWER table shown in Figure 10-38. This table includes the data from the appropriate fields for all of the records in PROSPECT. As the final part of this first step, you should use the [**Menu**] **T**ools **R**ename command to change the name of **ANSWER** to **MAILLIST**.

Figure 10-38

```
Viewing Answer table: Record 1 of 10                              Main
PROSPECT┬─Prospect Number─┬─First Name─┬─Last Name─┬─Address─
        │                 │            │           │
        │                 │     9      │    9      │    9


ANSWER┬─First Name─┬─Last Name─┬─Address─────────┬─City────
   1  │  Barry     │  Sumpter  │  567 Cards Way  │  Louisville
   2  │  Bill      │  Johnson  │  42 Old Rock Rd.│  Memphis
   3  │  Billy     │  Thompson │  1234 S. 3rd St.│  Louisville
   4  │  David     │  Jones    │  123 Yale Ct.   │  New Haven
   5  │  Fred      │  Foote    │  123 Brattle St │  Cambridge
   6  │  Guy       │  Greene   │  123 Park Place │  Louisville
   7  │  Jim       │  Morrison │  100 W. 73rd St │  New York
   8  │  John      │  Smith    │  555 Main Street│  Louisville
   9  │  Rodney    │  McCray   │  9999 Easy St.  │  Houston
  10  │  William   │  Bedford  │  222 N.E. Pkwy  │  Memphis
```

Now you are ready to add the records from CUSTOMER to MAILLIST. Since CUSTOMER and MAILLIST have slightly different structures, you cannot use the [Menu] Tools More Add command to combine them. If you want to put these two tables together, you'll need to use an insert query.

To begin, use the [**Menu**] **A**sk command to create new query forms for the CUSTOMER and MAILLIST tables. When these query forms come into view, move to the space under the name of the MAILLIST form (the form for the table into which you want the records inserted) and type **insert**. This entry tells Paradox that this query will insert records into the MAILLIST table.

Now you must enter examples in the two query forms that tell Paradox how to insert the data from CUSTOMER into MAILLIST. To begin, move to the First Name field of MAILLIST, press [**Example**], and type **FN**. Then move to the First Name field of CUSTOMER, press [**Example**], and type **FN**. (Of course, you can use any example you want to use to relate these fields, as long as you enter the same example in both fields. We chose FN for convenience.)

Now, continue in this way, entering example pairs in the corresponding fields of CUSTOMER and MAILLIST until you have entered examples in the First Name, Last Name, Address, City, State, and Zip fields of both tables. Of course, you must use a different example for each pair of fields. Figure 10-39 shows the completed query.

Figure 10-39

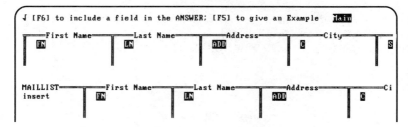

When you press **[Do-It!]** to process the query, Paradox will insert the data from the indicated fields of CUSTOMER into MAILLIST. In addition, the same entries will be entered in a table called INSERTED. Figure 10-40 shows the INSERTED table on the screen. Figure 10-41 shows the completed MAILLIST table.

Figure 10-40

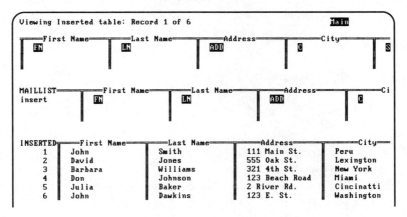

Figure 10-41

When you process an insert query, Paradox uses the examples you have defined in the two query forms to determine how to insert the entries for the source table into the target table. In this case, Paradox used the examples to transfer the data from the First Name field of CUSTOMER to the First Name field of MAILLIST, from the Last Name field of CUSTOMER to the Last Name field of MAILLIST, and so on.

Notes

As you have seen, insert queries allow you to transfer data from one table to another, even if the two tables have different structures. In fact, you can even use insert queries to insert data into an alphanumeric field in one table that is shorter than the alphanumeric field from which the data is inserted. If the target field is short enough, Paradox will trim the entries from the source table automatically as it inserts them in the target table.

You cannot, however, use an insert query to insert data from an alphanumeric field in one table into a number, dollar, or date field in another table, or from a number, dollar, or date field into an alphanumeric field. If you attempt to link two fields of different types with an example in an insert query, Paradox will highlight the second occurrence of the example and display the message *Expression in this field has the wrong type* when you try to process the query.

Insert Queries and Key Fields

If the target table of an insert query has a key field, things can be a good deal trickier. Let's consider a couple of simple examples.

Suppose that you want to use an insert query to insert the records from the CUSTOMER table directly into the PROSPECT table. Remember that the Prospect Number field in the PROSPECT table is a key field. To make this insertion, you might create an insert query like the one in Figure 10-42. Notice that this query includes examples that link the First Name, Last Name, Address, City, State, and Zip fields in the two tables, but that the Prospect Number and Cust Number fields are not linked.

Figure 10-42

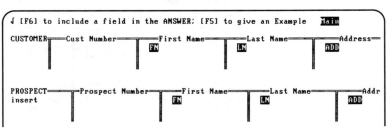

Figure 10-43 shows the screen after the query is processed. Figure 10-44 shows the resulting PROSPECT table. Notice that there are now 11 records in PROSPECT where there were only ten before. The trouble is that there should be 16 records in PROSPECT: the ten that were there, plus the six from CUSTOMER.

Figure 10-43

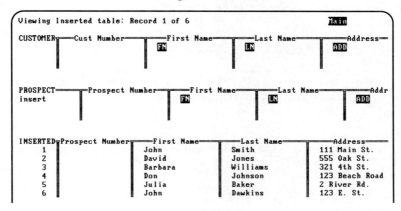

Figure 10-44

PROSPECT	Prospect Number	First Name	Last Name	Address
1		John	Dawkins	123 E. St.
2	1	John	Smith	555 Main Street
3	4	Jim	Morrison	100 W. 73rd St
4	5	Bill	Johnson	42 Old Rock Rd.
5	6	Fred	Foote	123 Brattle St
6	7	David	Jones	123 Yale Ct.
7	8	Billy	Thompson	1234 S. 3rd St.
8	9	Rodney	McCray	9999 Easy St.
9	10	William	Bedford	222 N.E. Pkwy
10	11	Barry	Sumpter	567 Cards Way
11	12	Guy	Greene	123 Park Place

Here's what happened: When you processed the query, Paradox began to add the records from CUSTOMER to PROSPECT. Since you did not link the Cust Number field to the Prospect Number field, the records from CUSTOMER were brought into PROSPECT without a Prospect Number field entry. Remember, though, that Prospect Number is a key field. This means that each entry in this field must be unique. If Paradox inserted all four records from CUSTOMER into PROSPECT, there would be six records in PROSPECT with the same key field entry: a blank. For this reason, Paradox only inserts one record from CUSTOMER into PROSPECT.

The real problem is that Paradox does not give you any indication of what has happened. If you look at the INSERTED table that results from this query, you'll see that it contains all of the records from CUSTOMER, leading you to believe that the insert query was processed properly. In addition, Paradox has not placed the excluded records into a KEYVIOL table, even though a key violation has clearly occurred.

Now let's look at an even more troublesome case. Suppose that you again want to combine CUSTOMER directly into PROSPECT, and that you create the insert query shown in Figure 10-45 to accomplish this task. This query is identical to the one in Figure 10-42 except that it includes a pair of examples that link the Prospect Number and Cust Number fields.

Figure 10-45

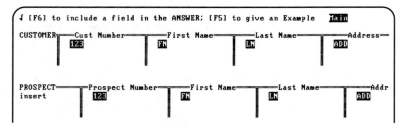

Figure 10-46 shows the PROSPECT table after this query has been processed. If you look closely, you will see that Paradox has *replaced* the entries from PROSPECT with the Prospect Number field entries 1, 2, 3, 4, 5, and 6 with the six records from CUSTOMER!

Figure 10-46

```
Viewing Prospect table: Record 1 of 13                    Main

PROSPECT┬Prospect Number┬─First Name─┬─Last Name─┬─Address─────
   1   │               │ John       │ Dawkins   │ 123 E. St.
   2   │      1        │ John       │ Smith     │ 111 Main St.
   3   │      2        │ David      │ Jones     │ 555 Oak St.
   4   │      3        │ Barbara    │ Williams  │ 321 4th St.
   5   │      4        │ Don        │ Johnson   │ 123 Beach Road
   6   │      5        │ Julia      │ Baker     │ 2 River Rd.
   7   │      6        │ John       │ Dawkins   │ 123 E. St.
   8   │      7        │ David      │ Jones     │ 123 Yale Ct.
   9   │      8        │ Billy      │ Thompson  │ 1234 S. 3rd St.
  10   │      9        │ Rodney     │ McCray    │ 9999 Easy St.
  11   │     10        │ William    │ Bedford   │ 222 N.E. Pkwy
  12   │     11        │ Barry      │ Sumpter   │ 567 Cards Way
  13   │     12        │ Guy        │ Greene    │ 123 Park Place
```

Apparently, when an insert query encounters a conflict between an entry in a field of a source table and an entry in the corresponding key field of the target table, it simply replaces the target table record with the source table record. Once again, there is no indication that this has occurred. The INSERTED table shows the six records from CUSTOMER, just as it would if the query had worked correctly. And, once again, Paradox has not entered any records into a KEYVIOL table, nor has it entered the old versions of the records from PROSPECT into a CHANGED table. In other words, the old records are unrecoverable.

The moral of all this? As with the Edit command, you should be very careful when you use insert queries to change tables that have key fields. The difficulties that you are likely to encounter may far outweigh the benefits of using the command.

Inserting from Two Tables

You can insert records only into one table at a time. You can, however, insert data from more than one table at a time into a target table. To see how this works, let's use a very simple example. Suppose you have created two tables, FIRST and LAST, that contain the first and last names of your friends. You want to insert these names into a table called NAMES. Figure 10-47 shows these tables.

Figure 10-47

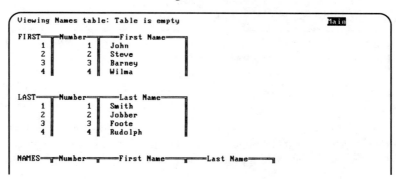

To do this, first use the [**Menu**] **A**sk command to create three query forms: one for FIRST, one for LAST, and one for NAMES. When the query forms are in view, move to the space under the form name in the NAMES query form and type **insert**.

Next, you must enter examples in the fields of the three query forms that tell Paradox how to insert data into NAMES. To begin, enter the same example–we'll use the letter N–into the Number field of all three tables. Next, enter an example into the First Name field of the FIRST query form and enter the same example into the First Name field of the NAMES table. Finally, enter an example into the Last Name field of the LAST query form and into the Last Name field of the NAMES table. Figure 10-48 on the next page shows you the completed query.

When you press [**Do-It!**] to process this query, Paradox will insert the entries from the First Name field of the FIRST table into the First Name field of the NAMES table and from the Last Name field of the LAST table into the Last Name field of the NAMES table. Figure 10-49 shows the NAMES table after the query is processed.

Figure 10-48

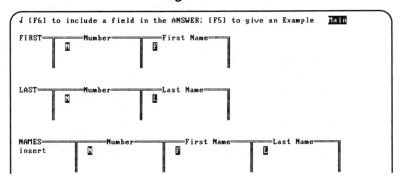

Figure 10-49

```
Viewing Names table: Record 1 of 4                    Main
NAMES──┬─Number─────┬─First Name─────┬─Last Name──
   1   │    1       │   John         │   Smith
   2   │    2       │   Steve        │   Jobber
   3   │    3       │   Barney       │   Foote
   4   │    4       │   Wilma        │   Rudolph
```

There is a fine point that you must understand about multitable insert queries. As long as each source table contributes unique fields to the target table, everything will work fine. What you cannot do with an insert query, however, is have two or more source tables, each of which contributes the same fields to the target table. For example, you could not create an insert query that would insert data from both PROSPECTS and CUSTOMER into MAILLIST at once. You must use two separate queries (one for each source table) to make this insertion.

Conclusion

In this chapter, you've learned about several of Paradox's most sophisticated commands. You've seen how the Add command can be used to append the records in one table to another table, and how to update the records in one table using those in another. You've learned how to use Subtract to delete from one table the records that it has in common with another table. You've seen how the MultiEntry and MultiAdd commands can be used to distribute records from one table into two or more tables. In addition, you've learned how to use insert queries to perform specialized multitable operations.

In the next two chapters, we'll show you how to create reports from the data in your Paradox tables.

Chapter 11
Report Fundamentals

In the preceding chapters of this book, we've shown you a variety of ways to manipulate the information in a Paradox table. As you performed these manipulations, you saw the results on the screen of your computer. You often will want to share the information in your Paradox tables with people who don't have access to Paradox, however. To do this, you'll need to create printed copies of your work.

The next two chapters of *The Paradox Companion* deal with reporting. In this chapter, we'll introduce you to the basic features of the Paradox report generator. In Chapter 12, we'll cover more advanced topics, like summary statistics, grouping, managing reports, and using the Paradox Custom Configuration Program to customize the report generator.

Instant Reports

Paradox's [Instant Report] key provides the easiest way to print a hard copy of a table. When you press the [Instant Report] key ([Alt]-[F7]) while viewing a table or form, Paradox automatically sends a default report for that table to your printer. In most cases, this report will be a tabular listing of the information in the table–a "standard" report.

For example, if you want to print a copy of the information contained in the 65-record, nine-field table named LISTINGS shown in Figure 11-1 on the next page, you would first issue the **[Menu]** View command, type **LISTINGS**, and press ↵ to bring LISTINGS to the workspace. Then, after making sure your printer is connected and turned on, press the **[Instant Report]** key ([Alt]-[F7]). As soon as you press this key, Paradox will display the message *Sending report to printer...* in the lower-right corner of the screen and will print the report shown in Figure 11-2 on page 331.

The report shown in Figure 11-2 is a simple tabular listing of the information in the LISTINGS table. Each record is printed on a single line of the page, and the entries from each field are printed in their own columns. The contents of the alphanumeric fields from the table appear left-aligned in the report and the contents of the numeric fields appear right-aligned, just as they do in a table. At the top of each column, Paradox has printed the name of the corresponding field in the table, followed by a dashed line. The order of columns in the report matches the field order in the *structure* of the table–not necessarily the order of the fields in the image. This is Paradox's standard report format.

Figure 11-1 The LISTINGS Table

Viewing Listings table: Record 1 of 65   Main   Viewing Listings table: Record 1 of 65   Main

LISTINGS	Address	Town	Owner	List Date	Style	Price	Sq Ft	BRs	Baths
1	123 Abby Ct.	Louisville	Kones,D	11/02/85	Ranch	32,950.00	1500	3	1
2	426 St. James Ct.	Louisville	Jones,S	11/05/85	Ranch	19,500.00	950	2	1
3	766 Baird St.	Louisville	Black,G	11/08/85	Colonial	139,950.00	2600	4	2.5
4	222 Big Ben Dr.	Louisville	Roberts,D	11/08/85	Other	53,500.00	1900	3	1.5
5	666 Montana Ave.	Louisville	Saul,H	11/09/85	Cape Cod	55,000.00	1900	3	1
6	509 Morocco Dr.	E'Town	Smith,B	11/10/85	Cape Cod	62,500.00	1875	3	1.5
7	987 Allan Dr.	Louisville	Newsome,K	11/12/85	Cape Cod	68,000.00	1900	4	2
8	549 Billtown Rd.	Louisville	Bizer,B	11/14/85	Ranch	72,500.00	2000	3	2
9	343 Market St.	Louisville	Bivins,D	11/15/85	Ranch	42,900.00	1675	3	1
10	198 Main St.	J'Town	Green,L	11/15/85	Other	27,500.00	800	3	1
11	885 Jefferson St.	J'Town	Zith,M	11/18/85	Ranch	55,000.00	1500	3	1
12	913 Whitney Dr.	North Hill	Kulp,R	11/20/85	Cape Cod	99,500.00	1800	4	2
13	363 Dower Ct.	North Fork	Culp,A	11/21/85	Cape Cod	189,000.00	2100	4	2
14	620 Windsong Ct.	Louisville	Pank,E	11/22/85	Colonial	250,000.00	4000	6	3.5
15	4500 Hempstead Dr.	Louisville	Pape,C	12/04/85	Colonial	150,000.00	2600	4	2.5
16	#6 Brandon Way	Louisville	Abrams,L	12/08/85	Ranch	67,000.00	2250	4	1.5
17	6610 Vermin Dr.	Louisville	Russ,J	12/10/85	Ranch	75,000.00	2100	3	1.5
18	712 Clifton Ct.	Louisville	Thomas,T	12/10/85	Ranch	30,000.00	1500	3	1
19	5432 Miller Rd.	Louisville	Young,R	12/15/85	Other	17,500.00	800	2	1
20	#12 Circle Ct.	Louisville	White,Y	12/19/85	Other	18,000.00	800	2	1
21	1222 Dee Rd.	South Fork	Smith,P	12/19/85	Ranch	22,950.00	950	3	1
22	222 Earl Ave.	J'Town	Wray,A	12/22/85	Ranch	51,000.00	1200	3	1
23	9827 Rowan St.	J'Town	Coad,B	12/27/85	Ranch	47,950.00	1100	3	1
24	3355 Bank St.	J'Town	Cobb,D	1/03/86	Ranch	37,500.00	1500	3	1
25	77 Portland Ave.	North Hill	Coe,A	1/05/86	Ranch	20,000.00	1500	3	1
26	99 Cardinal Hill Rd.	North Hill	Brand,B	1/05/86	Cape Cod	70,000.00	2000	3	1.5
27	#10 Old Mill Rd.	Louisville	Stern,M	1/07/86	Ranch	75,000.00	2150	4	1.5
28	5532 Mud Creek Dr.	Louisville	Hall,W	1/10/86	Ranch	12,000.00	950	2	1
29	4444 Normie Ln.	Louisville	James,J	1/11/86	Cape Cod	120,000.00	2400	5	2.5
30	3490 Bold Rd.	Louisville	Taft,H	1/15/86	Colonial	275,000.00	3000	5	3.5
31	#82 Rudd Rd.	Louisville	Lum,I	1/16/86	Cape Cod	88,950.00	2100	4	2
32	6712 Shelby St.	Louisville	Wood,B	1/16/86	Ranch	92,500.00	2400	4	2
33	7235 Shiloh Dr.	E'Town	Allan,J	1/17/86	Ranch	95,000.00	2750	4	2.5
34	8989 Big D Ln.	South Fork	Adkins,G	1/18/86	Ranch	17,000.00	1200	2	1
35	1001 Spring St.	North Hill	Frier,F	1/22/86	Other	45,000.00	1700	3	1.5
36	6935 Shiloh Dr.	E'Town	Grebe,C	1/25/86	Cape Cod	81,000.00	2000	3	2
37	4989 Adler Way	Louisville	Dole,V	1/30/86	Cape Cod	76,500.00	2000	3	1.5
38	5670 Beech St.	Louisville	Smith,P	2/02/86	Cape Cod	65,950.00	1800	3	1
39	#62 Billy Bone Ct.	Louisville	Taylor,A	2/04/86	Ranch	34,500.00	1600	3	1.5
40	3323 Mt. Holly Dr.	Louisville	Grizz,D	2/10/86	Ranch	22,100.00	1200	3	1
41	9989 Midway Rd.	Louisville	Maier,O	2/11/86	Ranch	61,250.00	1875	3	2
42	435 Oxted Ln.	Louisville	O'Neal,P	2/12/86	Ranch	53,790.00	1900	3	1
43	22 N. Ridge Ct.	Louisville	Nunn,A	2/15/86	Colonial	200,000.00	2900	5	3
44	654 Nora Ln.	Louisville	Orwick,S	2/18/86	Cape Cod	48,000.00	1600	3	1
45	659 Ridge Rd.	Louisville	Pulley,F	2/24/86	Ranch	30,000.00	1500	3	1
46	14 Short Rd.	Louisville	Quire,I	3/01/86	Ranch	52,300.00	1600	3	1
47	721 Zabel Way	Louisville	Stich,L	3/02/86	Ranch	47,950.00	1500	3	1
48	581 Yale Dr.	Louisville	Winer,L	3/05/86	Ranch	78,000.00	2100	4	1.5
49	854 Unseld Blvd.	Louisville	Volk,H	3/07/86	Other	87,000.00	2500	4	1.5
50	#5 Ashby St.	J'Town	Wagner,H	3/08/86	Other	97,000.00	2400	4	2.5
51	1989 Eastern Pkwy.	Louisville	Klink,C	3/11/86	Ranch	26,950.00	1100	2	1
52	9819 Wilson Ave.	J'Town	Crane,B	3/11/86	Ranch	28,000.00	1200	3	1
53	956 Volar Ln.	J'Town	Lamb,M	3/13/86	Ranch	18,000.00	1200	2	1
54	5372 Tyson Pl.	Louisville	Goode,J	3/16/86	Ranch	35,000.00	1500	3	1.5
55	9849 Taylor Blvd.	J'Town	Dukes,J	3/16/86	Ranch	32,950.00	1750	3	1
56	185 Pages Ln.	J'Town	Cowan,M	3/20/86	Other	15,500.00	1000	2	1
57	3752 St. Dennis	Louisville	Levine,J	3/22/86	Cape Cod	67,950.00	2500	3	2
58	20 Seebolt Rd.	Louisville	Priest,S	3/29/86	Other	28,500.00	950	3	1
59	2216 Lacey St.	North Hill	Beat,A	4/01/86	Cape Cod	94,999.00	2700	4	2.5
60	6262 Kenwood Dr.	North Hill	Beck,U	4/05/86	Ranch	71,650.00	2000	4	1.5
61	9222 Meadow Pl.	South Fork	Baxter,H	4/10/86	Ranch	85,000.00	2100	3	2
62	6791 Lotus Ave.	South Fork	Howell,T	4/12/86	Ranch	75,600.00	2000	3	2
63	586 Ansa Way	Louisville	Noel,C	4/15/86	Colonial	69,500.00	2200	4	1.5
64	99 N. Central Blvd.	Louisville	Stevens,R	4/16/86	Ranch	49,000.00	2500	3	1.5
65	4233 Mix Ave.	Louisville	Martin,D	4/18/86	Cape Cod	49,500.00	1900	3	1.5

Paradox will always print every record from any table. In this case, for example, Paradox has printed all 65 records from the LISTINGS table. Unless you specify that the report be grouped (a topic we'll discuss in Chapter 12), Paradox will print the records in the same order as they appear in the table from which you print them.

In addition to printing the 65 records from this table in the standard report, Paradox also has printed a title line at the top of the report. This title line contains the current date, the report title (in this case, *Standard report*), and the page number.

You also will notice that this report had to be printed on four separate pages. Unless your tables are very small, the printout of those tables will occupy more than one page.

Paradox can print from only a single table at a time. It cannot draw information from more than one table into a report as a part of the reporting process. If you want to include information from two or more tables in a single report, you must use a query to combine information from those tables into a single table and print from the new table.

Figure 11-2 A Standard Report

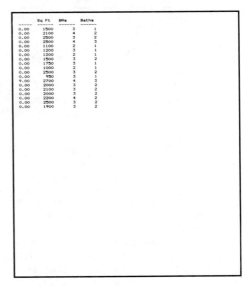

Report Specifications

When you pressed the [Instant Report] key, Paradox didn't just send an image of the current table to your printer–it added some explanatory text to the report, adjusted the spacing of the report, and so forth. The result was the standard report for the LISTINGS table. When Paradox printed this report, it did so according to the layout defined in the standard report specification (or report spec) shown in Figure 11-3. A report spec is a template that defines the arrangement of information in a Paradox report. Paradox automatically sets up a standard report spec for any table that you create.

Figure 11-3 A Standard Report Specification

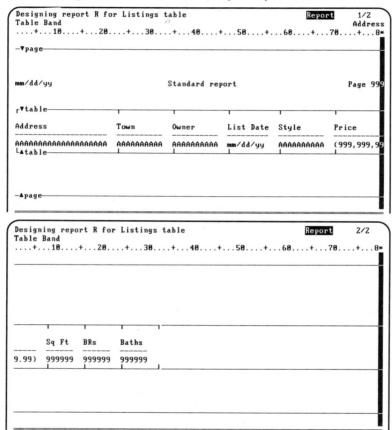

Report specifications are the most fundamental element of Paradox reporting. Whenever Paradox prints information from a table, it does so according to the layout of the information in a report spec. Normally, printing a Paradox report is a two-step process. First, you design a report spec that shows Paradox how you want the report to look (you can design up to ten report specs for any table). Then you tell Paradox to print the table according to that spec. When you first create a table, Paradox automatically designs a standard report specification for that table and designates it as the default report specification for that table. Whenever you press the [Instant Report] key while viewing a table, Paradox prints from the default spec for that table. Unless you have modified the standard report spec (a process that we'll explain later), Paradox will print it whenever you press the [Instant Report] key.

Every report spec contains the same essential components: elements, bands, and page-widths. We'll use the standard LISTINGS table report spec shown in Figure 11-3 to explain what these components are and how they work.

Elements

If you examine the standard report shown in Figure 11-2 closely, you'll see that it contains two types of information: entries from the fields in the source table (and from other special fields) and literal text. All Paradox reports contain one or both of these types of information. These two types of information come from two different types of elements in the report specification: field masks and literals.

Field Masks

Paradox uses special tools called field masks to represent the fields from a table in a report specification. The exact appearance of these masks depends on the type of field they represent. Masks that represent numeric fields appear as a series of the digit 9. For example, Paradox uses the mask 999999 to represent the BRs field in the report spec shown in Figure 11-3. Masks that represent alphanumeric fields appear as a series of the letter A. For example, Paradox uses the mask AAAAAAAAAA to represent the Owner field in the standard spec. Dollar ($) fields are represented with a series of 9s, like number fields, but also include parentheses, commas, and decimal points. The masks for date fields are generic representations of the form in which Paradox will display the date. For example, the mask mm/dd/yy instructs Paradox to print the date May 10, 1986, as 5/10/86, while the mask Month dd, yyyy instructs Paradox to print the same date as May 10, 1986. Paradox can print a date in any of eight different forms.

The length of a mask determines how much space Paradox allows each entry it prints from the field represented by that mask. If a mask is ten characters long, for example, Paradox will devote ten spaces to the entries from the field represented by that mask when it prints the report. Entries from alphanumeric fields will be left-aligned within their mask, while entries from numeric fields will be right-aligned.

In a standard report spec, the length of each mask is determined by the type and/or length of the field it represents, as defined in the structure (not necessarily the display image) of that field. The mask width for an alphanumeric field will equal the length designation for that field in the table's structure. Paradox will use a mask that is six characters wide for any numeric or short number field, a mask that is sixteen characters wide for a dollar field, and a mask that is eight characters wide for a date field. We'll show you how to adjust the length of a field mask later in this chapter.

In addition to using masks to draw information from the fields of a table, Paradox uses masks to place six kinds of special information in a report: the current date, the current time, the current page number, the current record number, the results of calculations, and summary statistics. In the standard report spec shown in Figure 11-3, for example, the mask mm/dd/yy at the left edge of the spec represents the current date, and the mask 999 at the right edge of the spec represents the current page number. We'll explore time fields, calculated fields, and summary fields later in this chapter and in Chapter 12.

Literal Text

In addition to field masks, any report spec can (and usually will) contain descriptive text. Unlike masks, which draw information from the fields of a table or place other variable information into a report, any text included in a report spec will be printed literally in the report. For this reason, nonmask entries in a report spec are called literals.

Paradox has included several literals in the report specification shown in Figure 11-3. For example, it has typed the literal *Standard report* at the top of the report specification. Additionally, Paradox has included the name of each field as a literal immediately above the mask that represents each field. The dashed lines that appear immediately below the field names also are literals.

Bands

As you have seen, the masks and literals that you include in a report specification determine what information will appear in a report. The placement of those elements within the report specification determines where they will appear in that report. Since the literal *Page* and the page number mask 999 appear to the right of the literal *Standard report* in the report spec shown in Figure 11-3, for example, the page number information will appear to the right of the title in the printed report. Additionally, since the literals *Address* and -------------------- are positioned above the mask for the Address field, Paradox will print those literals before it prints the entries from the Address field.

The position of one mask or literal relative to another mask or literal is not the only factor that determines where that element will appear in a report. The band in which that element appears also affects where it will be printed. A band is a section of a report template that is responsible for producing a certain portion of a report. A report spec's bands are defined by the horizontal lines that run across the spec. The lines that mark the beginning of a band will be marked with the symbol ▼ and the name of that band. For example, the topmost line in Figure 11-3 (the one with the legend ▼*page*) signals the beginning of the page band. The lines that signal the end of a band will be marked with the symbol ▲ and the name of the band. For example, the line with the legend ▲ *table* signals the end of the table band.

All standard Paradox reports (and most other reports) contain three bands: the report band, the page band, and the table band. The arrangement of the bands in a report spec divides all but the table band into two parts: a top and a bottom, which are sometimes called a header and a footer. Each section of each band is responsible for printing a different part of the report.

The Report Header

The report header is the section of the report band that appears above the top border of the page band. Literals and masks that are situated in this section will be printed only once, at the top of the report. You'll want to use this section of a report spec for information you want Paradox to print only at the top of the first page of a report, like an overall report title or like the date or time of printing. In the standard report spec shown in Figure 11-3, the report header section contains only a single blank line. This causes Paradox to skip one line at the top of the first page of the report.

The Report Footer

The report footer is the section of the report band that appears below the bottom border of the page band. The masks and literals that you include in this section of the report spec will be printed only once, on the last page of a report, immediately after the last record that Paradox prints, but before the page footer (a band we'll discuss in a few paragraphs). You'll want to use this section for information that you want Paradox to print only once, at the end of the report, such as a grand total of the entries in a column. In the standard report spec shown in Figure 11-3, the report footer consists of a single blank line. This causes Paradox to print a single blank line after it prints the 65th record in LISTINGS.

The Page Header

The table band of the standard report spec shown in Figure 11-3 divides the page band into two sections: a page header and a page footer. The page header is the section of the page band that appears above the upper border of the table band. The masks and literals you include in this section of a report specification will be printed once at the top of each page in the report. In addition to providing a place for titles, dates, and so forth at the top of each page, the page header is the only means of adding a top margin to each page.

In a standard report like the one shown in Figure 11-2, the page header will occupy six lines: three blank lines, a line that contains information (a current date mask, the literal *Standard report*, the literal *Page*, and a page number mask), and then another two blank lines. This page header instructs Paradox to skip three lines at the top of each page as a top margin, print a line of information, then skip another two lines.

The Page Footer

The page footer is the section of the page band that extends below the bottom border of the table band. Paradox prints any masks or literals you place in this section at the bottom of each page of the report. For example, you could use a summary mask in the page footer to print the total of the entries from a certain field on each page. Importantly, the page footer provides the only means of specifying a bottom margin for a report. The page footer of a standard report consists of four blank lines, which causes Paradox to leave a four-line margin at the bottom of each page.

The Table Band

The central portion of any standard report is the table band. The masks and literals that you include in this section will be printed between the bottom of the page header and the top of the page footer, as many times as will fit on that page. Although the table band is not overlayed by any other band, it contains two functional sections: a header and a body. The header consists of the rows of the table band above the first mask in that band. Any information on these lines will be printed once on the page, much like the page header, immediately below the last line of the page header. In a standard report, Paradox will print a blank line, then a line of field names, then a line of dashes once on each page.

The body of the table band begins with the first row that contains a field mask and ends with the bottom of the table band. Paradox will print the information in this section of the table band once for every record in the table, in the order that those records appear in the table (unless you have grouped them—a topic we'll cover in Chapter 12). In this case, for example, Paradox will print the *123 Abby Ct.* record first, the *426 St. James Ct.* record second, the *766 Baird St.* record third, and so forth. On each "pass" through a report, the field masks in the table band refer to a different record in the table that Paradox is printing.

Although in a standard report the lower section of the table band consists of a single row and contains only field masks, the table bands of your custom reports can occupy more than one row and can contain literals as well as field masks. If you added a blank line at the end of the table band of the report spec shown in Figure 11-3, for example, Paradox would leave a blank line between each pair of records that it prints, rather than printing them one after another with no lines in between. We'll show you how to add lines, literals, and masks to a report specification later in this chapter.

Columns in the Table Band

If you look closely at the table band, you'll notice that Paradox has placed small hash marks on the lines that define the top and bottom borders of that band. These marks divide the table band into columns. As you can see, Paradox has created one column in the table band for each of the fields in the source table. Paradox has placed one field mask, one column header, and one dashed line within each column. As you will see later, because the table band is divided into columns, it is easy to rearrange the fields in the report and adjust the spacing between the columns of the report. For now, just realize that the table band of any report spec will be divided into columns.

Other Bands

The standard report that Paradox automatically creates for any table consists of only the report, page, and table bands. When we discuss grouping in Chapter 12, however, you'll see that a report spec can contain yet another type of band: a group band. Group bands allow you to separate the information in a report into groups, based on a number of factors. Any group bands in a report spec (there can be up to 16 nested within any spec) fit on layers between the page band and the table band. Later in this chapter, we'll introduce yet another type of band–the form band. A form band is the equivalent of the table band in a different type of report–a free-form report.

How Many Records Print on a Page?

Together with the Length setting (a topic we'll discuss fully at the end of this chapter), the number of nonmask lines in a report spec determine how many records Paradox will print on each page of a report. Unless you specify otherwise, Paradox assumes that you are printing on standard eleven-inch long paper, and that your printer can print six lines per inch. Consequently, Paradox will print 66 lines per page.

Because all standard reports have the same layout, they should print the same number of records per page. Determining how many single-line records Paradox will print on a single page is a matter of subtraction. On the first page of the report, Paradox will skip one line for the report header. Next, Paradox will use six lines for the page header. The first three lines of the table band (a blank line and two lines of text) will use up three more lines on the page. Finally, the page footer uses up another four lines. Subtracting the total of these lines (14) from the total number of lines available on the first page (66) tells you that Paradox should print 52 records on that page. Paradox also should be able to print 52 records on the last page since it will have a one-line report footer but no report header. Because all but the first and last pages will have neither a report header nor a report footer, Paradox should be able to print 53 records on those pages.

Unfortunately, Paradox does not follow these rules in determining how many records it will print on a page. As you can see in Figure 11-2, for example, Paradox prints only 46 records on the first page of the report–not 52. A bug in Paradox Release 1.1 is responsible for this oddity. For some reason, Paradox skips a number of lines equal to the number of lines in the page header after it prints the page footer at the bottom of each page. In the case of a standard report, whose page header section always consists of six lines, Paradox will print six extra blank lines at the bottom of each page. Consequently, it prints six less records than it should (46 instead of 52) on the first page. When you print from a report spec that has an eight-line page header, Paradox will add an extra eight blank lines to each page, and so forth. To print as many records as possible on each page, then, you should keep your page headers as small as possible.

Page-widths

In addition to dividing a report specification in bands, Paradox also divides it into page-widths. Paradox uses vertical lines in bright inverse video, like the ones shown in Figure 11-3, to mark the ends of the page-widths in report specs. Very simply, page-widths are the graphic representations of the width of the printed pages in a report. All the page-widths in a report specification must be of the same width. Since most printers can print 80 characters on a line, the default width for page-widths is 80 characters. The position of the masks and literals in a report spec determines on which page they will be printed.

When Paradox designs the standard report for a table, it includes as many 80-character wide page-widths as are necessary to accommodate the fields of the table laid side by side. As you can see in Figure 11-3, for example, the default report spec for the LISTINGS table requires two page-widths because there is not enough room to fit all nine fields onto one page, given the default widths of their masks. Because of the system it uses to place fields in a standard report, Paradox often splits fields onto two pages. In this case, for example, the first part of the Price field appears in the first page-width, and the second part is positioned in the second page-width. As you can see in Figure 11-2, Paradox prints part of each entry from the Price column on different pages of the report. We'll show you later how to push a divided field onto a single page-width (and thus onto a single page of the printed report), either by adjusting the width of the column that contains the field or by adjusting the size of the page-width.

The Order of Printing

Any time that a report spec contains more than a single page-width, or a table contains more records than fit on a single page, or both, Paradox will print the table on multiple pages. As you can see in Figure 11-2, for example, the standard report for the LISTINGS table occupies four pages. Very simply, Paradox always prints the first page-width for all records in the table first, the second page-width for all the records next, and so forth. Because the page header information is contained within the first page-width of the report, Paradox only prints it on the first and second pages of the report—the ones that are printed from the first page-width.

Other Features

If you look again at Figure 11-3, you may notice a number of status messages at the top of the screen. The message at the left edge of the screen tells you the current operation: *Designing report R for Listings table*. The left edge of the second line of the screen is the Band indicator. In this area, Paradox displays the band in which the cursor is positioned. The message *Table Band* on the second line of Figure 11-3 indicates that the cursor is in the table band.

At the right side of the first line of the screen, Paradox displays the word *Report* in reverse video. This message indicates that you are in the report mode. To the right of this Mode indicator, Paradox displays the message *1/2*. This Page-Width indicator tells you that the cursor is in the first page-width of a two-page-width report.

Paradox uses the right edge of the second line of the screen as the Field Mask indicator. Whenever the cursor is positioned on a mask in a report spec, Paradox displays the name of the field represented by that mask in this area. In Figure 11-3, for example, the word *Address* indicates that the cursor is positioned on the mask that represents the Address field. Because Paradox uses generic characters like *A*s and *9*s for field masks, this indicator provides the only sure way to determine which field a mask represents.

Paradox displays a stylized horizontal ruler on the third line of the report spec screen. This ruler assists you in placing and centering masks and literals on the screen. In Figure 11-3, the horizontal ruler confirms that Paradox has set page-widths of 80 characters for this standard report.

Custom Reports

The standard report spec that Paradox creates for any table is useful in many reporting situations. In many cases, however, you'll want to create custom reports that are far more complex than the simple ones produced by the standard spec. The power of Paradox's report generator makes it easy to create this kind of report.

Creating a Report Specification

As we explained at the beginning of this chapter, Paradox automatically designs a standard report specification for every table it creates and makes that spec the default for the table. To create a custom report for a table, you must design a custom report specification. Including the default specification, up to ten report specifications can be associated with any table at once.

Creating a custom report specification is a five-step process. To begin, you must press the [**Menu**] key and choose **R**eport to reveal the Report menu shown in Figure 11-4. The Output command on this menu lets you send a report to a printer, the screen, or a file. The Design command lets you design a new report for a table. The Change command lets you make changes in an existing report.

Figure 11-4 The Report Menu

```
Output  Design  Change                                            Main
Send a report to the printer, the screen, or a file.
```

Because you want to design a new report, you should choose **D**esign from this menu. When you issue this command, Paradox will prompt you to supply the name of a table. You can do this either by typing the name and pressing ↵ or by pressing ↵ to reveal a list of names, pointing to one, and pressing ↵ again. In this case, we'll choose LISTINGS.

Once you have specified the table for which you want to create the report spec (the one whose records you want to print), Paradox will reveal the menu shown in Figure 11-5. As you can see, this menu contains ten choices: the letter *R* and the numbers 1 to 9. Each item on this menu represents one of the ten possible report specifications that can be associated with the table. (You may notice that this menu is very similar to the one you saw in Chapter 5 when you were creating forms.)

Figure 11-5 The Design Menu

```
R  1  2  3  4  5  6  7  8  9                                     Main
Standard report
```

The report stored under the letter *R* is the one that Paradox will print whenever you press the [Instant Report] key while you are viewing a table. When you first create a table, Paradox creates a standard report specification for that table and stores it under the letter *R*. That's why Paradox displays the prompt *Standard report* below the Design menu when you highlight the *R* option. Unless you have designed a report spec for the table previously, no reports will be associated with the other nine options (1-9). For that reason, the prompt *Unused report* will appear below the menu when you position the cursor on any of those choices.

When you see the Design menu, you should select the number (or letter) under which you want to store the report spec you are about to design. If you choose the number of any report you have designed already, Paradox will present the choices Cancel or Replace. If you choose Cancel, Paradox will return you to the Design menu and let you make another choice. If you choose Replace, Paradox will delete the old report spec to make room for the new one you will create. Until you already have designed nine custom report specifications for a table, you probably will want to choose an unused number rather than overwriting an existing spec. In this case, we'll select the number **1**.

Once you have selected the number under which you want to store the report spec, Paradox will prompt you to supply a description for the report. This step is optional. If you do enter a description (which may be up to 40 characters in length), it will appear on the second line of the menu when you highlight the number of the report specification. Also, Paradox will automatically place it in the page header of the report spec you are designing, just as it places the description *Standard report* in the page header of any standard report. If you choose not to enter a description, these areas will remain blank. In this case, we'll enter the description **Custom Report #1**.

After you enter a description for the report (or press ↵ to bypass this step), Paradox will display another menu that offers two options: Tabular and Free-form. Your choice from this menu determines the structure of the basic report spec Paradox will create for you. If you choose Tabular, Paradox will present a tabular report spec. Tabular report specs are well-suited for printing information in the table in a rigid columnar format. The standard report spec that Paradox automatically creates for any table is always tabular. On the other hand, free-form report specs are best suited for printing information in a less structured format. You would use a free-form report spec to print mailing labels and form letters, for example.

If your report will be tabular (row and column) in nature, like the standard report, you should choose the **T**abular option. Next, Paradox will present the report spec shown in Figure 11-6. As you can see, this specification looks like the standard report for the LISTINGS table, except that the description *Custom Report #1* instead of *Standard report* appears centered in the page header of the first page-width.

Once Paradox presents a new report spec, you can modify it in an almost unlimited number of ways. For example, you can delete, place, and move masks and literals, add and delete bands, add and delete page-widths, and so forth. Before you can do these things, however, you need to learn how to move around within a report specification.

Figure 11-6 A New Tabular Report Spec

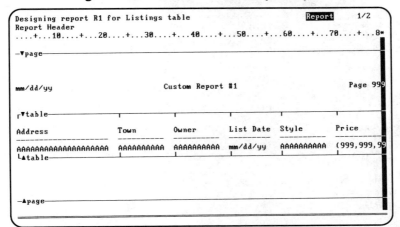

Moving Around in a Report Specification

When Paradox first displays a report specification screen, the cursor will be at the left edge of the first line of that screen. You can use the cursor keys on the numeric keypad, either by themselves or in combination with the [Ctrl] key, to move the cursor around the report specification screen.

These keys and key combinations do pretty much the same thing in the report mode as they do in the forms mode: → moves the cursor one space to the right, ↓ moves it one row down, and so forth. Because the pages of a form are situated vertically and the pages (page-widths) of a report are situated horizontally, however, the actions of the [Pg Up], [Pg Dn], [Ctrl]-[→], and [Ctrl]-[←] keys differ. In a report spec, the [Ctrl]-[→] key moves the cursor one-half screen to the right or to the right edge of the rightmost page-width in the spec, whichever comes first. Similarly, the [Ctrl]-[←] key moves the cursor one-half screen to the left or to the left edge of the leftmost page-width in the spec. The [Pg Dn] key moves the cursor down one screen or to the bottom edge of the page-width, whichever comes first, and the [Pg Up] key moves the cursor up one screen or to the top of the current page-width.

The Vertical Ruler

As you can see in Figures 11-3, and 11-6, Paradox automatically displays a horizontal ruler on the third line of any report specification. This ruler lets you know where the cursor is positioned relative to the left edge of the leftmost page-width in the report spec. In addition to this horizontal ruler, Paradox offers an optional vertical ruler. When you press the **[Vertical Ruler Toggle]** key ([Ctrl]-[V]), Paradox will display the vertical ruler shown in Figure 11-7. As you can see, this ruler is an Inverse Video band at the left edge of the screen that numbers each row. This ruler makes it easy to determine where the cursor is positioned relative to the first row of the report spec. When you press [Vertical Ruler Toggle] again, the ruler will disappear.

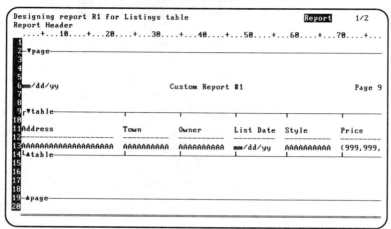

Figure 11-7 The Vertical Ruler

Printing Quick Copies of a Report

In most cases, the process of designing and printing a report will go something like this: First, you'll use the Report Design command to create a new report spec; second, you'll modify that spec; third, you'll press [Do-It!] or issue the [Menu] DO-IT! command to save the report; and fourth, you'll print from the saved spec. (We'll describe the process of printing from a saved report spec later in this chapter.)

In some cases, you'll want to print copies of a report while designing the spec for that report. Paradox gives you a couple of ways to do this. The easiest way to print is simply to press the [Instant Report] key while you are designing the report. As you learned earlier, pressing the [Instant Report] key while you are viewing a table causes Paradox to print the default report for that table (the one stored under the letter *R*). If you press [Instant Report] from within the report generator, however, Paradox will print a report from the report spec you are viewing. As you will see, the [Instant Report] key gives you an easy way to determine how a report will look as you are designing it.

The [Menu] Output command provides the second way to print a report from the spec you are editing within the report generator. When you issue this command, Paradox will present a menu with three options: Printer, Screen, and File. If you choose Printer, Paradox will direct the report whose spec you are viewing to your printer, as it does when you press [Instant Report]. The Screen and File options allow you to preview a report on the screen or send it to a text file, respectively. We'll discuss these options later.

Adding and Deleting Lines

Any new tabular report spec will occupy 20 lines of the screen and contain as many page-widths as are necessary to accommodate all of the fields in the source table. However, you can add or delete lines to make the report specification as small as one line or as large as 2000 lines.

Deleting Lines

To delete a line from a report spec, just move the cursor to the left edge of that line and press the [**Report Delete Line**] key ([Ctrl]-[Y]). When you press this key, Paradox will delete the current line and will squeeze the remaining lines up one row. If the line contains any field masks or literals, they will be removed from the report. For example, suppose you press [Report Delete Line] while the cursor is at the left edge of the fourth row of the page header band in the report spec shown in Figure 11-7. Figure 11-8 shows the result. This action removes the title line from the report, reducing the size of the page header by one line.

Figure 11-8 Deleting a Line from a Report Spec

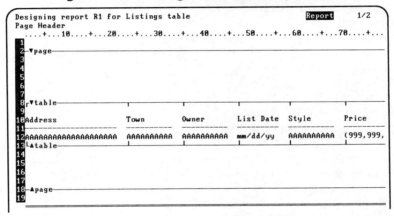

You also can use the [Report Delete Line] key to erase part of the characters on a line. When you press [Report Delete Line] while the cursor is anywhere but at the left edge of a line, Paradox will erase the character the cursor is on and all the characters to its right on the same line. Figure 11-9 shows the result of pressing [**Report Delete Line**] while the cursor is on the *C* in the title *Custom Report #1* in the report spec in Figure 11-7.

Figure 11-9 Deleting Part of a Line

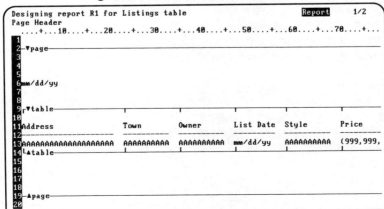

Paradox will just beep if you press the [Report Delete Line] key while the cursor is on a field mask or on a line that marks the border of a band.

Adding Lines

The ↵ key makes it possible to add new blank lines to a report spec. To add a new line at the end of a report spec, just move the cursor anywhere to the right of the rightmost character on the last line of the spec and press ↵. Unfortunately, adding a new line anywhere else in a report spec is not quite as simple. Unless the cursor is positioned to the right of the last character on the last line of the script, the action of the ↵ key depends on whether Paradox is in the overwrite or insert mode.

The Overwrite and Insert Modes

Most text editors, including the Paradox Report Editor, offer two different editing modes: overwrite and insert. When you first enter the Report Editor, Paradox will be in the overwrite mode. While Paradox is in this mode, you cannot use the ↵ key to add new lines anywhere except at the end of a report spec. If you press ↵ while the cursor is within a line other than the border of a band, Paradox will move the cursor to the beginning of the next line. If you press ↵ while the cursor is on a line that marks the border of a band, Paradox will just beep.

To enter a blank line in the middle of a report spec, Paradox must be in the insert mode. To place Paradox in this mode, just press the [Ins] key. When you press this key, Paradox will display the mode indicator *Ins* to the right of the inverse-video Report indicator in the upper-right corner of the screen.

Adding Lines in the Middle of a Spec

Once Paradox is in the insert mode, you can use the ↵ key to add new blank lines anywhere within a report spec. If you press ↵ while the cursor is positioned beyond the rightmost character in any line (except on a line that marks a border), Paradox will add a new blank line below that line and position the cursor at the beginning of that new line. Figure 11-10 shows the result of pressing ↵ while the cursor is positioned to the right of the field mask for the Baths field while Paradox is in the insert mode. As you can see, Paradox has added a new line at the end of the table band. If you printed from this report spec, Paradox would skip one line between every record.

Pressing ↵ in the insert mode when the cursor is positioned in the beginning or middle of a line produces different results. If you press ↵ while the cursor is positioned at the beginning of any line, Paradox will insert a line above that line. For example, if you press ↵ while the cursor is at the beginning of the first line in the spec shown in Figure 11-10, Paradox will add a new line at the top of the report header.

Figure 11-10 Adding a Row to the Table Band

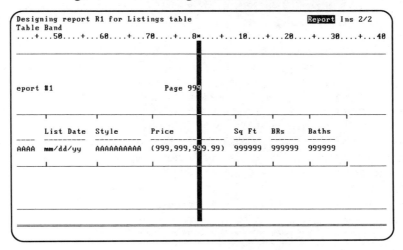

If you press the ↵ key in the insert mode while there are field masks or literals to the cursor's right, Paradox will add a new line below the current one and move the text to the right of the cursor to that new line. If the cursor is in the middle of a literal, Paradox will split it onto two lines. If the cursor is on a field mask, however, Paradox will beep and will not add a new line or split the mask.

However, Paradox does not allow you to break a line of the table band onto two different lines. If you press the ↵ key while the cursor is positioned anywhere in the table band other than at the beginning or end of a line, Paradox will simply move the cursor to the beginning of the next row without inserting a new row. This prevents you from accidentally destroying the columnar integrity of the tabular report. Paradox also moves the cursor to the beginning of the next row without inserting a new row if you press the ↵ key while the cursor is on a line that marks the border of a band.

Working with Page-widths

When Paradox presents you with a new report spec, that spec will consist of as many 80-character page-widths as are necessary to accommodate the fields from the source table. In the case of the LISTINGS table, Paradox creates a report spec that consists of two page-widths. The number of page-widths in any report spec is not fixed, however. Just as you can add lines to and delete lines from a report spec, you can add page-widths to and delete page-widths from a report spec. You also can adjust the size of page-widths.

Deleting a Page-width

Paradox allows you to delete the rightmost page-width from any multiple-page-width report spec. To delete a page-width, press the [**Menu**] key and issue the **S**etting **P**ageLayout **D**elete command. When you issue this command, Paradox will present you with two choices: Cancel and OK. If you choose Cancel, Paradox will not delete any page-widths and will display the previous menu. If you select OK, Paradox will delete the last (rightmost) page-width in the report spec and everything on it.

Importantly, any field masks that cross the page boundary from the previous page-width will also be deleted from the leftmost page. Additionally, Paradox will remove from the report spec any column of the table band that crosses a boundary onto the page-width you are deleting. For example, Figure 11-11 shows the result of issuing the **[Menu] S**etting **P**ageLayout **D**elete **OK** command from within the two-page-width report spec shown in Figure 11-10. As you can see, the Page-Width indicator now reads *1/1*, indicating that the report spec consists of a single page-width. Additionally, because the column of the table band that contains the Price field mask crosses the border between the first and second page-widths, Paradox has eliminated that column and its contents from the first page of the report. As we'll show you later, you can prevent this by altering the size of the page-widths in a report before you delete one.

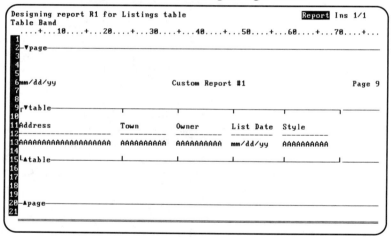

Figure 11-11 Deleting a Page-width

(If you are following along on your computer, you should issue the **[Menu]** **C**ancel **Y**es command at this point to abandon the report spec, then issue the **[Menu]** **R**eport **D**esign command to bring up a new spec for the LISTINGS table.)

Adding a Page-width

The [Menu] Setting PageLayout Insert command tells Paradox to insert a new page-width to the right of the last page-width. When you issue this command, Paradox will insert a blank page-width that is the same size as the other page-widths in the report. The Page-Width indicator will reflect the addition of the new page. In a few pages, we'll show you how to fill a new page-width with information by adding columns, field masks, literals, and so forth.

Resizing a Page-width

In addition to inserting and deleting page-widths, you can also alter the size of the page-widths in a spec. As we stated earlier, the page-widths in any new report will be 80 characters wide, and every page-width in a report must be of the same size.

In the case of the report spec shown in Figure 11-6, the default 80-column width of each page-width causes the sixth column of each table band to be split between the first and second pages. Therefore, Paradox prints part of the dashed-line literal and Price field entry on one page, and part on another. You can correct this problem by adjusting the page-widths in the report spec. In this case, you could reduce the width of each page-width to 69 characters so that the first five columns of the report are printed on one page, and the remaining four columns are printed on another page. If you have a wide-carriage printer, however, you probably will want to increase the size of the page-width to 132 characters, so the report consists of a single large page-width.

To alter the size of the page-widths in this report, issue the **[Menu] Setting P**ageLayout **W**idth command. When Paradox prompts you for a new page-width, press **[Ctrl]-[Backspace]** to delete the current setting (80), then type a new width. If you select **69** and press ↵, Paradox will revise the layout of the report as shown in Figure 11-12. When Paradox prints from this spec, it will print the first five columns on one page, and the remaining four columns on the next. Because you reduced the width of the page-widths, Paradox added a third page-width to the spec. You probably will want to use the [Menu] Setting PageLayout Delete command to remove this unneeded page from the spec. (Notice the Page-Width indicator at the top of the screen displays *1/3*.)

Figure 11-12   Decreasing the Size of a Page-width

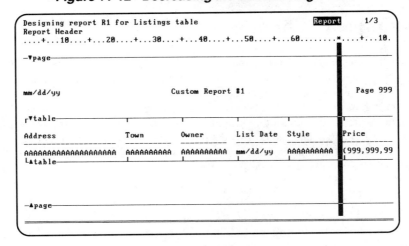

If you issue this command again and specify a width of **132**, Paradox will present the screen shown in Figure 11-13. When Paradox prints from this report, it will place all nine columns of the report on a single page. For this wide setting to work, you must be printing on a wide-carriage printer, or be printing in compressed print. (We'll show you how to alter print styles at the end of this chapter.)

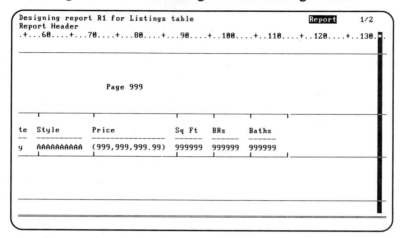

Figure 11-13   Increasing the Size of a Page-width

Importantly, Paradox did not delete the second page-width from the report spec when you increased the Page-Width setting to 132. The second page-width is still in the report spec although it contains no fields and no literals. Since you don't need this page-width any longer, you probably will want to remove it from the report spec. Also, notice that Paradox did not re-center the title with respect to the expanded page-width. If you want the title to be centered, you must edit it, using tools we'll present later in this chapter.

Working with Literals

Earlier in this chapter, you learned that report specifications can contain descriptive text that will be printed literally in reports. For example, the report spec in Figure 11-6 (and any other new tabular spec) contains a number of literals. In this case, Paradox has entered the report description *Custom Report #1* on the fourth line of the page header at the middle of the first page-width. In addition, Paradox has entered the name from one field in the LISTINGS table and dashed lines as literals in each of the columns of the table band. Once Paradox has created this or any other spec, you can delete existing literals from it or add new literals to it.

Entering Literals

For the most part, entering a literal into a report spec is as simple as moving the cursor to where you want the literal to be and then typing characters from the keyboard. To add the title *This Is a Tabular Report:* at the left edge of the report header for the basic LISTINGS spec shown in Figure 11-6, for example, you would move the cursor to the first character on the first (in this case, only) line of the report header section and type **This Is a Tabular Report**. So that the line would not be printed right at the top of the page, you would add a few blank lines above it by moving the cursor to the beginning of the line, pressing **[Ins]** to enter the insert mode, and pressing ↵.

Inserting and Overwriting

The way that Paradox places what you type into the report spec is affected by your choice of either the overwrite or insert mode. When you first enter the report mode, Paradox will be in the overwrite mode. While Paradox is in this mode, any characters that you type will replace other literals on the same line. If you place the cursor on the C in *Custom* on the fourth line of the report spec shown in Figure 11-6 and type **Special**, for example, your screen will look like Figure 11-14. As you can see, the letters in the word *Special* have overwritten the letters in *Custom*. The result is not an acceptable title.

Figure 11-14 Overwriting a Literal

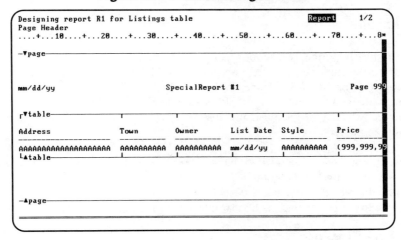

In most cases, you'll want to press the [Ins] key to place Paradox in the insert mode prior to typing literals into a report spec. The *Ins* indicator in the upper-right corner of the screen tells you when Paradox is in the insert mode. While Paradox is in the insert mode, it will push any literals or field masks that are under or to the right of the cursor, one space to the right for each character that you type. If you position the cursor on the C in the literal *Custom Report #1* in the report spec shown in Figure 11-6, press the **[Ins]** key to enter the insert mode, and type **Special** and then a space, your screen will look like the one shown in Figure 11-15. As you can see, Paradox has pushed the words *Custom Report #1* to the right as it inserted the text that you typed.

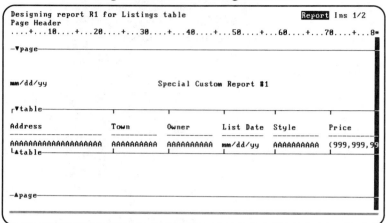

Figure 11-15 Inserting a Literal

Restrictions

There are three important restrictions that prevent you from placing literals into a report spec. First, you cannot type a literal on top of a field mask. If you attempt to do this in either the overwrite or insert mode, Paradox will just beep at you. Second, although Paradox will let you push a literal or field mask over a page-width boundary in the middle of a report, it will not let you push any element beyond the right border of the rightmost page-width in the report.

Third, when you enter a literal into the table band, Paradox will not allow you to type beyond the right edge of the column in which the literal begins, or to insert a literal so that another literal or field mask is pushed beyond the right boundary of a column. This restriction helps to preserve the columnar integrity of the report.

Deleting Literals

As you might expect, you also can delete literals from a report specification. To do this, you must use the [Backspace], [Del], or [Report Delete Line] ([Ctrl]-[Y]) keys. The [Backspace] key deletes the literal character to the left of the cursor. If Paradox is in the insert mode, it will drag the characters to the right of the cursor back to the left as you delete characters with this. If you press [Backspace] while Paradox is in the overwrite mode, however, the remaining characters on the line will stay in place.

The [Del] key provides the second way to delete literals from a report spec. When you press the [Del] key, Paradox will delete the literal character over which the cursor is positioned. If Paradox is in the insert mode, it will pull the characters to the right of the cursor one space to the left for each character it deletes. If Paradox is in the overwrite mode, however, the remaining characters on the line will stay in their original place.

The [Report Delete Line] key ([Ctrl]-[Y]) provides yet another way to delete literals from a report spec. This command allows you to delete either a full or partial line that contains literals, masks, or both.

Working with Columns

As you learned earlier, the table band of any tabular report specification is divided into columns. The separation of the table band into columns makes it easy to rearrange the information in, remove information from, and add information to a tabular report. The options under the [Menu] TableBand command allow you to erase, insert, resize, move, and copy the columns in the table band.

Rearranging Columns

When you use the [Menu] Report Design command to create a tabular report spec, Paradox creates one column in the table band for each field in the source table, and places masks for those fields into the columns in the order that the fields appear in the structure of the table. This default order will not always be the one in which you want to print the report, however. Fortunately, you can use either the [Rotate] key or the [Menu] TableBand Move command to rearrange the columns in the table band. Rearranging the columns in the table band changes the order of the fields in the printed report.

The [Rotate] Key

You can use the [Rotate] key ([Ctrl]-[R]) to move the column you select to the right edge of the table band and shift the remaining columns to the left. For example, suppose you want to move the List Date column in the report spec shown in Figure 11-13 all the way to the right of the table band. To do this, position the cursor anywhere within the List Date column (the one you want to move) and press [**Rotate**]. Instantly, Paradox will move the List Date column to the end of the table band so that the report spec looks like the one shown in Figure 11-16 on the next page. If you print from this revised specification, the List Date column will appear at the end of the report.

The TableBand Move Command

The TableBand Move command lets you move a column more precisely than does the [Rotate] key. Using this command, you can move a column from one place in a table band to any other position in that band in only two steps.

To demonstrate this command, suppose that you want to move the Sq Ft column in the report spec shown in Figure 11-16 to a position between the Style and Price columns. To do this, press the [**Menu**] key, select TableBand, and choose **M**ove. As soon as you issue this command, the cursor will change to a small blinking box, and Paradox will prompt you to use the arrow keys to place the cursor on the column you want to move. When you see this prompt, place the cursor anywhere in the column you want to move (in this case, the Sq Ft column) and press ↵.

Figure 11-16 Rotating Columns

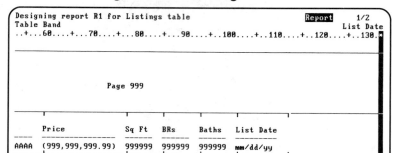

After you select a column to move, Paradox will prompt you to place the cursor on the new location for the column. The position you choose depends on the direction in which you are moving the column. If you are moving the column from right to left (as we are in this case), you should position the cursor in the column to the right of the place where you want the moved column. If you are moving a column to the right, position the cursor in the column to the left of the place where you want the moved column. In this case, since you are moving a column to the left, and you want to place it between the Style and Price columns, you should position the cursor in the Price column. When you press ↵, Paradox will move the column so that the report specification looks like the one shown in Figure 11-17.

Figure 11-17 Moving a Column

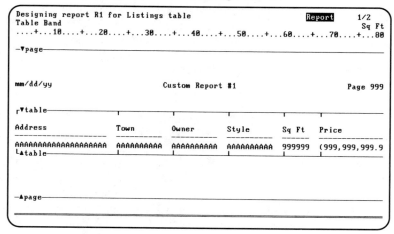

Erasing Columns

You can remove a column of information from a printed report by deleting the column of the table band that produces it. To delete a column from a table band, you must use the TableBand Erase command. For example, suppose you want to remove the Owner column from the report spec shown in Figure 11-17. To remove this column, issue the [**Menu**] TableBand Erase command. When Paradox prompts you to do so, place the cursor anywhere within the column you want to erase (in this case, Owner). When you press ↵, Paradox will remove that column from the table band. Figure 11-18 shows this result. The reports you print from this revised spec will not contain information from the Owner field of the LISTINGS table.

Figure 11-18   Removing a Column

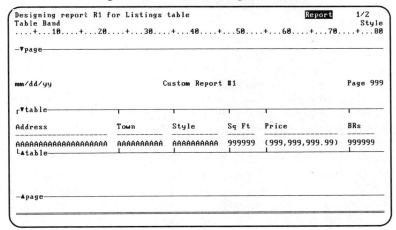

Inserting Columns

In addition to deleting columns from the table band, you also can add columns to it. To do this, you must use the [Menu] TableBand Insert command. When you issue this command, Paradox will insert a blank, fifteen-character wide column into the table band at the point you choose.

For example, suppose you want to place a new column between the Town and Style columns in the table band of the report spec shown in Figure 11-18. To do this, press the [**Menu**] key and issue the **TableBand Insert** command. As soon as you issue this command, the cursor will change to a small box, and Paradox will prompt you to place the cursor in the column to the right of the place where you want the new column. In this case, you should position the cursor within the Style column. When you press ↵, Paradox will insert the new column into the table band, and your report spec will look like the one shown in Figure 11-19.

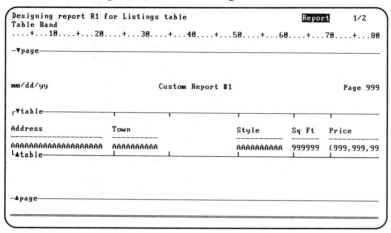

Figure 11-19 Inserting a Column

After you have inserted a new column into a report, you probably will want to enter a literal into it. You already know how to enter literals into a column. We'll show you how to place field masks in a report in a few pages. Of course, you also can use a new column purely for spacing purposes. Whenever Paradox inserts a new column into the table band, it pushes the remaining columns 15 spaces to the right.

If there are less than 15 empty spaces at the end of the rightmost page-width in a report spec when you attempt to insert a column, Paradox will beep and display the message *Not enough space here to insert a new column.* Before you can insert the column, you must add another page-width, increase the width of the existing page-widths, or erase one or more columns from the spec. Alternatively, you can decrease the width of one or more columns in the table band.

Resizing Columns

When you issue the [Menu] Report Design Tabular command, Paradox creates a standard report spec whose table band has as many columns as there are fields in the source table. The width of each column is determined by the name of the field that Paradox places in that column or by the width specification for that field in the structure of the table, whichever is greater. When you add a new column to a report spec, Paradox automatically sets its width at fifteen spaces. If you wish to change the width of any column in a table band, you must use the [Menu] TableBand Resize command.

For example, suppose you want to reduce the width of the new column in the report spec shown in Figure 11-19 to only five spaces. To do this, issue the **[Menu] T**able**B**and **R**esize command. As soon as you issue the command, Paradox will prompt you to place the cursor on the column you want to resize. Although you can place the cursor anywhere within the column, you'll want to position it at the column's right edge. In this case, move the cursor to the fifteenth space in the new column. When you press ↵,

Paradox will prompt you to use the → and ← keys to increase or decrease the width of the column, respectively. In this case, you should press the ← key ten times. Each time you press this key, Paradox will adjust the width of the column on the screen. When you press ↵, Paradox will lock the column at its new width, as shown in Figure 11-20.

Figure 11-20 Resizing a Column

```
┌─────────────────────────────────────────────────────────────────────────┐
│ Designing report R1 for Listings table              Report    1/2       │
│ Table Band                                                              │
│ ....+...10....+...20....+...30....+...40....+...50....+...60....+...70....+...80 │
│ ─▼page─                                                                 │
│                                                                         │
│                                                                         │
│ mm/dd/yy                       Custom Report #1              Page 999   │
│                                                                         │
│  ┌▼table─────────────────────────────────────────────────────────────┐  │
│                                                                         │
│  Address              Town           Style      Sq Ft   Price       BR  │
│  ──────────────────   ──────────     ────────── ──────  ─────────── ──  │
│  AAAAAAAAAAAAAAAAAA   AAAAAAAAA      AAAAAAAAA  999999  (999,999,999.99) 99 │
│  └▲table─────────────────────────────────────────────────────────────┘  │
│                                                                         │
│                                                                         │
│                                                                         │
│ ─▲page─                                                                 │
│                                                                         │
└─────────────────────────────────────────────────────────────────────────┘
```

Paradox places two restrictions on your ability to resize a column. First, you cannot reduce the width of a column to any less than the number of characters in the longest literal or field mask in that column. Second, you cannot increase the width of a column so that it pushes the remaining columns in the table band beyond the right edge of the rightmost page-width in the report spec.

Copying Columns

The final thing you can do with a column of a table band is make a copy of it. To do this, you must use the [Menu] TableBand Copy command. This command allows you to make an exact copy of any column in a table band and place that copy elsewhere in that band. In reports that occupy more than a single page-width, you may wish to place a copy of one column in each page. That way, the information printed on each page will make sense even if you don't glue the page-widths together.

For example, suppose you created a two-page report spec like the one in Figure 11-12. Now, you want the Address column to appear at the left edge of both page-widths of the report spec. To do this, you must insert a copy of that column between the Style and Price columns. To copy this column, press the [Menu] key and issue the TableBand Copy command. As soon as you issue this command, Paradox will change the cursor to a blinking box and will prompt you to indicate the column you want to copy. In this case, you should move the cursor to any position within Address. When you press ↵, Paradox will prompt you to position the cursor in the column to the right of the place where you want to insert the copy. In this case, you should move the cursor into the Price column. When you press ↵ again, Paradox will place a copy of the Address column at the left edge of the second page-width, as shown in Figure 11-21.

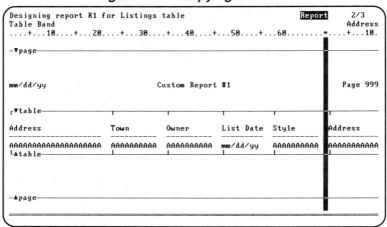

Figure 11-21 Copying a Column

As it does when you insert a column, Paradox will not allow you to copy a column unless the table band has enough free room to accommodate the copy. If you try to copy a column within a table band that lacks sufficient space to contain the copy, the message *Not enough space here for copy* will appear in the lower-right corner of the screen. You can circumvent this problem by resizing or erasing existing columns, increasing the size of the existing page-widths, or adding an additional page-width to the report spec.

Working with Field Masks

Field masks are the means by which Paradox extracts information from the fields of a table (as well as other special information) for use in a report. When you design a new report, like the one shown in Figure 11-6, Paradox will include one field mask in it for each field in the source table, as well as two special masks: one for the current date, and one for the current page number. In this section, we'll show you how to insert, delete, format, and resize field masks.

The Field option on the menu you see when you press [Menu] from within the report generator controls the manipulation of field masks in a report spec. When you select this option, Paradox will present you with three choices: Erase, Reformat, and Place. The Erase option allows you to delete a field mask from a spec. The Reformat option allows you to adjust the length and other display attributes of a field mask. The Place option allows you to add a field mask to a report spec.

Erasing a Field

When you issue the [Menu] Report Design Tabular command, Paradox creates a report spec that includes a field mask for every field in the source table plus one for the current date and one for the page number. To erase a single field mask, you must use the [Menu] Field Erase command. By removing a field mask from a report spec, you remove the information supplied by that field from the resulting report.

For example, suppose that you don't want the current date to appear at the top of each page of the report produced by the spec shown in Figure 11-6 on page 341. To remove the date from the report, you must remove the current date mask from the report spec. To do this, press the [**Menu**] key and issue the Field Erase command. As soon as you issue this command, Paradox will prompt you to move the cursor to the field you want to erase. To remove the current date field from the page header of this report, position the cursor anywhere on that mask. When you press ↵, Paradox will remove the mask from the report spec. Figure 11-22 shows this result. As you can see, Paradox has removed the current date mask from the fourth line of the report spec, but has not pulled the remaining element on that line back to the left. Whenever you delete a field mask from a line, Paradox will leave the remaining elements on that line in place, whether you are in the overwrite or insert mode.

Figure 11-22 Erasing a Field Mask

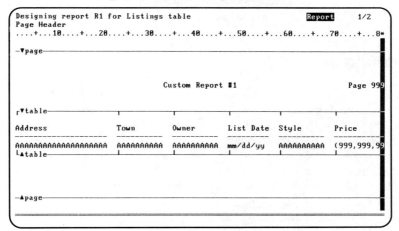

When Paradox designs a report, it places masks for each of the fields in the source table into their own columns of the table band. Because each field mask is in its own column, you can use the [Menu] TableBand Erase command to remove any field from the report. In some cases, however, you may wish to erase the field mask but leave the column in place. To do this, you must use the [Menu] Field Erase command.

For example, suppose that you want to erase the mask for the Owner field from the third column of the table band in the report spec shown in Figure 11-22. To do this, issue the [Menu] TableBand Erase command, position the cursor on the Owner mask, and press ↵. Figure 11-23 shows the result. As you can see, Paradox has erased the Owner mask from the third column of the table band, but has left that column (and the literals it contains) in place. At this point, you probably would want to use the [Del] or [Backspace] keys to erase those literals to produce a blank column.

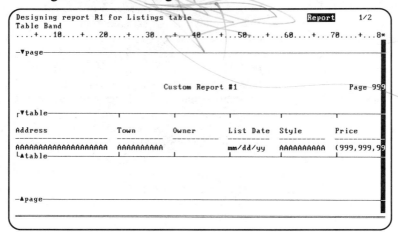

Figure 11-23 Erasing a Field Mask in the Table Band

Formatting a Field

The length and appearance of the mask for any field determines the way that the information extracted by that mask will appear in the printed report. For an alphanumeric field, the length of the mask determines the number of characters Paradox will print from the entries in that field. For example, the mask AAAAAAAAAA causes Paradox to allocate ten spaces for the entries in the field to which the mask refers. If an entry is shorter than the mask, Paradox will pad it with spaces in the report. If an entry is longer than the mask, Paradox will truncate the entry, displaying only as many characters as the mask is long.

The length of the masks for number, short number, and dollar fields has a more profound effect than just controlling the amount of space allocated to each entry. If any entry in a numeric or short number field is longer than the mask that represents it, Paradox will print that entry as a series of asterisks. Because the default mask for a number field is only six characters long, any number field entry that contains more than six digits will appear as a series of asterisks in a standard report. The masks for these fields also determine whether the printed form of the entry will contain commas or decimal points and how they will deal with signs. For example, the default mask for a dollar field specifies the use of commas, two digits to the right of the decimal place and the use of parentheses for negative numbers.

The mask for a date field determines in which of eight different forms that date will be printed. The default mask for a date field instructs Paradox to print the entries from a date field in mm/dd/yy form, even if the dates are in dd-Mon-yy form in the source table. The default mask for a dollar field instructs Paradox to include commas and parentheses when it prints the entries from that field in a report.

In many cases, the default mask that Paradox uses for a field will not produce exactly the look you want when that field is printed. Fortunately, Paradox provides a command–Field Reformat–that lets you change the size and/or appearance of the mask for any field. Reformatting a field is a three-step process. First, you issue the [Menu] Field Reformat command. Second, you point to the field you want to reformat. Third, you specify how you want the field to be formatted. The things you can do in this third step are determined by what type of field the mask represents.

Alphanumeric Fields

If the field you select is alphanumeric, the Field Reformat command will allow you to change its length. Because the default length of the field mask for an alphanumeric field is equal to the maximum number of characters that that field can hold, you probably won't want to increase its length very often. You may want to decrease the length of an alphanumeric field mask if all of the entries in that field are shorter than the maximum.

For example, suppose you've created a new report spec like the one in Figure 11-6 and you want to reduce the length of the Style mask from ten to only eight characters–the maximum number of characters in any entry in that field. To do this, issue the **[Menu] Field Reformat** command, position the cursor anywhere within the Style mask, and press ↵. Paradox will then move the cursor to the last character in the mask and prompt you to adjust its length. Each time you press →, Paradox will add another *A* to the mask. Each time you press ←, Paradox will remove an *A* from the mask. In this case, you'll want to press ← twice to reduce the length of the mask to eight characters. When you press ↵, Paradox will lock the mask at this new length, as shown in Figure 11-24.

Figure 11-24 Reformatting an Alphanumeric Field

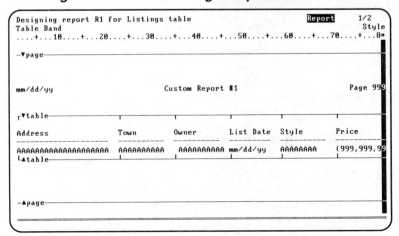

Date Fields

When Paradox places a date field in a report spec, it always uses the mask mm/dd/yy, which causes the dates to be printed in simple mm/dd/yy form. If you wish, you can use the [Menu] Field Reformat command to select an alternative format for date fields. The eight available formats are: mm/dd/yy; Month dd,yyyy; mm/dd; mm/yy; dd-Mon-yy; Mon yy; dd-Mon-yyyy; and mm/dd/yyyy.

For example, suppose you want to convert the current date mask in the page header of the report spec shown in Figure 11-24 into Month dd, yyyy form. To do this, issue the [Menu] Field Reformat command and point to the current date field. When you press ↵, Paradox will display a menu that contains the eight date forms. When you see this menu, you should choose the form in which you want the date to appear. In this case, you should choose the second form: Month dd, yyyy. When you press ↵, Paradox will replace the existing date mask with the new form you have chosen. Figure 11-25 shows this result. When Paradox prints from the spec, the date will appear in Month dd, yyyy form at the top of each page printed from the first page-width.

Figure 11-25   Reformatting a Date Field

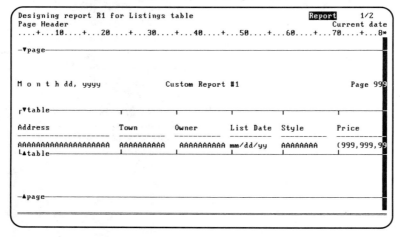

Number, Short Number, and Dollar Fields

You also can use the [Menu] Field Reformat command to change the way entries from numeric (number, short number, and dollar) fields are displayed. This command allows you to adjust the number of digits displayed to the left and right of the decimal place, to control the display conventions for positive and negative numbers, and to control the insertion of commas.

Specifying a Number of Digits

For example, suppose that you want to display the entries from the Price field in the table band of the spec shown in Figure 11-25 with six digits to the left of the decimal place, and none to the right. To reformat this field, issue the **[Menu] F**ield **R**eformat command and position the cursor on the Price mask. When you press ↵, Paradox will present three choices: Digits, Sign-Convention, and Commas. To change the number of digits, choose **D**igits. As soon as you make this choice, Paradox will move the cursor to the last character in the mask and prompt you to specify the number of digits you want to the left of the decimal place. To add digits, press the → key. To reduce the number of digits, press the ← key. Paradox will not allow you to increase the number of digits to more than 12, or decrease it to less than one. In this case, press ← three times to specify six digits to the left of the decimal place.

As soon as you press ↵ to select the number of digits to the left of the decimal point, Paradox will prompt you to select the number of digits you want to the right of that point. You can press → to add digits or ← to reduce the number of digits. To eliminate the decimal point and the two digits to its right in the example, press ← three times, then press ↵. Figure 11-26 shows the reformatted field.

Figure 11-26   Reformatting a Dollar Field

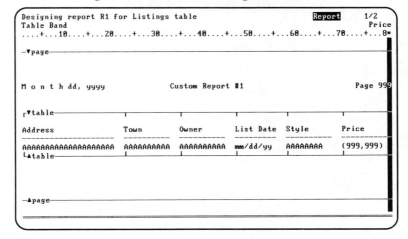

Specifying a Sign-Convention

In addition to altering the number of digits in the mask for a numeric field, you can control the use of signs. When you issue the [Menu] Field Reformat command, point to a numeric field, and select Sign-Convention, Paradox will present you with three choices: Unsigned, ParenNegative, and AlwaysSign. If you choose Unsigned (the default for number and short number fields), positive numbers will appear without a sign, but negative numbers will be prefaced with a minus sign (-). If you choose ParenNegative (the default for dollar fields), positive numbers will be printed without a sign, but negative numbers will be enclosed in parentheses. To show this format, Paradox will enclose the mask in parentheses. If you select AlwaysSign, Paradox will print a - sign in front of the negative numbers, print a + sign in front of the positive numbers, and display a +/- sign in front of the mask.

Specifying the Use of Commas

Paradox also lets you control the printing of commas in numeric fields. When you issue the [Menu] Fields Reformat command and choose Commas, Paradox will present you with two choices: NoCommas and Commas. If you choose NoCommas (the default for number and short number fields), Paradox will print the entries from the field without commas. If you choose Commas, however (the default for dollar fields), Paradox will include comma separators in the printed report and in the field mask.

Other Fields

Paradox also lets you reformat three special fields: page number fields, record number fields, and current time fields. When you issue the [Menu] Field Reformat command and select a page number or record number field, Paradox will only let you adjust the number of digits to the left of the decimal place. When you select a current time field, Paradox will let you choose from one of two formats: hh:mm pm and hh:mm:ss. You'll learn more about these types of fields in the next section of this chapter.

A Caution

Because reformatting a field often adds characters to its mask, the position of a mask within a report spec can restrict the way in which it can be formatted. As you know, a field mask cannot extend beyond the right boundary of a column in the table band, cannot extend beyond the right border of the rightmost page-width in a spec, and cannot overlap another mask or a literal. If the format you choose causes any of these things to happen, Paradox will not reformat the mask.

Placing Fields

In addition to removing fields and formatting the fields, you can place field masks into a spec. Paradox allows you to place four different types of field masks into any report spec: regular, special, calculated, and summary. Regular masks draw information from the fields of a table. Special fields allow you to include the current date, the current time, the current page number, or the current record number in your reports. Calculated fields allow you to place the result of a calculation in a report. Summary fields command Paradox to calculate a summary statistic (such as an average, sum, or count) and place it in the report. In this section, we'll cover the first three types of fields. We'll save our discussion of summary fields for Chapter 12.

Regular Fields

Placing a regular field in a table allows you to draw information from a field of the table for which the report is designed. Because Paradox includes a field mask for every field in a table and places it in its own column when you first design a tabular report, you probably won't place a regular field in a tabular report very often. However, you will occasionally want to place a regular field in a group header, or reinsert a field that you have previously deleted from the report spec back into the table band. As we'll explain later in this chapter, however, you'll frequently use a combination of the Field Erase and Field Place commands to move regular fields in a free-form report.

Although you can place regular fields into any band, you'll usually place them only in the table band of a tabular report, the form band of a free-form report, or the group band of either type of report. You probably won't want to place a regular field in a page or report band of a report spec. If you place a regular field in the page header, Paradox will draw information from the first record that it prints on that page. If you place a regular field in a page footer, Paradox will draw information from the last record on the current page. If you place a regular field in a report header or report footer, Paradox will draw information from the first and last records respectively that it prints in the report.

Every field mask in a table band must be positioned in a column. For this reason, placing a field mask into a table band usually is a two-step process: First, you add a new column to the table band, then place a field mask in that column. You can place a field mask into an existing column, either by itself (if you have deleted the original mask from that column, for example) or in addition to other mask(s) in that column.

As an example of placing a regular field mask into a table band, suppose you want to replace the Owner field mask that you deleted from the spec in Figure 11-22 to produce the mask shown in Figure 11-23. Since the column in which the mask was situated still exists, you don't need to add a column to the table band before replacing this mask.

To replace this mask, begin by issuing the **[Menu]** **F**ield **P**lace command. From the list of field types that Paradox presents, choose **R**egular. As soon as you make this choice, Paradox will display a list of the fields in the table for which you are designing the report. You should choose the field you want to place from this list. In this case, select **O**wner. After you make this selection, Paradox will prompt you to position the cursor where you want to place the field. In this case, you'll want to move the cursor to the beginning of the fourth row of the third column of the table band. When you press ↵, Paradox will place a mask for that field at the position of the cursor.

The next step of the placement process depends on what type of field the mask represents: number, dollar, short number, date, or alphanumeric. If you are placing an alphanumeric field, as we are in this case, Paradox will display the mask as a series of *A*s. Once Paradox presents this mask, you can adjust the number of characters in the mask. In this case, we'll press ↵ to accept the default length so that the spec again will look like the one in Figure 11-22.

If you are placing a number field, Paradox will display twelve 9s and let you adjust the number of digits to the right and left of the decimal place. If you are placing a short number field, Paradox will display six 9s and let you adjust the number of digits. Unlike a number field, a short number field can have only six digits to the left of the decimal. If you are placing a dollar field, Paradox displays a mask like (999,999,999.99) and lets you adjust the number of digits on both sides of the decimal place. If you are placing a date field, Paradox presents you with a menu of the eight possible date formats. The form you choose is the one that Paradox will place in the report spec.

Special Fields

In addition to placing regular fields in a report specification, you also can place any of four different special fields: a current date field, a page number field, a current time field, and a record number field. In fact, Paradox places two of these fields–current date and page number–in the page header of every new report it creates. Like the current date and page number fields, the other two special fields–current time and record number–do not draw information from the source table. The current time field stamps your report with the time at which the report is printed. The record number field allows you to number the records in a report.

Current Date Fields

A current date field commands Paradox to print the current date. Although you can place this field in any part of a report, you commonly will place it in the report header, the page header, the page footer, or the report footer. To place a current date field in a report, just issue the **[Menu]** **F**ield **P**lace command, select **D**ate, and choose which of the eight forms you want Paradox to use. When you press ↵, Paradox will place the field at the current location of the cursor.

Current Time Fields

A current time field stamps a report with the time it was printed, in much the same way a current date field stamps it with the date. Like a current date field, you probably will place a current time field only in the report or page bands. To place a current time field in a report spec, just issue the **[Menu]** **F**ield **P**lace command, select **T**ime, and choose from the two time forms that Paradox presents: hh:mm pm and hh:mm:ss. When you press ↵, Paradox will place the current time mask in the form you select at the current position of the cursor.

Page Number Fields

The special page number field lets you number the pages in a printed report. Because this mask numbers the pages in a report, you'll always want to place it in either the page header or page footer. To place a page number field in your report, issue the **[Menu]** **F**ield **P**lace **P**age command and move the cursor to where you want to place the field. When you press ↵, Paradox will place a three-character mask into the spec and let you adjust its width between a minimum of one character and a maximum of six characters.

Record Number Fields

The fourth special field, record number, allows you to number the records that Paradox prints in a report. Because this field assigns a number to each record, you'll want to use it only within the table band. In most cases, in fact, you'll want to place it in a separate column of that band.

For example, suppose that you want Paradox to number the records that it prints from the LISTINGS table report spec shown in Figure 11-26. To begin, use the [Menu] TableBand Insert command to add a new column at the beginning of the report. Once you have added this column, issue the [Menu] Field Place command and choose #Record. When you issue this command, Paradox will present two alternatives: Overall and PerGroup. Unless you have grouped the report (a topic we'll cover in Chapter 12), your choice here is not important. As soon as you make a selection, Paradox will ask you where to position the mask. In this case, you should point to the first space in the fourth row of the table band and press ↵. If you wish, you may then use the arrow keys to increase or decrease the width of the mask to as many as six or as few as one digit. In this case, just press ↵. Then enter the literals *Record #* and -------- so that the report spec looks like the one shown in Figure 11-27. When you print from this spec, Paradox will number the records in the report, as shown in Figure 11-28 on the next page.

Figure 11-27 A Record Number Field

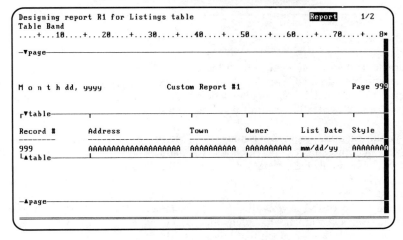

Calculated Fields

Calculated fields are the third type of fields you can place in a report spec. Like the calculated fields that you can place in a form, the calculated fields you include in a report will be based on formulas that draw information from other fields of the table. When you include a calculated field in the table band of a report, Paradox will perform the calculation for each record in the table and will print the result in the report.

Figure 11-28   A Report with Numbered Records

```
    May 19, 1986          Custom Report #1                  Page   1


    Record #    Address              Town         Owner      List Date  Style
    --------    -------              ----         -----      ---------  -----
       1        123 Abby Ct.         Louisville   Kones,D    11/02/85   Ranch
       2        426 St. James Ct.    Louisville   Jones,S    11/05/85   Ranch
       3        766 Baird St.        Louisville   Black,G    11/08/85   Colonial
       4        222 Big Ben Dr.      Louisville   Roberts,D  11/08/85   Other
       5        666 Montana Ave.     Louisville   Saul,H     11/09/85   Cape Cod
       6        589 Morocco Dr.      E Town       Smith,B    11/10/85   Cape Cod
       7        987 Allan Dr.        Louisville   Newsome,K  11/12/85   Cape Cod
       8        549 Billtown Rd.     Louisville   Bizer,B    11/14/85   Ranch
       9        343 Market St.       Louisville   Bivins,D   11/15/85   Ranch
      10        198 Main St.         J Town       Green,L    11/15/85   Other
      11        885 Jefferson St.    J Town       Zith,M     11/18/85   Ranch
      12        913 Whitney Dr.      North Hill   Kulp,R     11/20/85   Cape Cod
      13        363 Dower Ct.        North Fork   Culp,A     11/21/85   Cape Cod
      14        620 Windsong Ct.     Louisville   Pank,E     11/22/85   Colonial
      15        4500 Hempstead Dr.   Louisville   Pape,C     12/04/85   Colonial
      16        #6 Brandon Way       Louisville   Abrams,L   12/08/85   Ranch
      17        6610 Vermin Dr.      Louisville   Russ,J     12/10/85   Ranch
      18        712 Clifton Ct.      Louisville   Thomas,T   12/10/85   Ranch
      19        5432 Miller Rd.      Louisville   Young,R    12/15/85   Other
      20        #12 Circle Ct.       Louisville   White,Y    12/19/85   Other
      21        1222 Dee Rd.         South Fork   Smith,P    12/19/85   Ranch
      22        222 Earl Ave.        J Town       Wray,A     12/22/85   Ranch
      23        9827 Rowan St.       J Town       Coad,S     12/27/85   Ranch
      24        3355 Bank St.        J Town       Cobb,D     1/03/86    Ranch
      25        77 Fortland Ave.     North Hill   Coe,A      1/05/86    Ranch
      26        99 Cardinal Hill Rd. North Hill   Brand,B    1/05/86    Cape Cod
      27        #10 Old Mill Rd.     Louisville   Stern,M    1/07/86    Ranch
      28        5532 Mud Creek Dr.   Louisville   Hall,W     1/10/86    Ranch
      29        4444 Normie Ln.      Louisville   James,J    1/11/86    Cape Cod
      30        3498 Bold Rd.        Louisville   Taft,H     1/15/86    Colonial
      31        #82 Rudd Rd.         Louisville   Lum,I      1/16/86    Cape Cod
      32        6712 Shelby St.      Louisville   Wood,B     1/16/86    Ranch
      33        7235 Shiloh Dr.      E Town       Allan,J    1/17/86    Ranch
      34        8989 Big D Ln.       South Fork   Adkins,G   1/18/86    Ranch
      35        1001 Spring St.      North Hill   Frier,F    1/22/86    Other
      36        6935 Shiloh Dr.      E Town       Grebe,C    1/25/86    Cape Cod
      37        4989 Adler Way       Louisville   Dole,V     1/30/86    Cape Cod
      38        5678 Beech St.       Louisville   Smith,P    2/02/86    Cape Cod
      39        #62 Billy Bone Ct.   Louisville   Taylor,A   2/04/86    Ranch
      40        3323 Mt. Holly Dr.   Louisville   Grizz,D    2/10/86    Ranch
      41        9909 Midway Rd.      Louisville   Maier,O    2/11/86    Ranch
      42        435 Oxted Ln.        Louisville   O'Neal,P   2/12/86    Ranch
      43        22 N. Ridge Ct.      Louisville   Nunn,A     2/15/86    Colonial
      44        654 Nora Ln.         Louisville   Orwick,S   2/18/86    Cape Cod
      45        659 Ridge Rd.        Louisville   Pulley,F   2/24/86    Ranch
      46        14 Short Rd.         Louisville   Quire,I    3/01/86    Ranch
```

An Example

For example, suppose you want to print the columnar report shown in Figure 11-29 from the records in the LISTINGS table. As you can see, this report is a basic tabular report in which we have included a calculated field that computes the price per square foot of each piece of real estate–the result of dividing each record's Price entry by its Sq Ft entry.

To create this report, begin by issuing the [Menu] Report Design command, typing **LISTINGS**, and pressing ↵. Next, choose the number under which you want to store the report (we'll use number **2**), type a description like **Price Per Square Foot**, and select Tabular as the report type. Once you complete these steps, issue the [Menu] Setting PageLayout Width command, press [Ctrl]-[Backspace], type **132**, and then press ↵ to increase the width of the page-widths to 132 characters. Now issue the [Menu] Setting PageLayout Delete command to delete the second page-width from the spec. At this point, your screen will look much like Figure 11-13.

Once you have created this spec, you'll need to add a column at the end of the table band to hold the calculated field. To insert this column, issue the [Menu] TableBand Insert command, move the cursor beyond the last column in the table band, and press ↵. Having created this column, you probably will want to add a column header to it, just like the ones in the other columns. To do this, move the cursor to the beginning of the second row of the new column and type **Price Per Sq Ft**, then move to the beginning of the third row of that column and type a series of 15 dashes.

Report Fundamentals

Figure 11-29 A Report with a Calculated Field

```
5/17/86              Price Per Square Foot                  Page   1


Address         Town         Owner         List Date  Style       Price         Sq Ft   BRs   Baths   Price Per Sq Ft
-------         ----         -----         ---------  -----       -----         -----   ---   -----   ---------------
123 Abby Ct.        Louisville   Kones,D       11/02/85  Ranch        32,950.00      1500    3     1         21.97
426 St. James Ct.   Louisville   Jones,S       11/05/85  Ranch        19,500.00       950    2     1         20.53
766 Baird St.       Louisville   Black,G       11/08/85  Colonial    139,950.00      2600    4     3         53.83
222 Big Ben Dr.     Louisville   Roberts,D     11/08/85  Other        53,500.00      1900    3     2         28.16
666 Montana Ave.    Louisville   Saul,H        11/09/85  Cape Cod     55,000.00      1900    3     1         28.95
589 Morocco Dr.     E'Town       Smith,B       11/10/85  Cape Cod     62,500.00      1875    3     2         33.33
987 Allan Dr.       Louisville   Newsome,K     11/12/85  Cape Cod     60,000.00      1900    4     3         31.58
549 Billtown Rd.    Louisville   Bizer,R       11/14/85  Ranch        72,500.00      2000    3     2         36.25
347 Market St.      Louisville   Bivins,D      11/15/85  Ranch        42,900.00      1675    3     1         25.61
198 Main St.        J'Town       Green,L       11/15/85  Other        27,500.00       800    3     1         34.38
885 Jefferson St.   J'Town       Zith,M        11/18/85  Ranch        55,000.00      1500    3     1         36.67
913 Whitney Dr.     North Hill   Kulp,R        11/20/85  Cape Cod     99,500.00      1800    4     2         55.28
363 Dower Ct.       North Fork   Culp,A        11/21/85  Cape Cod    109,000.00      2100    4     2         51.90
620 Windsong Ct.    Louisville   Fank,E        11/22/85  Colonial    250,000.00      4000    6     4         62.50
4500 Hempstead Dr.  Louisville   Pape,C        12/04/85  Colonial    150,000.00      2600    4     3         57.69
#6 Brandon Way      Louisville   Abrams,L      12/08/85  Ranch        67,000.00      2250    4     2         29.78
6610 Vermin Dr.     Louisville   Russ,J        12/10/85  Ranch        75,000.00      2100    3     2         35.71
712 Clifton Ct.     Louisville   Thomas,T      12/10/85  Ranch        30,000.00      1500    3     1         20.00
5432 Miller Rd.     Louisville   Young,R       12/15/85  Other        17,500.00       800    2     1         21.88
#12 Circle Ct.      Louisville   White,Y       12/19/85  Other        10,000.00       800    2     1         12.50
1222 Dee Rd.        South Fork   Smith,P       12/19/85  Ranch        22,950.00       950    3     1         24.16
222 Earl Ave.       J'Town       Wray,A        12/22/85  Ranch        51,000.00      1200    3     1         42.50
9827 Rowan St.      J'Town       Coad,B        12/27/85  Ranch        47,950.00      1100    3     1         43.59
3355 Bank St.       J'Town       Cobb,D        1/03/86   Ranch        37,500.00      1500    3     1         25.00
77 Portland Ave.    North Hill   Coe,A         1/05/86   Ranch        20,000.00      1500    3     1         13.33
99 Cardinal Hill Rd. North Hill  Brand,B       1/05/86   Cape Cod     70,000.00      2000    3     2         35.00
#10 Old Mill Rd.    Louisville   Stern,M       1/07/86   Ranch        75,000.00      2150    3     2         34.88
5532 Mud Creek Dr.  Louisville   Hall,W        1/10/86   Ranch        12,000.00       950    3     2         12.63
4444 Normie Ln.     Louisville   James,J       1/11/86   Cape Cod    120,000.00      2400    5     3         50.00
3498 Bold Rd.       Louisville   Taft,H        1/15/86   Colonial    275,000.00      3800    5     4         72.37
#82 Rudd Rd.        Louisville   Lum,I         1/16/86   Cape Cod     88,950.00      2800    4     2         31.77
6712 Shelby St.     Louisville   Wood,B        1/16/86   Ranch        92,500.00      2400    4     2         38.54
7235 Shiloh Dr.     E'Town       Allan,J       1/17/86   Ranch        95,000.00      2750    4     3         34.55
8989 Big D Ln.      South Fork   Adkins,G      1/18/86   Ranch        17,000.00      1200    2     1         14.17
1001 Spring St.     North Hill   Frier,F       1/22/86   Other        45,000.00      1700    3     2         26.47
6935 Shiloh Dr.     E'Town       Grebe,C       1/25/86   Cape Cod     81,000.00      2000    3     2         40.50
4989 Adler Way      Louisville   Dole,V        1/30/86   Cape Cod     76,500.00      2000    3     2         38.25
5678 Beech St.      Louisville   Smith,F       2/02/86   Cape Cod     65,950.00      1800    3     2         36.64
#62 Billy Bone Ct.  Louisville   Taylor,A      2/04/86   Ranch        34,500.00      1600    3     1         21.56
3323 Mt. Holly Dr.  Louisville   Grizz,D       2/10/86   Ranch        22,100.00      1200    3     1         18.42
9909 Midway Rd.     Louisville   Maier,O       2/11/86   Ranch        61,250.00      1875    3     2         32.67
435 Onted Ln.       Louisville   O'Neal,F      2/12/86   Ranch        53,790.00      1900    3     1         28.31
22 N. Ridge Ct.     Louisville   Nunn,A        2/15/86   Colonial    200,000.00      2900    5     3         68.97
654 Nora Ln.        Louisville   Orwick,S      2/18/86   Cape Cod     40,000.00      1600    3     1         25.00
659 Ridge Rd.       Louisville   Pulley,F      2/24/86   Ranch        30,000.00      1500    3     1         20.00
14 Short Rd.        Louisville   Quire,I       3/01/86   Ranch        52,300.00      1600    3     1         32.69
```

You now are ready to place the calculated field in the new column. To do this, begin by issuing the **[Menu] F**ield **P**lace **C**alculated command. As soon as you issue this command, Paradox will prompt you to enter the expression you want it to calculate. Because you want Paradox to divide each record's entry in the Quantity field by its entry in the Price field, type the formula **[Price]/[Sq Ft]**, then press ↵.

After you have supplied an expression for the field, move the cursor to the location where you want Paradox to place the field (in this case, the beginning of the fourth row of the new column) and press ↵. Because one of the fields referenced by the expression is a dollar field, Paradox presents the default mask for a dollar field: (999,999,999.99). At this point, Paradox will let you specify the number of characters to the left and right of the decimal place. In this case, press ← seven times then press ↵ to specify three digits to the left of the decimal place, then press ↵ again to accept two digits to the right of the decimal. Figure 11-30 on the next page shows the result of this process.

As you can see, the message *[Price]/[Sq Ft]* appears in the upper-right corner of the screen while the cursor is positioned on this new field. This message indicates that the field is a calculated field and lets you know what expression it contains.

If you press [Instant Report] at this point, Paradox will produce the report shown in Figure 11-29. As you can see, Paradox has divided each record's Price field entry by its Sq Ft field entry, and printed the results in the last column of the report.

Figure 11-30   A Report Spec with a Calculated Field

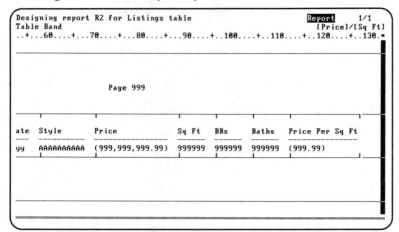

Notes

The expression you supply for any calculated field can be up to 40 characters long. It can contain field names (which must be enclosed in brackets), mathematical operators (like *, /, (), and +), literal strings (like *"Mr. "*), and literal numbers (like *65*). For example, you could use an expression like *"Mr. "+[Last Name]* to concatenate the literal string *"Mr. "* to the contents of a [Last Name] field. Similarly, you could use an expression like *65-[Age]* to subtract each entry in an [Age] field from the value 65. Paradox automatically checks every expression you enter. If the expression is not valid, Paradox will beep and let you try again.

Placing Multiple Fields in a Column

In most cases, each of the columns in the table band of your tabular report specs will contain only a single field mask. This convention makes it easy to use Paradox's TableBand commands (like Move, Copy, and Erase) to modify the appearance of a tabular report. You can place more than one field mask in any column of a table band, however. For example, you could place a mask for every field of a table side by side, or stack them one on top of another in a single column. In fact, you can place the same field in two or more places within the same report spec—even within the same column of a table band. To create nontabular arrangements of this sort, however, you probably will want to start with a free-form report format.

Designing Free-form Reports

So far, we have shown you how to design tabular reports. As you have seen, the tabular format is well suited for creating columnar reports. However, this format is too restrictive for use in creating less structured kinds of reports, such as mailing labels, form letters, and invoices. Fortunately, Paradox's free-form reporting format is ideally suited for these types of reports.

Both free-form and tabular report specs have a report band, a page band, and, optionally, one or more group bands. Additionally, you can use the same commands to add, delete, and resize page-widths, and to place, erase, and format field masks in both free-form and tabular report specs. Furthermore, you can move around both specs in the same way and can enter literals in the same way.

The principal difference between a free-form report spec and a tabular report spec is the substitution of a form band for the table band. When you print from a free-form report spec, Paradox prints the contents of the form band once for every record in the table—just as it does for the contents of the table band in a tabular report. Unlike a table band, however, a form band is not divided into columns. The noncolumnar structure of the form band provides a less-restrictive workspace for the design of nontabular reports.

A second difference between the tabular and free-form report specs is the absence of a TableBand option on the Free-form menu. Because free-form reports do not have table bands, this option is unnecessary in the free-form environment.

The other difference between the tabular and free-form reports is the presence of two special options—LineSqueeze and FieldSqueeze—on the free-form Setting menu. These commands allow Paradox to close up blank lines and spaces in a report. You'll understand the usefulness of these commands when we show you how to create mailing labels later in this section.

Designing a Free-form Report

Designing a free-form report spec is no more difficult than designing a tabular spec. For example, suppose you want to create a free-form report based on the data in the NAMES table shown in Figure 11-31 on the next page. First, issue the [**Menu**] **R**eport **D**esign command, then select the name of the table for which you want to design the report. In this case, we'll choose **NAMES**. Now, select a number under which to store the report spec. We'll choose the number **1**. Next, enter a description for the report (in this case, **Sample Free-form Report**). Finally, instead of choosing Tabular when Paradox prompts you for the report type, choose Free-form. Figure 11-32 shows the resulting spec.

Notice that this basic free-form report spec looks quite a bit like the tabular report specs that we have worked with throughout this chapter, except for the substitution of a form band for the table band, and the arrangement of the field masks within the form band. Although this band contains a mask for every field in the table, as well as a literal that names each field, the arrangement of this information is not the same as it is in a tabular report. Specifically, the field name literals and field masks are stacked one above the other on consecutive rows of the form band, rather than one after another across the page.

You can print a free-form report by pressing [Instant Report] while you are working within its spec. Figure 11-33 shows the first page of the report Paradox will print if you press [Instant Report] while you are looking at the free-form report spec in Figure 11-33. As you can see, Paradox skips one line at the top of the page for the report header, prints

Figure 11-31 The NAMES Table

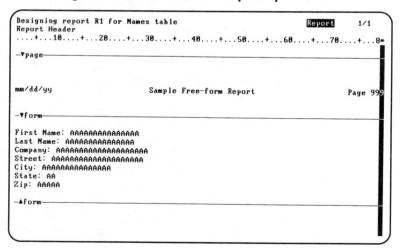

Figure 11-32 A Free-form Report Specification

the current date, the report title, and the page number on the fifth line of the page, then skips two more lines to reach the top of the form band. Because the first line of the form band is blank (as it always will be in a new free-form report), Paradox skips yet another line (the eighth line on the page). On the next seven lines of the page, Paradox prints the names of and entries in the fields of the first record in the NAMES table. Because the last line of the form band is blank (as it always will be in a new free-form report), Paradox skips another line (the sixteenth line on the page). Next, Paradox makes another pass through the form band, first skipping another line (the first line of the band) and then printing the entries from the second record in the table.

Figure 11-33 A Basic Free-form Report

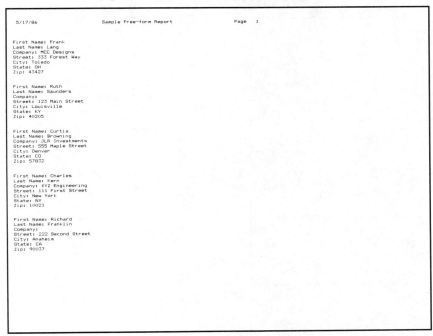

Paradox should continue in this fashion until it prints the last whole record it can print on the page before reaching the four-line page footer specified by the report spec. Paradox will not split records onto two pages of a report. Accordingly, it should print six records on the page. As you can see, however, it prints only five. The reason? The same bug that we discussed earlier in the section entitled "How Many Records Print on a Page?"

Importantly, you should note that Paradox prints the single blank line from the top of the form band before each record it prints, not just once as it does for a blank line or a line of text at the top of the table band in a tabular report. Unlike table bands in tabular report specs, form bands are not divided into header and body sections. Accordingly, Paradox will print every line of a form band for each record in a table.

Mailing Labels

As a more useful example of a free-form report, suppose you want to print the names and addresses from the NAMES table on 4" wide x 1 3/8" deep continuous-feed labels, as shown in Figure 11-34. To do this, start with the new free-form report spec shown in Figure 11-32. After bringing this spec to the screen, use the [Report Delete Line] key ([Ctrl]-[Y]) to delete the single line of the report header, the six lines of the page header (including the line that contains the report title and special masks), the four lines of the page footer, and the single line of the report footer. After you delete these lines, all that will be left of the report spec will be the nine lines of the form band.

Figure 11-34
Mailing Labels

```
Frank          Lang
MCC Designs
333 Forest Way
Toledo         , OH  43427
```

```
Ruth           Saunders
123 Main Street
Louisville     , KY  40205
```

```
Curtis         Browning
JLR Investments
555 Maple Street
Denver         , CO  57832
```

```
Charles        Kern
XYZ Engineering
111 First Street
New York       , NY  10023
```

```
Richard        Franklin
222 Second Street
Anaheim        , CA  90037
```

```
John           Smith
SSC Computers
897 Oak Street
Phoenix        , AZ  85217
```

```
Nancy          Moody
LMN Medical
456 Madison Avenue
Tampa          , FL  33601
```

```
Patti          Irwin
DFC Publishing
246 Monroe Street
Atlanta        , GA  30325
```

```
Kyle           Jones
192 Hill Street
Dallas         , TX  45723
```

```
Thomas         Spencer
PDQ Printers
100 Lake Street
Macon          , GA  31024
```

Figure 11-36
Squeezed Mailing Labels

```
Frank Lang
MCC Designs
333 Forest Way
Toledo, OH  43427
```

```
Ruth Saunders
123 Main Street
Louisville, KY  40205
```

```
Curtis Browning
JLR Investments
555 Maple Street
Denver, CO  57832
```

```
Charles Kern
XYZ Engineering
111 First Street
New York, NY  10023
```

```
Richard Franklin
222 Second Street
Anaheim, CA  90037
```

```
John Smith
SSC Computers
897 Oak Street
Phoenix, AZ  85217
```

```
Nancy Moody
LMN Medical
456 Madison Avenue
Tampa, FL  33601
```

```
Patti Irwin
DFC Publishing
246 Monroe Street
Atlanta, GA  30325
```

```
Kyle Jones
192 Hill Street
Dallas, TX  45723
```

```
Thomas Spencer
PDQ Printers
100 Lake Street
Macon, GA  31024
```

Once you have deleted these lines from the report spec, you are ready to design the labels. To begin, press the **[Ins]** key to enter the insert mode. Then use the **[Del]** or **[Backspace]** keys to delete all the literals from the form band. Next, move the cursor to the left edge of the Last Name mask, press **[Backspace]** to pull the field up to the line that contains the First Name mask, and press the **[Spacebar]** once to put a space between the two field masks. Then move the cursor to the left edge of the Zip field, press **[Backspace]** to pull that field onto the line that contains the State mask, and then press the **[Spacebar]** twice to place two spaces between the two fields. Next, position the cursor at the left edge of the line that now contains the State and Zip fields, press **[Backspace]** to pull those masks onto the line that contains the City field, then type a comma and press the **[Spacebar]**. Finally, use the ↵ key to insert one blank line at the top of the form band and two blank lines at the bottom so that it contains a total of nine lines. Figure 11-35 shows the finished report specification.

Figure 11-35   The Mailing Labels Spec

```
Changing report R1 for Names table                    Report      1/1
Page Header
....+...10....+...20....+...30....+...40....+...50....+...60....+...70....+...8*
—▼page—
—▼form—


AAAAAAAAAAAAAA AAAAAAAAAAAAAA
AAAAAAAAAAAAAAAAAAAA
AAAAAAAAAAAAAAAAAAAA
AAAAAAAAAAAAAA, AA  AAAAA



—▲form—
—▲page—
```

Before you print labels from this spec, you now should issue the **[Menu]** Setting PageLayout Length command and set the page length to **C**. This setting, which we'll explain in more detail in a few pages, tells Paradox to print the report continuously without page breaks. After you align the top of the first label with the print head in your printer and turn it on, you can press **[Instant Report]** to print the labels shown in Figure 11-35. Because you have deleted all but the lines in the form band, Paradox does not skip any lines at the beginning or end of the report or at the beginning or end of each page. Since the top of each label is 1 1/2 inches away from the top of the next label, and most printers print six lines to the inch, the nine-line form band assures that the addresses will be properly spaced on the labels.

The FieldSqueeze and LineSqueeze Options

If you look at the labels displayed in Figure 11-34, you'll see a couple of problems. First, there appears to be too much space between the first and last names on the third line of the labels and between the City field and the literal comma on the sixth line of the labels. Second, Paradox has left a blank line in the labels for those records that have an empty Company field.

The FieldSqueeze Option

As we explained earlier, Paradox allocates as many spaces to a field in a report as there are characters in its field mask. For example, because the mask for the First Name field in the mailing label spec is 15 characters long, Paradox always leaves 15 spaces for it at the beginning of the third line of each label. For this reason, and because we left a single space between the First Name and Last Name masks, Paradox always begins printing the Last Name entry on the seventeenth space of the line, regardless of the actual length of the First Name entry it prints on that line. This same principle is responsible for the gaps between the City field and the comma on the sixth line of each label.

Fortunately, Paradox offers a command that solves this problem: [Menu] Setting RemoveBlanks FieldSqueeze. After you issue this command, Paradox will allocate only as much space to a field as there are characters in that field–not always as many characters as there are in that field's mask. To turn off this attribute, issue the [Menu] Setting RemoveBlanks FieldSqueeze No command.

The LineSqueeze Option

The second problem with these labels is the blank fourth line that Paradox leaves in the labels of records that have an empty Company field. The [Menu] Setting RemoveBlanks LineSqueeze command takes care of this problem. When you issue this command and choose the Yes option, Paradox gives you two choices: Fixed and Variable. Both of these options will cause Paradox to squeeze out any blank lines that result from empty fields in reports. The difference between them is what they do with the lines they remove. The Fixed option causes Paradox to add any lines that it squeezes out of the form band back at the bottom of that band. This preserves the proper spacing for your fixed-form reports, like mailing labels. On the other hand, the Variable option causes Paradox to throw away the lines that it squeezes out of the form band, thus reducing the number of lines of the report.

Figure 11-36 on page 372 shows how the labels will print after you issue the [**Menu**] Setting **R**emoveBlanks FieldSqueeze **Y**es and [**Menu**] Setting **R**emoveBlanks LineSqueeze **Y**es **F**ixed commands. As you can see, Paradox has closed up the gaps between the fields on each line and has removed the blank fourth line from the labels for the records with an empty title field, without disturbing the spacing of the labels.

Notes

Because the fields in the NAMES table were in the order in which we wanted them to appear in the mailing labels, we were able to use the [Backspace] key to pull them into mailing label form. You probably will not be as lucky, however. In many cases, you will have to use a combination of the [Menu] Field Erase and [Menu] Field Place commands to move field masks into the proper order. The [Menu] Field Erase command allows you to remove a field mask from one place in a report spec, while the [Menu] Field Place command allows you to put it back in another location. The order in which you use these commands to move a field is not important.

The open nature of a free-form report spec lends itself to the development of other noncolumnar reports. For example, the report spec shown in Figure 11-37 shows a simple form letter based on the entries in the NAMES table. As you can see, the top portion of this spec is identical to our simple mailing labels. In the salutation, we reused the Last Name field. The remainder of the letter is composed of literals we typed into the spec. Of course, you could place fields within the body of the letter.

Figure 11-37 A Simple Form Letter

```
Changing report R2 for Names table                          Report Ins 1/1
Form Band,Field Squeeze,Line Squeeze
....+...10....+...20....+...30....+...40....+...50....+...60....+...70....+...8*
-▼page
-▼form
M o n t h dd, yyyy

AAAAAAAAAAAAAAA AAAAAAAAAAAAAA
AAAAAAAAAAAAAAAAAAA
AAAAAAAAAAAAAAAAAAA
AAAAAAAAAAAAAA, AA  AAAAA

Dear AAAAAAAAAAAAAAA:

We are pleased to announce the grand opening of our third store at 1775
Main Street, Louisville, Kentucky 40214.

I hope you will be able to stop by on May 17, 1986 to help us celebrate.  We
will be giving away some real neat door prizes, and everything in the store
will be marked down 10%.

See you there!

Sincerely,
```

Cancelling and Saving Report Specs

Once you have designed a report specification, you probably will want to save it for future use. You can do this by pressing the [Do-It!] key or by issuing the [Menu] DO-IT! command while you are viewing the report spec you want to save. When you do this, Paradox will save the spec to disk in a special report file. The first part of the name of the report file will be the name of the table for which you created the report. The first character of the extension will be the letter *R*, and the second character of the extension will be the report's number (1 to 9). The default report for any table (the one stored under the letter *R*) will have only the single-character extension *R*.

However, you do not have to save a report spec that you are designing or changing. If you do not want to save the changes you have made to a spec, just press the [Menu] key from within the report generator and choose Cancel. If you choose Yes when Paradox presents the choices Yes and No, Paradox will return you to the main mode without saving any changes you made to the spec. If you choose No, however, Paradox will remain within the report generator. You also can cancel the editing of a report spec by pressing [Ctrl]-[Break]. When you press this key, Paradox will return you to the main mode without saving the changes you made to the spec, just as if you had issued the [Menu] Cancel Yes command.

Revising Existing Reports

In this chapter, we have outlined a three-step process for creating a report. First, you use the [Menu] Report Design command to bring a new report spec to the screen. Second, you use any of the editing techniques described in this chapter (adding literals, deleting masks, and rearranging columns, for example) to customize the basic spec. Finally, you issue the DO-IT! command to save the spec.

You can change a report spec once you have designed it. To do this, you must use the [Menu] Report Change command. When you issue this command, Paradox will ask you to name the table. After you choose a table, Paradox will present a menu that lists the numbers of the existing reports for the table. If you have designed and saved reports only under numbers 1 and 2, for example, Paradox will present the options R, 1, and 2. (The R option always will be listed since it always contains a report spec.)

As soon as you select the report you want to change, Paradox will display the description of that report, and will give you the opportunity to change it. Changing the description does not change the appearance of the report. Paradox does not place the new description in the page header of the report spec. As soon as you press ↵, Paradox will present the report spec for the table. The spec will look exactly as it did when you last saved it, except that the word *Changing* will replace the word *Designing* at the top of the screen.

When you want to change an existing report, be sure to choose Change rather than Design from the Report menu. If you issue the [Menu] Report Design command and select an existing report, Paradox will present two options: Cancel and Replace. If you choose Replace, Paradox will erase the existing report stored under that number and will present you with the new basic report (either Tabular or Free-form) that you choose. Choosing Cancel spares the existing report and returns you to the previous menu.

Printing Reports

Throughout this chapter, we have presented examples of a variety of different reports. In those examples, we concentrated more on the fundamentals of designing the report spec than we did on the process of printing the report. Now, we'll explain the process of printing a report in detail.

Printing a Saved Report

In the previous parts of this chapter, we showed you how to use the [Instant Report] key to print a report. If you press [Instant Report] while you are viewing a table, Paradox will print a report from that table using the spec stored under the letter *R*. Unless you have modified this report, it will be the standard tabular report for the table. If you press [Instant Report] while you are viewing a report spec, however, Paradox will print according to the layout of that spec. Issuing the [Menu] Output Printer command from within the report generator has the same effect.

Once you have saved a report spec, you can print from that spec while you are in the main mode. To do this, issue the **[Menu] R**eport **O**utput command. When you issue this command, Paradox will prompt you for the name of the table whose records you want to print. You may respond by pressing ↵ to reveal a listing of the tables in the current directory and then by choosing a table from that list, or you may type the name of the table and press ↵. If the table is not in the current directory, you must specify the path to its file.

Once you have selected a table, Paradox will present a menu that lists the available reports for that table. This menu will consist of the letter *R* plus the numbers of any reports you have designed and saved. If you have supplied a description for a report, Paradox will display the description of that report immediately below the menu when you highlight its number. As soon as you select a report spec, Paradox will prompt you to specify a destination for the report: Printer, Screen, or File. If you choose Printer, Paradox will send the report to your printer. The Screen and File options allow you to preview the report on the screen and save the report in an ASCII text file, respectively. We'll discuss these alternative print destinations in a few pages.

Cancelling the Printing of a Report

Once you instruct Paradox to print a report, you'll usually let it print that report to completion. In some cases, however, you'll want Paradox to stop printing before it has printed the entire report. To cancel printing in the middle of a report, just press [Ctrl]-[Break]. When you do this, Paradox will briefly display the message *Cancelling report output...*, will cancel the printing of the report, will advance the paper to the top of the next page, and will return you to the cursor's original position. If your printer has a buffer, it may take several seconds for printing to stop once you've issued this command.

Print Settings

Unless you tell it otherwise, Paradox assumes that you will print a report on 8 1/2" by 11" continuous-feed paper, and that your printer will print ten characters per inch across a page and six lines per inch down the page. You may want to print on different sized paper, print on cut sheets, print in a different type style, and so forth. You can adjust Paradox's print settings to adjust for these conditions.

Adjusting the Width of a Page

The width of the page-widths in a report spec determines how many characters Paradox will print across each line of a page. As you have seen, Paradox sets 80 character page-widths for all new report specs. The [Menu] Setting PageLayout Width command allows you to adjust this width. If you have a wide carriage printer, for example, you probably will want to adjust the page-widths in your reports to 132 characters, as we did to produce the spec that is shown in Figure 11-13. Importantly, any elements (either literals or masks) that are split by the border of a page-width will be printed partially on one page and partially on another page. Unless you plan to actually "glue" the pages of the report together, you probably will want to adjust the placement of the information in your report so that it does not overlap a page-width boundary. Alternatively, you can adjust the widths of the page-widths so that they do not divide any element in your report.

Adjusting the Length of a Page

Unless you tell it otherwise, Paradox assumes that your printer will print six lines per inch and that you will print on paper eleven inches long. If you plan to print a report on paper of a different height, or if your printer prints more than six lines per inch, or both, you will need to adjust the Length setting for that report. To do this, issue the **[Menu] Setting P**ageLayout **L**ength command while you are working with the spec for the report whose settings you want to adjust. When you issue this command, Paradox will display the prompt *New page length:* at the top of the screen, followed by the current Length setting for that report (probably 66). Once you see this prompt, press **[Backspace]** or **[Ctrl]-[Backspace]** to erase the old setting, type in a new number, and press ↵. If you are printing on legal-sized paper, for example, you might specify a length of 84.

The minimum page length that Paradox will accept is two lines; the maximum is 2000 lines. If you want Paradox to disregard page breaks entirely, you should specify a Length setting of C. This setting, which instructs Paradox to print continuously, is useful for printing mailing labels.

Adjusting the Left Margin

In addition to adjusting the width of a page, you can adjust the margin that Paradox leaves at the left edge of each page. Unless you specify otherwise, Paradox will not leave any left margin; it will start printing at the left edge of each page. The [Menu] Setting Margin command allows you to adjust the left margin of a report. When you issue this command, Paradox will display the prompt *Margin size:* followed by the current left margin (usually 0). When you see this prompt, you should erase the old margin, type a new one, and press ↵. When you do this, Paradox will move the elements in your report spec to the right (or to the left if you decreased the margin). Figure 11-38 shows the result of adding a ten-space left margin to the report spec shown in Figure 11-13. As you can see, Paradox has inserted ten spaces at the left edge of each row of the spec.

Importantly, because the [Menu] Setting Margin command acts by inserting or deleting space at the left edge of the first page-width in a report spec, it controls the left margin of only the first page-width in the report. Also, because the Margin command moves the information in a report, it can cause the information in a report to be split between two page-widths. Paradox will not insert a margin if the insertion would push any element beyond the right edge of the rightmost page-width in the spec.

Figure 11-38   A Ten-character Left Margin

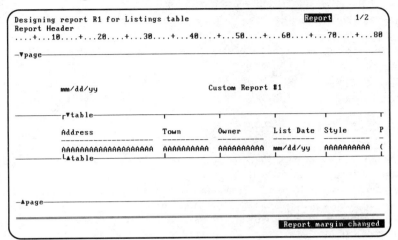

Setup Strings

Most printers are able to print in a variety of different type styles (such as bold, italic, compressed, expanded, and so forth). The most common way to change the style in which your printer prints is to send it a special code called a setup string. The [Menu] Setting Setup command allows you to change the style in which Paradox prints a report by instructing it to send a setup code to your printer before it begins printing that report.

To specify the style in which a report should be printed, you issue the **[Menu]** Setting Setup command while you are working with the spec for that report. When you issue this command, Paradox will present two choices: Predefined and Custom. If you choose Predefined, Paradox will present a list of predefined setup strings for a variety of different printers. (As we will explain in Chapter 12, you can use the PCCP to add strings to this list or delete strings from it.) Figure 11-39 shows such a list. If you choose one of these strings, Paradox will display the message *Setup string recorded* and will assign that string to the report spec. The next time you print from that spec, Paradox will use the print style you specified.

Figure 11-39   The Predefined Menu

```
Select a predefined setup string:                    Report    1/2
Small-IBMgraphics   Reg-IBMgraphics  Small-Epson-MX/FX  Small-Oki-92/93 ▶
```

In Paradox, setup strings must consist of a backslash followed by the ASCII number of the character you want to send. For example, the string \015 represents the character [Ctrl]-[O], which has the ASCII code 015. If you are using an Epson or Epson-compatible printer, sending this character to your printer will cause your report to be printed in compressed print. You should check your printer manual for the codes that will work with your printer.

The Custom option allows you to assign a custom setup string to a report. When you issue the **[Menu] S**etting **S**etup **C**ustom command, Paradox will display the prompt *Setup string:*, followed by the setup string currently assigned to the report (if you have chosen a predefined string, it will show up here). When you see this prompt, you can edit the default string (if any) to specify the print attributes that you want Paradox to use for the current report. If you want your Epson printer to print eight lines per inch, for example, you would type \027\048. (Accordingly, you'll want to use the [Menu] Setting PageLayout Length command to set the page length for the report to 88.)

Waiting between Pages

Unless you tell it otherwise, Paradox will assume that you will print your reports on continuous-feed paper. If you will be printing a report on cut sheets, you'll have to tell Paradox to wait for you to insert a new sheet of paper into the printer after it prints each page. To do this, you must use the **[Menu] S**etting **W**ait **Y**es command. When you issue this command, Paradox will assign the Wait attribute to the report spec that you currently are designing or editing. The next time you print from that spec, Paradox will stop at the end of each page and display the prompt *End of page Press any key to continue...* in the upper-left corner of the screen. As soon as you press any key (preferably after inserting a new sheet of paper), Paradox will print the next page.

Notes

When you use any one of the five commands described above, Paradox assigns the relevant attribute only to the report spec you are editing when you issue the command. The attributes that you assign to one report spec do not affect the printing of any other report–even other reports for the same table.

The settings that you assign to a report spec go into effect immediately. If you make a change to one of these settings while you are editing a report spec, and then press the [Instant Report] key, Paradox will print using the new setting. However, unless you use the [Do-It!] key or the [Menu] DO-IT! command to save the report spec, Paradox will not save those attributes with the spec. Consequently, Paradox will not use the attributes the next time it prints from that spec.

Finally, in addition to letting you change the print settings for an individual report, Paradox allows you to change the default value of these print settings. For example, if you usually want Paradox to print 88 lines per page, you could change the default Length setting from 66 to 88. We'll show you how to do this at the end of Chapter 12.

Alternative Print Destinations

Up until this point, we have sent reports to a printer. Although a printer is the most common destination for a report, Paradox can send a report to two alternative devices: to the screen of your computer and to a file. Your choice between Printer, Screen, and File on the Report Output menu determines where Paradox will send a report.

Printing to the Screen

When you issue the [Menu] Output command, select a table, select a report spec, and choose Screen, Paradox will display the message *Sending report to screen...* and send the report to the screen of your computer. Paradox sends the report to the screen of your computer in the same order that it would send it to your printer: the pages of the first page-width first, the pages of the second page-width second, and so forth. Because Paradox cannot display an entire page of most reports on the screen at one time, it breaks the report into even smaller sections. Pressing any key on the keyboard brings successive sections of the report into view. As you move through the report, Paradox displays a prompt in the form *Now Viewing Page x of Page-width x* at the top of the screen to let you know what part of the report you are viewing.

For example, Figure 11-40 shows the result of issuing the Output Screen command and specifying the report spec shown in Figure 11-6. As you can see, Paradox is displaying the first part of the first page of the report on the screen. Each time you press any key, Paradox will display a new section of the report. When Paradox reaches the end of the report, it will return you to where you were before you issued the command.

Figure 11-40 Printing to the Screen

```
Now Viewing Page 1 of Page Width 1
Press any key to continue


  5/19/86                      Standard report                    Page    1


  Address              Town            Owner       List Date  Style        Price
  ---------------      -----------     --------    ---------  ---------    ------
  123 Abby Ct.         Louisville      Kones,D     11/02/85   Ranch         32,95
  426 St. James Ct.    Louisville      Jones,S     11/05/85   Ranch         19,50
  766 Baird St.        Louisville      Black,G     11/08/85   Colonial     139,95
  222 Big Ben Dr.      Louisville      Roberts,D   11/08/85   Other         53,50
  666 Montana Ave.     Louisville      Saul,H      11/09/85   Cape Cod      55,00
  589 Morocco Dr.      E'Town          Smith,B     11/10/85   Cape Cod      62,50
  987 Allan Dr.        Louisville      Newsome,K   11/12/85   Cape Cod      60,00
  549 Billtown Rd.     Louisville      Bizer,B     11/14/85   Ranch         72,50
  343 Market St.       Louisville      Bivins,D    11/15/85   Ranch         42,90
  198 Main St.         J'Town          Green,L     11/15/85   Other         27,50
  885 Jefferson St.    J'Town          Zith,M      11/18/85   Ranch         55,00
  913 Whitney Dr.      North Hill      Kulp,R      11/20/85   Cape Cod      99,50
  363 Dower Ct.        North Fork      Culp,A      11/21/85   Cape Cod     109,00
```

Importantly, Paradox will only display the first 80 characters of any page-width on the screen when it previews a report. If you preview a report whose page-widths exceed 80 characters, therefore, you will be able to see only part of each page.

Printing to a File

In addition to letting you direct a report to a printer or to the screen of your computer, Paradox also lets you send a report to a text file. This option makes it possible to transfer the information from a Paradox report into another program that can read ASCII text files. When you issue the Output File command, Paradox will present you with the prompt *File Name:*. In response to this prompt, you should type the name of the file in which you want to store the report. If you want to store the file in a directory other than the current one, you must preface the file name with the name of that directory. If you do not specify an extension, Paradox will add .RPT to the name.

As soon as you press ↵, Paradox will display the message *Sending report to filename.RPT...* at the bottom of the screen as it writes the report into the file you named. Paradox will store the report in the file exactly as it would appear if you printed it to a printer. This means that the file will be divided into pages, just like the printed report. If you want to print a continuous stream of information, you should make the report a single large page-width and specify a Length setting of C.

Conclusion

In this chapter, we've demonstrated the basics of printing reports from a Paradox table. First, we showed you how to print an instant report. Next, we explained the concept of a report specification with bands, field masks, and literals. Then we showed you how to design a custom report specification. Finally, we showed you how to print reports.

In the next chapter, we'll cover several advanced reporting topics. In that chapter, we'll show you how to place summary fields, how to group reports, and how to use the PCCP to change Paradox's default report settings.

Chapter 12

Other Reporting Topics

In Chapter 11, we showed you how to use Paradox's Instant Report capability and how to design and use custom tabular and free-form reports. In this chapter, we'll cover advanced topics, including using summary statistics in reports, grouping reports, and using the Paradox Custom Configuration Program to change Paradox's default report settings. We'll also show you how to use the Tools menu commands to manage reports.

Summary Fields

Summary fields compute and display statistics on the entries in the fields in a report. For example, a summary field in an ORDERS table report might display the total dollar value of the orders in the report, or the average size of the orders in the report. On the other hand, a summary field in a CUSTOMER table report might display the total number of customers in the report.

To place a summary field in a report, you choose the Field Place Summary command from the Report menu. When you issue this command, Paradox will display a menu with two options: Regular, which allows you to summarize a regular field, and Calculated, which allows you to summarize the results of calculations.

Regular Summary Fields

Selecting Regular tells Paradox that you want to summarize the information in one of the regular fields you have included in the table band of your report. When you choose Regular, Paradox will first display a list of the regular fields in the report and ask you to select the field you want to summarize. You should select the field on which you want to group the report from the list.

The Type of Summary

Once you select a field, Paradox will display the menu shown in Figure 12-1. The choice you make from this menu determines what action the summary field will perform. For instance, if you select Sum, the summary field you are defining will total the entries in the specified field of the report. If you choose Average, the summary field will average the entries in that field. Choosing High or Low will cause the summary field to return the maximum or minimum value from the field. Choosing Count creates a summary field that counts the entries in the field.

Figure 12-1 The Summary Regular Menu

If you're summarizing a date field or an alphanumeric field, the Sum option will not be available. Average summaries are available for date, but not alphanumeric, fields.

PerGroup and Overall

After you select the type of the summary field, Paradox will display a menu that offers two options: PerGroup and Overall. Choosing PerGroup tells Paradox that the summary field should operate on only the records in the current group. (We'll tell you how to group records later in this chapter.) Choosing Overall tells Paradox to calculate a cumulative statistic. Whenever Paradox prints an Overall summary field, it will compute the selected statistic for all of the records printed on the report up to that point. This option lets you include running statistics (such as running totals or moving averages) in your reports.

Positioning Summary Fields

Next, Paradox will prompt you to set the position of the summary field. As with other types of fields, the placement of a summary field determines the position of that field on each page of your printed report. In general, you should always place summary fields in a footer (either a group footer, a page footer, or a report footer) below the column you want to summarize. If you place a summary field in the page footer, then the summary will be printed at the bottom of each page. Similarly, if you position the summary field in the report footer of the report spec, Paradox will print the summary statistic once at the end of the report.

If you select the PerGroup option from the PerGroup/Overall menu, you will place the summary field in a group footer. The summary field will compute a statistic for the records that appear in that group. (We'll cover grouping in the next part of this chapter.)

If you choose Overall from the PerGroup/Overall menu, then you can place the field in a group footer, the page footer, or the report footer. Whenever Paradox prints an Overall summary field, it will compute the requested statistic for all of the records in the report up to the position of the summary field. For instance, if you place an Overall summary field in the page footer of the report spec, then the summary field on each page of the report will display the cumulative statistic for that page and all previous pages, and will appear in the page footer section of each page.

An Example

For example, suppose you want to create a report for the LISTINGS table that includes the following summaries: on each page, a running total of the number of records in the report up to that point; at the end of the report, the sum and average of all entries in the Price field for the entire report.

To begin, issue the **[Menu] R**eport **D**esign command, type **LISTINGS**, and press ↵. When Paradox prompts you for a report number, choose **3**. Next, type **Summary Report** for the report description and select **T**abular as the report type. When the report specification screen appears, issue the **[Menu]** **S**etting **P**ageLayout **W**idth command, press **[Ctrl]-[Backspace]** to erase the current default, and type **132**. This step sets the page width of the new report to 132 characters, eliminating problems with split fields. Next, issue the **[Menu] S**etting **P**ageLayout **D**elete command to delete the second page-width from the report. Figure 12-2 shows the report specification.

Figure 12-2 A Report Specification

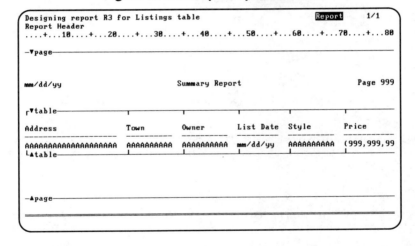

Now you are ready to begin placing summary fields. Let's start with the summary field that computes the running total of the number of records in the report. To place this field, issue the **[Menu] F**ield **P**lace **S**ummary **R**egular command. After you issue this command, Paradox will prompt you to select the field you want to summarize. When you see this prompt, select the **P**rice field. Next, you will see the menu shown in Figure 12-1. Since you want this summary field to compute a count, you should select **C**ount. Next, Paradox will ask you whether the summary field should be an Overall or a PerGroup summary. Since this summary field will compute a running count, you should choose **O**verall.

Next, Paradox will prompt you to place the field in the report. When you see this prompt, move the cursor to the page footer, position it at column 29, and press ↵. After you place the field, Paradox will prompt you to adjust the number of digits to display in

the field. You should press the ← key to reduce the number of digits to two, then press
↵. Paradox now will prompt you to set the number of decimal places for the field. To
accept the default setting (no decimal places), just press ↵. Finally, you should type a
literal next to the new field that identifies it. To do this, move the cursor to the
beginning of the line that contains the summary field and type **Total Listings:**. Figure
12-3 shows the report specification screen as it will look after the summary field is added.

Figure 12-3 Placing the Summary Field

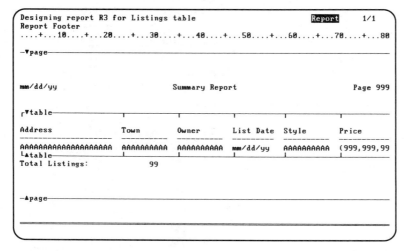

Now you are ready to place the remaining summary fields in the report. Before you do
anything else, move the cursor to the report footer, press **[Ins]** to enter the insert mode,
press ↵ to insert a new row, and then press **[Ins]** again. You'll need this row to hold
your last summary field.

When the new row is in place, you can place the field that will compute the total of the
Price field for every record in the report. To do this, issue the **[Menu] F**ield **P**lace
Summary **R**egular command again. When Paradox prompts you for the field you want to
summarize, choose **P**rice. Since you want this summary field to compute the sum of the
entries in the Price field, choose **S**um when you see the Summary Type menu. Since
you want this summary field to operate on every record in the report, you should select
Overall when Paradox presents the PerGroup/Overall menu.

When Paradox prompts you to place the field in the report, move the cursor to the first
row in the report footer, position it in column 71, and press ↵. As you recall, by
placing the summary field in the report footer, you are telling Paradox to base its value
on all of the entries in the report. Next, Paradox will prompt you to set the number of
digits in the field. You should press ← four times to set the number of digits at 8, and
then press ↵. When Paradox prompts you to set the number of decimal places, press ←
three times to remove all decimals and then press ↵. Finally, move the cursor to the left
and type **Total Price of Listings:**.

Now let's place the summary field that will compute the average price for the records in the report. To do this, issue the **[Menu] F**ield **P**lace **S**ummary **R**egular command and select **P**rice as the field to summarize. When Paradox prompts you for the type of summary field, select **A**verage. When you see the Overall/PerGroup menu, choose **O**verall. Now, use the cursor keys to move the cursor to column 74 in the second row of the report footer, press ↵ to place the field, use the ← key to set the number of digits to 6, press ↵, then press ↵ again to set the number of decimals to two. Finally, move the cursor to the space under the letter *T* in the word *Total* and type the literal **Average Price:** into the report spec to identify the new summary field.

When you have placed all of these summary fields, your report spec will look like Figure 12-4. Now press **[Instant Report]** to print the report. After you do this, Paradox will send the report to the printer. This is shown in Figure 12-5 on the next page. As you can see, Paradox has printed a running count of the number of records in the report at the bottom of each page. At the end of the report, Paradox has printed the total and average price of all records.

Figure 12-4   Summary Fields

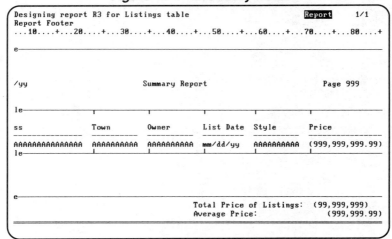

Calculated Summary Fields

Calculated summary fields allow you to compute and display summary statistics that are based on the results of mathematical expressions. The most common use of calculated summary fields is to compute and display summary statistics for calculated fields.

When you place a calculated summary field in a report, you first define a formula that Paradox will evaluate once for every record in the report. The expression may include Paradox's mathematical operators, literal characters, and references to fields. If you are using the summary field to compute statistics for a calculated field, the formula you define will be identical to the formula you used to define the calculated field. After you specify the formula, you tell Paradox which summary statistic you want to compute.

Figure 12-5 The Printed Report

```
5/20/86                  Summary Report              Page    1

Address              Town          Owner         List Date   Style       Price         Sq Ft    BRs    Baths
-------              ----          -----         ---------   -----       -----         -----    ---    -----
123 Abby Ct.         Louisville    Kones,D       11/02/85    Ranch        32,950.00    1500     3      1
426 St. James Ct.    Louisville    Jones,S       11/05/85    Ranch        19,500.00     950     2      1
766 Baird St.        Louisville    Black,G       11/08/85    Colonial    139,950.00    2600     4      3
222 Big Ben Dr.      North Hill    Roberts,D     11/08/85    Other        53,500.00    1900     3      2
666 Montana Ave.     Louisville    Saul,H        11/09/85    Cape Cod     55,000.00    1900     3      1
589 Morocco Dr.      E'Town        Smith,B       11/12/85    Cape Cod     62,950.00    1875     3      2
987 Allan Dr.        Louisville    Newsome,K     11/12/85    Cape Cod     60,000.00    1900     4      2
549 Billtown Rd.     Louisville    Bizer,B       11/14/85    Ranch        72,500.00    2000     3      2
343 Market St.       Louisville    Bivins,D      11/15/85    Ranch        42,900.00    1675     3      1
198 Main St.         J'Town        Green,L       11/15/85    Other        27,500.00     800     3      1
885 Jefferson St.    J'Town        Zith,M        11/18/85    Ranch        55,000.00    1500     3      1
913 Whitney Dr.      North Hill    Kulp,R        11/20/85    Cape Cod     99,500.00    1800     4      2
363 Dower Ct.        North Fork    Culp,P        11/21/85    Cape Cod    109,000.00    2100     4      2
620 Windsong Ct.     Louisville    Pank,E        11/22/85    Colonial    250,000.00    4000     6      4
4500 Hempstead Dr.   Louisville    Pape,C        12/04/85    Colonial    150,000.00    2600     4      3
#6 Brandon Way       Louisville    Abrams,L      12/08/85    Ranch        67,000.00    2250     4      2
6610 Vermin Dr.      Louisville    Russ,J        12/10/85    Ranch        75,000.00    2100     3      2
712 Clifton Ct.      Louisville    Thomas,T      12/12/85    Ranch        30,000.00    1500     3      1
5432 Miller Rd.      Louisville    Young,R       12/15/85    Other        17,500.00     800     2      1
#12 Circle Ct.       Louisville    White,Y       12/19/85    Other        10,000.00     800     2      1
1222 Dee Rd.         South Fork    Smith,P       12/19/85    Ranch        22,950.00     950     3      1
222 Earl Ave.        J'Town        Wray,A        12/22/85    Ranch        51,000.00    1200     3      1
9827 Rowan St.       J'Town        Coad,B        12/27/85    Ranch        47,950.00    1100     3      1
3355 Bank St.        J'Town        Cobb,D        1/03/86     Ranch        37,500.00    1500     3      1
77 Portland Ave.     North Hill    Coe,A         1/05/86     Ranch        20,000.00    1500     3      1
99 Cardinal Hill Rd. North Hill    Brand,B       1/05/86     Cape Cod     70,000.00    2000     3      2
#10 Old Mill Rd.     Louisville    Stern,M       1/07/86     Ranch        75,000.00    2150     3      2
5532 Mud Creek Dr.   Louisville    Hall,W        1/10/86     Ranch        12,000.00     950     2      1
4444 Normie Ln.      Louisville    James,J       1/11/86     Cape Cod    120,000.00    2400     5      2
3498 Bold Rd.        Louisville    Taft,H        1/15/86     Colonial    275,000.00    3800     5      4
#82 Rudd Rd.         Louisville    Lum,I         1/16/86     Cape Cod     88,950.00    2800     4      2
6712 Shelby St.      Louisville    Wood,B        1/16/86     Ranch        92,500.00    2400     4      2
7235 Shiloh Dr.      E'Town        Allan,J       1/17/86     Ranch        95,000.00    2750     4      3
8989 Big D Ln.       South Fork    Adkins,G      1/18/86     Other        17,000.00    1200     2      1
1001 Spring St.      North Hill    Frier,F       1/22/86     Other        45,000.00    1700     3      2
6935 Shiloh Dr.      E'Town        Grebe,C       1/25/86     Cape Cod     81,000.00    2000     3      2
4989 Adler Way       Louisville    Dole,V        1/30/86     Cape Cod     76,500.00    2000     3      2
5678 Beech St.       Louisville    Smith,P       2/02/86     Cape Cod     65,950.00    1800     3      2
#62 Billy Bone Ct.   Louisville    Taylor,A      2/04/86     Ranch        34,500.00    1600     3      1
3323 Mt. Holly Dr.   Louisville    Grizz,D       2/10/86     Ranch        22,100.00    1200     3      1
9909 Midway Rd.      Louisville    Maier,O       2/11/86     Ranch        61,250.00    1875     3      2
435 Oxted Ln.        Louisville    O'Neal,P      2/12/86     Ranch        53,790.00    1900     3      1
22 N. Ridge Ct.      Louisville    Nunn,A        2/15/86     Colonial    200,000.00    2900     5      3
654 Nora Ln.         Louisville    Orwick,S      2/18/86     Cape Cod     40,000.00    1600     3      1
659 Ridge Rd.        Louisville    Pulley,F      2/24/86     Ranch        30,000.00    1500     3      1
14 Short Rd.         Louisville    Quire,I       3/01/86     Ranch        52,300.00    1600     3      1
Total Listings:      46
```

```
5/20/86                  Summary Report              Page    2

Address              Town          Owner         List Date   Style       Price         Sq Ft    BRs    Baths
-------              ----          -----         ---------   -----       -----         -----    ---    -----
721 Zabel Way        Louisville    Stich,L       3/02/86     Ranch        47,950.00    1500     3      1
581 Yale Dr.         Louisville    Winer,L       3/05/86     Ranch        78,000.00    2100     4      2
854 Unseld Blvd.     Louisville    Volk,H        3/07/86     Other        87,000.00    2500     3      2
#5 Ashby St.         J'Town        Wagner,H      3/10/86     Other        97,000.00    2500     4      3
1989 Eastern Pkwy.   Louisville    Klink,C       3/11/86     Ranch        26,950.00    1100     2      1
9819 Wilson Ave.     J'Town        Crane,B       3/11/86     Ranch        28,000.00    1200     2      1
956 Volar Ln.        J'Town        Lamb,M        3/13/86     Ranch        18,000.00    1200     2      1
5372 Tyson Pl.       Louisville    Goode,J       3/16/86     Ranch        35,000.00    1500     3      2
9849 Taylor Blvd.    J'Town        Dukes,J       3/17/86     Ranch        32,950.00    1750     3      1
185 Pages Ln.        J'Town        Cowan,M       3/20/86     Other        15,500.00    1000     2      1
3752 St. Dennis      J'Town        Levine,J      3/22/86     Cape Cod     67,950.00    2500     3      2
28 Seebolt Rd.       Louisville    Priest,S      3/29/86     Other        28,500.00     950     3      1
2216 Lacey St.       North Hill    Beat,A        4/01/86     Cape Cod     94,999.00    2700     4      2
6262 Kenwood Dr.     North Hill    Beck,U        4/05/86     Ranch        71,650.00    2000     3      2
9222 Meadow Pl.      South Fork    Baxter,H      4/10/86     Ranch        85,000.00    2100     3      2
6791 Lotus Ave.      South Fork    Howell,T      4/12/86     Ranch        75,000.00    2000     3      2
586 Ansa Way         Louisville    Noel,C        4/15/86     Colonial     69,500.00    2200     4      2
99 N. Central Blvd.  Louisville    Stevens,P     4/16/86     Ranch        49,000.00    2500     3      2
4233 Mix Ave.        Louisville    Martin,D      4/18/86     Cape Cod     49,500.00    1900     3      2
                                                 Total Price of Listings: 4,274,589
                                                 Average Price:              65,762.91






Total Listings:      65
```

For example, in Chapter 11, you created a report that includes a calculated field, *Price Per Sq Ft*, which computes the price per square foot of each listing in the LISTINGS table. The values in this field are computed by dividing the Price field entries for each record by the Sq Ft entries for those records, using the formula *[Price]/[Sq Ft]*.

Now suppose you want to add a summary field to this report that computes the average price per square foot for all of the records in the report. To begin, issue the **[Menu] R**eport **C**hange command, specify LISTINGS as the table with which you want to work, and select the report number under which you saved the report (if you followed the example in Chapter 11, the number **2**). Figure 12-6 shows the report spec on the screen.

Figure 12-6 A Calculated Field

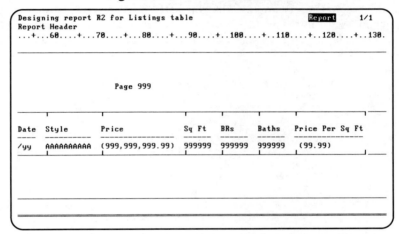

Next, issue the **[Menu] F**ield **P**lace **S**ummary **C**alculated command. After you issue the command, Paradox will display the prompt shown in Figure 12-7. When you see this prompt, you must enter an expression that tells Paradox on what to base the summary statistic you want it to compute. Since you want this summary field to compute the average of the entries in the *Price Per Sq Ft* field, you should use the same formula here that you used to define that field: **[Price]/[Sq Ft]**. When you have entered the expression, press ↵.

Figure 12-7 The Expression Prompt

```
Expression:                                                Report    2/2
Calculation from fields in a record -- e.g. [Quan] * [Unit-Price].
```

Next, Paradox will display the same Type menu shown in Figure 12-1. From this menu, you should select the type of statistic that you want the summary field to compute (Sum, Average, Count, High, or Low). Since you want this summary field to display the average price per square foot, when you see this menu, you should select **A**verage.

Next, Paradox will display the familiar PerGroup/Overall menu. As before, the choice you make from this menu determines the scope of the summary field. In this case, since you want the summary to operate on every record, you should choose Overall.

Now, Paradox will prompt you to place the summary field. You should use the cursor keys to move the cursor to the report footer, position it directly under the first character in the Price/Sq Ft field mask, and press ↵ to place the field. When Paradox prompts you to adjust the number of digits and decimal places to show, press ← to reduce the width of the field to two digits, press ↵, then press ↵ again to accept the default number of decimal places. Finally, type the literal **Average Price Per Square Foot:** in front of the field.

After you do this, your screen will look like Figure 12-8. Now, press [**Instant Report**] to print the report shown in Figure 12-9. As you can see, the summary field we placed in the report footer displays the average value of the [Price]/[Sq Ft] calculations for every record in the report.

Figure 12-8 A Calculated Summary Field

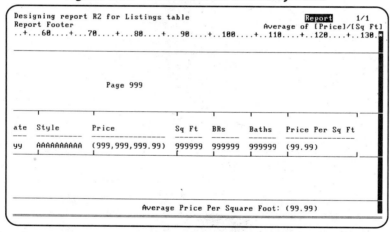

Of course, you can also create calculated summary fields that compute Sum, Count, High, and Low statistics. All you have to do is choose the appropriate option from the Summary Field Type menu while you are defining the summary field.

While you frequently will use calculated summary fields to compute statistics for the calculated fields in your reports, you can include a calculated summary field in a report that includes no calculated fields. For example, if the report spec in Figure 12-8 did not include the calculated field Price Per Sq Ft, you could still place the calculated summary field in the report spec. Even when you use a calculated summary field to summarize a calculated field, the formula that defines the summary field is independent of the formula that defines the calculated field.

Figure 12-9 The Printed Report

```
5/20/86                    Price Per Square Foot                 Page   1


Address              Town           Owner          List Date  Style      Price       Sq Ft   BRs   Baths   Price Per Sq Ft
-------              ----           -----          ---------  -----      -----       -----   ---   -----   ---------------
123 Abby Ct.         Louisville     Kones,D        11/02/85   Ranch       32,950.00   1500    3     1        21.97
426 St. James Ct.    Louisville     Jones,S        11/05/85   Ranch       19,500.00    950    2     1        20.53
766 Baird St.        Louisville     Black,G        11/08/85   Colonial   139,950.00   2600    4     3        53.83
222 Big Ben Dr.      Louisville     Roberts,D      11/08/85   Other       53,500.00   1900    3     2        28.16
666 Montana Ave.     Louisville     Saul,H         11/09/85   Cape Cod    55,000.00   1900    3     1        28.95
589 Morocco Dr.      E'Town         Smith,B        11/10/85   Cape Cod    62,500.00   1875    3     2        33.33
987 Allan Dr.        Louisville     Newsome,K      11/12/85   Cape Cod    60,000.00   1900    4     2        31.58
549 Billtown Rd.     Louisville     Bizer,B        11/14/85   Ranch       72,500.00   2000    3     2        36.25
343 Market St.       Louisville     Bivins,B       11/15/85   Ranch       42,900.00   1675    3     1        25.61
198 Main St.         J'Town         Green,L        11/15/85   Other       27,500.00    800    3     1        34.38
885 Jefferson St.    J'Town         Zith,M         11/18/85   Ranch       55,000.00   1500    3     1        36.67
913 Whitney Dr.      North Hill     Kulp,R         11/20/85   Cape Cod    99,500.00   1800    4     2        55.28
363 Dower Ct.        North Fork     Culp,A         11/21/85   Cape Cod   109,000.00   2100    4     2        51.90
620 Windsong Ct.     Louisville     Pank,E         11/22/85   Colonial   250,000.00   4000    6     4        62.50
4500 Hempstead Dr.   Louisville     Pape,C         12/04/85   Colonial   150,000.00   2600    4     3        57.69
#6 Brandon Way       Louisville     Abrams,L       12/08/85   Ranch       67,000.00   2250    4     2        29.78
6610 Vermin Dr.      Louisville     Russ,J         12/10/85   Ranch       75,000.00   2100    3     2        35.71
712 Clifton Ct.      Louisville     Thomas,T       12/10/85   Ranch       30,000.00   1500    3     1        20.00
5432 Miller Rd.      Louisville     Young,R        12/15/85   Other       17,500.00    800    2     1        21.88
#12 Circle Ct.       Louisville     White,Y        12/19/85   Other       10,000.00    800    2     1        12.50
1222 Dee Rd.         South Fork     Smith,P        12/19/85   Ranch       22,950.00    950    3     1        24.16
222 Earl Ave.        J'Town         Wray,A         12/22/85   Ranch       51,000.00   1200    3     1        42.50
9827 Rowan St.       J'Town         Coad,B         12/27/85   Ranch       47,950.00   1100    3     1        43.59
3355 Bank St.        Louisville     Cobb,D          1/03/86   Ranch       37,500.00   1500    3     1        25.00
77 Portland Ave.     North Hill     Coe,A           1/05/86   Ranch       20,000.00   1500    3     1        13.33
99 Cardinal Hill Rd. North Hill     Brand,B         1/05/86   Cape Cod    70,000.00   2000    3     2        35.00
#10 Old Mill Rd.     Louisville     Stern,M         1/07/86   Ranch       75,000.00   2150    3     2        34.88
5532 Mud Creek Dr.   Louisville     Hall,W          1/10/86   Ranch       12,000.00    950    2     1        12.63
4444 Norme Ln.       Louisville     James,J         1/11/86   Cape Cod   120,000.00   2400    5     3        50.00
3498 Bold Rd.        Louisville     Taft,H          1/15/86   Colonial   275,000.00   3800    5     4        72.37
#82 Rudd Rd.         Louisville     Lum,I           1/16/86   Cape Cod    88,950.00   2800    4     2        31.77
6712 Shelby St.      Louisville     Wood,B          1/16/86   Ranch       92,500.00   2400    4     2        38.54
7235 Shiloh Dr.      E'Town         Allan,J         1/17/86   Ranch       95,000.00   2750    4     3        34.55
8989 Big D Ln.       South Fork     Adkins,G        1/18/86   Ranch       17,000.00   1200    2     1        14.17
1001 Spring St.      North Hill     Frier,F         1/22/86   Other       45,000.00   1700    3     2        26.47
6935 Shiloh Dr.      E'Town         Grebe,C         1/25/86   Cape Cod    81,000.00   2000    3     2        40.50
4989 Adler Way       Louisville     Dole,V          1/30/86   Cape Cod    76,500.00   2000    3     2        38.25
5678 Beech St.       Louisville     Smith,P         2/02/86   Cape Cod    65,950.00   1800    3     2        36.64
#62 Billy Bone Ct.   Louisville     Taylor,A        2/04/86   Ranch       34,500.00   1600    3     1        21.56
3323 Mt. Holly Dr.   Louisville     Grizz,D         2/10/86   Ranch       22,100.00   1200    3     1        18.42
9909 Midway Rd.      Louisville     Maier,O         2/11/86   Ranch       61,250.00   1875    3     2        32.67
435 Oxted Ln.        Louisville     O'Neal,P        2/12/86   Ranch       53,790.00   1900    3     1        28.31
22 N. Ridge Ct.      Louisville     Nunn,A          2/15/86   Colonial   200,000.00   2900    5     3        68.97
654 Nora Ln.         Louisville     Orwick,S        2/18/86   Cape Cod    40,000.00   1600    3     1        25.00
659 Ridge Rd.        Louisville     Pulley,F        2/24/86   Ranch       30,000.00   1500    3     1        20.00
14 Short Rd.         Louisville     Ouire,I         3/01/86   Ranch       52,300.00   1600    3     1        32.69
```

```
5/20/86                    Price Per Square Foot                 Page   2


Address              Town           Owner          List Date  Style      Price       Sq Ft   BRs   Baths   Price Per Sq Ft
-------              ----           -----          ---------  -----      -----       -----   ---   -----   ---------------
721 Zabel Way        Louisville     Stich,L         3/02/86   Ranch       47,950.00   1500    3     1        31.97
581 Yale Dr.         Louisville     Winer,L         3/05/86   Ranch       78,000.00   2100    4     2        37.14
854 Unseld Blvd.     Louisville     Volk,H          3/07/86   Other       87,000.00   2500    3     2        34.80
#5 Ashby St.         J'Town         Wagner,H        3/10/86   Other       97,000.00   2500    4     3        38.80
1989 Eastern Pkwy.   Louisville     Klink,C         3/11/86   Ranch       26,950.00   1100    2     1        24.50
9819 Wilson Ave.     J'Town         Crane,B         3/11/86   Ranch       28,000.00   1200    3     2        23.33
956 Volar Ln.        J'Town         Lamb,M          3/13/86   Ranch       18,000.00   1200    2     1        15.00
5372 Tyson Pl.       Louisville     Goode,J         3/16/86   Ranch       35,000.00   1500    3     2        23.33
9849 Taylor Blvd.    J'Town         Dukes,J         3/17/86   Ranch       32,950.00   1750    3     2        18.83
185 Pages Ln.        J'Town         Cowan,M         3/20/86   Other       15,500.00   1000    2     1        15.50
3752 St. Dennis      J'Town         Levine,J        3/22/86   Cape Cod    67,950.00   2500    3     2        27.18
28 Seebolt Rd.       Louisville     Priest,S        3/29/86   Other       28,500.00    950    3     1        30.00
2216 Lacey St.       North Hill     Beat,A          4/01/86   Cape Cod    94,999.00   2700    4     3        35.18
6262 Kenwood Dr.     North Hill     Beck,U          4/05/86   Ranch       71,650.00   2000    3     2        35.83
9222 Meadow Pl.      South Fork     Baxter,H        4/10/86   Ranch       85,000.00   2100    3     2        40.48
6791 Lotus Ave.      South Fork     Howell,T        4/12/86   Colonial    75,600.00   2000    3     2        37.80
586 Ansa Way         Louisville     Noel,C          4/15/86   Colonial    69,500.00   2200    4     2        31.59
99 N. Central Blvd.  Louisville     Stevens,P       4/16/86   Ranch       49,000.00   2500    3     2        19.60
4233 Mix Ave.        Louisville     Martin,D        4/18/86   Cape Cod    49,500.00   1900    3     2        26.05
                                                                                     Average Price Per Square Foot:  32.42
```

Grouping Your Data

The Group command on the Report menu allows you to group the information in your reports. Grouping is a quick and easy way to organize the records in your table for reporting purposes. When you group a report on a field, Paradox will sort the records in the report on that field, thereby grouping together all records with a common entry in the grouping field. Once you have grouped a report, you can compute summary statistics based on the entries in each group. While you can group either tabular or free-form reports, the Group command is much more commonly used with tabular reports.

When you issue the [Menu] Group command while you are designing or changing a report specification, Paradox will display the menu shown in Figure 12-10. As you can see, this menu has five commands: Insert, which allows you to insert groups in the report; Delete, which allows you to delete a group; Headings, which allows you to specify when group headings will be printed; SortDirection, which allows you to select ascending or descending sort order for a group; and Regroup, which lets you change a grouping after it has been placed in the report. We will discuss each of these commands in the sections that follow.

Figure 12-10   The Group Menu

```
Insert  Delete  Headings  SortDirection  Regroup           Report    1/2
Insert a new group based on a field, range, or number of records.
```

Inserting Groups

To place a group in a report specification, you choose the Insert command from the Group menu. The next menu, which is shown in Figure 12-11, displays the types of groups you can insert. The Field command lets you insert a group based on a regular field. The Range command lets you insert a group based on a range of values. The NumberRecords command lets you create groups that contain a specific number of records. We'll cover each of these options in this part of the chapter.

Figure 12-11   Group Types

Field Groups

Field groups allow you to sort and group the records in your reports according to the entries in a particular field. When you group a report on a field, Paradox will sort the records in the report so that the entries in the grouping field are in order, and will group together all records with the same entry in the grouping field.

Grouping on an Alphanumeric Field

For example, suppose you want to create a report for the LISTINGS table that is grouped according to the entries in the Style field. To create this report, first issue the **[Menu] R**eport **D**esign command, type **LISTINGS**, and press ↵. Next, select a report number (we'll use **4**), enter a report description like **Listings By Style,** and select **T**abular as the report type. Then use the **[Menu] S**etting **P**ageLayout **W**idth command to change the width of the page-widths to **132** characters, and then the **[Menu] S**etting **P**ageLayout **D**elete command to delete the second page-width.

When the new report specification screen comes into view, issue the **[Menu] G**roup **I**nsert command. Since you want to group the report on the entries in a field, when you see the Group menu, choose the **F**ield option. Next, Paradox will display a list of the regular fields of the LISTINGS table and prompt you to select the one on which you want to group the report. When you see this list, select the **S**tyle field.

Next, Paradox will prompt you to place the group in the report. When you insert a group into a report spec, you are actually adding a new band–a group band–to the spec. You can only place group bands in two places: within the page band or within another group band. Since there are no other groups in the report you are creating, you will want to place the new group in the page band. To do this, move the cursor to anywhere in the page band header or footer, and press ↵. Your screen should now look like Figure 12-12.

Figure 12-12   Inserting a Group

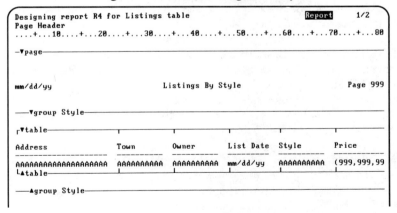

If you look at Figure 12-12, you see that the report spec now has a new band, *group Style*, which surrounds the table band. Notice the blank rows at the top and bottom of the new band. These blank rows are the header and footer for the new group band *group Style*. As in this case, when you first create a new group band, the group header and group footer will be single blank lines. Later in this chapter, we will show you how to enter literals, regular fields, and summary fields into group headers and footers.

If you try to place a group anywhere other than within the page band or within another group band, the error message *Cursor must be within the page band or a group band to insert a new group* will appear at the bottom of the screen. If you see this message, move the cursor to the page band and press ↵ again.

To see how the addition of the group affects the printed report, press [**Instant Report**]. The printed report is shown in Figure 12-13.

If you study this report, you'll see that the records in the report have been sorted so that the Style field entries are in ascending order: Cape Cod first, Colonial second, Other third, and Ranch fourth. In addition, notice that Paradox has grouped the report so that all of the records with the same Style field entry are clustered together, and has separated the groups with two blank lines. As you might have guessed, these blank lines are the empty group header and group footer. If you don't want the groups in your report to be separated in this way, just use the [Report Delete Line] key ([Ctrl]-[Y]) to delete the blank header and footer lines from the report spec.

Grouping on Numeric Fields

As you might expect, you can also group reports on numeric (number, short number, and dollar) fields. For example, suppose you want to create a new report for the LISTINGS table which is grouped on the BRs field. To create this report, first issue the [**Menu**] **R**eport **D**esign command, type **LISTINGS**, and press ↵. Next, select a report number (we'll use **5**), enter a report description like **Listings By Number Of Bedrooms**, and select **T**abular. Then use the [**Menu**] **S**etting **P**age**L**ayout **W**idth command to change the width of the page-widths to **132** characters, and then the [**Menu**] **S**etting **P**age**L**ayout **D**elete command to delete the second page-width.

When the new report specification screen comes into view, issue the [**Menu**] **G**roups **I**nsert command and choose the **F**ield option. Next, Paradox will display the regular fields of the LISTINGS table and prompt you to select the one on which you want to group the report. When you see this list, select the **BR**s field. Now Paradox will prompt you to place the group in the report. To place this group, move the cursor to anywhere in the page header and press ↵. Your screen should look like Figure 12-14 on page 396.

Now, press [**Instant Report**]. Figure 12-15 on page 397 shows the first page of the report. As you can see, the records in this report have been sorted so that those records with the smallest BRs field entries (2) are at the beginning of the report and those with the largest BRs field entries are at the end. In addition, Paradox has grouped the report so that all of the records with the same BRs field entry are clustered together and has separated the groups with two blank lines.

Other Reporting Topics   395

Figure 12-13   The Printed Report

```
5/17/86                 Listings By Style              Page   1


Address              Town          Owner         List Date   Style       Price         Sq Ft   BRs   Baths
-------              ----          -----         ---------   -----       -----         -----   ---   -----

#82 Rudd Rd.         Louisville    Lum,I          1/16/86    Cape Cod     88,950.00    2800     4     2
2216 Lacey St.       North Hill    Beat,A         4/01/86    Cape Cod     94,999.00    2700     4     3
363 Dower Ct.        North Fork    Culp,A        11/21/85    Cape Cod    109,000.00    2100     4     2
3752 St. Dennis      J'Town        Levine,J       3/22/86    Cape Cod     67,950.00    2500     3     2
4233 Mix Ave.        Louisville    Martin,D       4/18/86    Cape Cod     49,500.00    1900     3     2
4444 Normie Ln.      Louisville    James,J        1/11/86    Cape Cod    120,000.00    2400     5     3
4989 Adler Way       Louisville    Dole,V         1/30/86    Cape Cod     76,500.00    2000     3     2
5678 Beech St.       Louisville    Smith,P        2/02/86    Cape Cod     65,950.00    1800     3     2
589 Morocco Dr.      E'Town        Smith,B       11/16/85    Cape Cod     62,500.00    1875     3     2
654 Nora Ln.         Louisville    Orwick,S       2/18/86    Cape Cod     40,000.00    1600     3     1
666 Montana Ave.     Louisville    Saul,H        11/09/85    Cape Cod     55,000.00    1900     3     1
6935 Shiloh Dr.      E'Town        Grebe,C        1/25/86    Cape Cod     81,000.00    2000     3     2
913 Whitney Dr.      North Hill    Kulp,R        11/20/85    Cape Cod     99,500.00    1800     4     2
987 Allan Dr.        Louisville    Newsome,K     11/12/85    Cape Cod     60,000.00    1900     4     2
99 Cardinal Hill Rd. North Hill    Brand,B        1/05/86    Cape Cod     70,000.00    2000     3     2

22 N. Ridge Ct.      Louisville    Nunn,A         2/15/86    Colonial    200,000.00    2900     5     3
3498 Bold Rd.        Louisville    Taft,H         1/15/86    Colonial    275,000.00    3800     5     4
4500 Hempstead Dr.   Louisville    Pape,C        12/04/85    Colonial    150,000.00    2600     4     3
586 Ansa Way         Louisville    Noel,C         4/15/86    Colonial     69,500.00    2200     4     2
620 Windsong Ct.     Louisville    Pank,E        11/22/85    Colonial    250,000.00    4000     6     4
766 Baird St.        Louisville    Black,G       11/08/85    Colonial    139,950.00    2600     4     3

#12 Circle Ct.       Louisville    White,Y       12/19/86    Other        10,000.00     800     2     1
#5 Ashby St.         J'Town        Wagner,H       3/10/86    Other        97,000.00    2500     4     3
1001 Spring St.      North Hill    Frier,F        1/22/86    Other        45,000.00    1700     3     2
185 Pages Ln.        J'Town        Cowan,M        3/20/86    Other        15,500.00    1000     2     1
198 Main St.         J'Town        Green,L       11/15/85    Other        27,500.00     800     3     1
222 Big Ben Dr.      Louisville    Roberts,D     11/08/85    Other        53,500.00    1900     3     2
28 Seebolt Rd.       Louisville    Priest,S       3/29/86    Other        28,500.00     950     3     1
5432 Miller Rd.      Louisville    Young,R       12/15/85    Other        17,500.00     800     2     1
854 Unseld Blvd.     Louisville    Volk,H         3/07/86    Other        87,000.00    2500     3     2

#10 Old Mill Rd.     Louisville    Stern,M        1/07/86    Ranch        75,000.00    2150     3     2
#6 Brandon Way       Louisville    Abrams,L      12/08/85    Ranch        67,000.00    2250     3     2
#62 Billy Bone Ct.   Louisville    Taylor,A       2/04/86    Ranch        34,500.00    1600     3     1
1222 Dee Rd.         South Fork    Smith,P       12/19/85    Ranch        22,950.00     950     3     1
123 Abby Ct.         Louisville    Kones,D       11/02/85    Ranch        32,950.00    1500     3     1
14 Short Rd.         Louisville    Quire,I        3/01/86    Ranch        52,300.00    1600     3     1
1989 Eastern Pkwy.   Louisville    Klink,L        3/11/86    Ranch        26,950.00    1100     2     1
222 Earl Ave.        J'Town        Wray,A        12/22/85    Ranch        51,000.00    1200     3     1
3323 Mt. Holly Dr.   Louisville    Grizz,D        2/10/86    Ranch        22,100.00    1200     3     1
```

```
5/17/86                 Listings By Style              Page   2


Address              Town          Owner         List Date   Style       Price         Sq Ft   BRs   Baths
-------              ----          -----         ---------   -----       -----         -----   ---   -----

3355 Bank St.        J'Town        Cobb,D         1/03/86    Ranch        37,500.00    1500     3     1
343 Market St.       Louisville    Bivins,D      11/15/85    Ranch        42,900.00    1675     3     1
426 St. James Ct.    Louisville    Jones,B       11/05/85    Ranch        19,500.00     950     2     1
435 Oxted Ln.        Louisville    O'Neal,P       2/12/86    Ranch        53,790.00    1900     3     1
5372 Tyson Pl.       Louisville    Goode,J        3/16/86    Ranch        35,000.00    1500     3     2
549 Billtown Rd.     Louisville    Bizer,B       11/14/85    Ranch        72,500.00    2000     3     2
5532 Mud Creek Dr.   Louisville    Hall,W         1/10/86    Ranch        12,000.00     950     2     1
581 Yale Dr.         Louisville    Winer,L        3/05/86    Ranch        44,000.00    2100     4     2
6262 Kenwood Dr.     North Hill    Beck,U         4/05/86    Ranch        71,650.00    2000     3     2
659 Ridge Rd.        Louisville    Pulley,F       2/24/86    Ranch        30,000.00    1500     3     1
6610 Vermin Dr.      Louisville    Russ,J        12/10/85    Ranch        75,000.00    2100     3     2
6712 Shelby St.      Louisville    Wood,B         1/16/86    Ranch        92,500.00    2400     4     2
6791 Lotus Ave.      South Fork    Howell,T       4/12/86    Ranch        75,600.00    2000     3     2
712 Clifton Ct.      Louisville    Thomas,T      12/10/85    Ranch        30,000.00    1500     3     1
721 Zabel Way        Louisville    Stich,L        3/02/86    Ranch        47,950.00    1500     3     1
7235 Shiloh Dr.      E'Town        Allan,J        1/17/86    Ranch        95,000.00    2750     4     3
77 Portland Ave.     North Hill    Coe,A          1/05/86    Ranch        20,000.00    1500     3     1
885 Jefferson St.    J'Town        Zith,M        11/18/85    Ranch        55,000.00    1500     3     1
8989 Big D Ln.       South Fork    Adkins,G       1/18/86    Ranch        17,000.00    1200     2     1
9222 Meadow Pl.      South Fork    Baxter,H       4/10/86    Ranch        85,000.00    2100     3     2
956 Volar Ln.        J'Town        Lamb,M         3/13/86    Ranch        18,000.00    1200     2     1
9819 Wilson Ave.     Louisville    Crane,B        3/11/86    Ranch        28,000.00    1200     3     1
9827 Rowan St.       J'Town        Coad,B        12/27/85    Ranch        47,950.00    1100     3     1
9849 Taylor Blvd.    J'Town        Dukes,J        3/17/86    Ranch        32,950.00    1750     3     1
99 N. Central Blvd.  Louisville    Stevens,P      4/16/86    Ranch        49,000.00    2500     3     2
9909 Midway Rd.      Louisville    Maier,O        2/11/86    Ranch        61,250.00    1875     3     2
```

Figure 12-14   Inserting the Group

```
Designing report R5 for Listings table              Report     1/1
Page Header
....+...10....+...20....+...30....+...40....+...50....+...60....+...70....+...80
 ─▼page─────────────────────────────────────────────────────────────────────

 mm/dd/yy                 Listings By Number Of Bedrooms           Page 999

  ───▼group BRs──────────────────────────────────────────────────────────
    ┌▼table─────────────┬──────────┬──────────┬──────────┬──────────┐
    Address              Town       Owner      List Date  Style      Price
    ───────────────────  ──────────  ──────────  ──────────  ──────────  ──────────
    AAAAAAAAAAAAAAAAAA   AAAAAAAA   AAAAAAAA   mm/dd/yy   AAAAAAAA   (999,999,99
    └▲table─────────────┴──────────┴──────────┴──────────┴──────────┘
  ───▲group BRs──────────────────────────────────────────────────────────
```

Grouping on a Date Field

As you might expect, Paradox also allows you to group reports on date fields. All you have to do is issue the **[Menu] G**roup **I**nsert **F**ield command, select a date field, and place the group band in the page band header. When you print the report, Paradox will sort the report so that the records with the earliest date field entries are at the beginning of the report and those with the latest date field entries are at the bottom.

Range Groups

You can also group your reports according to ranges. When you group a report on ranges, Paradox will group together all the records in the report with grouping field entries that fall within the range you define. Exactly how you can group ranges of records, however, depends on the type of the field you select as the grouping field.

Date Fields

When you issue the **[Menu] G**roup **I**nsert **R**ange command and select **D**ate as the type of field to group, Paradox will display the menu shown in Figure 12-16.

Figure 12-16   The Range Menu for Date Fields

If you choose the Day option from this menu, Paradox will group together all of the records in the report that have the same day value in the selected date field. If you choose Week, Paradox will group records together that occur in the same week. Specifying a Month range will group together dates that occur in the same month. Selecting Year will group together records that occur in the same year.

Other Reporting Topics   397

Figure 12-15   The Printed Report

```
5/19/86             Listings By Number Of Bedrooms         Page   1


Address              Town         Owner        List Date  Style       Price         Sq Ft   BRs   Baths
-------------------  -----------  -----------  ---------  ---------   -----------   -----   ---   -----

#12 Circle Ct.       Louisville   White,Y      12/19/85   Other        10,000.00     800     2      1
185 Pages Ln.        J'Town       Cowan,M       3/20/86   Other        15,500.00    1000     2      1
1989 Eastern Pkwy.   Louisville   Klink,C       3/11/86   Ranch        26,950.00    1100     2      1
426 St. James Ct.    Louisville   Jones,S      11/05/85   Ranch        19,500.00     950     2      1
5432 Miller Rd.      Louisville   Young,R      12/15/85   Other        17,500.00     800     2      1
5532 Mud Creek Dr.   Louisville   Hall,W        1/10/86   Ranch        12,000.00     950     2      1
8989 Big D Ln.       South Fork   Adkins,B      1/18/86   Ranch        17,000.00    1200     2      1
956 Volar Ln.        J'Town       Lamb,M        3/13/86   Ranch        18,000.00    1200     2      1

#10 Old Mill Rd.     Louisville   Stern,M       1/07/86   Ranch        75,000.00    2150     3      2
#62 Billy Bone Ct.   Louisville   Taylor,A      2/04/86   Ranch        34,500.00    1600     3      1
1001 Spring St.      North Hill   Frier,F       1/22/86   Other        45,000.00    1700     3      2
1222 Dee Rd.         South Fork   Smith,P      12/19/85   Ranch        22,950.00     950     3      1
123 Abby Ct.         Louisville   Kones,D      11/02/85   Ranch        32,950.00    1500     3      1
14 Short Rd.         Louisville   Quire,I       3/01/86   Ranch        52,300.00    1600     3      1
198 Main St.         J'Town       Green,L      11/15/85   Other        27,500.00     800     3      1
222 Big Ben Dr.      Louisville   Roberts,D    11/08/85   Other        53,500.00    1900     3      2
222 Earl Ave.        J'Town       Wray,A       12/22/85   Ranch        51,000.00    1200     3      1
28 Seebolt Rd.       Louisville   Priest,S      3/29/86   Other        28,500.00     950     3      1
3323 Mt. Holly Dr.   Louisville   Grizz,D       2/10/86   Ranch        22,100.00    1200     3      1
3355 Bank St.        J'Town       Cobb,D        1/03/86   Ranch        37,500.00    1500     3      1
345 Market St.       Louisville   Bivins,D     11/15/85   Ranch        42,950.00    1675     3      1
3752 St. Dennis      J'Town       Levine,J      3/22/86   Cape Cod     67,950.00    2500     3      2
4233 Mix Ave.        Louisville   Martin,D      4/18/86   Cape Cod     49,500.00    1900     3      2
435 Oxted Ln.        Louisville   O'Neal,P      2/12/86   Ranch        53,790.00    1900     3      1
4989 Adler Way       Louisville   Dole,V        1/30/86   Cape Cod     76,500.00    2000     3      2
5372 Tyson Pl.       Louisville   Goode,J       3/16/86   Ranch        35,000.00    1500     3      2
549 Billtown Rd.     Louisville   Bizer,B      11/14/85   Ranch        72,500.00    2000     3      2
567B Beech St.       Louisville   Smith,P       2/02/86   Cape Cod     65,950.00    1800     3      2
589 Morocco Dr.      E'Town       Smith,B      11/10/85   Cape Cod     62,500.00    1875     3      2
6262 Kenwood Dr.     North Hill   Beck,U        4/05/86   Ranch        71,650.00    2000     3      2
654 Nora Ln.         Louisville   Orwick,S      2/18/86   Cape Cod     40,000.00    1600     3      1
659 Ridge Rd.        Louisville   Pulley,F      2/24/86   Ranch        30,000.00    1500     3      1
6610 Vermin Dr.      Louisville   Russ,J       12/10/85   Ranch        75,000.00    2100     3      2
666 Montana Ave.     Louisville   Saul,H       11/09/85   Cape Cod     55,000.00    1900     3      1
6791 Lotus Ave.      South Fork   Howell,T      4/12/86   Ranch        75,600.00    2000     3      2
6935 Shiloh Dr.      E'Town       Grebe,C       1/25/86   Cape Cod     81,000.00    2000     3      2
712 Clifton Ct.      Louisville   Thomas,T     12/10/85   Ranch        30,000.00    1500     3      1
721 Zabel Way        Louisville   Stich,L       3/02/86   Ranch        47,950.00    1500     3      1
77 Portland Ave.     North Hill   Coe,A         1/05/86   Ranch        20,000.00    1500     3      1
854 Unseld Blvd.     Louisville   Volk,H        3/07/86   Ranch        87,000.00    2500     3      2
885 Jefferson St.    J'Town       Zith,M       11/18/85   Ranch        55,000.00    1500     3      1
9222 Meadow Pl.      South Fork   Baxter,H      4/10/86   Ranch        85,000.00    2100     3      2
9819 Wilson Ave.     J'Town       Crane,B       3/11/86   Ranch        28,000.00    1200     3      1
```

```
5/19/86             Listings By Number Of Bedrooms         Page   2


Address              Town         Owner        List Date  Style       Price         Sq Ft   BRs   Baths
-------------------  -----------  -----------  ---------  ---------   -----------   -----   ---   -----

9827 Rowan St.       J'Town       Coad,B       12/27/85   Ranch        47,950.00    1100     3      1
9849 Taylor Blvd.    J'Town       Dukes,J       3/17/86   Ranch        32,950.00    1750     3      1
99 Cardinal Hill Rd. North Hill   Brand,B       1/05/86   Cape Cod     70,000.00    2000     3      2
99 N. Central Blvd.  Louisville   Stevens,P     4/16/86   Ranch        49,000.00    2500     3      2
9909 Midway Rd.      Louisville   Maier,O       2/11/86   Ranch        61,250.00    1875     3      2

#5 Ashby St.         J'Town       Wagner,H      3/10/86   Other        97,000.00    2500     4      3
#6 Brandon Way       Louisville   Abrams,L     12/08/85   Ranch        67,000.00    2250     4      2
#82 Rudd Rd.         Louisville   Lum,I         1/16/86   Cape Cod     88,950.00    2800     4      3
2216 Lacey St.       North Hill   Beat,A        4/01/86   Cape Cod     94,999.00    2700     4      3
363 Dower Ct.        North Fork   Culp,A       11/21/85   Cape Cod    109,000.00    2100     4      2
4500 Hempstead Dr.   Louisville   Pape,C       12/04/85   Colonial    150,000.00    2600     4      3
581 Yale Dr.         Louisville   Winer,L       3/05/86   Ranch        78,000.00    2100     4      2
586 Ansa Way         Louisville   Noel,C        4/15/86   Colonial     69,500.00    2200     4      2
6712 Shelby St.      Louisville   Wood,B        1/16/86   Ranch        92,500.00    2400     4      2
7235 Shiloh Dr.      E'Town       Allan,J       1/17/86   Ranch        95,000.00    2750     4      3
766 Baird St.        Louisville   Black,G      11/08/85   Colonial    139,950.00    2600     4      3
913 Whitney Dr.      North Hill   Kulp,R       11/20/85   Cape Cod     99,500.00    1800     4      2
987 Allan Dr.        Louisville   Newsome,K    11/12/85   Cape Cod     60,000.00    1900     4      2

22 N. Ridge Ct.      Louisville   Nunn,A        2/15/86   Colonial    200,000.00    2900     5      3
3498 Bold Rd.        Louisville   Taft,H        1/15/86   Colonial    275,000.00    3800     5      4
4444 Normie Ln.      Louisville   James,J       1/11/86   Cape Cod    120,000.00    2400     5      3

620 Windsong Ct.     Louisville   Fank,E       11/22/85   Colonial    250,000.00    4000     6      4
```

For example, suppose you want to design a report for the LISTINGS table that is grouped by month on the List Date field. To do this, issue the [Menu] Report Design command, type **LISTINGS**, select report number **9**, type the description **Listings By Month**, and select Tabular as the report type. When the report specification screen appears, issue the [Menu] Group Insert Range command, and select List Date. Then use the [Menu] Setting PageLayout Width command to change the width of the page-widths to **132** characters, and then the [Menu] Setting PageLayout Delete command to delete the second page-width.

When you see the menu in Figure 12-16, choose **Month**. After you do this, Paradox will prompt you to place the group in the report. As before, you should move the cursor to the page header band and press ↵. Figure 12-17 shows the report specification with the new *group List Date,range=Month* band in place. Now, press [**Instant Report**]. Figure 12-18 shows the first page of the resulting report. Notice that the report is arranged so that all of the records with date field entries in the same month are grouped together.

Figure 12-17 The Completed Screen

```
Designing report R9 for Listings table          Report    1/1
Page Header
....+...10....+...20....+...30....+...40....+...50....+...60....+...70....+...80
 ─▼page─────────────────────────────────────────────────────────────────────────


 mm/dd/yy                       Listings By Month                  Page 999

  ────▼group List Date,range=Month───────────────────────────────────────────
 ┌─▼table─────────────────────────────────────────────────────────────────┐

 Address              Town        Owner       List Date  Style      Price
 ────────────────     ─────────   ─────────   ─────────  ─────────  ─────────
 AAAAAAAAAAAAAAAAAA   AAAAAAAAA   AAAAAAAAA   mm/dd/yy   AAAAAAAAA  (999,999,99
 └─▲table─────────────┴───────────┴───────────┴──────────┴──────────┴────────┘
  ────▲group List Date,range=Month───────────────────────────────────────────
```

Numeric Fields

You can also group a report based on ranges of entries in numeric fields. When you ask Paradox to create a range group on a number, dollar, or short number field, it will display the prompt shown in Figure 12-19. This prompt allows you to specify the interval (range) that Paradox should use to group your report. Paradox uses the interval you specify to create a series of "bins" into which the records in the report are grouped. For example, if you specify an interval of 100, Paradox will place all records with an entry of 0 to 100 in one group, the records with values from 101 to 200 in a second group, and so on. If the field contains negative values, they will be similarly grouped using the interval you specify.

Figure 12-18 The Printed Report

```
5/17/86                    Listings By Month              Page   1


Address          Town         Owner        List Date  Style     Price         Sq Ft    BRs     Baths
-------          ----         -----        ---------  -----     -----         -----    ---     -----
123 Abby Ct.     Louisville   Kones,D      11/02/85   Ranch      32,950.00    1500     3       1
426 St. James Ct.Louisville   Jones,S      11/05/85   Ranch      19,500.00     950     2       1
222 Big Ben Dr.  Louisville   Roberts,D    11/08/85   Other      53,500.00    1900     3       2
766 Baird St.    Louisville   Black,G      11/08/85   Colonial  139,950.00    2600     4       3
666 Montana Ave. Louisville   Saul,H       11/09/85   Cape Cod   55,000.00    1900     3       1
589 Morocco Dr.  E'Town       Smith,B      11/10/85   Cape Cod   62,500.00    1875     3       2
987 Allan Dr.    Louisville   Newsome,K    11/12/85   Cape Cod   60,000.00    1900     4       2
549 Billtown Rd. Louisville   Bizer,B      11/14/85   Ranch      72,500.00    2000     3       2
198 Main St.     J'Town       Green,L      11/15/85   Other      27,500.00     800     3       1
343 Market St.   Louisville   Bivins,D     11/15/85   Ranch      42,900.00    1675     3       1
885 Jefferson St.J'Town       Zith,M       11/18/85   Ranch      55,000.00    1500     3       1
913 Whitney Dr.  North Hill   Kulp,R       11/20/85   Cape Cod   99,500.00    1800     4       2
363 Dower Ct.    North Fork   Culp,A       11/21/85   Cape Cod  109,000.00    2100     4       2
620 Windsong Ct. Louisville   Pank,E       11/22/85   Colonial  250,000.00    4000     6       4

4500 Hempstead Dr.Louisville  Pape,C       12/04/85   Colonial  150,000.00    2600     4       3
#6 Brandon Way   Louisville   Abrams,L     12/08/85   Ranch      67,000.00    2250     4       2
6610 Vermin Dr.  Louisville   Russ,J       12/10/85   Ranch      75,000.00    2100     3       2
712 Clifton Ct.  Louisville   Thomas,T     12/10/85   Ranch      30,000.00    1500     3       1
5432 Miller Rd.  Louisville   Young,R      12/15/85   Other      17,500.00     800     2       1
#12 Circle Ct.   Louisville   White,Y      12/19/85   Other      10,000.00     800     2       1
1222 Dee Rd.     South Fork   Smith,P      12/19/85   Ranch      22,950.00     950     3       1
222 Earl Ave.    J'Town       Wray,A       12/22/85   Ranch      51,000.00    1200     3       1
9827 Rowan St.   J'Town       Coad,B       12/27/85   Ranch      47,950.00    1100     3       1

3355 Bank St.    J'Town       Cobb,D       1/03/86    Ranch      37,500.00    1500     3       1
77 Portland Ave. North Hill   Coe,A        1/05/86    Ranch      20,000.00    1500     3       1
99 Cardinal Hill Rd.North Hill Brand,B     1/05/86    Cape Cod   70,000.00    2000     3       2
#10 Old Mill Rd. Louisville   Stern,M      1/07/86    Ranch      75,000.00    2150     3       2
5532 Mud Creek Dr.Louisville  Hall,W       1/10/86    Ranch      12,000.00     950     2       1
4444 Normie Ln.  Louisville   James,J      1/11/86    Cape Cod  120,000.00    2400     5       3
3498 Bold Rd.    Louisville   Taft,H       1/15/86    Colonial  275,000.00    3800     5       4
#82 Rudd Rd.     Louisville   Lum,I        1/16/86    Cape Cod   88,950.00    2800     4       2
6712 Shelby St.  Louisville   Wood,B       1/16/86    Ranch      92,500.00    2400     4       2
7235 Shiloh Dr.  E'Town       Allan,J      1/17/86    Ranch      95,000.00    2750     4       3
8989 Big D Ln.   South Fork   Adkins,G     1/18/86    Ranch      17,000.00    1200     2       1
1001 Spring St.  North Hill   Frier,F      1/22/86    Other      45,000.00    1700     3       2
6935 Shiloh St.  E'Town       Grebe,C      1/25/86    Cape Cod   81,000.00    2000     3       2
4989 Adler Way   Louisville   Dole,V       1/30/86    Cape Cod   76,500.00    2000     4       2

5678 Beech St.   Louisville   Smith,P      2/02/86    Cape Cod   65,950.00    1800     3       2
#62 Billy Bone Ct.Louisville  Taylor,A     2/04/86    Ranch      34,500.00    1600     3       1
```

Figure 12-19 The Range Prompt

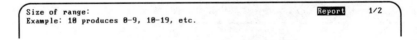

For example, suppose you want to design a report for the LISTINGS table that is grouped by ranges on the Price field. (You want to group the records with Price field entries from 0 to 50,000 together, the records with Price entries between 50,001 and 100,000 together, and so on.) To create this report, issue the [Menu] Report Design command, type **LISTINGS**, select a report number (we'll use **7**), type the report description **Listings By Price Range**, and select Tabular. Then use the [Menu] Setting PageLayout Width command to change the width of the page-widths to **132** characters, and the [Menu] Setting PageLayout Delete command to delete the second page-width.

When the report specification screen appears, issue the [Menu] Group Insert Range command and select Price as the field to group. Paradox then will prompt you for the size of the range. When you see this prompt, type **50000** and press ↵. When Paradox prompts you to indicate where you want to insert the group, move the cursor to the page header and press ↵. After you do this, Paradox will insert the new band *group List price, range=50000* into the report spec.

Now, press **[Instant Report]**. Figure 12-20 shows the first page of the resulting report. As you can see, Paradox has grouped the records in the report using the interval you specified. Note that the first group contains all of the records with Price field entries from 0 to 50000; the next group contains all of the records with entries from 50,001 to 100,000, and so on.

Figure 12-20   The Printed Report

```
5/17/86              Listings By Price Range           Page  1

Address            Town         Owner        List Date  Style      Price       Sq Ft   BRs   Baths
-------            ----         -----        ---------  -----      -----       -----   ---   -----

#12 Circle Ct.     Louisville   White,Y      12/19/85   Other      10,000.00    800    2     1
5532 Mud Creek Dr. Louisville   Hall,W        1/10/86   Ranch      12,000.00    950    2     1
185 Pages Ln.      J'Town       Cowan,M       3/20/86   Other      15,500.00   1000    2     1
8989 Big D Ln.     South Fork   Adkins,G      1/18/86   Ranch      17,000.00   1200    2     1
5432 Miller Rd.    Louisville   Young,R      12/15/85   Other      17,500.00    800    2     1
956 Volar Ln.      J'Town       Lamb,M        3/13/86   Ranch      18,000.00   1200    2     1
426 St. James Ct.  Louisville   Jones,S      11/05/85   Ranch      19,500.00    950    2     1
77 Portland Ave.   North Hill   Coe,A         1/05/86   Ranch      20,000.00   1500    3     1
3323 Mt. Holly Dr. Louisville   Grizz,D       2/10/86   Ranch      22,100.00   1200    3     1
1222 Dee Rd.       South Fork   Smith,P      12/19/85   Ranch      22,950.00    950    3     1
1989 Eastern Pkwy. Louisville   Klink,C       3/11/86   Ranch      26,950.00   1100    2     1
198 Main St.       J'Town       Green,L      11/15/85   Other      27,500.00    800    3     1
9819 Wilson Ave.   J'Town       Crane,B       3/11/86   Ranch      28,000.00   1200    3     1
28 Seebolt St.     Louisville   Priest,S      3/29/86   Other      28,500.00    950    3     1
659 Ridge Rd.      Louisville   Pulley,F      2/24/86   Ranch      30,000.00   1500    3     1
712 Clifton Ct.    Louisville   Thomas,T     12/10/85   Ranch      30,000.00   1500    3     1
123 Abby Ct.       Louisville   Kones,D      11/02/85   Ranch      32,950.00   1500    3     1
9849 Taylor Blvd.  J'Town       Dukes,J       3/17/86   Ranch      32,950.00   1750    3     1
#62 Billy Bone Ct. Louisville   Taylor,A      2/04/86   Ranch      34,500.00   1600    3     1
5372 Tyson Pl.     Louisville   Goode,J       3/16/86   Ranch      35,000.00   1500    3     2
3355 Bank St.      J'Town       Cobb,D        1/03/86   Ranch      37,500.00   1500    3     1
654 Nora Ln.       Louisville   Drwick,S      2/18/86   Cape Cod   40,000.00   1600    3     1
343 Market St.     Louisville   Bivins,D     11/15/85   Ranch      42,900.00   1675    3     1
1001 Spring St.    North Hill   Frier,F       1/22/86   Other      45,000.00   1700    3     2
721 Zabel Way      Louisville   Stich,L       3/02/86   Ranch      47,950.00   1500    3     1
9827 Rowan St.     J'Town       Coad,B       12/27/85   Ranch      47,950.00   1100    3     1
99 N. Central Blvd. Louisville  Stevens,P     4/16/86   Ranch      49,000.00   2500    3     2
4233 Mix Ave.      Louisville   Martin,D      4/18/86   Cape Cod   49,500.00   1900    3     2

222 Earl Ave.      J'Town       Wray,A       12/22/85   Ranch      51,000.00   1200    3     1
14 Short Rd.       J'Town       Quire,I       3/01/86   Ranch      52,500.00   1600    3     1
222 Big Ben Dr.    Louisville   Roberts,D    11/08/85   Other      53,500.00   1900    3     2
435 Oxted Ln.      Louisville   O'Neal,P      2/12/86   Ranch      53,790.00   1900    3     1
666 Montana Ave.   Louisville   Saul,H       11/09/85   Cape Cod   55,000.00   1900    3     2
885 Jefferson St.  J'Town       Zith,M       11/18/85   Ranch      55,000.00   1500    3     1
987 Allan Dr.      Louisville   Newsome,K    11/12/85   Cape Cod   60,000.00   1900    4     2
9909 Midway Rd.    Louisville   Maier,O       2/11/86   Ranch      61,250.00   1875    3     2
589 Morocco Dr.    E'Town       Smith,B      11/10/85   Cape Cod   62,500.00   1875    3     2
5678 Beech St.     Louisville   Smith,P       2/02/86   Cape Cod   65,950.00   1800    3     1
#6 Brandon Way     Louisville   Abrams,L     12/08/85   Ranch      67,000.00   2250    4     2
3752 St. Dennis    J'Town       Levine,J      3/22/86   Cape Cod   67,950.00   2500    3     2
586 Ansa Way       Louisville   Noel,C        4/15/86   Colonial   69,500.00   2200    4     2
99 Cardinal Hill Rd. North Hill Brand,B       1/05/86   Cape Cod   70,000.00   2000    3     2
6262 Kenwood Dr.   North Hill   Beck,U        4/05/86   Ranch      71,650.00   2000    3     2
```

Alphanumeric Fields

You can also group reports by ranges based on the entries in alphanumeric fields. When you issue the **[Menu] G**roup **R**ange command and select an alphanumeric field, Paradox will display the prompt shown in Figure 12-21. As you can see, this prompt allows you to define the number of characters from each entry in the grouping field that Paradox will use to group the report. If you enter a 1 in response to this prompt, Paradox will group all of the entries that begin with the same first letter. If you type 2, Paradox will group all of the entries that begin with the same two letters, and so on.

Figure 12-21   The Range Menu

```
Number of initial characters in range:                  Report    1/1
Use 1 to group by first letter, 2 to group by first two letters, etc.
```

Grouping a Specific Number of Records

You can also instruct Paradox to group a specific number of records together, regardless of the entries in the fields of those records. To create this type of group, you issue the [Menu] Group Insert NumberRecords command and specify the number of records you want Paradox to include in each group. When you group a report in this way, Paradox will not sort the report. Instead, it will simply create groups that contain the number of records you specify.

For example, suppose you want to design a report that prints the records in the LISTINGS table in groups of three. To do this, issue the [Menu] Report Design command, type **LISTINGS**, select a report number (we'll use **8**), type the description **Listings By Threes**, and select Tabular as the report type. Then use the [Menu] Setting PageLayout Width command to change the width of the page-widths to **132** characters, and the [Menu] Setting PageLayout Delete command to delete the second page-width.

When the report specification screen appears, issue the [Menu] Group Insert NumberRecords command. After you issue the command, Paradox will prompt you to enter the number of records to group. When you see this prompt, type **3** and press ↵. Next, Paradox will prompt you to place the group in the report spec. When it does, you should move the cursor to the page header and press ↵. Figure 12-22 shows the screen with the *group records=3* band in place.

Figure 12-22   The Report Specification Screen

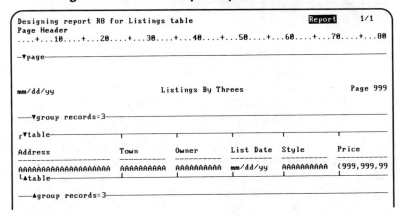

Figure 12-23 shows the first page of the report that Paradox will produce when you print this report spec. As you can see, the records in this report are separated into groups of three. Notice that the report is not sorted.

Figure 12-23 The Printed Report

```
5/17/86              Listings By Threes              Page   1

Address            Town          Owner        List Date   Style       Price          Sq Ft    BRs    Baths
-------            ----          -----        ---------   -----       -----          -----    ---    -----
123 Abby Ct.       Louisville    Kones,D      11/02/85    Ranch        32,950.00     1500      3       1
426 St. James Ct.  Louisville    Jones,S      11/05/85    Ranch        19,500.00      950      2       1
766 Baird St.      Louisville    Black,G      11/08/85    Colonial    139,950.00     2600      4       3

222 Big Ben Dr.    Louisville    Roberts,D    11/08/85    Other        53,500.00     1900      3       2
666 Montana Ave.   Louisville    Saul,H       11/09/85    Cape Cod     55,000.00     1900      3       1
589 Morocco Dr.    E'Town        Smith,B      11/10/85    Cape Cod     62,500.00     1875      3       2

987 Allan Dr.      Louisville    Newsome,K    11/12/85    Cape Cod     60,000.00     1900      4       2
549 Billtown Rd.   Louisville    Bizer,B      11/14/85    Ranch        72,500.00     2000      3       2
343 Market St.     Louisville    Bivins,D     11/15/85    Ranch        42,900.00     1675      3       1

198 Main St.       J'Town        Green,L      11/15/85    Other        27,500.00      800      3       1
885 Jefferson St.  J'Town        Zith,M       11/18/85    Ranch        55,000.00     1500      3       1
913 Whitney Dr.    North Hill    Kulp,R       11/20/85    Cape Cod     99,500.00     1800      4       2

363 Dower Ct.      North Fork    Culp,A       11/21/85    Cape Cod    109,000.00     2100      4       2
620 Windsong Ct.   Louisville    Fank,E       11/22/85    Colonial    250,000.00     4000      6       4
4500 Hempstead Dr. Louisville    Pape,C       12/04/85    Colonial    150,000.00     2600      4       3

#6 Brandon Way     Louisville    Abrams,L     12/08/85    Ranch        67,000.00     2250      4       2
6610 Vermin Dr.    Louisville    Russ,J       12/10/85    Ranch        75,000.00     2100      3       2
712 Clifton Ct.    Louisville    Thomas,T     12/10/85    Ranch        30,000.00     1500      3       1

5432 Miller Rd.    Louisville    Young,R      12/15/85    Other        17,500.00      800      2       1
#12 Circle Ct.     Louisville    White,Y      12/19/85    Other        10,000.00      800      2       1
1222 Dee Rd.       South Fork    Smith,P      12/19/85    Ranch        22,950.00      950      3       1

222 Earl Ave.      J'Town        Wray,A       12/22/85    Ranch        51,000.00     1200      3       1
9827 Rowan St.     J'Town        Coad,B       12/27/85    Ranch        47,950.00     1100      3       1
3355 Bank St.      J'Town        Cobb,D       1/03/86     Ranch        37,500.00     1500      3       1

77 Portland Ave.   North Hill    Coe,A        1/05/86     Ranch        20,000.00     1500      3       1
99 Cardinal Hill Rd. North Hill  Brand,B      1/05/86     Cape Cod     70,000.00     2000      3       2
#10 Old Mill Rd.   Louisville    Stern,M      1/07/86     Ranch        75,000.00     2150      3       2
```

Changing the Sort Order

As we have said, the default sort order for grouped reports is Ascending. If you wish, you can use the [Menu] Group SortDirection command to change the order of the sort from ascending to descending.

For example, suppose you have created the sort specification in Figure 12-14. As you can see, this spec instructs Paradox to group the report by the entries in the BRs field. Now suppose you want to change the sort order for this report from ascending to descending. To do this, issue the **[Menu] G**roup **S**ortDirection command. After you issue the command, Paradox will prompt you to position the cursor on the group you want to change. When you see this prompt, position the cursor in the *group BRs* band and press ↵. Paradox then will display a menu with two options: Ascending and Descending. To change the default setting, issue the **D**escending command. Now press **[Instant Report]**. Figure 12-24 shows the first page of the resulting report. As you can see, this report is sorted in descending, rather than ascending, order.

Group Headers and Footers

Earlier in our discussion of grouping, we pointed out that Paradox automatically creates a group header and group footer for each group you place in a report. So far, we have just left the header and footer empty as we printed grouped reports. As hinted earlier,

Figure 12-24 The Printed Report

```
5/19/86              Listings By Number Of Bedrooms        Page   1

Address              Town         Owner        List Date  Style       Price         Sq Ft  BRs   Baths
-------              ----         -----        ---------  -----       -----         -----  ---   -----

620 Windsong Ct.     Louisville   Pank,E       11/22/85   Colonial    250,000.00    4000   6     4

22 N. Ridge Ct.      Louisville   Nunn,A       2/15/86    Colonial    200,000.00    2900   5     3
3498 Bold Rd.        Louisville   Taft,H       1/15/86    Colonial    275,000.00    3800   5     4
4444 Normie Ln.      Louisville   James,J      1/11/86    Cape Cod    120,000.00    2400   5     3

#5 Ashby St.         J'Town       Wagner,H     3/10/86    Other        97,000.00    2500   4     3
#6 Brandon Way       Louisville   Abrams,L     12/08/85   Ranch        67,000.00    2250   4     2
#82 Rudd Rd.         Louisville   Lum,I        1/16/86    Cape Cod     88,950.00    2800   4     2
2216 Lacey St.       North Hill   Beat,A       4/01/86    Cape Cod     94,999.00    2700   4     3
363 Dower Ct.        North Fork   Culp,A       11/21/85   Cape Cod    109,000.00    2100   4     2
4500 Hempstead Dr.   Louisville   Pape,C       12/04/85   Colonial    150,000.00    2600   4     3
581 Yale Dr.         Louisville   Winer,L      3/05/86    Ranch        78,000.00    2100   4     2
586 Ansa Way         Louisville   Noel,C       4/15/86    Colonial     69,500.00    2200   4     2
6712 Shelby St.      Louisville   Wood,B       1/16/86    Ranch        92,500.00    2400   4     2
7235 Shiloh Dr.      E'Town       Allan,J      1/17/86    Ranch        95,000.00    2750   4     3
766 Baird St.        Louisville   Black,B      11/08/85   Colonial    139,950.00    2600   4     3
913 Whitney Dr.      North Hill   Kulp,R       11/20/85   Cape Cod     99,500.00    1800   4     2
987 Allan Dr.        Louisville   Newsome,K    11/12/85   Cape Cod     60,000.00    1900   4     2

#10 Old Mill Rd.     Louisville   Stern,M      1/07/86    Ranch        75,000.00    2150   3     2
#62 Billy Bone Ct.   Louisville   Taylor,A     2/04/86    Ranch        34,500.00    1600   3     1
1001 Spring St.      North Hill   Frier,F      1/22/86    Other        45,000.00    1700   3     2
1222 Dee Rd.         South Fork   Smith,P      12/19/85   Ranch        22,950.00     950   3     1
123 Abby Ct.         Louisville   Kones,D      11/02/85   Ranch        32,950.00    1500   3     1
14 Short Rd.         Louisville   Quire,I      3/01/86    Ranch        52,300.00    1600   3     2
198 Main St.         J'Town       Green,L      11/15/85   Other        27,500.00     800   3     1
222 Big Ben Dr.      Louisville   Roberts,D    11/08/85   Other        53,500.00    1900   3     2
222 Earl Ave.        J'Town       Wray,A       12/22/85   Ranch        51,000.00    1200   3     1
28 Seebolt Rd.       Louisville   Priest,S     3/29/86    Other        28,500.00     950   3     1
3323 Mt. Holly Dr.   Louisville   Grizz,D      2/10/86    Ranch        22,^100.00   1200   3     1
3355 Bank St.        J'Town       Cobb,D       1/03/86    Ranch        37,500.00    1500   3     1
343 Market St.       Louisville   Bivins,D     11/15/85   Ranch        42,900.00    1675   3     1
3752 St. Dennis      J'Town       Levine,J     3/22/86    Cape Cod     67,950.00    2500   3     2
4233 Mix Ave.        Louisville   Martin,D     4/18/86    Cape Cod     49,500.00    1900   3     2
435 Oxted Ln.        Louisville   O'Neal,P     2/12/86    Ranch        53,790.00    1900   3     1
4989 Adler Way       Louisville   Dole,V       1/30/86    Cape Cod     76,500.00    2000   3     2
5372 Tyson Pl.       Louisville   Goode,J      3/16/86    Ranch        35,000.00    1500   3     2
549 Billtown Rd.     Louisville   Bizer,R      11/14/85   Ranch        72,500.00    2000   3     2
5678 Beech St.       Louisville   Smith,P      2/02/86    Cape Cod     65,950.00    1800   3     2
589 Morocco Dr.      E'Town       Smith,B      11/10/85   Cape Cod     62,500.00    1875   3     2
6262 Kenwood Dr.     North Hill   Beck,U       4/05/86    Ranch        71,650.00    2000   3     2
```

however, Paradox allows you to make entries in the group header and footer. You often will enter literals and regular fields in your group headers and summary fields in your group footers.

Group headers are similar to page headers. Anything that you type in a group header will be printed at the top of each group. You will usually make entries in the group header that describe the entries in the group. Likewise, group footers are similar to page footers and report footers. Anything that you type in a group footer will be printed at the end of each group. The group footer is the best spot for summary fields that compute statistics about the group.

An Example

For example, suppose you have created the report specification like the one shown in Figure 12-12. As you can see, this report spec instructs Paradox to group the report on the Style field. Now suppose you want to define a group header and group footer. To begin, move the cursor to the group header and then press **[Ctrl]-[Home]** to move it to the left side of the screen. When the cursor is in place, type **Style:**. Now issue the **[Menu] Field Place Regular** command. When Paradox prompts you for the field you want to place, select the Style field, then move the cursor to a space just to the right of the literal *Style:* and press ↵ once to place the field, and again to set its length.

Now you're ready to place a summary field in the group footer that displays the average price of the records in each group. To do this, first type **Average Price:** in the group footer for the *group Style* band. Next, issue the **[Menu] F**ield **P**lace Summary **R**egular command and select **P**rice as the field to summarize. At the next prompt, select **A**verage as the type of summary. Since you want to compute a summary for only the records in the current group, when Paradox displays the PerGroup/Overall menu, you should choose **P**erGroup. Next, place the field in the group footer next to the prompt *Average Price:* and adjust the digits and decimals as you wish.

Figure 12-25 shows the completed report specification. If you press **[Instant Report]** to output this report spec, Paradox will create the report whose first page is shown in Figure 12-26. As you can see, Paradox has grouped the records in this report according to their Style field entries. In addition, Paradox has included a group header consisting of the literal *Style:* and the current Style field entry at the top of each field, and a footer consisting of a summary statistic at the bottom of each group. Since you selected PerGroup when you placed the summary statistic, the statistic at the foot of each group computes the average price of just the records in that group.

Figure 12-25 The Group Header and Footer

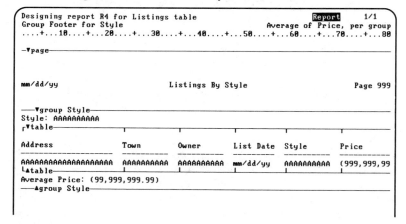

Notes

Notice that there is redundant information in the report in Figure 12-26. Since Paradox is printing the appropriate Style field entry for each group in the group header, you no longer need it to print the Style field entry for each record. To remove these entries, you can issue the **[Menu] T**ableBand **E**rase command and remove the **S**tyle column from the table band. Figure 12-27 shows the first page of the report that Paradox will create if you output this report spec after deleting the Style field column.

Figure 12-26 The Printed Report

```
5/17/86              Listings By Style              Page   1


Address              Town          Owner        List Date  Style        Price        Sq Ft   BRs   Baths
-------              ----          -----        ---------  -----        -----        -----   ---   -----
Style: Cape Cod
#82 Rudd Rd.         Louisville    Lum,I         1/16/86   Cape Cod      88,950.00    2800    4     2
2216 Lacey St.       North Hill    Beat,A        4/01/86   Cape Cod      94,999.00    2700    4     3
363 Dower Ct.        North Fork    Culp,A       11/21/85   Cape Cod     109,000.00    2100    4     2
3752 St. Dennis      J'Town        Levine,J      3/22/86   Cape Cod      67,950.00    2500    3     2
4233 Mix Ave.        Louisville    Martin,D      4/18/86   Cape Cod      49,500.00    1900    3     2
4444 Normie Ln.      Louisville    James,J       1/11/86   Cape Cod     120,000.00    2400    5     3
4989 Adler Way       Louisville    Dole,V        1/30/86   Cape Cod      76,500.00    2000    3     2
5678 Beech St.       Louisville    Smith,P       2/02/86   Cape Cod      65,950.00    1800    3     2
589 Morocco Dr.      E'Town        Smith,B      11/10/85   Cape Cod      62,500.00    1875    3     2
654 Nora Ln.         Louisville    Orwick,S      2/18/86   Cape Cod      40,000.00    1600    3     1
666 Montana Ave.     Louisville    Saul,H       11/09/85   Cape Cod      55,000.00    1900    3     1
6935 Shiloh Dr.      E'Town        Grebe,C       1/25/86   Cape Cod      81,000.00    2000    3     2
913 Whitney Dr.      North Hill    Kulp,R       11/20/85   Cape Cod      99,500.00    1800    4     2
987 Allan Dr.        Louisville    Newsome,K    11/12/85   Cape Cod      60,000.00    1900    4     2
99 Cardinal Hill Rd. North Hill    Brand,B       1/05/86   Cape Cod      70,000.00    2000    3     2
Average Price:       76,056.60
Style: Colonial
22 N. Ridge Ct.      Louisville    Nunn,A        2/15/86   Colonial     200,000.00    2900    5     3
3498 Bold Rd.        Louisville    Taft,H        1/15/86   Colonial     275,000.00    3800    5     4
4500 Hempstead Dr.   Louisville    Pape,C       12/04/85   Colonial     150,000.00    2600    4     3
586 Ansa Way         Louisville    Noel,C        4/15/86   Colonial      69,500.00    2200    4     2
620 Windsong Ct.     Louisville    Pank,E       11/22/85   Colonial     250,000.00    4000    6     4
766 Baird St.        Louisville    Black,G      11/08/85   Colonial     139,950.00    2600    4     3
Average Price:      180,741.67
Style: Other
#12 Circle Ct.       Louisville    White,Y      12/19/85   Other         10,000.00     800    2     1
#5 Ashby St.         J'Town        Wagner,H      3/10/86   Other         97,000.00    2500    4     3
1001 Spring St.      North Hill    Frier,F       1/22/86   Other         45,000.00    1700    3     2
185 Pages Ln.        J'Town        Cowan,M       3/20/86   Other         15,500.00    1000    2     1
198 Main St.         J'Town        Green,L      11/15/85   Other         27,500.00     800    3     1
222 Big Ben Dr.      Louisville    Roberts,D    11/08/85   Other         53,500.00    1900    3     2
28 Seebolt Rd.       Louisville    Priest,S      3/29/86   Other         28,500.00     950    3     1
5432 Miller Rd.      Louisville    Young,R      12/15/85   Other         17,500.00     800    2     1
854 Unseld Blvd.     Louisville    Volk,H        3/07/86   Other         87,000.00    2500    3     2
Average Price:       42,388.89
Style: Ranch
#10 Old Mill Rd.     Louisville    Stern,M       1/07/86   Ranch         75,000.00    2150    3     2
#6 Brandon Way       Louisville    Abrams,L     12/08/85   Ranch         67,000.00    2250    4     2
#62 Billy Bone Ct.   Louisville    Taylor,A      2/04/86   Ranch         34,500.00    1600    3     1
1222 Dee Rd.         South Fork    Smith,P      12/19/85   Ranch         22,950.00     950    2     1
123 Abby Ct.         Louisville    Kones,D      11/02/85   Ranch         32,950.00    1500    3     1
14 Short Rd.         .ouisville    Quire,I       3/01/86   Ranch         52,500.00    1600    3     1
1989 Eastern Pkwy.   Louisville    Klink,C       3/11/86   Ranch         26,950.00    1100    2     1
222 Earl Ave.        J'Town        Wray,A       12/22/85   Ranch         51,000.00    1200    3     1
3323 Mt. Holly Dr.   Louisville    Grizz,D       2/10/86   Ranch         22,100.00    1200    3     1
```

Figure 12-27 The Printed Report

```
5/17/86              Listings By Style              Page   1


Address              Town          Owner        List Date  Price        Sq Ft   BRs   Baths
-------              ----          -----        ---------  -----        -----   ---   -----
Style: Cape Cod
#82 Rudd Rd.         Louisville    Lum,I         1/16/86    88,950.00    2800    4     2
2216 Lacey St.       North Hill    Beat,A        4/01/86    94,999.00    2700    4     3
363 Dower Ct.        North Fork    Culp,A       11/21/85   109,000.00    2100    4     2
3752 St. Dennis      J'Town        Levine,J      3/22/86    67,950.00    2500    3     2
4233 Mix Ave.        Louisville    Martin,D      4/18/86    49,500.00    1900    3     2
4444 Normie Ln.      Louisville    James,J       1/11/86   120,000.00    2400    5     3
4989 Adler Way       Louisville    Dole,V        1/30/86    76,500.00    2000    3     2
5678 Beech St.       Louisville    Smith,P       2/02/86    65,950.00    1800    3     2
589 Morocco Dr.      E'Town        Smith,B      11/10/85    62,500.00    1875    3     2
654 Nora Ln.         Louisville    Orwick,S      2/18/86    40,000.00    1600    3     1
666 Montana Ave.     Louisville    Saul,H       11/09/85    55,000.00    1900    3     1
6935 Shiloh Dr.      E'Town        Grebe,C       1/25/86    81,000.00    2000    3     2
913 Whitney Dr.      North Hill    Kulp,R       11/20/85    99,500.00    1800    4     2
987 Allan Dr.        Louisville    Newsome,K    11/12/85    60,000.00    1900    4     2
99 Cardinal Hill Rd. North Hill    Brand,B       1/05/86    70,000.00    2000    3     2
Average Price:       76,056.60
Style: Colonial
22 N. Ridge Ct.      Louisville    Nunn,A        2/15/86   200,000.00    2900    5     3
3498 Bold Rd.        Louisville    Taft,H        1/15/86   275,000.00    3800    5     4
4500 Hempstead Dr.   Louisville    Pape,C       12/04/85   150,000.00    2600    4     3
586 Ansa Way         Louisville    Noel,C        4/15/86    69,500.00    2200    4     2
620 Windsong Ct.     Louisville    Pank,E       11/22/85   250,000.00    4000    6     4
766 Baird St.        Louisville    Black,G      11/08/85   139,950.00    2600    4     3
Average Price:      180,741.67
Style: Other
#12 Circle Ct.       Louisville    White,Y      12/19/85    10,000.00     800    2     1
#5 Ashby St.         J'Town        Wagner,H      3/10/86    97,000.00    2500    4     3
1001 Spring St.      North Hill    Frier,F       1/22/86    45,000.00    1700    3     2
185 Pages Ln.        J'Town        Cowan,M       3/20/86    15,500.00    1000    2     1
198 Main St.         J'Town        Green,L      11/15/85    27,500.00     800    3     1
222 Big Ben Dr.      Louisville    Roberts,D    11/08/85    53,500.00    1900    3     2
28 Seebolt Rd.       Louisville    Priest,S      3/29/86    28,500.00     950    3     1
5432 Miller Rd.      Louisville    Young,R      12/15/85    17,500.00     800    2     1
854 Unseld Blvd.     Louisville    Volk,H        3/07/86    87,000.00    2500    3     2
Average Price:       42,388.89
Style: Ranch
#10 Old Mill Rd.     Louisville    Stern,M       1/07/86    75,000.00    2150    3     2
#6 Brandon Way       Louisville    Abrams,L     12/08/85    67,000.00    2250    4     2
#62 Billy Bone Ct.   Louisville    Taylor,A      2/04/86    34,500.00    1600    3     1
1222 Dee Rd.         South Fork    Smith,P      12/19/85    22,950.00     950    2     1
123 Abby Ct.         Louisville    Kones,D      11/02/85    32,950.00    1500    3     1
14 Short Rd.         Louisville    Quire,I       3/01/86    52,500.00    1600    3     1
1989 Eastern Pkwy.   Louisville    Klink,C       3/11/86    26,950.00    1100    2     1
222 Earl Ave.        J'Town        Wray,A       12/22/85    51,000.00    1200    3     1
3323 Mt. Holly Dr.   Louisville    Grizz,D       2/10/86    22,100.00    1200    3     1
```

This last example points out a very important fact about groups: You can group a report on a field that is not included in the report. In the example, we deleted the Style field from the report. As you can see, Paradox still grouped the report correctly.

Also notice that, because you have defined a header and footer for the group in the report spec in Figure 12-25, Paradox no longer separates the groups in the report with blank lines. If you want to add blank lines back into the report between each group, just move the cursor to the group footer or group header of the report spec and press ↵ to insert a blank row. Once you add a blank row to the group header or footer, the groups in the report will again be separated by blank lines.

You can place as many summary fields in the group footer as you want. In addition, you can use any of the five types of summaries in a group footer. For example, you could add another summary to the report spec in Figure 12-25 that computes the maximum value in the Price field for the records in each group. All you'd have to do is insert a blank row in the group footer, type a literal like *Maximum Price:* in the new row, and then use the [Menu] Field Place Summary Regular command to insert the new summary.

Whenever a group is split between two pages, Paradox will repeat the group header for that group at the top of the second page. By using the [Menu] Group Headings command, you can change the default setting so that the group headings will not be printed on spillover pages. After you issue the [Menu] Group Headings command, Paradox will prompt you to place the cursor on the group you want to change. When you see this prompt, move the cursor to the group header and press ↵. After you do this, Paradox will display a menu with two options: Page and Group. You should select Group from this menu to change the default setting. After you do this, the Band indicator line at the top of the screen will read *headings per group*. From that point on, Paradox will not print spillover group headers.

Nesting Groups

You can have up to sixteen levels of groups in your reports. Adding additional groups to a report spec causes Paradox to create groups within groups in your printed reports. The highest level group serves as the primary sort key for the report. The next group serves as the secondary sort key, the third group as the third sort key, and so on.

An Example

For example, suppose you want to create a report for the LISTINGS table that is grouped on two fields: Style and BRs. You want to use Style as the main group so that the records in the report will be arranged into Style groups. You want to use BRs as a secondary group so that the records in each Style group are arranged into ascending order based on the entries in the BRs field.

To create this report, first issue the [**Menu**] **R**eport **D**esign command, type **LISTINGS**, and press ↵. Next, select a report number (we'll use **9**), enter a report description like **Listings By Style And Bedrooms**, and select **T**abular. Then use the [**Menu**] **S**etting **P**ageLayout **W**idth command to change the width of the page-widths to **132** characters, and the [**Menu**] **S**etting **P**ageLayout **D**elete command to delete the second page-width.

When the new report specification screen comes into view, issue the [**Menu**] **G**roups **I**nsert **F**ield command. Next, Paradox will display the regular fields of the LISTINGS table and prompt you to select the one on which you want to group the report. When you see this list, select the **S**tyle field. Next, Paradox will prompt you to place the group in the report. To place this group, move the cursor to the page header and press ↵.

Now you are ready to insert the second group. To do this, issue the [**Menu**] **G**roups **I**nsert **F**ield command again. When Paradox displays the regular fields of the LISTINGS table, select the **BR**s field. Next, Paradox will prompt you to place the group in the report. To place this group, move the cursor to anywhere within the *group Style* band and press ↵. Your screen should now look like Figure 12-28. Notice that the new band, *group BRs*, is enclosed by, or nested in, the *group Style* band. Because the *group BRs* band is nested inside the *group Style* band, Paradox will use the Style field as the primary grouping field. Within each Style group, the records in the report will be arranged in ascending order based on the BRs field.

Figure 12-28   Nested Groups

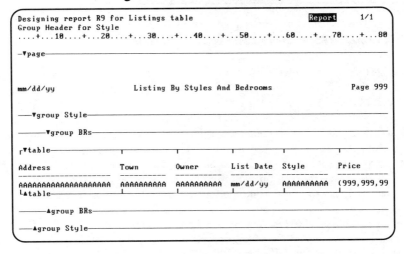

When you have defined the report spec, press [**Instant Report**] to create the printed report whose first page is shown in Figure 12-29. As you can see, the records in this report have been grouped by their Style field entries. Within each Style field group, the records are arranged so that the BRs field entries are in ascending order.

Figure 12-29 The Printed Report

```
5/17/86              Listings By Style And Bedrooms          Page   1

Address              Town         Owner         List Date  Style        Price            Sq Ft   BRs   Baths
-------              ----         -----         ---------  -----        -----            -----   ---   -----

3752 St. Dennis      J'Town       Levine,J      3/22/86    Cape Cod      67,950.00       2500    3     2
4233 Mix Ave.        Louisville   Martin,D      4/18/86    Cape Cod      49,500.00       1900    3     2
4989 Adler Way       Louisville   Dole,V        1/30/86    Cape Cod      76,500.00       2000    3     2
5678 Beech St.       Louisville   Smith,P       2/02/86    Cape Cod      65,950.00       1800    3     2
589 Morocco Dr.      E'Town       Smith,B       11/10/85   Cape Cod      62,500.00       1875    3     2
654 Nora Ln.         Louisville   Orwick,S      2/18/86    Cape Cod      40,000.00       1600    3     1
666 Montana Ave.     Louisville   Saul,H        11/09/85   Cape Cod      55,000.00       1900    3     1
6935 Shiloh Dr.      E'Town       Grebe,C       1/25/86    Cape Cod      81,000.00       2000    3     2
99 Cardinal Hill Rd. North Hill   Brand,B       1/05/86    Cape Cod      70,000.00       2000    3     2

#82 Rudd Rd.         Louisville   Lum,I         1/16/86    Cape Cod      88,950.00       2800    4     2
2216 Lacey St.       North Hill   Beat,A        4/01/86    Cape Cod      94,999.00       2700    4     3
363 Dower Ct.        North Fork   Culp,A        11/21/85   Cape Cod     109,000.00       2100    4     2
913 Whitney Dr.      North Hill   Kulp,R        11/20/85   Cape Cod      99,500.00       1800    4     2
987 Allan Dr.        Louisville   Newsome,K     11/12/85   Cape Cod      60,000.00       1900    4     2

4444 Normie Ln.      Louisville   James,J       1/11/86    Cape Cod     120,000.00       2400    5     3


4500 Hempstead Dr.   Louisville   Pape,C        12/04/85   Colonial     150,000.00       2600    4     3
586 Ansa Way         Louisville   Noel,C        4/15/86    Colonial      69,500.00       2200    4     2
766 Baird St.        Louisville   Black,G       11/08/85   Colonial     139,950.00       2600    4     3

22 N. Ridge Ct.      Louisville   Nunn,A        2/15/86    Colonial     200,000.00       2900    5     3
3498 Bold Rd.        Louisville   Taft,H        1/15/86    Colonial     275,000.00       3800    5     4

620 Windsong Ct.     Louisville   Pank,E        11/22/85   Colonial     250,000.00       4000    6     4


#12 Circle Ct.       Louisville   White,Y       12/19/85   Other         10,000.00        800    2     1
185 Pages Ln.        J'Town       Cowan,M       3/20/86    Other         15,500.00       1000    2     1
5432 Miller Rd.      Louisville   Young,R       12/15/85   Other         17,500.00        800    2     1

1001 Spring St.      North Hill   Frier,F       1/22/86    Other         45,000.00       1700    3     2
198 Main St.         J'Town       Green,L       11/15/85   Other         27,500.00        800    3     1
```

Using Summaries in Nested Groups

If you wish to, you can enter summary statistics in the group footers of nested groups to create several levels of summary statistics in your reports. For example, suppose you want to compute the average of the Price field entries in each BRs subgroup, and also the average of the Price field entries for each Style group. To do this, first issue the **[Menu] F**ield **P**lace **S**ummary **R**egular command, select **P**rice as the field to summarize, and select **A**verage from the Summary Type menu. To restrict the scope of the summary to the current group, you should choose PerGroup when Paradox displays the PerGroup/Overall menu. Finally, place the field in the group footer for the group Style band, and type the literal **Average Price for Style:** into the footer next to the summary field.

Now, repeat the steps above to create a new Average summary field on the Price field. This time, however, when Paradox prompts you to position the field, place it in the group footer for the group BRs band. Finally, type the literal **Average Price:** into the band next to the summary, as shown in Figure 12-30.

Now, you should press **[Instant Report]** to print the report whose first page is shown in Figure 12-31. As you can see, Paradox has included two levels of summaries in the report: one for each BR subgroup, and one for each Style group.

Other Reporting Topics   409

Figure 12-30   Summaries in Nested Groups

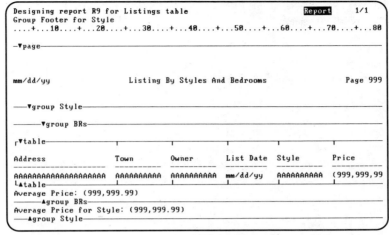

Figure 12-31   The Printed Report

Notes

As we mentioned previously, you can include up to 16 groups in a report spec. Inserting the third and subsequent groups is no different from inserting the second; you just issue the [Menu] Group Insert command, supply the appropriate information, and place the field within the appropriate group band. Each new group you insert adds a new level of grouping to the report.

In a small table such as this, secondary groupings may not make a great deal of difference in the printed report. However, when you are working with a large table, adding groups can help you analyze the data and spot trends.

Group Repeats

In all of the grouped reports created so far, Paradox has printed the entries in the grouping field for every record in the report. In the report in Figure 12-26 on page 405, which is grouped on the Style field, Paradox has repeated the Style field entry for every record in the report.

Sometimes you will want Paradox to print only the first entry in the grouping field for each group. To make this change, you can issue the [Menu] Setting GroupRepeats command. When you do this, Paradox will display a menu with two options: Retain and Suppress. The default selection, Retain, causes Paradox to print every occurrence of the grouping field, as shown in Figure 12-26. The other option, Suppress, causes Paradox to print only the first entry in the grouping field for every group.

Figure 12-32 shows the first page of a report created with GroupRepeats set to Suppress. Notice that Paradox has printed only the first entry in the grouping field for every group.

Figure 12-32   The Printed Report

GroupsofTables and TableofGroups

If you look at the grouped reports we've created so far, you'll see that the literals that define the columns in the table band are printed once at the top of each page of the report. If you wish, you can change the default setting so that the column titles are printed at the top of each group. To do this, issue the [**Menu**] **S**etting **F**ormat command. Paradox then will display a menu that offers two options: TableofGroups and GroupsofTables. The default setting, TableofGroups, prints the literals that define the columns in the Table band once at the top of each page of the report. The GroupsofTables option causes Paradox to print the field headers one time for each group.

Figure 12-33 shows an example of a report created with the GroupsofTables option. Notice that the literals that define the columns in the table band are now printed at the top of each group.

Figure 12-33   The GroupsofTables Format

The PAGEBREAK Keyword

In most cases, Paradox will move to the bottom of the page and print the contents of the page footer only after it has printed as many records as it can fit on a page. However, you can use the keyword PAGEBREAK to jump Paradox to the bottom of a page prematurely. This keyword must be typed in all capital letters, be positioned at the left edge of the report spec, and be on a line by itself. You will almost always enter the PAGEBREAK keyword in a group footer.

When Paradox encounters this keyword in a report spec, it will jump immediately to the end of the current page, where it will print the contents of the page footer (if any). It will begin printing the report at the top of the next page. If you have placed the PAGEBREAK keyword in a group footer (as you nearly always will) Paradox will begin the next page with the first record in the next group.

Groups and Record Number Fields

As you may recall from Chapter 11, when you place a record number field in a report specification, Paradox offers two options: Overall and PerGroup. The option you choose determines how the records in the report will be numbered. The Overall command tells Paradox to number the records consecutively from the beginning of the report. The PerGroup command tells Paradox to number the records within each group, starting with 1 at the beginning of each group.

If you place a record number field in a report as an Overall field, there is no way to change it to a PerGroup field. If you want to change an Overall record number field into a PerGroup record number field, you must delete and then replace the record number field.

The Regroup Command

The [Menu] Group Regroup command allows you to redefine a group you have already defined. This command allows you to change everything about a group–including its type and the field it groups–except for the position of the group relative to other groups in the report. To redefine a group, you just issue the [Menu] Group Regroup command. Paradox then will prompt you to place the cursor on the group you want to regroup. When you see this prompt, move the cursor to the group header or group footer of the group band you want to change, and press ↵. After you do this, Paradox will display the Group menu. From this point, redefining the group is exactly like inserting a new group. You can change the group any way you want–the only thing you cannot do is change the position of the group relative to other groups in the report.

Deleting Groups

Deleting a group from a report is as easy as issuing the [Menu] Group Delete command. After you issue the command, Paradox will prompt you to place the cursor on the group you wish to delete. When you see this prompt, move the cursor to the group header or group footer of the group to be deleted and press ↵. After you select the group that you want to delete, Paradox will prompt you to confirm the delete by displaying a Cancel/OK menu. If you select Cancel from the menu, Paradox will return to the previous menu so that you can make another selection. If you issue the OK command, however, Paradox will delete the group from the report.

Once you delete a group, the only way to replace it is to issue the [Menu] Group command and start over from scratch.

Grouping Free-form Reports

As you might expect, Paradox allows you to create groups in your free-form reports. While you will probably find more uses for groups in tabular reports, there are a few clever uses for groups in free-form reports.

For example, you could use a group to force Paradox to print the mailing label report you created in Chapter 11 for the NAMES table in zip code order. To do this, first issue the **[Menu] R**eport **C**hange command, specify **NAMES** as the table with which you want to work, and select the report number under which you saved the mailing label report (if you followed the example, this report will be saved under number **1**).

When the report spec comes into view, issue the **[Menu]** **G**roup **I**nsert **F**ield command, select the **Z**ip field, and place the group in the page band. When you have placed the group, your screen will look like Figure 12-34.

Figure 12-34   Grouping the Mailing Labels

```
Changing report R1 for Names table                          Report   1/1
Page Header
....+...10....+...20....+...30....+...40....+...50....+...60....+...70....+...8*
 —▼page
   —▼group Zip

 —▼form


     AAAAAAAAAAAAAA AAAAAAAAAAAAAA
     AAAAAAAAAAAAAAAAAA
     AAAAAAAAAAAAAAAAAA
     AAAAAAAAAAAAA, AA   AAAAA



 —▲form
   —▲group Zip
 —▲page
```

As in tabular reports, when you insert a group in a free-form report, Paradox automatically inserts a group header and a group footer around each group. Since this can affect the spacing in the printed report, you may want to eliminate these lines before you print the report. To remove the group header, just move the cursor to the blank line at the top of the *group Zip* band and press **[Report Delete Line]** ([Ctrl]-[Y]). Then move the cursor to the blank group footer and press **[Report Delete Line]** again. Figure 12-35 on the next page shows the report spec without the group header and footer. Now when you print the report, Paradox will print the mailing labels in zip code order.

As with tabular reports, you can insert up to 16 groups in a free-form report. Each additional group you create adds another level of grouping to the report.

If you wish, you can place literal text, regular fields, and summary fields in the group header and group footer of a free-form report. However, you are far more likely to use the group header and group footer in this way in tabular reports.

Figure 12-35 Grouping the Mailing Labels

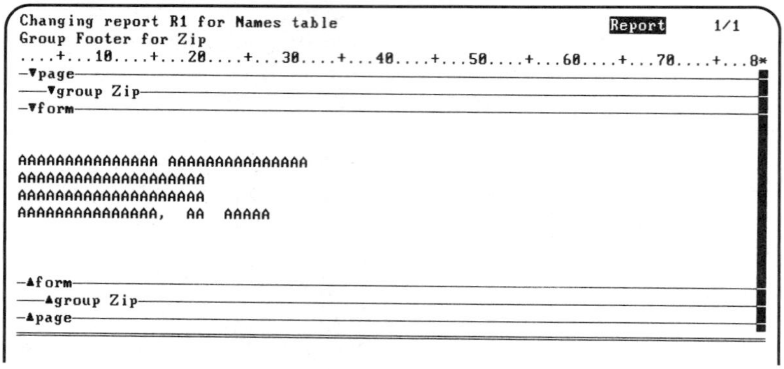

```
Changing report R1 for Names table                    Report      1/1
Group Footer for Zip
....+...10....+...20....+...30....+...40....+...50....+...60....+...70....+...8*
─▼page─────────────────────────────────────────────────────────────────────────
   ─▼group Zip────────────────────────────────────────────────────────────────
─▼form─────────────────────────────────────────────────────────────────────────


AAAAAAAAAAAAAA AAAAAAAAAAAAAA
AAAAAAAAAAAAAAAAAAA
AAAAAAAAAAAAAAAAAAA
AAAAAAAAAAAAAA, AA  AAAAA


─▲form─────────────────────────────────────────────────────────────────────────
   ─▲group Zip────────────────────────────────────────────────────────────────
─▲page─────────────────────────────────────────────────────────────────────────
```

Managing Reports

As you begin to design more and more reports, you will need to know how to manage those reports. For example, you will want to make copies of reports, rename reports, and delete obsolete reports. In this part of the chapter, we'll show you how to use the commands on the Tools menu to manage your reports. Since the commands that you use to copy, rename, and delete reports are nearly identical to the commands you used to manage tables and forms, we'll only cover them briefly here.

Copying Reports

You can use the [Menu] Tools Copy command to make copies of your reports. For example, suppose you want to make a copy of report 1 for the NAMES table. To do this, issue the **[Menu] T**ools **C**opy **R**eport command, type **NAMES** and press ↵. When Paradox displays the menu of report numbers for the NAMES table, select report number **1** and press ↵. Then, when Paradox prompts you to choose a report number for the copy, choose the number under which you want to save the copy (for instance, **5**) and press ↵. After you assign a report number to the copy, Paradox will make the copy and return you to the Main menu.

You will notice that the report number assigned to the report you are copying is not on the list of available destinations. This prevents you from assigning the same report number to the original and the copy.

If you select a report number for the copy that is the same as an existing report, Paradox will display a Cancel/Replace menu at the top of the screen. If you select Replace, Paradox will replace the existing report with the copy. If you assign the name **R** to the copy and then select Replace from the Cancel/Replace menu, Paradox will replace the default report with the copy.

Renaming Reports

You can use the [Menu] Tools Rename Report command to rename reports. For example, suppose you design a new report for the NAMES table and assign it the number 2. Now suppose you want to rename the report (assign it a new report number). To do this, issue the **[Menu] T**ools **R**ename **R**eport command, type **NAMES** and press ↵. Paradox then will display a menu of the existing reports for NAMES. When you see this menu, you should select the report number you want to rename (number **2**). Next, Paradox will display the Report Number menu from which you can choose a new name. When you see this menu, enter the new number for the report (we'll use number **6**.) After you do this, Paradox will rename the report.

If you select a report number as the new name that is already assigned to an existing report, Paradox will display a Cancel/Replace menu at the top of the screen. If you select Replace from this menu, Paradox will replace the existing report with the renamed report. If you assign the name *R* to the report and then select Replace from the Cancel/Replace menu, Paradox will replace the default report with the renamed report.

Deleting Reports

You can use the [Menu] Tools Delete Report command to delete reports. For example, suppose you design report number 1 for the NAMES table, and that report subsequently becomes obsolete. To delete the report, issue the **[Menu] T**ools **D**elete **R**eport command, type **NAMES**, and press ↵. After you do this, Paradox will display a menu of the existing reports for NAMES. When you see this menu, select the report number you want to delete (in this case, report number **1**.) Once you select a report, Paradox will delete it and return to the main workspace.

You should exercise caution when you issue the [Menu] Tools Delete command. Once an object is deleted, there is no way to recover it.

Changing the Report Default Settings

As you have seen, Paradox has default values for many of the report generator settings. You can, of course, change the default settings from within the report generator for each report you design. In addition, however, Paradox allows you to change the default report settings permanently. To do this, you must use the Paradox Custom Configuration Program (PCCP).

Entering the PCCP

To run the PCCP from within Paradox, first make sure that the script *Custom* is on the default directory. Then issue the **[Menu] S**cripts **P**lay command, type **Custom**, and press ↵. After a moment, Paradox will display the PCCP menu on the screen.

Making Changes

The Reports option on the PCCP menu allows you to set your own report defaults. After you choose this option, you will see the menu shown in Figure 12-36. As you can see, this menu has seven options: PageWidth, LengthOfPage, Margin, Wait, GroupRepeats, SetupStrings, and Exit. Each of these options (except for Exit) is the counterpart of a command within the report generator. The difference is this: When you issue these commands from within the report generator, you are setting values for the report on which you are working; when you issue them from within the PCCP, the values you enter become the default values for all reports.

Figure 12-36 The Reports Menu

```
PageWidth  LengthOfPage  Margin  Wait  GroupRepeats  SetupStrings  Exit
Change the default width of the printed report page.
```

You can use the PageWidth option to change the default width of your reports. If most of your reports are printed on a wide-carriage printer, you might want to change the default page width from 80 to 132 characters. To do this, issue the PageWidth command from the PCCP Reports menu. After you issue the command, Paradox will display the current default value and prompt you to change it. When this prompt appears on your screen, you can press [Backspace] to erase the current default value, type a new default value between 10 and 2000 (in this case 132), and press ↵.

You can use the LengthOfPage option to change the default page length of your reports from 66 lines to any length between 2 and 2000 lines. For example, suppose you typically print 88 lines on each page (eight lines per inch). To change the default setting to 88 lines, you would choose LengthOfPage from the Reports menu, press [Backspace] twice to erase the default, and then type 88. When you press ↵, the PCCP will lock in your setting.

The LengthOfPage command offers another option–Continuous–which instructs Paradox to print your reports in one continuous stream without any break between pages. If you like to print your reports in continuous fashion, you can select this option. However, keep in mind that setting the length to Continuous will cause Paradox to ignore the literals and fields you have placed in the page header and footer.

You can use the Margin option on the PCCP Report menu to change the default left margin on the first page width of your reports. The standard default setting is 0; you can change the setting to any value between 0 and 255. To make a change to this setting, you choose Margin from the Report menu, press [Backspace] to erase the current default, and type the new setting.

You can also use the PCCP to change the default setting for GroupRepeats. As you may recall, the GroupRepeats setting controls whether Paradox will print every entry in the grouping field or only the first entry in each group. To change this default, choose

GroupRepeats from the PCCP Reports menu. Paradox then will display a menu with two options: Retain and Suppress. Retain is the standard default setting. To change the default setting, you should choose the Suppress option.

The Wait option on the PCCP Reports menu allows you to change the default Wait setting. The Wait setting determines whether Paradox will pause and wait for you to insert a new sheet of paper after it prints each page, or will simply go ahead and begin printing the new page. When you choose Wait from the Reports menu, the PCCP will present two options: No and Yes. If you choose No, Paradox will not wait after it prints each page. If you choose Yes, Paradox will wait after printing each page.

The SetupStrings option on the PCCP's Reports menu allows you to customize any of Paradox's default setup strings. The default setup strings are the strings Paradox displays when you issue the [Menu] Setting Setup Predefined command from within the report generator. When you choose the SetupStrings option from the Reports menu, Paradox will display a table like the one shown in Figure 12-37. As you can see, this table displays the default setup strings for the currently supported printers.

Figure 12-37   The Default Setup Strings

```
Press [F1] for help, [F2] to save your changes, or [Esc] to cancel.
To choose a default, place an asterisk at the end of name of desired string.
SETUPS========Name=============================Setup String========
    1     Small-IBMgraphics         \027W\000\015
    2     Reg-IBMgraphics           \027W\000\018
    3     Small-Epson-MX/FX         \015
    4     Small-Oki-92/93           \015
    5     Small-Oki-82/83           \029
    6     Small-Oki-192             \029
    7     HPLaserJet                \027&l00\027(0U\027(s1p10v0s0b5T
    8
```

Once you see the SETUPS table, you can delete any setup strings that do not apply to you, or that add new strings to the list. To delete a string, place the cursor on the row containing the string you wish to delete and press **[Del]**. To add a new string to the table, just create a blank row in the table, then type a name for the new string in the Name column and the string itself in the Setup String column. The name you enter can be up to 20 characters long and must not include blank spaces. The string you define can be up to 50 characters long. You can enter as many setup strings as you want.

Of course, you can also modify one of the existing strings (either by deleting a part of it or adding to it). All you have to do is move the cursor to the appropriate record in the Setup String field and edit the entry using normal editing techniques. If you wish to designate a particular string as the default, type an asterisk (*) after its name in the Name field. If you define a default setup string, Paradox will employ that string whenever you print (provided you do not specifically choose another string).

When you have made the changes you want to the SETUPS table, you can press **[Do-It!]** to return to the PCCP Reports menu.

Leaving the PCCP

After you have made all the changes you want, issue the Exit command from the Reports menu and return to the PCCP Main menu. Then issue the DO-IT! command or press [Do-It!]. When the PCCP has saved your new default settings, the DOS prompt will appear on the screen. The changes you made will take effect when you next load Paradox.

Conclusion

In this chapter, we have shown you how to use summary fields and how to group your reports. In addition, we've shown you how to use the Tools menu commands to copy, rename, and delete reports, and how to use the PCCP to change Paradox's report defaults.

In the next chapter, we will begin our discussion of the Paradox Applications Language (PAL). In that chapter, we'll show you how to create simple scripts.

Chapter 13
Simple Scripts

In the previous chapters of this book, we have explored many of Paradox's capabilities. By now, you know how to use queries and how to create sophisticated forms and reports. If Paradox's capabilities stopped with what you already know, it would be a very powerful data base manager indeed. Paradox does a lot more, however. In addition to these basic features, Paradox is also programmable.

Paradox programs are called scripts. The simplest scripts are nothing more than recorded keystrokes that are stored in a text file. You can create scripts by asking Paradox to record your keystrokes as you choose commands, press function keys, or type information from the keyboard. You can also create scripts without recording them by using the PAL Script Editor.

When you play a script, Paradox "types" each keystroke that you have saved in the file in much the same way that a player piano plays from a scroll of music. When Paradox plays a script, the keys on your computer's keyboard don't move, but Paradox does perform the same actions that it would if it actually had pressed those keys.

Simple scripts are most useful for recording relatively short keystroke sequences that you repeat over and over, or for recording complex or tedious sequences that must always be performed correctly. Because scripts don't have to point and type like you do, they can perform a task much more quickly than you can. Because Paradox never makes a typo while playing a script, you can use scripts to perform important tasks and know they will be performed correctly.

On a more advanced level, Paradox offers a complete programming language called PAL (Paradox Applications Language). By using PAL commands and functions, you can develop scripts that employ such programming devices as variables, arrays, conditional tests, loops, custom menus, and subroutines. You can use these PAL tools to develop complete turnkey applications, like an integrated accounting system, a time and billing system, or an order entry/invoicing system. You also can use PAL more casually, however, to add power to your manual work within Paradox.

PAL and Paradox are closely related. Any script, from a simple recording to a sophisticated PAL program, works with the tables, forms, and queries on the Paradox workspace, just as you do. In a sense, a script is a Paradox user that you control. Once you tell it what to do, a script will manipulate the objects on the Paradox workspace for you quickly, automatically, and consistently.

In the next five chapters, we'll explore the ways that you can program Paradox. In this chapter, we'll show you how to record keystrokes in a script, how to play a script, and how to edit a script. In Chapter 14, we'll move beyond simple recording and introduce commands, variables, and equations. In Chapter 15, we'll present another powerful PAL component: functions. Chapter 16 will explore a number of essential PAL techniques, such as displaying information on the PAL "canvas," soliciting user input, looping, and printing. Finally, in Chapter 17, we'll explore such advanced topics as arrays, macros, and procedures.

Recording Scripts

The simplest scripts are ones that duplicate actions that you can perform from the keyboard of your computer. This kind of script can be used to automate tedious and repetitive tasks, thus freeing you from the chore of typing each command over and over. The easiest way to create this type of script is to record the keystrokes as you type them.

An Example

Suppose that you want to record a script named Empsort that sorts the EMPLYEE table shown in Figure 13-1 into ascending order based on the entries in the Salary field. To begin recording, press the **[Menu]** key and choose Scripts to reveal the menu shown in Figure 13-2. As you can see, this menu lists five items: Play, BeginRecord, QuerySave, ShowPlay, and Editor. We'll explain the purpose of each of these options as we move through this chapter.

To create the script Empsort, first choose **BeginRecord** and type **Empsort** to identify the file in which you want Paradox to record your keystrokes. As soon as you press ↵ to lock in the name, Paradox will flash the message

      Beginning recording of Empsort

in the message area at the bottom-right corner of the screen. This message indicates that Paradox will begin recording the script with your next keystroke. During a recording session, Paradox will display the letter *R* in the upper-right corner of the screen, indicating that your keystrokes are being recorded. (This message is obscured when Paradox displays the Main menu, however.)

As soon as Paradox is ready, you should perform the task that you want it to record, just as you would if Paradox were not recording it. In this case, you should issue the **M**odify **S**ort command. (The Main menu should be visible, so you don't have to press the [Menu] key.) After you issue the Modify Sort command, Paradox will prompt you for the name of the table you want to sort. When you see this prompt, either type the table

Figure 13-1 The EMPLYEE Table

```
Viewing Emplyee table: Record 1 of 16                          Main
 EMPLYEE   Emp Number    Last Name     First Name   SS Number       Addre
    1          1         Jones         David        414-74-3421     4000 St. Ja
    2          2         Cameron       Herb         321-65-8765     2321 Elm St
    3          3         Jones         Stewart      401-32-8721     4389 Oakbri
    4          4         Roberts       Darlene      417-43-7777     451 Lone Pi
    5          5         Jones         Jean         413-07-9123     4000 St. Ja
    6          6         Williams      Brenda       401-55-1567     100 Owl Cre
    7          7         Myers         Julie        314-30-9452     4512 Parksi
    8          8         Link          Julie        345-75-1525     3215 Palm C
    9          9         Jackson       Mary         424-13-7621     7021 Clark
   10         10         Jakes, Jr.    Sal          321-65-9151     3451 Michig
   11         11         Preston       Molly        451-00-3426     321 Indian
   12         12         Masters       Ron          317-65-4529     423 W. 72nd
   13         13         Robertson     Kevin        415-24-6710     431 Bardsto
   14         14         Garrison      Robert       312-98-1479     55 Wheeler
   15         15         Gunn          Barbara      321-97-8632     541 Kentuck
   16         16         Emerson       Cheryl       404-14-1422     8100 River
```

```
Viewing Emplyee table: Record 1 of 16                          Main
 Date of Birth   Date of Hire   Exemptions    Salary
   10/06/42        6/01/84          3          70,000.00
   11/24/29        6/01/84          4          50,000.00
    3/21/50        7/01/84          1          47,000.00
    9/24/60       11/01/84          3          14,000.00
    5/14/43       12/01/84          0          33,999.99
    1/12/20        1/01/85          5          40,000.00
    2/06/48        2/01/85          1          32,000.00
    6/03/33        4/01/85          2          30,000.00
    8/12/56        4/01/85          3          21,000.00
    5/23/59        5/01/85          6          34,000.00
    4/17/66        7/01/85          1          14,750.00
   12/30/44        7/01/85          0          38,000.00
    3/16/25        7/15/85          1          37,000.00
    5/09/45       10/01/85          4          32,000.00
    5/18/50       11/01/85          2          17,500.00
    7/30/66        1/01/86          2          12,000.00
```

Figure 13-2 The Scripts Menu

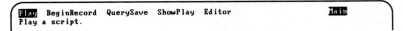

```
Play  BeginRecord  QuerySave  ShowPlay  Editor            Main
Play a script.
```

name **EMPLYEE** or press ↵ and choose that name from the list. After you select EMPLYEE as the table to sort, choose Same to command Paradox to place the sorted result back in EMPLYEE.

As soon as you select Same, Paradox will present the sort specification screen for the EMPLYEE table. To specify an ascending sort on the Salary field, use the ↓ key to position the cursor beside the field name Salary, then type the number **1**. Figure 13-3 shows the resulting sort specification screen.

Figure 13-3   The Sort Specification Screen

```
Sorting Emplyee table                                    Sort          R

  Number fields to set up sort order (1, 2, etc.). If you want a field sorted
    in descending sequence, follow the number with a "D" (e.g., "2D").
              Ascending is the normal sequence and need not be indicated.

              Emp Number
              Last Name
              First Name
              SS Number
              Address
              City
              State
              Zip
              Phone
              Date of Birth
              Date of Hire
              Exemptions
          1 ◄ Salary
```

After you have specified the sort order, you can command Paradox to perform the sort in one of two ways. First, you can press the **[Do-It!]** key [F2]. Alternatively, you can issue the **[Menu]** DO-IT! command. In either case, Paradox will sort EMPLYEE into ascending order based on the values in the Salary field and will display the result on the screen. Figure 13-4 shows the sorted EMPLYEE table.

Once you have performed the task that you wanted to record, you should stop recording. To do this, again issue the **[Menu]** Scripts command. This time, instead of displaying the five-item menu shown in Figure 13-2, Paradox will display the menu shown in Figure 13-5. This special four-item Scripts menu will appear only when you issue the Scripts command while Paradox is recording or playing a script. The End-Record option tells Paradox to stop recording and save the keystrokes it recorded into the .SC file you specified. The Cancel option also instructs Paradox to stop recording but not to save the recorded keystrokes. The Play option allows you to play one script while you are recording another. The QuerySave option allows you to save a query into a script. We'll discuss the Play and QuerySave options later. In this case, choose End-Record to stop recording and save the script.

Figure 13-4   The Sorted EMPLYEE table

```
Viewing Employee table: Record 1 of 16                    Main    R
 EMPLYEE   Emp Number    Last Name    First Name   SS Number     Addre
    1         16         Emerson      Cheryl       404-14-1422   8100 River
    2          4         Roberts      Darlene      417-43-7777   451 Lone Pi
    3         11         Preston      Molly        451-00-3426   321 Indian
    4         15         Gunn         Barbara      321-97-8632   541 Kentuck
    5          9         Jackson      Mary         424-13-7621   7821 Clark
    6          8         Link         Julie        345-75-1525   3215 Palm C
    7          7         Myers        Julie        314-38-9452   4512 Parksi
    8         14         Garrison     Robert       312-98-1479   55 Wheeler
    9          5         Jones        Jean         413-07-9123   4000 St. Ja
   10         10         Jakes, Jr.   Sal          321-65-9151   3451 Michig
   11         13         Robertson    Kevin        415-24-6710   431 Bardsto
   12         12         Masters      Ron          317-65-4529   423 W. 72nd
   13          6         Williams     Brenda       401-55-1567   100 Owl Cre
   14          3         Jones        Stewart      401-32-8721   4389 Oakbri
   15          2         Cameron      Herb         321-65-8765   2321 Elm St
   16          1         Jones        David        414-74-3421   4000 St. Ja

Viewing Employee table: Record 1 of 16                    Main    R
 Date of Birth   Date of Hire    Exemptions      Salary
    7/30/66         1/01/86          2          12,000.00
    9/24/60        11/01/84          3          14,000.00
    4/17/66         7/01/85          1          14,750.00
    5/18/50        11/01/85          2          17,500.00
    8/12/56         4/01/85          3          21,000.00
    6/03/33         4/01/85          2          30,000.00
    2/06/48         2/01/85          1          32,000.00
    5/09/45        10/01/85          4          32,000.00
    5/14/43        12/01/84          0          33,999.99
    5/23/59         5/01/85          6          34,000.00
    3/16/25         7/15/85          1          37,000.00
   12/30/44         7/01/85          0          38,000.00
    1/12/20         1/01/85          5          40,000.00
    3/21/50         7/01/84          1          47,000.00
   11/24/29         6/01/84          4          50,000.00
   10/06/42         6/01/84          3          70,000.00
```

Figure 13-5   Four-item Scripts Menu

```
Cancel  End-Record  Play  QuerySave                       Main    R
End recording of current script and keep it.
```

Notes

The names of your scripts can be up to eight characters in length and may contain any characters that are acceptable in DOS file names. When Paradox prompts you to specify a name, you should type only the name, not an extension. As soon as you press ↵, Paradox will set up a file using the name you supplied and will add the extension .SC, which identifies the file as a script file.

If you enter the name of an existing .SC file when Paradox prompts you for the new script's name, Paradox will present a menu with two options: Cancel and Replace. If you choose Cancel, Paradox will allow you to choose another name. If you choose Replace, Paradox will overwrite the existing script file.

Issuing Commands

While you are recording a script, you can issue commands just as you normally would: either by pointing to the command name and pressing ↵ or by typing the first letter in the name of the command. As you will see, Paradox records the commands you issue in the same way no matter how you select them.

The same is true for selecting tables and other objects. While you are recording, you can select a table or other object either by typing its name and pressing ↵ or by pressing ↵ and selecting the table or object name from the list that Paradox displays. Either way, the recorded script will look the same.

If you are in the habit of pressing the [Menu] key while the current menu already is visible at the top of the screen, then you may be in for a surprise when you view your recorded scripts. Because the Paradox screen flashes briefly and Paradox then redisplays the menu in these situations, you might assume that it is recording the [Menu] key. If you view a script in which you have pressed the [Menu] key redundantly, however, you'll see that Paradox records the keystroke as Esc rather than Menu. Apparently, pressing the [Menu] key when Paradox already is displaying a menu is equivalent to pressing the [Esc] key. Although this redefinition of keys has no effect on the performance of a script, you may wish to delete any unnecessary occurrences of [Esc] in your recorded scripts.

It is important that you understand that while you're recording a script, all of the commands you issue affect the objects on the Paradox workspace, just as they would if you were not recording. In this example, for instance, Paradox actually sorted the EMPLYEE table as we recorded a script we'll use later to sort the table again. Always be aware that the actions you take while you are recording a script affect the workspace in the same way that they do when you are not recording.

Recording Instant Scripts

The [Instant Script Record] key ([Alt]-[F3]) gives you an alternative way to begin recording a script. When you press this key, Paradox sets up a file named INSTANT.SC in the current directory. It will use this file to store special representations of the keystrokes that you type during the recording session. After you have pressed this key, Paradox will record your keystrokes in the file INSTANT.SC, beginning with the next keystroke that you type.

If there already is a file named INSTANT.SC on the current directory when you press the [Instant Script Record] key, Paradox will overwrite that file, destroying the existing script. You can prevent this from happening, of course, by using the [Menu] Tools Rename Script command to change the name of a previously recorded instant script before you press [Instant Script Record]. In general, you'll want to be sure to rename any script you create with [Instant Script Record] as soon as possible after you create the script.

In addition to allowing you to begin recording quickly, there are other benefits of using the [Instant Script Record] key to begin recording. First, you can stop recording and save the script by pressing the same key again. Second, you can invoke this command at any time, no matter where you are in the Paradox menu structure. To issue the [Menu] Scripts BeginRecord command, the Main menu must be accessible. Third, as we'll show you later, you can play an instant script just by pressing the [Instant Script Play] key.

There is one situation in which you should not press the [Instant Script Record] key, however: while the Scripts menu is in view. If you issue the [Menu] Scripts command any time other than when you are recording or playing a script, Paradox will display the five-item Scripts menu shown in Figure 13-2. If you issue the [Menu] Scripts command during the recording or playing of a script, however, you will see the four-item menu shown in Figure 13-5. Only the four items on this menu should be available to you during the recording or playing of a script.

If you issue the [Menu] Scripts command to reveal the five-option Scripts menu and then press [Instant Script Record], however, the regular Scripts menu will still be available to you. This menu contains four commands that should not be accessible during script play or recording, but which you will now see: BeginRecord, QuerySave, ShowPlay, and Editor. If you choose any of these commands while you are recording a script, you may cause a system error, which will result in a keyboard lockup and the possible loss of data. To avoid these problems, do not press the [Instant Scripts Record] key while the Scripts menu is visible.

Viewing a Script

Now that you have recorded your first script, let's take a look at the recorded script so that we can see just what Paradox has recorded. The first step in viewing (or editing) a script is to load it into a text editor. You probably will find PAL's built-in Script Editor to be the most convenient text editor to use for this task. You can view or edit a script within any word processor that can read an ASCII text file, however.

To view a script within the PAL Editor, issue the **[Menu] Script Editor** command. When you choose Editor, Paradox will present you with two choices: Write and Edit. The Write option allows you to compose a script from scratch, instead of recording it. We'll show you how to do that later in this chapter. In this case, we're interested in the Edit option, which allows you to view and/or edit a previously recorded (or written) script. When you choose Edit, Paradox will prompt you to specify the name of the script you want to edit. You may specify the script by typing its name or by pressing ↵ and, by either typing or pointing, choosing the name from a list. In this case, we'll type the name **Empsort** and press ↵.

As soon as you select the script you want to edit, Paradox will read that script from its .SC file and present it to you on the screen within the PAL Script Editor. As you can see, Figure 13-6 shows the script that we recorded in the previous paragraphs in the PAL

Editor. Within this editing environment, you can either edit the script or just view it. In this case, we'll just look at the script to see how Paradox has recorded each keystroke.

Figure 13-6 The Empsort Script

```
Changing script Empsort                                              Script
....+...10....+...20....+...30....+...40....+...50....+...60....+...70....+...80
{Modify} {Sort} {Emplyee} {Same} Down Down Down Down Down Down
Down Down Down Down Down Down "1" Do_It! Menu {Scripts} {End-Record}
```

Script Elements

A recorded script can contain three types of elements: menu items, special keys, and text. The script shown in Figure 13-6 contains all three of these elements.

Menu Selections

As you recall, our first action after starting the recording of the script was to choose Modify from the Main menu and Sort from the Modify menu. As you can see, Paradox has recorded these items as {Modify} and {Sort}, respectively–simply the names of the menu items surrounded by braces. Paradox uses the { } form to record anything that you choose from a menu, including commands and the names of tables, forms, and scripts that you select while issuing a command.

For example, the third item in our script is {Emplyee}. This item represents the name of the table that you want Paradox to sort. You could have selected this name in any one of three ways: by typing its name, by pressing ↵ and typing the first letter of its name, or by pressing ↵ and pointing to it. No matter how you selected it, Paradox would represent it in brace form within the script.

Similarly, the last line in the script is the recorded representation of the [Menu] Scripts End-Record command. This command appears in the script as a result of choosing Scripts End-Record to end the recording of the script. This command will always be the last line of any script that you create with the PAL recorder. It serves no purpose in the script, but it will not cause any problem when you play the script. You may wish to use the editing techniques that we cover later in this chapter to remove this command from your scripts, however.

Choosing Menu Items

As we mentioned earlier, the way you choose an item from a menu doesn't affect the way that Paradox records that item. The command is recorded in the same way whether you point to the command and press ↵ or type the first letter in the command name. In the example, Paradox did not care whether you selected Modify by typing M or by pressing the → key four times and then pressing ↵. Either way, the command would be recorded as {Modify}.

The same is true for the tables and other objects you specify while recording a script. When Paradox prompts you to supply an object's name, such as a table, you can either type the name and press ↵ or press ↵ and choose the name from the list Paradox displays. Either way, only the name of the object you select–and not the keystrokes you use to select it–will be recorded.

This rule has some important implications for your scripts. For one thing, it means that you cannot record a generic script. A generic script is a script that operates on whatever table happens to be active when you play it. To create generic scripts, you must either edit a recorded script or write the script from scratch. We'll show you how to create generic scripts at the end of this chapter.

Special Keys

The fifth through sixteenth commands in the example script are recorded representations of the ↓ key (remember that you used this key to move the cursor to the Salary field in the sort specification). As you can see, Paradox entered the word *Down* in the script each time you pressed the ↓ key.

Paradox always uses unquoted, unbraced words to represent any "special" key you press during the recording of a script. These special keys include the ten special function keys, the [Alt]-function key combinations, the cursor movement keys, and keys like ↵ and [Backspace]. For example, Paradox records the [Menu] key ([F10]) as Menu, the [Do-It!] key ([F2]) as Do-It!, the [Field View] key ([Alt]-[F5]) as FieldView, the [Rotate] key ([Ctrl]-[R]) as Rotate, and the ↵ key as Enter. Table 13-1 shows a complete listing of how Paradox represents these special keys in a recorded script.

Table 13-1 Key Representations in Scripts

Special Function Keys		Numeric Keypad Keys		[Ctrl] Key Combinations	
[F1]	Help	[Home]	Home	[Ctrl]-[Break]	CtrlBreak
[F2]	Do_It!	[End]	End	[Ctrl]-[Home]	CtrlHome
[F3]	UpImage	[Pg Up]	PgUp	[Ctrl]-[End]	CtrlEnd
[F4]	DownImage	[Pg Dn]	PgDn	[Ctrl]-←	CtrlLeft
[F5]	Example	←	Left	[Ctrl]-→	CtrlRight
[F6]	Check	→	Right	[Ctrl]-[Backspace]	CtrlBackspace
[F7]	FormKey	↑	Up	[Ctrl]-[Pg Up]	CtrlPgUp
[F8]	ClearImage	↓	Down	[Ctrl]-[Pg Dn]	CtrlPgDn
[F9]	EditKey	↵	Enter	[Ctrl]-[D]	Ditto
[F10]	Menu	[Tab]	Tab	[Ctrl]-[E]	Editor
[Alt]-[F3]	InstantRecord	[Ins]	Ins	[Ctrl]-[R]	Rotate
[Alt]-[F4]	InstantPlay	[Del]	Del	[Ctrl]-[V]	VertRuler
[Alt]-[F5]	FieldView	[Esc]	Esc	[Ctrl]-[Y]	DeleteLine
[Alt]-[F6]	CheckPlus	[Shift]-[Tab]	ReverseTab	[Ctrl]-[F]	FieldView
[Alt]-[F7]	InstantReport				
[Alt]-[F8]	ClearAll				
[Alt]-[F10]	PalMenu				

Some special function keys duplicate the action of commands on the Paradox menus. In these cases, the alternative that you choose affects the appearance of the script but not its outcome. Once you've filled in a sort specification, for example, you can command Paradox to perform the sort either by pressing the [Do-It!] key ([F2]) or by issuing the [Menu] DO-IT! command. If you press [Do-It!], then Paradox will record the command as Do_It!. On the other hand, if you select DO-IT! from the Sort menu, Paradox will store the command as Menu {DO-IT!}. Although these two alternatives achieve the same result, they do so by different mechanisms. One commands Paradox to press a key, while the other commands Paradox to choose a command from a menu. Similarly, you can edit a table either by pressing the [Edit] key ([F9]) or by issuing the [Menu] Modify Edit command. If you press [Edit] during the recording of a script, the recorded script will contain the representation EditKey. If you press the [Menu] key and choose Modify Edit, the script will contain the keystroke sequence Menu {Modify} {Edit} {filename}.

Literal Characters

The next item in the script, "1", is an example of text–the third type of element that can be found in a recorded script. This item corresponds to the number 1 that we typed into the sort specification form next to the field name *Salary*. Any time you type one or more characters into a table, a form, a report, a query, or a sort specification while you are recording, Paradox will enclose that character in quotes in the recorded script. If you had typed 1D to specify a descending sort, for example, Paradox would have recorded "1D". If you had entered the edit mode and typed the entry *123 Main Street* into the Address field, Paradox would have included "123 Main Street" in the recorded script. Any time that you perform any action other than choosing a menu item or pressing a special key, Paradox will record that action as text.

Mistakes

With the exception of the way it standardizes the choices you make from menus, Paradox is quite literal in the way it records your keystrokes. For this reason, any keys that you mistakenly press during the recording of a script will show up in the script. For example, suppose you move to a field of a table and type an entry like *Jones* without first entering the edit mode. Although Paradox will display the message

      Press the Edit key [F9] if you want to make changes

and will not enter the change into the table, it will record the text *{Jones}* and the key representation *Enter* in the script. Each time you play a script that contains this kind of error, Paradox will repeat your error. To remove the mistake, you must edit it out of the script. We'll show you how to edit a script in a few pages.

Returning to Paradox

When you're finished viewing (or editing) a script, you may do one of three things to stop editing and return to Paradox. If you want to return to the Paradox workspace without saving any changes, issue the **[Menu]** Cancel command and choose the **Yes** option. When you issue this command, Paradox will exit from the Paradox Script Editor and return you to the main Paradox workspace. If you have made any changes to the script, they will be forgotten. If you choose No instead of Yes after choosing Cancel, you will remain within the Script Editor.

If you have made changes to the script (we'll show you how to do this later) and you want to save them into the .SC file, you can issue the [Menu] DO-IT! command or just press the [Do-It!] key. When you do either of these things, Paradox will save the edited script and return you to the Paradox workspace. If you have not made any changes to the script, choosing either of these options will have the same effect as choosing the Cancel Yes option.

Playing Scripts

The principal reason for recording a script is to enable Paradox to perform a repetitive task automatically. Once you've recorded a script, therefore, you'll probably want to play it. When you play a script, Paradox reads and executes the commands stored in that script, one at a time. Because Paradox doesn't actually press keys, it can perform a task much faster than you can. Because Paradox always reads exactly what it has recorded, it never presses an incorrect key–unless you have done so during the recording of the script.

There are many ways to play a script. In most cases, you will issue the [Menu] Scripts Play command and then select the name of the script from a list. You can accomplish the same thing by pressing the [PAL Menu] key ([Alt]-[F10]) to reveal the PAL menu, choosing Play, and specifying the name of the script. If the script file is named INSTANT.SC (as it will be if you create it with the [Instant Script Record] key), you can play it by pressing the [Instant Script Play] key ([Alt]-[F4]). If you are viewing (or editing) a script, you can play it by pressing the [Menu] key to reveal the Scripts Editor menu, then select Go.

Each of these four commands plays a script "at speed." Whenever you issue one of these commands, Paradox actually does two things. First, it appears to freeze the current image on the screen. Then it reads the series of commands from the script file and executes them, one at a time. When the script is finished, Paradox unfreezes the screen to reveal the changed Paradox workspace.

The PAL Canvas

Notice we said that Paradox *appears* to freeze the screen when you play a script. In fact, the frozen image is not the Paradox workspace, but a copy of the workspace image painted onto a new workspace called the PAL canvas. The PAL canvas is an alternative workspace that is dropped in front of the Paradox workspace whenever you begin playing a script. With few exceptions, this canvas remains in place, obscuring the main Paradox workspace, until the script is finished.

Because Paradox paints this workspace with the image that was on the Paradox workspace when you began playing the script, it appears as though you're looking at the "frozen" Paradox workspace. As we'll explain in Chapter 16, however, PAL offers commands that let you clear this canvas and display your own messages during the execution of a script. For now, just realize that you'll be seeing the PAL canvas, not the Paradox workspace, whenever you play a script.

An Example

Suppose you want to play the script shown in Figure 13-6. To do this, issue the [**Menu**] **S**cripts **P**lay command and then select the name of the script that you want to play (in this case, **E**mpsort). You can select the script either by typing its name or by pressing ↵ and selecting its name from the list that Paradox displays. When you issue this command, Paradox will drop the PAL canvas, paint it with the current image of the screen, and begin to issue the stored commands. First, Paradox will choose Modify Scripts from the Main menu, select the EMPLYEE table, and specify that the results be placed in the same table. Paradox then will move down the sort specification and "type" a 1 to the left of the field name *Salary*. Next, Paradox will press the [Do-It!] key and perform the sort. Finally, Paradox will execute the [Menu] Scripts End-Record command.

Watching a Script Play

The ShowPlay option on the Scripts menu provides yet another way to play a script. Unlike the [Menu] Go and [Menu] Scripts Play commands and the [Instant Script Play] key, the ShowPlay command does not drop the PAL canvas prior to the execution of a script. As a result, it lets you watch while the script manipulates the Paradox workspace. When you issue the [Menu] Scripts ShowPlay command and specify a script, Paradox will present two choices: Fast and Slow. If you choose Fast, Paradox will execute the script relatively rapidly. Because it redraws the screen after each change it makes to the workspace, however, it takes nearly twice as long as normal to play a script in this mode. If you choose Slow, Paradox plays the script at about the same speed that you typically would issue the commands yourself. Although it sometimes can be fun to watch the execution of a script, you usually will want to take advantage of the faster execution that results when the Paradox workspace is obscured by the PAL canvas.

Notes

Paradox is able to execute the commands in a script quite rapidly for at least two reasons. First, even though Paradox does have to read the script from disk, it can do that a great deal faster than even the fastest typist can manipulate the keyboard. Because Paradox doesn't actually have to press keys, it can execute commands much faster than you can. Second, because the screen image doesn't change as a script is played, Paradox doesn't use time redrawing the screen each time it issues a command. Paradox redraws the screen, showing the result of all its actions, only after it has completely executed the script.

Saving Queries

In Chapters 8 and 9, you learned just how important queries are in Paradox. You also learned that Paradox does not save a query specification automatically with the other objects in a family. To save a query, you must issue the **[Menu]** Scripts QuerySave command. To bring a query back to the workspace, you must use the **[Menu]** Scripts Play command, and select the name of the query.

The commands for saving and retrieving queries are located on the Scripts menu because Paradox saves queries as scripts. For this reason, you can view and edit scripts in the Paradox Script Editor in the same way that you can view and edit a recorded script. In the following paragraphs, we'll show you what a recorded query looks like. In the next section of this chapter, we'll show you how to edit a query once you have saved it.

Saving a Query

Suppose you want to design and save a query that returns the entries from the Last Name and Salary fields of the records in the EMPLYEE table with Salary field entries that are greater than $35,000. To design this query, first use the **[Menu]** Ask command to create a blank query for the **EMPLYEE** table. Then use the **[Check Plus]** key to select the Last Name field, use the **[Check Mark]** key to select the Salary field, and type the condition **>35000** into the Salary field. When you finish, your query will look like the one shown in Figure 13-7.

Figure 13-7   An Example Query

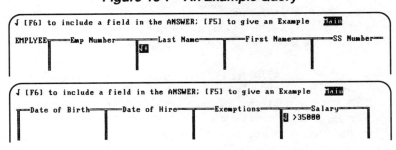

Once you have designed a query, you can execute it with the [Do-It!] key. The query will remain defined until you use the [Clear Image] or [Clear All] key to remove it from the workspace. When you clear the query from the screen, however, it will cease to exist. Unless you save a query before you remove it from the workspace, you will need to recreate it if you want to use it again.

As you learned in Chapter 8, you can save a query by issuing the [Menu] Scripts QuerySave command and specifying a name for the .SC file in which you want the query to be saved. To save the example query, issue the **[Menu]** Scripts **QuerySave** command and type the name **Highpay.** When you press ↵, PAL will save the query into the script file named HIGHPAY.SC.

Viewing the Saved Query

Because Paradox saves a query as a script, you can view or edit a saved query from within the PAL Script Editor or any other text editor that you wish to use. To load our example query into the Paradox Editor, we'll issue the [Menu] Script Editor Edit command, type the name of the script that contains the query, **Highpay**, and press ↵–exactly the same steps that you would use to view or edit any other script. Figure 13-8 shows the script form of our query.

Figure 13-8   The Query Script

```
Changing script Highpay                                      Script
....+...10....+...20....+...30....+...40....+...50....+...60....+...70....+...80
Query
      Emplyee : Last Name  :   Salary   :
              : CheckPlus  : Check >35000 :
              :            :             :
              :            :             :
Endquery
```

As you can see, the query script shown in Figure 13-8 looks something like the query in Figure 13-7 that it represents. There are four major differences between a query and its script representation, however. First, the script version of a query contains only the fields that are selected with a check or check plus and those fields that contain selection conditions–not every field in the query. For example, the script representation of the query shown in Figure 13-8 contains only two fields: Last Name (a selected field) and Salary (a selected field that contains a selection condition).

The second difference between the query and its script representation is the notation used to mark selected fields. As you know, Paradox uses the check mark and check plus symbols to mark selected fields in a query on the workspace. In the saved version of a query, however, Paradox replaces these symbols with the words *Check* and *CheckPlus*. In the saved query shown in Figure 13-8, for example, Paradox has placed the word *CheckPlus* in the Last Name field, and has placed the word *Check* in the Salary field.

The third difference between a query and its script version is the way that examples are represented. On the workspace, Paradox displays examples in inverse video. In a script, however, Paradox denotes examples by preceding them with an underline (_). For instance, the example zzz would be represented as _zzz in a script. Because the script shown in Figure 13-8 does not contain any examples, its script version does not use this underline notation.

The fourth difference between the query and its script version is the presence of the words *Query* and *EndQuery* at the beginning and end of the script. These two special words are PAL commands that must enclose the script version of a query. The Query command alerts Paradox that the lines that follow contain the script representation of a query. The EndQuery command marks the end of that query. In Figure 13-8, you also can see that a single blank line follows the Query command and another blank line precedes the EndQuery command. These blank lines also are essential parts of the script representation of a query.

Playing a Saved Query

You can play a saved query in much the same way that you play any other script. The result is somewhat different, however. Instead of pressing keys and issuing commands, Paradox loads the query back onto the workspace in its "unabridged" form. Once the query is back on the workspace, you can process it by pressing the [Do-It!] key, just as if it had never been saved.

In some cases, you may wish to bring a query to the workspace and execute it automatically. To do this, you must edit the saved query and add a Do_It! command directly after the word EndQuery in the query script. We'll show you how to do this in the next section of this chapter.

Recording Queries: An Alternative Approach

You usually will create a query script by designing a query in the Paradox workspace and then using the [Menu] Scripts QuerySave command to write that query into a script. Although this is the preferred method of saving a query, it is not the only way. Instead of saving a predesigned query, you can record the process of designing the query in the same way as you record any other keystrokes. For example, the script

> Menu {Ask} {Emplyee} Right Right CheckPlus Right Right Right Right Right
> Right Right Right Right Right Right Check ">35000"

automates the process of designing the query shown in Figure 13-7–the same one represented by the query script shown in Figure 13-8.

Even though these two methods achieve the same result, you probably will want to save most of your queries with the QuerySave command for a couple of reasons. First, Paradox can execute a Query/EndQuery representation faster than it can read and execute the series of keystrokes necessary to design a query. Second, the graphic nature of the Query/EndQuery form makes it easier for you to see and understand what the query is doing when you view and edit the script that contains the query. It also makes the query easier to edit once it is in a script.

Editing Scripts

So far, we have shown you how to record a script and save a query into a script. We also have shown you how to view a script in the Paradox Script Editor. In most cases, you'll want to do more than just view a script once you bring it into the Editor, however. Usually, you'll want to change it in some way. We'll refer to the process of adding to, deleting from, or replacing parts of a script as editing the script.

As we mentioned earlier, the first step in editing a script is to load it into the Paradox Script Editor or another text editor. As you will see, the Script Editor is not as powerful as most stand-alone word processing programs. The Editor has only an extremely basic ability to move and copy parts of a script, for example, and no search-and-replace capability. Despite these shortcomings, you probably will want to use the PAL Editor to edit most of your recorded scripts, at least until you become a fairly proficient script writer, for one principal reason: The PAL Script Editor allows you to edit a script without leaving Paradox.

Loading a script into the PAL Editor is a simple process. All you need to do is issue the [Menu] Script Editor Edit command and select the name of the script that you want to edit. You may select a script by typing its name and pressing ↵. Alternatively, you may press ↵ to reveal a list of script names and then choose one of these by typing the first letter in its name or by pointing to its name and pressing ↵ again. To load the script Empsort into the Editor, issue the **[Menu]** **S**cript **E**ditor **E**dit command and type the script name **Empsort**. When the script is loaded into the Editor, your screen should look like Figure 13-6.

Moving Around in the PAL Editor

Paradox uses an underline as the cursor in the PAL Editor, just as it does in all other environments. This cursor always marks the point that will be affected by the next key you press. Just as you might expect, you can use the standard cursor movement keys to reposition the cursor within the Script Editor. Each time you press the → key, Paradox will move the cursor one space to the right. Each time you press the ← key, Paradox will move the cursor one space to the left. Each time you press the ↑ or ↓ keys, Paradox will move the cursor one line up or down, respectively.

You can use other keys and combinations to move the cursor in increments greater than a single space or line. When you press the [Ctrl]-→ or [Ctrl]-← combinations, Paradox will move the cursor one entire screen to the right or left. The [Pg Up] and [Pg Dn] keys move the cursor up and down one screen at a time. The [Home] key moves the cursor vertically to the first line of the script, while the [End] key moves it vertically to the bottom line of the script. The [Ctrl]-[Home] and [Ctrl]-[End] combinations move the cursor to the first or last character on the current line.

The actions of these keys and combinations in the Script Editor are similar to their actions in the report generator. The two workspaces are a bit different in nature, however. First, the Script Editor workspace is not divided into page widths, as is the report generator workspace. Second, the width of the workspace in the Script Editor is fixed at 132 characters. Third, Paradox sets the bottom border of the Script Editor just below the last line of commands in the script you are editing.

Paradox will not allow you to move the cursor beyond the boundaries of the Script Editor workspace, nor will it allow the cursor to wrap around from one edge of the Editor workspace to the other. If you press → when the cursor is in the 132nd space on a line, or ← when the cursor is in the first space, Paradox will just beep at you. The same thing happens if you try to move beyond the upper border or below the current position of the bottom border of the workspace.

The Horizontal and Vertical Rulers

If you look again at Figures 13-6 or 13-8, you'll see a row of periods, plus signs, and numbers across the third line of the Script Editor screen. This row of symbols is the horizontal ruler. Each symbol on this ruler marks one "column" in the Script Editor. The horizontal ruler is useful for determining where the cursor is positioned within the current row, relative to the left edge of the workspace. The horizontal ruler is always visible whenever you are within the Paradox Script Editor.

In addition to this horizontal ruler, the Script Editor features a vertical ruler. This ruler, shown in Figure 13-9, allows you to determine in what row of the Script Editor the cursor is positioned. Although Paradox displays the horizontal ruler whenever you are within the Script Editor, it will not display the vertical ruler unless you command it to do so by pressing [Ctrl]-[V]. When you first press this key combination, the vertical ruler will appear. When you press [Ctrl]-[V] again, it goes away. Whether you use this ruler or not is purely a matter of personal preference.

Figure 13-9 The Vertical Ruler

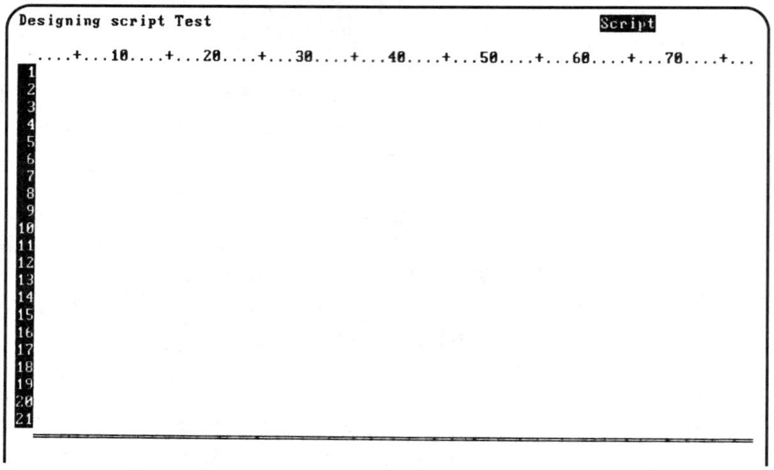

```
Designing script Test                                    Script
       ....+...10....+...20....+...30....+...40....+...50....+...60....+...70....+...
      1
      2
      3
      4
      5
      6
      7
      8
      9
     10
     11
     12
     13
     14
     15
     16
     17
     18
     19
     20
     21
```

Overwrite Mode Versus Insert Mode

Most text editors give you a choice of two editing modes: Overwrite and Insert. The PAL Script Editor is no exception. Your choice of mode is important when you are typing on a line that already contains characters. For example, suppose you type a character while the cursor is positioned on another character in a script. If the Script Editor is in the overwrite mode, it will replace the current character with the character you type. If the Script Editor is in the insert mode, however, it will place the character you type at the position of the cursor, and will move the remaining characters to the right. The result is an insertion, rather than a replacement of text.

Paradox always will be in the overwrite mode when you first enter the Script Editor. To change to the insert mode, you must press the [Ins] key. Whenever Paradox is in the insert mode, it will display the message *Ins* in the upper-right corner of the screen. Unless this indicator is present, Paradox will be in the overwrite mode. If you do a lot of word processing, you probably will not like Ansa's selection of Overwrite as the default editing mode.

Adding Lines to the Script Editor

You can add new blank lines to the workspace and thereby increase its size by pressing the ↵ key. If the cursor is positioned at the end of the last line when you press ↵, PAL will add a new blank line to the end of the script. The result of pressing the ↵ key from other locations within a script depends on whether you are in the insert or overwrite mode. If you press ↵ while the cursor is anywhere other than at the end of the last line while the Script Editor is in the overwrite mode, PAL will move the cursor to the beginning of the next line without inserting a new line into the script.

Pressing ↵ while the Script Editor is in the insert mode always adds new lines to a script. If the cursor is positioned at or beyond the last character on any line while the Script Editor is in the insert mode, pressing ↵ adds a new blank line below that line. If the cursor is positioned in the middle of a line when you press ↵, PAL will insert a new line below the current one and will move the text located to the right of the cursor to that new line. If the cursor is at the beginning of a line when you press ↵, PAL will insert a new line above the current position of the cursor.

Deleting Characters and Lines

There are three ways to remove text from a script. First, you can position the cursor on the character you want to delete and press [Del]. Whenever you press this key, PAL deletes the character on which the cursor is positioned and pulls the remaining text on the line one space to the left. Alternatively, you can position the cursor to the right of the character you want to delete and press [Backspace]. However, the action of the [Backspace] key is also affected by your choice of the overwrite or insert mode. If the Script Editor is in the overwrite mode, the characters to the right of the cursor remain in place as you press the [Backspace] key. The result is a gap in the line of the script. If the Editor is in the insert mode, Paradox "pulls" the characters to the right of the cursor one space to the left each time you press the [Backspace] key. While you are in the insert mode, then, you can combine the text from two adjacent lines by pressing [Backspace] from the beginning of the lower line.

Paradox also provides a way to delete whole and partial lines at a time. When you press [Ctrl]-[Y] from within the Script Editor, Paradox will delete all characters from the position of the cursor to the right end of the line. If the cursor is on the first character of the line, this combination erases the entire line and moves the remaining lines up one row. If the cursor is on any other character of the line, Paradox will erase only a portion of that line. If you press [Ctrl]-[Y] while the cursor is beyond the last character on the line, Paradox will just beep.

Modifying Our Example Script

Once you have loaded a script into the PAL Script Editor, making changes to that script is as easy as moving the cursor and typing. In this case, we'll make two changes to the Empsort script. First, we'll remove the superfluous command *Menu {Scripts} {End-Record}* from the end of the script. Then we will specify a descending rather than an ascending sort order.

We'll use the [Ctrl]-[Y] combination to remove the *Menu {Scripts} {End-Record}* sequence from the Empsort script. To do this, position the cursor on the *M* in *Menu* (or the space before it) on the second line of the script, then press **[Ctrl]-[Y]**. Instantly, Paradox will delete the commands Menu {Scripts} {End-Record} from the script.

Next, we'll make the script specify a descending rather than ascending sort based on the entries in the Salary field. To do this, move the cursor to the quote that follows the 1 in the string "1". Then look for the *Ins* indicator in the upper-right corner of the screen to determine if the Editor is in the insert mode. If not, press the **[Ins]** key. Then simply type the letter **D** (for descending) so that the string becomes "1D". When you finish making these changes, your screen should look like the one in Figure 13-10.

Figure 13-10   The Revised Empsort Script

```
Changing script Empsort                                        Script  Ins
....+...10....+...20....+...30....+...40....+...50....+...60....+...70....+...80
{Modify} {Sort} {Emplyee} {Same} Down Down Down Down Down
Down Down Down Down Down Down  "1D" Do_It!
```

Ending the Edit

Once you have made all the changes to a script that you want to make, you can stop editing in any of three ways. If you want to save the changes into the .SC file and then return to the Paradox workspace, you can issue the [Menu] DO-IT! command or just press the [Do-It!] key. If you want to return to the Paradox workspace without saving the changes, you can issue the [Menu] Cancel command and choose the Yes option. When you issue this command, Paradox will forget all of the changes you have made. The script will continue to exist in its original, unedited form. If you choose No instead of Yes after choosing Cancel, Paradox will not end the editing session.

If you issue the [Menu] Go command, Paradox will first save the changes you made to the script, just as it does when you choose the DO-IT! command. As soon as the changes have been saved, however, Paradox will play the revised script. If you plan to play the edited script after you save it (and you frequently will want to do this), choosing DO-IT! will save you time and keystrokes. In this case, just press **[Do-It!]** to end the editing of this script. As soon as PAL resaves the query into EMPORT.SC, overwriting the old version, it will return you to the Paradox workspace.

Another Example

For another example, let's make some changes to the query stored in the script Highpay. First, we'll change the selection condition *>35000* to *>40000*. Then we'll add the key representation *Do_It!* to the end of the script so that Paradox will execute the query automatically when you play the script.

To edit the Highpay script in this way, issue the [**Menu**] Scripts Editor Edit command and select **Highpay**. At this point, your screen should look like the one shown in Figure 13-8. To change the selection condition from *>35000* to *>40000*, just position the cursor on the 3 and type **40**. Because Paradox will be in the overwrite mode when you first enter the Editor, this action replaces the characters 35 with the characters 40.

Now we'll add the key representation Do_It! to the bottom of the script. This will make the query "self-executing." To do this, move the cursor to the final line of the script, and to the right of the last character on that line. (The fastest way to do this is to press the **[End]** key to move to the last line, then the **[Ctrl]-[End]** combination to move to the right edge of that line.) Once the cursor is in position, press ↵ to add a new blank line at the end of the script. Then type **Do_It!** (remember, no brackets) on this line so that the script looks like the one shown in Figure 13-11.

Figure 13-11 The Revised Highpay Script

```
Changing script Highpay                                          Script
....+...10....+...20....+...30....+...40....+...50....+...60....+...70....+...80
Query
         Emplyee : Last Name :  Salary   :
                 : CheckPlus : Check >40000 :
                 :           :              :
                 :           :              :
Endquery
Do_It!
```

To end the editing process, press **[Do-It!]** or issue the **[Menu]** DO-IT! command.

Combining Two Scripts

If you press the [Menu] key while editing a script, you'll see the six-item Script Editor menu shown in Figure 13-12. The first item on this menu, Read, allows you to read a copy of one script from the disk into the script you currently are editing. The ability to combine two scripts allows you to record a complex series of commands in parts, then combine the parts into the finished script. This command also allows you to reuse lines of previously recorded or written scripts in new scripts that perform similar functions.

Figure 13-12 The Script Editor Menu

```
Read  Go  Print  Help  DO-IT!  Cancel                            Script
Read contents of another script into this script starting at the cursor.
```

To show you how the Read command works, let's combine the revised Empsort script shown in Figure 13-10 into the revised Highpay script shown in Figure 13-11. The result will be a script that first creates a two-field ANSWER table of employees whose salary is greater than $40,000 per year, then sorts the ANSWER table into descending salary order. (To achieve this result, we will have to make a few additional changes once we combine the two scripts.)

The first step in this process is to read the revised Empsort script into Highpay. To begin, use the [Menu] Script Editor Edit command to load the Highpay script into the Editor. When the script is in view, move the cursor to the point within Highpay where you want Paradox to insert the Empsort script. In this case, we want Paradox to place the contents of Empsort after the last command in Highpay. To do this, just place the cursor anywhere in the last line of Highpay (the line that contains only the key representation Do_It!). The position of the cursor within the line is not important. Whenever you issue the Read command, Paradox will insert the imported script immediately after the line that contains the cursor, no matter where the cursor is positioned within that line.

Once you have positioned the cursor, issue the [Menu] Read command and select **Empsort**, either by typing and pressing ↵ or by pressing ↵ and choosing the name from the list. As soon as you select this script, Paradox will insert it into the script you are editing, starting on the line immediately below the cursor. Figure 13-13 shows the combined script.

Figure 13-13 The Combined Script

```
Changing script Highpay                                    Script
....+...10....+...20....+...30....+...40....+...50....+...60....+...70....+...80
Query

     Emplyee  : Last Name  :   Salary  :
              : CheckPlus  : Check >40000 :
              :            :              :
              :            :              :
              :            :              :
Endquery
Do_It!
{Modify} {Sort} {Emplyee} {Same} Down Down Down Down Down Down
Down Down Down Down Down Down "1D" Do_It!
```

This combined script needs some modification before it will do what we want it to do. Currently, the commands we combined into this script from Empsort direct Paradox to sort the EMPLYEE table, not the ANSWER table. Modifying these commands to sort ANSWER is a relatively easy process, however. First, move the cursor to the first letter of the word *Emplyee* in the tenth line of the script and press [Del] seven times to delete it. Then press the [Ins] key to enter the insert mode, and type the name **Answer**.

Next, remove all but one of the Down commands from the script. Because Salary is the second of only two fields in the ANSWER table, a single Down command is all that is needed to move the indicator to the Salary line of the sort specification. When you finish making these changes, the combined script will look like the one in Figure 13-14.

Figure 13-14 The Revised Combined Script

```
Changing script Highpay                                    Script Ins
....+...10....+...20....+...30....+...40....+...50....+...60....+...70....+...80
Query

     Emplyee  : Last Name  :   Salary  :
              : CheckPlus  : Check >40000 :
              :            :              :
              :            :              :
              :            :              :
Endquery
Do_It!
{Modify} {Sort} {Answer} {Same} Down "1D" Do_It!
```

Once you have made these modifications to the script, you can resave it, play it, or both. In this case, we will save and play the script all at once by pressing the [**Menu**] key and choosing **Go**. When we execute this script, Paradox will extract the Last Name and Salary information from all records in the EMPLYEE table whose salary exceeds $40,000, then sort the ANSWER table into descending salary order. Figure 13-15 displays this result.

Figure 13-15 The Sorted ANSWER Table

```
Viewing Answer table: Record 1 of 3                              Main
EMPLYEE┬──Emp Number──┬──Last Name──┬──First Name──┬──SS Number──
       │              │              │              │
       │              │              │              │

ANSWER─┬──Last Name──┬──Salary──
   1   │  Jones      │  70,000.00
   2   │  Cameron    │  50,000.00
   3   │  Jones      │  47,000.00
```

Creating Generic Scripts

Because Paradox interprets the choices you make from a menu when it records your keystrokes, rather than recording each →, ←, and ↵, the resulting scripts are specific to the objects that you operated on during the recording. This is great for certain kinds of scripts, including saved queries and scripts not specific to any Paradox object (such as scripts that change directories). However, in many cases you'll want to create generic scripts–scripts that perform some specific action on whatever table happens to be active. Fortunately, it is not too difficult to create generic PAL scripts.

For example, suppose you want to create a script that displays the structure of whatever table was active when you played the script. To create this script, use the [**Menu**] **V**iew command to bring any table to the workspace. In this case, we'll use this command to make EMPLYEE the current table. Once the table is in view, issue the [**Menu**] **S**cripts **B**eginRecord command to begin to record the script. In this case, we'll record the script under the name Struct. Once Paradox has begun recording, issue the [**Menu**] **T**ools **I**nfo **S**tructure command and press ↵ twice: once to reveal the list of tables in the current directory and again to select the first table from that list. Because Paradox always places the name of the current table at the beginning of the list, pressing ↵ twice selects that table (in this case, EMPLYEE). As soon as you select this table, Paradox will display its structure on the screen. Finally, issue the [**Menu**] **S**cripts **E**nd-Record command to stop the recording.

Figure 13-16 shows the completed script after you've loaded it into the Script Editor. As you can see, Paradox didn't record the commands *Enter Enter* when you pressed ↵ twice as you were recording the script. Instead, it recorded *{Emplyee}*, the name of the specific table that you selected when you pressed ↵ twice. For this reason, the recorded script is specific to the EMPLYEE table. Each time you play this script, Paradox will display the structure of EMPLYEE, no matter which table happens to be current at the time.

Figure 13-16 The STRUCT Script

```
Changing script Struct                                          Script
....+...10....+...20....+...30....+...40....+...50....+...60....+...70....+...80
Menu {Tools} {Info} {Structure} {Emplyee} Menu {Scripts} {End-Record}
```

Fortunately, some minor editing can transform this table-specific query into one that will display the structure of whatever table is current when you run the script. To make this script generic, press the **[Ins]** key to enter the insert mode and use the **[Backspace]** or **[Del]** keys to erase the {Emplyee} command. Then type **Enter Enter** so that the script looks like the one shown in Figure 13-17.

Figure 13-17 The Generic STRUCT Script

```
Changing script Struct                                          Script Ins
....+...10....+...20....+...30....+...40....+...50....+...60....+...70....+...80
Menu {Tools} {Info} {Structure} Enter Enter Menu {Scripts} {End-Record}
```

When you play this revised script, Paradox will issue the [Menu] Tools Info Structure command, just like the unedited version. Instead of selecting {Emplyee}, however, this script will press ↵ twice, selecting the first table in the list. Since Paradox always places the name of the current table at the beginning of the list of table names, this script will display the structure of the current table. If the cursor is currently in the CUSTOMER table, for example, PAL will display the structure of that table.

Writing Scripts from Scratch

Up to this point in the chapter, we have shown you how to create, view, and edit a recorded script. Although recording keystrokes is not the only way to create a script, it is the preferred method for new Paradox users. This is true for one main reason: You do not need to know how Paradox represents keystrokes in a script to record a script. As you continue recording and editing scripts, however, you will become relatively familiar with the keystroke representations and syntax of a script. As you develop this expertise, you may prefer to begin writing scripts from scratch rather than recording them. In fact, once you begin using PAL commands in your scripts, you will almost always write rather than record.

In many ways, writing a script from scratch is similar to editing a recorded script. The major difference, of course, is that you don't have a base from which to begin. To write a script from scratch, you issue the [Menu] Script Editor Write command, supply the name of the script you want to write, and begin typing the keystroke representations that you want the script to contain. Of course, you can use any text editor to write a script. Just as when you edit scripts, however, you probably will want to use the PAL Editor to write most of your scripts.

An Example

To demonstrate the process of writing a script in the PAL Script Editor, let's write a script that changes the current directory to c:\paradox\examples. We'll begin the process by entering the PAL Script Editor. To enter the Editor, issue the [Menu] Script Editor command, just as you did to edit a script. Instead of choosing Edit, however, choose Write. As soon as you select this option, Paradox will present the prompt *Enter name for new script:* and will wait for you to enter a name. In response to this prompt, you should type the name under which you want Paradox to store the script you are writing. In this case, we'll use the name **Chngdir**.

Unlike most other situations within Paradox, you must type a name in response to this prompt; you cannot press ↵ to view a list of existing scripts. If you type the name of an existing script, PAL lets you choose whether you want to replace it. If so, you should select **R**eplace. If not, you can select Cancel and choose a new name.

As soon as you select a name for the new script, Paradox will present you with the screen shown in Figure 13-18. As you can see, this workspace is exactly like the one that we used earlier to edit our recorded scripts, except that it is empty and is only one line deep. This is how the Script Editor will look whenever you begin writing a new script. Once you are within this space, you can press ↵ to add new lines to it, move around with the various cursor keys, and, of course, write a script.

Figure 13-18 The Empty Script Editor

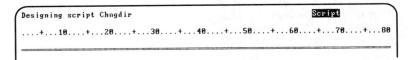

To perform the task of changing the directory from the keyboard, you would issue the [Menu] Tools More Directory command, press [Ctrl]-[Backspace] to erase the name of the current directory, type c:\paradox\examples, press ↵, and then choose OK. To automate this task within a script, you would write the commands

   Menu {Tools} {More} {Directory} CtrlBackspace {c:\\paradox\\examples} {OK}

The first command, Menu, tells Paradox to press the [Menu] key. The next three words, {Tools} {More} {Directory}, instruct Paradox to issue the Tools More Directory command. The next word, CtrlBackspace, represents the simultaneous pressing of the [Ctrl] and [Backspace] keys.

The next word, {c:\\paradox\\examples}, tells Paradox to "type" *c:\paradox\examples*–the name of the new directory. As you can see, we have used double backslashes in this command. In the context of a script, the backslash is a special character that commands Paradox to treat the next character literally. You will better understand the usefulness of this character as you read through the remaining PAL chapters. For now, realize that whenever you want to include a backslash in a script, you must type two backslashes.

The final command in the script, {OK}, answers the Cancel/OK prompt and commands Paradox to go ahead and change the directory.

Once you have written a script, you can save it to disk and exit from the Editor by pressing the **[Do-It!]** key or by issuing the DO-IT! command from the Script Editor menu. If you don't want to save the script, you can issue the [Menu] Cancel command to return to the Paradox workspace. If you want to save the script and then execute it all in one step, you should select Go from the Script Editor menu.

Syntax and Conventions

In the example scripts we have shown you so far, we have used certain conventions involving syntax, spacing, and capitalization. Some of these conventions are necessary for the proper execution of a script, while others just make the script easier to write and understand. In either case, you'll find it easier to write scripts once you understand the rules and conventions that are explained below.

Spacing

When Paradox records a script, it leaves a single space between adjacent commands on each line. Although you'll probably want to adhere to this convention when you write a script, it is not necessary to do so in all cases. Specifically, you don't need to use a space between a menu selection and any other command. For instance, Menu{View} and {Modify}{Sort} are acceptable command sequences. Because menu selections are surrounded by braces, Paradox can tell where one command ends and the other begins.

If neither of the two adjacent commands is a menu selection, however, you must separate the commands with a space. Otherwise, Paradox will not understand the command. For example, Paradox will accept the command sequence Down Down, but it will not understand the sequence DownDown.

Although Paradox sometimes cares whether you use no spaces as opposed to one space between commands, it is not particular regarding the use of multiple spaces. Paradox always will allow multiple spaces where only one or none is required. For example,

    Down   Down

is an acceptable sequence. However, you'll find that the use of extra spaces does nothing more than reduce the number of commands that you can see on the screen at one time.

Multiple Commands on Each Line

When Paradox records a script, it usually places several commands on each line. This convention, which squeezes more commands on the screen at the same time, allows you to view a larger portion of a script at once. Although you can write each command on a different line if you wish, that practice makes a script harder to read and understand when you are viewing and editing it.

In the next three chapters, we will present some special PAL commands that must appear alone on a line and others that may not be followed by any command on the same line. Even when this is not required, you probably will want to use only one command per line in most situations once you start developing advanced PAL programs.

Blank Lines in Scripts

In most cases, Paradox doesn't care about the presence of blank lines in a script. The exception to this rule is that certain special PAL commands that occupy multiple lines sometimes are very sensitive to the presence of blank lines. The script representation of a query is one case in which blank lines matter. Unless you leave a blank line after the Query command and another blank line before the EndQuery command, Paradox will not be able to understand the query. Paradox doesn't care whether you leave more than one blank line in these places, however.

As you read the next four chapters, you will see other examples where blank lines are allowed or not allowed. If a blank line is required, be sure to include it in the script. You also might want to use blank lines even when they are not required to make the flow of your script more understandable.

Capitalization

When Paradox records a script, it capitalizes the first letter of each menu item and capitalizes the representations of special keys, as listed in Table 13-1. These capitalization patterns are conventions, not rules. As long as you spell each menu item and special key representation correctly, Paradox doesn't care how these are capitalized. These conventions make a script easier for you to read and understand, however.

Capitalization does make a difference in the script representations of queries, however. Just as in a query on the workspace, Paradox is sensitive to the case of selection conditions in the script representation of a query.

In all other cases, including special PAL commands, functions, and references to field names and variables (subjects we'll discuss in Chapter 14), case makes no difference, except for readability. As you'll see throughout the next few chapters, however, we like to follow certain conventions when we write a script. First, the initial letter of each command or object name chosen from a menu should be capitalized, but the remaining letters should be lower case. Second, the names of all special PAL commands and functions (subjects we'll cover in Chapters 15 and 16) should be in all capital letters. Third, the name of variables (covered in Chapter 14) should be in lower-case form.

A Tip

Writing a script from scratch requires a high degree of familiarity with the layout of Paradox's numerous menus. If you forget a command sequence while writing a script, you'll have to save the incomplete script, work through the menus from the keyboard until you find the command you are looking for, then reload the script into the Editor and complete the script. If you have worked with Paradox for a while, the structure of the various menus probably will be pretty well engrained in your mind. If you have trouble remembering the location of various commands, however, you might want to develop a written "tree" that lists the commands on each menu and keep it handy when you write your scripts.

Script Errors

Unfortunately, not all scripts run properly when you play them, no matter how much you wish that they would. Typical causes of faulty scripts include misspellings of keystroke representations, references to objects that do not exist, and so forth. When Paradox encounters an error in a script that it is playing, it stops the script and presents the menu shown in Figure 13-19. In addition, the message *Script error – select Cancel or Debug from menu* appears in inverse video at the bottom of the screen. If you choose Cancel from this menu, Paradox will "lift" the PAL canvas and return control of the workspace to you. However, because Paradox will have executed the commands that came prior to the error, the workspace may be different than it was when you started.

Figure 13-19 The Debugger Prompt

The second option, Debug, allows you to enter the PAL Debugger. The PAL Debugger is a special environment in which you can spot and sometimes correct script-stopping errors. To understand how the Debugger works, suppose that you have asked PAL to play the following script:

Menu {Tools} {More} {Drectory} CtrlBackspace {c:\\paradox\\examples} {OK}

As you can see, the representation of the menu item Directory is misspelled in this script. When Paradox reaches this point in the script, it will stop processing the script and display the *Script error...* message. If you choose Debug at this point, Paradox will enter the PAL Debugger and present you with the screen shown in Figure 13-20.

Figure 13-20   The PAL Debugger

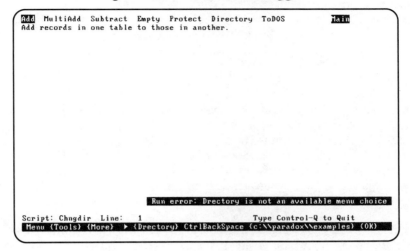

As you can see in this figure, PAL displays the line of the script that contains the error in inverse video at the bottom of the screen. (In this case, PAL displays the entire script since it is only one line long.) The normal video message on the second line from the bottom of the screen tells you which script you are debugging and where you are within that script. In this case, the message

> Script: Chngdir   Line: 1

indicates that you are debugging the first line of the script named Chngdir. Within the line that it is debugging, PAL flashes a solid arrow to mark the error. In this case, PAL positions the arrow to the left of the keystroke representation {Drectory}. The inverse video message on the fourth line from the bottom of the screen helps to explain the error to which PAL is pointing. In this case, the message

> Run error: Drectory is not an available menu choice

points out the misspelling of the item Directory.

Once PAL has pointed out the script error, you can take a number of actions, depending on what the error is. In most cases, you will want to write down the error, leave the Debugger, edit the script to change the error, and then play the script again. To do this, you could press **[Ctrl]-[Q]** to leave the Debugger, then issue the **[Menu]** Script Editor Edit command and type the name of the script that contains the error–in this case you would type the name **Chngdir**.

Alternatively, you can press the **[PAL Menu]** key ([Alt]-[F10]) while you still are within the Debugger to reveal the Debugger menu, which is shown in Figure 13-21. If you choose the **E**ditor option from the end of this menu, PAL will exit from the Debugger, clear the workspace, and present the error-containing script within the Script Editor.

Once the script is in the Editor, Paradox will position the cursor on the line that contains the error, automatically.

Figure 13-21 The Debugger Menu

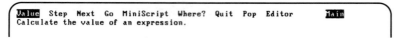

Once you enter the Editor in either of these ways, you can correct the error using the techniques you learned earlier in this chapter. In this case, you would move the cursor to the *r* in the word *Drectory*, press **[Ins]** to enter the insert mode, and type **i**. After you have corrected the script, you can end the edit by pressing the **[Do-It!]** key (or choosing DO-IT! from the Script Editor menu). Then you can play the corrected script by issuing the Menu {Scripts} {Play} command. Alternatively, you can choose Go from the PAL Editor menu to both save the changes and run the corrected script.

In Chapter 17, we'll explore the PAL Debugger in greater depth. In that chapter, we'll show you that there are two different types of script errors: run errors and syntax errors. As you will see, it often is possible to correct run errors temporarily from within the Debugger, then continue with the execution of the script, either continuously or one command at a time. For now, you should understand the basic way that you can use the Debugger to point out the errors that Paradox encounters when it executes a script.

Conclusion

In this chapter, we have introduced you to the power of Paradox scripts. First, we showed you how to record your keystrokes into a simple script. Then we showed you what a recorded script looks like. Next, we explained how Paradox represents a query in a script. Finally, after showing you how to play a script, we showed you how to edit a script, and how to write a script from scratch. We also explained the basics of debugging a script.

Simple recorded scripts like the ones presented in this chapter barely scratch the surface of the potential powers of programming Paradox. Although recorded scripts allow you to perform tasks quickly, they can't do anything more than you can from the keyboard. In the next four chapters, we'll move beyond the limited realm of keystroke representations into the world of PAL.

Chapter 14

PAL Basics

As you saw in Chapter 13, scripts are powerful tools that allow you to automate any of the tasks that you do within Paradox. However, scripts that contain only representations of keystrokes, whether recorded or written, can do nothing more than you can do from the keyboard yourself. The Paradox Applications Language (PAL) takes you beyond the limited power of these simple scripts. PAL is a complete, structured programming language that is designed specifically to work with Paradox. PAL allows you to use variables, set up loops, develop customized menus, solicit user input, and so forth in your scripts. These powerful features allow you to develop complex automated applications that go way beyond the scope of the simple scripts presented in Chapter 13.

Although a PAL program can do much more than a simple listing of keystrokes can, it is still a script. In fact, all PAL programs are scripts, and all scripts are PAL programs. The difference between them is one of complexity. The simple scripts presented in Chapter 13 are PAL programs that contain only representations of keystrokes. Because those keystroke representations are components of the Paradox Applications Language, however, those simple scripts are PAL programs.

The principal difference between advanced PAL programs with listings of keystrokes and the PAL programs presented in Chapter 13 is power. Unlike the simple scripts presented in Chapter 13, advanced scripts use special PAL commands and functions instead of or in addition to keystroke representations. Because advanced PAL programs are scripts, however, you write and play them in exactly the same way that you write and play a simple script. In this chapter, we'll assume a working knowledge of writing and playing scripts as we introduce the basic concepts and tools essential to PAL programming.

PAL Commands

PAL's 68 special commands are the principal tools you will use to create advanced PAL programs. These commands can be divided into the following six functional groups: input/output commands, system control commands, program control commands, workspace-manipulating commands, variable-manipulating commands, and menu-equivalent commands. **Input/output commands** allow PAL to request and receive input from a user, to display information on the screen during the execution of a script, and, finally, to send information to a printer. The commands in this group include ACCEPT,

SHOWMENU, ??, and PRINTER. **System control commands** allow PAL to do things like enter the Debugger, redefine the function of specific keys, and pause the execution of a script. Commands in this group include DEBUG, SETKEY, and SLEEP. **Program control commands** control the execution of a script based on the result of a conditional test. Commands in this group include IF, WHILE, SCAN, and SWITCH. **Workspace-manipulating commands** do things like move the cursor within an object, make entries into a table, and choose items from menus. Commands in this group include MOVETO, KEYPRESS, and SELECT. **Variable-manipulating commands** allow you to assign values to variables and arrays. Commands in this group include =, COPYTOARRAY, and RELEASE. **Menu-equivalent commands** provide streamlined ways to perform tasks that you can do with keystroke representations. Commands in this group include VIEW, EDIT, ADD, SORT, SETDIR, and DOS.

Command Basics

Before we begin examining individual PAL commands, let's look at the structure and syntax of commands in general. In this brief section, we'll look at the three components of a PAL command: command names, arguments, and keywords.

Command Names

A command's name is a word that identifies the command and, at least in most cases, gives you a rough idea of what that command does. For example, the CREATE command creates a table, the ACCEPT command solicits input from the keyboard, and the MESSAGE command displays a message on the screen.

Throughout the remainder of this book, we'll always present the names of PAL commands in upper-case form. This convention makes our scripts easier to read and understand. It does not have any effect on the way PAL reads and executes the commands, however. For example, PAL evaluates the commands VIEW "Emplyee", View "Emplyee", and view "Emplyee", in exactly the same way.

Arguments

Arguments are the second component of most PAL commands. A command's arguments tell it what objects to act upon, what to display, how many times to perform the action, how long to wait, etc. In the command *VIEW "Emplyee"*, for example, the argument *"Emplyee"* specifies which table PAL should bring onto the workspace. Likewise, in the command *SLEEP 3000*, the argument *3000* tells PAL to wait for three seconds.

Different commands require different types of arguments. Some commands, like VIEW, require string expressions as their arguments. Some commands, like SLEEP, require numeric expressions. Some commands accept date expressions as their arguments, while others accept logical expressions. By expression, we mean a literal value, a variable, a reference to a field, a formula, or a function.

A string expression is either a literal string (like "Emplyee"), a reference to an alphanumeric field, a variable that contains a string value, or a formula or function that returns a string value. Similarly, a numeric expression is a literal number (like 3000), a variable that contains a numeric value, a reference to a numeric field, or a formula or function that returns a numeric value. Likewise, any expression that is, contains, or returns a date value is a date expression, and any expression that is, contains, or returns a logical value is a logical constant. No matter which of these five types of expressions you use as the argument of a command, it must be of the type the command expects. You will learn more about these expressions later in this chapter and in Chapter 15.

Keywords

In addition to a command name and one or more arguments, some PAL commands contain one or more keywords. Keywords are special words that are required for the proper execution of the command, but are not the command name itself. For example, the word ENDQUERY is a keyword that is required by the QUERY command. Similarly, in the command *IF x=y THEN x=x+1 ELSE x=x+2*, THEN and ELSE are keywords that work in conjunction with the command name IF. Like command names, all keywords will be capitalized in the example scripts presented in this book. Although this capitalization isn't required, it does make a script easier to read.

Menu-equivalent Commands

Because menu-equivalent commands do things that you already know how to do with keystroke representations, they are a good place to begin learning PAL. Table 14-1 lists PAL's 20 menu-equivalent commands. As you can see, the names of most of these commands are spelled exactly like the menu items they represent. Some of these commands, like VIEW, PLAY, and EXIT, have exactly the same effect as choosing the items that they represent (View, Play, and Exit) from the Paradox menus. Other commands, like SORT, select the corresponding menu item and allow you to supply related information, all in a single step.

In almost all cases, these commands provide a more efficient way to program a task than does the use of keystroke representations. The "shorthand" nature of these commands and their ability to accept complex expressions as arguments are the two main reasons to choose them over keystroke representations. In the next few pages, we'll explain each of PAL's menu-equivalent commands and give an example of the use of each one.

Table 14-1 Menu-equivalent Commands

PAL Command	PAL Keystroke Sequence
ADD	Menu {Tools} {More} {Add}
CANCELEDIT	Menu {Cancel} {Yes}
COPY	Menu {Tools} {Copy} {Table}
CREATE	Menu {Create}
DELETE	Menu {Tools} {Delete} {Table}
DOS	Menu {Tools} {More} {ToDOS}
EDIT	Menu {Modify} {Edit}
EMPTY	Menu {Tools} {More} {Empty}
EXIT	Menu {Exit} {Yes}
INDEX	Menu {Tools} {QuerySpeedup}
MOVETO	Menu {Image} {GoTo}
PICKFORM	Menu {Image} {PickForm}
PLAY	Menu {Scripts} {Play}
PROTECT	Menu {Tools} {More} {Protect} {Password} {Table}
RENAME	Menu {Tools} {Rename} {Table}
REPORT	Menu {Report} {Output}
SETDIR	Menu {Tools} {More} {Directory}
SORT	Menu {Modify} {Sort}
SUBTRACT	Menu {Tools} {More} {Subtract}
VIEW	Menu {View}

The VIEW Command

VIEW is PAL's command equivalent to choosing View from Paradox's Main menu. The form of this command is

>   VIEW *tablename*

where the mandatory argument, *tablename*, is a string expression that specifies the name of a table stored in the current directory.

This command brings the specified table into view. For example, the command *VIEW "Emplyee"* will bring a table named EMPLYEE into view. This command is the equivalent of the keystroke sequence *Menu {View} {Emplyee}*.

The CREATE Command

PAL's CREATE command allows you to create a new table on the Paradox workspace. This command is the equivalent of issuing the [Menu] Create command, supplying a name for the new table, filling in the STRUCT table, and pressing [Do-It!]. The form of this command is:

>   CREATE *tablename fieldname:type1...fieldname n:type n*

The *tablename* argument supplies the name of the new table. The subsequent *fieldname:type* pairs identify the names and types of each column that you want to include in the table. Since a table can have up to 255 fields, this command will accept up to 255 *fieldname:type* pairs. An asterisk to the right of any field's type designates it as a key field. All arguments of this command must be string expressions.

For example, the command *CREATE "Test" "Name:L25" "Birthday:D*"* will create a table with two fields: Name and Birthday. Birthday will be a key field. This command is the equivalent of the keystroke sequence

> Menu {Create} {Test} "Name" Enter "L25" Enter
> "Birthday" Enter "D*" Do-It!

An optional form of this function, which lets you create a table with the same structure as an existing table, is shown below:

> CREATE *tablename* LIKE *tablename*

As in the first form of the function, the first *tablename* argument supplies a name for the new table. The second *tablename* argument, which must follow the keyword LIKE, specifies the table whose structure you want to copy. This command is similar to the [Menu] Borrow command on the Paradox Create menu.

The EDIT Command

The EDIT command is a substitute for the keystroke sequence *Menu {Modify} {Edit}*. The form of this command is

> EDIT *tablename*.

The mandatory argument *tablename* identifies the table you want to edit. The *tablename* argument must be a string expression.

This command brings the specified table into view and enters the edit mode. For example, *EDIT "Emplyee"* will bring the table named EMPLYEE into view and will put Paradox in the edit mode. This command is equivalent to the keystroke sequence *Menu {Modify} {Edit} {Emplyee}* and the sequence *Menu {View} {Emplyee} EditKey*.

The DELETE Command

The DELETE command instructs PAL to delete the family of objects that you specify. The form of this command is

> DELETE *tablename*

where the single argument is the name of the table whose family you want to delete. The *tablename* argument must be a string expression.

Unlike the [Menu] Tools Delete command, the DELETE command does not allow you to delete only a form, a report, a script, speedup files, a settings sheet, or a validity checking file for a table; it always deletes every object associated with the table that you name. For example, the command *DELETE "Emplyee"* will delete the table EMPLYEE and its family of objects. This command is equivalent to the keystroke sequence *Menu {Tools} {Delete} {Table} {Emplyee} {OK}*.

The COPY Command

The PAL COPY command is equivalent to the recorded keystrokes Menu {Tools} {Copy} {Table}. The form of this command is

COPY *source destination*

where *source* is the name of the table that you want to copy, and *destination* is the name of the new table. Both arguments must be string expressions.

The COPY command copies a table and its family of objects into a new table whose name you provide. For example, the command *COPY "Test" "TestCopy"* performs the same action as the keystroke sequence *Menu {Tools} {Copy} {Table} {Test} {TestCopy}*.

The EXIT Command

The EXIT command ends the current Paradox session and returns you to DOS. The form of this function is simply EXIT; it requires and accepts no arguments. The EXIT command is equivalent to the keystroke sequence Menu {Exit} {Yes}.

The SORT Command

The SORT command provides an alternative way to sort a table on the basis of the entries in any number of fields. The typical form of this command is

SORT *sourcetable* ON *field1 D, field2 D,* ...TO *destinationtable.*

The first argument, *tablename*, identifies the table that you want to sort. The next argument or arguments, which must follow the keyword ON, specify the fields on which you want to sort that table. The final argument, which must follow the keyword TO, specifies the table in which Paradox should store the sorted result. All of this command's arguments must be string expressions.

Many of the components of this command are optional. For example, you should follow a field name with the keyword *D* only if you want that field sorted in descending order. If you want to place the results of the sort within the same table that you sorted, you must omit the keyword TO and the *destination* argument. (This portion of the command is required, of course, if the table being sorted contains a key field). If you leave out the keyword ON and the *fieldname* argument(s), Paradox will sort the table into ascending order on the basis of the entries in every field, starting with the leftmost field in the table.

As you can see, this PAL command substitutes for the full process of issuing the [Menu] Modify Sort command, filling out the sort specification, and pressing the [Do-It!] key. For example, assuming that LastName and Age are the first and third fields of a table named TEST, the command

    SORT "Test" ON "Age" D, "LastName" TO "Sorted"

produces the same result as the recorded keystroke sequence

    Menu {Modify} {Sort} {Test} {Sorted} "2" Down Down "1D" Do_It!

The RENAME Command

PAL's RENAME command allows you to rename any family of Paradox objects. This command is the equivalent of the recorded keystroke with the sequence *Menu {Tools} {Rename}*. The form of this command is

    RENAME *currentname newname*

where the first argument is the current name of the family's table, and the second argument is the new name. Both arguments must be string expressions.

Unlike the [Menu] Tools Rename command, PAL's RENAME command doesn't let you selectively rename only a report, form, or script; it always renames an entire family of objects. For instance, the command *RENAME "Workers" "Emplyee"* changes the name of the WORKERS table and its related forms, reports, and indices to EMPLYEE, just as the keystroke sequence *Menu {Tools} {Rename} {Table} {Workers} {Emplyee}* does.

The PICKFORM Command

PAL's PICKFORM command is a substitute for the keystroke sequence *Menu {Image} PickForm*. The form of this function is

    PICKFORM *formnumber*

where *formnumber* is a number from 1 through 9 or the letter *F*. This argument, which must be a string expression, specifies which of the current table's forms you want to view and make active. Just like the PickForm option, this command acts upon the current table (the one that the cursor is in when you issue this command).

This command brings the selected form into view. For example, the command PICKFORM "2" will bring the second form for the active table into view. This command is equivalent to the keystroke sequence *Menu {Image} {PickForm}{2}*.

The EMPTY Command

PAL's EMPTY command clears all records from the table that you specify. The form of this command is

> EMPTY *tablename*

where *tablename* is a string expression that specifies the name of the table whose records you want to erase. For example, the command *EMPTY "Emplyee"* will delete every record from the EMPLYEE table. This command is equivalent to the sequence *Menu {Tools} {More} {Empty} {Emplyee} {OK}*.

The CANCELEDIT Command

PAL's CANCELEDIT command allows you to cancel the current editing session without saving any changes. This command, which accepts no arguments, is identical in action to pressing [Menu] during an edit and choosing Cancel Yes. In other words, the solitary command CANCELEDIT is equivalent to the keystroke sequence *Menu {Cancel} {Yes}*. This command makes sense only while you are editing a table.

The INDEX Command

The INDEX command allows you to create a pair of secondary indexes on any field in a table. The form of this command is

> INDEX *table* ON *field*

where the first argument is the name of the table you want to index, and the second argument is the name of the field on which you want to index that table. Both arguments must be string expressions.

Like the [Menu] Tools QuerySpeedup command, this command creates a pair of secondary index files for the table specified by the first argument. Unlike the QuerySpeedup command, however, which chooses the appropriate field for you, the INDEX command requires you to specify the field on which you want to index the table. The query for the table you want to index does not have to be on the workspace when you issue the INDEX command, as it does when you issue the QuerySpeedup command.

For example, if you wanted to create a secondary index on the Salary field of the EMPLYEE table, you would use the command *INDEX "Emplyee" ON "Salary"*.

The DOS Command

DOS is the PAL command equivalent of the [Menu] Tools More ToDOS command or the recorded keystroke sequence *Menu {Tools} {More} {ToDOS}*. This command, which does not accept an argument, instructs PAL to exit to DOS temporarily. As soon as you type *exit* at a DOS prompt and press ↵, however, you will return to the unchanged Paradox workspace. (For more on the ToDOS command, see Chapter 6.)

The ADD Command

ADD is the PAL command equivalent of the [Menu] Tools More Add command. This command allows you to append the records from one table to another table. The form of this command is

ADD *table of records to add   table to add to*

where the first argument is the name of the table from which you'll be reading, and the second argument is the name of the table to which you are appending. Both arguments must be string expressions.

For example, suppose you want to add the records in a table named MARSALES to the table named SALEHIST. You could use either the command *ADD "MarSales" "SaleHist"* or the keystroke sequence *Menu {Tools} {More} {Add} {MarSales} {SaleHist}*.

For the add to be successful, of course, the type of each column in the table being appended must be the same as the type of the column to which it will be appended. (For more on the [Menu] Tools More Add command, see Chapter 10.)

The SUBTRACT Command

The action of PAL's SUBTRACT command is equivalent to that of the [Menu] Tools More Subtract command. The form of this command is

SUBTRACT *table of records to subtract   table to subtract from*

The first argument must be the name of the table that contains the records to subtract from the table named in the second argument. As with the Add command, both arguments must be string expressions.

For example, suppose you want to subtract the records contained in the table named EXPIRED from the records in SUBSCRPT. You could do this with the command *SUBTRACT "Expired" "Subscrpt"* or the stored keystroke sequence *Menu {Tools} {More} {Subtract} {Expired} {Subscrpt}*.

The REPORT Command

REPORT is PAL's command equivalent of the [Menu] Report Output command. This command instructs PAL to print from the table you specify, using the report template that you specify. The syntax of this command is

> REPORT *table report specification*

The first argument must be the name of the table from which you want to print. The second argument, which must be a number from 1 through 9 or the letter *R*, identifies the report specification from which Paradox should print. In addition, both arguments must be string expressions.

For example, to print from report specification #2 of the table named EMPLYEE, you could use either the command *REPORT "Emplyee" "2"* or the stored keystroke sequence *Menu {Report} {Output} {Emplyee} {2} {Printer}*.

The REPORT command always sends information to a printer. You must use keystroke representations if you want to send a report to the screen or to a text file.

The SETDIR Command

SETDIR is PAL's command equivalent of the [Menu] Tools More Directory command. This command allows you to change the active drive and/or directory from within a script. The form of this command is

> SETDIR *directory.*

The single argument, which must be a string expression, specifies the directory that you want to make current.

Suppose you want to change the current directory to c:\paradox\examples. To do this, you could use the command *SETDIR "c:\\paradox\\examples"*.

Because the backslash (\) is a special character that tells PAL to treat the next character literally, two backslashes are needed to represent a single backslash. This command is the equivalent of the recorded keystroke sequence

> Menu {Tools} {More} {Directory} CtrlBackSpace {c:\\paradox\\examples} {OK}

If the current drive was c:\paradox, you could use the command *SETDIR "examples"* or the keystrokes *Menu {Tools} {More} {Directory} {examples} {OK}* instead.

The PLAY Command

PLAY is PAL's command equivalent of the [Menu] Scripts Play command (and the Play option on the PAL menu, which we'll discuss later). This command instructs PAL to play the script that you specify. The form of this command is simply

PLAY *scriptname*

where the single argument is the name of a script. Again, the single argument must be a string expression.

For example, to play a script named Abc, you could use either the command *PLAY "Abc"* or the keystroke sequence *Menu {Scripts} {Play} {Abc}*. In Chapter 16, we'll show you more examples of the use of the PLAY command.

The PROTECT Command

PROTECT is PAL's command equivalent for the [Menu] Tools More Protect Password command. This command allows you to encrypt and password-protect a Paradox table. Unlike its menu equivalent, the PROTECT command can be used only to protect a table, not a script. The form of the PROTECT command is

PROTECT *tablename password*

where the first argument (a string expression) is the name of the table you want to encrypt, and the second argument (also a string expression) is the password for that table.

To assign the password *abracadabra* to EMPLYEE, for example, you could use either the command *PROTECT "Emplyee" "abracadabra"* or the keystroke sequence

Menu {Tools} {More} {Protect} {Password} {Table} {Emplyee} {abracadabra} {abracadabra}.

As you can see, the PROTECT command provides a much briefer way to encrypt a table than the keystroke series.

The MOVETO command

PAL's MOVETO command allows you to move the cursor around within the Paradox workspace. The effect of the simplest form of this command

MOVETO RECORD *number*

is equivalent to that of the [Menu] Image GoTo Record command–it moves the cursor vertically to the record you specify within the current table. The single argument must be a number (not a string) that specifies the number of the destination record. For example, the command *MOVETO RECORD 15* moves the cursor to the fifteenth record of the current table, all within the current field. The recorded keystroke sequence *Menu {Image} {GoTo} {Record} {1}* would do the same thing.

Another form of the MOVETO command allows you to move to a specified field of the current image. This form of the command

    MOVETO [*field*]

is the command equivalent of the Menu {Image} {GoTo} {Field} command. Because the argument of this form of the MOVETO command must be a field reference (a subject we won't cover until later in this chapter), we'll delay our discussion of this until that point. Similarly, we'll delay our discussion of two remaining forms of the MOVETO command until Chapter 17.

Other Commands

PAL's other five types of commands–input/output, system control, program control, workspace manipulating, and variable manipulating–let you do more than just provide an alternative way to select items from the Paradox menus. Instead, they add real programming features, such as the use of variables, conditional testing, looping, user input, and so forth, to your scripts. We'll discuss most of these commands in context in Chapters 15 and 16.

For now, we'll explore the use of variables in a PAL script. In particular, we'll show you how the use of variables further distinguishes PAL's menu-equivalent commands from the keystroke sequences they represent.

Variables

Variables are another fundamental component of PAL programs. A variable is a "storehouse" for a number, text, or date value. Once you store a value in a variable, you can use that variable, instead of the literal value, as the argument of a PAL command. For example, if you store the string *Emplyee* in a variable named x, you could use either the command *VIEW "Emplyee"* or the command *VIEW x* to bring the EMPLYEE table to the workspace. As you will see, the use of variables, which are essential components of conditional testing and the acceptance of user input, contribute significantly to the power of a PAL program.

Assigning a Value to a Variable

PAL's = command lets you assign a value to a variable. The syntax of this command is

    variable=expression

where *variable* is the name of the variable in which PAL will store the value of the expression that follows the command. A variable name may be up to 132 characters long and may contain letters, numbers, and the characters . , $, ! , and _ . The name must begin with a letter, however. For example, a, xyz, prodname, a$B!c_123 are valid variable names, but 1abc is not.

Additionally, the name of a variable cannot contain spaces and should not be the same as any of PAL's keywords or function names. PAL makes no distinction between upper and lower-case letters in a variable name. For example, ABC, Abc, and aBC all refer to the same variable.

The expression to the right of the = command may take any of five forms. The simplest uses of the = command are ones in which the expression is a literal value–either a value, a string, or a date. For example, the command *x=123* stores the value 123 in the variable named *x*. The command *y="Emplyee"* stores the string *Emplyee* in the variable named *y*, and the command *z=11/24/58* stores the date 11/24/58 in the variable named *z*.

Although literal values are the simplest form of expression for an = command, they are not the ones you will use most often. The principal use for variables is to store values that may change each time you execute a script, such as the result of a formula or function, an entry from a table, or information input by the user during the execution of a program. We'll show you how to access and store information from these sources at the end of this chapter and in Chapter 15.

The Lifespan of Variables

The first time you use the = command to assign a value to a variable, PAL actually does two things: it "defines" the variable, then it stores a value in that variable. Defining a variable means bringing it into existence, a process that involves allocating a small amount of memory to that variable. Once PAL has defined a variable, that variable remains in existence until you do one of two things: end the current Paradox session or "undefine" the variable with the RELEASE VARS command.

The RELEASE VARS Command

RELEASE VARS is a PAL command that allows you to undefine variables selectively. The form of the RELEASE VARS command is

    RELEASE VARS *variable name(s)*

where the argument(s) are string expressions that specify the names of the variable(s) that you want to release. For example, the command *RELEASE VARS x* would release the variable named *x*, while the command *RELEASE VARS x,y,z* would release the variables *x*, *y*, and *z*.

You can use the special argument ALL with the RELEASE command, like this

    RELEASE VARS ALL

to undefine every variable that has been defined since the beginning of the current Paradox session. Importantly, releasing a variable doesn't just erase the value that is stored in that variable–it destroys the variable itself, freeing the RAM that was allocated to it.

If you do not release a variable during the course of a program, it will remain in existence until you end the current Paradox session. Exiting to DOS temporarily by means of the ToDOS option or the DOS or RUN commands has no effect on any variables.

The SAVEVARS Command

PAL offers a special command, SAVEVARS, that allows you to save the current values of any or all defined variables. The form of this command is

    SAVEVARS *variable name(s).*

Like the argument(s) of the RELEASE VARS command, the argument(s) of this command may be a single variable name, a list of names separated by commas, or the keyword ALL.

When PAL executes this command, it creates a script named Savevars. This script contains one = command for each currently defined variable, linking it to its current value. For example, suppose you have defined three variables during the current Paradox session: x, which stores the number 123; y, which holds the string *testing*; and z, which contains the date 11/24/58. If PAL read the command *SAVEVARS x*, it would save the command *x=123* in a script named Savevars. If PAL read the command *SAVEVARS x,y* in a script, it would save the commands *x=123* and *y="testing"* in that script. If PAL read either the command *SAVEVARS x,y,z* or *SAVEVARS ALL* in a script, it would save the commands *x=123*, *y="testing"* and *z=11/24/58*.

Each time PAL executes a SAVEVARS command, it replaces the former contents of the Savevars script. It does not append the new statement to the end of the existing script.

Once you've used the SAVEVARS command to save the current value of each currently defined variable into a script, you can recover those values later. You can do this within the same Paradox session or in a subsequent Paradox session simply by playing the Savevars script. For example, you could issue the [Menu] Scripts Play command and choose Savevars, or you could include the command *PLAY "Savevars"* in a script.

When you play a Savevars script, PAL will read each = command in sequence. If a variable named in the Savevars script has not yet been defined in the current Paradox session, the = command defines it and assigns it a value. If the variable already exists, the = command assigns it a new value. Consequently, you may wish to edit the Savevars script before running it to remove the = command for any variables whose values you do not want to overwrite.

Assigning a New Value to a Variable

Although a variable usually will remain in existence during an entire Paradox session, it doesn't have to store the same value for that entire length of time. Whenever you use the name of an existing variable to the left of a = command, PAL assigns a new value to that variable, replacing the old value. For example, suppose that you had stored the string *Emplyee* in the variable named *abc* early in a script. While *abc* contains the string *Emplyee*, the command *VIEW abc* would bring the table named EMPLYEE to the workspace. If PAL later read the command *abc="Jobs"*, however, it would replace the string *Emplyee* stored in *abc* with the string *Jobs*. The next time PAL executed the command *VIEW abc*, it would display the table named JOBS instead of EMPLYEE.

Variable Types

PAL variables can store four types of information: numbers, strings, dates, and logical constants. The first three types correspond to kinds of information that you can store in fields of a table. The fourth type, logical constants, can be stored only in a variable.

The kind of information that a variable holds controls where it can be used. If a variable holds a string, it can be used in situations where PAL expects a string argument. If a variable holds a date, it can be used whenever PAL expects a date, and so forth. In this sense, PAL assigns a type to a variable when it stores a value in that variable.

A variable's type is not permanent, however. Each time you assign a new value to a variable, PAL changes that variable's type so that it is compatible with the new data. For example, suppose you store the string *Emplyee* in the variable named *x* when you first define that variable. While *x* contains this string, it is an alphanumeric variable and can be used only in situations where a string is appropriate. If PAL reads the command *x=123* later in the macro, however, it will assign the number 123 to *x* and change the type of the variable *x* from alphabetic to numeric. While *x* contains this value, it can be used only when PAL expects a numeric value.

Referring to Entries in a Table

Another fundamental PAL technique is the ability to refer to entries in Paradox tables from within scripts. To refer to an entry, you must use one of the following special forms:

>   []
>   [*fieldname*]
>   [*tablename->*]
>   [*tablename->fieldname*]

Each of these four forms lets you refer to a table in a slightly different way. The simplest form, [], refers to the current field of the current record in the current table–in other words, the record/field intersection in which the cursor is positioned when PAL processes the command. The next form, [*fieldname*], refers to the named field of the current record in the current table. When you use this form, the position of the cursor determines the table and record, but not the field from which to pull the entry. The third form, [*tablename->*], refers to the field of the record that was current the last time you viewed or edited the specified table. The hyphen (-) and greater than sign (>) must follow the name of that table. The fourth form, [*tablename->fieldname*], refers to the specified field of whatever record the cursor was in when you last viewed or edited the specified table. In all cases, an image of the referenced table must be on the Paradox workspace.

Typically, you will use table references in four important ways in your PAL scripts: to store an entry in a variable, to make an entry into a table, as the argument of certain PAL commands, and as the argument of certain PAL functions. In this section, we will show you how to use table references in the first three of these ways. We will show you how to use references as the arguments of functions in Chapter 15.

Storing an Entry in a Variable

Storing an entry in a variable is as simple as using one of these reference forms as the argument of an = command. For example, suppose you want to store the contents of the Last Name field of the second record of the EMPLYEE table (shown in Figure 14-1) in a variable named x. To do this, you could use the script

```
VIEW "Emplyee"
Right Right Down
x=[]
```

The VIEW command brings the EMPLYEE table to the workspace, if it is not there already, and positions the cursor in the first field of the first record. The next three commands, *Right*, *Right*, and *Down*, move the cursor to the Last Name field of the second record. The final command, *x=[]*, stores a copy of the entry over which the cursor is positioned in a variable named x. In this case, PAL stores the string *Cameron* in the variable x.

You can assign this entry to x with any of the other three reference forms as well. For example, you could use the script

```
VIEW "Emplyee"
Down
x=[Last Name]
```

This script brings the EMPLYEE table to the workspace, moves to the first field of the second record, and then uses the command *x=[Last Name]* to pull the value from the Last Name field of that record.

Figure 14-1 The EMPLYEE Table

```
Viewing Emplyee table: Record 1 of 16                          Main
EMPLYEE──Emp Number──────Last Name───First Name────SS Number──────────Addre
    1  │     1         │ Jones      │ David      │ 414-74-3421 │ 4000 St. Ja
    2  │     2         │ Cameron    │ Herb       │ 321-65-8765 │ 2321 Elm St
    3  │     3         │ Jones      │ Stewart    │ 401-32-8721 │ 4389 Oakbri
    4  │     4         │ Roberts    │ Darlene    │ 417-43-7777 │ 451 Lone Pi
    5  │     5         │ Jones      │ Jean       │ 413-07-9123 │ 4000 St. Ja
    6  │     6         │ Williams   │ Brenda     │ 401-55-1567 │ 100 Owl Cre
    7  │     7         │ Myers      │ Julie      │ 314-38-9452 │ 4512 Parksi
    8  │     8         │ Link       │ Julie      │ 345-75-1525 │ 3215 Palm C
    9  │     9         │ Jackson    │ Mary       │ 424-13-7621 │ 7821 Clark
   10  │    10         │ Jakes, Jr. │ Sal        │ 321-65-9151 │ 3451 Michig
   11  │    11         │ Preston    │ Molly      │ 451-00-3426 │ 321 Indian
   12  │    12         │ Masters    │ Ron        │ 317-65-4529 │ 423 W. 72nd
   13  │    13         │ Robertson  │ Kevin      │ 415-24-6710 │ 431 Bardsto
   14  │    14         │ Garrison   │ Robert     │ 312-90-1479 │ 55 Wheeler
   15  │    15         │ Gunn       │ Barbara    │ 321-97-8632 │ 541 Kentuck
   16  │    16         │ Emerson    │ Cheryl     │ 404-14-1422 │ 8100 River
```

If the EMPLYEE table is anywhere on the workspace, and the cursor was in the second record when you last viewed or edited that table, the command *x=[Emplyee->Last Name]* also would assign the string *Cameron* to *x*. If the cursor was in the Last Name field of the second record when you last viewed the EMPLYEE table, and EMPLYEE was still on the workspace, the command *x=[Emplyee->]* would do the same thing.

Making an Entry into a Table

In addition to using table references to extract entries from a table, you can use them to make entries into a table. To do this, you must use a modified form of the = command. Instead of placing the table reference to the right of the = command, as you did to extract an entry, you must place the reference to the left of the command. The expression to the right of the = command tells PAL what to place in the referenced cell. To make an entry into a table in this or any other way, of course, the table must be in the edit mode.

For example, suppose you want to change the entry in the Last Name field of the second record in EMPLYEE from *Cameron* to *Jones*. To do this, you could use the script:

    EDIT "Emplyee"
    Home CtrlHome
    Right Right Down
    []="Jones"

This script brings the EMPLYEE table to the workspace in the edit mode. If the table is on the workspace already and the cursor is not in the upper-left corner of the table, the Home CtrlHome commands are needed to move it there. The Right Right Down commands then move the cursor to the Last Name field of the second record. Finally, the statement *[]="Jones"* enters the string *Jones* into that cell, replacing the former entry, *Cameron*. The script

```
EDIT "Emplyee"
Home CtrlHome
Down
[Last Name]="Jones"
```

uses another reference form to achieve the same effect.

Now suppose that you want to copy the entry from the Last Name field of the second record in the EMPLYEE table to the Last Name field of the fourth record in that table. To do this, you could use the script

```
EDIT "Emplyee"
Home CtrlHome Down
x=[Last Name]
Down Down
[LastName]=x
```

The first two statements bring the EMPLYEE table to the workspace in the edit mode and move the cursor to the second record. The third statement in this script, *x=[Last Name]*, stores that record's Last Name field entry (the string *Cameron*) in the variable *x*. The two Down statements move the cursor to the fourth record in the table. Finally, the command *[Last Name]=x* enters the contents of *x* (the string *Cameron*) into the Last Name field of that record. You cannot perform this task without the use of a variable.

Using References as Arguments

Some PAL commands expect field references as their arguments. One form of the MOVETO command, whose basic form we discussed earlier in this chapter, is a good example. When PAL encounters a MOVETO command in the form

MOVETO [*field and/or table reference*]

it will move the cursor to the specified field of the specified table.

For example, suppose that you want to move the cursor to the Address field of the fifth record in the EMPLYEE table. To do this, you could use the script

```
VIEW "Emplyee"
Down Down Down Down
MOVETO [Address]
```

The VIEW command brings the EMPLYEE table to the workspace and positions the cursor in the leftmost field of the first record. The four Down commands move the cursor down to the first field of the fifth record. Finally, the MOVETO [Address] command instructs PAL to move the cursor to the Address field within that record.

You also can use other reference forms as the argument of a MOVETO command. For example, the command *MOVETO [Jobs->]* moves the cursor to the last position it occupied in the JOBS table, and the command *MOVETO [Jobs->Description]* moves the cursor to the Description field of the record that the cursor was in when you last viewed or edited that table. For either of these commands to work, of course, an image of the referenced table (JOBS) must be on the workspace.

Formulas

PAL offers four value operators: +, -, *, and /. These operators allow you to manipulate numbers, strings, and dates, whether presented in literal form or stored in a variable or table. Any combination of values linked with operators is called a formula. In the following section, we'll explain the rules for the use of these operators and present some examples of their use.

Operating on Numbers

The most common use of PAL's operators (and the one with which you're probably familiar) is for adding, subtracting, multiplying, and dividing numbers. The simplest case of this usage is to manipulate literal numbers and store the result in a variable. When PAL reads the command $x=1+2$, for example, it adds 1 and 2 and stores the result (3) in the variable x. Likewise, the commands $x=1-2$, $x=1*2$, and $x=1/2$ subtract 1 from 2, multiply 1 by 2, and divide 1 by 2, respectively, and store the results in x.

The Precedence of Operators

You can use several operators in the same formula, of course. When you do, however, PAL doesn't necessarily evaluate the formula from left to right. For example, PAL will not return the value 0 when it evaluates the formula *1+2-3*4/5*. Instead, it will perform the multiplication first, the division next, the addition third, and the subtraction last. As a result, PAL returns the value .6 when it evaluates this formula. If a formula contains more than multiple occurrences of the same operator, PAL evaluates them in the order that they appear in the formula (left to right).

You can use parentheses to override this default order of precedence. For example, when PAL reads the formula *1+(2-3)*4/5*, it subtracts 3 from 2 before it evaluates any other operation, and, as a result, returns the value .2. When a formula contains more than one set of unnested parentheses, it processes the operation(s) within the leftmost set of parentheses first. For example, when PAL evaluates the formula *(1-2)*(3+4)*, it performs the subtraction first, the addition next, and the multiplication last, returning the result -7.

If the formula contains nested parentheses, PAL evaluates the operations in the innermost set of parentheses first, then works its way out. For example, the formula *(1-(2*3))/4*, returns the value -1.25 because PAL performs the multiplication first, the subtraction next, and the division last.

Operating on Dates

In addition to operating on numbers, PAL can operate on dates. When you use PAL to operate on dates, however, a few important restrictions apply. First, you can use only the + and - operators to operate on dates. Second, the value to the left of the operator must be a date. When PAL acts upon a date with the + operator, the value to the right of that operator must be a number. When PAL acts upon a date with the - operator, the value to the right of that operator may be either a number or a date.

When you use the + operator to add a number to a date, the result is a future date. For example, the formula *11/24/58+100* returns the date 3/04/59. When you use the operator to subtract a number from a date, the result is an earlier date. For example, the formula *11/24/58-100* returns the date 8/16/58. When you use the - operator to subtract one date from another, the result is the number of days that have elapsed between the two dates. When PAL evaluates the formula *11/24/58-8/16/58*, for instance, it returns the value 100, the number of days between the two dates.

Operating on Strings

PAL also can operate on strings–although in a much more limited way than it can operate on either numbers or dates. In fact, the only operation that you can perform on strings is to add one to the other. The process of adding two strings is called concatenation. For example, when PAL evaluates the command *y="John"+" "+"Smith"*, it stores the string *John Smith* in the variable *y*. You cannot add a number or date to a string or act upon any string with the -, *, or / operators.

Variables and Field References in Formulas

In the examples of formulas that we've presented so far, we've used literal numbers, dates, and strings. In your actual work with PAL, however, literal values will not be the most common component of your formulas. In most cases, you'll use variables and references to the table entries in your formulas much more often than you'll use literal values.

You can use a variable or field reference in a formula anywhere you would use the type of information that they store. Wherever you would use a number, for example, you can use a variable that stores a number or a reference to a numeric field. Wherever you would use a literal string, you can use a variable that contains a string or a reference to an alphanumeric field. Wherever you would use a date in a formula, you can use a variable that stores a date or a reference to a date field instead.

There are a variety of ways to combine literal values, variables, and field references in a formula. For example, the command *z=65-[Age]*, will store in the variable *z* the result of subtracting the contents of the Age field of the current record from 65. The command *[Full Name]=[First Name]+" "+[Last Name]* concatenates the entries from a record's First Name and Last Name fields, plus a separating space, and places the result in that record's Full Name field.

Modifying the contents of a variable is another common use for a formula. You often will use a command like *x=x+1* to increment the counter in a looping routine, for instance. Each time PAL executes this command, it will increase the value of *x* by 1. As you read through the remainder of this chapter and the three chapters that follow, you will see numerous examples of the use of formulas in PAL programs.

Conditional Testing

Conditional testing is another fundamental programming technique that is an essential component of PAL programming. A conditional test is a value that is compared to another value with any of six special operators: =, >, <, >=, <=, or <>. Unlike conventional formulas, conditional tests do not return a value. Instead, however, they return one of two conditional constants: True or False. The values on either side of these conditional operators may be literal values, variables, field references, or functions. You typically will use conditional tests within the context of PAL commands like IF, WHILE, and SWITCH.

Simple Conditional Tests

For example, the conditional test *x<5* will be true if *x* is storing a number less than 5. If *x* stores a number greater than or equal to 5, however, the conditional test will be false.

Conditional tests can work on strings as well as numbers. For example, the test *x="Emplyee"* will be true whenever *x* stores the string *Emplyee*, and the test *x<>"Emplyee"* will be true when *x* stores anything but that string. You typically will use only these two operators to compare strings. If you use any of the other operators (like > and <), PAL assigns values to the strings according to alphabetical order and compares them on the basis of those values. *A* is less than *B*, for example, and *B* is less than *C*. Lower-case letters have a higher value than their upper-case equivalents. For instance, *a* is greater than *A*, *b* is greater than *B*, and so forth. The value order of alphabetic characters is equivalent to the order into which Paradox arranges them in an ascending sort.

You also can use conditional operators to compare dates. For example, the conditional test *[DOB]>11/24/58* will be true if the DOB field entry of the current record contains a date more recent than November 24, 1958. You can use any conditional operator to compare two dates.

Logical Operators

In addition to these six conditional operators, PAL offers three logical operators that can act upon the outcome of conditional tests: AND, OR, and NOT. The AND and OR operators combine two conditional tests into a single test. When two conditional tests are combined with an AND operator, both tests must be true for the combined test to be true. For example, the combination *x>5 AND y<3* will be true only if the value stored in *x* is greater than 5 and the value stored in *y* is less than 3. If either of these conditional tests is false, or if both of them are false, the combined test will be false.

When two conditional tests are joined with the OR operator, the combined test will be true if either of the component tests is true, or if both are true. For example, the test *x>5 OR y<3* will be true in three cases: when the value stored in *x* is greater than 5, when the value stored in *y* is less than 3, and when both *x* is greater than 5 and *y* is less than 3. An OR combination will be false only when both components are false.

PAL's NOT operator negates a conditional test, thus reversing its result. Unlike the AND and OR operators, NOT works on a single conditional test instead of joining a pair of tests. For example, the conditional test *NOT x>5* is true when the value stored in *x* is 5 or less. This simple test is equivalent to the test *x<=5*. As another example, the test *NOT (x>5 AND y<3)* will be true when *x* is less than or equal to 5, when *y* is greater than or equal to 3, or both. The test is equivalent to the test *x<=5 OR y>=3*. The parentheses are necessary in this case to override PAL's default precedence for logical operators: NOT, AND, then OR.

Conclusion

In this chapter, we have introduced you to several of the building blocks essential to the development of advanced PAL scripts. First, we introduced PAL commands by demonstrating the use of PAL's 17 menu-equivalent commands. Next, we introduced the concept of variables and showed you how to use them to hold values and strings and how to use them as the arguments of PAL commands. Then we showed you how to make references to the entries in a Paradox table from within a script. Finally, we showed you how to combine literals, variables, and table references into formulas and how to develop conditional tests. In the next chapter, we'll present PAL's special functions–the last fundamental component of PAL programming.

Chapter 15

PAL Functions

In Chapter 14, you learned about the first two important elements of PAL: PAL commands and variables. In this chapter, we'll introduce you to the third important element of PAL: Functions.

Functions are special built-in tools that make calculations and return information about PAL and Paradox. Some functions allow you to make calculations that would be difficult or impossible to make using conventional formulas. For example, the SQRT() function calculates the square root of a number and the CNPV() function computes the present value of the column entries of a table. Other functions allow you to obtain information about PAL and Paradox. For example, the DRIVESPACE() function returns the number of bytes of free disk space, and the TABLE() function returns the name of the table in which the cursor is positioned.

Although there are a number of ways to categorize PAL's functions (the PAL Manual simply lists them alphabetically), we prefer to divide them into eight groups, based on their purposes: mathematical functions, geometric functions, statistical functions, financial functions, date/time functions, string functions, informational functions, and logical functions. We'll examine the functions in each of these groups in this chapter. Before we do that, however, let's take a moment to master a few concepts that are basic to working with PAL functions.

Function Basics

Most functions have two elements: the function name and the argument. Function names are descriptive terms, like CSUM, CNPV, and IMAGENO, that identify the task that the function performs. The argument tells PAL on what you want the function to operate. For example, in the function

   ABS(-123)

ABS is the function name and -123 is the argument. This function tells PAL to compute the absolute value of the number -123, and thus returns the value 123.

Arguments

The arguments of PAL functions must be PAL expressions. As you recall from Chapter 14, an expression is one of the following five items: a literal value, a reference to a variable, a reference to a field, a formula, or a function. All expressions are of one of four types: numeric, string, date, or logical. A numeric expression is an expression that has a numeric value. A string expression is one that has a string value. A date expression is one that has a date value. A logical expression has a logical value.

Different functions require different types of arguments. For example, the ABS() function, which computes the absolute value of a number, must have a numeric expression as its argument. On the other hand, the MONTH() function, which returns the month of a date as a number, requires a date expression as its argument. No matter what kind of expression (literals, variables, field references, and so forth) you use as the argument of a function, it must be of the correct type.

Some functions require more than one argument. For example, the function FV(*amount,rate,term*), which computes the future value of a constant stream of cash flows at a particular rate, requires three arguments: *amount*, *rate*, and *term*. All of these arguments must be numeric expressions.

Some functions, such as PI() and RECNO(), don't take any arguments. Even though these functions do not take an argument, you still must include a pair of parentheses after the function name whenever you use them.

Using Functions

Like equations, all PAL functions return one of four types of values: numbers, strings, dates, or logical constants. You can use a function in any situation where you would use a literal value, a variable, a reference, or an equation that contains or returns the same type of information.

Frequently you'll store the results of functions in variables. For example, the command

    x=ABS(-100)

stores the value 100 in the variable *x*. Once this command has stored the value 100 in *x*, other commands in the script can use that variable as the basis for other computations.

In other cases, you will use a function in a conditional test. For example, the script

    IF x<ABS(y)
       THEN x=x+1
    ENDIF

uses an ABS() function within the conditional test of an IF command. Similarly, the script shown in Figure 15-1 uses an ATLAST() function as the conditional test of a WHILE command, and an ISBLANK() function as the conditional test of an IF command.

Figure 15-1

```
Designing script Functns                                    Script
....+...10....+...20....+...30....+...40....+...50....+...60....+...70....+...80
WHILE NOT ATLAST()
   IF []=ISBLANK()
      THEN []=0
   ENDIF
   Down
ENDWHILE
```

You can also store the result of a function directly in a table. For example, the function LN() computes the natural logarithm of a number. The command

[NatLog]=LN([Numfield])

places the natural logarithm of the value in the Numfield field of the current record into the NatLog field of the current record.

Mathematical Functions

Although PAL's mathematical functions probably are not its most useful group of functions, they're the simplest in form and, thus, easiest to understand. These functions act upon numeric expressions, and all return numeric values. There are eleven functions in this group: ABS(), BLANKNUM(), EXP(), INT(), LN(), LOG(), MOD(), POW(), RAND(), ROUND(), and SQRT(). Table 15-1 shows the forms of these functions.

Table 15-1 Mathematical Functions

Function	Returns	Example	Returns
ABS(*value*)	Absolute value of *value*	ABS(-100)	100
BLANKNUM()	Blank numeric value (not 0)		
EXP(*value*)	Constant e (2.71828) raised to the value power	EXP(4.605)	100
INT(*value*)	Integer portion of *value*	INT(123.999)	123
		INT(-123.99)	-123
LN(*value*)	Natural logarithm of *value*	LN(100)	4.605
LOG(*value*)	Base 10 logarithm of *value*	LOG(1000)	3
MOD(*dividend,divisor*)	Remainder of *dividend/divisor*	MOD(7,2)	1
POW(*value,power*)	*Value* raised to *power*	POW(10,2)	100
RAND()	Random number between 0 and 1		
ROUND(*value,decimals*)	*Value* rounded to *decimal* places	ROUND(2.765,2)	2.77
		ROUND(100.99,0)	101
		ROUND(123.9,-1)	120
SQRT(*value*)	Square root of *value*	SQRT(100)	10

For the most part, the form and purpose of each of these functions should be clear from the table. Each of these functions performs a common mathematical task and returns a numeric value. Although we have used literal values in the arguments in the examples, you will more often use variables and field references when you actually use these functions in your scripts.

The only one of these tools that is tricky at all is BLANKNUM(). BLANKNUM() returns a blank numeric value. A blank numeric value is not the same as a value of 0. If you enter the value 0 into a numeric field, that field will contain the value 0. If you leave a record's numeric field empty, however, that field contains a blank numeric value. The principal use of this function is for returning a record's numeric field to its original blank state. If the cursor is positioned over a value in a numeric field, for example, the equation *[]=BLANKNUM()* will replace the value with a blank numeric value.

Geometric Functions

Geometric functions compute trigonometric values like the sine, cosine, and tangent of an angle. These functions are like mathematical functions in that they return numeric values and act upon numeric expressions. There are eight functions in this group: ACOS, ASIN, ATAN, ATAN2, COS, PI, SIN, and TAN. Table 15-2 shows the use of these functions.

Table 15-2 Geometric Functions

Function	Returns	Example	Returns
ACOS(*cosine*)	Angle with cosine *cosine*	ACOS(.5)	1.047197551196
ASIN(*sine*)	Angle with sine *sine*	ASIN(.5)	.5235987755982
ATAN(*tangent*)	Angle with tangent *tangent*	ATAN(1)	.7853981633974
ATAN2(*cosine,sine*)	Angle with cosine *cosine* and sine *sine*	ATAN2(1,1)	.7853981633974
COS(*angle*)	Cosine of *angle*	COS(2)	-.416138735681
PI()	π	PI()	3.141592653589
SIN(*angle*)	Sine of *angle*	SIN(2)	.9093048415109
TAN(*angle*)	Tangent of *angle*	TAN(3)	-.142546543074

The argument of the SIN(), COS(), and TAN() functions must be a numeric expression that specifies the measure of an angle in radians, not degrees. The result of these functions is the sine, cosine, or tangent of the specified angle.

PAL's ASIN(), ACOS(), ATAN(), and ATAN2() functions are called inverse geometric functions. The argument of the ASIN(), ACOS(), and ATAN() functions should be the sine, cosine, and tangent, respectively, of the angle you want to measure. These functions return the measure of the angle whose sine, cosine, or tangent equals the specified value. The ATAN2() function returns the measure of an angle when given both its sine and cosine. The value of the arguments in these functions must be greater than or equal to -1 or less than or equal to 1.

Statistical Functions

PAL's statistical functions compute common statistics, such as the average (mean), sum, and standard deviation. Statistical functions can be divided into two groups: simple statistical functions and columnar statistical functions. The first group, simple statistical functions, includes only two functions: MAX() and MIN(). The second group, columnar statistical functions, includes the functions CSUM(), CAVERAGE(), CCOUNT(), CMAX(), CMIN(), CSTD(), and CVAR().

MAX() and MIN()

PAL's MAX() function compares two numeric values and returns the greater of the two. Similarly, the MIN() function compares two numeric values and returns the lesser of the two. The forms of these functions are

MAX(*value1*,*value2*)
MIN(*value1*,*value2*)

The arguments *value1* and *value2* are the values you want to compare. These arguments can be any numeric expression. The result of the MAX() function is the greater of *value1* or *value2*; the result of MIN() is the lesser of the two values.

For example, the function MAX(10,1) returns the number 10. The function MIN(3,2) returns the value 2. PAL does not care which value you use as the first argument in the MAX() and MIN() functions. In other words, the function MAX(4,6) is identical to the function MAX(6,4). Both functions return the value 6. If both arguments of either function are equal, then PAL returns that value. For example, the function MIN(10,10) returns the value 10.

Columnar Statistical Functions

PAL offers a group of functions that compute statistics about the entries in a specified column of a table. The functions in this group are CMAX(), CMIN(), CSUM(), CAVERAGE(), CCOUNT(), CSTD(), and CVAR().

Table 15-3 shows the form of each of these functions. As you can see, each of these functions takes two arguments: table and field. The table and field arguments identify the table and field that contain the values on which you want the function to operate. These arguments must be string expressions that specify the name of the table and field for which the statistic should be calculated.

Table 15-3 Columnar Statistical Functions

Function	Returns
CMAX(*table,field*)	Maximum value in *field* of *table*
CMIN(*table,field*)	Minimum value in *field* of *table*
CAVERAGE(*table,field*)	Average of values in *field* of *table*
CSUM(*table,field*)	Sum of values in *field* of *table*
CCOUNT(*table,field*)	Count of entries in *field* of *table*
CSTD(*table,field*)	Standard deviation of values in *field* of *table*
CVAR(*table,field*)	Variance of values in *field* of *table*

The CMAX() and CMIN() Functions

PAL's CMAX() and CMIN() functions return the maximum and minimum values from the specified numeric field of a table. For example, suppose you want to determine the maximum and minimum salaries of the people listed in the EMPLYEE table, which is shown in Figure 15-2. As you can see, the Salary field contains the annual salary of each of the 16 people listed in this table. To determine the maximum salary in a script, you would use the function *CMAX("Emplyee","Salary")* which would return the value 70000.00. To determine the minimum salary, you would use the function *CMIN("Emplyee","Salary")*, which would return the value 12000.00.

Figure 15-2 The EMPLYEE Table

Viewing Emplyee table: Record 1 of 16   Main

EMPLYEE	Emp Number	Last Name	First Name	SS Number	Addre
1	1	Jones	David	414-74-3421	4000 St. Ja
2	2	Cameron	Herb	321-65-8765	2321 Elm St
3	3	Jones	Stewart	401-32-8721	4389 Oakbri
4	4	Roberts	Darlene	417-43-7777	451 Lone Pi
5	5	Jones	Jean	413-07-9123	4000 St. Ja
6	6	Williams	Brenda	401-55-1567	100 Owl Cre
7	7	Myers	Julie	314-38-9452	4512 Parksi
8	8	Link	Julie	345-75-1525	3215 Palm C
9	9	Jackson	Mary	424-13-7621	7821 Clark
10	10	Jakes, Jr.	Sal	321-65-9151	3451 Michig
11	11	Preston	Molly	451-00-3426	321 Indian
12	12	Masters	Ron	317-65-4529	423 W. 72nd
13	13	Robertson	Kevin	415-24-6710	431 Bardsto
14	14	Garrison	Robert	312-98-1479	55 Wheeler
15	15	Gunn	Barbara	321-97-8632	541 Kentuck
16	16	Emerson	Cheryl	404-14-1422	8100 River

Viewing Emplyee table: Record 1 of 16   Main

Date of Birth	Date of Hire	Exemptions	Salary
10/06/42	6/01/84	3	70,000.00
11/24/29	6/01/84	4	50,000.00
3/21/50	7/01/84	1	47,000.00
9/24/60	11/01/84	3	14,000.00
5/14/43	12/01/84	0	33,999.99
1/12/20	1/01/85	5	40,000.00
2/06/48	2/01/85	1	32,000.00
6/03/33	4/01/85	2	30,000.00
8/12/56	4/01/85	3	21,000.00
5/23/59	5/01/85	6	34,000.00
4/17/66	7/01/85	1	14,750.00
12/30/44	7/01/85	0	38,000.00
3/16/25	7/15/85	1	37,000.00
5/09/45	10/01/85	4	32,000.00
5/18/50	11/01/85	2	17,500.00
7/30/66	1/01/86	2	12,000.00

Importantly, the CMAX() and CMIN() functions ignore blank entries. If the sixteenth entry in the Salary field was blank, for example, the function *CMIN("Emplyee","Salary")* would not return the value 0; it would return 14000.00–the lowest nonblank value.

The CSUM() Function

PAL's CSUM() function totals the entries in the numeric field specified by its argument. For example, to determine the total annual salary of the people listed in the EMPLYEE table, you could use the function *CSUM("Emplyee","Salary")*, which would return 523249.99. Like the CMIN() and CMAX() functions, CSUM() ignores blank entries.

The CCOUNT() Function

PAL's CCOUNT() function returns the number of nonblank entries in a field. Unlike PAL's other columnar financial functions, CCOUNT() can act upon the entries in any type of column. For example, the function *CCOUNT("Emplyee","Last Name")* returns the value 16 since there are sixteen entries in the Name field of EMPLYEE. If one of the entries in this column had been blank, however, this function would return the value 15.

The CAVERAGE() Function

The CAVERAGE() function calculates the mean of the values in the specified field of the specified table. The mean is a simple average derived by dividing the sum of the entries in a column by the count of those entries. For example, the function *CAVERAGE ("Emplyee","Salary")* returns the value 32702.12.

Whenever you use the CAVERAGE() function, remember that PAL does not include blanks in the count. As a result, a CAVERAGE() function that acts upon a column that contains blanks will return a higher average than it would if the blanks were filled with zeros. If the third record of the Salary field in the EMPLYEE table was blank, for example, the function *CAVERAGE("Emplyee","Salary")* would return the value 31750.00. If that field contained the value 0 instead, however, the function would return the value 29765.62.

The CSTD() and CVAR() Functions

PAL's CSTD() and CVAR() functions calculate the standard deviation and variance of the values in a column, respectively. For example, you could use the function *CSTD("Emplyee","Salary")* to calculate the standard deviation of the entries in the Salary field of the EMPLYEE table, 14737.08, and the function *CVAR("Emplyee","Salary")* to calculate the variance of those entries, 217181394.86.

Financial Functions

PAL features four basic financial functions: PV, FV, PMT, and CNPV. These functions allow you to calculate the present and future values of an ordinary annuity, the periodic payments required to amortize a loan, and the net present value of a series of unequal cash flows, respectively.

The PV() Function

PAL's PV() function allows you to calculate the present value of a constant stream of periodic cash flows (also called an ordinary annuity). The form of the PV() function is

>PV(*payment, rate, term*)

where *payment* is the amount of the periodic cash flow, *rate* is the rate of interest at which you want to discount the annuity, and *term* is the number of periods across which you will receive cash flows.

The result of the PV() function is the present value of the periodic payments that you will receive across the stated term, discounted at the specified rate. For instance, suppose you have an opportunity to invest in an annuity that will pay you $500 per year for the next ten years. Assuming a discount rate of 7.5% per year, you could use the function *PV(500,.075,10)* to compute the present value of the annuity: $3432.04.

Importantly, PAL's PV() function assumes that the cash flows occur at the end of each period, not at the beginning. In the example above, for instance, PAL assumed that the first $500 flow occurred one year from the date of the analysis, the second flow occurred two years from the date of the analysis, and so forth. This type of cash flow is termed an annuity in arrears.

The FV() Function

PAL's second financial function, FV(), calculates the future value of a stream of equal cash flows. FV() has the form

>FV(*amount,rate,term*)

where *amount* is the periodic investment you plan to make, *rate* is the average rate of return you think the investment will earn, and *term* is the number of periodic investments you will make. These arguments must be numeric expressions. The result of the function is the future value of the investment.

This function is perfectly suited for analyzing a constant-contribution savings plan, like an IRA. Suppose you want to know how much an IRA that you start one year from today will be worth in 40 years if you contribute $2000 to it each year, assuming a 10%

rate of interest. You could use the function *FV(2000,.1,40)* to calculate that the IRA would be worth some $855,185.10 when you retire. Like the PV() function, FV() assumes that the cash flows occur at the end of each period.

The PMT() Function

PAL's third financial function is PMT(). This function calculates the periodic payment necessary to amortize a conventional note, like an auto loan or a mortgage. The form of this function is

PMT(*principal,rate,term*)

The first argument, *principal*, is the amount borrowed. The second argument, *rate*, is the periodic rate of interest. The third argument, *term*, is the term of the loan. These arguments must be numeric expressions. The result of the function is the payment that will amortize the principal amount across the term at the stated interest rate.

For example, suppose that you want to calculate the monthly payment on a thirty-year, 10.5%, $100,000 mortgage. You could use the function *PMT(100000,.105/12,30*12)* to calculate the monthly payment of $914.74.

The CNPV() Function

Like the PV() function, CNPV() calculates the present value of a stream of cash flows. Unlike the PV() function, however, the cash flows do not all have to be of the same amount. Also unlike the PV() function, the cash flows for the CNPV() function must be arranged in a column of a Paradox table. The form of the CNPV() function is

CNPV(*table,field,rate*)

The first two arguments, *table* and *field*, identify the table and the field of that table which contains the series of cash flows. The third argument, *rate*, specifies the rate of interest you want to use to discount the cash flows. The first two arguments must be string expressions; the third argument must be a numeric expression.

To calculate the present value of evenly spaced unequal cash flows, you first must enter those flows into a table. Because the cash flows for this function are entries in a column of a table, you can use it to calculate a net present value–a present value calculation that takes into account cash disbursements as well as cash receipts. For example, suppose that for a cash outlay of $1000 one year from today, you are guaranteed cash inflows of $100 two years from today, $200 three years from today, $300 four years from today, $400 five years from today, and $500 six years from today. Given a 10% rate of interest, what is the net present value of the investment? To perform this calculation, you would create and fill in the table shown in Figure 15-3. As you can see, this table, named NPV2, consists of only one field, Cashflows, and contains six records–one corresponding to each of the cash flows associated with the investment. To calculate the net present value of this cash flow stream, you could use the function *CNPV("Npv","Cashflows",.10)*, which returns the value $59.32.

Figure 15-3 The NPV Table

```
Viewing Npv table: Record 6 of 6                            Main
   NPV        Cashflows
    1         (1,000.00)
    2           100.00
    3           200.00
    4           300.00
    5           400.00
    6           500.00
```

Like PAL's PV() and FV() functions, the CNPV() function assumes that the cash flows occur at the end of each period, not at the beginning.

Date/Time Functions

PAL's eight date/time functions either generate date/time values or extract information from date/time values. For example, the TODAY() function returns the date value of the current day from your computer's system clock, the TIME() function returns the current time of day as a string, and the YEAR() function returns the year portion of a date value.

Table 15-4 shows the form of each of PAL's date/time functions. The date value arguments in these functions must be a date expression: a literal date value (such as 11/24/58), a reference to a variable or field that contains a date value, or a formula or function that returns a date value.

Table 15-4 Date/Time Functions

Function	Returns	Example	Returns
BLANKDATE()	Blank *date value*	BLANKDATE()	
DAY(*date value*)	Number 1-31 representing day of *date value*	DAY(10/06/86)	6
		DAY(11/24/86)	24
DOW(*date value*)	String representing day of week of *date value*	DOW(10/06/86)	Mon
		DOW(10/07/86)	Tue
MONTH(*date value*)	Number 1-12 representing month of *date value*	MONTH(10/06/86)	10
		MONTH(3/21/86)	3
MOY(*date value*)	String representing month of year of *date value*	MOY(10/06/86)	Oct
		MOY(3/21/86)	Mar
TIME()	String representing current time	TIME()	
TODAY()	Today's date	TODAY()	
YEAR(*date value*)	Number representing year of *date value*	YEAR(10/06/57)	57
		YEAR(3/21/86)	86

The BLANKDATE() Function

The BLANKDATE() function returns a blank date value. A blank date value is the entry that Paradox stores in an empty date field. The principal use of this function is for returning the date field of a record to its original blank state. If the cursor is positioned over a value in a date field, for example, the equation *[]=BLANKDATE()* will replace that value with a blank date value.

The DAY(), MONTH(), and YEAR() Functions

PAL's DAY() function acts upon a date expression and returns its day portion as a value between 1 and 31. For example, the function *DAY(11/24/58)* returns the value 24. The date value argument can be in either MM/DD/YY or DD-Mon-YY form. For example, the function *DAY(24-Nov-58)* is identical to *DAY(11/24/58)* and would also return 24.

PAL's MONTH() function returns a value from 1 through 12 that represents the month portion of a date value. For example, the function *MONTH(11/24/58)* returns the value 11, and the function *MONTH(10/6/57)* returns the value 10.

PAL's YEAR() function returns a numeric value that identifies the year represented by a date expression. For example, the function *YEAR(11/24/58)* returns the value 1958.

The DOW() and MOY() Functions

The DOW() function returns a string that identifies a date's day of the week of a date. The seven possible results of this function are *Mon*, *Tue*, *Wed*, *Thu*, *Fri*, *Sat*, and *Sun*. For example, the function *DOW(11/24/58)* returns the string *Mon*, indicating that November 24, 1958, was a Monday.

PAL's MOY() function returns a string that identifies the month of the year represented by a Paradox date value. The MOY() function returns one of the following 12 strings: *Jan*, *Feb*, *Mar*, *Apr*, *May*, *Jun*, *Jul*, *Aug*, *Sep*, *Oct*, *Nov*, or *Dec*. For example, the function *MOY(11/24/58)* returns the string *Nov*.

The TIME() Function

PAL's TIME() function returns the current time of day as a string in the form *hh:mm:ss*. Because this function draws its information from your computer's system clock, it requires and accepts no arguments. The result returned by this function depends on the time of day at which PAL evaluates it. The TIME() function uses the 24-hour, or military, clock convention.

If PAL encounters the function TIME() in a script at exactly 10:30 A.M., the function will return the string *10:30:00*. Similarly, if PAL encounters the function TIME() in a script at 1:03:54 in the afternoon, it will return the string *13:03:54*. It is important that you understand that the TIME() function does not return a time value–it returns a string that represents the current time.

The TODAY() Function

PAL's TODAY() function returns the current date in the form of a Paradox date value. Like the TIME() function, TODAY() extracts its information from your computer's system clock. For that reason, it accepts no arguments. Unlike the TIME() function, however, TODAY() returns a Paradox date value–not a string. If PAL evaluated the function TODAY() on April 15, 1986, for example, it would return the date value 4/15/86. Similarly, if PAL evaluated the equation *TODAY()-4/1/86* on April 15, 1986, it would return the value 14.

PAL's String Functions

String functions are the next group of PAL functions that we'll discuss. The thirteen functions in this group all operate upon string (alphanumeric) expressions or convert other types of expressions into strings. We first will look at a collection of simple string functions. Next, we'll look at functions that convert strings into dates or values. Finally, we'll examine PAL's complex string functions.

Simple String Functions

PAL's simple string functions allow you to do things like convert a string of upper-case letters into lower-case form or determine the length of a string. The functions in this group are ASC(), CHR(), LEN(), LOWER(), and UPPER(). As you can see, Table 15-5 shows the forms of these functions.

Table 15-5 Simple String Functions

Function	Returns	Example	Returns
ASC(*character*)	ASCII code of *character*	ASC("a")	97
CHR(*ASCII code*)	Character with stated *ASCII code*	CHR(100)	d
LEN(*string*)	Length of *string*	LEN("ABC")	3
LOWER(*string*)	Converts *string* to all lower case	LOWER("ABC")	abc
UPPER(*string*)	Coverts *string* to all upper case	UPPER("abc")	ABC

The ASC() and CHR() Functions

PAL's ASC() function returns the ASCII code that represents the character specified by its argument. The function's argument can be a single character (like *a* or *#*) or a special key representation (like *Backspace* or *F3*). Normal characters return a code from 0 to 255. For example, the function *ASC("A")* returns the value 65, the function *ASC("*")* returns the value 42, and the function *ASC("z")* returns the value 122. Special keys return negative numbers. The function *ASC("F1")* returns the value -59, for example, and the function *ASC("Up")* returns the value -72.

PAL's CHR() function is the inverse of the ASC() function–it returns the character that corresponds to the ASCII code specified by its argument. The single argument of the CHR() function must be an integer value from 0 to 255. For example, the function *CHR(65)* returns the string *A*, while the function *CHR(42)* returns the string ***. The argument of CHR() must be a positive number. The CHR() function will not convert negative ASCII codes to their special key representations.

The LEN() Function

The LEN() function allows PAL to determine the length of a string. The argument of this function usually will be a string expression. If you use a numeric or date expression as the argument of this function, however, PAL will treat it as a string and evaluate the function normally. The result of the function is the length of the string. For example, the function *LEN("hello")* returns the value 5, as does the function *LEN(12345)*.

The LOWER() and UPPER() Functions

PAL's LOWER() function converts the string you specify to all lower-case form. The function's argument must be a string expression. The result of the function is the same string with all letters in lower case. For example, the function *LOWER("HELLO")* returns the string *hello*. Similarly, if the Color field of the current record contains the string *RED*, the function *LOWER([Color])* will return the string *red*.

PAL's UPPER() function converts its string argument into a string in upper case. The single argument of this function also must be a string expression. For example, suppose that you want to convert the string entry stored in the variable *x* into all upper-case form. To do this, you would use the function *UPPER(x)*. If *x* contains the string *hello*, this function would return the string *HELLO*. If the argument already is in all upper-case form, the UPPER() function does not change it.

String Conversion Functions

String conversion functions either convert strings into values or dates, or values or dates into strings. There are three functions in this group: NUMVAL(), STRINGVAL(), and DATEVAL(). Table 15-6 shows the form of each of these functions.

Table 15-6 String Conversion Functions

Function	Returns	Example	Returns
DATEVAL(*string*)	Converts *string* into a date value	DATEVAL("12/31/86")	12/31/86
NUMVAL(*string*)	Converts *string* into a value	NUMVAL("123")	123
STRVAL(*value*)	Converts *value* into a string	STRVAL(123)	"123"

The NUMVAL() Function

PAL's NUMVAL() function converts a numeric string into a label. The argument of the function must be a string expression that specifies a numeric string. For example, suppose that you want to store the contents of the current record's alphanumeric Zip field as a value in the variable *x*. The command *x=NUMVAL([Zip])* would do the trick. If the current record's Zip entry is the string *12345*, this command would store the value *12345* in the variable *x*.

The STRVAL() Function

PAL's STRVAL() function is the inverse of the NUMVAL() function. NUMVAL() converts a numeric string into a value; STRVAL() converts a value into a numeric string. The single argument of STRVAL() must be a numeric expression, a date expression, or a conditional test. For example, the function STRVAL(123) returns the string *123*; the function *STRVAL(11/24/58)* returns the string *11/24/58*. If the argument is a logical constant, the function returns either the string *True* or the string *False*. For example, the function *STRVAL(10=10)* returns the string *True*.

The DATEVAL() Function

PAL's DATEVAL() function converts an alphanumeric entry in one of four forms into a date value. The argument of this function must be a string expression in the form MM/DD/YY, MM/DD/YYYY, DD-Mon-YY, or DD-Mon-YYYY. For example, if the current field contains the string *10/6/57*, the command *x=DATEVAL([])* will store the date entry *10/6/57* in the variable *x*.

Complex String Functions

The next group of string functions includes the functions SUBSTR(), FILL(), SPACES(), FORMAT(), MATCH(), and SEARCH(). These functions are more complex and powerful than those we have looked at so far.

The SUBSTR() Function

The SUBSTR() function allows PAL to extract a substring from a string, given a starting position and the number of characters to be extracted. The form of this function is

    SUBSTR(*string,start position,characters*)

where *string* is the string from which you want to extract some characters, *start position* specifies the position of the first character to be extracted, and *characters* specifies the number of characters to be extracted. The first argument must be a string expression. The other two arguments must be numeric expressions.

For example, suppose that you want to extract the fifth through seventh characters from the entry in the Phone field of the current record. To do this, you could use the function *SUBSTR([Phone],5,3)*. If the current record's Phone field entry was the string *501-555-1212*, this function would extract the string *555*–the three characters beginning with the fifth character in the entry.

The Fill() Function

PAL's FILL() function allows you to generate repeating strings of a single character. The form of this function is

FILL(*character,length*)

where *character* is the character that you want to repeat and *length* is the number of times you want it to be repeated. For example, the function FILL("=",20) would produce the string ====================.

The SPACES() Function

PAL's SPACES() function is a special case of the FILL() function. Whereas FILL() creates a repeating string of whatever character you specify, the SPACES() function creates a repeating series of space characters. The form of this function is

SPACES(*number*)

where the single argument specifies the number of spaces that you want in the string. For example, the function *SPACES(10)* creates a series of ten spaces, as does the function *SPACES(x)* if *x* has been assigned the value 10.

When used in conjunction with the LEN() function, SPACES() can be used to line up entries that appear on the PAL canvas (a concept we'll discuss in Chapter 16). If you want an entry to end on the twentieth column of the PAL canvas, for example, you could use the command *?? SPACES(20-LEN([])),[]*. The SPACES() function in this command creates a number of spaces equal to 20 minus the length of the entry in the current field.

The Format() Function

PAL's FORMAT() function allows you to convert alphanumeric, numeric, date, and logical expressions into formatted strings. Using this function, for example, you can convert any value into a string of the length you specify, change the case of alphanumeric values, and convert numeric values into strings that include + and - signs, parentheses, or $ symbols. You also can use the FORMAT() function to convert date values to any of eight different string forms or to convert the logical constants True and False into the strings *Yes* and *No* or *On* and *Off*.

The form of the FORMAT function is

FORMAT(*format code(s)*,*expression*)

where *format codes* are a series of one or more format codes and the *expression* argument is the value to be formatted. Table 15-7 lists the available format codes and the types of data to which they apply. As you can see, many of the possible format codes can be used only on numeric values; some can be used only on alphanumeric, date, or logical values; while a few can be used on all types of values.

Table 15-7 FORMAT Function Codes

Code	Function	Data Types
Wx	Controls display width	All
Wx.y	Controls total # of digits and # of digits to right of decimal	N
AL	Left justified	All
AR	Right justified	All
AC	Centered	All
CU	Upper case	A
CL	Lower case	A
CC	First letter of word capitalized	A
E$	Print floating $ sign	N,S,$
EC	Use comma separators	N,S,$
EZ	Use leading zeros	N,S,$
EB	Substitute blanks for zeros	N,S,$
E*	Substitute *s for zeros	N,S,$
S+	Use leading + or - sign	N,S,$
S-	Use - if negative	N,S,$
SP	Enclose - numbers in ()	N,S,$
SD	Use DB for +, CR for -	N,S,$
SC	Use CR if -	N,S,$
D1	MM/DD/YY	D
D2	Month DD, YYYY	D
D3	MM/DD	D
D4	MM/YY	D
D5	DD-Month	D
D6	Mon YY	D
D7	DD-Mon-YYYY	D
D8	MM/DD/YYYY	D
LY	Use Yes for True, No for False	L
LO	Use On for True, Off for False	L

For example, the function *FORMAT("D2",11/24/58)* converts the date value *11/24/58* into the string *November 24, 1958*. The argument D2 in this function tells PAL to convert the second argument into a string in date format 2. The function *FORMAT("CC","testing")* returns the string *Testing*.

As another example, suppose that x=3 and y=5. While the conditional test *x=y* would return the logical constant *False*, the function *FORMAT("LY",x=y)* would return the string *No*. In this example, the argument LY tells PAL to evaluate the second argument and return Yes if the argument is True and No if it is false.

Adjusting the Width

Two of the most-used format codes control the number of characters in the string result of the FORMAT function. The code W followed by a number adjusts the total number of characters in the string which the function returns. Depending on the number you specify and the length of the original value, this function can either truncate the value or pad it with blank spaces. For example, the function *FORMAT("W5",123)* will return the string " *123*", which begins with two blank spaces. (The quotation marks are included in the text only to indicate the leading spaces; they are not a part of the function's result.) Similarly, the function *FORMAT("W2","hello")* returns the string *he*.

Unfortunately, this function does not do a good job of truncating numeric values. When PAL evaluates the function *FORMAT("W3",12345)*, for example, it returns the three-character string ***–not the strings *123* or *345*. Unless you specify a length at least one character greater than the number of characters in the original value, the FORMAT function will return a string of asterisks.

A modification of the W code allows you to specify the number of digits to the right of the decimal place in the string that results when the FORMAT function works on a numeric value. The form of this code is *Wx.y*, where *x* is the total length of the string, and y is the number of digits to include to the right of the decimal place. This special form allows you to truncate digits from or add digits to the right of the decimal place. For example, the function *FORMAT("W7.2",123.456)* returns the string " *123.45*". The overall width of 7 (one greater than the number of actual characters in the result) is necessary to produce a recognizable value instead of a series of asterisks. Similarly, the function *FORMAT("W7.2",123)* returns the string " *123.00*".

Controlling Alignment

When you use the Wx code to increase the length of a numeric value, PAL usually will add extra spaces at the left of the resulting string. If you use the *Wx* code to increase the length of an alphanumeric value, however, PAL usually will add extra spaces to the right of that string. For example, the function *FORMAT("W10","abcd")* produces the ten-character string "*abcd*   ". Because the original value was a string, PAL added the padding to the right of that string.

You can use three additional codes–AL, AR, and AC–to control where PAL adds those extra spaces, however. The effect of these codes is to control the alignment of the nonspace characters in a string relative to the total width of the string. For example, the function *FORMAT("W10,AR","abcd")* produces the right-aligned string "   *abcd*". Similarly, the function *FORMAT("W10,AL",1234)* returns the string "*1234*   ", which is left aligned. On the other hand, the functions *FORMAT("W10,AC","abcd")* and *FORMAT("W10,AC",1234)* return the centered strings "   abcd   " and "   1234   ".

Formatting Numbers

You also can use the FORMAT function to convert numeric values into strings that include dollar signs, comma separators, + and - signs, or DB/CR notation. As you can see, the E codes control currency-related attributes, and the S codes control the use of signs. Since the attributes added by these codes increase the length of the original value, you always must use them in conjunction with a length-increasing Wx or Wx.y code. Otherwise, the function will return a string of asterisks. For example, although the function *FORMAT("W4,E$",123)* will produce the string *$123*, the function *FORMAT("E$",123)* returns the string ***.

Since the E attributes are not mutually exclusive, you can use more than one in the same FORMAT function. When you do this, however, you should use the letter *E* only once and follow it with one or more codes without comma separators. For example, you would use the function *FORMAT("W9.2,E$C",1234.56)*, which produces the string *$1,234.56*. Since the S codes are mutually exclusive, however, you should use only one within each FORMAT command. If you use more than one, the code furthest to the right will control the result.

The Match() Function

PAL's MATCH() function determines whether a given string matches a pattern, and if so, optionally returns the wildcard portion of that string. The first argument of this function must be the string that you want to test. The second portion must be the "pattern" to which you want to compare the first string. The final argument or arguments, which are optional, specify the variables in which you want to store portions of the original string.

The simplest form of this function compares a string to another string–not to a pattern. If the two strings are identical in all ways (except for capitalization, which MATCH() ignores), the MATCH() function will return the logical constant True. Otherwise, the function will return the constant False. For example, suppose that you want to determine if the entry in the current field matches the string *abc*. To do this, you could use the function *MATCH([],"abc")*. If the current field contains the string *abc*, *Abc*, *ABc*, *ABC*, *aBc*, *abC*, *aBC*, or *AbC*, this function will return the constant True. (This function differs from the equation *[]="abc"* in that it is not case-sensitive.)

Most of your MATCH() functions will be more complex than this, however. Instead of comparing a string to a string, they will compare a string to a pattern. Just like the patterns that you use within queries, these patterns can contain the wildcard symbols .. and @. As you recall, the @ character matches any single character, while the .. character matches any group of adjacent characters. For example, suppose that you wanted to see if the current entry begins with the letter *p* and ends with the letter *r*. To do this, you could use the function *MATCH([],p..r)*. If the current field contained the string *Paper*, *pour*, or *paupeR*, this function would return the constant True.

The most complex usage of the MATCH() function involves assigning the wildcard-matching portion(s) of the string to variables. For example, suppose you wanted to take the phone number entry *502-555-1212*, store the first three digits in the variable *areacode*, store the next three digits in the variable *exchange*, and store the remaining four digits in the variable *number*. To do this, you would use the function

MATCH("502-555-1212","..-..-..",areacode,exchange,number)

When PAL evaluates this function, it matches the string *502* to the first .. wildcard and stores it in the first variable, *areacode*. Then PAL matches the string *555* to the second .. and stores it in the second variable, *exchange*. Finally, PAL matches the string *1212* to the third .. and stores it in the variable *number*. In addition to assigning these strings to these variables, this function returns the constant True.

The SEARCH() Function

The SEARCH() function commands PAL to look for one string within another string. The form of this function is

SEARCH(*substring,string*)

where the *substring* argument is the string for which you want PAL to search and the *string* argument is the string in which you want it to search. If PAL finds a match for *substring* within *string*, it returns the position of the leftmost character of the match within *string*. If there is no match for the substring within the string, PAL returns the value 0. As with the MATCH() function, SEARCH() does not differentiate between upper and lower case. Unlike MATCH(), however, you cannot use wildcards within the search string.

For example, suppose that you want to determine if the entry in the current record's Name field contains the string *Smith*. To do this, you could use the function *SEARCH ("Smith",[Name])*. If the Name field contained the entry *John Smith*, this function would return the value *6*–the starting position of the substring *Smith* within the string *John Smith*. In the same situation, the function *SEARCH("John",[Name])* would return the value 1, and the function *SEARCH("Jones",[Name])* would return the value 0.

PAL's Informational Functions

PAL's informational functions return information about the status of the workspace and the operating environment in which Paradox is running. For example, the IMAGETYPE() function returns the type of the image in which the cursor currently is positioned, the DRIVESPACE() function returns the number of free bytes on the disk drive you specify, and the NFIELDS() function returns the number of fields in the table you specify. We'll present these functions in alphabetical order.

The ARRAYSIZE() Function

PAL's ARRAYSIZE() function returns the number of elements that can be stored in the named array. As you will learn in Chapter 16, an array is a variable that can store more than one entry. The form of this function is

ARRAYSIZE(*arrayname*)

where *arrayname* is the name of the array you want to test. The result of the function is the number of elements in the array *arrayname*. For example, suppose you use the command *ARRAY temprec[12]* to create a twelve-element array named *temprec*. In this case, the function *ARRAYSIZE(temprec)* will return the value 12.

The BANDINFO() Function

The BANDINFO() function lets PAL determine which band (section) of a report the cursor is located in when you are working in the Paradox report generator. The function takes no arguments.

BANDINFO() returns the contents of the Band indicator–the message on the second line at the upper-left corner of the report generator screen–as a string. If the cursor is in the Table band, for example, the message *Table* will appear in this area, and the function BANDINFO() will return the string *Table Band*.

The COL() Function

PAL's COL() function returns the column position of the cursor on the PAL canvas. This function takes no arguments. The possible results of this function, 0-79, correspond to the 80 columns visible on the screen. If the cursor is positioned at the left edge of the screen, the COL() function will return the value 1. If the cursor is positioned at the right edge of the screen, this function will return the value 79. The usefulness of this function will become more apparent in Chapter 16 when we show you how to interact with the user during a PAL script.

The COLNO() Function

The PAL function COLNO() returns the columnar position of the cursor within the current image on the Paradox workspace. This function takes no arguments.

If the cursor is within the image of a table, this function returns the offset of the field in which the cursor is positioned, relative to the leftmost column in the table (the record number column). For example, if PAL reads the function COLNO() in a script when the cursor is anywhere in the First Name field of the EMPLYEE table, it will return the value 3. Although the record number column does not appear when you view a table through a form, PAL still counts it when it evaluates this function.

The CURSORCHR() Function

PAL's CURSORCHAR() function returns the single character over which the cursor is positioned in the form mode, the report mode, or in the Script Editor. This function has no meaning in any other situation. For example, if the cursor is positioned over the first letter of the command *WHILE* in a script, the function CURSORCHAR() will return the string *W*.

The CURSORLINE() Function

PAL's CURSORLINE() function is similar to the CURSORCHAR() function. While the CURSORCHAR() function returns the current character in the Forms, Report, and Script Editors, however, the CURSORLINE() function returns all the text from the present position of the cursor to the end of the line. If the cursor is positioned on the first letter of the line *VIEW "Emplyee"* in the Script Editor, for example, the CURSORCHAR() function will return the string *VIEW "Emplyee"*. As we'll explain in Chapter 17, you can use this function in conjunction with the TYPEIN command to "cut and paste" text within a script, report, or form.

The DIRECTORY() Function

The DIRECTORY() function allows PAL to determine which directory Paradox currently is using. When PAL reads this function, it returns the specification of the current directory. If c:\paradox\examples is the active directory, for example, the function DIRECTORY() will return the string *c:\paradox\examples*.

You can use this function within an IF command to test the current directory and change it if it is not the one you want. For example, the script

```
IF DIRECTORY()<>"c:\paradox\examples"
   THEN Menu {Tools} {More} {Directory} {c:\\paradox\\examples} {OK}
ENDIF
```

will change the current directory to c:\paradox\examples only if that directory were not already the current one.

The DRIVESPACE() Function

PAL's DRIVESPACE() function returns the amount of free space remaining on the drive that you specify. The form of this function is

DRIVESPACE(*drive*)

where the argument is the single-letter designator of the drive you want to check. For example, if drive C has 2,345,678 bytes of free space, the command *DRIVESPACE("C")* will return the value 2345678. Because the case of the *drive* argument does not matter, the function *DRIVESPACE("c")* would return the same result.

The FIELD() Function

PAL's FIELD() function returns the name of the field in which the cursor currently is positioned. This function is meaningful only when the cursor is in a table, form, or query. If the cursor is positioned in the Last Name field of the EMPLYEE table, for example, the function *FIELD()* will return the string *Last Name*. If the cursor is in the leftmost field of a table (the one that contains the record numbers) when PAL evaluates this function, it will return the string #.

The FIELDINFO() Function

PAL's FIELDINFO() function returns the name of the field that the cursor currently is touching. This function only works when you are in the Forms and Report Editors. When the cursor touches a field that you have placed in a report, PAL displays the name of that field in the Field indicator at the right edge of the second line at the top of the screen. The FIELDINFO() function returns the contents of this Field indicator area. If your screen looks like Figure 15-4, for example, the function FIELDINFO() will return the string *First Name*.

Figure 15-4   The FIELDINFO() Function

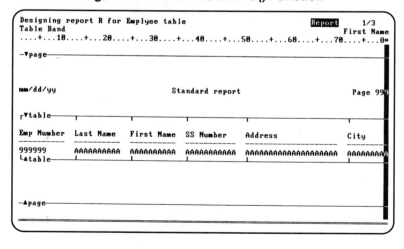

The FIELDNO() Function

PAL's FIELDNO() function returns the position of the field you specify within the structure of the table you specify. Unlike the COLNO() function, which returns the position of a column in the display image of the table, the FIELDNO() function returns the absolute position of a field according to the STRUCT table for that table. The results of these two functions will be the same only if you have not rotated the order of the columns in the table's display image.

The FIELDNO() function requires two arguments, as shown below:

FIELDNO(*field,table*)

The first argument must be a string or string variable that specifies the field whose position you want to check. The second argument must be a string or string variable that specifies the name of the table that contains that field. Although this table may be on the workspace, it does not have to be. If it is in other than the current directory, however, you must specify its complete path.

If c:\paradox\examples is the current directory, for example, and the table named EMPLYEE is stored in that directory, you would use the function *FIELDNO("Last Name","Emplyee")* to determine the position of the Last Name field within that table. If c:\paradox\examples is not the current directory, however, you would use the function FIELDNO("Last Name","c:\\paradox\\examples\\Emplyee").

The FILESIZE() Function

PAL's FILESIZE() function, whose form is

FILESIZE(*filename*)

returns the number of bytes of disk space occupied by the file named by its argument, *filename*. If the file you want to inspect is not in the current directory, you must include the path and/or drive name in the argument. In all cases, you must include the file's extension as a part of the argument. For example, you would use the function *FILESIZE("c:\\paradox\\examples\\abc.db")* to determine the size of data base file ABC, if that file is stored in the c:\paradox\examples directory, and c:\paradox\examples is not the current directory.

The IMAGENO() Function

The IMAGENO() function returns the position of the current image relative to the other images currently on the Paradox workspace. If the cursor is in the first image on the workspace (the one that Paradox makes current when you press the [Up Image] key until you hear a beep), this function will return the value 1. If the cursor is within the third image, this function will return the value 3, and so forth.

This function is useful for controlling the movement of the cursor between images. For example, the script

```
WHILE IMAGENO()>1
  UpImage
ENDWHILE
```

moves the cursor to the first image on the workspace.

The IMAGETYPE() Function

The IMAGETYPE() function allows you to determine, from within a script, in what type of image the cursor currently is positioned. If the current image is a table or a form, this function returns the string *Display*. If the current image is a query, this function returns the string *Query*. If the cursor is not within an image (if the workspace is blank or Paradox is in the Report, Form, or Script Editors), this function returns the string *None*.

The MENUCHOICE() Function

PAL's MENUCHOICE() function returns the currently highlighted menu selection as a string. For example, if the cursor is highlighting the selection report on the main Paradox menu, when PAL reads the command *x=MENUCHOICE()*, it will store the string *Report* in the variable *x*.

The MONITOR() Function

The PAL function MONITOR() allows PAL to determine the type of monitor for which you have configured Paradox. If you have configured Paradox for use with a color monitor, the MONITOR() function returns the string *Color*. If you have configured Paradox for a black-and-white monitor for use with a graphics card, this function will return the string *B&W*. If you have configured Paradox for use with a monochrome monitor (no graphics capability), this function will return the string *Mono*.

By using this function in conjunction with PAL's IF and STYLE commands, you can direct PAL to display messages in different styles, depending on what type of monitor Paradox is using when it plays the script.

The NFIELDS() Function

PAL's NFIELDS() function allows you to determine how many fields are contained within the table that you name. The form of this function is

NFIELDS(*tablename*)

where *tablename* is a string expression that specifies the name of a table. If the table is in the current directory, the argument can simply be the name of that table. If the table you want to test is in another directory, then you must specify the complete path, remembering to use double backslashes.

For example, suppose the four-field table named JOBS is stored in c:\paradox\examples. If c:\paradox\examples is the current directory, then the function *NFIELDS("Jobs")* will return the value 4. On the other hand, if c:\paradox\exmples is not the current directory, you would need to use the function *NFIELDS("c:\\paradox\\examples\\Jobs")*.

The NIMAGES() Function

PAL's NIMAGES() function returns the number of images (tables, forms, and queries) currently on the Paradox workspace. If the workspace contains two table images, two form images, and two queries, for example, the NIMAGES() function would return the value 6.

The script

```
WHILE IMAGENO()<NIMAGES()
   DownImage
ENDIF
```

uses the NIMAGES() function to move the cursor to the last image on the workspace. As long as the number of the current image (the result of the IMAGENO() function) is less than the total number of images on the workspace (the result of the NIMAGES() function), PAL will move to the next image. Because the conditional test will be false only when the cursor is within the final image, PAL will continue to press [Down Image] until that point.

The NKEYFIELDS() Function

PAL's NKEYFIELDS() function allows you to determine how many key fields a particular table contains. The form of this function is

NKEYFIELDS(*tablename*)

where *tablename* is a string expression that specifies the name of the table whose key fields you want to count. If the table is not stored in the current directory, then you must include the path within the argument. For example, suppose that the table named ORDERS, stored in the directory c:\paradox\examples, contains two key fields. If c:\paradox\examples is the current directory, then the function *NKEYFIELDS("Orders")* would return the value 2.

The NPAGES() Function

The NPAGES() function allows PAL to calculate the number of pages in the current form or report. When you are viewing or editing a form, this function returns the number of pages in that form. When you are editing a report specification, this function returns the number of page widths that the report contains. If you are viewing the EMPLYEE table through a three-page form, for example, the function NPAGES() will return the value 3.

The NRECORDS() Function

PAL's NRECORDS() function allows PAL to calculate the number of records in the table that you specify. The form of this function is

   NRECORDS(*tablename*)

where *tablename* is a string expression that specifies the name of the table whose records you want to count. If the table is not in the current directory, then you must include the full path to the table within the argument of the function.

For example, suppose that the table named PROSPECT, located in the directory c:\paradox\examples, contains 1234 records. If c:\paradox\examples is the current directory, then the function *NRECORDS("Prospect")* will return the value 1234. If c:\paradox\examples were not the current directory, however, this function would result in a script error. To count the records in this table, you would instead need to use the function *NRECORDS("c:\paradox\examples\Prospect")*.

The NROWS() Function

The NROWS() function returns the number of rows in the current image. Unlike NRECORDS(), the NROWS() function calculates the display size of an image, not the size of the table itself. Also unlike NRECORDS(), the NROWS() function operates upon the current image, not upon any table that you name. NROWS() therefore accepts no arguments.

For example, suppose that you use the [Menu] Image TableSize command to reduce the display image of the 250-record table PEOPLE so that only four records are visible at one time. If PAL reads the function NROWS() while the cursor is in the table image of PEOPLE, it will return the value 4.

The PAGENO() Function

PAL's PAGENO() function returns the number of the current page width when you are editing a report and returns the number of the current page when you are designing or using a form. This function has no meaning in any other context. This function takes no arguments.

For example, if the cursor is within the third page of a form, the function PAGENO() will return the value 3. If the cursor is in the fourth page width of a report, this function will return the value 4.

The PAGEWIDTH() Function

The PAL function PAGEWIDTH() calculates the width, in characters, of the pages in the current report specification. If the cursor is in a report whose pages are 80 characters wide, for example, the function PAGEWIDTH() will return the value 80.

The RECNO() Function

The RECNO() function returns the position of the record in which the cursor is positioned in the current display image (table or form), with respect to the first record in the table. Because the RECNO() function works on the current display image, it does not require or accept any arguments.

As an example of this function, suppose that you use the [Menu] View command to bring a table named DATES to the workspace and make it the current image. Then you press ↓ fifty times to position the cursor on the fifty-first record. If PAL reads the RECNO() function at this point, it will return the value 51.

The ROW() Function

PAL's ROW() function is the mate of the COL() function. Where COL() returns the cursor's horizontal position in the PAL canvas, ROW() returns its vertical position in the canvas. For example, suppose you use the command @10,20 to position the cursor at the intersection of row 10 and column 20 of the PAL canvas. If PAL reads the function ROW while the cursor is in this position, the function will return the value 10. (We'll explain how to position the cursor on the PAL canvas in Chapter 16.)

The ROWNO() Function

PAL's ROWNO() function returns the row position of the cursor within the current image. ROWNO() is closely related to COLNO(), which returns the column position of the cursor within the current image.

For example, suppose that you issue the [Menu] View command to bring a table to the workspace. Like any default-sized table, this one displays 21 records at a time. If you press the [Pg Dn] key, the cursor will be in the twenty-second record, which will be displayed on the first row of the table image, as shown in Figure 15-5. If PAL evaluates the ROWNO() function at this point, it will return the value 1. Although the cursor is in the twenty-second record of the table, it is in the first row of the image.

Figure 15-5   The ROWNO() Function

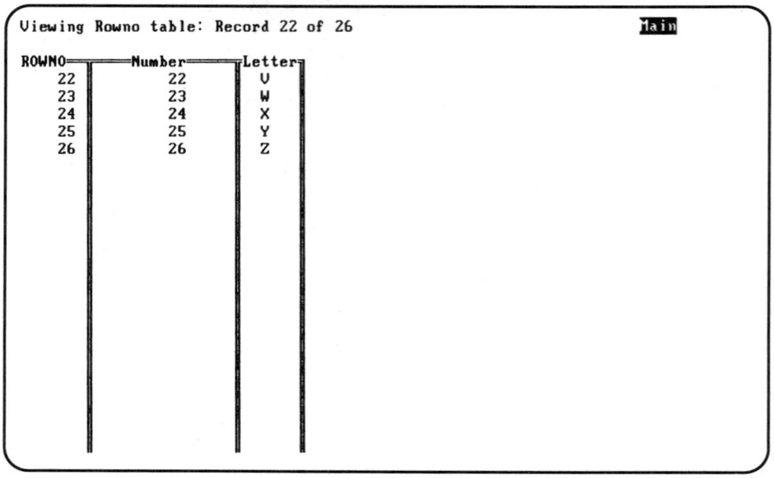

```
Viewing Rowno table: Record 22 of 26                    Main
 ROWNO      Number       Letter
   22         22            U
   23         23            W
   24         24            X
   25         25            Y
   26         26            Z
```

The SDIR() Function

PAL's SDIR() function returns, as a string, the complete drive/directory in which the script currently being played is located. This function takes no arguments. SDIR() is useful when you have called a script from a directory other than the one that is current. For example, suppose that you issue the [Menu] Scripts Play command and type c:\paradox\examples\script1 while c:\paradox is the current directory. If Script1 contains the function SDIR(), it will return the string *c:\paradox\examples*–the directory from which the current script was called. In the same situation, the DIRECTORY() function will return the string *c:\paradox*–the default directory.

The SYSMODE() Function

The SYSMODE() function allows PAL to determine which mode Paradox currently is in. Very simply, this function returns whatever message is in the Mode indicator at the upper-left corner of the screen. Depending upon which mode Paradox is in when PAL evaluates this function, it will return one of nine strings: *Create, DataEntry, Edit, Form, Main, Report, Restructure, Script,* or *Sort*. For example, if your screen looks like the one shown in Figure 15-6, the function SYSMODE() will return the string *Main*.

Figure 15-6 The SYSMODE() Function

```
Viewing Emplyee table: Record 1 of 16                    Main
EMPLYEE┬─Emp Number─┬─Last Name─┬─First Name─┬─SS Number─┬═Addre
   1   │     1      │ Jones     │ David      │414-74-3421│4000 St. Ja
   2   │     2      │ Cameron   │ Herb       │321-65-8765│2321 Elm St
   3   │     3      │ Jones     │ Stewart    │401-32-8721│4389 Oakbri
   4   │     4      │ Roberts   │ Darlene    │417-43-7777│451 Lone Pi
   5   │     5      │ Jones     │ Jean       │413-07-9123│4000 St. Ja
   6   │     6      │ Williams  │ Brenda     │401-55-1567│100 Owl Cre
   7   │     7      │ Myers     │ Julie      │314-30-9452│4512 Parksi
   8   │     8      │ Link      │ Julie      │345-75-1525│3215 Palm C
   9   │     9      │ Jackson   │ Mary       │424-13-7621│7821 Clark
  10   │    10      │ Jakes, Jr.│ Sal        │321-65-9151│3451 Michig
  11   │    11      │ Preston   │ Molly      │451-00-3426│321 Indian
  12   │    12      │ Masters   │ Ron        │317-65-4529│423 W. 72nd
  13   │    13      │ Robertson │ Kevin      │415-24-6710│431 Bardsto
  14   │    14      │ Garrison  │ Robert     │312-98-1479│55 Wheeler
  15   │    15      │ Gunn      │ Barbara    │321-97-8632│541 Kentuck
  16   │    16      │ Emerson   │ Cheryl     │404-14-1422│8100 River
```

The TABLE() Function

PAL's TABLE() function returns the name of the current table image as a string. Because this function works on the current image (which must be a table, form, or query), it accepts no arguments. For example, if the cursor is within the EMPLYEE table when PAL reads the command *table=TABLE()*, PAL will store the string *Emplyee* in the variable *table*.

The TYPE() Function

PAL's TYPE() function returns the type of the expression used as its argument. The form of this function is

    TYPE(*expression*)

where *expression* is the expression whose type you want to know. This expression can be a variable, equation, function, field reference, or a literal value, string, or date. If the argument of the TYPE() function is a numeric expression, it will return the string *N*. If the argument is a string expression, this function returns the letter *A*, followed by the number of characters in the string. If the argument is a date expression, it returns *D*.

You can use this function in a variety of ways. For example, when the cursor is positioned over the alphanumeric entry *Smith* in a table image, the function *TYPE([])* returns the string *A5*. Similarly, the function *TYPE(x)* returns the string *N* if x contains the value *1234.56* and the function *TYPE(11/24/58)* returns the string *D*.

The VERSION() Function

The VERSION() function allows PAL to determine what version of Paradox it is working in. This function accepts no arguments. If you are working in Paradox 1.0, this function will return the numeric value 1. If you are working in Version 1.1, this function will return the numeric value 1.1. As you know, some PAL commands and functions are available only in Version 1.1. By using this function to determine what version you are working in before you play a script, you can avoid the script error that will result when Paradox 1.0 reads a 1.1 command or function.

The WINDOW() Function

PAL's final informational function is WINDOW(). This function returns the contents of the message window at the bottom-right corner of the screen as a string. Because PAL erases the text that appears in the message window as soon as you press another key, this function provides the only way to capture these messages for future use. For example, suppose you run the script:

```
VIEW "Emplyee"
Right BackSpace
x=WINDOW()
```

This script tells Paradox to press the [Backspace] key without first entering the edit mode. When you run this script, PAL will store in the variable *x* the error message *Press the Edit key [F9] if you want to make changes*–the result of pressing the [Backspace] key while you are not in the edit mode.

PAL's Logical Functions

Logical functions are the only group of PAL functions that we have not yet discussed. Unlike the functions in the seven groups we have examined so far, the functions in this group do not return numeric, string, or date values. Instead, they return one of two logical constants: True or False. Because they return only these two logical results, these functions can stand alone as the conditional tests of IF and WHILE commands.

The ATFIRST() and ATLAST() Functions

PAL's ATFIRST() and ATLAST() functions determine whether the cursor currently is positioned within the first or last record in a table. Because these functions operate on the table in which the cursor is positioned, they accept no arguments. The ATFIRST() function returns the logical constant True if the cursor is in the first record of the table image, and False if it is in any other record. Similarly, the result of ATLAST() is True if the cursor is in the last record, and False if it is anywhere else. As you will see in Chapter 16, these functions are useful when you want PAL to step through a table one record at a time, stopping at the first or last record in the table.

The BOT() and EOT() Functions

PAL's next two logical functions, BOT() and EOT(), are similar but not identical to ATFIRST() and ATLAST(). BOT(), which stands for **B**eginning **O**f **T**able, returns the constant True when you attempt to move beyond the first record in a table with a MOVETO RECORD or SKIP command (not with the keystroke representation Up). Likewise, EOT(), which stands for **E**nd **O**f **T**able, returns the constant True when you try to move beyond the last record in a table, using the MOVETO RECORD or SKIP commands (not with the keystroke representation Down). You'll learn more about these functions in our discussion of the WHILE command in Chapter 16.

The CHARWAITING()/ GETCHAR() Functions

If you type a character while PAL is playing a script, your computer will not pass that character on to PAL immediately. In fact, PAL will not receive the character until it reads a command or function in the script that instructs it to accept input from the user. The CHARWAITING() function allows PAL to determine whether a character is currently being held in your computer's keyboard buffer. The CHARWAITING() function does not accept any arguments.

You'll commonly use the CHARWAITING() function in conjunction with another PAL function: GETCHAR(). The GETCHAR() function instructs PAL to retrieve a character from the keyboard buffer, if one is waiting there, or to pause until a character is typed, if one is not waiting.

For example, the script shown in Figure 15-7 demonstrates a simple use of GETCHAR() and CHARWAITING() functions. The IF command on the first line of this script instructs PAL to determine if a character is waiting in the keyboard buffer. If so, the CHARWAITING() function is True, and PAL evaluates the command *x=GETCHAR()*. This command instructs PAL to retrieve the character from the buffer and store it in the variable *x*.

Importantly, the GETCHAR() function returns the ASCII value (0-255) of the character it retrieves, not the character itself. The ASC() function in the command *IF x=ASC("q")* converts the character *q* into an ASCII value so that PAL can compare it to the value stored in the variable *x*. If the character in the buffer is a *q*, PAL will read the command QUIT and, therefore, exit from the script. If the character is anything but *q*, PAL will play the script named Subrout1.

Figure 15-7   An Example of the CHARWAITING() Function

```
Designing script Charwait                                    Script
....+...10....+...20....+...30....+...40....+...50....+...60....+...70....+...80
IF CHARWAITING()
  x=GETCHAR()
  IF x=ASC("q")
    THEN QUIT
  ENDIF
PLAY "Subrout1"
ENDIF
```

The DRIVESTATUS() Function

PAL's next logical function, DRIVESTATUS(), determines whether the drive you name is prepared to read or write information. The form of this function is

>DRIVESTATUS(*drive letter*)

where the *drive letter* argument is a string expression that specifies the disk drive you want to check.

The DRIVESTATUS() function returns the logical constant True unless the drive designated in its argument does not exist or is not operational. This function will return the constant False if there is no disk in the drive you name, for example, or if the door of that drive is not closed. If you have a dual-floppy system, the function *DRIVESTATUS("C")* will return the constant False.

The ISASSIGNED() Function

PAL's ISASSIGNED() function determines if a variable is currently defined; that is, whether or not the variable exists. (This function also tests for the existence of arrays and procedures–topics that we'll cover in Chapter 16.) The form of this function is

>ISASSIGNED(*variablename*)

where the single argument *variablename* is the name of a variable (or array or procedure). For example, if you have defined the variable *x* during the current session, the function *ISASSIGNED(x)* will return the constant True. If you have not defined the variable, or if you have used the command *RELEASE VARS x* after defining it, this function will return the constant False.

The ISBLANK() Function

PAL's ISBLANK() function checks to see if a variable, field, or array stores a blank value, or if a procedure returns a blank value. The form of this function is

ISBLANK(*argument*)

where *argument* is a reference to a variable, a field, an array element, or a procedure. If *argument* stores or returns a blank value, the ISBLANK() function will return the constant False. If *argument* stores anything other than a blank value, the ISBLANK() function will return the logical constant True.

The script shown in Figure 15-8 demonstrates a simple use of the ISBLANK() function. This script begins by entering the edit mode and moving the cursor to the Amount field of the first record in the current table. The *WHILE NOT EOF()* command tells PAL to execute the commands that come between that command and the ENDWHILE command until it reaches the end of the table (actually until it tries to move beyond the end of the table). The command *IF []=ISBLANK()* tests to see whether the current field is blank. If so, PAL enters the value 0 into it, moves down to the next row, and repeats the process. If the field contains other than a blank value, PAL moves down one row without replacing the entry.

Figure 15-8   An Example of the ISBLANK() Function

```
Designing script Blank                                    Script  Ins
....+...10....+...20....+...30....+...40....+...50....+...60....+...70....+...80
EditKey
MOVETO [Amount]
Home
WHILE NOT EOF()
   IF []=ISBLANK()
      []=0
   ENDIF
   SKIP 1
ENDWHILE
```

The ISEMPTY() Function

PAL's ISEMPTY() function tests whether the table you specify is empty or whether it contains records. The form of this function is

ISEMPTY(*tablename*)

where the single argument is the name of a table. If the table is not in the current directory, then you must include the directory and path in the argument. (Because the backslash is a special character which means "interpret the next character literally," you must use two backslashes in the path designation wherever you normally would use only one.) If the sixteen-record table named EMPLYEE is in the current directory, for example, the function *ISEMPTY("Emplyee")* will return the value False.

The ISFIELDVIEW() Function

PAL's ISFIELDVIEW() function determines whether Paradox is in the special field view mode (the result of pressing the [Field View] key ([Alt][F5]) while Paradox is in the table or edit mode). If so, the function will return the logical constant True. If not, the function will return the constant False. Because this function refers to the current table, it does not accept any arguments.

For example, the script

         IF NOT ISFIELDVIEW()
            THEN FieldView
         ENDIF

places Paradox in the field view if it is not already in that mode.

The ISFORMVIEW() Function

The ISFORMVIEW() function tests whether PAL is displaying the current table in the form view or in the table view. If the current image is a form, this function returns the logical constant True. If the current image is a table, the function returns the logical constant False. For example, the ISFORMVIEW() function in the script

         VIEW "Emplyee"
         Menu {Image} {PickForm} {F}
         x=ISFORMVIEW()

will return the logical constant True.

The ISFILE() and ISTABLE() Functions

PAL's ISFILE() and ISTABLE() functions both determine whether a given file exists. PAL's ISFILE() function checks for the existence of a specified file of any type on the current directory. The form of this function is

         ISFILE(*filename*)

where the *filename* argument is the name of the file whose existence you want to verify. If the file is not in the current directory, then you must specify the directory as well as the file. (Remember to use two backslashes wherever you normally would use only one.) The *filename* argument should include the full name of the file, including any extension.

For example, if the script file MENU.SC is in the directory c:\paradox\scripts, then the function *ISFILE("c:\\paradox\\scripts\\menu.sc")* will return the constant True. If the file does not exist, if it is on a different directory, or if you forget to include the file name extension .SC in the function's argument, the function will return the constant False.

The ISTABLE() function checks for the existence of Paradox table (.DB) files. The form of this function is

>ISTABLE(*filename*)

where the *filename* argument is the name of the file whose existence you want to check. As with ISFILE(), if the file is not in the current directory, then you must specify the directory as well as the file. Because the ISTABLE() function only looks for .DB files, there is no need to specify an extension.

For example, if a file named EMPLYEE.DB were in the directory c:\paradox\data, the function *ISTABLE("c:\\paradox\\data\\emplyee")* would return the logical constant True, as would the function *ISFILE("c:\\paradox\\data\\emplyee.db")*.

The ISINSERTMODE() Function

PAL's ISINSERTMODE() function does pretty much what you might think—it determines whether Paradox is in the insert or the overwrite mode while you are working in the Report, Form, or Script Editors. For example, the script

>IF NOT ISINSERTMODE()
>   THEN Ins
>ENDIF

toggles Paradox to the insert mode if it is in the overwrite mode.

The PRINTERSTATUS() Function

The PRINTERSTATUS() function determines whether your printer is ready to receive information from Paradox. This function accepts no arguments. If your printer is connected to the correct port, turned on, filled with paper, and in the ready mode, this function will return the logical constant True. If any of these conditions are not met, this function will return the constant False.

This command is useful within any script that prints a report. In the script shown in Figure 15-9, for example, this function tells PAL to prompt you if your printer is not ready. (We'll explain how the MESSAGE command works in Chapter 16).

Figure 15-9 An Example of the PRINTERSTATUS() Function

```
Designing script Prtready                                    Script  Ins
....+...10....+...20....+...30....+...40....+...50....+...60....+...70....+...80
IF NOT PRINTERSTATUS()
  THEN
    MESSAGE "Make sure printer is ready, then press any key"
    x=GETCHAR()
ENDIF
REPORT "Emplyee" "R"
```

Conclusion

In this chapter, we have explored another fundamental component of PAL programming: Functions. As you have seen, functions are special tools that allow you to calculate or extract information that would be difficult or impossible to obtain with variables and field references alone. We began the chapter by examining PAL's mathematical and geometric functions. Then we moved on to statistical functions and financial functions. Finally, we explored PAL's date/time, string, informational, and logical functions.

In the next two chapters of this section, we'll assume that you have a working knowledge of the PAL building blocks which we have presented in Chapters 13, 14, and 15. In Chapter 16, we'll present a number of PAL commands in the context of essential PAL programming techniques. In Chapter 17, we'll explore some other PAL topics, like the use of procedures, arrays, macros, and the PAL Debugger.

Chapter 16
Fundamental PAL Techniques

In the previous three chapters of this section, we have presented the basic building blocks you need to create PAL programs: the Script Editor, keystroke representations, commands, variables, equations, and functions. In this chapter, we'll use those building blocks as we demonstrate some fundamental PAL programming techniques. In the process, we'll present a number of the PAL commands that we passed over in our initial coverage of commands in Chapter 14.

Using the PAL Canvas

In Chapter 13, we introduced you to the PAL canvas. Whenever PAL begins to play a script, it obscures the Paradox workspace with the PAL canvas. When PAL "drops" the PAL canvas at the beginning of the execution of a script, it "paints" that canvas with an exact image of what is on the Paradox workspace at the time.

In many cases, the initial image will remain on the PAL canvas for the entire duration of the script play. This initial image does not need to stay on the PAL canvas during script play, however. By using various PAL commands, you can erase the initial image from the PAL canvas and replace it with the messages and prompts of your choice.

Clearing the PAL Canvas

PAL's CLEAR command allows you to erase all or part of the image displayed on the PAL canvas. The most basic form of this command is simply the word CLEAR. When PAL reads this command in a script, it immediately erases all information from the PAL canvas. For example, suppose you play a script with the single command *CLEAR* while the screen looks like Figure 16-1. As soon as PAL begins playing this script, it drops the PAL canvas and paints it with the image you see in Figure 16-1. Then the CLEAR command erases that image from the PAL canvas so that your screen is completely blank.

Figure 16-1 A Sample Screen

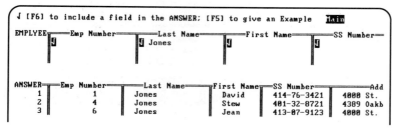

Once you have cleared the PAL canvas, it will remain empty for the entire execution of the script unless you use other PAL commands to write information onto it. (Because PAL executes this simple one-command script almost instantaneously, however, the cleared PAL canvas will be visible for only a fraction of a second before the PAL canvas is lifted to again reveal the Paradox workspace.)

Clearing Part of the PAL Canvas

Although you will most often use the CLEAR command to erase the entire PAL canvas, you can use special forms of this command to clear only selected portions. If you follow the CLEAR command with the keyword EOL (for end of line), as in *CLEAR EOL*, PAL will erase the current line from the cursor position all the way to the right edge of the PAL canvas. If the cursor is at the left edge of the screen, this command will erase the entire line. If the cursor is in another column, this command will erase a partial line.

Another form of the CLEAR command allows you to clear a rectangular portion of the PAL canvas. When you follow the CLEAR command with the keyword EOS (for end of screen), PAL erases a rectangle whose upper-left corner is marked by the current cursor position and whose lower-right corner is the lower-right corner of the screen.

Positioning the Cursor on the PAL Canvas

As we have said, you can display messages, prompts, menus, and the results of calculations on the PAL canvas during the execution of a script. To write messages on the PAL canvas, you use commands like ?, ??, and TEXT, which we'll demonstrate in a few pages. The place on the canvas where these messages appear depends on where the cursor is when PAL reads the commands. Therefore, before we show you how to display messages, we'll show you how to position the cursor on the PAL canvas.

Positioning the cursor on the PAL canvas is the job of the @ command. The form of this command is

> @row,column

where *row* and *column* are numbers that specify the row and column to which you want to move the cursor. These arguments may be any PAL expression that returns a numeric value. The row argument can be any number from 0 to 24, where 0 is the first row on the canvas and 24 is the last row. The column argument can be any number from 0 to 79, where 0 is the first (leftmost) column and 79 is the last (rightmost) column.

When PAL encounters an @ command in a script, it moves the cursor to the indicated position on the screen. For example, the command *@11,39* moves the cursor to the intersection of row 11 and column 39 of the PAL canvas–approximately in the center of the screen.

Writing on the PAL Canvas

Three commands–?, ??, and TEXT–allow you to write information on the PAL canvas at the location you specify. Two other commands–MESSAGE and RETURN–write information into the message area at the lower-right corner of the screen.

The ? and ?? Commands

PAL's ? and ?? commands are the most fundamental of all the commands that display information on the PAL canvas. The forms of these functions are

> ? *argument 1,argument 2,...,argument n*
> ?? *argument 1,argument 2,...,argument n*

where the arguments are any type of PAL expression. These functions can accept an unlimited number of arguments or none at all.

When PAL reads a ? command, it moves the cursor to the beginning of the next line of the PAL canvas and displays the value(s) of its argument(s) there. For example, when PAL executes the script

> CLEAR
> @10,20
> ? "This is a message"

it first clears the PAL canvas and moves the cursor to the intersection of row 10 and column 20. Then it moves to the left edge of row 11 and displays the message *This is a message* there.

The ?? command, on the other hand, displays the value(s) of its argument(s) at the current cursor position; it does not skip down a row before writing to the canvas. For example, when PAL executes the script

    CLEAR
    @10,20
    ?? "This is a message"

it will clear the PAL canvas and move the cursor to the intersection of row 10 and column 20, just as in the previous example. It then will write the string *This is a message* at that point instead of advancing to the beginning of the next line and displaying the message there.

When PAL finshes executing a ? or ?? command, the cursor will be positioned on the space to the right of the last character that PAL wrote onto the canvas. For example, after PAL executes the previous script, the cursor will be positioned at the intersection of row 10 and column 37–immediately to the right of the letter *e* in *message*.

Nonstring Arguments

In the examples of the ? and ?? commands, we used literal strings as arguments. In actual use, the ? and ?? commands can accept as arguments any kind of PAL expression: literal values, literal dates, variables, references, equations, and functions. For example, the two commands *?? 5* and *?? "5"* both would produce the same result–the character 5 displayed on the PAL canvas at the current position of the cursor. Similarly, when PAL reads the command *?? 11/24/58*, it will display the string *11/24/58* at the current cursor position.

In some situations, you may want to use the ? and ?? commands to display the contents of variables or the entries in a table on the screen. For example, if the variable *x* contains the value 1234.56, the command *?? x* will display *1234.56* at the current position of the cursor on the PAL canvas. If *x* contains the string *This is a test*, this command will display the string *This is a test*. If *x* contains the date 11/24/58, this command will display the string *11/24/58* at the position of the cursor.

Displaying entries from a table on the PAL canvas is also easy. For example, if the entry in the Age column of the fifth record in a table named PEOPLE contains the value 27, the script

    CLEAR
    VIEW "People"
    MOVETO RECORD 5
    @10,20
    ?? [Age]

will display the string *27*, beginning at the intersection of row 10 and column 20 of the otherwise empty PAL canvas.

You also can use equations and functions as the arguments of PAL's ? and ?? commands. When you do, PAL displays not the equations or functions but rather their results on the PAL canvas. For example, the script

```
x=1
y=2
CLEAR
@10,20
? x+y
```

will display the result 3 at the beginning of row 10 of the PAL canvas.

Multiple Arguments

Instead of using the ? and ?? commands to display only a single label, value, or date on the screen, you can and often will want to join many messages together on a single line. The easiest way to do this is to include multiple arguments in the ? or ?? commands. When PAL executes a ? or ?? command that has multiple arguments, it displays those arguments (or their results) back-to-back on the PAL canvas with no spaces in between.

When you use more than one argument with ? or ??, you must separate them from one another with commas. Because PAL's ? and ?? commands convert all types of expressions into strings for display purposes, the various expressions for a single command do not need to be of the same type.

For example, suppose that you want PAL to calculate the sum of the values stored in the variables *x* and *y* and display the result to the right of the text *The sum of x and y is* at the intersection of row 10 and column 20. To do this, you might use the script

```
x=1
y=2
CLEAR
@10,20
?? "The sum of x and y is ",x+y,"."
```

This script clears the PAL canvas, positions the cursor at the intersection of row 10 and column 20, and writes the sentence *The sum of x and y is 3*. As you can see, this message is composed of three parts. The first argument causes PAL to type the words *The sum of x and y is* followed by a single space. Since the next argument is an equation, PAL evaluates it and displays the result, 3, to the right of the first string. PAL then displays the final argument, a literal period, to the right of that result.

Long Messages

Sometimes, the information that is displayed on the screen by a ? or ?? command will not fit on one line. When this happens, PAL will break the message when it reaches the 80th column of the PAL canvas, then it will move the cursor to the beginning of the next line and will continue typing there. For example, Figure 16-2 shows the result of playing the script

```
CLEAR
@1,50
?? "Now is the time for all good men to come to the aid of their country."
```

Figure 16-2 A Long Message

```
                                            Now is the time for all good m
en to come to the aid of their country.
```

Formatting the Display

In Chapter 13, we introduced the FORMAT() function as a way to convert values into formatted strings. Another important use of this function is to alter the way the ? and ?? commands display messages on the PAL canvas. As you recall, the FORMAT function allows you to alter the display of any type of expression: numeric, alphanumeric, date, and logical. Using this function, for example, you can control the width and alignment of any type of value, the case of alphanumeric values, and the use of signs, parentheses, and currency notation for numeric values. You also can use the FORMAT() function to control the form in which dates are displayed and to make the logical constants True/False display as either Yes/No or On/Off.

Without the use of the FORMAT() function, the ? and ?? commands display values verbatim, exactly as they appear in the function or as they are stored in the variable or field. If the variable *x* holds the value 7654.321, for example, the command *?? x* will write 7654.321 onto the screen at the present position of the cursor. But suppose that you want PAL to display the value with a leading $ sign, a comma separating the hundreds from the thousands, and only two digits to the right of the decimal place, like this: $7,654.32. If you want to display the value in this way, you can use the command *?? FORMAT("W9.2,E$C",x)*. You can use the FORMAT() function as the argument of a ? or ?? command to format messages in an almost endless variety of ways. For example, while the command *? [State]* displays the contents of the current record's State field exactly as it appears in the table, the command *? FORMAT("CU",[State])* will display it in all-capital form.

The TEXT Command

PAL's TEXT command provides yet another way to write information onto the PAL canvas. Unlike the ? and ?? commands, the TEXT command can write only literal text onto the screen. It cannot display the contents of variables or fields, nor the results of equations and functions. It does allow you to write multiple-line blocks of text to the screen with a single command, however.

The TEXT command actually is a combination of two commands: TEXT and ENDTEXT. The form of this command is

    TEXT
    one or more lines of text
    ENDTEXT

When PAL encounters a TEXT command in a script, it writes to the screen a literal copy of the characters that come between that command and the next ENDTEXT command. PAL always begins writing at the current position of the cursor. For the TEXT command to work properly, the text must begin on a line subsequent to the one that contains the TEXT command–never on that same line.

For example, consider the script

    CLEAR
    @11,0
    TEXT
    PAL APPLICATION #1
    Press any key to continue...
    ENDTEXT

When PAL runs the script, it will clear the screen, position the cursor in the first column of row 11, and type the message

    PAL APPLICATION #1
    Press any key to continue...

Because PAL automatically assumes that what comes between a TEXT command and an ENDTEXT command is literal text, there is no need to enclose it in quotation marks. If you do, in fact, PAL will print the quotation marks on the screen. Likewise, if you include blank lines between the TEXT and ENDTEXT commands, PAL will leave blank lines on the screen.

If the cursor is not in the first column of the screen when PAL comes to a TEXT command, it will print the first line of the text beginning at the position of the cursor. The second and subsequent lines will be printed beginning in column 1, however. For this reason, you will usually want to position the cursor in column 0 before you issue a TEXT command. If you want to position the text toward the center of the screen, you should include leading spaces on each line of text.

Because the TEXT command is not able to evaluate formulas or functions, you cannot use the FORMAT() function to customize the text that it displays.

The SLEEP Command

The information displayed by PAL's ?, ??, and TEXT commands disappears when PAL finishes playing the current script, when the screen is cleared, or when it is overwritten by other information at the same location. In some cases, this means that PAL will erase the information almost as soon as it is written on the screen. You can prolong the duration of these messages on the screen, however, by using PAL's SLEEP command.

The SLEEP command allows you to pause the execution of a script for the period of time that you specify. The form of this command is

    SLEEP *time in milliseconds*

where the *time in milliseconds* argument is a numeric expression with a value between 0 and 30000. Because the argument represents a number of milliseconds (1/1000ths of a second), a value of 1000 will produce a one-second delay, a value of 15000 will produce a fifteen-second delay, and a value of 30000 will produce the maximum thirty-second delay.

For example, suppose that you want the message *This message will last for 5 seconds* to appear on the screen for five seconds. To do this, you would use the script

    CLEAR
    @11,30
    ?? "This message will last for 5 seconds"
    SLEEP 5000

The CLEAR command erases the PAL canvas. The command @11,30 moves the cursor toward the middle of the screen where the ?? command displays the message *This message will last for 5 seconds*.

If the script ended at this point, PAL would erase this message as soon as it appeared. Because the SLEEP command delays the end of the script for five seconds, however, this message remains for that period of time.

Styling the Display

The STYLE command allows you to change the style in which the results of the ?, ??, and TEXT commands are displayed. If you are using Paradox on a computer system with a monochrome monitor, you can use this command to display information in reverse video, bright characters, blinking characters, or combinations of these three styles. If your system has a color monitor, however, you can command Paradox to display text in any of 256 background and foreground color combinations.

Because STYLE is a command, not a function, you can't use it as the argument of another command like ? or ??. Instead, you must include it in the script ahead of the command that displays the text you want to style. Once PAL reads a STYLE command, the style settings within that command remain in effect for the remainder of the script unless you include other STYLE commands that change or cancel those settings.

The REVERSE, INTENSE, and BLINK Keywords

If you are using a monochrome monitor, you can use the STYLE command with three keywords–REVERSE, INTENSE, and BLINK–to format the messages you write to the screen with ?, ??, and TEXT. REVERSE causes the message to be written in inverse (reverse) video. INTENSE causes the message to be written in high-intensity video. BLINK causes the message to be written in blinking characters.

For example, suppose you want PAL to display the text *This is plain video* in normal unstyled text, starting at the intersection of row 2 and column 20 on the PAL canvas, display the text *This is reverse video* in reverse video two lines below it, the text *This is intense video* two lines below that, and the text *This is blinking video* two lines below that. To do this, you would use the script shown in Figure 16-3.

Figure 16-3 The STYLE Command

```
Designing script Styles                                      Script
....+...10....+...20....+...30....+...40....+...50....+...60....+...70....+...80
CLEAR
@2,20
?? "This is plain video"
STYLE REVERSE
@4,20
?? "This is reverse video"
STYLE INTENSE
@6,20
?? "This is intense video"
STYLE BLINK
@8,20
?? "This is blinking video"
SLEEP 10000
```

The CLEAR command that starts the script erases the PAL canvas. Then, the command @2,20 positions the cursor at the intersection of row 2 and column 20, where PAL writes *This is plain video* without any embellishment. The command *STYLE REVERSE* that follows turns on the Reverse Video attribute for all text that PAL subsequently writes to the canvas. The *@4,20* command positions the cursor at the intersection of row 4 and column 20. Then the command *?? "This is reverse video"* writes *This is reverse video* on the screen. Because we turned on the Reverse attribute prior to writing this text, PAL displays it in reverse video. The command @6,20 positions the cursor in row 6.

The *STYLE INTENSE* command in this script does two things: it cancels the previously assigned Reverse attribute and it activates the Intense Video attribute. All text that PAL writes to the screen after it reads this command will be intense, but will not be in reverse video. The ?? command writes the string *This is intense video* to the screen in intense video. Similarly, the command *STYLE BLINK* cancels the previously assigned Intense attribute and activates the Blink Video attribute. Then the ?? command writes the string *This is blinking video* to the screen in blinking video. Figure 16-4 shows the result of this script on the screen. (Unfortunately, the Blink and Intense styles cannot be represented well in a figure.)

Figure 16-4 An Example of the STYLE Command

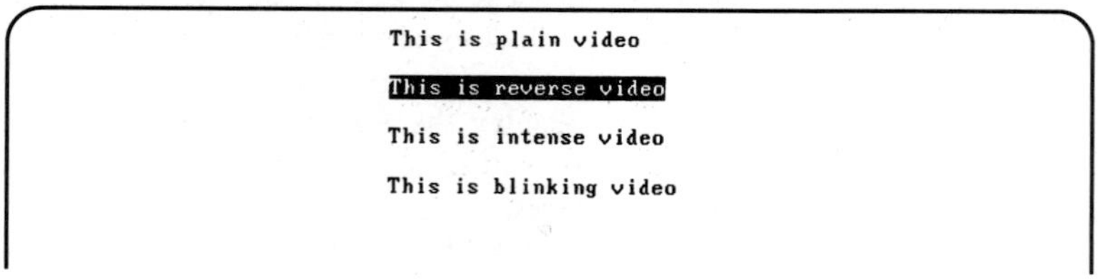

```
This is plain video
This is reverse video
This is intense video
This is blinking video
```

As you have seen, using a new STYLE command to select a different attribute cancels the current attribute. To cancel the current attribute and return to plain text, just use the STYLE command without an argument. For example, the script

```
STYLE
@10,20
?? "This is plain video again"
```

would turn off any active display attributes and display the line *This is plain video again* in plain video.

Although you commonly will use only one of these style attributes at a time, you can use them together to create combined effects. To do this, just follow the STYLE command with more than one keyword. For example, the command *STYLE REVERSE,BLINK* tells PAL to display reverse video blinking video. Similarly, the command *STYLE BLINK,INTENSE* instructs PAL to display bright binking text.

You can use the keywords REVERSE, INTENSE, and BLINK to control the display of text on a color monitor as well. On a color system, however, the STYLE REVERSE command will display green characters on a cyan background, and the STYLE INTENSE command will display bright green characters on the normal black background.

The ATTRIBUTE Keyword

If you have a color monitor, PAL offers you a wide variety of styles in addition to the ones available for a monochrome system. In fact, you can use any of 256 combinations of foreground and background colors. To access these styles, you must use the alternative form of the STYLE command shown below:

> STYLE ATTRIBUTE *color code*

The *color code* argument is a numeric expression with a value between 0 and 255. The value of the expression determines what combination of background and foreground colors PAL uses. For example, the command *STYLE ATTRIBUTE 5* instructs PAL to write text in magenta characters on a black background, the command *STYLE ATTRIBUTE 73* tells PAL to display light blue characters on a red background, and the command *STYLE ATTRIBUTE 115* instructs PAL to display cyan characters on a light grey background.

Color codes from 128 to 255 use the same color combinations as their lower-level counterparts, but also produce blinking text. For example, using the code 133 (which is equivalent to the lower-level code 5) produces blinking magenta characters on a black background. Appendix A at the end of the *PAL User's Guide* contains a complete listing of the colors produced by these 256 codes.

Unlike the Reverse, Intense, and Blink attributes, these color codes cannot be used in combination with each other. If you include more than one code following a STYLE ATTRIBUTE command, in fact, a script error will occur. Furthermore, you cannot use these color attributes in conjunction with the reverse, intense, or blink operators.

You can use these color attributes on a monochrome monitor, however. Although this will not allow you to see colors, it give you access to another display attribute: the underline. For example, the command STYLE ATTRIBUTE 1 produces underlined text on a monochrome (nongraphics) monitor, and the command STYLE ATTRIBUTE 9 produces high-intensity underlined text. See Appendix A in the *PAL User's Guide* for a listing of the effects of these codes on a monochrome monitor.

STYLE and TEXT

Although we used the ? and ?? commands in our examples of STYLE, you can also use the STYLE command to change the display attributes of the information displayed by the TEXT command. To do this, just include a STYLE command in your script before the TEXT/ENDTEXT combination. Because this command affects any information subsequently written to the screen, it affects the information displayed by the TEXT command, just as it affects the information written by the ? and ?? commands.

The MESSAGE Command

PAL's MESSAGE command provides another way to display information on the PAL canvas. Unlike the ?, ??, and TEXT commands, MESSAGE does not allow you to control where the information appears on the screen. Instead, the MESSAGE command always displays the information you specify in inverse video in the message area at the lower-right corner of the screen.

Like ? and ??, the MESSAGE command can display literal values, the information stored in variables and fields of a table, or the results of formulas and functions. The form of the MESSAGE command is

MESSAGE *argument 1,argument 2,...,argument n*

Each argument (all but the first are optional) may be any valid PAL expression. When you use multiple arguments, PAL will display them back-to-back on the screen. PAL will not insert a space in between the text from each argument unless you include a literal space in the string.

For example, suppose you want PAL to display the message *This is a test* in the message area, as shown in Figure 16-5. To do this, you would use the command MESSAGE "This is a test". If *x* contained the value 25, you could use the command MESSAGE "The value of x is ",*x* to display the message *The value of x is 25* as shown in Figure 16-6.

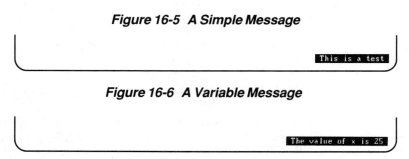

Figure 16-5 A Simple Message

Figure 16-6 A Variable Message

As you can see, PAL makes the message area only large enough to accommodate the information that it is displaying. PAL always begins the message area at the right edge of line 23 of the screen and expands it to the left as needed. In most cases, your messages will be less than 78 characters long–the maximum number that can fit on a single message line. PAL will accept messages of up to 255 characters in length, however. When a message exceeds 78 characters in length (so that it is too long to fit on one line), then PAL expands the message area so that the whole message is displayed. For example, Figure 16-7 shows how PAL displays a long message.

Figure 16-7 A Long Message

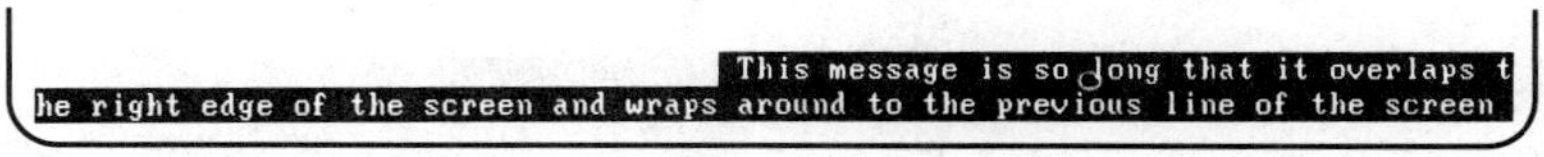

```
                              This message is so long that it overlaps t
he right edge of the screen and wraps around to the previous line of the screen
```

Because the MESSAGE command can display the results of functions, you can use the FORMAT() function to alter the appearance of information in the message area. For example, if the variable *x* contains the value 25, you could use the command

>   MESSAGE "The value of x is ",FORMAT("W6.2,E$",x)

to display the message *The value of x is $25.00*.

The RETURN Command

PAL provides yet another way to display information on the PAL canvas: the RETURN command. Although the ability of this command to display information on the screen is only one of the many things this command can do, it is an important one nonetheless. The form of this command is

>   RETURN *expression*

where the optional argument is a PAL expression of any type.

The first effect of the RETURN command is to cancel the execution of the script that PAL is currently playing. If the current script is a subroutine or procedure that has been called by another script (subjects that we'll discuss later), PAL returns to the calling script. If PAL is within the main script (the one you commanded PAL to play), PAL will return you to the Paradox workspace.

If you specify an argument for the RETURN command, PAL will display the value of that argument in the reverse-video message area at the bottom-right corner of the screen—much like the MESSAGE command does. Unlike the result of the MESSAGE command, however, the result returned by the RETURN command is not erased when script play ends. Instead, it remains in view until you press the next key.

The RETURN command is useful in scripts that simply return the value of a variable or the result of an equation or function. For example, suppose you want to calculate the future value of investing $1000 per year for the next 20 years at 9% interest. You could use the script *RETURN FV(1000,.09,20)*. Because the result of the RETURN command remains on the screen after the end of the script play, no SLEEP command is necessary.

Interacting with the User

The scripts we have presented so far manipulate the objects on the Paradox workspace and display information on the PAL canvas. As you become more experienced with PAL, however, you'll find situations in which you want the user to interact with the script. For example, you may want the user to supply a value, browse or edit a table, or make a selection from a custom menu. Three special PAL commands–ACCEPT, WAIT, and SHOWMENU–make this interaction possible.

The ACCEPT Command

The ACCEPT command instructs PAL to pause the execution of a script while you type information from the keyboard. As soon as you press ↵, PAL will store your input in a variable and continue with the script. The simplest form of this command is

ACCEPT *type* TO *variable*

The *type* argument specifies the type of information that PAL should accept. This argument may be any of the following strings: A*x*, where *x* is a number from 1 to 255 that defines the length of the entry ACCEPT will accept; *N*; *$*; *S*; or *D*. Each of these type strings corresponds to one of Paradox's field types: *N* to number, *$* to dollar, and so on. The type that you specify limits the type of entry you can make in response to an ACCEPT statement, just as a field's type controls what you can enter into that field.

The *variable* argument, which must follow the keyword TO, must be a valid variable name. If the variable you specify has not been defined previously, PAL will create it automatically.

For example, suppose you want PAL to accept a number from the keyboard and return its square root. To do this, you could use the script shown in Figure 16-8.

Figure 16-8 The ACCEPT Command

```
Changing script Accept                                      Script Ins
....+...10....+...20....+...30....+...40....+...50....+...60....+...70....+...80
CLEAR
@1,20
?? "Enter a number, please: "
ACCEPT "N" TO x
@3,20
?? "The square root of ",x," is ",SQRT(x)
SLEEP 5000
```

The first two commands in this script clear the PAL canvas and position the cursor at the intersection of row 1 and column 20. The third command displays the prompt *Enter a number, please:* at the current position of the cursor. The next command, *ACCEPT "N" TO x*, tells PAL to wait while you type a number from the keyboard. As you press keys, the letters you type will appear at the current position of the cursor. Because you specified the Numeric type, PAL will just beep if you attempt to type a letter. As soon as you press ↵, PAL will store your response in the variable x and continue with the macro. If you type 100 in response to this prompt, for example, PAL will store the numeric value 100 in x.

Finally, the command @3,20 moves the cursor to line 3, and the ?? command calculates the square root of the number you input (in this case, the square root of 100 is 10) and displays the message *The square root of 100 is 10* in reverse video in the message area. Because this message will disappear as soon as PAL finishes playing the script, the SLEEP command is required to keep it visible (in this case, for five seconds).

Mandatory Input

Although the first argument of an ACCEPT command assures that you can enter only information of the specified type, it does not require that you make an entry. If you press ↵ in response to an ACCEPT command without first typing an entry, PAL will store a blank value of the specified type in the destination variable.

Fortunately, there is a way to force the user to make an entry in response to an ACCEPT command. If you include the keyword REQUIRED in the ACCEPT command after the type argument but before the keyword TO, PAL will not let you just press ↵ without making an entry. For example, the command *ACCEPT "N" REQUIRED TO z* requires that you make a valid numeric entry. If you try to press ↵ in response to this command, PAL will display the message *Expecting a non-blank value* in the message area and will wait for you to make a valid entry. PAL will not continue playing the script until you type a nonblank entry of the proper type.

Specifying a Default

Another optional argument of the ACCEPT command instructs PAL to present a default entry to the user. When you specify a default, PAL will display it on the screen at the current position of the cursor. If you press ↵ while this default is visible, PAL will store that default in the specified variable. To override the variable, you can press [Ctrl]-[BackSpace] to erase it entirely and then type a new response. Alternatively, you can press the [Backspace] key to erase some characters, type more characters to add to the default or do a combination of the two.

For example, suppose that you want PAL to ask the user for a value but also present the value 2000 as a default. To do this, you could use the script

```
CLEAR
@10,20
?? "Amount to invest? "
ACCEPT "N" DEFAULT 2000 to z
```

The first three commands clear the canvas, position the cursor at the intersection of row 10 and column 20 and display the prompt *Amount to invest?* at that point. The DEFAULT 2000 argument of the ACCEPT command then displays the characters 2000 to the right of that prompt. If you press ↵ at this point, PAL will store the value 2000 in the variable *z*. If you want to enter a different value, you should press [Ctrl]-[Backspace] to erase the default, then type the new entry.

Specifying Minimum and Maximum Values

Other optional arguments allow you to specify a minimum or maximum acceptable response to an ACCEPT command. To specify a minimum acceptable value, you must include the keyword MIN, followed by a value representing the minimum acceptable value, between the type argument and the keyword TO. Likewise, to specify a maximum acceptable response, you must use the keyword MAX, followed by a value representing the maximum acceptable value.

For example, suppose you want PAL to solicit a value between 0 and 4000 and store it in the variable *ira*. To do this, you would use the command *ACCEPT "N" MIN 0 MAX 4000 TO ira*. The MIN 0 argument commands PAL to accept no response lower than 0, while the MAX 4000 response commands it not to accept a value greater than 4000. If you typed the value 3500 in response to this command and pressed ↵, PAL would store that value in the variable *ira*. If you entered a value greater than 4000 or less than 0, however, PAL would display the message *Value between 0 and 4000 is expected* in the message area and would wait for you to modify your response.

Specifying a Picture

PAL also lets you specify a picture or pattern to which the response to an ACCEPT command must conform. To do this, you must include the keyword PICTURE (followed by the pattern to which the input must conform) between the type argument and the keyword TO.

The characters that you can use to specify the picture are exactly the same as the ones you can use to specify a picture for entry of information into a field of a table. The # represents any single digit, the ? accepts any letter, the @ accepts any character, the & accepts a letter and converts it to upper case, and the ! accepts any character and converts letters to upper case. A semicolon (;) tells PAL to interpret the next character literally and an asterisk (*) followed by a number tells PAL to repeat the next character. Characters enclosed in brackets ([]) are an optional part of the pattern, and characters enclosed in braces ({ }) are grouped together. Commas (,) are used to separate alternatives. Other characters appear literally in the string. (For a more complete discussion of pictures, see Chapter 4.)

For example, suppose that you want the user to enter a Social Security number in the form 404-74-1421 and have PAL store that entry in the variable *ss*. To do this, you would use the command *ACCEPT "A11" PICTURE "###-##-####" TO ss*. The argument *A11* specifies an eleven-character alphanumeric string. The argument *PICTURE "###-##-####"* tells PAL that the input must be in the form of three numbers, a hyphen, two numbers, another hyphen, and then four more numbers. After you type the first three numbers, PAL will fill in the - automatically, then wait for another two numbers. After you enter those numbers, PAL will insert another hyphen. As soon as you type four more numbers and press ↵, PAL will store the entry in the variable *ss*. If you press ↵ before completing the entry, or if you type any character other than a number, PAL will just beep.

Using a Lookup Table

The final optional argument for the ACCEPT command allows you to use a lookup table to check the validity of an entry. To utilize this feature, you must include the keyword LOOKUP, followed by the name of a table between the type code and the keyword TO. The first column of the table that you specify must contain the list of acceptable entries.

For example, suppose you want to use the ACCEPT command to solicit a valid state abbreviation from the user of the script. To do this, you would create the table named STATES shown in Figure 16-9, then use the command *ACCEPT "A2" LOOKUP "States" TO state*. When PAL evaluates this command, it will pause and wait for a two-letter response. As soon as you press ↵, PAL will check the response against the entries in the first column of the STATES table. If PAL finds an exact match for the entry within that table, it will store the entry in the variable *state*. If PAL cannot find a match, it will display the message *Not one of the possible values for this field* in the message area and wait for you to modify your response.

Figure 16-9 The STATES Table

```
Viewing States table: Record 1 of 51                           Main
   STATES═╤═State Abbreviation═╤══════State Name══════
       1  ║  AL                ║  Alabama
       2  ║  AK                ║  Alaska
       3  ║  AZ                ║  Arizona
       4  ║  AR                ║  Arkansas
       5  ║  CA                ║  California
       6  ║  CO                ║  Colorado
       7  ║  CT                ║  Connecticut
       8  ║  DE                ║  Delaware
       9  ║  DC                ║  District of Columbia
      10  ║  FL                ║  Florida
      11  ║  GA                ║  Georgia
      12  ║  HI                ║  Hawaii
      13  ║  ID                ║  Idaho
      14  ║  IL                ║  Illinois
      15  ║  IN                ║  Indiana
      16  ║  IA                ║  Iowa
      17  ║  KA                ║  Kansas
      18  ║  KY                ║  Kentucky
      19  ║  LA                ║  Louisiana
      20  ║  ME                ║  Maine
      21  ║  MD                ║  Maryland
      22  ║  MA                ║  Massachusetts
```

The WAIT Command

In most cases, the PAL canvas obscures the Paradox workspace for the entire execution of a script. When the script is finished playing, PAL lifts the canvas to reveal the altered Paradox workspace. However, there will be many cases in which you'll want to pause during the execution of a script and interact with an image on the Paradox workspace, for example, to enter or edit data. PAL's WAIT command makes this possible.

The WAIT command allows you to view, edit, or perform data entry on a table, form, or query during the execution of a script. When PAL encounters a WAIT command in a script, it lifts the PAL canvas and pauses the execution of the script. Depending on the form of the WAIT command and whether Paradox is in the edit or data entry mode, you will be able to move around in the current image, edit its entries, or make new entries.

The simplest form of the WAIT command is

> WAIT *TABLE/RECORD/FIELD* UNTIL *keys*

The first argument of the WAIT command must be one of the following three keywords: TABLE, RECORD, or FIELD. These keywords control your ability to move the cursor within the current image. The WAIT TABLE command allows you to move the cursor to any field of any record in the image. If you press any cursor movement key from within a WAIT TABLE command, PAL will move the cursor just as if you weren't within a script. The WAIT RECORD command restricts your movement to the record in which the cursor was positioned when PAL lifted the canvas. If you try to press ↑, ↓, [Pg Up], [Pg Dn], and so forth, while you're within a WAIT RECORD command, PAL will just beep at you. The WAIT FIELD command does not allow you to move the cursor from its current location–a single field of a single record. Pressing any cursor movement key from within this situation produces a beep.

The second required part of the WAIT command is the keyword UNTIL, followed by the representation of one or more keys. These key representations identify the key or keys you want to use to tell PAL to stop waiting and resume running the script. When you press the specified key, PAL exits from the WAIT command, drops the PAL canvas, and continues with the execution of the script. These key representations can be in any of the following forms: an ASCII or extended IBM code (like 56 or -42), a single character as a string (like *a* or *A*), a string that names a special function key (like *F2*), or the name that Paradox assigns to a key (like *Menu* or *CtrlBackspace*).

If you specify more than one key representation, you must separate them with commas. In addition, the cursor must be in a table, form, or query when you use the WAIT command. If the cursor is not within a table, form, or query when PAL reads a WAIT command, a script error will result.

For example, the commands *WAIT TABLE UNTIL "F2"*, *WAIT TABLE UNTIL "Do_It!"*, and *WAIT TABLE UNTIL -60* all allow you to move around an entire table until you press the [Do-It!] key ([F2]).

Importantly, upper and lower-case letters are not equivalent when you specify a single character as the UNTIL argument. For example, to end the command *WAIT RECORD UNTIL "A"*, you must hold down the [Shift] key and press A. Typing a lower-case *a* will not return you to the script. If you want to use either an upper or lower-case *a* to return you to the script, you must use the command *WAIT RECORD UNTIL "A","a"*.

Viewing or Editing?

What you can do to the current image while the WAIT command is in effect depends on which mode Paradox is in before PAL executes the WAIT command. If you have issued the [Menu] Modify Edit command or pressed the [Edit] key prior to the time PAL reads the WAIT command, you will be able to make or edit entries in the image you are viewing. For example, the script

        EDIT "Emplyee"
        MOVETO RECORD 5
        WAIT RECORD UNTIL "F2"

allows you to edit any entry within the fifth record of the EMPLYEE table. When you press [F2], the script will resume.

If you are in the data entry mode when the WAIT command is issued, you'll be able to enter new records into a table. For example, the script

        Menu {Modify} {DataEntry} {Emplyee}
        WAIT TABLE UNTIL "F2"
        Do_It!

allows you to enter new records into the EMPLYEE table. When you press [F2], PAL will resume the script. The Do_It! command will store the records in the EMPLYEE table. Notice that we've used the WAIT TABLE form of the command here. This allows the user to enter as many records as he wishes.

If you are not in the edit or data entry modes when PAL encounters a WAIT command, you can move the cursor within the "Restrict range" imposed by the command, but you will not be able to edit any of the entries in that range. For example, although the script

        VIEW "Emplyee"
        WAIT TABLE UNTIL "F2"

allows you to move the cursor around the entire EMPLYEE table, it does not let you edit any of the entries within that table.

Importantly, you cannot enter the edit or data entry modes once PAL executes the WAIT command. During the pause caused by a WAIT command, PAL will lock out all of the special function keys. For this reason, you cannot use either the [Edit] key ([F9]) or the [Menu] Modify Edit command to enter the edit mode. If you want the user to be able to edit the information in an image, and not just view it, then you must make sure that Paradox is in the edit mode before it reads the WAIT command.

Messages and Prompts

Two optional arguments, MESSAGE and PROMPT, allow you to display instructions on the screen during the pause caused by a WAIT command. In most cases, you will want to use at least one of these arguments to instruct the user what key(s) can be used to resume playing of the script.

MESSAGE

The most basic (although not most useful) of these arguments is the keyword MESSAGE. The MESSAGE argument is always followed by an expression that defines the message you want PAL to display. When PAL reads a WAIT command that contains the optional MESSAGE argument, it displays the value of the expression that follows the keyword MESSAGE in reverse-video in the message area.

For example, the script

```
EDIT "Emplyee"
End Down
WAIT RECORD MESSAGE "Add a new record, then
    press Do-It!" UNTIL"F2"
```

will produce the screen shown in Figure 16-10. As you can see, the cursor is positioned in a new record at the bottom of the table, and PAL is displaying the message *Add a new record, then press Do-It!* in the message area. This message instructs you to add a new record (the keyword RECORD restricts your movement to the current record, of course) and to press the [Do-It!] key to resume execution of the script.

As you learned earlier, any information that appears in the message area will disappear as soon as you press a key. In this case, PAL will erase this message as soon as you press the ➡ key to move to the Emp Number field. Because this message does not remain during the entire editing session, you may not know which key to press when you want to resume execution of the script.

Figure 16-10 The MESSAGE Argument

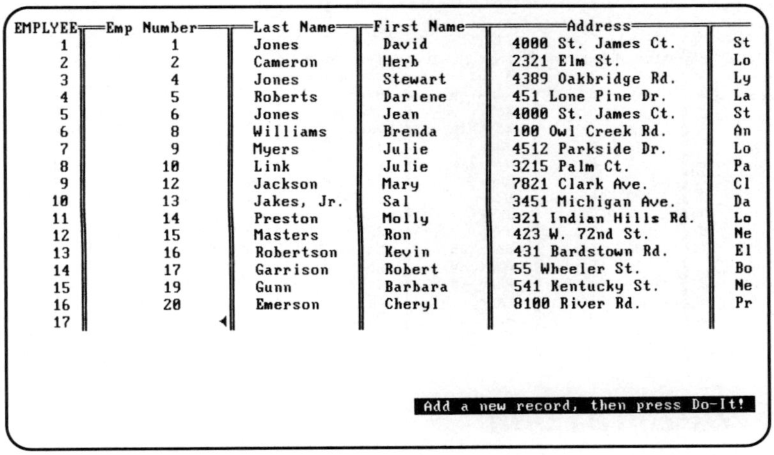

```
EMPLYEE  Emp Number   Last Name    First Name   Address
   1         1        Jones        David        4000 St. James Ct.   St
   2         2        Cameron      Herb         2321 Elm St.         Lo
   3         4        Jones        Stewart      4389 Oakbridge Rd.   Ly
   4         5        Roberts      Darlene      451 Lone Pine Dr.    La
   5         6        Jones        Jean         4000 St. James Ct.   St
   6         8        Williams     Brenda       100 Owl Creek Rd.    An
   7         9        Myers        Julie        4512 Parkside Dr.    Lo
   8        10        Link         Julie        3215 Palm Ct.        Pa
   9        12        Jackson      Mary         7021 Clark Ave.      Cl
  10        13        Jakes, Jr.   Sal          3451 Michigan Ave.   Da
  11        14        Preston      Molly        321 Indian Hills Rd. Lo
  12        15        Masters      Ron          423 W. 72nd St.      Ne
  13        16        Robertson    Kevin        431 Bardstown Rd.    El
  14        17        Garrison     Robert       55 Wheeler St.       Bo
  15        19        Gunn         Barbara      541 Kentucky St.     Ne
  16        20        Emerson      Cheryl       8100 River Rd.       Pr
  17

                                   Add a new record, then press Do-It!
```

PROMPT

Fortunately, the other optional argument of the WAIT command allows you to create more permanent messages. The form of this argument is

>PROMPT *message1,message2*

The keyword PROMPT may be followed by one or two arguments, each of which may produce a message of up to 80 characters in length. When PAL executes the WAIT command, it will display the first message across the top line of the screen, starting at the left edge of the screen. If the WAIT command includes a second message, it will appear on the second line of the screen, also left-justified. Unlike the information in the message area, these prompts will remain for the duration of the WAIT command.

For example, when PAL plays the script

>EDIT "Emplyee"
>End Down
>WAIT RECORD PROMPT "Add a new record to the table",
>   "Press Do-It! when you are finished" UNTIL "F2"

your screen will look like Figure 16-11. As you can see, the prompt *Add a new record to the table* appears at the top of the screen, and the prompt *Press Do-It! when you are finished* appears immediately below it.

Figure 16-11 The PROMPT Argument

```
Add a new record to the table
Press Do-It! when you are finished
 EMPLYEE   Emp Number    Last Name     First Name          Address
    1          1          Jones         David         4000 St. James Ct.      St
    2          2          Cameron       Herb          2321 Elm St.            Lo
    3          4          Jones         Stewart       4389 Oakbridge Rd.      Ly
    4          5          Roberts       Darlene       451 Lone Pine Dr.       La
    5          6          Jones         Jean          4000 St. James Ct.      St
    6          8          Williams      Brenda        100 Owl Creek Rd.       An
    7          9          Myers         Julie         4512 Parkside Dr.       Lo
    8         10          Link          Julie         3215 Palm Ct.           Pa
    9         12          Jackson       Mary          7821 Clark Ave.         Cl
   10         13          Jakes, Jr.    Sal           3451 Michigan Ave.      Da
   11         14          Preston       Molly         321 Indian Hills Rd.    Lo
   12         15          Masters       Ron           423 W. 72nd St.         Ne
   13         16          Robertson     Kevin         431 Bardstown Rd.       El
   14         17          Garrison      Robert        55 Wheeler St.          Bo
   15         19          Gunn          Barbara       541 Kentucky St.        Ne
   16         20          Emerson       Cheryl        8100 River Rd.          Pr
   17
```

Using WAIT in a Form

In the examples presented so far, we've used the WAIT command to view and/or edit the table image of a Paradox table. In many cases, however, you'll find it more useful to use the WAIT command to interact with the form image of a table, for the following reason. When you use the WAIT commands to view or edit a table image, you will be able to see up to 22 records at a time, even if you have restricted the movement of the cursor to only a single record or field with the WAIT RECORD or WAIT FIELD commands. If the table is in the form view, you will be able to see only a single record at a time. If you've used the WAIT TABLE command, you'll be able to press the [Pg Up] and [Pg Dn] keys to view other records through the form. If you've used the WAIT RECORD or WAIT FIELD commands, however, you will not be able to see any record other than the one you want to view or edit.

Typically, allowing user interaction through a form is a four-step process. First, you use the VIEW or EDIT commands to bring a table to the Paradox workspace. Second, you use the [Form Toggle] key or the [Menu] Image PickForm command to view that table as a form. (Because PAL disables the function keys during the execution of a WAIT command, the only way to WAIT in a form is to enter the form view of the table before PAL reads the WAIT command.) Third, if you plan to restrict movement of a single record or to restrict movement to a single field of that record, you'll want to move that record into view and move the cursor to the appropriate field within that record. Having done these three things, you are ready for PAL to execute the WAIT command. For example, the script

```
EDIT "Emplyee"
FormKey End PgDn
WAIT RECORD PROMPT "Add a new record to the table",
  "Press Do-It! when you are finished" UNTIL "F2"
```

will present the screen shown in Figure 16-12 and restrict you to adding a single record.

Figure 16-12 Using WAIT in a Form

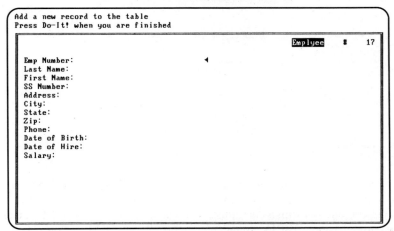

Multiple UNTIL Keys

At the beginning of this section, we showed you how to use more than one key to end the execution of a WAIT command. What we didn't show you is how to make PAL do different things depending on which key you press. When you press the key designated in the WAIT command, of course, PAL drops the PAL canvas and continues executing the script. PAL also saves the representation of the key you pressed within a temporary variable named *retval*, exactly as it appears in the WAIT command. For example, if you press the [Do-It!] key to end the command *WAIT TABLE UNTIL "F2"*, PAL will store the string *F2* in the variable *retval*. If you press the [Do-It!] key in response to the command *WAIT TABLE UNTIL "Do_It!"*, PAL will store the string *Do_It!* in *retval*.

By using this stored value within an IF statement, you can make PAL take different actions, depending on which key the user pressed to end the WAIT command. For example, suppose you want to modify the record-entry script shown above so that either the [Do-It!] or [Esc] keys will end the WAIT. If the user presses [Do-It!], then you want PAL to save the changes the user has made. If the user presses [Esc], however, you want PAL to end the edit without saving the changes and then end the script.

To achieve this effect, you would use the script shown in Figure 16-13. As you can see, the UNTIL argument of the WAIT command lists two keys: F2 and Esc. When you press either of these keys, PAL exits from the WAIT command and stores the keystroke in the variable *retval*. The IF/THEN/ELSE command directs PAL in one of two ways, depending on what is stored in *retval*. If *retval* contains the string *Esc*, PAL will issue the CANCELEDIT command, and then quit from the script. If *retval* contains the string *F2*, however, PAL will press the [Do-It!] key, thus saving the changes.

Figure 16-13 A WAIT Script

```
Changing script Wait                                              Script
....+...10....+...20....+...30....+...40....+...50....+...60....+...70....+...80
EDIT "Emplyee"
FormKey End PgDn
WAIT RECORD PROMPT "Add a new record to the table",
    "Press Do-It! when you are finished" UNTIL "F2","Esc"
IF retval = "Esc"
    THEN CANCELEDIT QUIT
    ELSE Do_It!
ENDIF
```

Custom Menus

In addition to soliciting input from the user with PAL's ACCEPT and WAIT commands, you also can use PAL to design custom menus. By using PAL's SHOWMENU command in conjunction with a conditional command like IF or SWITCH, you can create custom menus that look just like standard Paradox menus. When you choose an item from a custom menu, PAL will execute the set of commands that you have assigned to that item.

The basic form of PAL's SHOWMENU command is

    SHOWMENU
        choice 1:prompt 1,
        choice 2:prompt 2,
        ...,
        choice n:prompt n
    TO variable

As you can see, the keyword SHOWMENU is followed by a series of choice/prompt pairs. Each choice/prompt pair specifies a menu item that will appear on the custom menu and a prompt that PAL will display when you highlight that item in the menu. Each pair must be separated from the one that precedes it with a comma. (We find it convenient to place each pair on a separate line and to indent the pairs relative to the SHOWMENU command. It is not necessary to do so, however.) Although these choices and prompts usually will be literal strings, they can be any PAL expression.

The list of choice/prompt pairs that follow a WAIT command must end with the keyword TO, followed by the name of a variable. When you select an item from the custom menu, PAL stores that choice in the TO variable. If you choose a numeric value or date, PAL will store it as a string.

The number of choice/prompt pairs in the WAIT command determines how many items will appear on the menu. Although you can include a virtually unlimited number of choices in a menu, only about seven or eight will fit across the screen at a time, depending on their length. If you include more items in a menu than PAL can display across the screen at one time, it will display the symbol ▶ at the right edge of the menu. As you press → to move beyond the last visible choice, a new one will scroll into view and another one will scroll off the left edge of the screen.

Selecting an Item from a Custom Menu

You can select an item from a custom menu in exactly the same ways you select an item from a standard Paradox menu. First, you can use the →, ←, [Home], and [End] keys to position the highlight on the item you want to choose, then press ↵. Alternatively, you can select an item by typing the first letter in its name. If only one item begins with the letter you type, PAL will select that item. If more than one choice begins with the letter you type, PAL will present a limited menu that contains only the choices that begin with that letter. To select an item from this limited menu, you must move the highlight to it and press ↵.

When you select an item from a custom menu, PAL stores the string equivalent of that item in the TO variable. The method you use to choose that item does not affect the way it is stored. For example, suppose you choose the option Cancel from a custom menu. No matter whether you choose this option by pointing to it and pressing ↵ or by typing the letter *c*, PAL will store the string *Cancel* in the TO variable.

Once PAL displays a custom menu, you must do one of two things: select an item from that menu or press the [Esc] key. If you press the [Esc] key instead of selecting an item from the menu, PAL will store the string *Esc* in the TO variable. If you press any key other than a cursor movement key, the ↵ key, the [Esc] key, or the first letter of any menu choice, PAL will just beep.

A Simple Example

As an example of the SHOWMENU command, suppose you want PAL to present a menu with three choices: Alpha, Beta, and Gamma. If you choose Alpha from the menu, PAL will display the message *You selected Alpha* in the message window for five seconds. If you choose Beta, PAL will display the five-second message *You selected Beta*. If you pick Gamma, PAL will display the message *You selected Gamma*. To do this, you would use the script shown in Figure 16-14.

The CLEAR command that begins the script erases the PAL canvas. The SHOWMENU command then displays the three choices Alpha, Beta, and Gamma on the first line of the screen and places the highlight on the first option. On the second line, PAL displays the prompt that corresponds to the choice that currently is highlighted. Since Alpha is highlighted, PAL displays the prompt *Choice 1 of 3*. Figure 16-15 shows this menu.

Figure 16-14 A Simple Menu Script

```
Changing script Menu1                                    Script
....+...10....+...20....+...30....+...40....+...50....+...60....+...70....+...80
CLEAR
SHOWMENU
   "Alpha":"Choice 1 of 3",
   "Beta":"Choice 2 of 3",
   "Gamma":"Choice 3 of 3"
TO Choice
MESSAGE "You have selected "+Choice
SLEEP 5000
```

Figure 16-15 A Custom Menu

```
Alpha   Beta   Gamma
Choice 1 of 3
```

Now suppose that you choose Beta, either by using the arrow keys to position the highlight on that choice and pressing ↵ or by typing the letter *B*. Either way, PAL will store the string *Beta* in the variable *choice*. As soon as *choice* receives this string, PAL will evaluate the command *MESSAGE "You have selected "+Choice*. This causes PAL to concatenate the contents of *choice* to the literal string *You have selected* and display the result–the string *You have selected Beta*–in the message area. The final command, *SLEEP 5000*, instructs PAL to freeze the display for five seconds before it ends the script and lifts the PAL canvas.

The DEFAULT Option

When PAL executes a basic form of the SHOWMENU command, it automatically highlights the first item on the custom menu. If you press ↵ without moving the highlight, PAL will execute the commands that relate to the first item. If you want PAL to automatically position the highlight on an item other than the first one in the list, you must include the optional DEFAULT statement within the SHOWMENU command. The form of this statement, which must follow the last choice/command pair, is

> DEFAULT *choice*

where the argument *choice* is one of the items on the menu.

For example, suppose you want PAL to highlight the second option on the three-item menu shown in Figure 16-15 automatically. To do this, you should modify the script to look like Figure 16-16.

The statement *DEFAULT "Beta"* in this script instructs PAL to position the cursor on the choice Beta, the second item on the menu, when it first displays that menu. Figure 16-17 shows this result.

Figure 16-16 A Menu Default Script

```
Changing script Menu1                                    Script
....+...10....+...20....+...30....+...40....+...50....+...60....+...70....+...80
CLEAR
SHOWMENU
   "Alpha":"Choice 1 of 3",
   "Beta":"Choice 2 of 3",
   "Gamma":"Choice 3 of 3"
DEFAULT "Beta"
TO Choice
MESSAGE "You have selected "+Choice
SLEEP 5000
```

Figure 16-17 A Simple Menu

```
Alpha  Beta  Gamma
Choice 2 of 3
```

Using the SWITCH Command

In most cases, of course, you will want PAL to do more than just store your choice in a variable and display it for you. In fact, you probably will want PAL to execute a different sequence of commands for each possible menu choice. To do this, you must use a conditional testing function like IF or SWITCH to determine which item was selected and route the execution of the script accordingly.

The simplest form of the SWITCH command is

    SWITCH
        CASE condition 1:commands 1
        CASE condition 2:commands 2
        ...
        CASE condition n: commands n
    ENDSWITCH

where a series of cases are sandwiched between the words SWITCH and ENDSWITCH. Each CASE contains a conditional test/command pair. When PAL executes this command, it evaluates each conditional test, starting with the first one, until it finds one that is true. When that happens, PAL will issue the commands that correspond to that test, then exit from the SWITCH command without evaluating the remaining tests.

An Example

For example, suppose that your Paradox files are stored in three different directories: c:\paradox\ordentry, c:\paradox\glegder, and c:\paradox\acctspay, and you want to develop a menu-driven script that allows you to switch quickly from one directory to another. To do this, you could use a script like the one shown in Figure 16-18. As you can see, this script uses a SWITCH command to evaluate the menu choice.

Figure 16-18 A Menu Script with SWITCH

```
Changing script Menu2                                    Script
....+...10....+...20....+...30....+...40....+...50....+...60....+...70....+...80
CLEAR
SHOWMENU
   "Orders":"Change to Order Entry subdirectory",
   "GL":"Change to General Ledger subdirectory",
   "AP":"Change to Accounts Payable subdirectory",
   "Cancel":"Do not change directory"
TO choice
SWITCH
   CASE choice = "Orders":SETDIR "c:\\paradox\\ordentry\\" {OK}
   CASE choice = "GL":SETDIR "c:\\paradox\\gledger\\" {OK}
   CASE choice = "AP":SETDIR "c:\\paradox\\acctspay\\" {OK}
ENDSWITCH
```

When PAL plays this script, it presents the four-item menu shown in Figure 16-19 and waits for you to make a choice. When you make a selection (or press [Esc]), PAL will store that selection (or the string *Esc*) in the variable *choice*. Depending on which selection you choose, PAL will store one of four strings in the variable: *Orders*, *GL*, *AP*, or *Cancel*. As soon as you have made a selection, PAL will evaluate the SWITCH command in the following way. First, PAL will test to see if the variable *choice* contains the string *Orders*. If so, PAL will execute the command SETDIR *"c:\\paradox\\ordentry\\ {OK}"*, then exit from the SWITCH command without evaluating any of the other cases. If *choice* does not contain *Orders*, PAL will skip to the next case, *choice="GL"*. If this condition is true, PAL will execute the command SETDIR *"c:\\paradox\\gledger\\ {OK}"* and quit from the SWITCH command. If this condition is false, PAL will skip to the next case, *choice="AP"*. If this condition is true, PAL will evaluate the command SETDIR *"c:\\paradox\\acctspay\\ {OK}"* and then exit from the SWITCH command. If none of these conditions are true, PAL will exit from the SWITCH command without performing any actions.

Figure 16-19 A Custom Menu

```
Orders  GL  AP  Cancel
Change to Order Entry subdirectory
```

Although there is a fourth choice on the menu, Cancel, we have not included a CASE command to correspond to that choice. If none of the first three CASE statements are true, then you must either have selected the fourth choice, Cancel, or pressed the [Esc] key. In either case, you do not want PAL to change the directory. Because this script ends without providing instructions for either of these cases, the current directory will remain unchanged unless you choose one of the first three items from the menu.

When PAL exits from the SWITCH command, it continues playing the script with the commands (if any) that follow the keyword ENDSWITCH. Since the ENDSWITCH command is the last command in this script, PAL just quits from the script and returns you to the Paradox workspace. If other PAL commands had followed the keyword ENDSWITCH, PAL would have executed those commands.

The OTHERWISE Option

If you have included a CASE statement for each possible menu choice, or if you do not want any action to be taken when you select an item other than the ones for which you included CASE statements, then you can use the basic form of the SWITCH command. If you want PAL to perform the same action when you select any of several choices, however, you can use the optional keyword OTHERWISE within the SWITCH command. This argument must follow all CASE statements, but must precede the keyword ENDSWITCH.

As a modification to the example shown above, suppose that you want PAL to display the message *Directory not changed* in the message area for three seconds if the user selects Cancel from the menu or presses [Esc]. To do this, you would add the statement

OTHERWISE: MESSAGE "Directory not changed" SLEEP 3000

to the original SWITCH statement, as shown in Figure 16-20. When you play this script, PAL will present the menu shown in Figure 16-19 and store your response in the variable *choice*. If any of the three cases specified in the SWITCH command are true, PAL will change the directory and exit from the SWITCH command, skipping the remaining cases (if any) and the OTHERWISE statement. If none of the cases are true, however, PAL will execute the commands that follow the keyword OTHERWISE. In this case, these commands instruct PAL to display the message *Directory not changed* in the message area. After three seconds, PAL will exit from the SWITCH command.

Figure 16-20 The OTHERWISE Option

```
Changing script Menu2                                       Script
....+...10....+...20....+...30....+...40....+...50....+...60....+...70....+...80
CLEAR
SHOWMENU
  "Orders":"Change to Order Entry subdirectory",
  "GL":"Change to General Ledger subdirectory",
  "AP":"Change to Accounts Payable subdirectory",
  "Cancel":"Do not change directory"
TO choice
SWITCH
  CASE choice = "Orders":SETDIR "c:\\paradox\\ordentry\\" {OK}
  CASE choice = "GL":SETDIR "c:\\paradox\\gledger\\" {OK}
  CASE choice = "AP":SETDIR "c:\\paradox\\acctspay\\" {OK}
  OTHERWISE: MESSAGE "Directory not changed" SLEEP 3000
ENDSWITCH
```

Subroutine Calls and Branching

PAL's PLAY command gives you the ability to play one script from within another script. The form of this command is

    PLAY *scriptname*

where the single argument *scriptname* specifies the script you want to play. This argument may be a literal string, a reference to a variable or field that contains the name of a script, or a function or formula that returns the name of a script. For example, the command *PLAY "Script1"* commands PAL to play the script named Script1, as does the command *PLAY x* when the variable *x* contains the string *Script1*.

When PAL encounters a PLAY command, it reads the named script from disk and then executes it, step by step. If the script you want to play is in the current directory, then the argument of the PLAY command can be simply the name of the script. If the script is in a different directory, however, you must include the directory and/or drive name in the argument. If the script named *XYZ.SC* is stored in c:\paradox\scripts, for example, and c:\paradox\scripts is the current directory, then you can use the command *PLAY "xyz"* to play it. If c:\paradox\scripts is not the current directory, however, you would have to use the command *PLAY "c:\\paradox\\scripts\\xyz"* to execute it.

A PLAY command within a script can result in either a subroutine call or a branch. To explain what these two terms mean, and the difference between them, suppose that PAL encounters the command *PLAY "ScriptB"* while playing ScriptA. When this happens, PAL pauses the execution of ScriptA and begins playing ScriptB. If PAL reads a RETURN command or comes to the end of ScriptB without encountering a QUIT command, it jumps back to ScriptA and resumes executing it at the command that follows *PLAY "ScriptB"*. In this situation, ScriptB is a subroutine that is called by ScriptA. This use of a PLAY command is a subroutine call. IF PAL encounters a QUIT command within ScriptB, however, it will exit from the script instead of passing control back to Script A. This one-way routing is called branching.

A Simple Subroutine Call

The script named ScriptA shown in Figure 16-21 contains a subroutine call to the script named ScriptB shown in Figure 16-22. When PAL plays ScriptA, it clears the PAL canvas and positions the cursor at the intersection of row 10 and column 30, writes the message *This is ScriptA* to the canvas and pauses for three seconds. When PAL reads the command *PLAY "ScriptB"*, it searches the current directory for the script named ScriptB. If PAL finds that script, as it does in this case, it will clear the PAL canvas, reposition the cursor at the intersection of row 10 and column 30, then display the message *This is ScriptB*, and pause for another three seconds. Because SLEEP 3000 is the last command in ScriptB, PAL then returns to ScriptA and resumes execution with the command *CLEAR*–the command that immediately follows the PLAY command that called the subroutine. As soon as this statement erases the PAL canvas, PAL positions the cursor at the intersection of row 10 and column 30 again, displays the message *This is ScriptA again*, waits for three seconds, then ends the script and returns to the Paradox workspace.

Figure 16-21   Script A

```
Changing script Scripta                                          Script  Ins
....+...10....+...20....+...30....+...40....+...50....+...60....+...70....+...80
CLEAR
@10,30
?? "This is ScriptA"
SLEEP 3000
PLAY "ScriptB"
CLEAR
@10,30
?? "This is ScriptA again"
SLEEP 3000
```

Figure 16-22   Script B

```
Changing script Scriptb                                          Script
....+...10....+...20....+...30....+...40....+...50....+...60....+...70....+...80
CLEAR
@10,30
?? "This is ScriptB"
SLEEP 3000
```

A Simple Branch

Very simply, a branch is a subroutine call in which control is not passed back to the calling script. This happens when PAL encounters a QUIT command somewhere within the called script. As a simple example of a branch, suppose that ScriptB looked like the script in Figure 16-23 instead of the one in Figure 16-22. When you play ScriptA, PAL will clear the canvas and display the message *This is ScriptA* starting at the intersection of row 10 and column 20. After three seconds, PAL will branch to ScriptB, clear the screen, reposition the cursor, and display the message *This is ScriptB* for three seconds.

Figure 16-23   ScriptB (Revised)

```
Changing script Scriptb                                          Script
....+...10....+...20....+...30....+...40....+...50....+...60....+...70....+...80
CLEAR
@10,30
?? "This is ScriptB"
SLEEP 3000
QUIT
```

If ScriptB ended at this point, PAL would return to ScriptA. ScriptB contains another command, however: QUIT. This command ends the execution of both levels of script play, returning you to the Paradox workspace. Because PAL does not pass control back to ScriptA, this PLAY command results in a branch.

Ending a Subroutine Prematurely

As we have mentioned, reaching the end of a subroutine is only one of two ways to end the execution of a subroutine and pass control back to the calling script. The RETURN command provides the other way. In most cases, you will use this command within an IF statement to return to a calling script based on the result of a conditional test.

For example, suppose the script shown in Figure 16-24 is named DELETE.SC and a large script named MAIN.SC contains the command *PLAY "Delete"*. When PAL reads this command while playing MAIN.SC, it begins playing DELETE. The first two commands in DELETE clear the PAL canvas and position the cursor at the intersection of row 10 and column 20. The next two commands display the prompt *Name of table to delete?* at the current position of the cursor and wait for you to type a table name. As soon as you type any combination of up to eight characters and press ↵, PAL will store that entry in the variable *name*.

Figure 16-24 DELETE.SC

```
Designing script Delete                                    Script  Ins
....+...10....+...20....+...30....+...40....+...50....+...60....+...70....+...80
CLEAR
@10,20
?? "Name of table to delete? "
ACCEPT "A8" TO name
IF NOT ISTABLE(name)
   THEN RETURN
ENDIF
DELETE name
```

Next, the IF command tests the entry stored in *name* to see if it is a valid table name. If so, PAL will execute the DELETE *name* command, deleting the named table, then return control to the calling script (MAIN). If *name* does not contain a valid table name, however, PAL executes the RETURN command, passing control back to MAIN. This premature return prevents the execution of DELETE, which would result in a script error.

Using a Menu to Call Subroutines

One of the most common situations in which you'll call or branch to another script is from within a custom menu. The simple script displayed in Figure 16-25 shows an example of this use. The SHOWMENU command in this script presents the simple menu shown in Figure 16-26. When you choose an item from this menu, PAL will store your choice in the variable *choice*. The SWITCH command that follows uses your response to route PAL to one of three other scripts: A, B, or C. If you select *A* from the menu so that *choice* contains the string *A*, PAL will execute the command *PLAY "A"*. If you select *B*, PAL will execute the command *PLAY "B"*. If you select *C*, PAL will execute the command *PLAY "C"*. These commands instruct PAL to pause the execution of MAIN and start playing the scripts A, B, or C.

Figure 16-25 A Menu Calling Subroutines

```
Changing script Menu3                                    Script
....+...10....+...20....+...30....+...40....+...50....+...60....+...70....+...80
CLEAR
SHOWMENU
   "A":"Play Script A",
   "B":"Play Script B",
   "C":"Play Script C"
TO choice
SWITCH
   CASE choice = "A":PLAY "A"
   CASE choice = "B":PLAY "B"
   CASE choice = "C":PLAY "C"
ENDSWITCH
```

Figure 16-26 A Custom Menu

```
A  B  C
Play Script A
```

Whether these three PLAY commands call or branch to the script they name depends on whether or not that script contains a QUIT command. If PAL reads a QUIT command within the named script, it will exit from the script without returning to MAIN. If the named script does not contain a QUIT command, however, PAL will resume executing MAIN as soon as it reads a RETURN command or reaches the end of the subroutine.

The IF/THEN/ELSE Command

IF is PAL's most fundamental conditional testing command. This command instructs PAL to perform one of two actions, based on the result of a conditional test. Because this command is so common to PAL programming, we already have used it in several places within this and the past three chapters. So far, we have used only the basic form

> IF *conditional test* THEN *true commands* ENDIF

The first expression following the keyword IF must be a conditional test. As we explained in Chapter 14, a conditional test is an expression that returns one of two results: True or False. In many cases, a conditional test will consist of one expression that is compared to another expression by one of the following operators: =, >, <, >=, <=, or <>. In other cases, your conditional tests will be one of PAL's logical functions, like ISTABLE(), ATLAST(), or DRIVESTATUS(). You can even use the logical operators AND, OR, and NOT to combine different conditional tests or modify their results. (For more on conditional testing, see Chapter 14.)

The second part of any IF command must be the keyword THEN, followed by one or more commands. If the conditional test of the IF command is true, PAL will evaluate the commands that follow the keyword THEN. Once PAL has executed these commands, it will skip to the command that follows the keyword ENDIF and continue executing the script at that point. If the conditional test is false, however, PAL will not execute the THEN commands. Instead, it will exit from the IF statement and resume executing with the command that follows the keyword ENDIF.

The script shown in Figure 16-27 contains a simple use of the basic IF command. This script begins by clearing the PAL canvas, positioning the cursor at the intersection of row 10 and column 20, and displaying the prompt *Name of table to edit?* PAL then waits for you to type the name of a table, which it stores in the variable *x*. The IF command that follows tests to see whether the table you named exists. If the table does not exist, the conditional test *NOT ISTABLE(x)* will be true, and PAL will evaluate the commands that follow the keyword THEN. In this case, THEN is followed by the single command *PLAY "MakeTabl"* which calls a subroutine that lets you design the table you named. After PAL finishes with that subroutine, it returns to the command *EDIT x* that follows the ENDIF command and places that table in the edit mode. If the table you named exists, PAL skips the subroutine and goes directly to the *EDIT x* command.

Figure 16-27 The IF Command

```
Changing script If                                    Script
....+...10....+...20....+...30....+...40....+...50....+...60....+...70....+...80
CLEAR
@10,20
?? "Name of table to edit? "
ACCEPT A8 to x
IF NOT ISTABLE(x)
   THEN PLAY "MakeTabl"
ENDIF
EDIT x
```

The Advanced Form

As you have seen, the basic form of the IF command instructs PAL to perform special actions only when the conditional test is true. It does not specify a set of commands that should be executed exclusively when the conditional test is false. The advanced form of the IF command allows you to do this, however. This advanced form is:

> IF conditional test
>   THEN *true commands*
>   ELSE *false commands*
> ENDIF

When PAL evaluates this form of the IF command, it first evaluates the conditional test. If the conditional test is true, PAL evaluates the commands that follow the keyword THEN, then skips to the command following the ENDIF keyword. If the conditional test is false, PAL skips the THEN portion of the command, evaluates the commands that follow the keyword ELSE, and then skips the command following the ENDIF keyword.

The simple script shown in Figure 16-28 demonstrates a simple use of this advanced form of the IF command. When PAL plays this script, it clears the screen, prompts you to type a number, and stores your response in the variable *x*. PAL then asks you to type another number, and stores your response in the variable *y*. When PAL reads the IF command that follows, it first evaluates the conditional test *x>y*. If your first response is greater than your second response, this test will be true and PAL will evaluate the command that follows the keyword THEN. This MESSAGE command instructs PAL to display the message *x is greater than y* in the message area, substituting the stored values of *x* and *y* into the string. PAL then skips to the end of the IF command. Since SLEEP 3000 is the only command that follows the keyword ENDIF, PAL displays the message for three seconds and then ends the script.

Figure 16-28 The IF Command (Advanced Form)

```
Changing script If2                                       Script
....+...10....+...20....+...30....+...40....+...50....+...60....+...70....+...80
CLEAR
@10,20
?? "Type any number: "
ACCEPT "N" TO x
@12,20
?? "Type another number: "
ACCEPT "N" to y
IF x>y
  THEN MESSAGE x," is greater than ",y
  ELSE MESSAGE y," is greater than ",x
ENDIF
SLEEP 3000
```

If your first response (*x*) is less than your second response (*y*), however, PAL follows a different course of action. Instead of evaluating the THEN portion of the IF command, PAL evaluates the command that follows the keyword ELSE. This MESSAGE command instructs PAL to display the message *y is greater than x*, again substituting the stored values of *x* and *y* into the string. PAL then skips to the next command (SLEEP 3000), waits for three seconds, then returns you to the Paradox workspace.

While Loops

The WHILE command instructs PAL to execute a set of commands over and over for as long as a given condition is true. The form of this command is

> WHILE *conditional test*
>   *commands*
> ENDWHILE

The first argument of this function must be a conditional test. If the conditional test is true, PAL executes the sequence of commands that follow. These commands usually work with the objects on the Paradox workspace and alter the elements that are referred to by the conditional test. When PAL reaches the end of the command sequence, it returns to the beginning of the WHILE command and evaluates the conditional test again. As long as the conditional test is true, PAL continues with this cycle. If the conditional test is false, however, PAL immediately exits from the WHILE loop, skips to the command that follows the keyword ENDWHILE, and then resumes the execution of the script at that point.

An Example

The script shown in Figure 16-29 shows a simple example of a WHILE loop. This script begins by bringing the sixteen-record EMPLYEE table to the screen and positioning the cursor in the Last Name field of the first record in that table. The WHILE loop then commands PAL to present each entry from the Last Name field in the message window for one second. The conditional test for this command, *NOT EOT()*, tests to see whether PAL has tried to move beyond the end of the table. Since the cursor begins on the first record of this sixteen-record table, the test is true on the first pass. As a result, PAL executes the commands *MESSAGE []*, *SLEEP 1000*, and *SKIP 1*. The MESSAGE command displays the contents of the current field in the message window. The SLEEP command instructs PAL to keep the message there for one second. The SKIP command then instructs PAL to move the cursor down one row—in this case, to the Last Name field of the second record.

As soon as PAL finishes this first pass through the loop, it moves back to the top and reevaluates the conditional test. Since the cursor is in the second record of a 16-record table, the test *NOT EOF()* still is true. As a result, PAL displays the Last Name entry from the second record for one second, moves the cursor down one row, and jumps back to the top of the loop. PAL continues in this fashion to display the Last Name field entries from the third through fifteenth records. On the sixteenth pass through the loop, the cursor is positioned on the sixteenth (last) record in the table. After PAL displays the contents of the Last Name field of that record for one second, it again evaluates the SKIP 1 command. Because the cursor is in the last record of the table, this command triggers an end-of-file condition.

As PAL begins the seventeenth pass through the loop, then, the conditional test will be false. Consequently, PAL breaks from the loop and skips to the command that follows the end of the WHILE command. This MESSAGE command displays the message *End of table* in the message area.

Figure 16-29 The WHILE Command

```
Changing script While                                    Script
....+...10....+...20....+...30....+...40....+...50....+...60....+...70....+...80
VIEW "Employee"
Home
MOVETO [Last Name]
WHILE NOT EOT()
  MESSAGE []
  SLEEP 1000
  SKIP 1
ENDWHILE
MESSAGE "End of table"
SLEEP 3000
```

The LOOP Command

In most cases, PAL will execute all of the commands within a WHILE loop during each pass through that loop. In some cases, however, you may want PAL to return to the top of the loop prematurely. The LOOP command makes this possible. Whenever PAL encounters a LOOP command during the execution of a WHILE, SCAN, or FOR loop (we'll discuss SCAN and FOR later), it will return to the top of the loop without executing the commands that follow the LOOP command. If the conditional test is still true, PAL will make another pass through the loop.

The script shown in Figure 16-30 shows a simple use of LOOP. This script moves the cursor down the Quantity field of a table named ABC, replacing every blank entry with the numeric value 0. When it encounters a nonblank record, the command *IF NOT ISBLANK([])* is true. For this reason, PAL evaluates the commands *SKIP 1* and *LOOP* within the THEN statement. The SKIP 1 command moves the cursor down one record. The LOOP command then returns PAL to the top of the loop, ready for another pass. Because PAL never reaches the []=0 command, it does not replace the entry in the current field. PAL continues in this fashion until it reaches the end of the table at which point it exits from the script.

Figure 16-30 The LOOP Command

```
Designing script Loop                                    Script Ins
....+...10....+...20....+...30....+...40....+...50....+...60....+...70....+...80
EDIT "Abc"
Home
MOVETO [Quantity]
WHILE NOT EOT()
   IF NOT ISBLANK([])
      THEN SKIP 1 LOOP
   ENDIF
   []=0
   SKIP 1
ENDWHILE
MESSAGE "End of table"
SLEEP 3000
```

In most cases, there is a way to avoid the use of the LOOP command. In this example, for instance, you could replace the WHILE command with the one shown below:

> WHILE NOT EOT()
>   IF ISBLANK([])
>   THEN []=0
>   ENDIF
>   SKIP 1
> ENDWHILE

Instead of testing for the negative condition *NOT ISBLANK()*, the IF command within this loop tests for the positive condition *ISBLANK()*. This allows you to use one SKIP command instead of two and eliminates the need for the LOOP command.

The QUITLOOP Command

PAL's QUITLOOP command provides an alternative way to exit from a loop. Unlike the LOOP command, which breaks only the current pass through the loop, the QUITLOOP command breaks the loop entirely. When PAL encounters a LOOP command, it returns to the top of the loop and attempts to make another pass through it. When PAL encounters a QUITLOOP command, however, it jumps to the command that follows the loop and continues executing the script there, just as if the conditional test were false.

For example, suppose you want PAL to step down through a table, one record at a time, stopping when it reaches a blank entry or the end of the table, whichever comes first. To do this, you would use the WHILE loop

```
WHILE NOT EOT()
  IF ISBLANK([])
    THEN QUITLOOP
  ENDIF
  SKIP 1
ENDWHILE
```

The conditional test *NOT EOT()* will remain true until PAL tries to move beyond the bottom of the table. Each time PAL passes through this loop, it evaluates the continuing execution at the command *IF ISBLANK([]) THEN QUITLOOP ENDIF*. As long as the current entry is not blank, PAL will continue to execute the loop. If PAL encounters a blank before it reaches the end of the table, however, the test *ISBLANK ([])* will be true. Consequently, PAL will evaluate the command *QUITLOOP*, which breaks the loop. Because no commands follow the WHILE command, PAL will end the script as well.

Infinite Loops

In some situations, you may wish to create WHILE loops whose conditional tests are always true. PAL will continue to evaluate these loops until it encounters a QUITLOOP command. The easiest way to create this type of loop is to use the logical constant True as the conditional test of the WHILE command. However, you also can use an unchanging true test like 1=1, 2>1, or NOT FALSE as the conditional test.

One common use of this technique is to lock the user within a menu. In most cases, after PAL has executed the commands related to a selection on a custom menu, it will continue executing the script at the command that follows the SHOWMENU sequence. If you want the same menu to reappear so that the user can make another choice, you must enclose its SHOWMENU command within a WHILE True loop. So that the user can break from the loop, of course, you'll want to include a selection that issues the QUITLOOP command.

The script shown in Figure 16-31 demonstrates this technique. As you can see, this script is a SHOWMENU/SWITCH pair enclosed within a WHILE loop. The first command in this script, *WHILE True*, instructs Paradox to issue the commands contained within the loop repeatedly, stopping only when it encounters a QUITLOOP or QUIT command. The first command within the loop, SHOWMENU, instructs PAL to display a four-item custom menu.

As soon as you choose an item from this menu, PAL will store that selection in the variable *choice*. The SWITCH command that follows evaluates *choice*. If you select *B*, for example, PAL will evaluate the commands *MESSAGE "You picked A. Try again." SLEEP 2000 CLEAR*. These commands instruct PAL to display the message *You picked A. Try again.* for two seconds, and then clear the screen.

Typically, PAL will return to the menu once it evaluates your choice. Because this menu is enclosed within a WHILE loop, however, PAL will continue to redisplay the menu for as long as the conditional test is true. Because the conditional test is the logical constant True in this script, PAL will be locked into the menu until it encounters a QUITLOOP or QUIT command. A QUITLOOP command would break the loop, but continue execution of the script with the command that follows the keyword ENDWHILE. A QUIT command would cancel the execution of the entire script and return you to the Paradox workspace.

In this example, the C option provides the way out of the loop. If you select *C* from this custom menu, PAL will evaluate the command *QUITLOOP* that follows the command *CASE choice="C"*. When PAL executes this command, it immediately breaks from the loop and resumes execution of the script at the command following ENDWHILE. In this case, it reads the commands *MESSAGE "Returning to Paradox" SLEEP 3000,* which display the message *Returning to Paradox* in the message area for three seconds. Because these commands are the last ones in the script, PAL then ends the script and returns you to the Paradox workspace.

Figure 16-31 An Infinite Loop

```
Changing script Menu4                                      Script Ins
....+...10....+...20....+...30....+...40....+...50....+...60....+...70....+...80
WHILE True
   SHOWMENU
      "A":"Choice A",
      "B":"Choice B",
      "C":"Return to Paradox"
   TO choice
   SWITCH
      CASE choice="A":MESSAGE "You picked A. Try again." SLEEP 2000 CLEAR
      CASE choice="B":MESSAGE "You picked B. Try again." SLEEP 2000 CLEAR
      CASE choice="C":QUITLOOP
      CASE choice="Esc":MESSAGE "You pressed [Esc]. Try again." SLEEP 2000 CLEAR
   ENDSWITCH
ENDWHILE
MESSAGE "Returning to Paradox" Sleep 3000
```

FOR/ENDFOR Loops

In addition to WHILE, Paradox Release 1.1 offers another looping command: FOR. Like the WHILE command, the FOR command instructs PAL to execute a series of commands repeatedly. The FOR command repeats the specified commands as long as the value of its built-in counter is not greater than a value you specify.

The form of the FOR command is

> FOR *counter*
>   FROM *initial value*
>   TO *final value*
>   STEP *increment value*
>   *commands*
> ENDFOR

The first argument of this command, *counter*, is the name of the variable you want to use as the counter for the loop. The second argument, which must follow the keyword FROM, is a value expression that sets the initial value of the counter. The third argument, which must follow the keyword TO, specifies the value that the counter variable should not exceed. The fourth argument, which must follow the keyword STEP, tells PAL how much to increase (or decrease) the value of the counter variable after each pass through the FOR loop. The next commands are the ones that PAL will execute on each pass through the loop. The keyword ENDFOR signals the end of the loop.

The script shown in Figure 16-32 contains an example of a FOR/ENDFOR loop. This script presents the Last Name entries from the first ten records from the EMPLYEE table in the message window for one second each.

Figure 16-32 The FOR/ENDFOR Command

```
Changing script For                                              Script
....+...10....+...20....+...30....+...40....+...50....+...60....+...70....+...80
VIEW "Emplyee"
Home
MOVETO [Last Name]
FOR counter
  FROM 1
  TO 10
  STEP 1
  MESSAGE [] SLEEP 1000 SKIP 1
ENDFOR
MESSAGE "End of script"
SLEEP 2000
```

The first three commands in this script bring the EMPLYEE table to the workspace and position the cursor on the Last Name field of the first record. The FOR loop that follows is responsible for displaying each of the first ten entries from that field in the message window. This loop begins by designating *counter* as the counter variable. The statement *FROM 1* assigns counter the initial value of 1. The STEP 1 statement instructs PAL to add 1 to the value of counter after each pass through the loop. The TO 10 statement tells PAL to stop when the value of *counter* exceeds ten.

On the first pass through the loop, *counter* will store the value 1. Since one is less than ten, PAL will execute the commands *MESSAGE [], SLEEP 1000*, and *SKIP 1*. These commands display the contents of the first record's Last Name field for one second, then move the cursor down one row in the table. At the end of this pass, PAL increases the value of *counter* by one and moves back to the top of the loop. Before the second pass, then, *counter* contains the value 2. Since two still is less than ten, PAL makes another pass through the loop, displaying the contents of the second record's Last Name field.

PAL continues in this fashion, displaying the Last Name field of the third through tenth records. During the tenth pass through the report, PAL will increase the value of *counter* to eleven. Because eleven is greater than ten (the TO value), PAL breaks from the loop and continues executing the script with the commands that follow the keyword ENDFOR. The commands *MESSAGE "End of script"* and *SLEEP 2000*, instruct PAL to display the message *End of script* for two seconds. Because these commands are the last ones in the script, PAL stops at this point and returns to the Paradox workspace.

Alternative Forms

Although most uses of the FOR command will include FROM, TO, and STEP statements, these terms actually are optional. If you do not include the keyword STEP and a Step value, PAL will increment the counter by a value of 1 after each pass through the loop. In the example, we could have omitted the STEP statement without affecting the outcome of the script. If you do not include a FROM statement within the FOR command, you must assign an initial value to the counter variable from outside the loop. If this variable contains a value, PAL will use that value as the initial value of the counter variable. If the counter variable has not been assigned a value prior to the execution of a FOR command, and that FOR command does not contain a FROM statement, a script error will result.

If you omit the keyword TO and the TO value from a FOR command, PAL will continue to process the loop indefinitely. PAL's QUIT and QUITLOOP commands provide the only way to escape from such a loop. If PAL encounters a QUITLOOP command during a pass through a FOR loop, it will break the loop, but continue executing the script. If PAL encounters a QUIT command during the execution of a script, it will exit from the script entirely and return you to the Paradox workspace.

Scanning

In addition to WHILE and FOR, PAL offers one other looping command: SCAN. However, the applications for the SCAN command are much more limited than for either of these two other commands. Specifically, the SCAN command directs PAL to move down a field of a table one record at a time, starting at the top of the table, and to perform an action on each record. If you include an optional FOR argument (not to be confused with the FOR command), PAL will act only upon records that meet the specified selection conditions. Although this action can be duplicated by the WHILE and FOR commands, you will find that the SCAN command provides the most convenient way to perform this type of loop.

The form of the SCAN command is

>   SCAN
>   FOR *condition*
>   *commands*
>   ENDSCAN

where *commands* represents the list of commands that PAL will execute for each pass through the loop, and *condition* specifies the optional selection conditions. Because PAL always begins a scan with the first record in a table, there is no need to position the cursor within the first record before the scan begins.

An Example

The script in Figure 16-33 shows an example of a SCAN loop. This script steps through the currently empty Number field of a table named XYZ, filling it with the sequential series of ascending values 1, 2, 3, and so on. In addition, this script begins by bringing XYZ to the workspace or making it the current image, entering the edit mode, moving the cursor to the Number field of the first record, and assigning the value 1 to the variable *x*. Then the SCAN loop takes control. PAL will execute the commands in this loop once for each of the records in the table. On the first pass, the command *[]=x* enters the value of *x* (1) into the Number field of the first record, and the command *x=x+1* increases the value of *x* to 2. When PAL reaches the end of the first pass, it moves the cursor down one row to the Number field of the second record and enters the value 2. PAL continues in this fashion until it has entered a value into the Number field of every record in the table.

Figure 16-33 The SCAN Command

```
Designing script Scan                                          Script
....+...10....+...20....+...30....+...40....+...50....+...60....+...70....+...80
EDIT "Xyz"
MOVETO [Number]
x=1
SCAN
  []=x
  x=x+1
ENDSCAN
```

Another Example

Our first example of the SCAN command acted upon every record in the table. If your SCAN command contains a FOR argument, however, PAL will act upon only the records that meet the selection conditions that you specify. Although PAL only executes the commands enclosed within the SCAN command for the selected records, it still steps through every record in the table.

The script shown in Figure 16-34 demonstrates the use of a SCAN command that includes a FOR clause. This script steps through the Quantity field of a table named ABC, replacing every blank with the value 0. In addition, this script begins by bringing the ABC table to the Paradox workspace in the edit mode. The SCAN command that follows steps through the Quantity field, one record at a time. If the Quantity field of the current record is blank, PAL will execute the command *[Quantity]=0*, which enters the value 0 in the blank Quantity field. If the current record's Quantity field is not blank, PAL skips the *[Quantity]=0* command, moves to the next record, and tries again.

Figure 16-34 The SCAN/FOR Command

```
Designing script Scan2                                          Script
....+...10....+...20....+...30....+...40....+...50....+...60....+...70....+...80
EDIT "Abc"
SCAN
   FOR ISBLANK([Quantity])
   [Quantity]=0
ENDSCAN
```

In this script, we have demonstrated another feature of the SCAN command—the cursor does not need to be in the field that you are acting upon or the field to which the selection conditions apply. In this case, PAL stepped through whatever field the cursor was in when the script began. Because the argument of the ISBLANK command refers to the Quantity field, however, PAL tests that field—not the one the cursor is in. Similarly, because the command *[Quantity]=0* refers to the Quantity field, PAL places the value 0 in that field—not the field in which the cursor is positioned.

Printing

In addition to working with the information in tables from within scripts, you often will want to print from within a script. PAL gives you three ways to do this. First, you can print from a prepared report specification. Second, you can "echo" the information that is displayed on the PAL canvas to your printer. Third, you can print specific strings to the printer, one at a time.

Printing from a Report Specification

In most cases, you will print from within a script in exactly the same way you print manually from within Paradox—by choosing a previously designed report specification and commanding Paradox to print from it. There are two ways to do this from within a script. First, you can use the keystroke representation

Menu {Report} {Output} {*tablename*} {*report number*} {*Printer,Screen,File*}

where *tablename* is the name of the table from which you want to print, *report specification* is a number from 1 to 9 or the letter *R* that specifies the report specification to use, and *Printer*, *Screen*, or *File* tells PAL where to print the report. If you specify Printer, PAL will send the report to your printer. If you specify Screen, PAL will preview the report on the screen. If you specify File, PAL will print the report to the .RPT file that you specify.

PAL's REPORT command provides an easier and more flexible way to print from a report specification within a script. As explained in Chapter 14, the form of this menu-equivalent command is

REPORT *table report*

where *table* is a string expression that is, contains, or returns the name of the table you want to print, and *report* is either a value expression that is, returns, or contains an integer from 1 to 9 or a string expression that is, contains, or returns the string *R*. The ability to use variables, field references, equations, and functions instead of literal strings is the principal advantage of this command relative to keystroke representations.

In most cases, you probably will manipulate the information in a table before you print that information. For example, you may wish to sort the records before printing, print only those records that meet certain selection conditions, or combine information from two or more tables in the same report. This process of preparing the information for printing is an ideal task to automate in a script. For example, suppose that you want to select the SS Number and Salary fields of all the records from the EMPLYEE table with Salary field entries that exceed 30,000.00, arrange them into ascending salary order, and print them in a standard Tabular report. To do this, you could use the script shown in Figure 16-35.

As you can see, this script begins with the script version of a query that selects the SS Number and Salary field entries for the records in the EMPLYEE table with Salary field entries that exceed 30,000.00. The easiest way to create this query script is to create the query in Paradox, then use the [Menu] Scripts QuerySave command to save it as a script. The Do_It! command that follows the script query instructs PAL to execute this query, placing the results in a table named ANSWER. The command SORT "Answer" ON "Salary" sorts the records from the ANSWER table into ascending order based on the entries in the Salary field, and places the sorted results back into ANSWER. The final command, *REPORT "Answer" "R"*, commands PAL to print a standard Tabular report of the records in the sorted ANSWER table. This report is shown in Figure 16-36.

Figure 16-35 A Printing Script

```
Changing script Print                                    Script

....+...10....+...20....+...30....+...40....+...50....+...60....+...70....+...80
Query

    Emplyee : SS Number :    Salary    :
            :   Check   : Check >30000 :
            :           :              :
            :           :              :

Endquery
Do_It!
SORT "Answer" ON "Salary"
REPORT "Answer" "R"
```

Figure 16-36 The Printed Report

```
5/06/86                     Standard report                    Page    1


SS Number      Salary
-----------    ----------------
314-38-9452      32,000.00
312-98-1479      32,125.00
413-07-9123      33,999.99
321-65-9151      34,000.00
415-24-6710      37,000.00
317-65-4529      38,000.00
401-55-1567      40,000.00
401-32-8721      47,000.00
321-65-8765      50,000.00
414-76-3421      70,000.00
```

Instant Reports

If you want to print a standard Tabular report from within a script, you do not need to use PAL's REPORT command. Instead, you can use the special key representation *InstantReport*. When PAL reads this keystroke in a script, it will print the report stored in the R selection for the current table. Unless you change the R specification from its default state, it will contain the format for a simple Tabular report. Since *InstantReport* prints from the current table, you must be sure that the table you want to print is on the workspace and that the cursor is within it before PAL reads this keystroke representation.

Designing a Report Specification within a Script

Although you can design a report specification from within a script, we don't recommend it. If a script contains the instructions for creating a report specification, PAL would recreate the specification each time you played that script—an unnecessary and time-consuming task. Once you design a report specification, of course, you can use PAL's REPORT command to call upon it at any time.

Echoing Information to the Printer

PAL's PRINTER command provides a second way to print information from within a report. Once PAL reads a PRINTER ON command in a script, it will begin echoing to your printer all subsequent information displayed on the screen by the ?, ??, and TEXT commands. A PRINTER OFF command or the end of the script cancels this command.

As an example of the use of this command, suppose that you want to print the records in the EMPLYEE table in the form of simple mailing labels. To do this, you would use the script shown in Figure 16-37. The PRINTER ON command that begins this script assures that the information displayed by the following ? commands will be echoed to the printer. The SCAN command instructs PAL to execute the six ? commands that follow each record in the table, beginning with the first record. The first ? command tells PAL to skip to the beginning of a new line, both on the screen and on the printer, and print the first and last name of the current record. The next ? command skips to the beginning of the next line and displays and prints the contents of that record's Address field. The third ? command tells PAL to skip the beginning of a new line and print the contents of the City, State, and Zip fields for that record. The final three ? commands make PAL skip three blank lines. As soon as PAL finishes the first pass through this loop, it begins another, this time displaying and printing the selected fields of the second record. Once PAL has printed a label for each record in the table, it turns the printer off and exits from the script.

Figure 16-37 The PRINTER Command

```
Changing script Printer                                      Script Ins
....+...10....+...20....+...30....+...40....+...50....+...60....+...70....+...80
PRINTER ON
VIEW "Emplyee"
SCAN
   ? [First Name]," ",[Last Name]
   ? [Address]
   ? [City],", ",[State]," ",[Zip]
   ?
   ?
   ?
ENDSCAN
PRINTER OFF
```

In almost all situations, you'll find it easier to prepare a report in the Paradox report mode than to create it by echoing information to the printer. For example, skipping blank lines in mailing labels is a matter of issuing the [Menu] Settings RemoveBlanks LineSqueeze Yes Fixed command from within the report. Removing blank lines in an echoed report involves a complex nesting of IF commands. Overall, the principal use of the PRINTER command is to print the results or contents of variables, equations, and functions within a report. Unless you need to do this, however, you probably will want to use the REPORT command to output information to your printer.

The Print Command

PAL's PRINT command provides the third way to print information from within a script. This command instructs PAL to send information (literal values, the contents of variables and fields, and the results of equations and functions) to your printer or to a file directly without displaying it on the screen. The two forms of the PRINT command are

> PRINT *expression 1,expression 2,...,expression n-1,expression n*
> PRINT FILE *filename expression 1,expression 2,...,expression n-1,expression n*

The first form of this function sends information to a printer. The second form sends information to the file you name in the file name argument. If that file already exists, PAL appends the new information to the end of that file. If the file doesn't exist, PAL creates it.

Like the PRINTER command, the PRINT command is of limited usefulness. In most cases, you'll find it easier to design a report specification than to use multiple PRINT commands to send information to a printer or to a file.

One of the best uses for the PRINT command is sending special ASCII codes to your printer. You can use a backslash followed by any of the ASCII codes 0 to 254 to send any ASCII character to your printer. For example, since ASCII character 10 is the line feed character on an Epson printer, the command *PRINT "\010"* will send a line feed instruction to your printer. The most useful application of this technique is for sending print attribute codes to your printer prior to printing. For example, the command *PRINT "\027\015"* prepares your Epson printer to print in compressed print, and the command *PRINT "\027\048"* instructs it to print eight lines per inch.

You can also use four special characters—\n, \t, and \r—to send common characters to the printer. The string \n sends a line feed to the printer. The string \t sends a tab character to the printer. The string \f sends a form-feed character, and \r sends a carriage return.

If you do send literal text to the printer with the PRINT command, you'll need to be sure to include a \n character at the end of each line of text. Unlike the PRINTER command, PRINT does not automatically add a line feed at the end of each line it prints. For example, to print the contents of the First Name field of a table on the printer, you'd use the command *PRINT [First Name]"\n"*.

Passwords

Since most of your PAL programs will work with Paradox tables, and some of your tables will be password-protected, chances are good that you will encounter a situation in which you'll need to work with a protected table in a script. There are two ways to access a password-protected table from within a script. First, you can supply the password for each table as you call it to the workspace. If the table named ORDERS is protected with the password *abracadabra*, for example, you could use the keystroke sequence

> Menu {View} {Orders} {Abracadabra}

within your script to bring it to the workspace. You must use a similar sequence for each password-protected table you want to access within the script.

This keystroke-representation method works well if your script calls upon only one or so password-protected tables. If your script calls on several, however, you might want to take advantage of PAL's PASSWORD command. This command, which has the form

> PASSWORD *password 1,password 2,...,password n*

lets you supply passwords in advance for any protected tables you'll access during the script. Once these passwords have been supplied in the context of the PASSWORD command, PAL will allow you free access to the tables to which they apply.

For example, suppose you want to access three password-protected tables in the course of a script: ORDERS (which has the password *abracadabra*), CUSTOMERS (which has the password *shazaam*), and PRODUCTS (which has the password *open sesame*). To assure free access to these tables, you might include the command

> PASSWORD "abracadabra","shazaam","open sesame"

early in the script. Once PAL reads this command, it will not be necessary to supply the passwords for these three files when you first open them, as you normally would.

Revoking Passwords

As you learned in Chapter 6, once you supply the correct password for a file, Paradox will allow you to access that file again and again during the current Paradox session without supplying the password each time. If a script that has unprotected one or more files ends without exiting to DOS, then you will be able to access those files freely. Fortunately, PAL provides a command, UNPASSWORD, that allows you to "revoke" one or more of the passwords supplied during the play of a script. This command prevents unauthorized access to the table after the script is finished, without necessitating an exit from Paradox.

The form of the UNPASSWORD command is

> UNPASSWORD *password 1,password 2,...,password n*

where the expressions that follow the command are the passwords that you want to revoke. If your script contained the PASSWORD command used above, for example, you would need to use the command

UNPASSWORD "abracadabra","shazaam","open sesame"

near the end of the script to reprotect them before the end of script play.

Password-Protecting a Script

In addition to password-protecting tables, you'll probably want to password-protect any scripts that contain a PASSWORD command. Otherwise, anyone could use the [Menu] Scripts Editor Edit command to bring the script into the Script Editor, view the PASSWORD command, and learn the passwords for your files. You must password-protect a script in much the same way you password-protect a table. To password-protect a script, you issue the [Menu] Tools More Protect Password command. Instead of choosing Table, as you would to password-protect a table, you select Script and supply the name of the script you want to protect either by typing it and pressing ↵ or by pressing ↵ to reveal a list of scripts, highlighting the one you want to protect, and pressing ↵ again.

As soon as you supply the name of a script, PAL will prompt you to type a password. This password may be any string of up to 50 characters. As soon as you type the password and press ↵, PAL will prompt you to retype it. If you type it the same way again, PAL will accept the password and encrypt the script. If you type the password differently—if even the capitalization is not the same—PAL will reject it and will not assign the password to the script. If you want to protect the script, you must start the process over again.

Password-protecting a script does a number of things. First, it prevents anyone from viewing the script in the PAL Script Editor unless they know the password, or from viewing it in any other text editor. If you retrieve a password-protected script into a text editor like WordStar, it will appear as a jumbled mess of strange characters. If you try to bring it into the PAL Script Editor, PAL will prompt you for the script's password. If you know the password, PAL will bring the script into the editor. If you don't know the password, however, PAL will not let you see the script.

Importantly, password-protecting a script does not prevent you from playing it. No matter whether a script is password-protected or not, PAL will play it when you issue the [Menu] Scripts Play command, choose Play from the PAL menu, or use a PLAY command from within a script.

Password-protecting a script does prevent you from using the [Ctrl]-[Break] combination to cancel the execution of that script, however. If you press [Ctrl]-[Break] while PAL is playing a script that is not password-protected, PAL will stop the execution of that script and present you with the choices Cancel or Debug. If you choose Cancel, PAL will terminate the script and return you to the Paradox workspace. If you choose Debug, PAL will enter the PAL Debugger–a topic we'll cover thoroughly in the next chapter. If you press [Ctrl]-[Break] while PAL is playing a password-protected script, however, PAL will just continue playing that script.

Comments in Scripts

In addition to keystroke representations and commands, PAL programs can contain comments. Comments annotate a script, making it easier to understand what the script does when you view or edit it. Including a comment in a script is as easy as typing a semicolon and then typing the comment. The ; character signals PAL that a comment follows. When PAL encounters a semicolon in a script, it disregards all characters from the semicolon to the end of the line on which it appears. You can place a comment on a line by itself or on a line that contains other commands.

Figure 16-38 shows an example of a simple annotated script. As you can see, the first line of the script is a comment that tells you the name of the script and what it does. The comment at the end of each subsequent line explains the purpose of the commands on that line. For example, the comment *;bring EMPLYEE into view* explains the function of the command VIEW "Emplyee".

Figure 16-38 Comments in Scripts

```
Changing script Printer                                         Script Ins
....+...10....+...20....+...30....+...40....+...50....+...60....+...70....+...80
;script for printing mailing labels
PRINTER ON                              ;echos screen to printer
VIEW "Emplyee"                          ;bring EMPLYEE into view
SCAN                                    ;move through EMPLYEE record by record
    ? [First Name]," ",[Last Name]      ;prints first and last names
    ? [Address]                         ;prints address
    ? [City],", ",[State]," ",[Zip]     ;prints city, state, zip
    ?                                   ;blank lines
    ?
    ?
ENDSCAN                                 ;Loop to SCAN command
PRINTER OFF                             ;turn off printer echo
```

Although you usually can place a comment to the right of any line of commands, you should not place comments to the right of a TEXT command, the keyword ENDTEXT, or the text that falls between them.

Conclusion

In this chapter, we have explained a number of essential PAL programming techniques. We expect that you will use these techniques over and over as you begin to write your own scripts. If so, you may want to review this chapter from time to time to reinforce your understanding of these concepts and pick up any fine points that you missed.

In the final chapter of this book, we will demonstrate some advanced PAL programming techniques, such as keyboard macros, procedures, and arrays.

Chapter 17

Other PAL Features

In the previous four chapters, we have introduced you to the basics of PAL: recording, editing, and playing scripts; PAL commands, variables and equations; and functions. In this final chapter, we'll present several other important PAL features, including the Value command, miniscripts, macros, arrays, procedures, and the PAL Debugger.

The Value Command

The Value option on the PAL menu allows you to perform calculations quickly and easily. When you press the [PAL Menu] key ([Alt]-[F10]), Paradox will display the PAL menu shown in Figure 17-1. When you choose Value, the fourth item on this menu, Paradox will reveal the prompt and message shown in Figure 17-2. When you see this prompt, you can type any valid variable, field reference, equation, or function. When you press ↵, PAL will calculate the value of the expression you typed and display the result in the message area at the bottom-right corner of the screen.

Figure 17-1 The PAL Menu

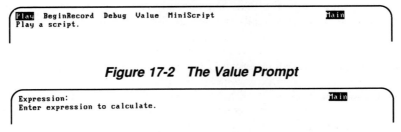

Figure 17-2 The Value Prompt

For example, suppose you want to know the product of multiplying 145 by 17. To make this calculation, press the [PAL Menu] key ([Alt]-[F10]), choose Value, and type **145*17**. When you press ↵, PAL will display the result of this formula, 2465, in the message area. Similarly, suppose you want to know the future value of investing $1000 per year for 20 years at 10% interest. To make this calculation, press **[PAL Menu]**, choose Value, type **FV(1000,.1,20)** and press ↵. After a moment, PAL will display the result, 57274.99949325, in the message area.

When you use the Value option to calculate a value, PAL actually creates and plays a temporary RETURN script. In the example above, for instance, PAL created and played the single-line script *RETURN 145*17*. The result of a VALUE command is exactly the same as if you had written the RETURN script in the Script Editor and played it yourself.

Miniscripts

The MiniScript command on the PAL menu allows you to create and play temporary, single-line scripts that are up to 50 characters long. When you issue this command, PAL will present the prompt shown in Figure 17-3. When you type one or more PAL commands onto this line and press ↵, PAL will execute those commands as a script.

Figure 17-3   The MiniScript Prompt

Miniscripts are useful for testing the effect of various PAL commands as you learn about PAL or for performing simple tasks that you cannot do from within Paradox, like storing the result of a calculation in a variable. For example, suppose you want to store the sum of the entries in the Salary field of the EMPLYEE table into the variable SalSum. To do this, you could press **[Pal Menu]**, choose the MiniScript command, and type **SalSum=CSUM("Emplyee","Salary")**. As soon as you press ↵, PAL will execute the script, storing the sum of the values in the Salary field in SalSum.

As we will show you later, you also will use miniscripts for two other purposes: to aid in debugging scripts and to create keyboard macros.

Because a miniscript is a script, PAL automatically checks it for errors as it plays. If PAL encounters an error in the miniscript, it will display the message *Script error–select Cancel or Debug from menu* in the message area, and will present the menu choices Cancel and Debug at the top of the screen. If you choose Cancel, PAL will return you to the Paradox workspace. (We'll cover the Debug option later in this chapter.)

PAL does not save miniscripts to disk. For that reason, you must retype a miniscript each time you want to play it. If you plan to use a script more than once or twice, you should create it as a regular script and not as a miniscript.

Keyboard Macros

Up to this point, we have played scripts in any of three ways: by issuing the [Menu] Scripts Play command, by choosing Play from the PAL menu, or by including a PLAY command in a script. It is possible to play a script simply by pressing a single key or a combination of two keys, however. To do this, you must use PAL's SETKEY command to link a key or key combination to a script. Once you have set up this link, you can play the script by pressing that key or combination of keys. These script/key combinations are called keyboard macros.

PAL's SETKEY command is the secret to creating a keyboard macro. The form of this command is

SETKEY *keycode commands*

The first argument, *keycode*, must be a keycode expression that specifies the key or combination that you want to use to play the script. As you'll recall from our discussion of the WAIT command in Chapter 16, you can specify a keycode in five ways. First, you can use a single-character string, like *a*, *Z*, or *?*. Second, you can use the ASCII number for that character (a numeric value from 0 to 255). Third, you can use a negative numeric value from -1 to -132 to represent characters from the "extended" IBM character set, including special function keys, arrow keys, and various [Alt] combinations (listed in Appendix B of the *PAL User's Guide*). Fourth, you can use the strings *F1*, *F2*, and so on, to represent regular function keys; *F11*, *F12*, and so on, to represent shifted function keys; *F20*, *F21*, and so on, to represent [Ctrl]-function key combinations; and *F30*, *F31*, and so on, to represent [Alt]-function key combinations. Finally, you can use the names PAL assigns to special keys, like Right, Rotate, and Check.

The second argument of this command, *commands*, is a list of one or more valid PAL commands. These can be PAL commands like SORT, WHILE, or PLAY, or they can be keystroke representations like Menu, {Scripts}, or {View}. Importantly, all of the commands that you want PAL to execute when you invoke the macro must be on the same line as the SETKEY command itself.

Defining a Macro

To create a macro, you must write a SETKEY script that tells PAL to link a series of commands to a key. Then you must play that script. When you play the SETKEY script, PAL sets up the relationship between the key and the commands specified by the SETKEY command.

Once you run a SETKEY script, the macro defined by that script will remain active until the end of the current Paradox session or until you undefine that macro. To return a macro-linked key to its normal function prior to the end of a Paradox session, you must use an abbreviated form of the SETKEY command: SETKEY *keycode*. The single argument should be the code of the key you want to return to its normal function. The absence of a set of commands following the keycode instructs PAL to "undefine" the macro and return the key to its original function.

A Simple Example

Suppose you want Paradox to display the structure of the current table whenever you press [Ctrl]-[S]. To do this, you should enter the Script Editor and compose the simple one-line script

SETKEY 19 Menu {Tools} {Info} {Structure} Enter Enter

After writing this script, press **[Menu]** and choose **G**o from the Script Editor menu to save and play the script. Playing the script activates the macro. When you subsequently press [Ctrl]-[S], PAL will issue the [Menu] Tools Info Structure command, will press ↵ once to reveal a list of table names, and will press ↵ again to select the first name from the list–the name of the current table. As a result, PAL will display the structure of the current table.

A More Complex Example

As we mentioned earlier, the commands that you want to link to a key must fit entirely on the same line as the SETKEY command. For a simple macro like the one explained above, this restriction is not a problem. In many cases, however, you'll want to link a key to a script that contains more commands than can fit on a single line. In these cases, you can link the key to a PLAY command that calls the script you want PAL to execute.

For example, suppose you want PAL to play the script *Newemply*, which is shown in Figure 17-4, when you press [Alt]-[Q]. To link this script to the [Alt]-[Q] key, you must write and play the script

SETKEY -16 PLAY "Newemply"

Once you play this script, pressing [Alt]-[Q] will execute the command PLAY *"Newemply"*, which instructs it to branch to the script named *Newemply*. Because Newemply contains a query followed by a *Do_It*! command, PAL will bring the query to the workspace, execute it, and end the script.

Figure 17-4 The Newemply Script

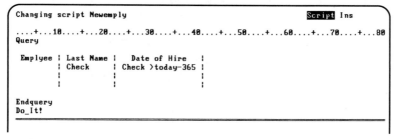

Other Macro Notes

Instead of using the Script Editor to create a SETKEY script, you can use the MiniScript command to create and play the script. To do this, press the [PAL Menu] key, choose the MiniScript command, and type the **SETKEY** script you want to play. When you press ↵, PAL will play the script, defining the macro.

Remember, though, that PAL does not save miniscripts. If you plan to use your SETKEY scripts over and over, you should write them using the PAL Editor. That way, all you have to do to redefine the macro in your next Paradox session is play the saved SETKEY script. If you use the MiniScript command to define these macros, you'll have to retype the SETKEY script at the start of the next Paradox session.

One useful programming technique is to combine your most-used macros into one script. By playing this one script at the beginning of each Paradox session, you can activate all of these macros at once for use throughout that session. If you have written your macros into separate scripts, you can use the Script Editor's Read command to combine them. To make this process really convenient, you can designate the macro-containing script as an auto-executing script (a process we'll discuss near the end of this chapter).

One final note: Although you can link a script to any key on your computer's keyboard, you should be careful which keys you actually use. Once you link a key to a script, PAL will execute that script whenever you press that key—when you are selecting an item from a menu, when you are typing an entry into a table, when you are creating a report or script, and so forth. If you link macros to keys that have special purposes in Paradox, such as ↵, →, [End], [Edit], and so on, you'll find yourself unable to issue the commands you want to issue once a macro is in effect. Therefore, we recommend that you link your scripts to keys and combinations that Paradox does not use for any other purpose. In most cases, we prefer to use the [Alt] or [Ctrl] combinations that Paradox does not use.

Arrays

In Chapter 14, we introduced the use of variables within a PAL script. In that chapter, you learned that each variable can hold a single value. In addition to these simple variables, PAL allows the use of a special type of variable called an array.

An array is a variable that can hold more than one value at a time (up to 15,000 values, in fact). The "pockets" that store the values in an array are called elements. Each element can hold one value of any type. You can store information into and retrieve information from an array either one element at a time or all at once.

COPYTOARRAY and COPYFROMARRAY

The principal use of an array is to store a group of related values. For example, you might use an array variable to store all of the entries from a record. In fact, PAL provides two commands, COPYTOARRAY and COPYFROMARRAY, that are designed specifically for storing the contents of a record in an array and writing the contents of an array back into a table. The COPYTOARRAY command creates an array that has one more element than the number of fields in the current table, then copies the table name and every entry from the current record into that array. The form of this command is

> COPYTOARRAY *arrayname*

where the single argument is the name of the array in which you want to store the record. The COPYFROMARRAY command copies the elements from an array (usually one created by the COPYTOARRAY command) back into a table. The form of this command is

> COPYFROMARRAY *arrayname*

where the single argument is the name of the array whose elements you want to access.

The script shown in Figure 17-5 demonstrates a basic use of the COPYTOARRAY and COPYFROMARRAY commands. This script moves the entries from a record you choose to another row within that table. (You must be viewing or editing a table when you run this script.) The first command in this script tests to see whether Paradox is in the edit mode. If not, PAL places it in the edit mode. The WAIT TABLE command causes PAL to display the prompts *Position the cursor on the record you want to move* and *Then press [Enter]* at the top of the screen, and lets you move the cursor freely within the current table.

Figure 17-5 COPYTOARRAY and COPYFROMARRAY

```
Changing script Arrays                                         Script
....+...10....+...20....+...30....+...40....+...50....+...60....+...70....+...80
IF NOT SYSMODE()="Edit"
   THEN EditKey
ENDIF
WAIT TABLE PROMPT "Position cursor on record you want to move",
   "Then press [Enter]" UNTIL "Enter"
COPYTOARRAY temp
Del
WAIT TABLE PROMPT "Position cursor at destination",
   "Then press [Enter]" UNTIL "Enter"
Ins
COPYFROMARRAY temp
```

When you position the cursor in any field of the record you want to move and press ↵, PAL will execute the command *COPYTOARRAY temp*, which creates an array named *temp* and copies the entries from the current record into it. The array that PAL creates will have one element for each field in the table, plus one to store the name of the table itself. The table name always occupies the first element in the array. The subsequent elements in the array store the entries from the fields of the record, in order, starting with the leftmost field.

For example, if the cursor is positioned anywhere in the third record of the table shown in Figure 17-6 when you press ↵, the COPYTOARRAY command will create a four-element array. The first element would hold the name of the table–the string value *Sample*. The second element would store the record's Date field entry–the date value *3/03/86*. The third element of the array would hold the entry from the third record's Number field–the numeric value *30*. The fourth element of the array would hold the entry from the third record's Name field–the string value *Smith*.

Figure 17-6   The SAMPLE Table

```
Viewing Sample table: Record 1 of 12                    Main
SAMPLE    Date       Number      Name
     1    1/01/86        10      Jones
     2    2/02/86        20      Williams
     3    3/03/86        30      Smith
     4    4/04/86        40      Brown
     5    5/05/86        50      White
     6    6/06/86        60      Black
     7    7/07/86        70      Michaels
     8    8/08/86        80      Ford
     9    9/09/86        90      Dow
    10   10/10/86       100      Cohen
    11   11/11/86       110      Johnson
    12   12/12/86       120      Cleaver
```

After PAL has created this array and copied the entries from the third record into it, PAL reads the command *Del*, which deletes the record whose contents it just copied into the array. Then PAL reads another WAIT command. This command instructs PAL to display the prompts *Position cursor at destination* and *Then press [Enter]*, then allows you to move the cursor freely within the table. As soon as you press ↵, PAL will read the command *Ins*, which causes it to insert a new record into the table at the current position of the cursor. Finally, PAL reads the command *COPYFROMARRAY temp*. This command instructs PAL to copy the contents of the array *temp* (the contents of the third record) back into the table in the proper fields, within the record in which the cursor is positioned. Figure 17-7 shows the result of moving the third record to the beginning of the SAMPLE table.

Figure 17-7   The Rearranged SAMPLE Table

```
Viewing Sample table: Record 1 of 12                    Main
SAMPLE    Date       Number      Name
     1    3/03/86        30      Smith
     2    1/01/86        10      Jones
     3    2/02/86        20      Williams
     4    4/04/86        40      Brown
     5    5/05/86        50      White
     6    6/06/86        60      Black
     7    7/07/86        70      Michaels
     8    8/08/86        80      Ford
     9    9/09/86        90      Dow
    10   10/10/86       100      Cohen
    11   11/11/86       110      Johnson
    12   12/12/86       120      Cleaver
```

Importantly, the field which is assigned to an element of an array is determined by the structure of a table, not by the order of the fields in its image. If you have rotated a table image prior to acting upon it with the COPYTOARRAY command, then the order of the fields in the image will not match the order of the elements in the array.

You also can use the COPYFROMARRAY command to place the elements from an array into a table other than the one from which they were extracted. For this process to be successful, however, the type (alphanumeric, date, number, etc.) of each field into which PAL will place the information from the array must match the type of value stored in the corresponding position in the array. Importantly, the destination table can have more fields than there are elements in the array, as long as the types of the first fields in the table match the types of values stored in the elements of the array.

Retrieving Individual Elements From an Array

Although you commonly will use the COPYFROMARRAY command to retrieve all the elements from an array at once, as we have in the example above, you also can operate on the elements in an array individually. To do this, you must use the reference form *arrayname[element]*, where *arrayname* is the name of an array and *element* is an expression that identifies the element that you want to reference. If the array was created using a COPYTOARRAY command, then the *element* argument can be either a numeric expression that identifies the element you want to access, or a string expression that specifies the name of the field from which that element was copied. If you create an array with an ARRAY command (we'll show you how to do this in a few paragraphs), you must identify the elements by number.

For example, suppose that you have created a four-element array *temp* (described above) by issuing the COPYTOARRAY command while the cursor is in the third record of the SAMPLE table. Having stored the third record in this array, suppose you want to retrieve its individual elements into four variables: w, x, y, and z. To copy the contents of the first element in the array–the table name SAMPLE–into w, you would use the command *w=temp[1]*. To copy the contents of the second element into x, you could use either the command *x=temp[2]* or the command *x=temp["Date"]*. To copy the contents of the third element into y, you could use either the command *y=temp[3]* or the command *y=temp["Number"]*. Similarly, you could copy the contents of the fourth element into z with either the command *z=temp[4]* or the command *z=temp["Name"]*. In this case, w would contain the string value *Sample*, x would contain the date value *3/03/86*, y would contain the numeric value *30*, and z would contain the string value *Smith*.

Throughout the last four chapters, we have told you that you can use five types of expressions–literal values, variables, field references, formulas, and functions–as the arguments of various PAL commands and functions. In fact, you also can use references to the individual elements in an array as arguments. For example, if the third element of the array named *temp* holds the value 30, the function *SQRT(temp[3])* will return the value 6.324. Similarly, the command *MESSAGE "The third element in temp holds the value ",temp[3]* will display the message *The third element in temp holds the value 30*.

Placing Individual Elements in an Array

Just as you can retrieve elements of an array individually, you also can store values into the elements of an array one at a time. For example, you would use the command *temp[3]=500* to place the numeric value *500* in the third element of the array *temp* (provided that *temp* already exists). If the third element of *temp* already contains a value (as it does in this case), that value will be overwritten by the new value you assign to it. The old and new values do not have to be of the same type, however. For example, you could use the command *temp[3]="thirty"* to replace the numeric value *30* with the string value *thirty*. Once you do this, however, you cannot use the COPYFROMARRAY command to enter the contents of the array back into the table from which it came.

Creating an Array Manually

Although you usually will use the COPYTOARRAY command to create your arrays, you also can define an array manually. To do this, you must use PAL's ARRAY command. The form of this command is

> ARRAY *arrayname[#]*

where *arrayname* is the name of the array you want to create, and # is the number of elements you want it to contain. To define a five-element array named *results*, for example, you would use the command *ARRAY results[5]*.

The ARRAY command does not automatically fill in an array when it is created. Once you have defined an array, you must use the = command to assign values to its individual elements. For example, you could use the commands *results[1]="John"*, *results[2]="Smith"*, *results[3]="123 Any Street"*, *results[4]="Indianapolis"*, and *results[5]="IN"* to store John Smith's name and address in the array *results*. The arrays you create with the ARRAY command can store any information you want to put in them. Unlike the first element of the arrays you create with the COPYTOARRAY command, the first element of a custom array does not have to hold a table name.

Undefining an Array

Once you define an array, that array remains defined until the end of the current Paradox session or until you specifically release it. As long as an array is defined, it uses up memory, whether it stores any values or not. You can use the RELEASE command to "undefine" an array in much the same way that you can use it to release a variable. In fact, you can even use the same form of the command–*RELEASE VARS*. To release individual arrays, you must use the form

> RELEASE VARS *array 1,...,array n*

where the argument(s) are the name(s) of the arrays you want to release. (You can mix array names and variable names within the same RELEASE command to release arrays and "normal" variables at the same time.) If you issue the *RELEASE VARS ALL* command, PAL will undefine all existing arrays and regular variables.

Procedures

Procedures are RAM-resident subroutines that you can define and use during the playing of any PAL script. A procedure can perform an action, return a value, or both. If the procedure performs an action only, then it is much like a typical subroutine that you call with a PLAY command from within a script. As we will explain, however, a procedure gives you three advantages relative to a subroutine: it can accept arguments, it can execute more quickly (remember–procedures are RAM-resident), and it can use private variables. An example of this is a procedure that deletes a record from a table.

If a procedure returns a value result, then we'll refer to it as a user-defined function. Like PAL's built-in functions, user-defined functions can accept arguments and return a value result based on those arguments. This type of procedure must end with a RETURN command, which returns the value of the procedure to the calling script. A procedure that calculates the median of a column of values is an example of this type of procedure.

Defining a Procedure

To define a procedure, you must use PAL's PROC/ENDPROC command within a script. The basic form of the PROC command is

> PROC *procedurename(parameter 1, parameter 2,...,parameter n)*
>   *commands*
> ENDPROC

The first argument of the PROC command must be the name you want to assign to the procedure, followed by a list of any variables that you will pass to the procedure when you call it. These variables are the *formal parameters* of the procedure. Like PAL's built-in functions, some procedures will require one or more arguments, and some will have none. Even if the procedure that you are defining will not require any arguments, you must include a set of parentheses after the name of the procedure in the PROC command.

Following the procedure name, you must list all of the commands you want PAL to execute when you call the procedure. The keyword ENDPROC marks the end of the PROC command.

Two Simple Examples

The simple script named PROC1 shown in Figure 17-8 defines a simple user-defined function. This function calculates the future value of investing a single lump sum of money today. For example, you could use this procedure to calculate the value 25 years from today of investing $100 today at a guaranteed annual rate of 10%. The first line of this script designates *CompVal* (for compound value) as the name of the procedure and specifies three parameters: *amount*, *rate*, and *term*. The second line of the script calculates the formula *amount*POW(1+rate,term)* and returns the result as the value of the procedure. The keyword *ENDPROC* marks the end of the procedure.

Figure 17-8   A Simple User-Defined Function

```
Designing script Proc1                                    Script
....+...10....+...20....+...30....+...40....+...50....+...60....+...70....+...80
PROC CompVal(amount,rate,term)
  RETURN amount*POW(1+rate,term)
ENDPROC
```

The script named PROC2 shown in Figure 17-9 defines a script that performs an action instead of returning a value. This procedure deletes the record designated by its second parameter from the table named by its first parameter. The first line of this script designates *Delrec* as the name of the procedure and specifies two parameters: *tabl* and *rec*. The second line commands PAL to bring the table named by the first parameter onto the Paradox workspace in the edit mode. The next command tells PAL to move the cursor to the record named by the second parameter. The next command tells PAL to delete that record. Then the *Do_It*! command completes the edit, and the keyword *ENDPROC* signals the end of the procedure.

Figure 17-9   A Procedure That Performs an Action

```
Designing script Proc2                                    Script
....+...10....+...20....+...30....+...40....+...50....+...60....+...70....+...80
PROC Delrec(tabl,rec)
  EDIT tabl
  MOVETO RECORD rec
  Del
  Do_It!
ENDPROC
```

Using Procedures

Once you have written a procedure script, using the procedure is a two-step process. First, you must load the procedure, then you must call the procedure.

Defining a Procedure

Defining a procedure is a simple matter of playing the script that contains the PROC command. When you play a procedure script, PAL reads the commands between the command PROC and the keyword ENDPROC and places them in RAM in a special "interpreted" form.

Unlike a macro, a procedure does not remain defined for the entire duration of a Paradox session. Instead, it remains active only during the play of the highest-level script in the script system that loaded the procedure. Once script play ends, the procedure no longer is active. For this reason, you'll need to play a procedure script within each script system in which you will call that procedure.

Calling a Procedure

Once you have played a procedure script, you can command PAL to execute that procedure at any time during the remainder of the play of the current script system. If the procedure returns a value, then you can use as you would a built-in PAL function or a formula. If the procedure performs an action, then you can use it in place of a series of PAL commands. In either case, you must call a procedure in the same way you would "call" a built-in function—by typing its name followed by a pair of parentheses that enclose the procedure's arguments, if any.

For example, suppose you want to use the CompVal procedure shown in Figure 17-8 to calculate the value in 25 years of investing $100 today at a guaranteed annual rate of 10%. To do this, you could use the simple script shown in Figure 17-10.

Figure 17-10 A Script That Calls a Procedure

```
Designing script Proccall                                    Script
....+...10....+...20....+...30....+...40....+...50....+...60....+...70....+...80
CLEAR
@10,20
PLAY "Proc1"
?? CompVal(100,.10,25)
SLEEP 5000
```

The first line clears the PAL canvas. The next line positions the cursor at the intersection of row 11 and column 20 of the screen. The third command, *PLAY "Proc1"*, instructs PAL to play the script shown in Figure 17-8. The effect of playing this script is to load the procedure *CompVal* into RAM in a compiled form.

Once CompVal has been loaded, PAL can evaluate the command *??CompVal (100,.10,25)*. This command instructs PAL to evaluate the user-defined function *CompVal*. When PAL evaluates this procedure, it first assigns the values of the arguments in the call to the parameters of the procedure. PAL assigns the first argument in the call to the first parameter, the second argument to the second parameter, and so on. In this case, PAL assigns the value 100 (the first value in the procedure call) to the variable *amount* (the first parameter of the procedure). PAL assigns the value .10 (the second argument in the call) to the variable *rate* (the second parameter in the procedure definition). Similarly, PAL assigns the value 25 to the parameter *term*.

Once PAL has assigned the values from the call to the variables in the procedure definition, it evaluates the procedure's key formula: *amount*POW(1+rate,term)*. Since *amount* equals 100, *rate* equals .10, and *term* equals 25, this formula returns the value 1083.470594338. Since this procedure call is the argument of a ?? command, PAL displays this result at the current position of the cursor. The final command in the script, SLEEP 5000, assures that this result will remain visible for five seconds.

In the example, we used literal values as the arguments in the call of the user-defined function CompVal. You also can use references to variables, references to fields, formulas, and functions as arguments, however.

Efficiency Considerations

The procedure-calling script shown in Figure 17-9 takes advantage of only one of the benefits offered by procedures: the ability to pass arguments. By programming a calculation within a user-defined function, you don't have to type in a complex formula each time you want to perform that calculation. Instead, you can perform that calculation again and again simply by calling that procedure and supplying the appropriate arguments. Because the parameters of the procedure are generic, it will return a different value depending on what values you pass to it.

A second benefit of programming a calculation within a procedure is speed. When you play a procedure script, PAL stores the commands from that script in RAM in a compiled (or preinterpreted) form. This saves time in two ways. First, PAL does not have to read the script from disk each time it executes that script. Second, PAL does not have to "interpret" the commands into a form that it can understand before executing them.

Unfortunately, you will not realize this increase in speed unless you call a procedure more than one time within a given script system. To call a procedure once within a script, you must do two things: play the procedure-containing script, and call the procedure. When PAL plays the procedure-containing script, it reads each command in the script, interprets it, and stores it in RAM. When you call the procedure, PAL executes the commands that it previously has read and interpreted.

The second and subsequent times that you call a procedure from within a script, however, PAL does not have to reread and reinterpret the commands in that procedure; it merely plays them. Consequently, PAL will execute a procedure much more rapidly the second and subsequent times the procedure is called during a script.

The script shown in Figure 17-11 allows you to use the CompVal procedure over and over again within the same script. Because the majority of this script is enclosed in a WHILE True loop, PAL will execute it until it encounters a QUIT or QUITLOOP command–as it will when you enter n (or N) in response to the final ACCEPT statement in the script. Because the command *PLAY "Proc1"* is outside the loop, however, PAL will load the procedure CompVal only once. Each time you supply a new set of values, PAL will execute the procedure without having to reread and reinterpret it.

Figure 17-11 Calling a Procedure More Than One Time

```
Changing script Proccal2                                    Script
....+...10....+...20....+...30....+...40....+...50....+...60....+...70....+...80
PLAY "Proc1"
WHILE True
  CLEAR
  @10,0
  ?? "Enter the amount to invest: "
  ACCEPT "N" TO x
  ? "Enter the annual rate of interest: "
  ACCEPT "N" TO y
  ? "Enter the number of years to hold the investment: "
  ACCEPT "N" TO z
  ? "Investing $",x," at ",y,"% will yield $",CompVal(x,y,z)," in ",z," years."
  ? "Calculate another? (y/n) "
  ACCEPT "A1" TO answer
  IF answer<>"y"
    THEN QUITLOOP
  ENDIF
ENDWHILE
```

Global and Private Variables

The third advantage of using procedures instead of subroutine scripts is the ability of a procedure to use private variables. Normally, when you use the = or ACCEPT commands to define a variable, that variable remains defined for the remainder of the current Paradox session or until you use a RELEASE VARS command to undefine it. The values of these variables are accessible from any part of any script during the session and can even be saved for use in future scripts with the SAVEVARS command. For these reasons, most variables are termed *global* variables.

The variables that you use in a PROC command to define a procedure (its formal parameters) are not global, however. Instead, they are private to the procedure itself. During the play of the procedure, PAL assigns values to these parameters based on the order of the values in the procedure call and uses those values to calculate a result, perform an action, or both. Once PAL has finished executing a procedure, however, it releases these formal parameter variables. Consequently, you cannot refer to a parameter of a procedure before or after PAL has executed that procedure.

For example, the variables *amount*, *rate*, and *term* in the procedure CompVal (shown in Figure 17-8) are private to that procedure. These variables are private because they are its formal parameters. Because they are private, you can only refer to them from within the procedure; you cannot refer to them in any way from outside of the procedure.

For example, suppose that after playing the script in Figure 17-11, which calls the CompVal procedure, you press [**PAL Menu**], choose **V**alue, and type **amount**. When you press ↵, Paradox will display the message *Variable amount has not been assigned a value*. This occurs because amount (like rate and term) is private to CompVal.

Importantly, the variables *x*, *y*, and *z* in the script in Figure 17-11 are global, not private. Remember–only variables that are defined within the PROC command in the script that defines a procedure are private to that procedure. Any variables that are defined in a script that calls a procedure (as are *x*, *y*, and *z*) will be global.

The fact that the variables used in the definition of a procedure are private to that procedure has one major advantage: You don't have to worry about these variables interfering with other variables elsewhere in the script. This means that you can use any procedure in any script without worrying about whether the variables in the procedure conflict with the variables in that script.

Other Private Variables

Although the parameter variables of a procedure are private to that procedure, any other variables in that procedure will be global. For example, in the procedure

```
PROC Adder(x,y)
    z=x+y
    Return z
ENDPROC
```

x and *y* are private to the procedure *Adder*, but *z* is global. Because *z* is global, you can reference it even after the procedure has been executed. In addition, the value assigned to *z* in the procedure will replace the value of any variable named *z* that you may have defined previously during the same Paradox session.

Fortunately, there is a way to make this kind of variable private. To do this, you must list the variables you want to make private after the keyword PRIVATE following the PROC command. This keyword must immediately follow the name and arguments of the procedure, and must precede the commands that you want the procedure to execute. For example, the script

```
PROC Adder(x,y)
    PRIVATE z
    z=x+y
    Return z
ENDPROC
```

makes *z* private to *Adder*. That way, the *z* used in *Adder* will not interfere with any public *z* used elsewhere in the script, and vice-versa.

The Retval Variable

The variable *retval* gives you a way to access the value of a procedure call. As you know, when you end a procedure with a RETURN command followed by an expression,

PAL returns the value of that expression to the calling script. In addition, PAL assigns that value to the temporary variable *retval*. When PAL plays the script shown in Figure 17-8, for example, it assigns the value 1083.470594338 to the variable *retval*.

Once PAL has assigned a value to *retval*, that value remains in effect until PAL assigns another value to retval (usually when you call another procedure), until you use the RELEASE VARS command to release it, or until you exit from Paradox. To access the value returned by the procedure later in the script, then, all you have to do is reference the variable *retval*.

Releasing Procedures

The memory-resident nature of procedures has advantages and disadvantages. The main advantage, of course, is speed of execution. The primary disadvantage is that procedures occupy precious memory that could be used for other things. Even though PAL automatically undefines all procedures when it ends the play of a system of scripts, there may be times when you need to remove a procedure from RAM while a script is playing.

Fortunately, two special versions of PAL's RELEASE command allow you to undefine procedures in much the same way that you would undefine a variable or an array. To clear every currently defined procedure from RAM, just include the command *RELEASE PROCS ALL* in your script. To release only selected procedures, you must use the command form

    RELEASE PROCS *proc1,proc2,...,procn*

where *proc1*, *proc2*, and so forth are the names of the procedures that you want to clear from RAM. For example, the command *RELEASE PROCS adder,compval* would remove the procedures *Adder* and *CompVal* from RAM.

Procedure Libraries

As you first begin to work with procedures, chances are that you'll store each procedure in its own script. That way, you can activate a specific procedure by playing the script that defines it. If you plan to use the procedure only within a single script system, you may include the PROC/ENDPROC commands directly within that system so that no PLAY command is necessary. Either way, you'll activate only one procedure at a time.

As you become more experienced with procedures, you probably will find yourself using more than one script within many of your PAL applications. In these cases, you may wish to combine several PROC statements within a single script file. That way, you can activate more than one procedure with a single PLAY command. When you issue the PLAY command, of course, PAL will read each command from within each PROC command, one at a time, interpret it, and store it in RAM. These groupings of PROC statements are a primitive form of procedure library.

PAL offers an even more advanced form of procedure library, however. Through the use of PAL's WRITELIB command, you can store one or more procedures on disk in a compiled form–not as a series of PROC/ENDPROC commands. Because PAL interprets the commands before they are stored, it can execute them as soon as it reads them from disk–it does not have to interpret them first. The result is a significant time savings for most large PAL applications.

Creating a Procedure Library

You must create a library before you can store any procedures in it. To create a procedure library, you must use PAL's CREATELIB command. The form of this command is

    CREATELIB *libraryname*

where *libraryname* is a string expression that specifies the name for the library you want to create. This name may be from one to eight characters in length and may contain any characters that DOS allows in a file name. If the library is not in the current directory, you must include the full path in the first argument. (Remember to use two backslashes wherever you normally would use only one). When you issue the CREATELIB command, PAL creates an empty library file with the name you specify, plus the file name extension .LIB. For example, you would use the command *CREATELIB "lib1"* to create a library named LIB1.LIB.

Writing Procedures to a Library

Once you have created a procedure library, you can store one or more procedures in it. To store a procedure in a library, you must use PAL's WRITELIB command. The form of this command is

    WRITELIB *libraryname proc1,...,procn*

where *libraryname* is a string expression that specifies the library into which you want to store the procedures, and *proc1,...,procn* are the names of the procedures you want to store in that library.

A procedure must be in RAM before you can store it in a procedure library. That means that PAL has to read the PROC command that defines the procedure you want to save within the same script system that contains the WRITELIB command that saves it. If your procedures are stored in individual .SC files, then saving a procedure to a library is a simple matter of designing and playing a script that contains two commands: a PLAY command that loads the procedure-defining script, and a WRITELIB command that saves that procedure into a library.

For example, suppose you want to save the procedure named CompVal defined by the script named PROC1 shown in Figure 17-8 into a library named *FCNS.LIB*. If FCNS.LIB did not yet exist, you would write and play the single-line script *CREATELIB "Fcns"*. (The best way to do this is with a miniscript.) Once the library exists, you would write and play the script

    PLAY "Proc1" WRITELIB "Fcns" CompVal

Again, you probably will want to use a miniscript to do this. When PAL plays this script, it first will play the script *Proc1*, which interprets the procedure *CompVal* and loads it into RAM. Once CompVal is in RAM, the command *WRITELIB "Fcns" CompVal* saves a compiled copy of CompVal into the procedure library FCNS.

You can use the WRITELIB command again and again to store additional procedures into a library. Each time you use the WRITELIB command to access a library that already contains one or more procedures, PAL will add the new procedure(s) to the library. Any procedure library can hold up to 50 procedures–more than you are likely to want to put in a single library.

Reading Procedures from a Library

Once you have written one or more procedures into a library, you can use PAL's READLIB command to retrieve one or more procedures from that library into RAM. The form of the READLIB command is

    READLIB *libraryname proc1,...,procn*

where *libraryname* is a string expression that specifies the library that contains the procedure(s) that you want to activate, and *proc1,...,procn* are the names of those procedures. If the library is not in the current directory, the argument must include the full path name.

For example, suppose you want to load the procedure named *CompVal* from the procedure library FCNS. To do this, you would issue the command *READLIB "Fcns" CompVal*, either as a part of a larger script or as a miniscript. When PAL executes this command, it reads the procedure *CompVal* from the FCNS library in the current directory. Because the procedures in a library are already interpreted, PAL does not have to interpret CompVal as it reads it into RAM. This saves time relative to retrieving a procedure from a script file–a process that involves both reading the procedure from disk and interpreting it.

Once the procedure is in RAM, you can call it in exactly the same way you would if you had read it from a script file. Of course, the procedure will remain active until the end of play of the current script system, or until you remove it with the RELEASE PROCS command, whichever comes first.

Taking an Inventory of the Contents of a Library

PAL's INFOLIB command allows you to inventory the contents of a procedure library. When PAL reads this command, it will display a temporary LIST table that catalogues the procedures in the library. Like the LIST tables you saw in Chapter 6, the LIST table that contains the procedure list includes two fields: Procedure and Size. The Procedure field lists the names of each procedure in the library. The Size field lists the number of bytes occupied by each procedure.

Removing Procedures from a Library

Although it is easy to add a procedure to a procedure library, it is next to impossible to remove a procedure from a library once it is stored. The only way to remove a procedure from a library is to exit to DOS, delete the .LIB file, use the CREATELIB command to recreate it, and then use the WRITELIB command to save all but the procedures you wanted to remove back into the library.

Autoloading Libraries

PARADOX.LIB is PAL's default autoload library. By autoload, we don't mean that PAL will load every procedure from PARADOX.LIB automatically whenever you load Paradox into your computer. Instead, we mean that PAL will look to that library if you call a procedure that it cannot find in RAM.

When you call a procedure, PAL first looks for that procedure in RAM. If PAL cannot find that procedure in RAM, it looks for a library named *PARADOX.LIB*. If that library exists, PAL will search for the procedure within that library. If PAL finds the procedure in PARADOX.LIB, it will read that procedure from disk and then execute it. If PAL cannot find the PARADOX.LIB library, or if PARADOX.LIB does not contain the procedure you called, a script error will result.

Although PARADOX.LIB is the default autoload procedure library, you can command PAL to look to another library instead. To do this, you must use the = command to store the name of the autoload library in the special variable *autolib*. For example, suppose you want PAL to look to a library named JOE when it cannot find a called procedure in RAM. To make this change, you would play the command *autolib="Joe"* prior to making the procedure call. Once you issue this command, PAL will look to JOE.LIB instead of PARADOX.LIB whenever you call a procedure that is not in RAM. JOE.LIB will remain the autoload library until PAL reads another *autolib=libname* command. When you begin a new Paradox session, however, PARADOX.LIB will be the default library.

The PAL Debugger

In Chapter 14, we introduced the PAL Debugger. The PAL Debugger is a useful tool that lets you test your scripts and identify errors within them. From within the PAL Debugger, you can step through a script one command at a time, viewing the results of each command as PAL executes it. In this way, you can identify errors within the script, and, in some cases, correct them.

Entering the Debugger from an Error

In Chapter 14, we showed you how PAL automatically checks for errors as it plays a script. If PAL encounters an error during the execution of a script, it will pause, display the message *Script error–select Cancel or Debug from menu* in the message area, and present the two choices Cancel and Debug at the top of the screen. If you choose Cancel, PAL will cancel the execution of the script and return you to the Paradox workspace. If you choose Debug, however, PAL will take you into the PAL Debugger.

When you enter the Debugger from an error, PAL does a number of things. First, it lifts the PAL canvas to reveal the Paradox workspace. Second, it displays the error-containing line of the script in reverse video across the bottom of the screen. Third, it displays the name of the script and the number of the line that it is debugging on the second line from the bottom of the screen. Fourth, it uses a solid right arrow (the Debugger cursor) to point to the error within that line. Fifth, it presents an explanation of that error in the message area. Figure 17-12 shows an example of this basic Debugger screen.

Figure 17-12 The Basic Debugger Screen

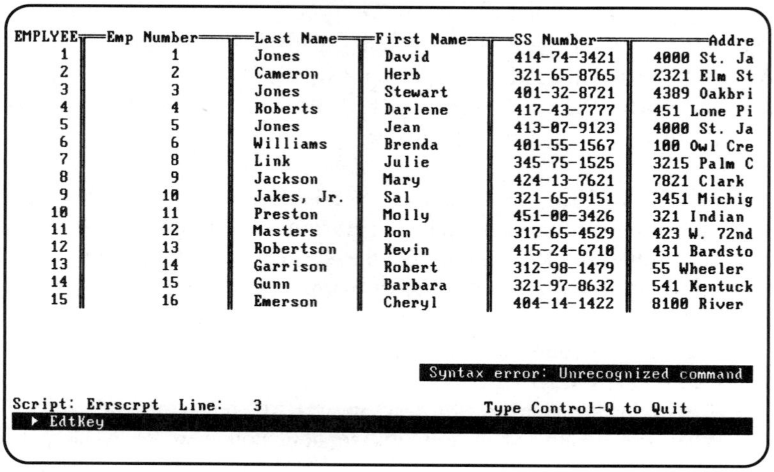

```
┌─────────────────────────────────────────────────────────────────────────┐
│EMPLYEE┬─Emp Number─┬─Last Name─┬─First Name─┬─SS Number─┬─────────Addre │
│   1   │     1      │  Jones    │   David    │414-74-3421│ 4000 St. Ja   │
│   2   │     2      │  Cameron  │   Herb     │321-65-8765│ 2321 Elm St   │
│   3   │     3      │  Jones    │   Stewart  │401-32-8721│ 4389 Oakbri   │
│   4   │     4      │  Roberts  │   Darlene  │417-43-7777│ 451 Lone Pi   │
│   5   │     5      │  Jones    │   Jean     │413-07-9123│ 4000 St. Ja   │
│   6   │     6      │  Williams │   Brenda   │401-55-1567│ 100 Owl Cre   │
│   7   │     8      │  Link     │   Julie    │345-75-1525│ 3215 Palm C   │
│   8   │     9      │  Jackson  │   Mary     │424-13-7621│ 7821 Clark    │
│   9   │    10      │  Jakes, Jr.│  Sal      │321-65-9151│ 3451 Michig   │
│  10   │    11      │  Preston  │   Molly    │451-00-3426│ 321 Indian    │
│  11   │    12      │  Masters  │   Ron      │317-65-4529│ 423 W. 72nd   │
│  12   │    13      │  Robertson│   Kevin    │415-24-6710│ 431 Bardsto   │
│  13   │    14      │  Garrison │   Robert   │312-98-1479│ 55 Wheeler    │
│  14   │    15      │  Gunn     │   Barbara  │321-97-8632│ 541 Kentuck   │
│  15   │    16      │  Emerson  │   Cheryl   │404-14-1422│ 8100 River    │
│                                                                         │
│                                       Syntax error: Unrecognized command│
│ Script: Errscrpt  Line:   3                   Type Control-Q to Quit    │
│     ▶ EdtKey                                                            │
└─────────────────────────────────────────────────────────────────────────┘
```

Types of Errors

PAL categorizes script errors into types: Syntax errors and run errors. A syntax error results when PAL is unable to recognize a command in a script. In most cases, this happens when you misspell a command, include an incorrect number of arguments or list them in the wrong order, or omit a keyword. For example, the misspelled command *EDT* would cause a syntax error, as would the use of the command *WHILE* without the keyword ENDWHILE. Whenever PAL has entered the Debugger as the result of a syntax error, the message in the message window will begin with the words *Syntax error:*.

A run error results when PAL encounters a command that has the correct syntax, but is used in the wrong context. For example, the command *[]=5*, which attempts to make an entry into a table, will cause a run error if PAL is not in the edit mode. Similarly, the command *PLAY "Abc"* will result in a run error if the file ABC.SC is not in the current directory. If the message in the Debugger's message window does not begin with the words *Syntax error*, then PAL has encountered a run error.

The important difference between these two types of errors is the extent to which you can recover from them within the PAL Debugger. If you encounter a syntax error, there's really nothing to do but exit from the Debugger and edit the script. If you encounter a run error, however, you generally can make a temporary correction and continue playing the script. Because syntax errors are more common and you can do less with them, we will cover them first. Then we will show you how to use the Debugger to recover from a run error.

Debugging Syntax Errors

A syntax error results when PAL is unable to recognize a command within a script due to a misspelling, missing keywords, an inappropriate number of arguments, and so forth. Unfortunately, there's not much you can do about a syntax error from within the Debugger, other than write down the explanation of the error, exit from the Debugger, and edit the script. To do this, you could press [Crtl]-[Q] to exit from the Debugger, cancel the execution of the script, and return to the workspace, then use the [Menu] Scripts Edit command to bring the script into the PAL Editor and correct the mistake.

Fortunately, there is an easier way to perform these actions. While you are looking at the Debugger screen, press the **[PAL Menu]** key ([Alt]-[F10]) to reveal the Debugger menu shown in Figure 17-13. If you choose Editor from this menu, PAL will exit from the Debugger, cancel the play of the script, clear the Paradox workspace, enter the Script Editor, load the flawed script, and position the cursor on the command that caused the error. You'll want to use this command to correct almost all syntax errors.

Figure 17-13 The Debugger Menu

```
Value  Step Next Go MiniScript Where? Quit Pop Editor        Main
Calculate the value of an expression.
```

Debugging Run Errors

Fortunately, the PAL Debugger gives you more flexibility to deal with run errors than it does with syntax errors. When you enter the Debugger due to a run error, you can exit from the Debugger, edit the script, and replay it, just as you would for a syntax error. In most cases, however, you can adjust for the error from within the Debugger and continue playing the script. After the script has played to completion, you can enter the Script Editor and edit the script to remove the error.

Figure 17-14   A Script That Causes a Run Error

```
Designing script Runerror                                           Script
....+...10....+...20....+...30....+...40....+...50....+...60....+...70....+...80
EDIT "Abc"
SCAN
 FOR ISBLANK([Quantity])
  [Quantity]=0
ENDSCAN
```

For example, suppose that the table ABC is in the directory c:\paradox\data, and that the current directory is c:\paradox\info. Because ABC is not in the current directory, if you play the script in Figure 17-14, PAL will balk at the command *EDIT "Abc"*, and a run error will occur. If you choose **Debug** from the Script Error menu PAL displays when it encounters the error, the screen shown in Figure 17-15 will appear. As you can see, PAL displays the line *EDIT "Abc"* at the bottom of the screen, points to that command, and presents the error message *Cannot find Abc table* in the message area.

Figure 17-15   Another Debugger Screen

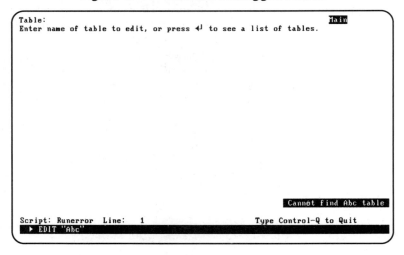

When PAL enters the Debugger, it lifts the PAL canvas to reveal the Paradox workspace and pauses the execution of the script at the point where the error occurred. For example, the prompt at the top of Figure 17-15 indicates that PAL has issued the [Menu] Modify Edit command and is waiting for the name of a table.

During this pause, you can use the Paradox menus, special keys, and even other scripts (usually miniscripts) to work with the objects on the Paradox workspace, just as if you weren't in a script at all. Once you use these techniques to adjust for the error, you can command PAL to resume the execution of the script.

Making the Command Usable: The Go Option

The error in the script in Figure 17-14 occurred because the table ABC was not in the current directory. There are two ways to deal with this problem. The first is to copy the table into the current directory. To do this, press the **[Esc]** key to exit from the Edit command back to the Main menu. Then issue the **[Menu]** **T**ools **C**opy **T**able command, specify the location and name of the table to copy (in this case, **c:\paradox\data\ABC**), and specify the name for the copy, **ABC**. When you press ↵, Paradox will copy ABC into the current directory. (Remember–you're doing all this from within the Debugger.)

Once ABC is in the current directory, you can resume playing the script. In this case, you'll want PAL to continue by executing the command *EDIT "Abc"*–the one that PAL is pointing to within the Debugger. To resume the play of the script with that command, just press the **[PAL Menu]** key to reveal the Debugger menu, and select the **G**o option. (You also can issue this command by pressing [Ctrl]-[G]). Either way, this command tells PAL to resume playing the script, starting with the current command. Since you have copied ABC into the current directory, PAL will be able to execute the command *EDIT "Abc"*. As long as the script does not contain any other errors, PAL will continue to play it through to the end, just as if it never had entered the Debugger.

"Replacing" the Command: The Next Option

The second way to deal with this problem is to supply a replacement for the command that contains the error. You can do this either from the keyboard or with a script. In this case, you could press **[Esc]** to return to the Main menu, issue the **M**odify **E**dit command, type **c:\paradox\data\ABC**, and press ↵. As soon as you issue this command, PAL will bring the ABC table to the Paradox workspace in the edit mode, which is exactly what the script command *EDIT "Abc"* was supposed to do.

Once you have made this correction, you can continue playing the script. Because you have executed a command that takes the place of the command that PAL is debugging, however, you will want to skip that command and resume execution of the script with the command that follows it. To skip the command to which PAL is pointing, press the **[PAL Menu]** key to reveal the PAL menu, then choose **N**ext. (You can also issue this command by pressing [Ctrl]-[N].) When you issue this command, PAL skips the command to which it currently is pointing (in this case, the one that caused the error) and points to the command that follows (in this case, SCAN). Once PAL has skipped the command that you have replaced, you can issue the **G**o command to resume the play of the script. Assuming that there are no more errors in the script, PAL will play it to completion. At that point, you can enter the Script Editor and correct the error within the script itself.

Using a Miniscript to Correct a Run Error

As we mentioned earlier, you can also correct a run error from within the Debugger by designing and playing a miniscript. The MiniScript option on the PAL Debugger menu makes this possible. For example, suppose you are running the script shown in Figure 17-14, and PAL has presented the Debugger screen shown in Figure 17-15. To correct the error, you could press the [PAL Menu] key to reveal the Debugger menu, choose MiniScript, and type the command COPY "c:\\paradox\\data\\ABC" "ABC".

When you press ↵, PAL will not play this command immediately, as it would if you had designed the miniscript outside of the Debugger. Instead, it will place the miniscript in the highlighted script line at the bottom of the screen. To play the miniscript, you must press [PAL Menu] and issue the Go command (or press [Ctrl]-[G]). When you do this, PAL will play the miniscript in its entirety, copying the table ABC into the current directory. When PAL finishes playing the miniscript, it will again present the error-causing command in the Debugger's script line and await your instructions. In this case, you'll want to choose Go from the Debugger menu (or press [Ctrl]-[G]) to resume the play of the script. Since you have copied ABC into the current directory, PAL will be able to play the current command, EDIT "Abc", and continue to execute the remainder of the script.

In most cases, using a miniscript to correct a run error is more time-consuming than using menu commands. For this reason, you probably will not use miniscripts within the Debugger all that often. When the run error is due to a problem with a PAL command, however, a miniscript provides the only way to correct it. For example, suppose PAL encounters the command FOR ISBLANK([Quntity]) within a SCAN statement. The misspelling of the field name Quantity results in a run error. To correct this error and continue playing the script, you first must issue the MiniScript command, type FOR ISBLANK([Quantity]) and press ↵. Then you must issue the [PAL Menu] Go command to play the miniscript. Finally, you must issue the Next command to skip the line of the original script that caused the error, then issue the [PAL Menu] Go command again to continue playing the script.

Entering the Debugger Voluntarily

Although you will enter the Debugger most commonly as the result of errors in your scripts, you can also enter it without encountering an error. There are three ways to do this. First, in any situation other than during the playing or debugging of a script, you can enter the Debugger by pressing the [PAL Menu] key ([Alt]-[F10]), choosing Debug from the PAL menu, and typing the name of a script. When you enter the Debugger in this way, PAL will present a screen much like the one shown in Figure 17-15. Because you did not enter the Debugger as the result of an error, however, PAL will display the first line of the script–which may not contain an error–at the bottom of the screen. Since no error has occurred, no error message will appear in the message area.

The second way to enter the Debugger is to include the PAL command DEBUG in a script. This command allows you to debug a script during the execution of that script. When PAL encounters a DEBUG command within a script, it suspends execution of that script and enters the Debugger, placing at the bottom of the screen the line that contains the command that follows the DEBUG command. The arrow will point to the command that follows the DEBUG command. Because PAL did not enter the Debugger as the result of an error, it will not display an explanation in the message area.

The third way to enter the Debugger is to press [Ctrl]-[Break] during the execution of a script. When you do this, PAL will pause the execution of the script and will present the options Cancel and Debug. If you choose Debug, PAL will enter the Debugger, place the line that it was executing at the bottom of the screen, and point to the command that it was about to execute when you interrupted the script. If you choose Cancel, PAL will return you to the main Paradox workspace. (Of course, [Ctrl]-[Break] will be inactive during the play of a password-protected script.)

The Step Command

Now that you know how to enter the PAL Debugger outside the context of an error, you probably are asking, "Why would I want to?" The answer is: To better understand the flow of your script. By using the Debugger menu's Step command, you can execute a script one command at a time, at your own pace. Because the PAL canvas is lifted while PAL is in the Debugger, you can view the effect of each command on the Paradox workspace as PAL executes it. When you issue the Step command, either by pressing the [PAL Menu] key to reveal the Debugger menu and choosing Step, or by pressing [Ctrl]-[S], PAL will execute the command to which the Debugger cursor currently is pointing. After PAL executes that command, it will move the Debugger cursor to the next command and await your instructions.

Other Debugger Commands

In addition to Go, Next, Step, MiniScript, Editor, and Quit, the Debugger menu contains three other useful commands: Value, Where?, and Pop. Although you probably will not use these three commands as often as you will the other six, they will come in handy in some programming situations.

The Value Command

The Value command on the Debugger menu does the same thing that the Value command on the PAL menu does; it lets you calculate the value of an equation or function or discern the current value of a variable. You can use the Value command from within the Debugger to determine the current value of a variable. For example, suppose you are debugging a script that uses a counter variable x. You can use the Value command to determine the current value of the counter variable from within the Debugger. To do this, you issue the Value command (either by choosing it from the PAL menu or by pressing [Ctrl]-[V]) and then type *x*. When you press ↵, PAL will display the current value of *x* in the message area.

The Where? Command

The Where? command on the Debugger menu allows you to determine where you are within a multiple-level script. When you issue this command (either by accessing the Debugger menu and choosing Where? or simply by pressing [Ctrl]-[W]), PAL will present a graphic representation of the levels of the script and pinpoint the level of the script that contains the command that PAL currently is debugging.

For example, suppose that PAL is playing a script named MAIN. This script contains the command *PLAY "SUB1"*, which calls a script SUB1. Also suppose that the script *SUB1* contains a WHILE command without a matching ENDWHILE keyword. When PAL comes to the end of SUB1, it will stop the play of the script and present the choices Cancel and Debug. If you choose Debug, PAL will present the Debugger screen. If you issue the Where? command at this point, your screen will look like the one shown in Figure 17-16. As you can see, PAL represents the levels of the script as a series of overlapping "pages." The upper level is the script MAIN. The second level is the script SUB1. The third level is the Debugger. The message *(You are here)* indicates that PAL currently is within the Debugger. As soon as you press any key, PAL will return you to the Debugger screen.

Figure 17-16   The Where? Command

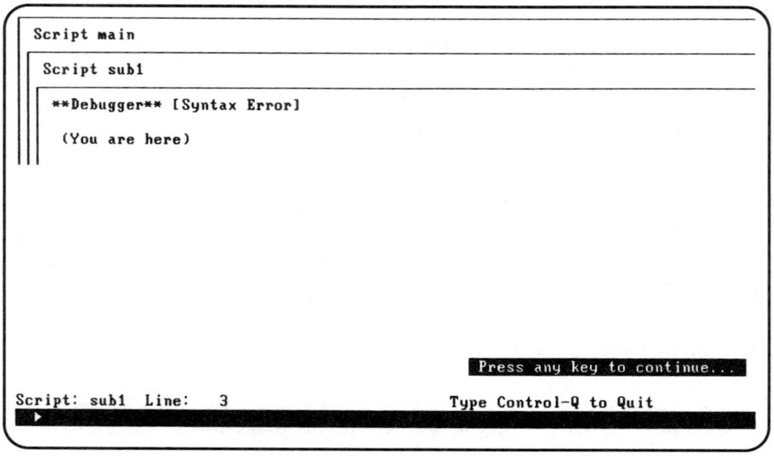

```
Script main
  Script sub1
    **Debugger** [Syntax Error]
      (You are here)




                                    Press any key to continue...
  Script: sub1  Line:   3             Type Control-Q to Quit
  ▶
```

The Pop Command

The Pop command is another tool that you can use to debug multiple-level scripts. This command causes PAL to jump out of the current subroutine, back to the command that follows the command that called the subroutine. Once you are back at the higher level script, you can use the Go command to continue playing the script. You can issue the Pop command either by choosing it from the Debugger menu or by pressing [Ctrl]-[P].

Printing Your Scripts

PAL's final debugging tool–printing a hard copy of a script–is not a part of the PAL Debugger. In fact, you cannot print a script while you are in the Debugger–you must be editing that script from within the PAL Script Editor to print it. To print a copy of the script that you are editing, you issue the [Menu] Print command or press the [Instant Report] key ([Alt]-[F7]). Either way, PAL will send a copy of the script to your printer. You can use the resulting hard copy to document and debug your scripts.

Tilde Variables

In the five PAL chapters of *The Paradox Companion*, we have used variables only within the context of PAL programs. However, you also can use variables within your Paradox queries. The ability to use variables in queries allows you to create selection conditions that are based on the results of PAL functions and formulas.

Using a variable as a selection condition within a query is as simple as prefacing that variable with a tilde (~) and entering it into the appropriate position in the query. Before you evaluate the query, of course, you should make sure that variable contains the value you want to use as the basis of the selection condition. You commonly will use a miniscript to assign values to selection-condition variables.

For example, suppose you want to select from the simple PEOPLE table shown in Figure 17-17 the records with Age entries that exceed the average of all the entries in the Age field. To do this, you need to do two things: Store the average of the Age field entries in a variable and design a query whose selection condition is based upon the tilde form of that variable. The order in which you perform these two tasks is not important.

Figure 17-17 The PEOPLE Table

```
Viewing People table: Record 1 of 10                        Main
PEOPLE         Name                Age
    1     Doug                      28
    2     Tom                       26
    3     Judy                      25
    4     Gena                      28
    5     Ken                       35
    6     Julie                     26
    7     Steve                     27
    8     Barbara                   36
    9     Denise                    31
   10     Pat                       21
```

In this case, we'll use a miniscript to calculate the average value of the entries in the Age column and store that result in a variable named *avg*. To do this, press the **[PAL Menu]** key ([Alt]-[F10]), choose MiniScript, and type **avg=CAVERAGE("People","Age")**. When you press ↵, PAL will evaluate this command and store the value 28.3 in the variable *avg*. To confirm that *avg* holds this value, you can issue the Value command, type **avg**, and press ↵.

After storing the average Age value in *avg*, you can design a query that uses the tilde form of that variable to select all records with Age field entries greater than that average. To design this query, issue the **[Menu]** Ask command and select the **PEOPLE** table. Once the blank query form appears on the screen, press the **[Check Mark]** key while the cursor is in the record number column to select both fields of the table. Then move the cursor to the Age column and type the selection condition **>~avg**. Figure 17-18 shows the completed query.

Figure 17-18   A Tilde-variable Query

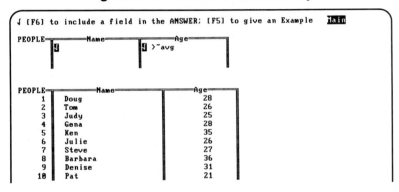

When you press **[Do-It!]** to execute this query, Paradox will present the ANSWER table shown in Figure 17-19. As you can see, Paradox has selected only the three records with Age field entries that exceed the value stored in *avg*: 28.3.

Because you can store the result of any PAL function or equation in a variable, and because the tilde symbol allows you to use any PAL variable within a query, you can design queries that select records based on the value returned by any PAL formula or function. Because the queries refer to variables, not literal values, they will select different sets of records each time the value of the variable changes. For example, if you add an eleventh record, with the Age field entry 100, to the PEOPLE table and again use a miniscript to calculate an average Age field entry, PAL will store the value 34.8 in *avg*. When you re-execute the query shown in Figure 17-18, Paradox will select only the fifth and eighth records from PEOPLE.

Figure 17-19 The ANSWER Table

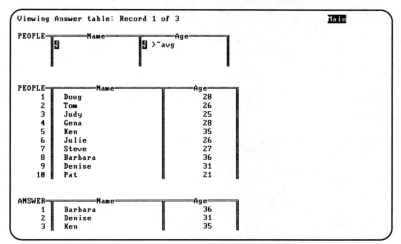

Auto-executing Scripts

Throughout the PAL section of this book, we have executed scripts either by choosing Play from the Scripts or PAL menus, or by including a PLAY command in a script. Either way, you had to instruct PAL explicitly to play the script. In certain circumstances, however, PAL will play a script automatically as soon as you load Paradox into your computer. We'll refer to a script that plays automatically as an auto-executing script.

INIT.SC Scripts

Whenever you load Paradox into your computer, PAL will look in the current directory for a script named INIT.SC. If PAL finds a script with that name, it will play that script as soon as Paradox has finished loading. This feature lets you create complete turnkey applications or automate housekeeping tasks, such as changing the current directory.

For example, Figure 16-20 in the previous chapter shows a script that you might want to set up as an auto-executing script. When PAL plays this script, it presents a menu that allows you to select the directory in which you want to work.

To make this script an auto-executing script, you need only give it the name INIT.SC. If you have already created the script, you can change its name by issuing the [Menu] Tools Rename Script command. Once you have changed the name of the script to INIT, Paradox will run it automatically whenever you load Paradox. When PAL runs the script, it will offer four choices: Orders, General Ledger, Accounts Payable, and Cancel. If you choose any of the first three options, PAL will issue a SETDIR command to change the current directory. If you choose Cancel, PAL will exit from the script without changing the directory. When Paradox is loaded, the active directory will be the one you specified.

Running a Script from DOS

Paradox provides yet another way to execute a script automatically as Paradox loads. Ordinarily, you will load Paradox into your computer by typing the word *paradox* at the DOS prompt. If you follow this command with the name of a script, however, Paradox will play that script as soon as Paradox has been loaded. For example, if the script named *START.SC* is in the Paradox directory (the one that holds your Paradox system files), then you can load Paradox and play that script automatically by typing **paradox start** at the DOS prompt.

If the script you want to play is not in the directory that holds your Paradox system files, you must preface the name of the script with its drive and/or directory. For example, if START.SC is in the directory c:\paradox\scripts, then you would type **paradox c:\paradox\scripts\start** or **paradox scripts\start** to play *START.SC*.

You can use this method in place of or in conjunction with an INIT script. If you type a script name at the DOS prompt, and the current directory contains a script named INIT.SC, PAL will play the INIT script before it plays the one you specified.

If either an INIT script or a script that you name at the DOS prompt ends with an EXIT command, then you will return to DOS after the play of the script is over. This technique allows you to create fully automated applications that never give full control of Paradox to the user. If you often name a certain script at the DOS command line, you may wish to include it in a simple .BAT file.

Other PAL Commands

In this and the previous four chapters of *The Paradox Companion*, we have presented most but not all of PAL's programming commands. In the final part of this chapter, we'll briefly discuss the nine commands that we missed: BEEP, ECHO, EXECUTE, KEYPRESS, LOCATE, MOVETO, RESET, RUN, and TYPEIN.

The BEEP Command

The BEEP command instructs PAL to issue a short beep. This command, which accepts no arguments, is useful for signaling the end of a script, drawing attention to a message, and so forth. For example, the script fragment

```
@10,0
?? "Enter a number between 1 and 10: "
BEEP BEEP BEEP
ACCEPT "N" to guess
```

uses three consecutive beeps to alert the user that he or she needs to make an entry.

The ECHO Command

In most cases, the PAL canvas obscures the workspace during the execution of a script. PAL's ECHO command lets you lift the PAL canvas and watch the script manipulate the Paradox workspace. The form of this command is

ECHO *speed*

where the single argument *speed* must be one of the following four keywords: NORMAL, FAST, SLOW, or OFF. The NORMAL option commands PAL to play the script at close to the speed it would play if it were not revealing the Paradox workspace at all. The SLOW option instructs PAL to play the script slower than normal. The FAST option causes PAL to play the script at about the speed you could issue commands from the keyboard. The ECHO OFF command tells PAL to drop the PAL canvas again. The effect of this command is much like that of the ShowPlay command.

The EXECUTE Command

PAL's EXECUTE command allows you to use string formulas to produce PAL command statements that PAL will execute just like any other PAL command. The form of this command is

EXECUTE *stringexpression*

where the argument of the command is a string expression (usually a formula) that returns a valid PAL command sequence.

The script shown in Figure 17-20 shows a common example of the use of this command. The first two statements in the script clear the PAL canvas, position the cursor at the beginning of row 10, and display the *Destination field?* prompt. The ACCEPT command stores your response (which should be a field name) as a string in the variable *fld*. If you type *Address*, for example, PAL will store the string *Address* in *fld*.

Figure 17-20   The EXECUTE Command

```
Designing script Exescrpt                                    Script
....+...10....+...20....+...30....+...40....+...50....+...60....+...70....+...80
CLEAR
@10,0
?? "Destination field? "
ACCEPT "A20" to fld
EXECUTE 'MOVETO ["+fld+"]"
```

Unfortunately, you cannot use this variable directly in the argument of a MOVETO command. If you use the command *MOVETO [fld]* within a script, for example, PAL will try to move the cursor to the field named *fld*–it will not recognize the word *fld* as the name of a variable.

To use this stored field name as the argument of a MOVETO command, you must use PAL's EXECUTE command. For example, the command *EXECUTE "MOVETO ["+fld+"]"* in the script in Figure 17-20 allows you to use the value *fld* in the MOVETO command. When PAL reads this command, it first evaluates the argument–the string formula *"MOVETO ["+fld+"]"*. Since *fld* contains the string *Address*, this formula returns the long string *MOVETO [Address]*. Since this string is the result of the argument of an EXECUTE command, PAL treats it just like a literal MOVETO command. As a result, PAL moves the cursor to the Address field of the current record.

The KEYPRESS Command

The KEYPRESS command allows PAL to type a character from within a script. The form of this command is

KEYPRESS *keycode*

where *keycode* is the PAL keycode expression representing the key PAL should press.

When used in conjunction with the GETCHAR() function and IF command, KEYPRESS allows you to set up keyboard filters that intercept and test every character typed from the keyboard. If a character typed is among the ones you have told KEYPRESS to look for, PAL will take the action you specify. If the character is not among the ones you are looking for, PAL will pass that character on to Paradox.

The script shown in Figure 17-21 demonstrates the use of the KEYPRESS command within a simple keyboard filter that disables the use of the [Help] key. The *ECHO NORMAL* command assures that you will be able to see what is happening on the Paradox workspace as you issue commands from the keyboard. The *WHILE True/ENDWHILE* command that encloses the remainder of the script assures that the macro will stay in effect for the duration of the current Paradox session. The command *x=GETCHAR()* tells PAL to wait for you to type a key and store the ASCII code for that key in the variable *x*. The IF statement that follows tests to see if you pressed the [Help] key. If so, PAL beeps but does not pass the keystroke on to Paradox. If you press any key but [Help], however, PAL will execute the command *KEYPRESS x*. The effect of this command is to pass the keystroke on to Paradox, just as if it never had trapped the key at all.

Figure 17-21   The KEYPRESS Command

```
Designing script Keyprssc                                    Script
....+...10....+...20....+...30....+...40....+...50....+...60....+...70....+...80
ECHO NORMAL
WHILE True
  x=GETCHAR()
  IF x=ASC("Help")
    THEN BEEP
    ELSE KEYPRESS x
  ENDIF
ENDWHILE
```

The LOCATE Command

PAL's LOCATE command allows PAL to search a table for a record that matches the entries you specify in one or more fields. If PAL finds a matching record, it will move the cursor to that record. This command has two forms. The first form,

> LOCATE *value*

searches for the first occurrence of its argument, *value*, among the entries in the current field of the current table, starting at the top of that field.

The second form of the LOCATE command is more complex than the first. This form

> LOCATE *value1,...,valuen*

searches for exact matches of its value arguments in the first *n* fields of the current table, starting at the top of that table. For example, if the cursor is in a table whose first two fields are First Name and Last Name, respectively, the command *LOCATE "John","Smith"* will search the table for the first record that has the entry *John* in its First Name column and the entry *Smith* in its Last Name column. Although you can include as many value arguments as the table has fields, you cannot skip fields. That is, if a LOCATE command has three arguments, PAL will search the first three fields of the table for matches.

You can use the keyword NEXT with either form of LOCATE. When you use this keyword, which must come between the LOCATE command and its value arguments, PAL will start the search not at the top of the current table, but at the current position of the cursor within that table. For example, if the cursor is in the Last Name field of the third record of a table when PAL reads the command *LOCATE NEXT "Smith"*, PAL will search for the entry *Smith* in the Last Name field, starting with the fourth record.

In addition to moving the cursor to a matching record, the LOCATE command assigns a value to the variable *retval*. If the LOCATE command finds a matching record, it places the logical constant True in the variable *retval*, in addition to moving the cursor to that record. If the LOCATE command does not find a matching record, it stores the value FALSE in that variable and does not move the cursor.

The MOVETO Command

In Chapter 14, we presented two forms of PAL's MOVETO command. There are two more forms of MOVETO. The third form

    MOVETO *imagenumber*

commands PAL to move the cursor to the image specified by the numeric expression *imagenumber*. The images are numbered from the top of the workspace to the bottom so that image number 1 is the top image on the workspace.

The fourth form of the MOVETO command is

    MOVETO *imagestring*

where *imagestring* is a string expression that specifies the name of the image to which you want to move. For example, the command *MOVETO "Emplyee"* moves the cursor to the EMPLYEE table, provided it is on the workspace. This command has the same effect as the form *MOVETO [Emplyee->]*.

The RESET command

PAL's RESET command cancels any activity currently in process on the workspace (such as editing a table or designing a report), returns Paradox to the main mode, and clears the Paradox workspace. The principal use of this command is to clear the workspace prior to executing a script. The RESET command does not alter the definitions of any procedures, variables, arrays, or macros.

The RUN Command

PAL's RUN command allows you to exit to DOS temporarily, run an external program, and then return to Paradox, all with a single command. The form of this command is

    RUN *commandline*

where *commandline* is the name of the program or utility you want to run. If the program is not in the current directory, you must specify the path to that directory (remember to use dual backslashes).

For example, the command *RUN "Format A:\"* will exit from Paradox and run the DOS utility program Format. When the Format command is finished, PAL will return you to Paradox. If more PAL commands follow, PAL will continue executing the script. If RUN is the last or only command in the script, PAL will return you to the Paradox workspace, exactly as you left it.

The optional keyword SLEEP instructs PAL to wait for a specified period of time after exiting from the external program before it returns you to Paradox. This delay is useful when you use the RUN command to issue a DOS command such as DIR and want to view the results for a few seconds. This keyword must precede the commandline argument and must be followed by a numeric expression that specifies the number of milliseconds you want PAL to wait. For example, the command *RUN SLEEP 5000 "Dir A:\"* displays a directory of the contents of drive A, then waits for five seconds before returning to Paradox.

The TYPEIN Command

PAL's TYPEIN command allows you to "type" the value of any expression into Paradox at the present position of the cursor. The form of this command is

TYPEIN *expression*

where *expression* is the expression whose value you want PAL to type. You can use this command in any situation where you normally would type characters from the keyboard.

The TYPEIN command lets you type the value of an expression into a form, report, or script–not just a table. For example, suppose the variable z contains the string *Sales Report for FY 1986*. You want to use this string as the title of a report you are designing. To enter this text into the report, just position the cursor where you want the text to appear, press **[PAL Menu]**, choose MiniScript, and type **TYPEIN z**. When you press ↵, PAL will type the contents of the variable z–the string *Sales Report for FY 1986*–at the current position of the cursor.

Conclusion

This chapter concludes our discussion of PAL programming. In this chapter, we presented some other important PAL features, like the Value command, miniscripts, macros, arrays, procedures, the PAL Debugger, and such powerful but infrequently used PAL commands as RESET and LOCATE.

Appendix

Importing and Exporting Files

If you are like many Paradox users, you probably also use other programs, such as Lotus 1-2-3, Symphony, PFS: File, or dBASE III. If this is true for you, the chances are good that, sooner or later, you'll need to export information from Paradox to another program or import data from another program into Paradox. For example, you may want to import a file from dBASE III into Paradox or export a table from Paradox to Lotus 1-2-3. Fortunately, Paradox makes it easy to export and import data.

In this appendix, we'll show you how to import and export data. We'll also discuss the relevant part of the Paradox Custom Configuration Program–the AsciiConvert command.

[Menu] Tools ExportImport

Paradox has the ability to import data from and export data to Lotus 1-2-3 (Release 1A and Release 2.0), Symphony (Release 1.0 and Release 1.1), dBASE (II, III, and III+), PFS: File (or the IBM Filing Assistant), VisiCalc, and ASCII text files. The command that allows you to import and export data is [Menu] Tools ExportImport. When you issue this command, you see a menu like the one in Figure A-1.

Figure A-1   The ExportImport Menu

```
Export  Import                                              Main
Convert from Paradox format to another file format.
```

As you can see, this menu offers two choices: Export and Import. The Export command lets you export data from Paradox to another program's file format. If you choose the Export command from the menu in Figure A-1, Paradox will display the menu shown in Figure A-2. This menu offers options for each of the programs to which Paradox can export files.

Figure A-2   The Export Menu

```
1-2-3  Symphony  Dbase  Pfs  Visicalc  Ascii              Main
Export to a .WKS or a .WK1 file.
```

The Import command lets you import data from another program's files into Paradox. If you choose Import from the ExportImport menu, Paradox will display the menu shown in Figure A-3. As you can see, this menu offers the same choices as the Export menu.

Figure A-3 The Import Menu

Lotus 1-2-3

Many Paradox users also use Lotus 1-2-3, the popular electronic spreadsheet. If you use 1-2-3, there will probably be times when you will want to export data from Paradox into 1-2-3 so that you can analyze that data or use it as the basis for a spreadsheet model. If you have built data bases in 1-2-3, you might want to import the data from those data bases into Paradox so that you can take advantage of Paradox's greater power.

Exporting a Table to Lotus 1-2-3

To export a table from Paradox to Lotus 1-2-3, you should issue the [Menu] Tools ExportImport Export command and select the 1-2-3 option. When you issue this command, Paradox will display the prompt shown in Figure A-4, which asks you which release of Lotus you are using.

Figure A-4 The 1-2-3 Version Prompt

When you see this prompt, you should select the option that matches your version of Lotus. Next, Paradox will prompt you to enter the name of the table to export. When the table prompt appears on your screen, you should type the name of the table you want to export and press ↵. When you do this, Paradox will prompt you to enter a name for the 1-2-3 file it is about to create. You now should type the name for that file and press ↵. If you are exporting the table to a file on a different drive or directory, type the name of the drive or directory before you type the file name. After you do this, Paradox will write the data in the table into a 1-2-3 file of the type you selected.

There are a few important rules to keep in mind about exporting tables to 1-2-3. As in Paradox, each column in the exported 1-2-3 worksheet is a field, and each row is a record. The field names from the Paradox table will become the column headers in row 1 of the worksheet. The first field from the Paradox table will be in column A of the 1-2-3 worksheet, the second field will be in column B, and so forth.

When you export a Paradox table to 1-2-3, Paradox uses the widths of the alphanumeric fields in the table to set the widths of the corresponding columns in the 1-2-3 worksheet. However, since numeric fields in Paradox do not have defined widths, Paradox does not change the width of the 1-2-3 worksheet columns that receive data from these types of fields. You can widen or narrow these columns using 123's commands.

Of course, 1-2-3's data management capabilities are not nearly as sophisticated as Paradox's. For that reason, such characteristics of your Paradox tables as key fields, secondary indexes, and field types will not be transferred to the 1-2-3 worksheet.

Because of the different formats of Lotus Release 1A and 2.0 files, you should be sure to select the correct version from the 1-2-3 menu. Although 1-2-3 2.0 will read 1-2-3 1A files, 1-2-3 1A will not read files that are in the 1-2-3 2.0 format. Of course, should you export a file to the wrong format, you can start over and export it to the correct format.

Importing a File from Lotus 1-2-3

Importing a file from 1-2-3 is just as easy as exporting a Paradox table to 1-2-3. To import a file from 1-2-3 into Paradox, you issue the [Menu] Tools ExportImport Import command and select 1-2-3 from the Import menu. When Paradox displays the Version menu, choose the option that matches the version of 1-2-3 you are using. Next, Paradox will prompt you to enter the name of the 1-2-3 worksheet file you want to import. If you are uncertain about the file name, you can simply press ↵ and Paradox will display a list of the 1-2-3 files on the current directory. When you see this list, you can choose the file you want by pointing to its name. After you select a file to import, Paradox will prompt you to enter a name for the Paradox table into which you want the data from the 1-2-3 worksheet imported. Paradox can only import 1-2-3 data into new tables; it cannot append imported data directly to an existing table. For that reason, when Paradox prompts you for the name of the Paradox table that will receive the imported data, you must type a new name. If the name you type conflicts with an existing name, Paradox will display the now familiar Cancel/Replace menu to alert you.

When you press ↵, Paradox will begin the conversion process. As it converts the file, Paradox will display the message *Converting filename.WKS to TABLENAME...* at the bottom of the screen. In addition, Paradox will display in the upper-left corner of the screen a series of messages that tell you where it is in the conversion process. After a few moments, Paradox will display the new table in the workspace. Also, a message at the bottom of the screen will tell you the total number of records converted.

When Paradox imports a table from Lotus, it follows certain rules. First, Paradox requires that the 1-2-3 worksheet contain nothing but a 1-2-3 data base and assumes that the field names for the data base are in the first row of the worksheet, and that the first field (column) of data is in column A. Most of your 1-2-3 data bases will conform to these rules. Paradox assumes the labels in the first row of the worksheet are the field names for the 1-2-3 data base and converts them to Paradox field names. Anything below the first row is assumed to be data. If the field names are not in the first row, Paradox will use the first row that contains text as the field names. Any rows above it are ignored.

As you may know, fields in 1-2-3 data bases do not have field types. Of course, the fields in Paradox tables do have types, so Paradox uses a few simple rules to determine the types of the field in the imported table. The type of each field in the imported table is based on the entries in the columns of the 1-2-3 worksheet. Any column that contains a label (text) will be converted to an alphanumeric field. A column that contains both numbers and dates will be converted to an alphanumeric field. A Number column formatted as currency or with two decimal places will be converted to a dollar field. All other Number columns will be converted to number fields. Columns that contain dates exclusively will be converted to date fields.

Symphony

The process of exporting tables to Symphony (Release 1.0 and Release 1.1) and importing Symphony worksheets into Paradox is very similar to exporting and importing 1-2-3 files. To export a table into a Symphony file, issue the [Menu] Tools ExportImport Export command and select the Symphony option from the Export menu. Then, select the appropriate version number, 1.0 or 1.1, from the Symphony menu. When you make this choice, Paradox will prompt you first for the name of the table you want to export and then for the name of the Symphony file into which you want to export the data. After you supply both names, Paradox will write the data from the table into a Symphony file with the specified file name. The rules that Paradox follows when exporting tables to Symphony are identical to those it uses for creating 1-2-3 files. Paradox uses the same rules for setting the field types of data imported from Symphony worksheets that it uses when you import 1-2-3 worksheets.

The file name extension that Paradox gives to the Symphony file it creates depends on which option you choose from the Version menu. If you choose option 1, Paradox will write the data into a Symphony 1.0 file with a .WRK extension. If you choose option 2, the file will be a Symphony 1.1 file with the file name extension .WR1. As when exporting 1-2-3 files, you should be careful to select the correct option.

You can also import Symphony worksheets into Paradox. To import a worksheet from Symphony, issue the [Menu] Tools ExportImport Import Symphony command. Then select the appropriate version number, 1.0 or 1.1, from the Symphony menu. Next, enter the name of the file to import, followed by a name for the new Paradox table. After you do this, Paradox will import the file.

dBASE II and III

Many Paradox users are former users of dBASE II or dBASE III. Other Paradox users work in organizations where some people still use dBASE. If you fit into either of these categories, it is likely that you will need to import data from or export data to dBASE at some point. We'll show you how to do that in this section.

Exporting Tables to dBASE II, III, or III+

Selecting Dbase from the Export menu allows you to export data from Paradox to dBASE II, dBASE III, or dBASE III+. After you issue the [Menu] Tools ExportImport Export command and choose the Dbase option, you will see the menu shown in Figure A-5. Option 1 on the menu allows you to export a table from Paradox to dBASE II. Option 2 allows you to export Paradox data into a dBASE III or III+ file. You should choose the option that matches the version of dBASE that you are using.

Figure A-5 The Dbase Menu

After you select the correct option, Paradox will prompt you to enter the name of the Paradox table that you want to export. Then, Paradox will prompt you to enter a name for the converted file. When you enter a file name, you do not need to add an extension. Paradox will automatically assign a .DBF extension for you.

When you export a Paradox table to a dBASE file, the Paradox field names will become the field names for the dBASE file. However, since field names in Paradox can be up to 25 characters long, but field names in dBASE can be only 10 characters long, any long field names in your Paradox table will be shortened.

Since dBASE II and III both offer field types that correspond to most of the Paradox field types, most of your data will not be changed during the conversion. The only exceptions are date and short number fields. dBASE II does not support date fields, so any date fields will be converted to character fields when you export to dBASE II. Neither version of dBASE supports short number fields. Any short number field you export to dBASE will be treated as a straight numeric field. Table A-1 summarizes the Paradox to dBASE field conversion rules.

Table A-1 Paradox to dBASE Field Conversion

Paradox Field Type	dBASE II Field Type	dBASE III/III+ Field Type
Alphanumeric	Character	Character
Number	Numeric	Numeric
Dollar	Numeric (2 Decimal Places)	Numeric (2 Decimal Places)
Short Number	Numeric	Numeric
Date	Character	Date

Importing dBASE Files

Importing data from dBASE II, III, or III+ data bases is just as easy as exporting tables to those programs. After you issue the [Menu] Tools ExportImport Import Dbase command, you will be prompted to select the dBASE version you are using (II, III, or III+). Then you will be prompted to enter the name of the dBASE file you want to import. Again, you do not need to enter an extension. After you type a file name and press ↵, Paradox will prompt you to enter a name for the new Paradox table in which you want to store the imported records. As when you import data from 1-2-3 files, you must always import data from dBASE files into a new Paradox table. Once you type a table name and press ↵, the file will be converted. After a few moments, the new Paradox table will be displayed in the workspace.

Table A-2 summarizes the rules for dBASE to Paradox field conversions. Paradox supports all of dBASE's field types, except for logical fields and memo fields. When you import a dBASE file that contains a logical field, that field will be converted into an alphanumeric field with a width of 1. The entries in this field will be the letters *T* and *F* (for True and False) or *Y* and *N* (for Yes and No). If the file being imported contains a memo field, only the first 255 characters in that field will be imported.

Table A-2   dBASE to Paradox Field Conversions

dBASE Field Type	Paradox Field Type
Character	Alphanumeric
Logical	Alphanumeric (Length=1)
Number	Number
Number (2 Decimal Places)	Dollar
Date (dBASE III and III+ Only)	Date
Memo (dBASE III and III+ Only)	Alphanumeric (Length=255)

PFS and IBM Filing Assistant

PFS: File, from Software Publishing Company, and its cousin the IBM Filing Assistant are two of the most popular simple data base managers. Many Paradox users started out with one of these tools and graduated to Paradox when their needs outgrew the power of these programs. So that these users can move their data up into Paradox, Ansa has given Paradox the ability to import (and export) files from PFS: File.

To export a table to PFS: File, issue the [Menu] Tools ExportImport Export command and choose Pfs. After you issue the command, you will be prompted to enter the name of the table you wish to export, followed by a name for the exported file. Unless you enter an extension, Paradox will automatically add .PFS to the file name you specify.

After you type the file name and press ↵, Paradox will export the table. The message *Converting TABLENAME to FILENAME.PFS...* will appear at the bottom of the screen. After a few moments, Paradox will return to the main workspace.

PFS: File has no specific data types; therefore, it treats every field as a character string. When you export a Paradox table to PFS: File, every field is converted to a character string. The field names from the Paradox table are preserved in PFS: File.

To import a file from PFS into Paradox, issue the [Menu] Tools ExportImport Import Pfs command. After you do this, Paradox will prompt you to enter the name of the file you want to import (remember to include the extension .PFS). After you enter the name of the file to be imported, Paradox will prompt you to enter a name for the new Paradox table into which the data will be imported. Once you type a name and press ↵, Paradox will import the file and display the new table in the workspace. Since PFS: File has no specific data (field) types, Paradox scans the records in the file to determine how the records will be imported. Table A-3 shows how Paradox assigns field types.

Table A-3 PFS to Paradox Field Conversions

PFS Character String	**Paradox Field**
Non-numeric characters	Alphanumeric
Numeric Characters	Number
Numeric Characters (2 Decimal Places)	Dollar
Characters in the YY/MM/DD or MM/DD/YY Format	Date
Attachment Pages	Alphanumeric (Length=255)

VisiCalc

Although VisiCalc, the "granddaddy" of all spreadsheet programs, is not widely used today, Paradox does have the ability to exchange data with VisiCalc. You can export Paradox tables to VisiCalc using the Data Interchange Format (DIF). To export a table into DIF format, issue the [Menu] Tools ExportImport Export Visicalc command. After you issue this command, Paradox will prompt you to enter the name of the table you want to export, followed by the name of the DIF file you want to write the data into (if you do not enter an extension for the file, Paradox will automatically assign it the extension .DIF). Once you type a file name and press ↵, Paradox will export the data in the table into the DIF file. After you have exported the table, you can exit from Paradox, load VisiCalc, and read the DIF file into VisiCalc.

When you export a Paradox table to a DIF file, Paradox field names are converted to column titles in row 1. Alphanumeric fields are converted to Text columns. Number, dollar, and short number fields are converted to Number columns. Date fields are converted to text in the MM/DD/YY format.

To import a file from VisiCalc (or any program which uses the DIF format), you must first use that program to create a DIF file that contains the data you want to import. Make sure that you give the name of the DIF file the extension .DIF; the file must have a .DIF extension in order to be imported.

Once you have created a DIF file that contains the data to be imported, load Paradox and issue the [Menu] Tools ExportImport Import Visicalc command. After you issue the command, Paradox will prompt you to enter the name of the DIF file you want to import. Next, Paradox will prompt you to enter a name for the new Paradox table that will receive the imported data. After you type a table name and press ↵, the file will be converted and displayed in the workspace.

Paradox imports DIF files by treating each tuple as a record and each vector as a field. If the Label feature of DIF hasn't been used to name columns, row 1 will be imported as the field names for the table. Table A-4 shows the conversion rules for importing DIF files.

Table A-4 DIF to Paradox Field Conversions

DIF Column	Paradox Field
Text	Alphanumeric
Numbers	Number
Numbers (2 Decimal Places)	Dollar
Text in the MM/DD/YY Format	Date

Importing and Exporting ASCII Files

In addition to being able to exchange data with the programs discussed so far, Paradox also can import and export ASCII files. ASCII files are simple files that contain only alphabetic and numeric characters. Many programs can create and read ASCII text files, so you can use Paradox's ability to export and import these files as a way to exchange information with programs other than those on the ExportImport menus.

Exporting a Paradox Table to an ASCII File

The [Menu] Tools ExportImport Export Ascii command lets you export a Paradox table to an ASCII file. After you issue this command, Paradox will display the menu in Figure A-6, which asks you if you want to export a delimited file or a text file. If you choose Delimited, Paradox will write the table into an ASCII text file in which the fields are separated by commas and alphanumeric values are enclosed in (delimited by) quotation marks ("). If you choose Text, Paradox will write the data in the table into an ASCII file in which each record in the table is one line in the file. You can only use the Text option if the table you're exporting contains only one field and that field is an alphanumeric field.

Figure A-6 The Ascii Export Menu

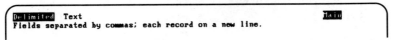

You will probably use the Delimited option to export a table and then import it into a mail-merge program or a word processor. Some programs of this type may work better if you use the [Menu] Report Output command to output a report to a file, rather than export the table. The choice of this technique is dependent on the program to which you are exporting the data.

Importing ASCII Files

Paradox lets you import ASCII files three different ways. You can import a delimited ASCII file into either a new table or into an existing Paradox table. In addition, you can import an undelimited ASCII text file in which each line of text becomes a record in a new table.

As you might expect, to import an ASCII file, you first issue the [Menu] Tools ExportImport Import Ascii command. When you issue this command, Paradox will display the menu shown in Figure A-7. The choices on this menu are Delimited, AppendDelimited, and Text.

Figure A-7 The Ascii Menu

```
Delimited AppendDelimited Text                              Main
Create a new table from an ASCII delimited text file.
```

Delimited Files

The Delimited option allows you to import a delimited ASCII file into a new Paradox table. When you choose this option, Paradox will prompt you to enter the name of the file you want to import, then for the name of the new table. Once you type a table name and press ↵, Paradox will convert the file and display it in the workspace.

If the ASCII file you are importing does not include field names, Paradox invents names for each of the fields in the table. The first field becomes Field-1, the second Field-2, and so on. If you wish, you can use the [Menu] Modify Restructure command to change the names of these fields to something more meaningful.

When Paradox imports a delimited file, it assumes that any entry that is enclosed in quotation marks is an alphanumeric entry. Any entry that is not enclosed in quotation marks will become a numeric entry. Paradox also assumes that the fields in the ASCII file are separated by commas.

Later in this appendix, we'll show you how to change the delimiter and separator that Paradox uses to determine field types. This feature allows you to import any ASCII file, regardless of the way it is delimited and separated.

Importing an ASCII File into an Existing Table

The Append Delimited option allows you to import a delimited ASCII file into an existing table. When you import an ASCII file into an existing Paradox table, Paradox does everything it can to convert the data in the ASCII file into Paradox data properly. However, if the file cannot be converted, the problem records will be placed in a temporary PROBLEMS table. The PROBLEMS table consists of three fields: a Line Number field, a Line field, and a Reason field. The Line Number field in the PROBLEMS table tells you the line in the ASCII file that caused the problem. The Line field shows you the first 80 characters in the line, and the Reason field gives you a brief explanation of the problem. With this information, you can edit the ASCII file and then import it. In some cases, you may find it easier to emport the file into a new table, restructure that table, and then add the records to the existing table.

If you are adding records from an ASCII file to an existing table that contains a key field, the imported records will be merged in the table in key-field sequence. However, if the imported record contains a key-field value that is the same as an existing value, the imported record will **replace** the existing record in the table. For this reason, we suggest that you always make a copy of the original table before you import the file.

Importing Unseparated ASCII Files

The Text option on the ASCII menu lets you import a file in which the fields are not separated. To do this, issue the [Menu] Tools ExportImport Import Ascii Text command. After you issue this command, Paradox will prompt you to enter the name of the file to import, and then for the name for the new table. After you do this, Paradox will convert the file and display it in the workspace.

Paradox imports unseparated ASCII files into tables with one alphanumeric field. Each line in the file is converted to one record in the table. If there are records in the file that cannot be converted, Paradox will display those records in a PROBLEMS table as described above.

The AsciiConvert Command

As you have learned, a delimiter is a character used to distinguish non-numeric fields in an ASCII file. A separator is the character used to separate fields in an ASCII file. When you use the [Menu] Tools More ExportImport command to exchange data between Paradox and delimited ASCII files, Paradox assumes that the default delimiter is a quotation mark and that the default separator is a comma. However, since different programs may use different delimiters and separators, Paradox allows you to change its default separator and delimiter settings. To do this, you must run the Paradox Custom Configuration Program (PCCP) and choose the AsciiConvert command. When you choose AsciiConvert from the PCCP menu, Paradox will display the menu shown in Figure A-8.

Figure A-8 The AsciiConvert Menu

```
Delimiters  Separator  ZeroFill  Exit
Change default delimiter or choose fields to be delimited
```

Changing the Delimiter

To change the default delimiters, you choose the Delimiters option. When you make this choice, Paradox will display a menu with two options: Choice and Always? These let you define a delimiter and decide which fields should be enclosed by the delimiter.

If you issue the Choice command, Paradox will display the default delimiter (if you have not previously made a change, the default will be a quotation mark) and prompt you to change it. To change the default delimiter, press the [Backspace] key to erase it, type a new delimiter, and press ↵.

The Always? option on the Delimiters menu allows you to define which fields should be delimited. When you issue this command, Paradox will display a menu with two options: AllFields and OnlyStrings (the default). The OnlyStrings setting tells Paradox to place delimiters around non-numeric fields only. The other option, AllFields, tells Paradox to place delimiters around all fields.

Changing the Separator

To change the default separator, choose the Separator command from the AsciiConvert menu. After you make this choice, Paradox will display the default separator (if you have not previously changed this setting, the default will be a comma) and prompt you to change it. To change the default, press [Backspace] to erase the current separator and type the new one.

The ZeroFill Option

The ZeroFill command on the AsciiConvert menu lets you control how blank numeric fields are exported into ASCII files. By default, Paradox exports blank numeric fields as blanks. If you wish, you can change the default to convert blank numeric fields to zeros for export. To do this, choose the ZeroFill command from the AsciiConvert menu and select the Zeroes option.

Conclusion

In this appendix, we've shown you how to import data from programs like Lotus 1-2-3, Symphony, dBASE II, dBASE III, and PFS: File into Paradox, and how to export data from Paradox and those programs. We've also shown you how to import and export ASCII files and how to change the default settings for ASCII files with the PCCP.

Index

A

@ command (PAL), 508-509
@ operator (queries), 217-218
ACCEPT command, 520-523
  default entries, 521
  lookup tables, 524
  mandatory input, 521
  minimum and maximum values, 522
  pictures, 522-523
ADD command, 457
Alphanumeric fields, 34
AND queries, 234-236
  combining AND and OR queries, 236-238
  see also Queries, AND queries
ANSWER table, 152-153, 194-196, 200-201, 268
  characteristics of, 200-201
  editing, 200
  field order, 268
  fields in, 198
  querying, 200
  renaming, 201
  saving, 201
ARRAY command, 565
Arrays, 561-566
  COPYTOARRAY and COPYFROMARRAY commands, 561-564
  defining manually, 565
  placing elements in, 561-563, 565
  retrieving elements from, 561-563, 565
  undefining, 565-566
ARRAYSIZE() function, 490
ASC() function, 482-483
Ask command, 191, 196
ATFIRST() function, 500
ATLAST function, 500
Auto-executing scripts, 585-586
Average operator, 278, 279

B

BANDINFO() function, 490
BEEP command, 587
Blank operator, 227-229, 263, 275
BLANKDATE() function, 481
Borders, 133-137
Borrow command, 40-41, 174
BOT() and EOT() functions, 501
Branching, 536, 537-539

C

Calc operator, 273-280
  calculating summary statistics, 278-280
  concatenation, 275, 276
  vs. changeto, 277
Calc queries, 273-278
Calculated fields, 128-130, 365-368, 389, 390
Calculated summary fields, 387-391
CANCELEDIT command, 456
CASE keyword, 533
CAVERAGE() function, 477
CCOUNT() function, 477
CHANGED table, 242-245, 262, 298
Changeto queries, 242-245
  changing several records, 244-245
  reversing, 243
  using examples, 262-263
CHARWAITING() function, 501-502
[Check Mark] key, 14, 194, 197, 202-209
CHR() function, 482-483
CLEAR command, 507-508
  EOL option, 508
  EOS option, 508
CMAX() function, 476-477
CMIN() function, 476-477
CNPV() function, 479-480
COL() function, 490
COLONO() function, 490
Comma format, 86
Commands,
  defined, 15
  issuing, 16
  see also individual command names
  PAL
    see also PAL commands

Commands by Name
Ask, 191, 196
Create, 29, 39-41
Exit, 28
Help, 22-23
Image, 80
Modify DataEntry, 41-44, 77
Modify Edit, 62-67, 111
Modify MultiEntry, 304-315
Modify Restructure, 165-166, 176
Modify Sort, 177-190
Move, 132, 145
Output File, 381-382
Output Screen, 381
Output Printer, 342, 376

Put, 117
Read, 440
Report Change, 376
Report Design, 339
Report Output, 377
Script Editor Edit, 434
Script Editor Write, 442, 443
Scripts BeginRecord, 420
Scripts Editor Edit, 425
Scripts End-Record, 422
Scripts Play, 246, 429
Scripts QuerySave, 199, 245-246, 431
Scripts ShowPlay, 430
Setting Format, 411
Setting GroupRepeats, 410
Setting Margin, 378
Setting PageLayout, 345-348
Setting PageLayout Width, 347, 377-378
Setting RemoveBlank FieldSqueeze, 374
Setting RemoveBlank LineSqueeze, 374
Setting Setup, 379-380
Setting Wait, 380
TableBand Copy, 355-356
TableBand Erase, 353
TableBand Insert, 353-354
TableBand Move, 351-352
TableBand Resize, 354-355
Tools Copy Form, 146-147
Tools Copy JustFamily, 152-153, 185
Tools Copy Report, 414
Tools Copy Table, 151-152
Tools Delete Form, 147-148
Tools Delete KeepSettings, 89
Tools Delete QuerySpeedup, 250
Tools Delete Report, 415
Tools Delete Table, 153-154, 180
Tools Delete ValCheck, 101
Tools Export/Import, 593-604
Tools Info, 154-158
Tools Info Family, 157-158
Tools Info Inventory, 155-156
Tools Info Inventory Files, 156-157
Tools Info Inventory Scripts, 156
Tools Info Inventory Tables, 156
Tools Info Structure, 154-155
Tools More Add, 76, 171-172, 175, 241, 289-301,
Tools More Directory, 162-163
Tools More Empty, 158-159
Tools More MultiAdd, 315-320
Tools More Protect Password, 159-160
Tools More Protect Password Script, 555-556
Tools More Protect Write-Protect, 161-162
Tools More Subtract, 301-304
Tools More ToDOS, 163-165
Tools QuerySpeedup, 248

Tools Rename Form, 148
Tools Rename Report, 415
Tools Rename Script, 424
Tools Rename Table, 150-151
Undo, 49-50
ValCheck, 89-101
ValCheck Clear All, 101
ValCheck Clear Field, 100
View, 51
Undo, edit mode, 67
? and ?? commands, 509-512
  formatting the display, 512
  multiple arguments, 511
  nonstring arguments, 510-511

Command line configuration, 27-28
Commands,
  Erase Area, 137-138
  Format, in forms, 112
  GoTo, 55-56, 112,
  Style, 138-142
Compaq computers, 24
Computed statistics, 287-288
Concatenation, 275, 276
Conditional tests, 469-470, 541
Configuring Paradox, 24
Conventions, 2-3
COPY command, 454
Copy protection, 7
COPYFROMARRAY command, 561-564
COPYTOARRAY command, 561-564
Copying JustFamily, 152-153
Copying tables, 151-152
Copying reports, 414
Count operator, 278, 279-280, 283-284
Create command, 29, 39-41, 166
CREATE command (PAL), 452-453
Create menu, 39
Creating tables, 29-41
  with queries, 265-270
CREATELIB command, 573
CSTD() function, 477
CSUM() function, 477
Cursor location indicator, 42
Cursor movement
  during data entry, 43-44
  during editing, 46
  in a form, 104-106
  in the field view, 47-48
  in the Forms Editor, 121
  in an image, 53
  in queries, 197
  in report specifications, 341
  in STRUCT table, 36-37
  moving between images, 59

CURSORCHR() function, 491
CURSORLINE() function, 491
CVAR() function, 477

D

Data entry, 41-44
  advanced techniques, 50
  editing during, 109-111
  ending, 44-45
  setting a default, 92-93
  special tricks, 101-102
  using a form, 107-111
  validity checks, 89-101
DataEntry/Edit menu, 112
Date fields, 35-36
  data entry, 102
  formats, 85
Date formats, 36
DATEVAL() function, 484
Date/time functions, 480-482
DAY() function, 481
DEBUG command, 581
Debugger, 576-583
  see also PAL Debugger
Debugger command, 446, 447
Debugger menu, 448
Debugging scripts, 446-448, 576-583
Delete queries, 240-241
  reversing a deletion, 241-242
  using examples in, 264-265
Deleting records, 48, 64, 240-241
Deleting rows, 38
Deleting reports, 415
Deleting tables, 153-154
DELETE command, 453-454
DELETED table, 240-241, 265
DIRECTORY() function, 491
Directory, changing, 162-163
Display-only fields, 128
DO-IT! command, 33, 39, 41, 44, 67
[Do-It!] key, 14, 39
Dollar fields, 35
  data entry, 102
  formats, 85
DOS, accessing from Paradox, 163-165
DOS command, 457
DOW() function, 481
DRIVESPACE() function, 491-492
DRIVESTATUS() function, 502

E

ECHO command, 587
EDIT command, 453
[Edit] Key ([F9]), 67-68
Editing scripts, 434-446

Editing tables, 62-67
  during data entry, 45-50
  field view, 47-48, 64, 110-111
  through a form, 109-112, 130
  Tools More Add command, 299-301
  validity checks, 89-101
EMPTY command, 456
Emptying tables, 158-159
Entering data, 41-44
  Modify MultiEntry command, 308-310
  using a form, 107-109
ENTRY table, 41-44, 308-310
  editing, 45-50
EOT and BOT functions, 501
Erase Area command, 137-138
Erase Borders command, 136
Erase Field command, 131
Examples, 253-273
  basics, 254
  characters to use, 255-256
  defining statement, 258
  editing, 254-255
  [Example] key, 253
  in changeto queries, 262-263
  in delete queries, 264-265
  in insert queries, 322-323
  in selection conditions, 258
  in single-table queries, 257-259
  two-table operations, 265-270
  vs. selection conditions, 255
  with the blank operator, 263, 275
  with the not operator, 263-264, 275
EXECUTE command, 587-588
EXIT command, 454
Exporting files, 593-604
Exporting/Importing files
  ASCII Files, 600-602
  AsciiConvert Command, 602-604
  dBase, 596-598
  Lotus 123, 594-596
  PFS:File, 598-599
  Symphony, 596
  VisiCalc (DIF Files), 599-60

F

Families, 152-153, 157-158
FAMILY table, 157-158
FIELD() function, 492
Field Erase command, 356-357
Field Place command, 363-389
Field Place Summary command, 383-385, 389
Field Reformat command, 358-359
Field names, 33
Field references, 468-469
Field types, 34-36

Field view, 47
    editing, 47-48, 64, 87
    in forms, 110-111
    to edit rounded fields, 87
Fields
    calculated fields, 128-130, 365-368, 389-390
    changing size, 81-83
    changing format, 84-86
    defined, 19
    display-only fields, 128
    formats, 84-87
    key fields, 71
    maximum length, 19
    moving, 87-88
    placing in a form, 117, 124-130
    record number fields, 130, 412
        #Record, 130, 365
    types, 34-36
    types in a form, 124-130
    viewing, 43
Files
    file name extensions, 20
    inventory, 156
    types, 20, 33, 89, 100, 101, 249-250, 382, 422-423
FIELDINFO() function, 492
FIELDNO() function, 492-493
FILESIZE() function, 493
FILL() function, 485
Financial functions, 478-480
Find queries, 238-239, 270-271
Fixed format, 85, 86
FOR command, 546-547
    keywords, 546-547
    alternative forms, 547
FOR loops, 546-547
Form view
    see also Forms
Formats, 84-87
FORMAT() function, 485-487, 512
Forms
    borders, 133-137
    calculated fields, 128-131
    changing, 146
    copying, 146-147
    creating, 113-142
    creating custom forms, 113-148
    cursor movement in, 104-106
    default form, 103-104
    deleting, 147-148
    deleting records, 111
    descriptions, 120-121
    design screen, 114
    designing, 113-142
    display-only fields, 128
    editing tables through, 109-112
    entering records through, 107-109
    erasing an area, 137-138
    field view, 110-111
    forms design screen, 114
    Forms Editor, 121-124
        replace and insert modes, 122-123
        word wrap, 123-124
    Image menu, 112
    inserting records, 111
    managing, 146-148
    multipage forms, 142-144
        deleting pages, 145-146
        designing, 142-144
        moving areas between pages, 144-145
    names, 114, 120
    numbers, 114, 119-120
    placing fields, 117-118, 124-125
    renaming, 148
    replacing the default form, 120
    style settings, 138-142
        Blink attribute, 140-141
        displaying field names, 138-139
        intensity, 140
        Reverse attribute, 141
        text and borders, 140
    using, 104-112
Forms Change command, 113, 146
Forms Design command, 113
Formulas, 467-468
Free-form reports, 368-375
    grouping, 413-414
Functions, 470-506
    see also PAL functions
FV() function, 478-479

G
General format, 85
Geometric functions, 474
GETCHAR() function, 501-502
Go command, 429
GoTo command, 55-56, 112
Greater than operator (>), 220, 221
Greater than or equal to operator (>=), 220, 221
Group menu commands, 392-414
Group statistics, 284-286
Group summaries
    in queries, 279
    in reports, 392-414
Grouping reports, 392-414
    see also Reporting, grouping

H
Hardware requirements, 5-6
Help command, 22-23

I

IBM color/graphics adapter, 24
IF/THEN/ELSE command, 530, 539-540
   advanced form, 540-541
Images, 20
   changing, 80-89
   form view, 21-22
   moving between images, 59
   removing images, 61-62
   table view, 21
   viewing more than one, 57-61
Image menu, 21, 80-89
   in forms, 112
Image ColumnSize command, 81-83
Image Format command, 84-87
Image GoTo command, 55-56
Image KeepSettings command, 89
Image Move command, 87-88
Image PickForm command, 118-119
Image TableSize command, 80
IMAGENO() function, 493-494
IMAGETYPE() function, 494
Importing files, 593-604
INDEX command, 456
Indexes
   deleting, 250
   primary, 248
   secondary, 248, 249
INFOLIB command, 575
Informational functions, 489
INIT.SC scripts, 585-586
Insert operator, 321-328
Insert queries, 241, 321-328
   and key fields, 324-327
   with two tables, 327-328
INSERTED table, 325-327
Installing Paradox, 7-9
   Release 1.0, 7
   floppy disk installation, 9
   hard disk installation, 8
   uninstalling Paradox, 9
Instant Reports, 329-330
Instant .SC File, 424-425
Instant Scripts, 424-425
ISASSIGNED() function, 502
ISBLANK() function, 503
ISEMPTY() function, 503
ISFIELDVIEW() function, 504
ISFILE() function, 504-505
ISFORMVIEW() function, 504
ISINSERTMODE() function, 505
ISTABLE() function, 504-505

K

Key fields, 71-78
   AND queries, 248
   defining, 71-72
   insert queries, 324-327
   Modify MultiEntry command, 311-314
   multiple key fields, 78
   Tools More Add command, 297-298
   Tools More MultiAdd command, 317-318
   vs. QuerySpeedup, 251
Key violations, 74-77, 295
Keyboard macros, 558-561
Keyed tables, 71-79
   editing, 77-78
   entering records into, 72-74
   restructuring, 175
   sorting, 189-190
   with multiple key fields, 78
KEYPRESS command, 588
KEYVIOL table, 74-77, 175, 247, 289, 295-296, 312-314
   Tools More MultiAdd command, 316-317, 319-320
   editing, 74-77
   key fields, 246-248

L

LEN() function, 483
Less than operator (<), 220, 221-222
Less than or equal to operator (<=), 220, 222
Like operator, 224-225
LIST table, 155-156
Loading Paradox, 10, 11
LOCATE command, 589-590
Logical ANDS and ORS, 231
Logical operators in PAL, 470
LOOP command, 543
Loops
   see also FOR loops
   see also WHILE loops
LOWER() function, 483

M

Macros, 558-561
Managing tables, 149-176
Map table, 306-320
MATCH() function, 488-489
Mathematical functions, 473-474
MAX() function, 475
Max operator, 278, 283
Memory requirements, 5, 6
Menu area, 11, 12
Menu indicator, 42
Menu-equivalent commands, 451-460
Menus
   custom, 530-535
   submenus, 18
      see also PAL custom menus
      see also SHOWMENU command

MENUCHOICE() function, 494
Message area, 12
MESSAGE command, 518-519
MIN() function, 475
Min operator, 278, 283
Miniscript command, 558
Miniscripts, 558
Modify DataEntry command, 41-44, 77, 107
Modify Edit command, 62, 111
Modify MultiEntry command, 304-315
    creating the source and map tables, 306-308
    creating the source table, 306-308
    Entry option, 308-310
    key fields, 311-314
    password protection, 314-315
    reusing the multientry system, 311
    Setup option, 307
Modify Restructure command, 165-166, 176
Modify Sort command, 177-190
    New option, 178, 180-181, 183
    Same option, 178, 180-181, 183
MONITOR() function, 494
MONTH() function, 481
Move command, 132, 145
MOVETO command, 459-460, 590
MOY() function, 481
Multitable operations, 289-328

N

NFIELDS() function, 494-495
NKEYFIELDS() function, 495
NIMAGES() function, 495
Normalized tables, 29-71, 268, 305
not operator, 225-227, 263-264, 275
NPAGES() function, 496
NRECORDS() function, 496
NROWS() function, 496
Number fields, 34
    data entry, 102
    formats, 85
    number record fields, 130, 365
Numeric keypad, 15
NUMVAL() function, 484

O

Objects, 20
.. operator, 216-217
OR queries, 231-234
    combining AND and OR queries, 236-238
    see also Queries, OR queries
Output File Command, 381-382
Output Screen Command, 381

P

PAGEBREAK keyword, 411-412
PAGENO() function, 496-497
PAGEWIDTH() function, 497

PAL, 419-592
    arrays, 561-566
    auto-executing scripts, 585-586
    basics, 449-470
    branching scripts, 536, 537-539
    canvas, 508-509
        see also PAL canvas
    commands
        see also PAL Commands by Name
    comments in scripts, 556
    conditional tests, 469
    custom menus, 529-534
        see also PAL commands
        see also SHOWMENU
    formulas, 467-470
        operating on numbers, 467
        operators, 467
        precedence of operators, 467-468
    functions, 470-506
        see also PAL functions
    keyboard macros, 558-561
    logical operators, 470
    making entries in tables, 465-466
    printing from within a script, 549-553
    printing scripts, 583
    procedures, 566-575
        see also PAL procedures
    programming techniques, 507-556
    referring to table entries, 463-464
    storing an entry in a variable, 464-465
    subroutines, 536-539
        the RETURN command, 538-539
        using menus to call, 538-539
    the ; character, 556
    tilde variables, 583-584
    types of errors, 576-577
    variables, 460-463
        arrays, 561-566
        assigning values, 460-461, 463
        lifespan, 461
        saving, 461-462
        types, 463
PAL calculator, 288
PAL canvas, 420, 507-508
    clearing the PAL canvas, 507-508
    positioning the cursor, 508-509
PAL commands, 419-592
    arguments, 450-451
    command names, 450
    input/output commands, 449-450
    keywords, 451
    menu-equivalent commands, 450, 451-460
    program control commands, 450
    system control commands, 450
    variable-manipulating commands, 450
    workspace-manipulating commands, 450

PAL Commands by Name
@, 508-509
=, 460-461
? and ??, 509-516
ACCEPT, 520-521
ADD, 457
ARRAY, 565
BEEP, 587
CANCELEDIT, 456
CLEAR, 507-508
COPY, 454
COPYFROMARRAY, 561-564
COPYTOARRAY, 561-564
CREATE, 452-453
CREATELIB, 573
DEBUG, 581
DELETE, 453-454
DOS, 457
ECHO, 587
EDIT, 453
EMPTY, 456
EXECUTE, 587-588
EXIT, 454
FOR, 546-547
   alternative forms, 547
IF/THEN/ELSE, 539-540
   advanced form, 540-541
INDEX, 456
INFOLIB, 575
KEYPRESS, 588
LOCATE, 589-590
LOOP, 543
MESSAGE, 518-519
MOVETO, 459-460, 590
PASSWORD, 554
PICKFORM, 455-456
PLAY, 459, 536
PRINT, 553
PRINTER, 552
PRIVATE, 571
PROC, 566-567
PROTECT, 459
QUERY, 432-433
QUIT, 537
QUITLOOP, 544
READLIB, 574
RELEASE, 565-566, 572
RELEASE VARS, 461-462
RENAME, 455
REPORT, 458
RESET, 590
RETURN, 519
RUN, 590-591
SAVEVARS, 461-462, 570
SCAN, 547-549
SETDIR, 458
SETKEY, 558-559
SHOWMENU, 530-531
SLEEP, 514
SORT, 454-455
STYLE, 515-517
SUBTRACT, 457
SWITCH, 530, 533-535
TEXT, 513-514
TYPEIN, 591
UNPASSWORD, 554-555
VIEW, 452
WAIT, 524-525
WHILE, 541-542
WRITELIB, 573-574
see also individual commands

   DEFAULT keyword, 532-533
   PAL custom menus, 530-535
     an example, 533-534
     making selections from, 531
     subroutines, 538-539
PAL Debugger, 446-447, 576-583
   debugging run errors, 577-578
   debugging syntax errors, 577
   entering voluntarily, 580-581
   types of errors, 576-577
   using a miniscript, 580
PAL Debugger menu, 576-582
   Editor, 576-580
   Go option, 579
   Miniscript, 580
   Next option, 579-580
   Pop option, 582-583
   Quit option, 576
   Step option, 581
   Value option, 581-582
   Where? option, 582
PAL Editor, 425-429
   see also Script Editor
PAL formulas, 467-470
   conditional tests, 541
   operating on dates, 468
   operating on numbers, 467
   operating on strings, 468
   operators, 467
   precedence of operators, 467-468
   variables and field references, 468-469
PAL functions, 470-506
   arguments, 472
   basics, 470-471
   date/time functions, 480-482
   financial functions, 478-480
   geometric functions, 474
   informational functions, 489

logical functions, 500
mathematical functions, 473-474
statistical functions, 475-477
string functions, 482-489
using functions, 472-473
see also individual functions

PAL Functions by Name
ARRAYSIZE(), 490
ASC(), 482-483
ATFIRST(), 500
ATLAST(), 500
BANDINFO(), 490
BLANKDATE(), 481
BOT(), 501
CAVERAGE(), 477
CCOUNT(), 477
CHARWAITING(), 501-502
CHR(), 482-483
CMAX(), 476-477
CMIN(), 476-477
CNPV(), 479-480
COL(), 490
COLNO(), 490
CSTD(), 477
CSUM(), 477
CURSORCHR(), 491
CURSORLINE(), 491
CVAR(), 477
DATEVAL(), 484
DAY(), 481
DIRECTORY(), 491
DOW(), 481
DRIVESPACE(), 491-492
DRIVESTATUS(), 502
EOT(), 501
FIELD(), 492
FIELDINFO(), 492
FIELDNO(), 492-493
FILESIZE(), 493
FILL(), 485
FORMAT(), 485-487, 512
    codes, 486
FV(), 478-479
GETCHAR(), 501-502
IMAGENO(), 493-494
IMAGETYPE(), 494
ISASSIGNED(), 502
ISBLANK(), 503
ISEMPTY(), 503
ISFIELDVIEW(), 504
ISFILE(), 504-505
ISFORMVIEW(), 504
ISINSERTMODE(), 505
ISTABLE(), 504-505
LEN(), 483

LOWER(), 483
MATCH(), 488-489
MAX(), 475
MENUCHOICE(), 494
MIN(), 475
MONITOR(), 494
MONTH(), 481
MOY(), 481
NFIELDS(), 494-495
NIMAGES(), 495
NKEYFIELDS(), 495
NPAGES(), 496
NRECORDS(), 496
NROWS(), 496
NUMVAL(), 484
PAGENO(), 496-497
PAGEWIDTH(), 497
PMT(), 479
PRINTERSTATUS(), 505-506
PV(), 478
RECNO(), 497
ROW(), 497
ROWNO(), 497-498
SDIR(), 498
SEARCH(), 489
SPACES(), 485
STRVAL(), 484
SUBSTR(), 484-485
SYSMODE(), 498-499
TABLE(), 499
TIME(), 481-482
TODAY(), 482
TYPE(), 499
UPPER(), 483
VERSION(), 499-500
WINDOW(), 500
YEAR(), 481

PAL keyboard macros, 558-561
PAL menu, 429, 557
PAL menu commands
    miniscript, 558
    value, 557-558
PAL pictures, 93-97
PAL procedure libraries, 572-575
    autoloading, 575
    creating, 573
    reading from, 574
    taking inventory, 575
    writing to, 573-574
PAL procedures, 566-575
    calling, 568-569
    defining, 566-567
    efficiency considerations, 569-570
    global and private variables, 570-572
    loading, 567-568

releasing, 572
using, 567-570
PAL Script Editor, 419, 425-429, 434-446
PAL variables,
   assigning values, 463
   lifespan, 461
   retval, 571-572
   saving, 461-462
   types, 463
Paradox
   features, 1
   Release 1.1, 4
Paradox Applications Language, 449
   see also PAL
Paradox Custom Configuration Program, 24-27
   see also PCCP
\paradox directory, 8, 10
PASSWORD command, 554
Password protection, 159-161
   Modify MultiEntry command, 314-315
   removing and changing password, 161
   scripts, 553-556
Patterns, 216-220
PCCP, 24-27
   changing the default directory, 163
   changing the default report settings, 415-418
   configuring Paradox, 24
   custom script, 163
   eliminating display problems, 24
PICKFORM command, 455-456
Pictures, 93-97
   picture characters, 93-97
PLAY command, 459, 536, 537-539
Playing scripts, 429
PMT() function, 479
Pop command, 582-583
PRINT command, 553
PRINTER command, 552
PRINTERSTATUS() function, 505-506
Printing
   cancelling, 377
   from within a report specification, 342
   from within a script, 549-553
   printing to a file, 381-382
   printing to the screen, 381
   scripts, 583
   setup strings, 379
   reports, 376-382
   see also Reporting
PRIVATE command, 571
Private variables, 570-572
PROBLEMS table, 171-172, 289
PROC command, 566-567
Procedures, 566-575
   see also PAL procedures

Procedure libraries, 572-575
   see also PAL procedure libraries
Programming techniques, 507-556
PROTECT command, 459
Protecting tables, 159-162
Put command, 117
PV() function, 478

Q

Queries, 191-251
   AND queries, 234-236
      in one field, 235-236
   ANSWER table, 200
   basics, 196-201
   blank operator, 227-229, 275
   calc operator, 273
   calc queries, 273-278
      see also Calc queries
   changeto queries, 242-245
   [Check Mark] key, 14, 194, 197, 202-209
   delete queries, 240-242, 264, 265
   deselecting all fields, 205
   duplicate records
      defined, 206-207
      in multifield queries, 208
      selecting, 206
   examples, 253-288
   [Example] key, 253
   filling in the query form, 192, 194
   find queries, 238-239
   index files for QuerySpeedup, 249-250
   insert queries, 321-328
   key fields, 246-248
      vs. Query Speedup, 251
   like operator, 224-225
   logical ANDS and ORS, 231
   not operator, 225-227, 275
   .. operator, 216-217
   OR queries, 231-234
      blank rows in, 233
      on different fields, 233-234
      selecting fields in, 232
   patterns, 216-220
   playing a saved query, 433
   processing, 194, 195
   query forms, 191-194, 196, 197
      making entries in, 197-198
   querying ANSWER, 200
   range operators, 220
   recording queries, 433-434
   reusing query forms, 198-199
   reversing a deletion, 241-242
   saving, 245-246, 431-434
   saving ANSWER, 201
   secondary indexes, 248, 249
   selecting duplicate records, 215

selecting fields, 202-209
selecting ranges of records, 220
selection conditions, 209-238
   defining, 209
   see also Selection conditions
   speeding up, 246-252
   .Y01 and .X01 files, 249-250
statistical operators, 278
   see also Statistical operators
today operator, 230-231
two-table queries, 272-273
using tilde variables, 583-584
.Y01 and .X01 files, 249-250
QUERY command, 432-433
Query forms, 191-194, 196-197
   clearing, 199
   creating, 191-192, 199
   deselecting fields, 202
   entering selection conditions, 209-238
   filling in, 192-194
   making entries in, 197-198
   multiple query forms, 197, 267-268
   reusing, 198-199
   selecting fields in, 197-200, 201-209
Query scripts, 431-434
QuerySpeedup, 246-252
QUIT command, 537
QUITLOOP command, 544

R

Range operators, 220-222
   alphanumeric fields, 223
   date fields, 223
   greater than (>), 220, 221
   greater than or equal to (>=), 220, 221
   less than (<), 220, 221, 222
   less than or equal to (<=), 220, 222
   not operator, 226
   patterns, 224
Read command, 440
READLIB command, 574
RECNO() function, 497
Record, 19
#Record fields, 130, 365
Record number column, 42
Recording scripts, 420-425
   see also Scripts recording
Records
   adding, 65-66
   changing with changeto queries, 242-244
   deleting, 64, 111, 240-241
   finding and editing, 239
   inserting, 111
   number showing, 80
Recovering disk space, 176

RELEASE command, 565-566, 572
   PROCS keyword, 572
   VARS keyword, 565-566
RELEASE VARS command, 461-462
Release 1.0, installing, 7
Release 1.1, installing, 7
RENAME command, 455
Renaming reports, 415
Renaming tables, 150-151
Report Change command, 376
REPORT command, 458
Report Design command, 339
Report GroupRepeats command, 416-417
Report LengthofPage command, 416
Report Margin command, 416
Report Output command, 377
Report PageWidth command, 416
Report SetupStrings command, 417
Report specifications, 329-375
   see also Reporting, report specifications
Reporting, 383-418
   adjusting the left margin, 378
   adjusting the page length, 378
   adjusting the page width, 377-378
   cancelling printing, 377
   changing default settings, 415-418
   copying reports, 414
   custom reports, 339-376
   deleting groups, 412
   deleting reports, 415
   field masks, 356
   formatting fields, 358-362
   free-form reports, 368-375
      FieldSqueeze/LineSqueeze, 373
      designing, 369-371
      grouping, 413-414
   fundamentals, 329
   grouping, 392-414
      free-form reports, 413-414
      GroupsofTables/TableofGroups, 411
      PAGEBREAK keyword, 411-412
      changing the group sort order, 402
      deleting the grouping field, 404, 406
      field groups, 392-414
      group headers and footers, 400-404
      group repeats, 410
      grouping numbers of records, 401-402
      inserting groups, 392-401
      nesting groups, 406-408
      placing summary fields in, 403-406, 408-410
      record number fields, 412
      summaries in nested groups, 406-408
      types, 392
   instant reports, 329-330
   mailing labels, 371-373

managing reports, 413-414
PAGEBREAK keyword, 411-412
page-widths, 345-348
print settings, 377
printing a saved report, 376
printing to a file, 381-382
printing to the screen, 381
record number fields, 412
records printed per page, 337
renaming reports, 415
report descriptions, 340
Report Design command, 339
report numbers, 339-340
report specifications, 331-375
    adding and deleting lines, 342-345
    bands, 334
    cancelling, 375
    columns, 351
    placing calculated fields, 365-368
    placing current date fields, 364
    placing current time fields, 364
    elements, 333
    field masks, 333-334
    field types, 363
    insert mode, 344-345
    literal text, 334
    multiple fields in a column, 368
    other bands, 336-337
    other features, 338-339
    overwrite mode, 344
    page footer, 335
    page header, 335
    page lengths, 378
    page number fields, 364
    page widths, 337-338, 345-347, 377-378
    placing fields, 362
    rearranging columns, 351
    record number fields, 365
    report footer, 335
    report header, 335
    saving, 375
    special fields, 364
    table band, 336
    vertical ruler, 341-343
revising reports, 376
setup strings, 379
summary fields, 383
    PerGroup and Overall, 384
    calculated summary fields, 387-391
    positioning in reports, 384
    regular, 383-387
    types, 383-384, 389
tabular reports, 329-368
    designing, 339-368
Report Wait command, 417
RESET command, 590

Restructuring tables, 165-176
    changing field types, 172-174
    changing field size, 168-172
    deleting fields, 167
    keyed tables, 175
    moving fields, 167-168
    recovering disk space, 176
    restructure menu, 174
RETURN command, 519, 558
Reversing a deletion, 241-242
ROW() function, 497
ROWNO() function, 497-498
RUN command, 590-591

S

SAVEVARS command, 461-462, 570
Saving queries, 431-434
SCAN command, 547-549
Scientific format, 86
Script Editor, 419, 425-429, 434-446
    adding lines, 436-437
    combining two scripts, 439-441
    cursor movement, 434-435
    deleting characters and lines, 437
    exiting from, 438
    insert mode, 436
    menu, 439
    overwrite mode, 436
    Read command, 440
    rulers, 435
    workspace, 435
    Write command, 442, 443
Script errors, 446-448
Script file, 422, 423
Scripts, 419-448
    auto-executing, 585-586
    comments in, 556
    creating generic scripts, 427, 441-442
    editing, 434-446
    ending the edit, 429, 438
    elements, 426
    errors, 446-448
    INIT.SC, 585-586
    instant, 424-425
    key representations, 427, 428
    mistakes, 428
    names, 423
    recording, 420-425
        issuing commands, 424
        the [Menu] key, 424
    renaming, 424
    running a script from DOS, 586
    saving, 431-434
    syntax and conventions, 444-446
    types of errors, 576-577
    viewing, 425-426

writing scripts, 442-448
\ character, 443
.SC files, 422-42
Scripts BeginRecord command, 420
Scripts Editor Edit command, 425
Scripts End-Record command, 422
Scripts menu, 420, 421
Scripts Play command, 246, 429
Scripts QuerySave command, 199, 245-246, 431
Scripts ShowPlay command, 430-431
SDIR() function, 498
SEARCH() function, 489
Selection conditions, 209-238
    blank operator, 263
    defining, 209
    exact-match, 209-214
    examples in, 258
    not selecting condition field, 214-215
    position in a query form, 209
    quotation marks, 211-212
    selecting fields, 214
    two or more conditions in a field, 235
SETDIR command, 458
SetDirectory command, 163
.SET file, 89
SETKEY command, 558-561
    keycode argument, 559
Setting Format command, 411
Setting GroupRepeats command, 410
Setting Margin command, 378
Setting PageLayout command, 345-348
Setting PageLayout Length command, 378
Setting PageLayout Width command, 347, 377-378
Setting RemoveBlank FieldSqueeze command, 374
Setting RemoveBlank LineSqueeze command, 374
Setting Setup command, 379
Setting Setup Custom command, 380
Setting Setup Predefined command, 379
Setting Wait Yes command, 380
Setup strings, 379
Short number fields, 35
SHOWMENU command, 530-531
SLEEP command, 514
SORT command, 454-455
Sorting, 177-190
    basics, 180-186
    defining the sort form, 178-179
    descending order, 181-182
    destination, 177-178
    keyed tables, 189-190
    multiple-field, 186-189
    repeating, 183
    reversing, 183-184
    sort menu, 184-185

    sort order, 181-182
    Tools Copy JustFamily command, 185-186
SPACES() function, 485
Special function keys, 13, 14
Statistical functions, 475-477
Statistical operators, 278-284
    all, 280
    average, 278
    count, 278
    field compatibility, 280-282
    group statistics, 284-286
    grouping multiple fields, 286
    in alphanumeric fields, 282
    in date fields, 282
    in numeric fields, 282
    in selection conditions, 283-284
    in two or more fields, 282-284
    max, 278
    min, 278
    scope, 280-282
    sum, 278
    unique, 280
    using computed statistics, 287-288
String conversion functions, 483
String functions, 482-489
STRUCT table, 31-33, 154-155, 166, 167, 168, 175
    editing, 37-38
STRVAL() function, 484
STYLE command, 515-517
    attribute keyword, 517
    BLINK keyword, 515-517
    INTENSE keyword, 515-517
    REVERSE keyword, 515-517
    with the TEXT command, 517
Style command, 138-142
Submenus, 18-19
Subroutines, 536-537
SUBSTR() function, 484-485
SUBTRACT command, 457
Subtracting records, 301-304
Sum operator, 278, 279
Summary fields, 383-391
    calculated, 387-391
    placing in reports, 384, 385-386, 390
    regular, 383-387
    types of summaries, 383-384,389
    see also Reporting, summary fields
SWITCH command, 530, 533-535
    CASE keyword, 533
    ENDSWITCH keyword, 533
    OTHERWISE keyword, 535
SYSMODE() function, 498-499

T

TABLE() function, 499

Table view, 21
TableBand Copy command, 355-356
TableBand Erase command, 353
TableBand Insert command, 353-354
TableBand Move command, 351-352
TableBand Resize command, 354-355
Tables, 29-70
    ANSWER, 152-153, 194, 195, 196, 200-201, 268
    CHANGED, 242-245, 262, 298
    copying, 151-152
        using a query, 205
        JustFamily, 151-152
    creating, 29-33, 68-70
    defined, 19
    defining, 32
    DELETED, 240-241, 265
    deleting, 153-154
    deleting a record, 38
    designing, 68-70
    editing, 62-67
    emptying, 158-159
    ENTRY, 41-44
    families, 20, 152-153, 157-158
    FAMILY, 157-158
    image, 51
    INSERTED, 325-327
    inserting a record, 37-38
    KEYVIOL, 74-77, 175, 247, 295-296
    keyed, 71-79
        see also Keyed tables
    LIST, 155-156
    names, 20, 33
    normalizing, 29-71, 268
    PROBLEMS, 171-172
    protecting, 159-162
    renaming, 150-151
    restructuring, 165-176
        see also Restructuring tables
    selecting, 16-18, 52
    sorting, 177-190
    STRUCT, 31-33, 154-155, 166, 167
        erasing an entry, 37
    temporary, 20
    viewing, 17, 51
    write-protecting, 161-162
Temporary tables, 20
TEXT command, 513-514
    ENDTEXT keyword, 513-514
Tilde variables, 583-584
TIME() function, 481-482
TODAY() function, 482
Today operator, 230-231
Tools Copy Form command, 146-147
Tools Copy JustFamily command, 152-153, 185
Tools Copy Report command, 414
Tools Copy Table command, 151-152, 166
Tools Delete Form command, 147-148
Tools Delete KeepSettings command, 89
Tools Delete QuerySpeedup command, 250
Tools Delete Report Command, 415
Tools Delete Table command, 153-154, 180
Tools Delete ValCheck command, 101
Tools Export/Import command, 593-604
Tools Info command, 154-158
Tools menu, 149
Tools More Add command, 76, 171-172 241, 243, 289-301
    basics, 289-290
    field types, 292
    keyed tables, 292-301
    NewEntries option, 76, 292, 293-298
    non-keyed tables, 290-292
    Update option, 76, 292, 298-301
    using to edit tables, 299-301
Tools More Directory command, 162-163
Tools More Empty command, 158-159, 291
Tools More MultiAdd command, 315-320
    key fields, 317-318
    KEYVIOL table, 316-317, 319-320
    NewEntries option, 315-318
    Update option, 318-320
Tools More Protect Password command, 159-160
Tools More Protect Password Script command, 555-556
Tools More Protect Write-Protect command, 161-162
Tools More Subtract command, 301-304
Tools More ToDOS command, 163-165
Tools More menu, 149-150
Tools QuerySpeedup command, 246, 248
Tools Rename Form command, 148
Tools Rename Report command, 415
Tools Rename Script command, 424
Tools Rename Table command, 150-151, 201
Two-table operations, 265-273
    queries, 272-273
TYPE() function, 499
TYPEIN command, 591

U

Undo command, 49-50, 67
Uninstalling Paradox, 9-10
UNPASSWORD command, 554-555
UPPER() function, 483

V

.VAL files, 100,101
ValCheck command, 89-101
Validity checks, 89-101
    clearing, 100-101
    .VAL files, 100,101

pictures, 93-97
  picture characters, 93-97
  required values, 98
  saving, 100
  setting a default value, 92-93
  setting a high value, 90
  setting a low value, 90-91
  table lookups, 98-99
Value command, 557-558, 581-582
Variables, 460-463
  global variables, 570-572
  in PAL formulas, 468-469
  private variables, 570-572
  retval, 571-572
  tilde, 583-584
  see also PAL variables
VERSION() function, 499-500
VIEW command (PAL), 452
View command, 51, 103
Viewing
  entries in narrow field, 83
  fields, 54
  images of several tables, 60-61
  multiple images, 57-60
  records, 55
  scripts, 429

W

WAIT command, 524-525
  FIELD keyword, 524
  in a form, 528-529
  MESSAGE keyword, 526-527
  multiple UNTIL keys, 529-530
  PROMPT keyword, 527-528
  UNTIL keyword, 524
Where? command, 582
WHILE command, 541-545
  ENDWHILE keyword, 541-545
  infinite loops, 544-545
Wildcard operators, 216-226
  @ operator, 217-218
  .. operator, 216-217
WINDOW() function, 500
Workspace, 12
WRITELIB command, 573-574
Write-protection, 161-162

Y

YEAR() function, 481
.Y01 and .X01 files, 249-250

Keys by Name
[Alt]-function keys, 15
[Backspace] key, 13
[Check Mark] ([F6]), 14, 194, 197, 202-209
[Check Plus] ([Alt]-[F6]), 15, 207-208

[Clear All] ([Alt]-[F8]), 15, 62, 191, 199
[Clear Image] ([F8]), 14, 61, 199
[Ctrl] key combinations, 13-14
[Ctrl]-[Break] key, 14
[Del] key, 15, 241
[Ditto] key ([Ctrl]-[D]), 14, 101-102
[Do-It!] key ([F2]), 14, 39
[Down Image] key ([F4]), 14, 59, 61, 197
[Edit] key ([F9]), 14, 57, 111
[Enter] key, 13
  see also ↵ key
[Esc] key, 13
[Example] key ([F5]), 14, 253
[Field View] ([Alt]-[F5]), 14, 15, 47-48, 64
[Form Toggle] key ([F7]), 14, 103
[Help] key ([F1]), 14
[Ins] key, 15
[Instant Report] key ([Alt]-[F7]), 15, 155, 329-330
[Instant Script Play] key ([Alt]-[F4]), 15, 425, 429
[Instant Script Record] ([Alt]-[F3]), 15, 424-425
[Menu] key ([F10]), 12, 14
[Num Lock] key, 15
[PAL Menu] key ([Alt]-[F10]), 15, 429, 557
[Quit] key ([Ctrl]-[Q]), 447
[Report Delete Line] ([Ctrl]-[Y], 14, 343
[Return] key
  see ↵ key,
[Rotate] key ([Ctrl]-[R]), 14, 88, 351-352
[Script Delete Line] key ([Ctrl]-[Y], 437
[ToDOS] key ([Ctrll]-[O]), 14, 164
[Undo] key ([Ctrl]-[U]), 14, 49
[Up Image] key ([F3]), 14, 59, 61, 197, 199
[Vertical Ruler Toggle] ([Ctrl]-[V]), 14, 341-343, 435
↑, ↓, →, ← keys, 36-37, 43-48, 53, 104-106, 121, 197, 341
↵ key, 13

Special Characters
character in PAL pictures, 93-94
? character in PAL pictures, 94
@ character in PAL pictures, 94
& character in PAL pictures, 94-95
! character in PAL pictures, 94-95
; character in PAL pictures, 96
; character, 556
* character in PAL pictures, 96
, character in PAL pictures, 96
[ ] characters in PAL pictures, 96
" " characters, 211-212
\ character, 443

For advanced tips and techniques, subscribe to The Cobb Group's *Paradox User's Journal*.

Send for your free copy today.
This complimentary issue includes a feature article on directory-changing scripts, shows you how to organize your Paradox tables, offers tips on loading quickly and naming tables–plus much more. ☑ Check the box below for your free copy–or call toll-free: 1-800-223-8720.

Also from The Cobb Group:

For Symphony users:
The Symphony User's Journal
Mastering Symphony, 2nd Edition
The Hidden Power of Symphony

For 123 users:
Douglas Cobb's 123 Journal
Douglas Cobb's 123 Upgrade Book

The Cobb Group Money-Back Guarantee
If for any reason you are not satisfied with a Cobb Group product, you may return it within 10 days for a full refund. Journals may be cancelled at any time for a refund of the balance of your subscription.

Need more information?
Call The Cobb Group toll-free: 1-800-223-8720
(In Kentucky, call 502-425-7756.)

----------------- FOLD HERE -----------------

Send for a FREE journal!

Order:

Paradox User's Journal
☐ Free Issue–no obligation
☐ 1 yr (12 issues) $70 (outside U.S. $90)
☐ 2 yr (24 issues) $120 (outside U.S. $155)

The Symphony User's Journal
☐ Free Issue–no obligation

Douglas Cobb's 123 Journal
☐ Free Issue–no obligation

☐ *Mastering Symphony, 2nd Ed.* Qty.___
    $24.95 + $1.50 handling* = $26.45 each
☐ *The Hidden Power of Symphony* Qty.___
    $22.95 + $1.50 handling* = $24.45 each

*Handling charges will vary outside U.S.
Call 1-800-223-8720 or 502-425-7756.

Send me information on:
☐ *Douglas Cobb's 123 Upgrade Book*
☐ Other Cobb Group products for Lotus 123

Ship To:
Name_____
Firm_____
Street Address (no PO Box #'s)_____
City_____ State_____ Zip_____
Type of Business_____ Phone (____)_____

Payment:
☐ US Check (payable to: The Cobb Group) $_____   ☐ Bill me (No book shipped without payment)
☐ VISA   ☐ AmExpress   ☐ MasterCard   Expiration_____
Card Number_____ Name_____
Cardholder's Signature_____
Total Amount of Order $_____ (In Kentucky, add 5% sales tax to your order)

Book orders must be prepaid before shipment. FOB destination. Books are shipped by U.P.S. within the continental U.S., by airmail outside the continental U.S. Foreign orders must be prepaid in U.S. funds. Allow 4-6 weeks for delivery of books.

Thank you for your order!

BUSINESS REPLY MAIL
FIRST CLASS PERMIT NO. 618 LOUISVILLE, KENTUCKY

POSTAGE WILL PAID BY ADDRESSEE

NO POSTAGE
NECESSARY
IF MAILED
IN THE
UNITED STATES

The Cobb Group, Inc.
PO Box 24480
Louisville, Kentucky
40224